ENOCH AND QUMRAN ORIGINS

ENOCH AND QUMRAN ORIGINS

New Light on a Forgotten Connection

Edited by

Gabriele Boccaccini

Associate Editors

J. Harold Ellens and James Alan Waddell

with the collaboration of

Jason von Ehrenkrook, Ronald Ruark, and Aaron Brunell

WILLIAM B. EERDMANS PUBLISHING COMPANY

GRAND RAPIDS, MICHIGAN / CAMBRIDGE, U.K.

Wm. B. Eerdmans Publishing Co.
255 Jefferson Ave. S.E., Grand Rapids, Michigan 49503 /
P.O. Box 163, Cambridge CB3 9PU U.K.

Printed in the United States of America

10 09 08 07 06 05   7 6 5 4 3 2 1

Library of Congress Cataloging-in-Publication Data

Enoch Seminar (2nd: 2003: Venice, Italy)
    Enoch and Qumran origins: new light on a forgotten connection /
    edited by Gabriele Boccaccini; associate editors, J. Harold Ellens and James Waddell
    with the collaboration of Ronald Ruark, Jason von Ehrenkrook, and Aaron Brunell.
        p.   cm.
    Includes bibliographical references.
    ISBN 0-8028-2878-7 (pbk.: alk. paper)
    1. Ethiopic book of Enoch — Criticism, interpretation, etc. — Congresses. 2. Bible.
O.T. Daniel — Criticism, interpretation, etc. — Congresses. 3. Book of Jubilees —
Criticism, interpretation, etc. — Congresses. 4. Qumran community — Congresses.
5. Essenes — Congresses. 6. Judaism — History — Post-exilic period, 586 B.C.–210 A.D.
— Congresses.   I. Boccaccini, Gabriele, 1958–   II. Title.

BS1830.E7E56   2005

                                    2005045106

www.eerdmans.com

*Special thanks to the
Department of Near Eastern Studies
of the University of Michigan,
the Frankel Center for Judaic Studies,
and the Michigan Center for Early Christian Studies
for making possible the Second Enoch Seminar in Venice
and the completion of this project*

Contents

Contents

Contents

PART FIVE: THE ENOCHIC-ESSENE HYPOTHESIS REVISITED

Contents

Abbreviations

AB	Anchor Bible
ABD	*The Anchor Bible Dictionary* (ed. Freedman, 6 vols., 1992)
AGJU	Arbeiten zur Geschichte des antiken Judentums und des Urchristentums
Ant.	Josephus, *Antiquitates Judaicae*
ANTZ	Arbeiten zur neutestamentlichen Theologie und Zeitgeschichte
AOAT	Alter Orient und Altes Testament
AOS	American Oriental Series
APOT	*The Apocrypha and Pseudepigrapha of the Old Testament* (ed. Charles, 1913)
BA	*Biblical Archaeologist*
BASOR	*Bulletin of the American Schools of Oriental Research*
BASP	*Bulletin of the American Society of Papyrologists*
BBR	*Bulletin for Biblical Research*
BETL	Bibliotheca ephemeridum theologicarum lovaniensium
BHS	*Biblia Hebraica Stuttgartensia*
BHWJ	Bericht der Hochschule für die Wissenschaft des Judentums
Bib	*Biblica*
BibOr	Biblica et orientalia
BJS	Brown Judaic Studies
BKAT	Biblischer Kommentar: Altes Testament
BZAW	Beihefte zur *ZAW*
BZNW	Beihefte zur *ZNW*
CahRB	Cahiers de la Revue biblique

CBQ	*Catholic Biblical Quarterly*
CBQMS	Catholic Biblical Quarterly–Monograph Series
ConBOT	Coniectanea biblica, Old Testament
CRINT	Compendia rerum iudaicarum ad novum testamentum
CSCO	Corpus scriptorum christianorum orientalium
DA	*Deir Alla* (texts and inscriptions)
DDD	*Dictionary of Deities and Demons in the Bible* (ed. Toorn, et al., 2nd ed. 1992)
DJD	Discoveries in the Judaean Desert
DSD	*Dead Sea Discoveries*
DSS	Dead Sea Scrolls
EJL	Early Judaism and Its Literature
ET	English translation
FAT	Forschungen zum Alten Testament
GCFI	*Giornale Critico della Filosofia Italiana*
GCS	Griechischen christlichen Schriftsteller
Hen	*Henoch*
HO	Handbuck der Orientalistik
HSM	Harvard Semitic Monographs
HSS	Harvard Semitic Studies
HTR	*Harvard Theological Review*
HUCA	*Hebrew Union College Annual*
IEJ	*Israel Exploration Journal*
JBL	*Journal of Biblical Literature*
JDS	Judean Desert Series
JJS	*Journal of Jewish Studies*
JQR	*Jewish Quarterly Review*
JR	*Journal of Religion*
JSHRZ	Jüdische Schriften aus hellenistisch-römischer Zeit
JSJ	*Journal for the Study of Judaism*
JSJSup	Journal for the Study of Judaism Supplement Series
JSNTSup	Journal for the Study of the New Testament–Supplement Series
JSOT	*Journal for the Study of the Old Testament*
JSOTSup	Journal for the Study of the Old Testament–Supplement Series
JSP	*Journal for the Study of the Pseudepigrapha*
JSPSup	Journal for the Study of the Pseudepigrapha Supplements
JTS	*Journal of Theological Studies*
KAI	*Kanaanäische und aramäische Inschriften* (ed. Koehler and Baumgartner)

KAR	*Keilschrifttexte aus Assur religiösen Inhalts* (ed. Ebeling, 1919-23)
KTU	Die keilalphabetischen Texte aus Ugarit
L.A.B.	*Liber Antiquitatum Biblicarum*
LCL	Loeb Classical Library
LXX	Septuagint
MGWJ	*Monatsschrift für Geschichte und Wissenschaft des Judentums*
MS(S)	manuscript(s)
MT	Masoretic Text
NCBC	New Century Bible Commentary
NTS	*New Testament Studies*
OBO	Orbis biblicus et orientalis
OTL	Old Testament Library
PAAJR	*Proceedings of the American Academy of Jewish Research*
PAM	Palestinian Archaeological Museum photos
PIBA	*Proceedings of the Irish Biblical Association*
PTSDSSP	Princeton Theological Seminary Dead Sea Scrolls Project
PVTG	Pseudepigrapha Veteris Testamenti graece
QD	Quaestiones disputatae
RB	*Revue biblique*
REJ	*Revue des études juives*
RevQ	*Revue de Qumran*
RHR	*Revue de l'histoire des religions*
RSR	*Recherches de science religieuse*
RTL	*Revue théologique de Louvain*
SBLEJL	Society of Biblical Literature Early Judaism and Its Literature
SBLMS	Society of Biblical Literature Monograph Series
SBLSCS	Society of Biblical Literature Septuagint and Cognate Studies
SBLSP	Society of Biblical Literature Seminary Papers
SBLTT	Society of Biblical Literature Texts and Translations
SBT	Studies in Biblical Theology
SC	Sources chrétiennes
SJLA	Studies in Judaism in Late Antiquity
SJOT	*Scandinavian Journal of the Old Testament*
SNTSMS	Society for New Testament Studies Monograph Series
SPB	Studia postbiblica
SR	*Sciences religieuses*
ST	*Studia theologica*
STDJ	Studies on the Texts of the Desert of Judah
SVTP	Studia in Veteris Testamenti pseudepigrapha

TDNT	*Theological Dictionary of the New Testament* (ed. Kittel and Friedrich, 1964-74)
TSAJ	Texts and Studies in Ancient Judaism
UF	*Ugarit-Forschungen*
USQR	*Union Seminary Quarterly Review*
VT	*Vetus Testamentum*
VTSup	Vetus Testamentum, Supplements
WMANT	Wissenschaftliche Monographien zum Alten und Neuen Testament
WO	*Die Welt des Orients*
WUNT	Wissenschaftliche Untersuchungen zum Neuen Testament
ZAW	*Zeitschrift für die alttestamentliche Wissenschaft*
ZNW	*Zeitschrift für die neutestamentliche Wissenschaft*

Introduction: From the Enoch Literature to Enochic Judaism

Gabriele Boccaccini

A book on Enoch and Qumran origins shows how dramatically our understanding of second temple Judaism has changed in contemporary scholarship. Such a topic would have been inconceivable only half a century ago, when Qumran had still to reemerge from the sands of the desert with its precious manuscripts and 1 Enoch was still struggling against the impediments of its "noncanonical" status and its dubious reputation as a bizarre and marginal pseudepigraphon.[1] After sharing a past of oblivion and marginality, Qumran and Enoch now seem to enjoy an exciting time of revival and a common destiny of success. The flourishing of Qumran studies is apparent, even outside academia; a flood of publications, exhibits, and television programs has made Qumran well known even on the popular level. Not as spectacular, with still too few serious attempts to popularize the achievements of scholarly research and catch the imagination of a general audience,[2] the march of 1 Enoch has been no less triumphant. Lost for centuries to Judaism and Christianity (with the only exception of the Ethiopic church), 1 Enoch has been slowly but surely regaining its proper position within second temple Jewish studies. In his recent commentary George Nickelsburg describes the document as "arguably the most important text in the corpus of Jewish literature from the Hellenistic and Roman periods."[3]

1. The article of J. Y. Campbell, "The Origin and Meaning of the Term Son of Man," *JTS* 48 (1947): 145-55, can well be taken as representative of such a prejudicial approach.
2. Notably, M. Barker, *The Book of Enoch and Its Influence on Christianity* (Nashville: Abingdon, 1988).
3. G. W. E. Nickelsburg, *1 Enoch* (Minneapolis: Fortress, 2001), 1.

Gabriele Boccaccini

1. Two Centuries of Enoch Studies

After the Scottish explorer James Bruce "rediscovered" the book of Enoch in 1773, the first scholarly task was to make the text available in critical editions and modern-language translations. Philologists like Richard Laurence, August Dillmann, and Johannes Flemming won the day.[4]

At the turn of the twentieth century, the work of Robert Henry Charles contributed to locate the text in the broader context of Jewish apocalyptic literature.[5] 1 Enoch's important role in second temple Judaism was fully recognized, although circumscribed by the canonical boundaries of intertestamental literature. Charles made it clear: "To the biblical scholar and to the student of Jewish and Christian theology 1 Enoch is the most important Jewish work written between 200 BC and 100 AD."[6] The document became a regular presence in the collections of the Old Testament Pseudepigrapha and in the introductions to Jewish apocalyptic literature.[7]

The predominantly Christian interest in the Pseudepigrapha, which fostered the early stages of the Enoch research, made it vulnerable to theological assumptions and to the spread of anti-Jewish and even anti-Semitic attitudes that so heavily characterized European (and American) culture between the wars. Documents like 1 Enoch, which in Jewish eyes had always remained the bizarre product of marginal sects detached from normative Judaism, appeared now more and more irrelevant also to the many Christian scholars whose primary task was to de-Judaize Christianity.

It took the Holocaust to shake even the most insulated consciences and lay the foundations for a different relationship between Christians and Jews. The discovery of the Dead Sea Scrolls in 1947 could not have been timelier. It proved how deeply the Jesus movement was rooted in the diverse and dynamic

---

4. R. Laurence, *Libri Enochi prophetae versio aethiopica* (Oxford: Parker, 1838); Laurence, *The Book of Enoch* (Oxford: Parker, 1821); A. Dillmann, *Das Buch Henoch übersetzt und erklärt* (Leipzig: Vogel, 1853); Dillmann, *Liber Henoch aethiopice* (Leipzig: Vogel, 1851); J. Flemming, *Das Buch Henoch* (Leipzig: Hinrichs, 1902).

5. R. H. Charles, *The Book of Enoch* (London: SPCK, 1917); Charles, *The Book of Enoch, or 1 Enoch, Translated from the Editor's Ethiopic Text, and Edited with the Introduction, Notes, and Indexes of the First Edition Wholly Recast, Enlarged, and Rewritten* (Oxford: Clarendon, 1912); Charles, *The Ethiopic Version of the Book of Enoch* (Oxford: Clarendon, 1906); Charles, *The Book of Enoch translated from Professor Dillmann's Ethiopic Text emended and revised . . . edited with Introduction, Notes, Appendices, and Indices* (Oxford: Clarendon, 1893).

6. Charles, *Book of Enoch translated*, vi.

7. R. H. Charles, ed., *The Apocrypha and Pseudepigrapha of the Old Testament*, 2 vols. (Oxford: Clarendon, 1912, 1913); E. Kautzsch, ed., *Die Apokryphen und Pseudepigraphen des Alten Testaments*, 2 vols. (Tübingen: Mohr, 1900).

environment of second temple Judaism. The discovery of the scrolls marked yet another important step in the study of 1 Enoch. The publication of the Qumran fragments by Josef Milik in 1976 emphasized the composite nature of 1 Enoch as an ancient collection of second temple Jewish texts.[8] The Jewishness of the document was now apparent to both Christian and Jewish scholars, as were its relevance and popularity in its own time.

With the publication of the scrolls came also a renewed interest in the Old Testament Pseudepigrapha and, with it, a new wave of editions and translations. The publication of the new English translation of 1 Enoch in 1983 by Ephraim Isaac in the James Charlesworth collection represents only the tip of the iceberg; in the same years, 1 Enoch was appearing in similar collections in Italy (Fusella and Sacchi, 1981), Spain (Corriente and Piñero, 1984), Germany (Uhlig, 1984), England (Knibb, 1984), and France (Caquot, 1987).[9] The Enoch literature quickly regained center stage. James VanderKam began exploring the literary growth of the traditions associated with the patriarch Enoch well beyond the boundaries of the Enoch corpus, while John Collins studied the contribution of 1 Enoch to the broader development of apocalypticism in the second temple period.[10]

In these last two decades, the most important development is that "the emphasis has shifted from the study of the Enoch texts to the study of the intellectual and sociological characteristics of the group behind such literature."[11] It has become apparent that the texts in 1 Enoch were the core of a distinctive movement of thought in second temple Judaism. The boundaries of such a movement overlapped yet did not coincide either with the broader complex of oral and literary traditions associated with the figure of Enoch (some of which

8. J. T. Milik, *The Books of Enoch: Aramaic Fragments of Qumran, Cave 4* (Oxford: Clarendon, 1976).

9. E. Isaac, "1 (Ethiopic Apocalypse of) Enoch," in *Old Testament Pseudepigrapha*, ed. James H. Charlesworth, vol. 1 (New York: Doubleday, 1983), 5-89; P. Sacchi and L. Fusella, "Libro di Enoc," in *Apocrifi dell'Antico Testamento*, ed. P. Sacchi, vol. 1 (Turin: UTET, 1981), 413-667; F. Corriente and A. Piñero, "Libro I de Henoc (etiopico y griego)," in *Apócrifos del Antiguo Testamento*, ed. A. Díez Macho, vol. 4 (Madrid: Cristiandad, 1984), 11-143; S. Uhlig, "Das äthiopischen Henochbuch," in JSHRZ, vol. 5.6 (Gütersloh: Mohn, 1984), 461-780; M. A. Knibb, "1 Enoch," in *The Apocryphal Old Testament*, ed. H. F. D. Sparks (New York: Oxford University Press, 1984), 169-319; A. Caquot, "Hénoch," in *La Bible: Écrits intertestamentaires*, ed. A. Dupont-Sommer and M. Philonenko (Paris: Gallimard, 1987), 465-625.

10. J. C. VanderKam, *Enoch and the Growth of an Apocalyptic Tradition*, CBQMS 16 (Washington, D.C.: Catholic Biblical Association of America, 1984); J. J. Collins, *The Apocalyptic Imagination: An Introduction to the Jewish Matrix of Christianity* (New York: Crossroad, 1984).

11. G. Boccaccini, "The Rediscovery of Enochic Judaism and the Enoch Seminar," in *The Origins of Enochic Judaism*, ed. G. Boccaccini (Turin: Zamorani, 2002 [= *Henoch* 24.1-2, 2002]), 9.

were used in different ideological frameworks) or with the broader corpus of Jewish apocalypses (some of which belonged to different, if not opposite, parties).

The contemporary research in 1 Enoch is a collective enterprise that involves scholars from different countries and different schools. It would be enough here to mention Florentino García Martínez, Michael Knibb, Klaus Koch, Helge Kvanvig, and Loren Stuckenbruck in Europe; John Collins, James Charlesworth, Martha Himmelfarb, Lawrence Schiffman, David Suter, and James VanderKam in the United States; Devorah Dimant, Hanan Eshel, Ithamar Gruenwald, and Michael Stone in Israel. Without diminishing in any way the contribution made by these scholars and many others to Enoch studies, special credit for the rediscovery of Enochic Judaism as an autonomous form of Judaism goes to Paolo Sacchi and George Nickelsburg.

In 1979 Sacchi launched the journal *Henoch,* publishing the first of an impressive series of articles which made 1 Enoch not only the prototype of the apocalyptic genre but also the core of a distinct variety of Judaism.[12] In 1990 Sacchi's *L'apocalittica giudaica e la sua storia* (ET: *Jewish Apocalyptic and Its History*) marked the first attempt at writing an intellectual history of the Enochic movement as a distinctive apocalyptic party within the broader context of second temple Judaism and ancient Jewish apocalypticism.[13] Sacchi identified the "essence" of such an intellectual movement in a particular concept of evil, understood as an autonomous reality antecedent to humanity's ability to choose, the result of a "contamination that has spoiled [human] nature," an evil that "was produced before the beginning of history."[14]

Nickelsburg's commentary on 1 Enoch also came in 2001 as the result of a long series of studies that the author had devoted to the subject since the late 1970s. He describes the Enoch movement as a form of Judaism in which "the Mosaic torah [was] not yet a universal norm."[15]

In the Enochic system of thought the two contradictory concepts of human responsibility and human victimization coexist between the Scylla of an

---

12. See G. Boccaccini, "Jewish Apocalyptic Tradition: The Contribution of Italian Scholarship," in *Mysteries and Revelations,* ed. J. J. Collins and J. H. Charlesworth (Sheffield: Sheffield Academic Press, 1991), 33-50.

13. P. Sacchi, *L'apocalittica giudaica e la sua storia* (Brescia: Paideia, 1990); ET: *Jewish Apocalyptic and Its History,* trans. W. J. Short (Sheffield: Sheffield Academic Press, 1997).

14. P. Sacchi, "Riflessioni sull'essenza dell'apocalittica: peccato d'origine e libertà dell'uomo," *Hen* 5 (1983): 57.

15. Nickelsburg, *1 Enoch,* 1. A useful survey on the role of the Mosaic law in 1 Enoch is in K. C. Bautch, *A Study of the Geography of 1 Enoch 17–19: No One Has Seen What I Have Seen* (Leiden: Brill, 2003), 289-99.

absolute determinism and the Charybdis of an equally absolute anti-determinism. "The Enochic corpus explains the origin and presence of sin and evil on earth in two ways: (1) sin and evil are the function of a primordial heavenly revolt whose results continue to victimize the human race; (2) responsibility for sin and evil lies with the human beings who transgress God's law."[16] Accept either of these extremes against the other and the entire Enochic system would collapse into the condemnation of God as the unmerciful source of evil or as the unjust scourge of innocent creatures.

While Sacchi's interest focused almost exclusively on intellectual issues, Nickelsburg's work offers some very interesting insights also regarding the sociology of the Enoch group. Although "the 108 chapters of 1 Enoch provide little explicit information about an Enochic community . . . some textual evidence points in the direction of a community or group. Collective terms like 'the righteous, the chosen, the holy' indicate a consciousness of community." The strongest evidence is given by the fact that "the Enochic literature . . . developed in stages, over three centuries, from a core narrative about the Watchers. To account for this ongoing, evolving tradition, one must posit concrete channels of transmission. . . . The texts themselves indicate a process of developing composition in the name of Enoch." It is therefore appropriate to speak of "a community or communities who believed that their possession of the divinely given wisdom contained in the Enochic texts, constituted them as the eschatological community of the chosen, who are awaiting the judgment and the consummation of the end time."[17] We do not know what this party was called, or what it called itself in antiquity. However, since this movement of dissent first coalesced around ancient myths with Enoch as their hero, the term "Enochic Judaism" seems quite appropriate and satisfactory as a modern label.

As for the identification of the Enochic authors, Nickelsburg thinks they can be described as "scribes" and that "it is possible, though not altogether certain, that at least some of the authors of the Enochic literature were also priests, indeed, disaffected members of the Jerusalem priesthood."[18] With David Suter, Nickelsburg also emphasizes Upper Galilee as the place where Enochic traditions possibly originated.[19]

16. Nickelsburg, *1 Enoch*, 46.

17. Nickelsburg, *1 Enoch*, 64.

18. Nickelsburg, *1 Enoch*, 67. Boccaccini ("The Priestly Opposition: Enochic Judaism," in *Roots of Rabbinic Judaism* [Grand Rapids: Eerdmans, 2002], 89-103) sees evidence in 1 Esdr 5:38-40 (Ezra 2:61-63; Neh 7:63-65) that priests who served in the second temple were indeed expelled from the priesthood during the late Persian period.

19. Nickelsburg, *1 Enoch*, 119, 238-47; cf. D. Suter, "Why Galilee? Galilean Regionalism in the Interpretation of 1 Enoch 6–16," *Hen* 25 (2003): 167-212.

In sum: it seems that we may now with some confidence talk of Enochic Judaism as a nonconformist, anti-Zadokite, priestly movement of dissent, active in Israel since the late Persian or early Hellenistic period (fourth century B.C.E.). At the center of Enochic Judaism was neither the temple nor the torah but a unique concept of the origin of evil that made the "fallen angels" (the "sons of God" also recorded in Gen 6:1-4) ultimately responsible for the spread of evil and impurity on earth. "The [Enochic] myths assert, deterministically on the one hand, that human beings are less the perpetrators than the victims of sin, which had its origin in the divine realm. On the other hand, they maintain that sin and evil originated not with God's permission, but as the result of a rebellious conspiracy that was hatched behind God's back."[20]

Taking up traditions that predate the postexilic origins of the movement,[21] Enochic Judaism gave them a different interpretation than that provided within the Zadokite tradition. The cosmic rebellion of the fallen angels was not simply, as in the Mosaic torah, one of the primeval sins that characterized the ancient history of humankind. By crossing the boundaries between heaven and earth, the evil angels led by Semyaz and Azazel broke apart the divisions set by God at the time of creation. According to the Book of the Watchers, it was the mother of all sins, the original sin which corrupted and contaminated God's creation and from which evil relentlessly continues to spring forth and spread. As God said to the angel Raphael: "The whole earth has been corrupted through the works that were taught by Azazel: to him ascribe all sin!" (1 En 6:8). In a cosmic battle the rebellious angels were defeated by the good angels and imprisoned in chains "in a hole in the desert which is in Dudael . . . [until] the day of the great judgment" (6:4-6). The giants, the monstrous offspring of the unnatural union between angels and women, were killed (10:9-10), but their immortal souls survived as the evil spirits and continue to roam about the earth (15:8-10). As disturbing as this idea can be, God's reaction limited but did not eradicate evil, until God will put an end to this evil world and will create a new world qualitatively different from, and discontinuous with, what was before.

The theological attempt to absolve the merciful God from being responsible for the presence of evil on earth leads to the conclusion that human beings are less the perpetrators than the victims of evil. Human freedom and responsibility are not denied, but the importance of divine grace is enhanced. Without

20. Nickelsburg, *1 Enoch,* 47.
21. Helge Kvanvig and Klaus Koch are the scholars that mostly have emphasized the ancient origins of Enochic traditions (see their contributions in Boccaccini, *The Origins of Enochic Judaism,* as well as in this volume).

God's intervention humans would be totally at the mercy of evil, but the rebellious power of evil limits the effectiveness of God's intervention. The very idea of a covenant between God and God's people is disrupted by the presence of the third party, the devil, who acts maliciously outside and against the rules of any covenant.

The autonomous party, of which 1 Enoch is evidence, was not a closed conventicle but had manifestly a large influence, so much so as to generate a broader movement of thought focused on the idea of the demonic origin of evil. Second temple Jewish documents such as Jubilees, the Testaments of the Twelve Patriarchs, the Life of Adam and Eve, 2 Enoch, the Apocalypse of Abraham, and 4 Ezra all contain citations of and allusions to Enoch texts and ideology. Profoundly influential in its own time, Enochic Judaism "will have a profound impact on the shape of emergent Christianity" (the Letter of Jude mentions the writings of the prophet Enoch as Scripture, and many church fathers would share this view), while becoming "increasingly alien to many of the rabbinic teachers and their communities as they consolidate their religion after the destruction of Jerusalem in 70 CE."[22]

2. The Enoch Seminar

The rediscovery of Enochic Judaism is undoubtedly one of the major achievements of contemporary research. The most recent and comprehensive introductions to second temple Judaism by Paolo Sacchi, Lester Grabbe, Gabriele Boccaccini, and George Nickelsburg give broad recognition to this ancient Jewish movement of dissent.[23] A glance at the textbooks and syllabi of courses in interbiblical, early Jewish and early Christian studies at universities and seminaries all around the world shows how rapidly Enochic Judaism is gaining acceptance even within the mainstream curriculum of undergraduate education.[24]

That we are at the beginning of a broad and promising field of research is proved by the enthusiasm with which specialists from America, Europe, and Israel have welcomed the invitation of the University of Michigan to join a series

22. Nickelsburg, *1 Enoch*, 1.

23. P. Sacchi, *History of the Second Temple Period* (Sheffield: Sheffield Academic Press, 2000); L. L. Grabbe, *Judaic Religion in Second Temple Judaism* (London: Routledge, 2000); Boccaccini, *Roots of Rabbinic Judaism*; G. W. E. Nickelsburg, *Ancient Judaism and Christian Origins: Diversity, Continuity, and Transformation* (Minneapolis: Fortress, 2003).

24. See, for example, J. S. Anderson, *The Internal Diversification of Second Temple Judaism* (Lanham, Md.: University Press of America, 2002).

of biennial seminars that step-by-step would cover the entire history of the movement, from its pre-Maccabean origins to its latest developments in Christianity and rabbinic Judaism. Launched in 2000 by the Department of Near Eastern Studies of the University of Michigan, in collaboration with the Frankel Center for Judaic Studies and the Michigan Center for Early Christian Studies, the Enoch Seminar has become the center and the engine of the contemporary renaissance of Enochic studies.

The first meeting of the Enoch Seminar was held in Sesto Fiorentino, Florence, Italy (19-23 June 2001), and was devoted to "The Origins of Enochic Judaism." In attendance were:

Gabriele Boccaccini, director (University of Michigan, USA)
Randal A. Argall (Jamestown University, USA)
Andreas Bedenbender (Humboldt University, Germany)
Alessandro Catastini (University of Rome, Italy)
James H. Charlesworth (Princeton Theological Seminary, USA)
Sabino Chialà (Monastero di Bose, Italy)
John J. Collins (Yale University, USA)
Michael A. Daise (William and Mary College, USA)
Devorah Dimant (Tel Aviv University, Israel)
Yaron Eliav (University of Michigan, USA)
Mark A. Elliott (University of Toronto, Canada)
Esther Eshel (Bar-Ilan University, Israel)
Hanan Eshel (Bar-Ilan University, Israel)
Florentino García Martínez (Groningen Qumran Institute, the Netherlands)
Claudio Gianotto (University of Turin, Italy)
Ithamar Gruenwald (Tel Aviv University, Israel)
Martha Himmelfarb (Princeton University, USA)
Sylvia Honigman (Tel Aviv University, Israel)
Michael A. Knibb (King's College London, England)
Klaus Koch (University of Hamburg, Germany)
Helge S. Kvanvig (University of Oslo, Norway)
Luca Mazzinghi (Theological University of Florence, Italy)
George W. E. Nickelsburg (University of Iowa, USA)
Mauro Perani (University of Bologna, Italy)
Pierluigi Piovanelli (University of Ottawa, Canada)
Stephen B. Reid (Austin Presbyterian Seminary, USA)
Liliana Rosso Ubigli (University of Turin, Italy)
Paolo Sacchi (University of Turin, Italy)

Brian Schmidt (University of Michigan, USA)
Loren T. Stuckenbruck (Durham University, England)
David W. Suter (Saint Martin's College, USA)
Eibert J. C. Tigchelaar (Groningen Qumran Institute, the Netherlands)
Ralph Williams (University of Michigan, USA)
Benjamin G. Wright III (Lehigh University, USA)
Adela Yarbro Collins (Yale University, USA)

Secretaries of the conference were J. Harold Ellens, James Waddell, and Adam
Chalom of the University of Michigan.

The second meeting of the Enoch Seminar was held in Venice, Italy (1-4
July 2003), and was devoted to "Enoch and Qumran Origins." Here is the list of
participants:

Gabriele Boccaccini, director (University of Michigan, USA)
Matthias Albani (University of Leipzig, Germany)
Jeff Anderson (Wayland Baptist University at Anchorage, USA)
Albert I. Baumgarten (Bar-Ilan University, Israel)
Andreas Bedenbender (Humboldt University, Germany)
Stefan Beyerle (Oldenburg University, Germany)
Piero Capelli (University of Venice, Italy)
James H. Charlesworth (Princeton Theological Seminary, USA)
Sabino Chialà (Monastero di Bose, Italy)
John J. Collins (Yale University, USA)
Michael A. Daise (William and Mary College, USA)
Philip R. Davies (University of Sheffield, England)
James R. Davila (University of St. Andrews, Scotland)
Marcello Del Verme (University of Naples, Italy)
Torleif Elgvin (Lutheran Theological Seminary, Norway)
Yaron Eliav (University of Michigan, USA)
Mark A. Elliott (University of Toronto, Canada)
Esther Eshel (Bar-Ilan University, Israel)
Hanan Eshel (Bar-Ilan University, Israel)
Ida Fröhlich (Catholic University, Hungary)
Florentino García Martínez (Groningen Qumran Institute, the Netherlands)
Claudio Gianotto (University of Turin, Italy)
Lester L. Grabbe (University of Hull, England)
Ithamar Gruenwald (Tel Aviv University, Israel)
Charlotte Hempel (England)

Matthias Henze (Rice University, USA)
Martha Himmelfarb (Princeton University, USA)
Michael A. Knibb (King's College London, England)
Klaus Koch (University of Hamburg, Germany)
Helge S. Kvanvig (University of Oslo, Norway)
Armin Lange (University of North Carolina at Chapel Hill, USA)
Eric W. Larson (Florida International University, USA)
Timothy H. Lim (University of Edinburgh, Scotland)
Corrado Martone (University of Turin, Italy)
George W. E. Nickelsburg (University of Iowa, USA)
Mauro Perani (University of Bologna, Italy)
Pierluigi Piovanelli (University of Ottawa, Canada)
Emile Puech (CNRS, France/EBAF, Israel)
Annette Yoshiko Reed (McMaster University, Canada)
John C. Reeves (University of North Carolina at Charlotte, USA)
Henry W. Rietz (Grinnell College, USA)
Liliana Rosso Ubigli (University of Turin, Italy)
Jacques van Ruiten (University of Groningen, the Netherlands)
Paolo Sacchi (University of Turin, Italy)
Lawrence H. Schiffman (New York University, USA)
David W. Suter (Saint Martin's College, USA)
Shemaryahu Talmon (Hebrew University of Jerusalem, Israel)
Eibert J. C. Tigchelaar (Groningen Qumran Institute, the Netherlands)
Patrick Tiller (USA)
James C. VanderKam (Notre Dame University, USA)
Megan Williams (University of Michigan, USA)
Ralph Williams (University of Michigan, USA)
Benjamin G. Wright III (Lehigh University, USA)

J. Harold Ellens, James Waddell, Ronald Ruark, Jason von Ehrenkrook, and Aaron Brunell of the University of Michigan served as secretaries of the conference.

The third meeting of the Enoch Seminar is scheduled at the Monastery of Camaldoli, Arezzo, Italy (6-10 June 2005), and will be entirely devoted to the study of the Book of the Parables (or Similitudes) of Enoch and to the problem of the Messiah "Son of Man." In 2007 the topic will be "Enoch and Christian Origins" (John the Baptist, Jesus, Paul, and the Synoptic tradition), while in 2009 we will explore the legacy of Enochic Judaism in the Jesus movement and in Jewish traditions after the destruction of the second temple in books like the Gospel of John, Revelation, 2 Baruch, 4 Ezra, and 2 Enoch (the title for the conference is "The Legacy of Enochic Judaism").

It is sufficient to review the list of participants to measure the international impact of these biennial meetings. Even more significant than the geographical distribution is the contribution of specialists from different fields — Old Testament, Dead Sea Scrolls, Jewish apocalypticism and mysticism, Old Testament pseudepigrapha, New Testament, Christian and rabbinic origins. The presence of Enoch texts among the Dead Sea Scrolls, the literary and ideological connections with Old and New Testament documents, and the uncountable ramifications of Enochic ideas and concepts in the many Judaisms of the second temple period, including early Christianity, make the study of Enoch literature a central issue for any specialist in ancient Judaism and Christian origins. The Enoch Seminar has become the laboratory for an interdisciplinary experiment that has no parallel in any other field, such as that of "biblical" studies, which has been for centuries so heavily shaped and constrained by canonical boundaries.

Not only has the Enoch Seminar provided an opportunity for meeting and discussion, it has also prompted in these last years a renewed interest in Enoch that has materialized in the writing of numerous books, articles, reviews, and dissertations. The Enoch Seminar itself has promoted the publication of collections of essays. The first was the 2002 volume *The Origins of Enochic Judaism* (Turin: Zamorani, 2002 [= *Henoch* 14.1-2, 2002]), in which twenty-three specialists explored the intellectual and sociological origins of Enochic Judaism as well as the early theology of the movement and its relations with the Zadokite priesthood and the Wisdom tradition. The current volume, *Enoch and Qumran Origins,* is the second major publication sponsored by the Enoch Seminar. A third publication project (*The Early Enoch Tradition,* edited by Gabriele Boccaccini and George Nickelsburg) is in the making, which deals specifically with the theology and sociology of the early Enoch movement. Recently two new English translations of 1 Enoch have been published: Daniel Olson, *Enoch: A New Translation* (North Richland Hills, Tex.: BIBAL, 2004), and George Nickelsburg and James VanderKam, *The Book of Enoch* (Minneapolis: Fortress, 2004). Much more is to come. A collection of essays on the Similitudes is planned as a result of the third meeting of the Enoch Seminar at Camaldoli, while we all look forward to the publication of the second volume of George Nickelsburg's commentary, which in collaboration with James VanderKam will cover the Astronomical Book and the Similitudes of Enoch, thus providing the most complete and detailed scholarly commentary on the book of Enoch since its "rediscovery" in the eighteenth century.

Gabriele Boccaccini

3. Enoch and Qumran Origins

How do the Dead Sea Scrolls affect our knowledge of Enoch literature? And how does the Enoch literature affect our understanding of Qumran? In particular, how does the study of Enoch challenge or modify the Essene Hypothesis, and to what extent does it support or dismiss alternative hypotheses, such as García Martínez's Groningen Hypothesis and Boccaccini's Essene-Enochic Hypothesis? These questions were the subject of the Venice meeting of the Enoch Seminar, and are the subject of the present volume.

When the Enoch Seminar met in Venice in July 2003, the first volume of Nickelsburg's commentary on 1 Enoch had just been published. This work can be taken as representative of the *status quaestionis,* if not of the consensus of contemporary scholarship on 1 Enoch and its relationship with Qumran studies on the eve of the Venice meeting. Thus, in a short paragraph Nickelsburg summarized the relationship between Enoch and the Qumran community: "Although there is no evidence that any of the Enochic text was composed at Qumran, the fragments from Cave 1 and Cave 4 indicate that the Enochic texts were favorites to this community. . . . Furthermore, references to community formation in CD 1 and 1QS 8 parallel some of the details in the Apocalypse of Weeks and suggest that the Qumran Community was a latter-day derivative of or successor to the community or communities that authored and transmitted the Enochic texts."[25]

If there was indeed such closeness between the Enoch tradition and Qumran, so much so that a parent-child relation can be posited, and if Enochic Judaism was an anti-Zadokite tradition, how can the idea of Qumran as a priestly Zadokite movement still be sustained?

The Zadokite high priests were in charge of the temple on the eve of the Maccabean revolt. Since in the sectarian scrolls the members of the Qumran sect refer to themselves as "sons of Zadok," the classical Essene Hypothesis maintained that the leadership at Qumran was provided by members of the priestly House of Zadok. Once they lost power and the Maccabees became the new dynasty of high priests, they would have retreated to the wilderness in protest.

25. Nickelsburg, *1 Enoch,* 65. That the Essene community at Qumran was the offspring of the Enochic party is the core of Boccaccini's Enochic-Essene Hypothesis (see G. Boccaccini, *Beyond the Essene Hypothesis: The Parting of the Ways between Qumran and Enochic Judaism* [Grand Rapids: Eerdmans, 1998]). Recently, this idea has been reiterated by David R. Jackson, who concludes his analysis of Enochic Judaism by claiming that "the Qumran sectarian works are works of Enochic Judaism" (see D. R. Jackson, *Enochic Judaism: Three Defining Paradigm Exemplars* [London: T&T Clark, 2004], 221).

The problem with such a reconstruction is that all ancient sources agree that the descendants of the Zadokite high priests fled not to Qumran but to Egypt, where they built a rival temple at Heliopolis. We should have in the first place more properly spoken of a split within the Zadokite family.

The Enoch literature provides yet another major difficulty. From the presence of many copies of Enoch texts in the Qumran library and from the many references to the Enoch literature in the sectarian scrolls, we know that the early Enoch tradition was held in great esteem at Qumran, especially in the earlier period of the origins of the community. If the Qumranites were a Zadokite movement, why did they preserve not only Zadokite texts (like the Mosaic torah) but also a large collection of anti-Zadokite texts?

Furthermore, the Enoch theology was very influential in the shaping of Qumran theology, no less than the covenantal Zadokite theology. If the Qumranites were a Zadokite movement, why did they share the Enochic idea that the second temple was since the beginning a contaminated temple led by an illegitimate priesthood? If the Qumranites were Zadokite, we would expect an apology for the temple before the Maccabean rise to power. Members of the House of Zadok would have never dismissed the legitimacy of the second temple without losing their own identity and undermining their claim to be the only legitimate priesthood.

Yet, while calling themselves the "sons of Zadok," the Qumranites seemed to despise everything the Zadokites had done, and held in great esteem the literature of their Enochic enemies. Should we face the impossible paradox of a Zadokite movement rooted in an anti-Zadokite ideology? Or should we read the references to the "sons of Zadok" typologically, as Philip Davies already suggested many years ago, and not as evidence of an actual genealogical relation?[26]

In this volume the reader will find different emphases on the role of Enoch at Qumran, and different assessments on the relationship between Enochians, Essenes, and Qumranites. There is no consensus on whether it was the Enochians who became the Essenes, or, more likely, whether they were a component of that large movement with which the Qumran community was in some way associated. Yet a new, shared awareness unites all the specialists who have worked in this project — the mystery of Essene and Qumran origins is largely hidden in the Enoch literature.

---

26. P. R. Davies, "Sons of Zadok," in *Behind the Essenes: History and Ideology in the Dead Sea Scrolls* (Atlanta: Scholars, 1987), 51-72.

4. This Volume

This volume was not planned as a celebration. The distinguished group of scholars who participated in the Venice meeting of the Enoch Seminar had four days of passionate and substantive meetings, which — hard to believe! — for the seven-to-eight hours of daily seminar duty made them totally oblivious to the tempting beauty of the hosting city and apparently happy with their secluded discussions. As the participants were all specialists who had published extensively in the field, they were asked to contribute short essays, exercising constructive criticism, highlighting the most controversial issues, stressing disagreement more than celebrating consensus, so that the discussion could target the substance of the problems.

After the conference all participants, including some members of the Enoch Seminar (namely, William Adler, Peter Flint, and Loren Stuckenbruck) who had been unable to attend the Venice meeting, were invited to revise their notes and express their thoughts (and afterthoughts) around five major topics, focusing on the work of the five specialists who were asked to respond. The first step was to assess the influence of the Enochic tradition on two documents that certainly played a central role in Qumran origins, that is, Daniel and Jubilees, by revisiting the work of John Collins and James VanderKam. Then the emphasis was placed on the piece of Enoch literature that appears to be closer to the time of Qumran origins, that is, the Apocalypse of Weeks — a work to which George Nickelsburg has devoted so much attention. Finally, we revisited two recent hypotheses on Qumran origins, García Martínez's Groningen Hypothesis and Boccaccini's Enochic-Essene Hypothesis, which both present Qumran as an outgrowth of the Enochic apocalyptic tradition.

The result is a very engaging and substantive discussion among forty-seven specialists from eleven countries (the United States, Canada, France, Belgium, the Netherlands, Italy, Germany, the United Kingdom, Norway, Hungary, and Israel). Reading this book offers a unique experience of total immersion in the contemporary scholarly debate, where questions prevail over answers and doubts over certainties, but where above all there exists an eagerness to understand and make sense of the often puzzling evidence.

I will leave to the reader and to the skill and experience of James Charlesworth in his summary and conclusions the task of assessing how deeply our knowledge in the field has advanced as a result of our discussions. Very little remains at this point to be said except to thank all distinguished specialists who have contributed to the volume, the Ph.D. students who have helped complete the editing process, and the publisher Eerdmans for adhering so enthusiastically to this project. For all of us it has been a fascinating intellectual journey — an experience that we hope the reader also will share and enjoy.

PART ONE

DREAM VISIONS AND DANIEL

Enoch's Dream Visions and the Visions of Daniel Reexamined

Matthias Henze

In his elegant book *The Sense of an Ending,* critic Frank Kermode describes how the human imagination is drawn again and again to moments we call crises in trying to give some order and design to the past, present, and future (Kermode 2000, 94). The perception is that the crisis at hand is somehow pre-eminent, more worrisome, and more significant than other crises, resulting in a feeling of urgency that fuels the apocalyptic mind. This powerful eschatological element which Kermode describes in modern English fiction is at work also, *mutatis mutandis,* in early Jewish apocalypses. The present essay is concerned with this sense of an ending in two contemporary compositions, the Enochic book of Dream Visions (1 En 83–90) and Daniel's apocalyptic visions (Dan 7–12), two apocalypses that show a significant degree of homogeneity.

There appears to be a steadily growing consensus in the field, anchored to no small degree upon the work of John Collins, that holds that Judaism in the late second temple period was rather diverse in nature and included not one but several apocalyptic groups. In his classic *Judaism and Hellenism,* Martin Hengel proposed that an organized group, the "assembly of the pious," or Hasidim (1 Macc 2:42; 7:12-13; 2 Macc 14:6), was the precursor of both the Essenes, and subsequently of the Qumran community, and of the Pharisees. It was this group that produced Dream Visions (1 En 83–90), the Apocalypse of Weeks (1 En 93:1-10; 91:11-17), the Epistle of Enoch (1 En 91–108), and the book of Daniel (Hengel 1974, 1:175-80; Tcherikover 1970, 197-203).

In response Collins, among others, argued in a number of publications that apocalypticism cannot be identified with any single group. While there is undoubtedly a tradition-historical continuity that links the Enochic and Danielic writings with the Qumran community, this by no means precludes the possibility that we are dealing with more than one group. Thus Collins writes, "Enoch is not invoked as a revelatory authority in the literature of the Dead Sea sect. This would be surprising if the books of Enoch that we have were produced by an early stage of the same movement. Moreover, other lines of continuity can be traced in the scrolls, for example, with the book of Daniel, and with Sadducean halakhic traditions. It is likely that the Dead Sea sect was fed by more than one tributary stream" (Collins 1998b, 29; 1998a, 70-79).

In subsequent publications Collins has brought his view about the nature of the groups that formed these "tributary streams" further into focus. Thus he writes in his article on pseudepigraphy and group formation, "I have argued that the groups in question should not be conflated. Rather we should postulate a multiplicity of groups in the early second century BCE, groups that were probably quite small and loosely structured" (Collins 1999, 55).

The differences between Hengel and Collins in their respective assessments of second temple Judaism should not be overdrawn. It is true that Hengel calls the Hasidim "a clearly defined Jewish party" and portrays them rather broadly as the parent movement of second temple Jewry, but he is also aware of a plethora of "other pietistic and conventicle-like splinter-groups who emerged from the Hasidim" (Hengel 1974, 175 and 179), a view not incompatible with that of Collins. In the end Collins's insistence that we are dealing with different groups of modest size, several of which have influenced the Qumran community, will undoubtedly find broad support.

I will take as my point of departure Gabriele Boccaccini's wonderfully challenging *Beyond the Essene Hypothesis*. Boccaccini understands his volume as a "study of the history of competing philosophical positions in antiquity." The two main representatives are, of course, Enochic and Zadokite Judaism, two distinct strands of Judaism which in his view follow ideologies that are "directly opposed" to one another (Boccaccini 1998, xiv, 72). Boccaccini is certainly right to point out that the texts under consideration reflect significant disagreement on such fundamental issues as the priesthood, the calendar, and the origin of evil. However, it is less clear to me that his "method of systematic analysis of middle Judaic documents" (8) fits the subject. In other words, there is a certain temptation to exaggerate alleged differences between the texts, hoping to arrive at a sociological description of two fundamentally opposed groups whose existence is merely postulated, when in fact we are first of all comparing texts, not sociological groups, and second, there is no reason why such different positions on theological issues could not have existed in a single group. I propose that there is little in the texts to suggest that the groups behind them were either "competing" or "opposed." To the contrary, the texts seem quite compatible, as were, I suspect, the groups who wrote them.

Numerous interpreters have pointed to the extensive parallels between Daniel 7 and the Animal Apocalypse (1 En 85–90). This is a well-plowed field in apocalyptic scholarship, to which many scholars have put their spade. Suffice it to say at this point that both texts, composed during the years 167-163 B.C.E. (Collins 1993, 61; Nickelsburg 2001, 361; Tiller 1993, 78-79), include pseudonymous dream visions featuring predators symbolizing rulers or kingdoms, an animal transformed into a man, animals with horns of extraordinary size, a throne set up for God to sit in judgment as books are opened before him, and animals being destroyed by fire (Goldingay 1989, 150).

The authors of Enoch's and Daniel's visions used related traditions. This is evident, furthermore, from the division of the period of apostasy in the Animal Apocalypse into four segments, a division similar to the four-kingdom schema in Daniel 2 and 7 (Nickelsburg 2001, 360), and from the depiction of the throne-room scene in Daniel 7:9-14 and 1 Enoch 14. Yet there are also differences: Boccaccini, among others, has thus proposed that the two texts stem from different parties, an argument supported by the different views he finds in the texts regarding the legitimacy of the second temple, the origin of evil, the role played by angels, a passive versus a militant support of the Maccabees, and the importance of the Mosaic torah (Boccaccini 1998, 81-86).

While Boccaccini's proposition of different authorial groups is shared by the majority of scholars, and rightfully so, it seems nonetheless that the differences between the texts have been exaggerated. The importance, or lack thereof, of the Mosaic torah, often seen to present a striking difference between Enochic and Danielic Judaisms, may serve as a good example. In her recent review article of Boccaccini's *Essene Hypothesis,* Hindy Najman responded to his claim that the Enochians completely ignore the Mosaic torah and the Jerusalem temple: "Indeed, the claim that Enochians 'ignored' the torah of Enoch's 'rival Moses' is supported only by an argument from silence: 1 Enoch's omission of the Mosaic covenant and the gift of torah. It is unclear what such omissions prove, especially since Boccaccini does not explain which traditions and laws were then thought to compromise Mosaic torah" (Najman 2002, 352-53).

Najman's point is well taken, and not only with respect to Boccaccini's work; it applies to our comparison of the Animal Apocalypse and Daniel's visions as well. It is of course true that the torah of Moses receives only scant attention in the Enochic corpus, but so also in Daniel, which barely refers to the law of Moses.

There are further methodological problems here. An evaluation of the two apocalypses cannot be based primarily on a comparison of long lists of what are deemed to be key features in the texts, drawn up somewhat arbitrarily by each interpreter. These lists of features are awkwardly reminiscent of similar lists compiled by scholars in the twentieth century in an effort to arrive at an agreement on what constitutes the apocalyptic genre, an approach that was rightfully rejected for being arbitrary and misleading (Hanson 1975, 6-7). Instead, a sound evaluation of the Enochic and Danielic apocalypses has to begin by considering the texts' overall form and purpose.

The most striking commonality between the apocalypses is their extensive use of literary forms that were not used in earlier writings, such as *ex eventu* prophecies and pseudonymous dream visions. As for the differences, Daniel shows no cosmological interest, and with the exception of Daniel 9, which is almost certainly secondary, the book is not covenantal. The calendar marks another important difference. It is equally important to ask about the purpose for which the visions were composed. Daniel's visions reflect a strong sense of an imminent end, no doubt propelled by the presently experienced persecutions, an aspect less pronounced in Enoch's visions.

I want to take my argument one step further, however, and propose as my second thesis that Enochic and Danielic strands of apocalyptic thought are not merely compatible, but merged at an early stage. The fluid nature of the material, as well as the ease with which the traditions were transmitted and blended, may well be indicative of how the apocalypticists themselves evolved intellectually and how they operated as groups.

Among the Dead Sea Scrolls are several writings that are associated with Daniel, though their precise link with the canonical book is a matter of contention and has to be established for each text individually. Especially relevant for our debate are the so-called Pseudo-Daniel texts from Cave 4. According to the current arrangement of the fragments by John Collins and Peter Flint, the first of the two texts (4Q243 and 244) has three parts: the opening episode introduces both Daniel and the alleged court setting; there then follows a review of history from the primeval period all the way to the Hellenistic age; and, in good apocalyptic fashion, the text concludes with what appears to be an eschatological finale (Collins 1996a).

In spite of the fragmentary state of the manuscript, it is possible to make a few tentative observations. Much like the Greek Additions to Daniel, Pseudo-Daniel may have been composed in the mid–second century B.C.E., possibly right around the time of the completion of the biblical book. Also like the Greek Additions, the texts do not appear to depend on the biblical book. In other words, Pseudo-Daniel and the additions are not later interpretations of an already-fixed Daniel tradition, but independent compositions that almost certainly stem from different circles.

The review of the primeval period in the first Pseudo-Daniel text includes a reference to Enoch. In his article on Daniel and Enoch in the Dead Sea Scrolls, Loren Stuckenbruck makes much of this. He points out that the first Pseudo-Daniel text shares several features with the Enochic tradition: (1) the designation of the righteous as "the elect" who "will be gathered together" (1 En 90:33; 93:10); (2) the presence of the demonic in biblical history; and (3) an interest in preexilic events, for which he finds the closest analogy not in the book of Jubilees, as Collins and Flint would have it, but in 1 Enoch 85–86. In the end Stuckenbruck suggests that the Pseudo-Daniel texts present "a blending of Danielic and Enochic traditions which takes a form found in neither Daniel nor the Animal Apocalypse" (Stuckenbruck 2001, 375).

The differences between the Enochic and Danielic texts did not deter the author of Pseudo-Daniel from using both traditions to create his own apocalyptic scenario. More importantly still, this happened right around the time when Hebrew/Aramaic Daniel reached its final form and, as virtually all scholars have suggested, it happened quite independently of the canonical book. The nature of the material suggests that we should not think of apocalyptic groups of the second century B.C.E. in terms of continuous and independent strands of traditions that are ultimately opposed to one another. After all, apocalyptic literature is characterized by a high degree of fluctuation and translatability, with later apocalypses constantly recycling language, imagery, and entire literary genres found in earlier material. The confluence of Danielic and Enochic traditions is most evident in the Similitudes of Enoch (1 En 37–71), and particularly in the "son of man," who figures prominently in the second parable (1 En 46:2, 3, 4; 48:2), and who is clearly influenced by Daniel 7 and the vision of the "one like a human being" arriving in a cloud to meet the Ancient of Days and to receive dominion.

This brings me to my third and final point. In the attempt to describe the diverse apocalyptic groups of the second century B.C.E., much has been made of what appears to be epithetical self-descriptions of these circles, such as "the lambs" in the Animal Apocalypse, "the chosen righteous" in the Apocalypse of Weeks, and "the wise" in Daniel. The epithets are cast in theological, not in sociohistorical, language. In effect, these deliberately vague terms disguise rather than reveal the true identity of their authors. The purpose of the epithets is both to legitimize the group in question by making the claim that they have been singled out by God to assume a unique role in the end time and to convey a message of hope that their struggle is not in vain.

The purpose of the epithets is not to reveal the group's identity beyond their theological self-understanding, which now becomes their dominant point of reference. The texts mention certain oppositions, though I am less certain about the nature of the opposition at the end of the second Pseudo-Daniel text; but the opposition implied in the epithets is between all of Israel that went astray and the group in question which was saved, not between rival splinter groups. Also, epithets, much like the Enochic and Danielic traditions discussed above, traveled: the same or related group designations were clearly used by more than one group. This is exemplified most clearly in the motif of "blindness," an expression of apostasy, in the second Pseudo-Daniel text ("these in blindness" in 4Q245 frg. 2 i 3), the Apocalypse of Weeks (1 En 93:8), the Animal Apocalypse (1 En 89:32, 41, [54], 74; 90:7, 26; Nickelsburg 2001, 380-81), and the blind people groping for the way in the opening column of the *Damascus Document* (1:9-10).

Related or identical epithets in different texts hardly point to one and the same group. Annette Reed has cautioned us in this volume not to conflate different forms of continuity. Textual continuities need not be identical with sociological continuities. The use of the same epithet in different texts is a case in point, as these were clearly used by more than one group. Moreover, the distinct character of text production, redaction, and transmission in ancient Judaism renders problematic any easy or uncritical equation of a given text with a single Jewish party.

In conclusion, Collins's description of the apocalyptic circles as small is certainly correct. I am less certain that they were "loosely structured." A general impression of apocalyptic conventicles would suggest otherwise. Also, in light of the fluid nature of the material, it must be asked how stable the groups were over time. Both Enoch and Daniel are composites to begin with, stemming from more than one group. Both books are the result of long processes of transmission. In the case of Daniel we know that the groups of tradents changed (Henze 2001). There are also significant methodological limitations: the data we work with are informative only to a certain degree (Nickelsburg 1983). What we have are allegorical dream reports cast in highly stylized language, not sociological descriptions of actual groups.

The Sociological Context of
the Dream Visions of Daniel and 1 Enoch

Patrick Tiller

One of the urgent topics for the study of Enochic literature is the question of the possible relationships between the groups that produced the visions of Daniel and Enoch. Very often we treat this as a theological question, certainly a legitimate approach. It is interesting and helpful to consider the relationships between the theologies of the various texts; but theologies are not groups. What I want to consider is the *sociological* question of the relationships between the producers of the literature.

Very little may be known with certainty about the social organization of pre-Maccabean Judea. It was ruled by Seleucid Syria as a part of the province Coele-Syria. There was a tradition of high priestly rule, and it seems that the high priest and his fellow priests usually functioned as imperial agents and as local leaders. The high priest had rivals, one of whom, Joseph the Tobiad, was able to gain the right in the previous century to collect imperial taxes for the Ptolemaic rulers in Egypt, if one accepts Josephus's story as even a little bit historical. By the time of Antiochus IV, however, the high priesthood had again become a lucrative and powerful position, as evidenced by the expensive and deadly struggles to obtain it. In addition, there was a council of elders, the *gerousia,* but its makeup and responsibilities are unknown.

High priestly rule was maintained both militarily and ideologically. The Syrian rulers no doubt supplied military support, but the high priest seems to have had some of his own troops as well (2 Macc 4:40; Josephus, *Ant.* 12.239-40). The ideology was traditional but needed to be maintained by the constant reinforcement of the performance of the temple cult and the teaching of sages such as Ben Sira. The book of Sirach provides us with the clearest, and possibly most biased, contemporary picture of the political-social structure of Seleucid Judea, since it attempts to prescribe as well as describe. It presupposes an orderly society over which the high priest and his fellow priests rule, with sages like Ben Sira serving as teachers of the people, advisers, judges, diplomats, and the like.

This picture is confirmed by the decree of Antiochus III, preserved in Josephus, *Antiquities* 12.138-44, which, within the Seleucid Empire, established Jerusalem as the center of a temple state led by a council of elders, and the priests with the scribes and temple singers as privileged aristocracy. James Ellis Taylor summarizes his conclusions about this decree: "Seleucid rule in Jerusalem rested on a series of privileges and benefactions that are fairly simple and direct in nature and easily paralleled in ancient political life" (Taylor 1979, 170). These privileges and benefactions were granted to the council of elders, the priests, and other temple personnel.

Ben Sira's portrait of Judea as a harmonious society that revolved around the political, economic, and religious rule of the high priest is, however, false. Seleucid rule was maintained in part by establishing competing and independent authorities, all of whom reported directly to the king. There is a hint of this competition in the fact that Antiochus's decree establishes the *gerousia*, the council of elders, as chief in the Jerusalem hierarchy, but by the time of Antiochus IV it is the high priest. The fact that provincial officials were dependent directly on the king and not on some local chief is illustrated by the Scythopolis Inscription published by Y. H. Landau (1966, 54-70, cited in Taylor 1979, 108) and studied in detail by Taylor in his dissertation (108-68). Taylor has shown that Ptolemy, the *strategos* and high priest of Coele-Syria and the addressee of Antiochus's decree concerning Jerusalem, functioned as governor with a supervisory role over all the sanctuaries in the land, including the one in Jerusalem. Yet, despite his apparently powerful position, Ptolemy had little or no authority over other local financial and logistical administrators *(dioiketai)*. The inscription is a record of correspondence with the Syrian king concerning disputes between Ptolemy and other agents of the empire, including local garrison commanders.

Sages were members of the privileged aristocracy that depended in part upon imperial and/or priestly benefactions for their position and stature in society. Inasmuch as their patrons had conflicting interests and loyalties, the interests and loyalties of the sages/scribes would also conflict (Horsley and Tiller 2002, 74-107). It is in this context that we should think about the social setting in which the dream visions in Daniel and 1 Enoch were produced.

These visions give very little clear evidence of the social location of their creators. Nevertheless, there are some hints that can reasonably be adduced.

The Animal Apocalypse positions itself within a group of elect Judeans around the beginning of the second century B.C.E. that began to proclaim its own version of piety, with no dependence on the "corrupt" temple, and engaged in some form of armed resistance (Tiller 1993, 109-26). Indications in both Sirach and 1 Enoch (especially book 5) show that Ben Sira and the Enochic sages operated in conscious opposition to each other (Wright 1997, 189-222; Argall 1995, 249-55). Both books present their authors as sages and teachers, with their own unique traditions. The Enochic sages write to oppose high priestly rule while Ben Sira writes to establish and uphold it. Both propose innovations over against the structure prescribed by Antiochus's decree, which seems to establish the *gerousia* over the priests and does not mention the high priest at all. The close literary (unless it is oral) relationship between the Book of the Watchers and Dream Visions probably indicates a succession of Enochic teachers who maintained and passed on the Enochic tradition. This is different from Jubilees, where traditions about Enoch are retold, but with less faithfulness to the traditions told in the name of Enoch.

The producers of Daniel seem to self-identify with the *maskilim,* whose task is to instruct people and lead them to righteousness and to accept martyrdom, and eventually to shine like the stars of heaven (Dan 11:33-35; 12:3). Although the biblical book of Daniel offers little evidence for a continuing tradition, the existence of Pseudo-Daniel fragments at Qumran attests the existence of more than one apocalyptic text that was written in Daniel's name. It is therefore possible that the several authors were associated in one way or another. Further, as Stuckenbruck (2001, 378-85) has pointed out, there is probably some direct literary or traditional dependence between the Book of the Giants (4Q530 2:15b-20) and Daniel 7:9-10, 28. This would imply that the tradents of the Danielic traditions and/or those of the Enochic traditions made use of each other's work.

The kind of community that we imagine might have produced the Enochic and Danielic literature depends on our model. If we think Enoch and Daniel are inscribed performances of oral tradition, then we can consider political or ethnic groups like villages or larger populations. For example, the early chapters of Daniel may represent oral traditions that circulated among the Jewish diaspora of the time. Another kind of group could be a community connected by religion. For example, most of the early Christian apocrypha are essentially written copies of performances of oral traditions that were developed and transmitted within the Christian churches. In both examples we have sociologically identifiable communities, with boundaries and rules of their own.

Nothing in either Enoch or Daniel, however, can be realistically taken as evidence for a community, unless by community one means only an aggregate of individuals with similar interests. However, when we speak of community or group, we usually have in mind an organized social structure with defined boundaries and constraints. Having a common hero and theology does not imply social structure. Horsley makes a similar argument concerning the Epistle of Enoch: "We should not think that 1 Enoch 92–105 is the product of a movement or group any more than we would understand the text of Sirach as testimony to Ben Sira heading a social movement" (Horsley 2000, 115). Nor does anything in either book argue for a kind of exclusive claim to election or advice to withdraw from the larger society.

Both books assume that the wise will function as teachers for many others who are not among the wise and that this teaching will be based on revealed wisdom. This is implied in the Animal Apocalypse and clearly stated both in Ben Sira and in the Epistle of Enoch (Nickelsburg 1982, 333-48). We do not know to what extent these teachers were able to gain a popular following, nor do we know whether any real social groups ever defined their boundaries in terms of adherence to the teachings of either "Enoch" or "Daniel." As we are reminded by Lester Grabbe, "there is no necessary connection between apocalypses and apocalyptic communities" (Grabbe 1989, 29). It is, in fact, difficult to imagine what sort of community or social movement could have been devoted to the cultivation of either Danielic or Enochic wisdom. It is far more likely that the sages who produced both sets of literature were members of a larger social group and that their teachings were largely compatible with the ideals of the group.

We know that the producers of the visionary literature and/or traditions understood themselves to function as teachers and as sages. That the writers of apocalyptic literature are connected with wisdom teachers is by now a commonplace assumption in scholarship (Smith 1978, 74; Collins 1984, 30; Grabbe 1989, 27-47). This is precisely the social function that Ben Sira claimed for himself in his book on wisdom. Nothing in Daniel, Enoch, or Sirach can be taken as evidence for the existence of a community, group, or movement. There is evidence only for the existence of a class of professional sages and teachers, trained in the traditions of their aristocratic or apocalyptic wisdom, whose politically charged teachings had an impact on their own and subsequent generations.

Dream Visions and Apocalyptic Milieus

Armin Lange

In his article "Pseudepigraphy and Group Formation in Second Temple Judaism," John Collins asks whether in the second century B.C.E. we encounter one apocalyptic movement or a multiplicity of small conventicle-like apocalyptic groups (Collins 1999; cf. 1998a, 70-79). Each of these supposed groups would relate to the pseudepigraphic namesake of their apocalyptic writings. Each of the apocalypses and pseudepigraphic prophecies Collins analyzes in his article would foretell the rise of an elect group. Apparently, the authors of the apocalyptic texts in question understood themselves as part of these elect groups.

Traditionally, the tradents behind both the Enochic and Danielic apocalypses as well as those behind the book of Jubilees were perceived as one and the same group, which was then identified as the so-called New Covenant, that is, the parent movement of the Qumran group (Hengel 1974, 1:175-180; cf. Collins 1999, 44n). Contrary to this view, Collins shows that in descriptions of the elect groups in the Enochic and Danielic apocalypses, more differences than parallels can be found. Here only a few examples of the differences observed by Collins are given (Collins 1999, 44-49, 55-58).

1. The self-designations of authors and tradents of the apocalypses in question are different. The Apocalypse of Weeks (1 En 93:1-10; 91:11-17) describes the "elect ones of righteousness from the eternal plant of righteousness" (e.g., 93:10). In the Book of the Watchers (1 En 1–36) they are designated "the plant of creation" (e.g., 11:16), and in the Animal Apocalypse (1 En 85–90), "small lambs." In the book of Daniel the authors and/or tradents describe themselves as *maskilim*.

2. The attitude toward the torah is different. The *Damascus Document* and

other Essene texts from the Qumran library attest to a penitential movement mainly concerned with the torah, while the figure of Enoch precedes the torah and the revelation supposedly given to him in the Enochic literature concerns matters about which the torah has little to say.

3. In contrast with the lambs of the Animal Apocalypse, the *maskilim* of the book of Daniel do not appear to take up arms and seem to regard the Maccabees as only "a little help" (Dan 11:34).

4. Pseudepigraphy is absent in the Essene texts from Qumran while it is abundant in Enochic and Danielic literature.

Therefore Collins argues against the existence of one apocalyptic movement and for a multiplicity of small conventicle-like apocalyptic groups. Collins's argument is based on well-analyzed evidence and his conclusions can hardly be rejected. But if in the second century B.C.E. there is not just one homogenous apocalyptic movement, it remains to be asked how the different apocalyptic conventicles related to each other. Is it possible that at least some of these groups shared a common milieu? This question is especially difficult as almost no sociological data are preserved. But an answer might be provided by an analysis of the imagery and visionary techniques employed by the different apocalypses in question. Such an approach might be all the more promising if from the same time several apocalypses are preserved. This would allow direct comparison of documents contemporary with each other. Therefore, this study will analyze the visionary techniques and symbolic codes in the Enochic and Danielic literature from the Maccabean era. Afterward I will turn to the book of Jubilees to ask whether the parallels between the Enochic and Danielic literature attest to an overall apocalyptic milieu.

Enochic Literature

The Enochic Animal Apocalypse (1 En 85–90) in the book of Dream Visions (1 En 83–90) is a good starting point.[1] This text presents itself as a symbolic dream vision received by Enoch. In symbolic cipher Enoch foresees the whole history of Israel from Adam and Eve until Judas Maccabeus. When it comes to the Animal Apocalypse, it is almost a truism of Enochic research that in this text earthly realities are symbolized by fauna and flora while otherworldly realities are symbolized by human figures or stars. For example, Israel's ancestors from Adam and Eve to Isaac and Rebecca are depicted as bovines (85:3–89:12). From Jacob onward Israel and the Israelites are depicted as sheep (89:12ff.). Rams represent the kings and

---

1. For the date of this document, see Tiller (1993, 61-82) and Nickelsburg (2001, 25-26).

rulers of Israel and Judah (see, e.g., Saul and David in 89:42-48; compare Judas Maccabeus as a horn of a ram in 90:9, 13). On the other hand, in 89:59ff., 90:1 the patron angels of the nations are described as shepherds (*APOT,* 255; Hengel 1974, 1:187; Tiller 1993, 324-326; Nickelsburg 2001, 390).[2] If someone moves from the earthly to the heavenly realm, this change in quality is symbolized by a change in shape. Thus, 86:1, 3 describes the fallen Watchers as stars which became bovines (cf. 86–88), and 89:1, 9 describes Noah as a bovine which became a human. Likewise, 89:36, 38 describes the transformation of Moses from sheep to human.[3]

The same symbolic system seems to have been employed in what is left of the Enochic Book of Giants.[4] In 4QEnGiants[b] (4Q530) II 3-20, the author incorporated two symbolic dreams by the giants Hahyah and 'Ohyah. In his dream the giant Hahyah sees trees representing the giants, trees threatened by water and fire. The giant 'Ohyah dreams of the ruler of the earth sitting down upon a throne, a scene strikingly reminiscent of Daniel 7. Again the earthly and the otherworldly realities are represented by either flora or a human being. Thus, the Book of Giants employs the same symbolic code as the Animal Apocalypse. So far we can say that the two compositions of the Enochic conventicle used the same imagery and visionary technique. But are this imagery and this visionary technique restricted to the Enochic book of Dream Visions?

Danielic Literature

To answer this question the Danielic literature, especially the book of Daniel,[5] needs to be analyzed. It is not necessary to repeat all of Collins's arguments

---

2. VanderKam (1984, 165-67; 1995, 85-89) has shown that the imagery used by the Animal Apocalypse is influenced by prophetic texts, especially Jer 25. But such an influence exerted by prophetic literature only explains why for its symbolic code the Animal Apocalypse chose the particular animals it used in 1 En 85–90 and does not argue against a shared symbolic code used by a wider group of apocalyptic conventicles.

3. For the transfigurations of Noah and Moses from animals to angels, see Porter (1983, 53), Collins (1998a, 68), Nickelsburg (2001, 375, 377, 381-82), and Tiller (1993, 259, 267, 295-96). For transfigurations of Moses and other prominent figures of Israelite history in ancient Jewish literature, see Charlesworth (1980), Himmelfarb (1991), and Moses (1996, 20-84).

4. The Enochic Book of Giants is much more difficult to date than the Animal Apocalypse or the book of Daniel. Stuckenbruck (1997a, 31) suggests that the Book of Giants "may have been written sometime between the Book of the Watchers and Daniel, that is, sometime between the late third century and 164 BCE." As a dating sometime close to or during the Maccabean era seems quite possible to me, I have included this text in my analysis.

5. For the Maccabean date of the book of Daniel, see Soggin (1989, 475-77), Collins (1993, 61), and Kaiser (1994, 171).

concerning why the two groups behind the Enochic and the Danielic literatures should be judged as different groups. It is enough to note that the two groups use different self-designations. In the Apocalypse of Weeks (1 En 93:1-10; 91:11-17) the Enochic group calls itself the eternal plant of righteousness or the elect ones from the eternal plant of righteousness (e.g., 93:10), emphasizing the ethical aim of this group. On the other hand, the group behind the book of Daniel seems to have called itself the *maskilim* ("instructors"; Dan 11:33, 35; 12:3, 10), emphasizing their sapiential character. Furthermore, in Maccabean times the Danielic and Enochic circles seem to have had different attitudes toward Judas Maccabeus and his comrades. While the Animal Apocalypse mentions Judas in positive terms (1 En 90:9-14), the book of Daniel does not refer to him at all. "Daniel's failure to indicate clear support for the Maccabees, then, was not necessarily entailed by the apocalyptic emphasis on the heavenly battle. Rather, it would seem that there were different positions within the Jewish resistance, and that of Daniel must be distinguished from that of the Maccabees and even from that of the Animal Apocalypse" (Collins 1993, 66-67).

Despite their origin from two different groups, texts deriving from the Enochic and the Danielic conventicles use the same symbolic cipher to depict the otherworldly and the earthly realities, that is, fauna and flora versus stars and human shapes. In Daniel 4 a huge tree symbolizes Nebuchadnezzar's reign[6] while birds and other animals represent his subjects. A holy Watcher, whose physical appearance is not described, descends from heaven and gives a command to cut the tree down. In Daniel 7:2-14 a sequence of four beasts, ten horns, and another horn represents a sequence of four kingdoms, ten Hellenistic kings, and Antiochus IV Epiphanes. In 7:9-14 the heavenly judgment and the following eschaton are described by using a cast of human figures. For example, in 7:9 there is an ancient one sitting on a throne and in 7:13 a figure "like a son of a man."[7] In Daniel 8 a ram with two horns (8:3-4) symbolizes the kings of Media and Persia, while the rest of the population is represented by "all beasts" (8:4). Following the Persian Empire in 8:5-12, the Hellenistic kingdoms are represented by a male goat with first one and then four horns. Out of one of these four horns grows a large horn representing Antiochus IV Epiphanes. And in 8:10-12 the heavenly reality is described in human or astronomical terms (stars; host of heaven; prince of the host). In 10:5-6, 18 the heavenly reality is again described in a human form, that is, as a man or someone who looked like a man.

6. As symbols for kingdoms, trees are also employed in 4QFour Kingdoms[a-b]. But this text is too deteriorated for a detailed analysis of its symbolic code.

7. For the debate about the figure "like a son of man," see Ferch (1979) and Kvanvig (1988, 345-602).

To what extent the vision described in 4Qapocryphal Daniel (4Q246) fits into this system remains unanswered.[8] In 4Q246 2:1 the text refers to *zyqy'* (the comets) seen in a vision. But as the preceding texts speak about the son of God, it remains unclear whether the kingdom of the people that, like comets, lasts only for a short time is entirely of human quality. Therefore, 4Qapocryphal Daniel is of no help in deciphering the symbolic code of the Danielic literature in Maccabean times.

As in the Enochic literature, the imagery described in the book of Daniel is found in symbolic dream visions (Dan 4 and 7) or in visions devised by the author of Daniel on the role model of dream visions. Thus, Enochic and Danielic literatures employ the same visionary technique, that is, the symbolic dream vision. In these dream visions, both Enochic and Danielic texts employ the same symbolic code.

A Common Apocalyptic Milieu?

In my opinion, the imagery and visionary technique shared by Danielic and Enochic texts are best explained by an apocalyptic milieu shared by both the Enoch and the Daniel conventicles. The imagery and visionary technique used even hint at the specific Jewish-Israelite tradition that influenced this apocalyptic milieu. In second temple Judaism the interpretation of allegoric dream visions was the domain of sages. A good example is the Reuben redaction of the Joseph story. In the fifth century B.C.E. the Reuben redaction[9] of this sapiential didactic tale[10] transforms Joseph into a dream diviner. That the Joseph story is not exceptional in its sapiential contextualization of dream divination is attested by another sapiential didactic tale, the sojourn of Abraham in Egypt in the Genesis Apocryphon (1QapGen 19:10–20:32).[11] In this text Abraham is described as a wise sage to whom Pharaoh sends some of his court officials for advice (1QapGen 19:24-27). In 1QapGen 19:14-21 this sage Abra-

---

8. Of 4Qpseudo-Daniel[a-b] (4Q243-44); 4Qpseudo-Daniel[c] (4Q245); 4Qapocryphal Daniel (4Q246); and 4QFour Kingdoms[a-b] (4Q552-53), only the text attested by 4Qapocryphal Daniel (4Q246) can be dated to the Maccabean period with any certainty (for the dating of apocryphal Daniel, see Puech 1996).

9. For the redactional history of the Joseph story and the date of its Reuben redaction, see Schmitt (1980).

10. For the genre of the Joseph story see Rad (1971) and Müller (1977).

11. For the genre of 1QapGen 19:10–20:32 see Lange (1996). For 1QapGen 19:10–20:32 as an independent textual tradition being incorporated into the Genesis Apocryphon, see Lange (1996, 192-98).

ham is described as having and subsequently interpreting a symbolic dream warning him of the coming dangers in Egypt. Therefore, as has been pointed out by Gerhard von Rad (1985, 337-63; 1993, 316-31) and Hans-Peter Müller (1969; 1972),[12] the supposed apocalyptic milieu was influenced by wisdom circles. This wisdom influence does of course not exclude a prophetic influence on apocalypticism.

If the Enochic and Danielic conventicles shared in a common apocalyptic milieu that was influenced by the Wisdom tradition, does this mean that other eschatological conventicles described by Collins share in the same milieu? To answer this question the book of Jubilees should be compared with Enochic and Danielic literatures.

Jubilees is from the same time period as the book of Daniel, the Enochic book of Dream Visions, and the Enochic Book of Giants.[13] But in other respects Jubilees is distinct from the Enochic and Danielic literatures. Given the prominence in second temple Judaism of Moses, the pseudepigraphic namesake of Jubilees, it seems improbable that the tradents behind Jubilees could have identified themselves in the same exclusive way with Moses as the Enochic and Danielic conventicles might have done with their pseudepigraphic namesakes. Furthermore, Jubilees in itself is not an apocalypse but rewritten Bible. But although Jubilees is not an apocalypse, chapter 23 certainly incorporates one. Different from the Enochic and Danielic literatures though, Jubilees 23:8-32 is not attributed to a visionary but is an excursus in the long dictate from the heavenly tablets given by the angel of the presence to Moses. And different from the book of Daniel and the Animal Apocalypse, in Jubilees 23:8-32 the history of the world is not narrated in a symbolic code.[14]

According to Jubilees 23:8-32, the increasing wickedness of the world results in shorter and shorter life spans until three-week-old babies have the appearance of someone a hundred years old. Only when the wicked return to the law does the decreasing life span of humans reverse itself. The Jubilees apocalypse lacks the imagery used in the book of Dream Visions or the book of Daniel. Furthermore, different from the Enochic and Danielic literatures, Jubilees seems to avoid the imagery of allegoric dreams. Where possible, it even con-

---

12. Müller supposes a magic-mantic wisdom tradition that would be distinct from more philosophically inclined wisdom traditions. Only the magic-mantic wisdom would have developed into apocalypticism.

13. For a Maccabean date of the book of Jubilees, see VanderKam (1977, 214-85).

14. In this respect, Jub 23:8-32 is reminiscent of apocalyptic texts written in Hasmonean times which also do not employ a symbolic code, i.e., the Apocryphon of Jeremiah — 4QapocrJer A (4Q383); 4Qpap apocrJer B? (4Q384); 4QapocrJer C^{a-f} (4Q385a, 387, 388a, 389-90, 387a); 4QpsDan^{a-b} ar (4Q243-44); and 4QpsDan^c ar (4Q245).

sciously deletes the allegoric dreams of the Joseph story. Otherwise, allegoric dreams are remodeled into theorematic dreams.

1. Jubilees 4:19 creates the impression that the Enochic book of Dream Visions and its Animal Apocalypse (1 En 85–90) are an easy-to-understand theorematic dream.

2. In its reiteration of Genesis 37, Jubilees 34:10-19 deletes Joseph's dreams in total (Gen 37:5-11).

3. Jubilees 39:16-18 condenses the dreams of the cupbearer and the baker (Gen 40:6-19) in a way that their allegoric character gets lost.

4. Jubilees 40:1-6 avoids the allegoric elements of the dreams of the pharaoh (Gen 41:1-36).

Thus, in using different imagery, the book of Jubilees is not only distinct from the Enochic and Danielic literatures, it tries to avoid the symbolic inventory of the Enochic-Danielic milieu totally; and even more, it avoids the allegoric visions which are narrated in its "biblical *Vorlage*" and which use the symbolic inventory of the Enochic and Danielic literatures.

As James VanderKam and others have argued repeatedly, the book of Jubilees comes from a priestly background. "This follows from the nature of the book with its heavy emphasis on priestly concerns, from the special attention devoted to the line of righteous men through whom the sacerdotal legislation was transmitted from earliest times, and from the extraordinary status of Levi among the sons of Jacob. . . . Jubilees adds numerous sections which betray the writer's priestly bent" (VanderKam 1992, 3:1030-31). Among the priestly topics thus inserted, VanderKam lists the Sabbath laws, the sacred calendar, properly celebrated festivals, sacrificial regulations, the prohibition of consuming blood, circumcision, and the avoidance of impurity and uncleanness.

This priestly background of the book of Jubilees argues for a different social setting than the apocalyptic milieu shared by the Enochic and Danielic groups. Jubilees thus uses different visionary techniques and does not employ a symbolic code for its apocalypse. And Jubilees comes from a different social setting than the Danielic and Enochic literatures. While the Danielic and Enochic literatures seem to come from different apocalyptic conventicles sharing a common apocalyptic milieu, at best Jubilees seems to be loosely affiliated with this apocalyptic milieu.

Conclusion

The comparison between the Enochic and Danielic literature from Maccabean times, on one hand, and the comparison of those texts with the book of Jubilees, on the other, both confirm and contradict Collins's idea that in second temple Judaism there was not one apocalyptic movement but a wide range of different apocalyptic conventicles. Both the Danielic and the Enochic conventicles use the same type of symbolic visions in their apocalypses, and both employ the same symbolic system to encode these visions. Both seem to be influenced by sapiential as well as prophetic traditions. But in the self-designations used as well as in their self-understanding, there are enough differences between the two circles behind the Danielic and Enochic literatures that both cannot derive from the same group. The most feasible explanations for both differences and similarities is that both groups belong to a wider apocalyptic milieu.

A comparison of Jubilees with the Enochic and Danielic literature shows that not all eschatological groups known from Maccabean times shared this apocalyptic milieu. Conventicles related to Mosaic parabiblical literature did not employ the same symbolic cipher or visionary technique to be found in the Enochic and Danielic literatures. On the contrary, Jubilees consciously tries to avoid symbolic visions and in 23:8-32 phrases its own apocalypse in a nonsymbolic way. Furthermore, the book of Jubilees originates from priestly circles and displays less interest in sapiential or prophetic traditions. It is thus feasible to suppose that the circles in which Jubilees originated did not share in the same apocalyptic milieu as the Enochic and Danielic literatures.

The Animal Apocalypse and Daniel

James R. Davila

In addressing the subject of Daniel and the Animal Apocalypse briefly, I wish to focus first on some basic parallels and differences between the two works which have led scholars to declare them both broadly apocalyptic but the products of two different parties or movements, and second, to say a little about the term "apocalyptic" itself. My comments have little in the way of originality, and I offer them in the hope of distilling some issues that may be helpful to have before us in the discussion which constitutes this volume.

First, the Animal Apocalypse and Daniel share some basic beliefs and themes, although in many cases the ideas are taken in different directions. These ideas include the Maccabean revolt as the culmination of the eschatological crisis, a final throne judgment, a physical resurrection of the dead, historical determinism exemplified in a review of future history, some form of eschatological redeemer, and the theory that Jeremiah's seventy years of exile in Jeremiah 25 have an esoteric meaning that needs to be decoded. Second, the two works disagree on some fundamental theological points and eschatological projections. The Animal Apocalypse sees human evil as originating in angelic rebellion, takes the Maccabees to be central to the eschatological redemption, advocates armed resistance to Antiochus, sees the offerings of the second temple as polluted by its priesthood, makes no mention of a rebuilt temple in the eschatologically reconstructed Jerusalem, refers to the conversion of the Gentiles, and fails to mention the Sinai covenant and the torah of Moses, even when telling the story of Moses at Sinai.

Daniel sees angelic evil as a danger, but one contained by God's power; ignores or dismisses the Maccabees or damns them with feigned praise; advocates passive resistance and martyrdom in the conflict with Antiochus; sees the offerings of the second temple as only temporarily polluted by the desecration by Antiochus; asserts that at the eschaton the desecrated temple will be restored and purified; says nothing about the conversion of the Gentiles; and treats the covenant and torah as important.

The evidence is pretty clear that the Animal Apocalypse and Daniel disagree on many significant issues. Their points of agreement are more generic and are generally nuanced rather differently. There is a shared matrix, but I am not enthusiastic about calling this apocalyptic, a term I regard as somewhere between useless and harmful. I am suspicious of many of the overarching terms we use which are basically scholarly constructs ("mysticism," "magic," "apocalyptic," "gnosticism," "parabiblical," and even, at least for the first century, "Judaism" or "Christianity"), and I am biased toward talking about specific phenomena we can actually point to or quantify, such as literary genres, *Gattungen,* types of prophetic oracles, types of psalms, life situations, texts, artifacts, and rituals.

So I am comfortable talking about apocalypses, since we have plenty of these on hand from antiquity; but I have my doubts that apocalyptic really describes anything very useful. It seems to mean second temple texts or movements that have an interest in things we find in apocalypses: heavenly ascents, angelic revelations, revelations of secret wisdom, restored monarchy, the final judgment, earthly or heavenly paradises, the afterlife, protest against (perceived) oppression, reapplying myth to the eschaton, and the like.

I cannot find a center to it all. For example, why are both the Book of the Watchers, which has almost no eschatological interest, and the book of Revelation, which is almost entirely eschatological, considered apocalyptic aside from the fact that they are both composed in the literary genre apocalypse? Moreover, if that is the only reason, what do we lose by just calling them both apocalypses? I would prefer to think of what people call apocalyptic as a motley collection of aspects of prophetic, sapiential, and recycled royal theologies that have as much in common with, say, late wisdom texts like Ben Sira, or liturgical/poetic material like the Hodayot or the Odes of Solomon, or scriptural exegesis such as the pesherim, as with each other. So I would encourage us all to try to focus on concrete phenomena we can point to rather than synthetic constructs of dubious value such as apocalyptic.

It has been pointed out in the discussion which constitutes this volume that the Book of the Watchers is not a good example for the point I am making, since it does in fact have a significant eschatological interest. 3 Baruch, the Apocalypse of Paul, the Apocalypse of Adam, and the core of 3 Enoch (1–15/16), which appears as a separate unit in some manuscripts, are better examples, since they do not include a future eschatology.

My point is that when we put works like these alongside Daniel and Revelation, it is difficult to see how they are apocalyptic apart from simply embodying the genre apocalypse. Apocalypses need not deal with future eschatology. They do always have divinely revealed secrets, but so do other genres such as pesherim, Sibylline Oracles, and even incantations. There is no center to the term "apocalyptic" apart from its function as an adjective applied to apocalypses. It is true that there was much interest in ancient Judaism and early Christianity in revealed heavenly secrets and speculations about future eschatology and the transcendence of death, but to call this "apocalyptic" is to use confusingly imprecise terminology.

Appendix

(a) Some Shared Beliefs and Themes in Daniel and the Animal Apocalypse

Animal Apocalypse	*Daniel*

The Maccabean revolt as the culmination of the eschatological crisis:

1 En 90:6-19	Dan 7:19-27; 8:23-26; 9:24-27; 11:29-45

A final throne judgment:

1 En 90:20-27 (of angels and people)	Dan 7:9-14 (of the fourth beast)

A physical resurrection of the dead:

1 En 90:33 (of the righteous)	Dan 12:2-3, 13 (of the righteous and wicked)

Historical determinism exemplified in a review of future history (debatable to what degree the determinist doctrines are equivalent)

An eschatological redeemer:

the snow-white bull (1 En 90:37-39)	One like a son of man (Dan 7:13-14).

Jeremiah's seventy years (Jer 25) decoded as:

seventy *shepherds* (the angels of the nations) oppressing postexilic Israel	Seventy *weeks* of years (Dan 9:1-2, 24-27)

(b) Some Disagreements between Daniel and the Animal Apocalypse

Animal Apocalypse	*Daniel*
Human evil originates in angelic rebellion (1 En 86:1-6)	Angelic evil is a danger but is contained by God's power (Dan 10:12-14, 20)
The Maccabees are central to eschatological redemption (1 En 90:6-19)	Ignores (Dan 7:19-27; 9:24-27), dismisses (Dan 8:24?), or damns the Maccabees with feigned praise (Dan 11:34?)
Advocates active armed resistance (1 En 90:6-19)	Advocates passive resistance and martyrdom (Dan 1–6; 11:32-34)
The offerings of the second temple are polluted by its priesthood (1 En 89:73-74)	The offerings are temporarily polluted by the desecration by Antiochus (Dan 8:9-15; 9:24, 27; 12:11-12)
At the eschaton Jerusalem (the house) will be torn down and rebuilt, but there is no mention of the rebuilding of the temple (the tower) (1 En 90:28-29)	At the eschaton the desecrated temple will be restored and purified (Dan 8:14)
Conversion of the Gentiles (1 En 90:30)	Nothing corresponding
No mention of the Sinai covenant even at Sinai! (1 En 89:28-37)	The covenant and torah of Moses figure importantly (Dan 9:4, 11, 13; 11:22, 28, 30, 32)

The Covenantal Theology of
the Apocalyptic Book of Daniel

Gabriele Boccaccini

Since I was a student of Paolo Sacchi at the University of Turin, I have been fascinated by Enoch's and Daniel's "parallel lives," as expressed in Dream Visions and in the book of Daniel. The two documents have been long separated by their different "canonical" status, but they are very nearly contemporary, both being dated to the first years of the Maccabean revolt between the murder of Onias III, the last legitimate Zadokite high priest, and the death of Antiochus Epiphanes. Both documents share the same literary genre (apocalypse) and the same worldview (apocalypticism), and — what is even more significant — substantially address the same questions.

In my *Middle Judaism* I devoted a long chapter to the relationship between Dream Visions and Daniel (Boccaccini 1991); the chapter was the revision of an article previously published in Italian in the journal *Henoch* (Boccaccini 1987). In those publications I raised what I introduced as "a fundamental question: Is [the] apocalyptic corpus also the expression of a single tradition of thought or have authors of various traditions of thought used the same literary genre to express their various convictions?" (1991, 128). My answer was that "an identical form could be used by different traditions and identical ideas (even the same worldview) could assume a different meaning (a role, a specific weight) in different contexts" (1991, 128). Daniel and Dream Visions were a case in point. The two apocalyptic writings could not be the product of the same group, as their ideologies were divergent if not opposite. If we kept denoting as "apocalyptic" the ideology of the group that produced Dream Visions, we would have reached the paradoxical conclusion that Daniel was not apocalyptic, and could even be labeled anti-apocalyptic. At that time it was still commonplace to talk of apocalypticism as if it were a single movement and to denote the Enochic tradition as "the" apocalyptic movement. Now we all agree, as Collins also has clearly stated, that "the Jewish apocalypses were not produced by a single apocalyptic movement but constituted a genre that could be utilized by different groups in various situations" (Collins 1998a, 280). On the other hand, the term "Enochic" is gradually and successfully replacing the term "apocalyptic" to denote the ideological tradition of Dream Visions. I suspect that if Sacchi had to republish today his book *Jewish Apocalyptic and Its History* (Sacchi 1997), he would retitle it, for the sake of clarity, *Enochic Judaism and Its History*. Thanks to this conceptual and terminological clarification, the paradox is now overcome: we may continue to label both Dream Visions and Daniel as apocalyptic texts, even though Dream Visions is Enochic and Daniel is not.

Provided that "Daniel does not belong to the same ideological tradition as Enoch" (Collins 1997, 295; cf. Reid 1989; Sacchi 1997, 23; Nickelsburg 2001, 68), there remains the problem of the relation between the apocalyptic group that composed Daniel and the one that composed Dream Visions. Were they related, complementary, or even antagonistic? In my view the crucial point remains the different understanding, in the two documents, of the problem of the origin of evil and the relation with the Mosaic torah. While at the center of Dream Visions is the idea of the superhuman origin of evil and the Mosaic torah is conspicuously absent, Daniel sees the degeneration of history as a consequence of the breaking of the Mosaic torah. This idea is explicitly stated in Daniel's prayer in chapter 9.

The smooth style of the Hebrew text — it is full of traditional phrases and free of Aramaisms — makes it likely that Daniel's prayer was not composed by the author of the rest of the chapter and was indeed a preexistent, autonomous literary unit. However, any attempt to claim that it was a later, secondary addition goes against the evidence. In the textual tradition we do not have a single manuscript or variant to support the idea that the prayer was added to the text. The prayer belongs either to the author or to a very early stage in the transmission of the text.

Besides, the linguistic connections between the prayer and its actual context in Daniel 9 are too many and too circumstantial to be merely accidental (Jones 1968; Gilbert 1972). The best we can say is, with Collins, that "although the prayer was not composed for the present context, it was included purposefully by the author of Daniel 9 and was not a secondary addition" (Collins 1993, 348). The real problem therefore is not the authenticity of the prayer but its relation with the overall ideology of the document. Daniel's prayer takes texts like Nehemiah 1:4-11, 9:6-37, or Ezra 9:5-15 as its model; it is "a communal prayer of confession, of a type widely used in the post-exilic period" (Collins 1998a, 108). Why was this piece of Zadokite covenantal theology included?

Collins claims that "the content of the prayer does not represent the theology . . . of the author of the book" (Collins 1993, 360; cf. Towner 1971, 213). He sees a sharp contrast "with the apocalyptic framework of Daniel"; the Zadokite idea that "the affliction of Jerusalem is a punishment for sin and will be removed if the people repent and pray" is irreconcilable with the apocalyptic view that "the course of events is predetermined . . . and people cannot change the course of events" (Collins 1998a, 108-9). Daniel's prayer would be no more than a literary topos, "an act of piety, which is appropriate as the prayer of the one who failed to understand at the end of chap. 8" (Collins 1993, 360; cf. Lacocque 1979, 177).

The centrality of the prayer and its theological implications cannot be so easily dismissed, however (Boccaccini 2002, 181-88). The argument cannot be based only on the assumption that the prayer does not fit in, as nothing similar is found in any other apocalyptic text. Have we not just said that apocalypticism was used by different ideologies and groups?

Whoever inserted it in the text did not see any contradiction between the prayer and the overall ideology of the text. Ancient authors were not less sophisticated than us; if the prayer of confession was such an inert topos in the Jewish literature of the second temple, why do we not find anything similar at the beginning of Dream Visions, where Enoch is experiencing an identical situation of dismay, yet his prayer is so markedly different (1 En 83–84)? Furthermore, Daniel's prayer occupies a key position at the core of the second section of the book. Why should the author of Daniel have wanted to waste such an important spot to accommodate a literary topos, one not even consistent with his own thought?

It is true that the apocalyptic parts of Daniel do not contain many covenantal patterns. After all, the apocalyptic imagery was born and first developed outside a covenantal framework. Before reading a text in the light of other texts, however, we have to try to make sense of it in its own terms. In Daniel 7 and 9 the author makes his point; he shares the apocalyptic worldview and accepts the Enochic idea that history is condemned to inexorable degeneration — an idea that is, yes, in sharp contrast with Zadokite Judaism. Yet, in spite of any similarities, a fundamental difference makes Daniel representative of yet a different party. Daniel opposes the Enochic doctrine of the superhuman origin of evil, and strenuously defends the tenets of Zadokite covenantal theology.

To Enoch the entire course of history is revealed, from the creation until the eschatological reign. History is a drama that unfolds with humankind as both protagonist and victim. "All of the men's deeds were shown to me, each in all of their parts" (1 En 90:41), says Enoch at the book's conclusion. The explanation of everything that has happened, is happening, and will happen is contained in Dream Visions, which establishes the superhuman origin of evil, sets the limits of human freedom, and indicates the characteristics of future salvation. The idea of causality within the unfolding of history corresponds to the Enochic idea of a world corrupted by an original sin of angels. For Dream Visions this sin effects its degenerative action in the succession of increasingly iniquitous kingdoms up until the cathartic intervention of God.

This concept appears completely extraneous to the author of Daniel. The vision of history in Daniel does not have the same comprehensive character seen in Dream Visions. The entire course of history is not revealed to Daniel, only the events that await Israel in the period immediately following the breaking of the covenant, that is, since the time in which revelation is imagined to have taken place. Nothing is said of the preceding history. Daniel's apocalyptic visions do not set themselves up as a tool for a universal and self-sufficient interpretation of reality. The events described do not make sense in themselves; their cause must be found elsewhere. We are told what is going to happen, not why.

Norman Porteous writes: "Without this prayer there would be something essential missing from the book of Daniel" (Porteous 1965, 136). I would say even more: without the prayer of Daniel 9, the book of Daniel as a whole would lack any internal logic. We simply would not understand the reason history is degenerating, which according to Daniel is because of the sin of Israel in breaking the torah. The consistency of the theological message of the book depends entirely on the establishment of a cause-and-effect relationship between the Zadokite idea of covenant and the Enochic theory of the degeneration of history.

Unlike his apocalyptic colleague and competitor, the author of Daniel does not blame angels, nor does he dismiss the validity of the covenant, as the old sages of sapiential Judaism had done before (Boccaccini 2002). What Daniel seeks in Jeremiah's prophecy is not the cause of the degenerative process of history, which, he already knows, is the sin of the people against the covenant, but the consequences the realization of the divine curse has on history and the individual. To pose the question about the duration of the exile means to question the possibility of a redemption of history once the punitive mechanism has been set in motion. It is to question the enduring effects of the covenant on the collective and the individual level in the new situation the people find themselves in — subject to the divine curse.

The angel responds to Daniel's doubts and reveals that the seventy years of Jeremiah's prophecy should in reality be understood as "seventy weeks of years," and that this span of time corresponds to the time necessary "to finish the transgression, to put an end to sin, and to atone for iniquity" (Dan 9:24).

That the prayer was included by the same hand that composed chapter 9 is proved by the fact that not only Daniel's prayer but also the angel's answer is consistent with the principles of Zadokite covenantal theology. According to Leviticus 26:3-45 (P), "peace in the land" is one of the blessings of the covenant (26:3-13), but "if you will not obey me . . . I will set my face against you, and you shall be struck down by your enemies; your foes shall rule over you" (26:14-17). The length of the punishment is subordinated to Israel's repentance: "If in spite of these punishments you have not turned back to me, but continue hostile to me, then I too will continue hostile to you: I myself will strike you sevenfold for your sins" (26:23-24; cf. 26:18, 21, 27-28). This is exactly what happened according to Daniel. Israel "broke the covenant" (26:15) and was punished by God with seventy years of exile, as announced by the prophet Jeremiah, but then Israel in spite of this did not turn back to God but continued to be hostile. As a result, God multiplied the punishment "sevenfold" and the seventy years became "seventy weeks of years" (Dan 9:24). God's punishment will culminate in the coming, in the last week, of a king who "shall make a strong covenant with many for one week, and for half of the week shall cause sacrifice and offering to cease; and the desolating abomination will be in their place, until the decreed destruction is poured out upon the desolator" (Dan 9:26-27).

The iniquitous king who in Daniel 9 signals the climax of God's punishment is undoubtedly the same figure already introduced in Daniel 7. His actions against God and God's people in both chapters are identical ("he shall speak words against the Most High and shall think to change the times and the law," Dan 7:25; cf. 8:9-12, 24-26; 9:26-27; 11:28-39), as are the duration of his apparent success ("a time, [two] times, and half a time," Dan 7:25 = 12:7; cf. 9:27) and his end ("he shall be consumed and destroyed," Dan 7:26; cf. 8:25; 9:27; 11:45). The emphasis is significant. In the two sections of Daniel, two different periodizations are used: history seen phenomenologically by humankind as a succession of kingdoms ("the four kingdoms") and history seen by God as the instrument of God's punishment ("the seventy weeks"). The common figure of the "iniquitous king" allows the two periodizations to be synchronized just as the visual and aural presence of clapboards allows the image and sound of a film to be synchronized exactly. The unity of the two sections is further strengthened by the role of the number four as the number for punishment. Four are the times God repeats the curse in Leviticus (Lev 26:18, 21, 23-24, 27-28); four are the subdivisions of the seventy weeks (7 + 62 + half a week + half a week); four are the times of the iniquitous king's persecution ("one time, two times, half a time"); four are the kingdoms.

From Leviticus 26 Daniel also learned that the righteous will suffer, and understood the reason of their suffering. "You shall have no power to stand against your enemies. . . . And those of you who survive shall languish in the land of your enemies because of the iniquities of their ancestors" (Lev 26:37-39). The punishment will in fact have an end, but only after the seventy weeks have passed. The period is necessary to expiate the guilt, and not even a righteous generation can change the course of the events.

Leviticus 26 ends with a word of hope. If the people would recognize not only that they broke the covenant but that they also continued to sin afterward, at the end God will deliver them from their enemies. "If they confess their iniquity and the iniquity of their ancestors, in that they committed treachery against me and, moreover, that they continued hostile to me . . . then I will remember my covenant with Jacob . . . Isaac . . . and Abraham . . . and I will remember the land" (Lev 26:40-45). This is what Daniel says will happen at the end of the seventy weeks (Dan 9:27).

In sum, Daniel 9 (Daniel's prayer *as well as* the angel's reply) advocates the view that the degeneration of history and the cosmic conflict are consequences of the breaking of the covenantal relationship between God and humankind. Daniel's covenantal theology is daring and highly innovative, yet still compatible with the Zadokite principles as expressed in Leviticus 26. Even the deterministic idea that the time of desolation is decreed is not inconsistent once this time is understood as punishment.

There is no contradiction between Daniel's prayer and the overall ideology of the book (Boccaccini 2002; cf. the contributions of Davila and Sacchi to the present volume). In his commentary on 1 Enoch, Nickelsburg also emphasizes the different attitude of Daniel and Dream Visions toward the Mosaic torah, and connects the "theology" of Daniel 9 directly to its warning in 11:30-32 "not to forsake the covenant" (Nickelsburg 2001, 68). This was the main goal and accomplishment of the author of Daniel, who utilized the apocalyptic imagery (an imagery he shared with Dream Visions) and consciously included it within the framework of a covenantal theology. The author of Daniel did it so successfully that for more than two thousand years most Jews have not seen any contradiction between apocalypticism and covenant, between the cosmic conflict and their obedience to the Mosaic torah. It was not by chance that the apocalyptic book of Daniel entered the rabbinic canon and the apocalyptic Dream Visions did not.

Comparing the Groups Behind Dream Visions
and Daniel: A Brief Note

Florentino García Martínez

If I understand correctly, the core of this debate — in which we are discussing a single aspect of the many-sided work of John Collins — is to ascertain whether or not there is a relationship, and if there is, of which sort, not between two concrete literary productions — the book of Daniel known in its rather different redactions (Hebrew/Aramaic versus Greek) and the Dream Visions known as a part of the books of Enoch — but between the groups, schools, traditions, or whatever else we want to call them, that are behind these literary compositions. If my understanding is correct, it seems to me obvious that we are comparing apples with pears, to put it bluntly.

As Collins has demonstrated, Daniel, in whatever redaction, is a conglomerate in which the Aramaic stories, the apocalyptic Hebrew sections, and even a separate piece as the prayer of chapter 9 (independently copied on 4Q116 [4QDan^e] as suggested by Ulrich in DJD) have been redacted together under the umbrella of the mythical Danil. Much in the same way the different components of the books of Enoch have been brought together under the equally mythical patriarch. If what we are looking for are the groups behind the collections, we should rather compare all the compositions which have been put under the same umbrella, which in the case of Daniel will include a large number of "pseudos" now known from Qumran or from other sources, and in the case of the Dream Visions not only the Enoch books but other compositions such as the Book of the Giants.

If the comparison is explored at this larger level, several of the problems will appear in a different perspective. For example, we will easily realize that the torah-centrism of the prayer of Daniel 9 is not stranger in the context of the whole than the explicit rebuttal of the celestial origin of evil expressed in the Epistle of Enoch (98:4).

In my opinion this observation forces us to conclude that tolerance for theological dissonance in the assumed groups is much larger than we (from our rather Cartesian frame of minds) are ready to allow.

I do not know if the type of documentation will allow us to deduce solid conclusions about these two groups or schools, but we do have another group about which we can be more assertive, namely, the *yaḥad*. There is no doubt about the active presence of elements in the *yaḥad* deriving from both Daniel and Dream Visions. And all of their diversity not only coexists side by side, but it contributes actively to the forming of a distinct entity by mingling together with another entity equally important but not fully represented in either of these two: a torah-centered form of Judaism of priestly origins that Gabriele Boccaccini likes to call Zadokite Judaism.

In a perceptive essay on the social setting of the *maskilim* of Daniel, Philip Davies has demonstrated that we have enough evidence to assert more than a simple literary dependence of the *yaḥad* group and the *maskilim* behind Daniel, that we also have more than circumstantial evidence of the presence of "Zadokite" elements in the group, and that the strong influence of the Enochic literature on the group is undeniable.

In my opinion it is this "ménage à trois" and not the legal or adulterous marriage of the Danielic and the Enochic groups that is at the basis of the parent group from which, in the best tradition of the Groningen Hypothesis, the Qumran split emerged.

The "One Like a Son of Man" (Dan 7:13) and the Royal Ideology

Matthias Albani

The identification of the "one like a son of man" (Dan 7:13) is a classical *crux interpretum* in Daniel exegesis. According to John Collins, three categories of explanations have been put forward since the emergence of critical scholarship: (1) an exalted human being, i.e., a king or a messianic figure, who fulfills the promises to David; (2) a collective symbol for the Jewish people; or (3) a heavenly being, e.g., the archangel Michael (Collins 1993, 308ff.).

In view of the apparently collective interpretation in Daniel 7:18, 27, there is no doubt that the "one like a son of man," here abbreviated "son of man," represents in some way the "people of the holy ones of the Most High," a collective symbol of the Jewish people. However, the question is whether the collective interpretation is a sufficient explanation, as the mysterious figure shows clearly individual traits too. The exalted royal messianic figure is an interpretation supported by the statement in Daniel 7:14 that "dominion and glory and kingship" was given to "one like a son of man." Thus, the promises still open to the Davidic dynasty (Pss 2:8-9; 89:27; 110) are fulfilled.

On the other hand, the four great beasts from the sea (Dan 7:3ff.) are symbols of kingdoms represented by individual kings, so we might expect the same in the eschatological kingdom of the "people of the holy ones of the Most High." Finally, there are also good reasons for the angelic interpretation: in the book of Daniel and elsewhere in the Hebrew Bible the throne of the Most High is usually surrounded by heavenly beings (Dan 7:10; 8:10f.) which are explicitly described in the context as humanlike beings (10:16, 18; cf. 8:15; 9:18; 10:5). Indeed, the expression "one like a son of man" means likeness to, but not necessarily identity with, a human being. The archangel Michael, "the great prince

47

who stands over your people" (Dan 12:1) as the heavenly representative of Israel in the book of Daniel, is therefore best conceived as "the one like a human being." In the words of Klaus Koch, he is the one "der als großer Gebieter die Zeit der Großreiche ablöst und das nachzeitliche Regiment übernimmt" (Koch 1995, 163).

All three interpretations emphasize important aspects of the controversial figure. Therefore the question arises whether the three sketched positions inevitably exclude one another or there is a common denominator which allows a synthesis of the three interpretations. The following presentation offers a proposal as to how such a synthesis could be conceivable.

The Earthly Son of God and the Heavenly Sons of God

The "one like a son of man" is given "dominion and glory and kingship" by the Most High (Dan 7:14) after depriving the hostile kingdoms of power (four great beasts from the sea). This is the eschatological fulfillment of the promises still open for the Davidic dynasty (Pss 2:8f.; 89:27; 110). Although in the book of Daniel the "one like a son of man" is never *expressis verbis* identified with the Messiah, his function in the eschatological hope of Daniel 7 runs parallel to the role of the royal Messiah in messianic expectations. He represents as "quasi king" the "people of the holy ones of the Most High" in the eschatological time. Therefore it is appropriate methodologically to consider first the son of man figure in the religio-historical picture of the Israelite royal ideology.

In this perspective we indeed can see a bridge between the angelic and the royal interpretation of the son of man: according to the Israelite royal ideology, the king was seen as the son of God who belongs in a sense to the divine world. Some biblical texts formulate the legitimization of the king with aid of father-son imagery. In Psalm 2:7 YHWH calls the enthroned Davidic king "my son" (cf. 2 Sam 7:14; Pss 89:27; 110:3[LXX]); God has set his son on Zion, on the holy mountain (Ps 2:6). In Psalm 89:27 we find the promise "I will make him the firstborn, the highest of the kings of the earth." The father-son imagery illustrates the king's closeness to YHWH and is connected with the enthronement act which is also presupposed in Daniel 7:9. The difficult text of Psalm 110:3b seems to refer to the king being born "from the womb of dawn"; that is, the king comes from the heavenly sphere. The Egyptians believed that the dawn-light bears the stars which have a close relation to the kings. In this sense verse 3b may be compared with the royal star that comes forth out of Jacob (Num 24:17). That means the "Davidic king was believed to have come forth from God's world to rule the people with Yhwh's help and to wage war against its enemies" (Laato 1997, 93). The king was seen as a "son of God" or as a "divine being" (*elohim*, Ps 45:6) sitting at the right hand of God (Ps 110:1). In the temple in Jerusalem, the "intersection point" between heaven and earth, he had access to God's world (cf. Isa 6).

Ezekiel 28:12ff. says the king of Tyre was originally on the holy mountain of God in Eden, walking among stones of fire (stars?), before he was cast from the mountain of God because of his hubris. He was an "anointed cherub," that is, an angelic heavenly being. This was probably the conviction of the Davidic kings too, because the temple of Jerusalem symbolizes among other things the garden of Eden, situated on the holy mountain of God (cf. Ps 48:1ff.; see also the report of the diplomatic exchange between Solomon and Hiram of Tyre on the building of the Jerusalem temple in 1 Kings 5:1-12, which could also imply a close relationship between Israelite and Tyrian royal ideologies and the associated temple concepts).

According to Isaiah 14:13, the heavenly beings on the mountain of God around the throne of the Most High are called "stars of God." This notion corresponds to the imagery of the "host of heaven" which surrounds the throne of God (1 Kings 22:19; cf. Judg 5:20). "The host of heaven connotes both the stars and the heavenly beings, either gods or angels. The stars were the visible manifestations of the heavenly beings. . . . At Ugarit the stars appear to be members of the divine council" (Collins 1993, 331). Similar to Ugaritic texts (cf. *KTU* 1.10 I 3f.), the members of the divine council are also called "sons of God" in the Hebrew Bible (Ps 89:7; cf. Gen 6:2; Ps 29:1; Job 1:6), which are identified with or closely related to the stars in Job 38:7. The Canaanite mount of congregation "on the farthest sides of the north," the place of the throne of the Most High surrounded by the "stars of God" (Isa 14:13), was in the Jerusalem temple theology obviously identified with the mount Zion (Ps 48:2f.), on which the temple of YHWH is situated (cf. Ps 46:4f.). In view of the royal ideology sketched here, there is good reason to assume that the Davidic king as earthly son of God was counted in a way among the heavenly sons of God on the mountain of God — or in other words, the "star of Jacob" belonging to the heavenly "stars of God." By the enthronement in the temple on the holy mountain, the Israelite king became a "mighty god" (Isa 9:6; cf. the "mighty ones" in Ps 103:20), namely, the "son" of his divine father YHWH (Pss 2:7; 110:3).

However, the failure of the Davidic monarchy (587 B.C.E.) and the rising monotheism since the time of exile deprived the kings of their divine nimbus. The royal claim for divineness was criticized as hubris. Divine kings such as "Helel, the son of dawn" were cast from the heavenly stars to the netherworld (Isa 14), from the mountain of God to the ground (Ezek 28; cf. 32). This prophetic message against the hubris of the heathen kings was also aimed at the Israelite royal ideology (cf. Ezek 21:30f. [English: 21:25f.]; Ps 82:6f.?). For example, in Ezekiel's new conception of the temple a divine "son of God" king has no longer any place, but only a "prince" who is largely disrobed of his former sacral dignity. Central ideas of the royal ideology were democratized in exilic-postexilic times (e.g., Gen 1:26f.; Ps 8:5f.).

The Earthly Righteous Ones and the
Heavenly Angels in the Book of Daniel

Centuries later, in the apocalyptic literature, some ideas of the royal pattern return *mutatis mutandis:* now the righteous Jewish people, not the kings, are associated with the stars or angels. According to Daniel 8:10f., the stars of the "host of heaven" appear as the adversaries of the "little horn," Antiochus IV, who exalted himself as high as the prince of the host by taking away the regular burnt offering and casting down the sanctuary of God. The stars of the heavenly host and the earthly members of the temple community are here seen in close relationship. In the time of the end the wise men "who lead many to righteousness" will be resurrected to everlasting life, shining like the stars (Dan 12:3; cf. 1 En 104:2-6). That means they will be exalted into the astral realm of angels or holy ones. It seems the earthly righteous ones are *sub specie aeternitatis* already counted among the heavenly holy ones (cf. 4Q491 frg. 11 col. 1:12-14?) who surround the throne of the Most High (Dan 7:10; cf. Ps 89:6, 8). "Everyone who is found written in the book" (Dan 12:1) shall be delivered in the final judgment (cf. 7:10). Thus, justice and righteousness are the continuum between this world and the other world of God.

That shows there is no insurmountable gap in apocalyptic imagination between just human beings and angels, between the earthly and the heavenly "holy ones," but rather a close affinity — similar to the old royal ideology which sees the just king, the representative of God on earth, as a quasi-divine being (Pss 2:7; 45:7). Indeed, the righteous ones in the book of Daniel play the role of the former just Israelite kings: they fulfill in a sense the function of the king by "leading many to righteousness" (Dan 12:3; see Daniel's counsel to the king in Dan 4:27[24]). Originally the Davidic kings had the task to realize justice and righteousness on earth (2 Sam 23:3; Ps 72). However, the Israelite kings failed in fulfilling their divine task (see Ezek 21:25ff. [German: 21:30ff.]; 34; Deuteronomistic history; etc.), and the heathen kings more than ever (cf. Isa 14; Ezek 28; 32). In the book of Daniel the succession of monarchies is a history of growing sin and iniquity culminating in the rule of King Antiochus IV (cf. Dan 7:2-8). Therefore the just people of Israel take the position of the kings, replacing the royal "sons of God" in the time of the end. One can speak here of a democratization of the old royal ideology.

This traditio-historical background is in my opinion the common denominator of the messianic and angelic interpretation of the "one like a son of man" in Daniel 7:13, because in the Israelite royal ideology, which was later transformed into messianic expectations, there is no basic contradiction between the royal Messiah (Ps 2:2) and heavenly beings like the archangel Michael. However, assuming that the sketched traditio-historical background is correct, why is the enthroned heavenly figure in Daniel 7:13 called "one like a son of man" and not "son of God"?

Antiochus IV, the Eschatological "Son of Dawn" as "Counterfigure" of the Heavenly Son of Man

The key for answering this question is in my opinion the figure of the wicked king Antiochus IV Epiphanes ("little horn") who embodies hubris and iniquity in the book of Daniel by exalting himself to the stars and as high as the prince of the host (Dan 8:11; cf. 11:36-37; 2 Macc 9:10). In fact, the king claimed divineness ("Epiphanes") in the same way as other Hellenistic rulers. "The Ptolemaic rulers were styled 'Savior God' *(theos sōtēr)* and 'Son of Helios' (*TDNT* 8:336). They could also trace their ancestry to Dionysus. The Seleucid rulers and the lesser Greek kings in the East claimed the title 'God' *(theos).* Seleucus's father was said to be Apollon" (Fossum 1992, 6:133). The ascent of the little horn to the stars and to the throne of the Most High has a clear biblical precedent in Isaiah 14:12-15 (Collins 1993, 332). The mythical story of the fall of "Helel ben Shachar" (Shining one, son of Dawn) is used in a song of taunt to celebrate the fall of the king of Babylon who aspired to set his throne "above the stars of God." "Son of Dawn" might be a royal title and another designation for "son of God." We find a related conception in the difficult text Psalm 110:3, which seems to speak of the king being born "from the womb of dawn." In Isaiah 14 we meet the classical motif of royal hubris which is also an important topic in the book of Daniel (cf. chaps. 4–5; 11).

From the Jewish point of view the heathen kings assume a divine position which is in conflict with the sovereignty of the only God (cf. Dan 4:35 [German: 4:32]). Therefore their rule is taken away by God and his people. This seems also to be the content of the apocalyptic Aramaic text 4Q246 from Qumran. "Son of God" or "son of the Most High" could be a pejorative term here (cf. Ps 82:6), referring to some Seleucid king (Antiochus IV?). Unfortunately the interpretation of the fragmentary text is not certain. "Son of God" could also be interpreted in a positive way as a functional equivalent to the "son of man" in Daniel 7. However, the structure of the text speaks in my opinion on behalf of the negative interpretation of the "son of God" title (see in this sense Puech 1996; and Steudel 1996).

Anyway, it is probable that the title "son of God" was viewed critically in orthodox Jewish circles because it was a reminder of the hubris of the Hellenistic kings who claimed divineness like the "son of dawn" in Isaiah 14:12 (Dan 8:11). Therefore the author of Daniel 7 avoided the royal designation "son of God" and instead used the rarer term "son of man," which occurs also in the Hebrew Bible in a royal context but implying humility, not arrogance. Psalm 80:17 says: "Let your hand be upon the man of your right hand, upon the son of man whom you made strong for yourself." The main theme of the psalm is the appeal to God for deliverance from the oppression of enemies and the prayer for Israel's restoration (80:3ff.). The "son of man" on the right hand is the king of Psalm 110 (cf. Pss 18:36[35]; 20:7[6]), who is enthroned by God at his right hand subjecting his enemies (cf. Ps 2:2ff., 8f.). The enthronement of the "son of man" and subjection/destruction of God's enemies are also the main topics of Daniel 7:9ff. Unlike the arrogant heathen kings who aspire to divine power, the "son of man" of Psalm 80 appears as a humble and obedient ruler whom God made strong (cf. also Ps 8:5-6). Interestingly enough, in the Targumim the "son of man" of Psalms 8:5[4] and 80:17 is interpreted as an eschatological messianic figure.

The "One Like a Son of Man" and the Archangel Michael

However, there is also a small but important difference between the royal "son of man" in Psalm 80 and the figure in question in Daniel 7:13. The enthroned eschatological ruler is called "*one like* a son of man." The likeness means that he is a heavenly figure. "It seems . . . that the son of man represents a stage of development in Jewish eschatology in which messianic expectations (with an imminent, earthly focus) were transformed to the transcendental dimension. The son of man is a functional equivalent of the messiah but is not identified with him" (Laato 1997, 266). In view of the failure of the old royal ideal of just rule (cf. Pss 72; 82:2-5), the royal hubris and the abuse of discretionary power (cf. Dan 3–5; 8:10f.; 11:36f.), apocalyptic Jewish circles no longer believed in a just earthly ruler but only in a transcendent realization of the king's ideal.

The eschatological opponents of the iniquitous Antiochus, who exalted himself to the stars, are the suffering Jewish righteous ones exalted by God to the angels or stars post mortem (Dan 12:3). Their representative is the archangel

Michael (12:1; cf. 10:13, 21), the "great prince," the protector of his people. Michael represents and defends the suffering "people of the holy ones of the Most High" (7:27), who receive the eternal kingdom (7:18). In doing so the archangel embodies the royal Israelite ideal of military and just power which rules in obedient accordance with God. As angel he is like a royal "son of man"; however, he is no earthly messianic king but a heavenly being. This eschatological heavenly ruler, "coming with the *clouds* of heaven," is the counterpart or "counterfigure" of the wicked earthly king Antiochus IV, the fallen "son of dawn" who tried to "ascend above the heights of the *clouds*" to be like the Most High (Isa 14:14). The "little horn" arrogates divineness and power to himself, but God's "horn" (Ps 89:18[17]), the "son of man," receives it from God, who makes him strong (Ps 80:17). The angelic "son of man" accepts God's supremacy like the other holy ones in the assembly of God (cf. Ps 89:6-7).

Perhaps the meaning of the angel name Michael is not accidentally chosen against this background: "Who is like God." This name of the eschatological angelic prince of Israel implies a humble and God-fearing rule which has the promise of eternal duration. Thus, the promises still open to the Davidic dynasty (cf. Pss 2:8-9; 89:4, 29; 110) are eschatologically fulfilled and surpassed.

"One Like a Son of Man": Innuendoes of a Heavenly Individual

Stefan Beyerle

What does the expression "one like a son of man" mean in Daniel 7:13? A collective symbol for the angelic host, Israel, the divine kingdom, the Davidic king, the Messiah, the high priest, an angel, e.g., Michael or Gabriel (Redditt 1999, 127)? In short, all these different possibilities of an identification lead to the following alternatives: Is this "one like figure" in heaven or on earth? Is the so-called son of man[1] an individual or does he symbolize a community? The answer to these questions, in general, sets the course for a decision on the traditio-historical background of the "son of man" sayings in the Gospels (Collins 1995; Dunn 1997). Recent German New Testament scholarship is rather skeptical about an ancient Jewish "son of man" tradition (Kreplin 2001).

In the following essay I will first examine the linguistic evidence. Second, the visionary setting in Daniel 7 and related sources is considered. The ambition of this study is not to add new evidence to a tangled and more and more tantalizing debate (Burkett 1999). I rather want to stress the peculiarity of the syntagmatic expression in Daniel 7:13 in the setting of a heavenly sanctuary.[2]

---

1. The translation of Aramaic *kebar 'enash* with "(one) like a son of man" is disputable. It simply designates one single person among mankind.

2. Janowski (2002) distinguishes "vertical" and "horizontal" concepts of sanctuaries in the whole ancient Near East.

The "Son of Man" as an Individual

Philology in combination with the examination of Aramaic parallels is a significant means to reconstruct the semantics of the expression *kebar 'enash* in the visionary context of Daniel 7 (Koch 1995, 2:140-72). Regarding the "Old Aramaic"[3] evidence, where the Deir Alla inscription speaks of the boisterousness of the "sons of men"[4] and where a text from *Sefire* uses *br 'nsh* in the indefinite sense[5] ("someone"), a more or less generic use is common to all witnesses.[6]

In the so-called Middle Aramaic period the sources from Qumran are of special interest. In comparison with the Old Aramaic, Klaus Koch stated a progressive individualization (Koch 1995, 2:158-59). Of special interest, and mostly neglected, is a passage from the Epistle of Enoch (1 En 93:13). Here the Qumran manuscript 4Q212 [4QEn[g] ar] 1, v, 20-21 (first century B.C.E.) reads: "Or who [among all the sons of m]en can [know and measure what is] the length and breadth of the entire earth?" (Milik 1976, 270; García Martínez and Tigchelaar 1997, 1:444-45). Through an interpretation of this question as a rhetorical one and through the possible implied answer "Enoch," the individual character of the expression "son of man" becomes apparent (Nickelsburg 2001, 252). But the individualization depends on the implied answer, and the literal sense of the passage marks a generic meaning of the "sons of men."

In some ways comparable is another example from the Middle Aramaic period. In 1QapGen 21:13, a paraphrase of Genesis 13:16, God promises Abram an offspring that "not one single man" is able to count (Fitzmyer and Harrington 1978, 118; García Martínez and Tigchelaar 1997, 1:44). Even if the number has shifted from plural to singular, both expressions in 1 Enoch and in the Genesis Apocryphon allude to the *br 'nwsh* as a generic term without denying that the expression could refer to an individual. The remaining references contrast the "sons of men" with the Watchers, e.g., in 1 Enoch (cf. 1 En 7:3: 4QEn[a] ar [4Q201] 3:18; 1 En 14:2: 4QEn[c] ar [4Q204] 6:11).[7] The Astronomical Book determines a certain place for mankind within a tripartite cosmography (cf. 1 En 77:3: 4QEnastr[b] ar [4Q209] 23:8).

---

3. The terminology and chronology of the phases of the Aramaic language are related to Fitzmyer (1979).

4. On the expression *br 'nsh* in a heavily damaged context of *DA* II,8, see Hoftijzer and Jongeling (1995, 1:85, 194).

5. On the context of *Sefire* 3:16, see Fitzmyer (1995, 138f.).

6. Also a Georgian inscription from the second century C.E. at Armazi, see *Armazi* 7-11: see *KAI*, 2nd ed., #276 (= 1:53; 2:328).

7. An individual interpretation seems plausible in the passage about the dead souls in 1 En 22:3: 4QEn[e] ar (4Q206) 2, ii, 1.

To sum up, a comparison of the idiom *kebar 'enash* in Daniel 7:13 with Aramaic sources only leads to possible allusions to an individual meaning, mostly depending on the reading of the context. However, within the vast majority of references, the generic sense predominates (see also 1QapGen 19:14-16).[8]

The Heavenly Setting in Daniel 7

First of all, the four beasts in Daniel 7 represent mundane kingdoms that contrast with a certain aspect of humanity as reflected in the expression "son of man."[9] Furthermore, in Daniel 7:14 the "son of man" is endowed with "dominion, glory and kingship." In Daniel 2:37 and 5:18 only God gives "glory" *(yeqar)*,[10] and in Daniel 7 "glory" is related only to the "son of man." Also the Qumran literature, as it is related to the Daniel traditions, refers to the "glory" as an attribute of a heavenly kingdom. In the Prayer of Nabonidus a Jewish exorcist asks the king to write down a proclamation of the "glory" of the "Most High God," with the purpose that the king will be cured from a "malignant inflammation" (see 4QPrNab ar [4Q242] 1-3, 5) (Collins 1996b, 88). The prehexaplaric Old Greek version of Daniel 7:14 has shortened the triad in favor of the (royal) "dominion" *(exousia)*.[11] The Greek text of the Daniel legends uses "dominion" again to contrast the heavenly *basileia* with the terrestrial kingdoms (cf., e.g., Dan 3:33 [4:3]; 4:23 [4:26]).

A more detailed understanding of the surroundings of the "son of man" can be examined through a comparison of the visionary elements in Daniel 7:9-10, 7:13-14 and the Book of the Giants, 1 Enoch 14, and Ezekiel 1. In 4QEnGiants[b] ar (4Q530) 2:16-19 the dream vision reports that a "ruler of the heavens" de-

---

8. A dream vision explains the reasons of Abram's deception before the pharaoh. Here the Genesis Apocryphon adds a midrashic explanation to Gen 12:9-20 (Bernstein 1998, 147; Kugel 1998, 255-57).

9. Also the winged lion and the small horn are described with human features (attitude and knowledge). On the contrast, see Keel (2000).

10. Klaus Koch reminds me of the prayer of David in 1 Chron 29:11-12, according to which "riches and honor *(kavod/doxa)*" come from God. In his commentary on the book of Daniel, Koch further compares all relevant parallels that deal with a certain royal ideology from Persian times (see Dan 2:37; 4:19, 27, 33; 5:18-19) and calls the "glory" an "aura of authority" that can be compared with the meaning of *kavod* in the Targumim. Furthermore, the bestowal of a mundane king with attributes such as glory, power, or might by (a) God reminds one of the iconography and inscriptions from Commagene. They were part of the sanctuaries that Antiochus I of Commagene had erected in the first century B.C.E., especially at Nimrud Dagh (Koch 1999, 189-97; Boyce and Grenet 1991, 309-52).

11. The Greek Papyri 967 reads v. 14 with an asterisk here (Geißen 1968, 24-25, 108-9).

scended and an angelic assembly sat together (Puech 2001, 19-47). Loren Stuckenbruck (2001) has listed all relevant correspondences with Daniel 7, as the plural of the "thrones,"[12] the "thousand thousands" or the recordings. The main difference between Daniel and the Giants can be seen in the theophany of 4QEnGiants[b] that is explicitly orientated toward earth. The reason for this earthbound orientation might be that the objects in the Book of Giants are the giants with their whereabouts on earth. The dream vision in the Book of Giants represents an older tradition compared with the much more elaborate eschatology in Daniel 7.[13]

The first vision in the book of Ezekiel is composed as a blueprint of a heavenly sanctuary. In Ezekiel 1:22-28 we hear about the four creatures carrying a dome upon their heads. On this dome stands a throne upon which a person with the appearance of a human being takes his place. Fire, rays, and brightness determine the heavenly *doxa*. Also related to this motif is the comparison of the throne with lapis lazuli. Comparable to that is a cosmology attested in a Marduk-Text from neo-Assyrian times (KAR 307). According to this text, the former god of Babylon, Marduk, is now enthroned as the heavenly God-King sitting on a socle made of lapis lazuli. While Marduk's shrine is in the middle heaven, the lower heaven is made of transparent jasper. This corresponds with the crystal-like shining dome in Ezekiel 1:22 (Hartenstein 2001). Therefore, the crystal dome in Ezekiel 1 functions as a socle for the heavenly throne made of lapis lazuli. As in Ezekiel, the motifs of brightness or *doxa* in Daniel 7 provide further allusions to an understanding of the theophany as a *heavenly* theophany.

The most compelling parallel to Daniel 7 is 1 Enoch 14, because only in these chapters do we find the combination of a throne vision with entering into the throne hall (Kvanvig 1988, 556-602; Kvanvig 1984; Nickelsburg 2001, 254-66). Instantly, the story of Enoch's ascent to the heavenly sanctuary in 1 Enoch 14:8-9 is composed of metaphors of brightness.[14] Here, thunder and lightning urged Enoch to the heavens, where he reached a building surrounded by tongues of fire. A few verses later, in 14:18-20, Enoch has reached the second house in heaven, where he saw a lofty throne with the appearance like crystal (*krystallinon*: Cod. Panopolitanus). The "Great Glory" (*hē doxa hē megalē*: Cod. Panopolitanus) was sitting on this throne, and beneath this throne were streams of flaming fire. Here also a heavenly scene is indicated. As George

---

12. Against this the throne scenes in the book of the Similitudes of Enoch speak of one throne for the "chosen one" or the "son of man" (Hannah 2003).

13. See, e.g., Bar 3:26-28 (Mussies 1999; Stuckenbruck 1997b).

14. This text is also attested in Aramaic (4QEn[c] ar [4Q204] 1, vi, 20-22) (García Martínez and Tigchelaar 1997, 1:416; Milik 1976).

Nickelsburg puts it in his commentary: "Our author's God is the transcendent, wholly other, heavenly King. . . . God's holiness and purity are indicated by such imagery as: icelike, snowlike, sunlike, glory, fire" (Nickelsburg 2001, 260).

A comparison of motifs attested in the visionary scenes of Daniel 7:9-10 and 7:13-14 leads to the conclusion that the "son of man" was part of an angel-like assembly in a heavenly sanctuary. He is characterized as an individual, subordinated to the enthroned God. The "son of man" receives royal and God-like features in order to distinguish him from all human beings. The "son of man" is transcendent and functions within a drama of apocalyptic eschatology. This heavenly individual would later be interpreted as the Messiah.

Response: The Apocalyptic Worldview of Daniel

John J. Collins

I do not propose to respond to every point raised in these papers. I am in essential agreement with the arguments of Matthias Henze and Stefan Beyerle. I will begin with the broader issues raised by James Davila and Gabriele Boccaccini, then comment briefly on some more specific issues raised by Matthias Albani and Patrick Tiller, and return to some broader issues raised by Armin Lange and Florentino García Martínez.

The Issue of Terminology

The issue of terminology raised by James Davila was debated intensively in the 1970s, and it is surprising that he shows no awareness of that debate. One of the early elements of consensus in that discussion was that the word "apocalyptic," used as a noun, was highly confusing. This point is still resisted in some quarters, most recently by Lester Grabbe (2003, 107-33), but it is fundamental to bringing any clarity to the discussion. (See my rejoinder to Grabbe: Collins 2003, 44-52.) As Davila rightly notes, it is necessary to begin with specific phenomena, and in the case of "apocalyptic" the place to begin is with the genre apocalypse. This point was made more than thirty years ago by Klaus Koch (Koch 1972), and provided the impulse for the study of the genre in Semeia 14 (Collins 1979) and for my own monograph, *The Apocalyptic Imagination*, in 1984. In light of the continued insistence of some scholars on speaking of "apocalyptic," the point bears repetition.

It is not at all clear to me, however, how Davila understands the genre.

The definition worked out in Semeia 14 included both formal elements (a narrative framework, revelation mediated by an otherworldly being to a human recipient) and a common content, on a fairly high level of abstraction (a transcendent reality that is both temporal, insofar as it envisages eschatological salvation, and spatial, insofar as it involves a supernatural world) (see Collins 1979, 9). Davila, however, "cannot find a center to it all." In part, his problem seems to be confusion over the word "eschatology." He does not explain his understanding of the word, but it does not seem to include the judgment and fate of individuals after death, precisely the common core of apocalyptic eschatology and the element that distinguishes apocalyptic eschatology from that of the prophets. Hence his bewildering statements that the Book of the Watchers "has almost no eschatological interest" (which he retracts in response to the discussion) and that such apocalypses as 3 Baruch and the Apocalypse of Paul "do not include a future eschatology." But the whole raison d'être of these texts is to consider life in light of the postmortem fate of the dead, which is to say, in light of eschatology. It seems to me that much of Davila's difficulty arises from a failure to appreciate the central importance of the judgment of the dead in all the Jewish and early Christian apocalypses.

It is also central to Daniel and to the Enoch apocalypses, including the Animal Apocalypse, although it is not correct to speak of physical resurrection, at least in the case of Daniel. The hope for resurrection and life with the angels, or the fear of eternal damnation, radically alters the horizon of life and the values that inspire action. The apocalyptic worldview (which is precisely the worldview shared by the apocalypses) is one where human beings rely on supernatural revelation, in a world that is the arena of struggle between supernatural powers, and where the ultimate stakes are eternal reward or punishment after death (see further Collins 1991, 15-17). Texts that share these assumptions about the world may still differ on all sorts of specific issues, as Davila quite rightly sees. But the fact that no two trees are identical does not mean that we cannot speak of a forest.

Apocalyptic and Covenantal Theology

Gabriele Boccaccini's paper also deals with a broad issue of the theology of Daniel. Boccaccini takes the prayer in chapter 9 as his point of departure. We agree that this prayer is covenantal (though I see no justification for labeling it "Zadokite"). We also agree that it is unlikely to have been composed by the author of the visions but that it was included in the book for a purpose. There our agreement ends. The difficulty here is not that nothing similar is found in any other apocalyptic text (that is not the case). The problem is that nothing similar is found in the visions of Daniel. Boccaccini asserts that "whoever inserted it in the text did not see any contradiction between the prayer and the overall ideology of the text," but this assumption gives little credit to the editor for sophistication. The logic of the prayer, and of covenantal theology (which is Deuteronomic rather than Zadokite), is that Jerusalem would be restored in response to repentance. The angel, however, tells Daniel that this is not so. The time of desolation is decreed. It will end at the appointed time regardless of repentance and prayer. This is an essential difference between Daniel's apocalyptic theology of history and the covenantal, Deuteronomic theology. Surely the editor was sophisticated enough to see the difference (on the prayer in its context, see further Collins 1993, 359-60). Postmodern literary critics tell us repeatedly how literary sources are "subverted" or "resignified" in works that cite them or allude to them. I would argue that the Deuteronomic prayer in Daniel 9 is subverted by the new apocalyptic context in which it is placed, and I see no reason to think that the subversion was inadvertent.

Boccaccini assumes that for Daniel "the degenerative process of history" results from the sin of the people against the covenant and the consequent implementation of the curses. But no passage from Daniel can be cited in support of this argument, outside of the prayer. The crisis in history in chapter 7 is not initiated by the people's sin but by the mythological beasts that arise from the sea. In chapters 8 and 11 it arises from the rebellion of the "little horn," who tries to rise above the stars and above every god. Boccaccini asserts that Daniel does not blame angels, but the adversaries in chapter 10 are the angelic "princes" of the various nations (compare the seventy shepherds in the Animal Apocalypse). To be sure, Daniel does not draw on the myth of the fallen angels that is fundamental to the Enoch tradition, but it draws on other myths that attribute the problems of the world to supernatural agents. The options for understanding the origin of evil were not limited to a choice between the specifically Enochic myth and covenantal theology.

I should note, however, that it was possible in ancient Judaism to employ covenantal theology within an apocalyptic framework. This is essentially what we find in the apocalypses of 4 Ezra and 2 Baruch from the end of the first century C.E. (although covenantal theology is problematized to a great degree in 4 Ezra). Also we find both covenantal theology and an apocalyptic worldview in sectarian texts from the Dead Sea Scrolls, such as *Serekh ha-Yaḥad*. The Mosaic covenant, however, does not provide the context for either the books of Enoch or the book of Daniel. The attempt to integrate these early apocalyptic traditions with covenantal theology marks a new development, which we can see in the book of Jubilees and in the Dead Sea Scrolls. The shift toward a torah-centered theology is one of the features of the sect described in the scrolls, which distinguishes it from earlier apocalyptic traditions. The manner in which that shift came about is a major issue in the religious and intellectual history of Judaism in the second (or early first) century B.C.E., which awaits further exploration, although a beginning has been made by Bedenbender (2000).

Royal Ideology and Heavenly Mythology

Matthias Albani enriches our understanding of the mythological background of Daniel by drawing attention to its continuity with the old royal ideology. It seems to me, however, that the choice of an angelic deliverer in Daniel rather than a messianic king is more significant than Albani allows. It may be that the royal traditions had been thoroughly democratized. In any case, Daniel expresses no interest in the line of David or in the restoration of the monarchy. The prominence of Michael, the heavenly deliverer, expresses the conviction that the salvation of Israel was not to be attained by human military action but by reliance on the heavenly world.

It is characteristic of apocalyptic literature that the description of such figures is not restricted to fixed formulae but allows for diversity of expression. Accordingly, there is no reason to ask why this figure is called "one like a son of man" rather than "son of God." An angelic figure could have been called a "son of God," but the use of this expression was never de rigueur. "One like a son of man" is not a title but a description of a visionary figure, and is not at all incompatible with understanding the figure in question as a heavenly "son of God." I see no reason to think that the title "son of God" was viewed critically because of its supposed association with the hubris of Hellenistic kings. It would be used as a messianic title by Jews in the following centuries, almost certainly in the disputed Aramaic text 4Q246, and beyond any dispute in the Gospels (cf. the close parallel to 4Q246 in Luke 1:35). If the author of Daniel chose not to use this expression in chapter 7, this more likely is due to the close association of the title with the Davidic kingship, an institution in which Daniel expresses no interest, than to any association with Hellenistic kingship.

Lack of interest in the Davidic monarchy is a trait shared by the writings attributed to Enoch and to Daniel. The Similitudes of Enoch, which are later than the other works in 1 Enoch by at least a century, perhaps by two, speak of a messiah (1 En 48:10; 52:4), but he is a heavenly figure, described in language borrowed from Daniel 7 ("that son of man"). Other, later, apocalypses, 4 Ezra and 2 Baruch, would accommodate a messianic king in their eschatological expectations. The Dead Sea Scrolls, too, had a place for a human, earthly deliverer as well as an angelic one, as we can see from the fragment of the War Rule preserved in 4Q285. There appears, however, to have been very little messianic expectation in the early second century B.C.E., when Daniel and most of the books of Enoch took shape. When messianic expectation revived in the first century C.E., in reaction to the Hasmonean kingship and the Roman conquest, it was incorporated into the apocalyptic worldview. Interestingly enough, we then find "son of God" language not only in 4Q246 but also in the apocalypse of 4 Ezra (7:28-29; 13:32, 37). On the history of messianism in this period, see further Collins 1995.

The Problem of Identifying Groups

Patrick Tiller is right to caution us against reconstructing groups for which we do not have adequate evidence. The brief discussion suffers, however, from lack of clarity as to what would constitute a group or community. So we are told that "nothing in either Enoch or Daniel . . . can be realistically taken as evidence for a community, unless by community one means only an aggregate of individuals with similar interests." But is this not at least part of what we mean by a group? We do not know whether the *maskilim* of Daniel were organized in any way, but they evidently shared some common understanding and purpose that was distinctive in their context. The "chosen righteous" in the Apocalypse of Weeks seem to be quite distinct from other Jews of their time. Moreover, the continuity between the various Enochic compositions would seem to suggest that there was some kind of group context in which this tradition was passed on. Granted that there is no necessary connection between apocalypses and apocalyptic communities, we still have to account for the references in apocalyptic texts to groups of people who were self-consciously different from other Jews of their time. We do not know how, or to what extent, these groups were organized, and the lack of concrete evidence about social formations remains one of the most frustrating aspects of this literature. This is not a reason, however, to deny that there were any such groups at all, even though any claims we make about them must of necessity be modest.

An Apocalyptic Milieu?

We can by now, I think, speak of a consensus that the old view of the Hasidim, as a group that embraced the authors of the Danielic and Enochic literature and the forebears of the sect known from the Dead Sea Scrolls, and others besides, is unsatisfactory. The differences between these writings, notably the different attitudes to the armed rebellion of the Maccabees, cannot be ignored. Florentino García Martínez has cautioned that we may be too Cartesian in our modern scholarly analyses. Ancient ideas of requirements of compatibility in theological discourse may have been different from ours. His point is well taken. Those who questioned the angelic origin of sin were not necessarily expelled from the Enoch community (assuming that there existed such a community from which one could be expelled). I do not think this point undercuts the idea that the Danielic and Enochic literature reflect distinct traditions, and presumably different "groups," however organized. But it should warn us against any tendency to polarize the various groups that were active in Judea in the early second century B.C.E. Later, in the Dead Sea Scrolls, we find intense polemic between sectarian groups (the followers of the Teacher versus the "seekers of smooth things"). There is no evidence of such polemic between the bearers of Enochic and Danielic tradition. To say that two groups were distinct is not to say that they were opposed to each other. The authors and tradents of this literature may well have regarded what they had in common as more important than the points on which they differed. Factions in a society are often united by a common enemy. In the case of Daniel and at least some of the Enochic writings, such as the Animal Apocalypse, the common enemy was the Seleucid king.

It is obvious that the writings attributed to Daniel and Enoch have much in common. This is why they are all categorized as "apocalyptic." I have written of the common elements in these writings as constituting an apocalyptic "worldview." Armin Lange prefers to speak of an apocalyptic "milieu." It is unfortunate that he does not clarify just what he means by this term, as it is open to different interpretations. Whether or not it contradicts my own view of distinct groups in any way depends on whether it is taken to mean an intellectual milieu, a world of shared ideas, or a social milieu, which would imply some form of association but not necessarily membership in a single organization.

The common milieu posited by Lange is attested primarily by shared symbolism and visionary technique. Daniel and the Animal Apocalypse do not allude to precisely the same myths, but they use mythological and visionary imagery in similar ways. Both use the literary form of dream visions, which is evidently indebted to Near Eastern traditions of dream interpretation. I would go further and point to shared beliefs about the way the world works. Both books assume that human life is influenced by angelic and demonic forces. Both assume that history is running a predetermined course, and both expect a definitive divine intervention, to be followed by a universal judgment and the transformation of the elect (in Daniel the *maskilim* shine like the stars; in the Animal Apocalypse they become white bulls). Despite this common conceptual framework, which I would call a worldview, the two books commend different courses of action. The Animal Apocalypse endorses the militancy of the Maccabees. Daniel at most regards the militants as "little help" (11:34), and it is not clear that he acknowledges them at all.

The common elements in the two books, then, point to a common intellectual milieu, or a world of shared beliefs and symbols, which finds expression in a shared literary genre. It is not clear that it requires a common social milieu, or any form of association, but at this point our evidence is simply inadequate. If both works were written in Jerusalem, or at least in Judea, we might expect some form of contact between the authors and tradents, especially since both books might be described as resistance literature, and so the authors had a common cause, whatever their differences. Moreover, they shared many presuppositions about the world, which would facilitate discussion of their differences. The two books are obviously products of a common situation, the persecution under Antiochus Epiphanes. But in the end we simply do not know whether the authors or tradents associated with each other in any way. We do know that both writings became part of the library of the sect known from the scrolls, and we may infer that they were not regarded as incompatible with each other.

Whether or not a book like Jubilees is assigned to the same "milieu" depends on the level of abstraction on which we wish to operate. Jubilees still shares what I have described as the apocalyptic worldview, but it attaches great importance to the torah of Moses in both its narrative and its halakic aspects. Appropriately, it is the name of Moses, rather than Enoch or Daniel, that is attached to it. It surely was not authored by the same people who wrote the books of Enoch or Daniel. Nonetheless, it is clearly influenced by the Enoch tradition and belongs at least in part to the same intellectual milieu. It is also a work of mixed genre, part revelation, part quasi-historical narrative.

Lange suggests that the common milieu of these writings, other than Jubilees, was related to the Wisdom tradition, as argued by von Rad and H.-P. Müller. The idea that apocalypticism is indebted to "mantic wisdom," as proposed by Müller, has received broad support, from myself among others. It must be admitted that the only aspect of mantic wisdom that figures prominently in these books is dream interpretation, which is then extended to provide a model for the interpretation of mysterious signs (such as the writing on the wall in Daniel) and even scriptures (Dan 9). Other forms of Babylonian divination are not acknowledged at all. It was to the merit of von Rad to recognize that this kind of interpretation constitutes a kind of wisdom, but he failed to distinguish this activity from the more familiar proverbial wisdom of Proverbs and Ben Sira. Indeed, Ben Sira had little patience with dreams and their interpretation, as can be seen from Sirach 34:1-8. It does not seem to me useful to bundle together mantic and proverbial wisdom under the single rubric of "the Wisdom tradition," as if the practitioners of each had anything to do with each other. Insofar as the use of mantic wisdom gives any clue of the social milieu of the apocalyptic literature, it does not suggest any affinity or association with sages of the type of Ben Sira.

Much remains obscure about the precise social settings of the apocalyptic writings, and this will probably remain the case unless new evidence becomes available. Nonetheless, I think some progress has been made over the last thirty years. This progress has been twofold. On the one hand, we have come to appreciate the nuances that distinguish the individual books and are no longer willing to lump them together without further ado. On the other, we have come to appreciate that these differences are not incompatible with shared symbolism, ideas, and literary techniques that distinguish these works from other writings of the time, such as Ben Sira or 1 Maccabees. Both the coherence of the corpus and the distinctive features of individual books must be kept in view. Finally, we must resist the temptation to construe difference as conflict. The books of Daniel and Enoch each had their distinctive emphases, but they were not engaged in ideological warfare with each other. Rather they were concerned with a common enemy of Gentile rule which was brought to a crisis point by the actions of Antiochus Epiphanes.

References to Part One

Argall, Randal A. 1995. *1 Enoch and Sirach: A Comparative Literary and Conceptual Analysis of the Themes of Revelation, Creation, and Judgment.* SBLEJL 8. Atlanta: Scholars.

Bedenbender, Andreas. 2000. *Der Gott der Welt tritt auf den Sinai. Entstehung, Entwicklung und Funktionsweise der frühjüdischen Apokalyptik.* ANTZ 8. Berlin: Institut Kirche und Judentum.

Bernstein, Moshe J. 1998. "Pentateuchal Interpretation at Qumran." In *The Dead Sea Scrolls after Fifty Years: A Comprehensive Assessment,* edited by Peter W. Flint and James C. VanderKam, 1:128-59. Leiden: Brill.

Boccaccini, Gabriele. 1987. "È Daniele un testo apocalittico? Una (ri)definizione del pensiero del libro di Daniele in rapporto al libro dei Sogni e all'apocalittica." *Hen* 9:267-302.

―――. 1991. "Daniel and Dream Visions: The Genre of Apocalyptic and the Apocalyptic Tradition." In *Middle Judaism: Jewish Thought, 300 BCE to 200 CE,* 126-60. Minneapolis: Fortress.

―――. 1998. *Beyond the Essene Hypothesis: The Parting of the Ways between Qumran and Enochic Judaism.* Grand Rapids: Eerdmans.

―――. 2002. *Roots of Rabbinic Judaism: An Intellectual History, from Ezekiel to Daniel.* Grand Rapids: Eerdmans.

Boyce, Mary, and Frantz Grenet. 1991. *A History of Zoroastrianism.* Vol. 3, *Zoroastrianism under Macedonian and Roman Rule.* HO I,8,2,2. Leiden: Brill.

Burkett, Delbert Royce. 1999. *The Son of Man Debate: A History and Evaluation.* SNTSMS 107. Cambridge: Cambridge University Press.

Charlesworth, James H. 1980. "The Portrayal of the Righteous as an Angel." In *Ideal Figures in Ancient Judaism: Profiles and Paradigms,* edited by John J. Collins and George W. E. Nickelsburg, 135-51. SBLSCS 12. Chico, Calif.: Scholars.

Collins, John J. 1984. *The Apocalyptic Imagination: An Introduction to the Jewish Matrix of Christianity.* New York: Crossroad.

———. 1991. "Genre, Ideology and Social Movements in Jewish Apocalypticism." In *Mysteries and Revelations: Apocalyptic Studies since the Uppsala Colloquium,* edited by John J. Collins and James H. Charlesworth, 11-32. JSPSup 9. Sheffield: Sheffield Academic Press.

———. 1993. *Daniel: A Commentary on the Book of Daniel.* Hermeneia. Minneapolis: Fortress.

———. 1995. *The Scepter and the Star: The Messiahs of the Dead Sea Scrolls and Other Ancient Literature.* AB Reference Library. New York: Doubleday.

———. 1996a. "Pseudo-Daniel Revisited." *RevQ* 17:111-31.

———. 1996b. "4QPrayer of Nabonidus ar." In *Qumran Cave 4, XVII: Parabiblical Texts, Part 3,* edited by George Brooke et al., 88. DJD 22. Oxford: Clarendon.

———. 1997. *Seers, Sybils, and Sages in Hellenistic-Roman Judaism.* JSJSup 54. Leiden: Brill.

———. 1998a. *The Apocalyptic Imagination: An Introduction to Jewish Apocalyptic Literature.* 2nd ed. Grand Rapids: Eerdmans.

———. 1998b. *Apocalypticism in the Dead Sea Scrolls.* New York: Routledge.

———. 1999. "Pseudepigraphy and Group Formation in Second Temple Judaism." In *Pseudepigraphic Perspectives: The Apocrypha and Pseudepigrapha in Light of the Dead Sea Scrolls,* edited by Esther G. Chazon and Michael E. Stone, 43-58. STDJ 31. Leiden: Brill.

———. 2003. "Prophecy, Apocalypse and Eschatology: Reflections on the Proposals of Lester Grabbe." In *Knowing the End from the Beginning: The Prophetic, the Apocalyptic, and Their Relationships,* edited by Lester L. Grabbe and Robert D. Haak, 44-52. London: T. & T. Clark.

———, ed. 1979. *Apocalypse: The Morphology of a Genre.* Semeia 14. Atlanta: Scholars.

Dunn, James D. G. 1997. "'Son of God' as 'Son of Man' in the Dead Sea Scrolls? A Response to John Collins on 4Q246." In *The Scrolls and the Scriptures: Qumran Fifty Years After,* edited by Stanley E. Porter and Craig A. Evans, 198-210. JSPSup 26. Sheffield: Sheffield Academic Press.

Ferch, Arthur J. 1979. *The Son of Man in Daniel Seven.* Andrews University Seminary Doctoral Dissertation Series 6. Berrien Springs, Mich.: Andrews University.

Fitzmyer, Joseph A. 1979. "The Phases of the Aramaic Language." In *A Wandering Aramean: Collected Aramaic Essays,* 57-84. SBLMS 25. Chico, Calif.: Scholars.

———. 1995. *The Aramaic Inscriptions of Sefire.* 2nd ed. BibOr 19A. Rome: Pontificio Istituto Biblico.

Fitzmyer, Joseph A., and Daniel J. Harrington. 1978. *A Manual of Palestinian Aramaic Texts, Second Century BC–Second Century AD.* BibOr 34. Rome: Pontificio Istituto Biblico.

Fossum, Jarl. 1992. "Son of God." In *ABD* 6:128-37.

García Martíncz, Florentino, and Eibert J. C. Tigchelaar, eds. 1997. *The Dead Sea Scrolls Study Edition.* Vol. 1, *1Q1–4Q273.* Leiden: Brill.

Geißen, Angelo, ed. 1968. *Der Septuaginta-Text des Buches Daniel: Kap. 5–12, zusammen mit Susanna, Bel et Draco sowie Esther Kap. 1,1a–2,15 nach dem Kölner Teil des Papyrus 967, Papyrologische Texte und Abhandlungen.* Vol. 5. Bonn: Habelt.

Gilbert, Maurice. 1972. "La prière de Daniel: Dn 9,4-19." *RTL* 3:284-310.

Goldingay, John E. 1989. *Daniel.* Waco, Tex.: Word.

Grabbe, Lester L. 1989. "The Social Setting of Jewish Apocalypticism." *JSP* 4:27-47.

—————. 2003. "Prophetic and Apocalyptic: Time for New Definitions — and New Thinking." In *Knowing the End from the Beginning: The Prophetic, the Apocalyptic, and Their Relationships,* edited by Lester L. Grabbe and Robert D. Haak, 107-33. London: T. & T. Clark.

Hannah, Darrell D. 2003. "The Throne of His Glory: The Divine Throne and Heavenly Mediators in Revelation and the Similitudes of Enoch." *ZNW* 94:68-96.

Hanson, Paul D. 1975. *The Dawn of Apocalyptic: The Historical and Sociological Roots of Jewish Apocalyptic Eschatology.* Philadelphia: Fortress.

Hartenstein, Friedhelm. 2001. "Wolkendunkel und Himmelsfeste: Zur Genese und Kosmologie der Vorstellung des himmlischen Heiligtums JHWHs." In *Das biblische Weltbild und seine altorientalischen Kontexte,* edited by Bernd Janowski and Beate Ego, 139-44. FAT 32. Tübingen: Mohr Siebeck.

Hengel, Martin. 1974. *Judaism and Hellenism: Studies in Their Encounter in Palestine during the Early Hellenistic Period.* Philadelphia: Fortress.

Henze, Matthias. 2001. "The Narrative Frame of Daniel: A Literary Assessment." *JSJ* 32, no. 1: 5-24.

Himmelfarb, Martha. 1991. "Revelation and Rapture: The Transformation of the Visionary in the Ascent Apocalypses." In *Mysteries and Revelations: Apocalyptic Studies since the Uppsala Colloquium,* edited by John J. Collins and James H. Charlesworth, 79-90. JSPSup 9. Sheffield: Sheffield Academic Press.

Hoftijzer, Jan, and Karel Jongeling, eds. 1995. *Dictionary of the North-West Semitic Inscriptions.* HO I,21,1. Leiden: Brill.

Horsley, Richard A. 2000. "Social Relations and Social Conflict in the Epistle of Enoch." In *For a Later Generation: The Transformation of Tradition in Israel, Early Judaism, and Early Christianity,* edited by Randal A. Argall, Beverly A. Bow, and Rodney A. Werline, 100-115. Harrisburg, Pa.: Trinity.

Horsley, Richard A., and Patrick Tiller. 2002. "Ben Sira and the Sociology of the Second Temple." In *Second Temple Studies III: Studies in Politics, Class, and Material Culture,* edited by Philip R. Davies and John M. Halligan, 74-107. JSOTSup 340. Sheffield: Sheffield Academic Press.

Janowski, Bernd. 2002. "Die heilige Wohnung des Höchsten: Kosmologische Implikationen der Jerusalemer Tempeltheologie." In *Gottesstadt und Gottesgarten: Zu Geschichte und Theologie des Jerusalemer Tempels,* edited by Othmar Keel and Erich Zenger, 24-68. QD 191. Freiburg: Herder.

Jones, Bruce William. 1968. "The Prayer in Daniel IX." *VT* 18:488-93.

Kaiser, Otto. 1994. *Grundriß der Einleitung in die kanonischen und deuterokanonischen*

Schriften des Alten Testaments. Vol. 2, *Die prophetischen Werke.* Gütersloh: Gütersloher.

Keel, Othmar. 2000. "Die Tiere und der Mensch in Dan 7." In *Hellenismus und Judentum: Vier Studien zu Daniel 7 und zur Religionsnot unter Antiochus IV,* edited by Othmar Keel and Urs Staub, 18-23. OBO 178. Fribourg and Göttingen: Universitätsverlag and Vandenhoeck.

Kermode, Frank. 2000. *The Sense of an Ending: Studies in the Theory of Fiction with a New Epilogue.* Oxford: Oxford University Press.

Koch, Klaus. 1972. *The Rediscovery of Apocalyptic.* SBT 33. Naperville, Ill.: Allenson.

———. 1995. "Das Reich der Heiligen und des Menschensohns: Ein Kapitel politischer Theologie." In *Die Reiche der Welt und der kommende Menschensohn: Studien zum Danielbuch, Gesammelte Aufsätze,* 2:140-72. Neukirchen-Vluyn: Neukirchener.

———. 1999. *Daniel.* BKAT XXII,3. Neukirchen-Vluyn: Neukirchener.

Kreplin, Matthias. 2001. *Das Selbstverständnis Jesu: Hermeneutische und christologische Reflexionen, historisch-kritische Analyse.* WUNT II/141. Tübingen: Mohr Siebeck.

Kugel, James L. 1998. *Traditions of the Bible: A Guide to the Bible as It Was at the Start of the Common Era.* Cambridge: Harvard University Press.

Kvanvig, Helge S. 1984. "Henoch und der Menschensohn: Das Verhältnis von Hen 14 zu Dan 7." *ST* 38:101-33.

———. 1988. *Roots of Apocalyptic: The Mesopotamian Background of the Enoch Figure and of the Son of Man.* WMANT 61. Neukirchen-Vluyn: Neukirchener.

Laato, Antti. 1997. *A Star Is Rising: The Historical Developments of the Old Testament Royal Ideology and the Rise of the Jewish Messianic Expectations.* Atlanta: Scholars.

Lacocque, André. 1979. *The Book of Daniel.* Atlanta: John Knox.

Landau, Y. H. 1966. "A Greek Inscription Found Near Hefzibah." *IEJ* 16:54-70.

Lange, Armin. 1996. "1QGenAp XIX10-XX32 as Paradigm of the Wisdom Didactive Narrative." In *Qumranstudien: Vorträge und Beiträge der Teilnehmer des Qumranseminars auf dem internationalen Treffen der Society of Biblical Literature, Münster, 25.-26. Juli 1993,* edited by Heinz-Josef Fabry, Armin Lange, and Hermann Lichtenberger, 191-204. Göttingen: Vandenhoeck & Ruprecht.

Milik, Jozef T. 1976. *The Books of Enoch: Aramaic Fragments of Qumran Cave 4, with the Collaboration of Matthew Black.* Oxford: Clarendon.

Moses, A. D. A. 1996. *Matthew's Transfiguration Story and Jewish-Christian Controversy.* JSNTSup 122. Sheffield: Sheffield Academic Press.

Müller, Hans-Peter. 1969. "Magisch-Mantische Weisheit und die Gestalt Daniels." *UF* 1:79-94.

———. 1972. "Magische Weisheit und Apokalyptik." In *Congress Volume Uppsala 1971,* 268-93. VTSup 22. Leiden: Brill.

———. 1977. "Die weisheitliche Lehrerzählung im Alten Testament und seiner Umwelt." *WO* 9:77-98.

Mussies, Gerard. 1999. "Giants." In DDD, 343-45.

Najman, Hindy. 2002. "Review of G. Boccaccini [1998], *Beyond the Essene Hypothesis*." *Association for Jewish Studies Review* 26, no. 2: 352-54.

Nickelsburg, George W. E. 1982. "The Epistle of Enoch and the Qumran Literature." *JJS* 33:333-48.

———. 1983. "Social Aspects of Palestinian Jewish Apocalypticism: 1 Enoch 92-105." In *Apocalypticism in the Mediterranean World and the Near East*, edited by David Hellholm, 641-54. Tübingen: Mohr Siebeck.

———. 2001. *1 Enoch 1: A Commentary on the Book of 1 Enoch, Chapters 1–36, 81–108*. Hermeneia. Minneapolis: Fortress.

Porteous, Norman W. 1965. *Daniel*. OTL. Philadelphia: Westminster.

Porter, Paul A. 1983. *Metaphors and Monsters: A Literary-Critical Study of Daniel 7 and 8*. ConBOT 20. Lund: Gleerup.

Puech, Émile. 1996. "246. 4QApocryphe de Daniel ar." *DJD* 22:164-84.

———. 2001. "4QLivre des Géants b ar." In *Qumran Grotte 4, XXII: Textes Araméens première partie: 4Q529-549*, edited by Émile Puech, 19-47. DJD 31. Oxford: Clarendon.

Rad, Gerhard von. 1971. "Josephsgeschichte und ältere Chokma." In *Studien zum Alten Testament*, 1:272-80. 4th ed. Munich: Kaiser.

———. 1985. *Weisheit in Israel*. 3rd ed. Neukirchen-Vluyn: Neukirchener.

———. 1993. *Theologie des Alten Testaments*. Vol. 2, *Die Theologie der prophetischen Überlieferungen Israels*. 10th ed. Gütersloh: Chr. Kaiser/Gütersloher.

Redditt Paul L. 1999. *Daniel*. NCBC. Sheffield: Sheffield Academic Press.

Reid, Stephen Breck. 1989. *Enoch and Daniel: A Form Critical and Sociological Study of Historical Apocalypses*. Berkeley: BIBAL.

Sacchi, Paolo. 1997. *Jewish Apocalyptic and Its History*. Sheffield: Sheffield Academic Press.

Schmitt, Hans-Christoph. 1980. *Die nichtpriesterliche Josephsgeschichte. Ein Beitrag zur neuesten Pentateuchkritik*. BZAW 154. Berlin and New York: De Gruyter.

Smith, Jonathan Z. 1978. *Map Is Not Territory: Studies in the History of Religions*. SJLA 23. Leiden: Brill.

Soggin, Jan Albert. 1989. *Introduction to the Old Testament: From Its Origins to the Closing of the Alexandrian Canon*. Translated by John Bowden. 3rd ed. OTL. Louisville: Westminster/John Knox.

Steudel, Annette. 1996. "The Eternal Reign of the People of God: Collective Expectations in Qumran texts (4Q246 vs 1QM)." *RevQ* 17:507-25.

Stuckenbruck, Loren. 1997a. *The Book of Giants from Qumran: Texts, Translation, and Commentary*. TSAJ 63. Tübingen: Mohr Siebeck.

———. 1997b. "The Throne-Theophany of the Book of Giants: Some New Light on the Background of Daniel 7." In *The Scrolls and the Scriptures: Qumran Fifty Years After*, edited by Stanley E. Porter and Craig A. Evans, 211-20. JSPSup 26. Sheffield: Sheffield Academic Press.

———. 2001. "Daniel and Early Enoch Traditions in the Dead Sea Scrolls." In *The*

Book of Daniel: Composition and Reception, edited by John J. Collins and Peter W. Flint, 2:368-86. VTSup 83.2. Leiden: Brill.

Taylor, James Ellis. 1979. "Seleucid Rule in Palestine." Ph.D. diss., Duke University.

Tcherikover, Victor. 1970. *Hellenistic Civilization and the Jews.* New York: Atheneum.

Tiller, Patrick A. 1993. *A Commentary on the Animal Apocalypse of 1 Enoch.* EJL 4. Atlanta: Scholars.

Towner, W. Sibley. 1971. "Retributional Theology in the Apocalyptic Setting." *USQR* 26:213.

VanderKam, James C. 1977. *Textual and Historical Studies in the Book of Jubilees.* HSM 14. Missoula, Mont.: Scholars.

———. 1984. *Enoch and the Growth of an Apocalyptic Tradition.* CBQMS 16. Washington, D.C.: Catholic Biblical Association of America.

———. 1992. "Jubilees, Book of." In *ABD* 3:1030-32.

———. 1995. *Enoch: A Man for All Generations.* Studies on Personalities of the Old Testament. Columbia: University of South Carolina Press.

Wright, Benjamin G. 1997. "Fear the Lord and Honor the Priest: Ben Sira as Defender of the Jerusalem Priesthood." In *The Book of Ben Sira in Modern Research: Proceedings of the First International Ben Sira Conference,* edited by Pancratius C. Beentjes, 189-222. BZAW Supplement Series 255. Berlin: De Gruyter.

PART TWO

ENOCH AND JUBILEES

Jubilees — Read as a Narrative

Helge S. Kvanvig

James VanderKam discusses various characteristics of the book of Jubilees. There are many ways to characterize the book as a whole: Targum, commentary, and rewritten Bible (VanderKam 2001a, 135f.). Each of these casts a light on how Jubilees relates to its basic sources, Genesis and Exodus. There should be no doubt that this is an essential perspective on the book. But at the same time, we cannot underestimate the fact that the material from Genesis and Exodus is reorganized in Jubilees into a narrative with its own distinctive qualities, as is implicit in VanderKam's reading of Jubilees as well. In the following I will discuss this implicit understanding in so many readings of Jubilees. How do we read Jubilees narratively?

When we regard Jubilees as a narration, the first distinction we have to make is between narrative and story. There are many technical terms one could use, but I choose "narrative" and "story" for their simplicity.[1] As a whole the book is a narrative, and in this narrative there is a story, linking the events in a chain. The narrative begins on Mount Sinai and ends on Mount Sinai (Jub 50:2). It organizes the content as a revelation given there to Moses by the Angel of Presence. Throughout the book we are repeatedly reminded through the addresses by this angel to Moses that this is the setting. We are in the narrative on Mount Sinai all the time. The story line is different. The story starts with the creation, moves through the various stages of the history of the ancestors of Is-

---

1. For this terminology, cf. Rimmon-Kenan (1989, 1-28). Mieke Bal characterizes the same level of a narrative as *fabula* (Bal 1985, 1-10). Cf. the discussion of differing terminology related to story and events in Hawthorn (1994, 198f.).

rael, and ends with Moses on Mount Sinai, with the curious effect that on the narrative level it is revealed to Moses what happened to him on the story level (cf. the break in narrative style from Jub 47:1).

Observing these two levels of the text, we are already struck by one feature. It is on the story level that Jubilees follows the pattern of Genesis and Exodus. Even though there are many differences, the organizing principle of following the actions of the forefathers is taken from the Mosaic torah. This is not the case with the narrative. The organization of the material on this level is solely the fiction of the author, stressing, as it seems, the unique authority of Moses as the direct human recipient of heavenly revelations. Therefore he appears both at the beginning and at the end of the book and is addressed throughout.

According to Aristotle's *Poetics*, the story, or *mythos* in his wording, consists of a beginning, a middle, and an end.[2] Jubilees is in this respect well organized. The importance of the Sabbath is emphasized both at the beginning and at the end of the story (Jub 2:16-33; 50:1-13). History moves forward to the election of Jacob and his descendants to keep the Sabbath commandment (2:19-22). The same numerical principle is underlying both creation and history. The creation consists of twenty-two kinds of works (cf. 2:15); history up to the election of Jacob consists of twenty-two leaders of humanity (2:23).

That Jacob is placed in this central position of the story comes as a surprise in comparison with his ambiguous role in the Mosaic torah; but all the negative traits in the biblical portrait of him are removed in Jubilees. Quantitatively the story of Jacob embraces most of the patriarchal period, from 19:13 to 45:6. He is thus put in direct relation to Abraham through Abraham's blessing at his birth (19:16-29), and there is only a short interplay between his death and the birth of Moses (47:1). At his birth his belonging to the genealogical line of the great ancestral heroes is emphasized, in accordance with his placement at the beginning of the story. He is blessed with the blessing of Adam, Enoch, Noah, and Shem (19:27).

The first great revealer in the story line of Jubilees is Enoch (4:17-26). It is therefore interesting to note that there are several features that connect Enoch and Jacob. The most important of them is that they both are connected to the central theme of Jubilees: sexual impurity. Enoch testifies against the Watchers who have defiled themselves with earthly women (4:22). This event is in Jubilees, unlike Genesis, the direct cause of the flood (5:1-4). The judgment of the Watchers and their gigantic offspring forms the paradigm for the judgment of

---

2. For Aristotle, cf. Halliwell (1995). Text in the *Poetics*, chap. 6, lines 15-30, p. 50, and chap. 7, lines 21-30, p. 54. For a discussion, cf. Halliwell (1998, 97-99, 138-39).

all humankind (5:6-18). Their great sin was that they transgressed the forbidden border of sexuality — they married whomever they chose (5:1). This is exactly what Jacob did not do — he chose wives within the borders of his own kin. It is crucial to recognize these interconnecting narrative links, if not the events at the beginning of the story, since in primeval time the latter seem to have nothing to do with what takes place later in the story when Israel is separated from the nations as God's chosen people.

According to Aristotle, a complex *mythos* has two features: the events are recorded *meta tade*, "one after another," and *dia tade*, "one because of another."[3] The first feature forms the episodic structure of the narrative, the other the logical or credible structure (Halliwell 1998, 96-106). The overall episodic structural element in Jubilees is not difficult to discern. All the events are placed in a scheme of 49 + 1 jubilees, one jubilee being forty-nine years. The chronology starts with Adam and Eve in Paradise (3:15) and ends with exodus, the Sinai revelation, and the entry into Canaan, which are placed in the fiftieth jubilee (48:1; 50:4).

The logical or credible structure of a narrative has as a presupposition that there is a tension in the story, something that threatens to cause the events to fall apart (Bal 1985, 19ff.). This obstacle has to be overcome in a way that seems logical or credible for the reader or listener. The plot of the story is accordingly linked to how the protagonists struggle to overcome obstacles that prevent them from achieving a desired end. What Israel is freed from at the end is what obstructs them on the journey. The question is whether this obstruction is formed as a theme that unites the different parts of the story. If we divide the fifty jubilees, we find the Watcher episode placed in the twenty-fifth jubilee. This incident functions in two ways in the narrative, both as a paradigm of evil and as the ultimate cause of evil.

The acts of the Watchers constituted the paradigm for three kinds of evil that humans should avoid: fornication, uncleanness, and injustice. These basic evils were all embedded in the acts of the Watchers and repeated by the sinners throughout history. The fornication is connected to illicit intercourse; uncleanness is connected to the transgression of sexual borders — they married whomever they chose — and injustice is connected to the violence and bloodshed of their offspring (7:20-25). To avoid these sins it was necessary for the Israelites and their ancestors to separate from the Gentiles and above all not to mix with them sexually. This theme is repeated throughout the book, particularly in the great speeches (20:1-10; 22:10-24; 25:1-23). It is also the main plot in the story of Jacob and Esau (26:1-29).

3. This is the distinguished feature of what Aristotle designates as a complex *mythos;* cf. *Poetics*, chap. 10, lines 11-20, pp. 62-64; cf. also the reflection in Ricoeur (1984, 40-42, 66-67).

Of special interest is the story about the rape of Dinah (Jub 30), because it is connected to the establishment of the Levite priesthood (31:13-17). The story of Dinah demonstrates that the law of sexual purity could be broken in two ways: by foreign men taking Israelite women, exemplified in the plot, and by Israelite men defiling themselves with foreign women, included in the admonition elaborating the story. Read in relation to the Watcher story, as we know it both from the book of Enoch and Jubilees, both paradigms apply: the Watchers could be seen as outsiders taking women belonging to the human family as insiders, or the Watchers could be seen as insiders, belonging to the heavenly realm, defiling themselves with human women as outsiders.[4]

The Watcher story is not only a paradigm for sin and evil, it also constitutes the root cause for the evil that haunts men. The evil acts of the Watchers and giants continue through the acts of the demons (7:27; cf. 10:1-14; 11:4-5; 17:15–18:2; 19:28; 48:2, 9, 12-18; 49:2). At the request of Mastema, the prince of evil, one-tenth of the evil spirits were left on the earth, the others had to share the fate of the Watchers, their fathers (10:5, 8-9). The effect of this heavily reduced force was, however, still formidable: every kind of error and sin, and every kind of transgression — to corrupt, to destroy, and to shed blood on the earth (11:5).

VanderKam maintains that even though the Watcher story is important in the primeval history, it plays a modest role in Jubilees as a whole (VanderKam 1999, 154; 1978, 1:229-51). This inference is correct if we look for direct references to or quotations from the Watcher story in the book as a whole. When we read Jubilees narratively, however, we see the role of the Watcher story differently. Both the episodic and the logical structure of the narrative draw heavily on it.

In the story line the Jacob narrative forms the central part. The basic theme of the Jacob story and the Watcher story is the same, sexual purity. In the overall structure of the book, freedom from evil is promised at the entrance into Canaan in the fiftieth jubilee; evil becomes a part of human destiny through the transgression of the Watchers in the twenty-fifth jubilee. In the logical structure the plot is based on how evil at the end of time will be conquered. In this context the Watcher story functions both as a paradigm for what evil is and as a foundational story for how evil became a part of human reality.

4. In the Book of the Watchers (1 En 6–16) the Watchers and giants could thus be both a mythical image read in the light of Greek invaders, as suggested by Nickelsburg (1977, 383-405; 2001, 169ff.), and a mythical image reflecting the impurity of Jewish priests, as suggested by Suter (1979, 115-35). In the first case they are outsiders violating the purity of Jewish women, like Shechem raping Dinah, and in the second case they are insiders violating their purity in sexual unity with foreign women. Cf. the discussion in Kvanvig (2002b).

This is one of the literary devices that distinguish Jubilees from Genesis and Exodus. In the Mosaic torah it is difficult to find an overall structure that combines the different parts or a basic plot starting in primeval time and running through history. This is exactly what we find in Jubilees: the story material from Genesis and Exodus is joined together in a much more comprehensive way through creating beginnings, endings, middles in the narrative, making plots, starting in the primeval history and developing through the history of the great ancestors.

A narrative is marked by a discordant concordance, according to Paul Ricoeur (1984, 42-45). There is something that holds the narrative together and something that tears it apart. This relates to the tension in the story, as we have seen, but often also to the composition as a whole, on the narrative level (Kvanvig 2002a, 79ff.). Read as a whole, Jubilees is very concordant. Nevertheless, there is a disturbing discordance in the narrative — in fact, in the very heart of it — connected to the role of Moses and the revelation of the divine torah.

There is a strange relationship between *intra*textuality and *inter*textuality at play in Jubilees. On the one hand the biblical torah is incorporated into the book, forming the backbone of the story elaborated there. On the other hand the biblical torah exists outside the book as a separate document that is quoted. How do we understand this enigmatic interplay between the intratextual torah and the intertextual torah?

According to VanderKam, the author makes explicit references to the biblical torah, the intertextual, in three passages: 2:24, 6:22, and 30:12 (VanderKam 2001a, 136f.). In these three places it is referred to as "the first law" or simply "the law." The references occur in contexts closely related to the main themes of the book: the Sabbath (2:24), the covenant (6:22), and the separation of the Israelites from the Gentiles (30:12). It is, however, never told how and under what circumstances the first law was revealed, nor what kind of authority is given to this law in relation to Jubilees itself. The first law is simply cited in three places as a known witness to the central issues revealed to the readers of Jubilees. VanderKam states that Jubilees presents itself as an absolutely authoritative work whose divine message compels acceptance and obedience. Nevertheless, he claims that the purpose of the author was not to replace the books of the Bible, but to save them from being misconstrued (12). How do we know this?

The enigma of the first law becomes even greater when we recognize the importance of sacred books in the history of humankind. The transmission of these books, starting with the first revealer Enoch and ending with the eternal priesthood of Levi, forms yet one more coherent feature of the book (4:17-21; 7:38-39; 8:11-12; 10:13-14; 12:25-27; 21:10; 32:24-26; 45:16). In the story line these books and the accompanying oral instructions formed the divine wisdom and laws according to which the chosen line of humanity lived. They followed these laws as they gradually grew and finally were witnessed to in Jubilees itself.[5] The author of Jubilees thus places his own book into the sequence of these books. Jubilees is the final and full revelation in the succession of divinely inspired books. Why is the Pentateuch missing in this line? Why are Enoch and Noah the great revealers of humankind and not Moses, to whom the first law was given? Why is it clearly stated that the succession of revelatory books before Jubilees ended with Levi (45:6) and not with the first law?

A comparison between the roles of Moses in the Bible and in Jubilees is, at this point, instructive. Both maintain that the ultimate revelation took place on Mount Sinai, but the fiction is very different. In the final shape of the Pentateuch, revelation is successively connected to the three covenants, forming three stages in the relation between God and his people: Noah (Gen 9), Abraham (Gen 17), and Moses (Exod 24). The three stages are connected to three different names of the divinity: Elohim in the primeval history, El Shaddai for Abraham (Gen 17), and YHWH for Moses (Exod 3 and 6). The climax of the story is thus Moses. To him is revealed the divine name at Horeb (Sinai); he is called as a prophet (Exod 3–4); he delivers the people from the bondage in Egypt, leading them through the Sea of Reeds (Exod 5–14); and he receives the divine torah at Mount Sinai (Exod 19ff.).

The fiction in Jubilees is ambiguous. Moses is introduced already at the beginning of the book. His role as the ultimate revealer is even more in focus than in the Mosaic torah. After this beginning we should expect the story line to be directed toward him at the end of the story as the climax of the whole. However, nothing is said about the revelation of the divine name to Moses, there is no calling of him, and Exodus is only summarily recorded. There is no dramatic language of revelation as in the Mosaic torah when the Israelites arrive at Sinai (Exod 19). There is, accordingly, a considerable gap between Moses presented on the narrative level in the introduction and Moses as he is recorded in the story itself. The role of Moses in the story, following the pattern of the Mosaic torah, is reduced to give room for the Moses of the narrative fiction unique to Jubilees.

This is clearly shown when the law is given to Moses at the beginning of the narrative. The setting of Jubilees 1 is taken from Exodus 24:12-18, in which God invites Moses to the top of the mountain to receive the stone tablets with the law and the commandments (Exod 24:12). In Jubilees 1:1-4 this setting is repeated and elaborated. Moses is invited to come to the mountain to receive the

---

5. Cf. the list of laws related to the chosen line in VanderKam (2001a, 100-109).

two stone tablets of the law and commandments. When he comes to the top, however, he is allowed to see "the division of all the times — both of the law and of the testimony" (1:4). Both the law and the testimony are words that Moses should write down in a book (1:5). This book is Jubilees itself. The law and commandments of Exodus as a part of the biblical torah do not appear in the text of Jubilees. The author makes use of the words of the Pentateuch to make the torah of the Pentateuch disappear.

This brings us back to the narrative design of Jubilees, how the fiction is based on an interplay between the intratextual and the intertextual torah. Moses is placed on Mount Sinai at the beginning of Jubilees not to institute a new covenant like the Moses of the Mosaic torah, but to renew the Noahitic covenant from primeval time (Jub 1:5). He does not receive the torah of the Mosaic torah, but Jubilees. Furthermore, Jubilees is not like the biblical torah in constituting a new torah, but a story about how the divine torah came into being in the past, including an elaboration and interpretation of this torah. Moses' arrival on the mountain does not foreshadow a new revelation, but heralds a reconsideration of the revelations already given. In short, in Jubilees the biblical Moses is placed at the start of the narrative as the ultimate witness of his own reduced significance.

In retrospect I will place this narrative reading of Jubilees into the broader framework of the discussions of Enoch scholars. There are two questions that need addressing. The first is whether it is possible or advisable to go behind the texts and try to reconstruct the collective bodies (groups, communities, milieus) responsible for the Enochic books. The second is what kind of criteria we should use when we talk about separate or rival collective bodies (and not simply about differing opinions between individual scribes, sages, or priests belonging to the same milieu).

In the first case, Jubilees presents an image of transmitting books within a special milieu. It even names those supposed to be responsible for the transmission of the books of the forefathers at the time of the author — the Levites! In addition, it presents an image of different kinds of heavenly revelations, the writing down of revelations, transmission of written documents, and instruction through oral teaching throughout history. I do not read these concrete images from the life within a community simply as historical fiction, but as a reflection of a practice known to the readers of the book. It reminds us that when there were scrolls, there had to be somebody who took care of and cherished the scrolls. In the case of the Enochic books this was done through many centuries in an ongoing tradition of commenting and revising. Jubilees shows us that there existed a "family of texts" that belonged to a "family of people," and that these two notions belong together.

The second issue deals with the kinds of criteria that should be applied to distinguish between collective bodies of various kinds and not simply between individuals broadly belonging to the same milieu. It is not difficult to imagine that different scribes belonging to the scribal milieu of the second temple could tell different stories from the past, or the same story in different ways, or that they could have different opinions about ethical or cultic rules. On the other hand, is it likely that three scribes that basically shared the same ideology or theology could give the following alternative versions of what happened on Mount Sinai? Moses comes to the mountain and receives the torah of the Pentateuch (as in the Mosaic torah), he receives Jubilees (as in the book of Jubilees), or he receives nothing (as in the Enochic Animal Apocalypse). When we consider the central role of the torah in this period, it is difficult to argue that it was not of major, dividing importance whether the biblical torah or Jubilees counted as the basic revelation, or that the scribe of the Animal Apocalypse simply forgot to mention that Moses received the torah, or that it was self-evident. This is even more significant since Jubilees draws heavily on the books of Enoch. In the Enochic Animal Apocalypse Moses received nothing, while in the Mosaic torah Enoch is a figure with no revelatory significance at all.

The same is the case with the recognition of the second temple. One can imagine that Danielic scribes, reworking and transmitting Danielic visions, were connected to the scribal milieu of the second temple, even though their apocalyptic worldview was very different from that of the scribes transmitting the biblical Pentateuch. This is possible because the scribes nevertheless shared the same view on the temple; but is it possible to think that a scribe, in one way or another attached to the temple, could totally dismiss the legitimacy of this temple as in the Animal Apocalypse and in the Apocalypse of Weeks?[6] I think for both the torah and the temple we are dealing with dividing lines not only between texts and individuals, but between collective bodies. The two different literary notions demand totally different attitudes and practices in daily life. In both cases Jubilees tries to bring the two opposite views together, but in a way closer to Enoch than to the biblical torah: Moses becomes the witness of a new torah that includes the Enochic material, and even though the critique of the second temple in Jubilees is cautious, it is certainly there.[7]

6. In the Animal Apocalypse the bread on the altar is unclean (1 En 89:73). In the Apocalypse of Weeks the only thing that can be said about the first generations of the second temple is that all their deeds will be perverse (1 En 93:9). The first temple is, however, highly praised (93:7-8).

7. In the prediction of history in the opening of the book, the second temple is not mentioned. The new temple described in Jub 1:17 is not the second temple, but the eschatological

There is a third aspect so obvious that it is often overlooked. In the discussion about groups and ideologies in the second temple period, the scope is often limited to Palestine and the religious and cultural worldview formed within what is constructed as Judaism. In this narrow perspective the Enoch literature, with its emphasis on primeval time as the time when the basic conditions of reality were laid down and the basic revelations about them were given, seems as something exotic compared to what is regarded as mainstream Judaism. In a broader religious perspective, however, it is possible to flip this picture. In the ancient religions that could influence Palestine in this period — Canaanite, Greek, Mesopotamian — the revelation of the foundational events is placed at the beginning. In this regard the Mesopotamian traditions are closest to Enoch because they have the concept of both great revealers in the beginning of history and the flood as the catastrophe forming reality which divides between mythical time and ancient legendary time (Kvanvig 2002b, 207f.). From this perspective it is the biblical torah which is exotic. To claim that the foundational events happened in primeval time was commonplace; to claim that they happened on a mountain in a desert in the midst of history was highly original.

In his contribution to the Enochic-Essene Hypothesis, Boccaccini listed four characteristics of the Enochic teaching: the origin of evil, the illegitimacy of the second temple, the calendar of 364 days, and the emphasis on the Watcher story. He could have included the relation to the torah — and closely connected to this issue is the whole question about where and how the foundational events and the revelations took place. In the Enoch traditions they happened in primeval time. There might be a connecting link here to what is said about the Essenes by the ancient historiographers. Philo, Josephus, and Pliny all treat the Essenes as an ancient movement. Josephus even states that Essene practice and doctrine came from a remote age, older than Greek philosophers. Pliny records a tradition that the Essenes had existed for thousands of years as an eternal people (Boccaccini 1998, 23f.). This does not, of course, conform to any historical reconstruction of either the Essenes or Enochians. It conforms, however, to the fiction of the Enochic books and the fiction of the transmission of these books in Jubilees. Even though both the Enochic books and Jubilees point to a specific phase in the second temple period for the origin of the community of the righteous (Nickelsburg 2001, 398ff.), they both claim that the revival is based on books and traditions going back to the beginning of history.

---

temple, which will be built after the transformation of the people into the plant of righteousness. The predictions in Jub 23:21 refer to the second temple and the cult performed there. In the temple the worshipers will mention the great name, but neither truly nor rightly. Moreover, they will defile the Holy of Holies.

The LXX and Enoch:
Influence and Interpretation
in Early Jewish Literature

Erik W. Larson

The purpose of this chapter is to explore the influence of the Old Greek translation of the book of Genesis (OGGen) on some of the subsequent Jewish apocryphal writings in Greek that mention Enoch or the fall of the Watchers in some way. As is well known, OGGen diverges from the Masoretic Text of the Bible (MT) in several distinctive ways in its rendering of Genesis 5:22-24 and 6:1-8, which form the nucleus around which the traditions about Enoch develop. For example, while MT states that "Enoch walked with God," a phrase used elsewhere in the Bible only of Noah (Gen 6:9) — though a similar phrase is used of Abraham (17:1) — OGGen renders this periphrastically as "Enoch pleased God." Moreover, whereas MT reads "and he was not, for God took him," OGGen translates "And he was not found because God translated him."

In 6:1-8, perhaps the most important difference between OGGen and MT is the translation of "sons of God" (6:2) by "angels of God." Although the manuscript evidence is divided over whether to read "angels of God" or "sons of God," I believe that the former is more likely to be the original reading here. The more literal "sons of God" does occur, nonetheless, in the Greek of 6:4.

OGGen dates to the third century B.C.E. (Holladay 1983, 52). After this, the most securely dated reference to Enoch in Greek occurs in the translation of Ben Sira around 130 B.C.E. The relevant verses are Sirach 16:7, 44:16-18, 49:14. The first verse deals with the period before the flood and speaks of the rebellion of the giants using the word *gigantes* as found in OGGen 6:4. Interestingly, the Hebrew of this verse reads "princes of old" *(nsyky qdm)*, which Patrick Skehan (Skehan and Di Lella 1987, 270) suggests was a conscious attempt by the author to avoid the mythological overtones of the Genesis passage and the Enochic literature. But the grandson has gone ahead and reestablished the connection with his use of "giants," probably influenced by OGGen.

Sirach 44:16 is a much disputed verse. It is omitted from the Masada manuscript and from the Syriac. But it is present in the Greek (both text types), MS B from the Cairo Genizah, and the Syro-Hexapla. Although some have been inclined to see the verse as a later interpolation, James VanderKam (1995, 105-6), Randal Argall (1995, 9-13), and Benjamin Wright (1997, 215) have each made their own case for its authenticity. I concur with their conclusion.

The Greek of this verse shows two similarities with OGGen. The Hebrew phrase *hthlk ʿm yyy* is rendered by *euērestēsen kyriō*, and *wylqḥ* is translated by *metetethē*. The latter may be contrasted with the second time Enoch's translation is mentioned in 49:14, however, where *nlqḥ* is glossed by *anelēmphthē*. This is clearly a more literal translation, though perhaps one may account for it by the fact that Elijah is referred to in 48:9 as *ho analēmphtheis en lailapi pyros kai en harmati hippōn pyrinōn*. Indeed, it appears that the details of Enoch's life are often filled out with ideas and phraseology from the lives of Elijah (who was taken like Enoch), Noah (who walked with God like Enoch; cf. below on Jubilees), and even Abraham to some extent (who also walked perfectly before the Lord; cf. Gen 17:1). However this may be, it is clear from the grandson's translation that by the second half of the second century B.C.E., OGGen had become a literary influence in Jewish literature written in Greek.

The next work to consider is the Wisdom of Solomon. This work was likely composed in Greek, though Charles Torrey (1945, 100ff.) once suggested that chapters 1–10 were translated from a Semitic original, either in the first century B.C.E. or in the first century C.E. Though Enoch is not named in this work, he is clearly referred to in 4:10-15. In verses 10 and 14 the phrases *euarestos theō* and *arestē . . . kyriō hē psychē autou* recall OGGen 5:22, 24. Enoch's translation is described in verse 10 by the verb *metetethē* as in OGGen 5:24, while in verse 11 a new verb, *hērpagē*, is introduced. The phrase *mē kakia allaxē synesin autou* may pick up on *eplēthunthēsan hai kakiai tōn anthrōpōn epi tēs gēs* in Genesis 6:5, and the statement in verse 14 *hoi de laoi idontes kai mē noēsantes mēde thentes epi dianoia to toiouto* may likewise echo the second part of 6:5. Thus, as was true with Greek Ben Sira, one sees a clear influence of OGGen on the text of the Wisdom of Solomon.

We come next to Jubilees. Jubilees is very important since it gives more attention to Enoch than does either of the other texts we have looked at so far. James VanderKam (1995, 110-21) has suggested that the text of Jubilees shows that its author knew at least four of the five Enochic works attested at Qumran, namely, the Book of the Watchers, the Astronomical Book, Dream Visions, and the Epistle of Enoch. It is clear from the scholarly discussion of these matters that some doubt direct literary knowledge and prefer to see a more subtle influence of nonliterary traditions.

We do not know much about the Greek version, and only snippets of it have been preserved by Christian writers. But the Ethiopic version was most certainly made from the Greek and can be used as a witness to it (VanderKam 1977, 6-7 and 94). Because so little of the Greek Jubilees has survived, it is difficult to hazard a guess as to the date of the translation, and one could suppose a time as early as the first century B.C.E. if it was made by Jews, or as late as the first or even second century C.E. if made by Christians (VanderKam 1977, 15; Scott 2002, 126-34).

Jubilees mentions Enoch's character in 10:17 where he is linked with Noah: "he [Noah] lived longer on the earth (than) other people except Enoch because of his righteousness in which he was perfect; because Enoch's work was something created as a testimony for the generations of eternity so that he should report all deeds throughout generation after generation on the day of judgment." In this instance the character of Enoch is described in terms drawn from Noah in Genesis 6:9, and clearly this is because both were said to have "walked with God." Earlier, the translation of Enoch is mentioned in 4:23 as follows: "He was taken from human society, and we led him into the Garden of Eden for (his) greatness and honor." The Ethiopic verb used is a passive form of the root *nash'a*, which could be a rendering of either of the Greek words *elēmphthē/anelēmphthē* or perhaps even *ērthē*. In any event, it is unlikely that the Greek read *metetethē* as in OGGen.

Regarding the fall of the Watchers, Jubilees 4:15 states, "He [Mahalalel] named him Jared because during his lifetime the angels of the Lord who were called Watchers descended to earth to teach mankind to do what is just and upright upon the earth." The comment "the angels of the Lord who were called Watchers" is arresting. I would suggest that the underlying Hebrew, which unfortunately is not preserved in any of the Qumran manuscripts for this verse, read "sons of God who were called Watchers" and that the Ethiopic is a literal translation of the Greek, which used "angels" in place of "sons," under the influence of OGGen. This is supported also by Jubilees 5:1, which is a paraphrase of Genesis 6:1-2 and uses "angels of the Lord" where MT has "sons of God" ("angels" occurs again in v. 6). Even if this hypothesis is accepted, the influence of OGGen on the story of Enoch in Jubilees is very slight.

One final work to be examined is Pseudo-Philo's *Liber antiquitatum biblicarum*. This work was likely written in the first century, but there is debate about whether it was written before or after 70 C.E. Many feel that it was originally written in Hebrew and then translated into Greek, and thence into Latin (Harrington in Perrot and Bogaert 1976, 75-77). But Louis Feldman (1971, xxv-

xxvii) suggests a Greek original. The Latin of the *Liber antiquitatum biblicarum* 1:15-16 reads:

> *Et vixit Enoch annos CLXV et genuit Matusalam. Et vixit Enoch postquam genuit Matusalam annos CC et genuit filios* quinque *et filias* tres. *Placuit autem Enoch Deo* in tempore illo *et non inveniebatur, quoniam transtulit illum Deus.*

The words in italics are directly dependent on the Bible, and one can see that the *Liber antiquitatum biblicarum* follows OGGen in both its phrases "Enoch pleased God" and "God translated him." It even follows the chronology of OGGen in having Enoch live 165 years before he begets children instead of 65 years as in the MT.

Interestingly, however, in 3:1, which summarizes Genesis 6:1-2, the *Liber antiquitatum biblicarum* uses "sons of God" instead of "angels of God" as in OGGen and Jubilees. It is possible that this reading is due to influence from the Vulgate, which indeed reads *filii Dei* here, but against this is the fact that in the three instances where the *Liber antiquitatum biblicarum* follows OGGen just noted, the readings go against the Vulgate and have not been changed.

Alternatively, there may be a theological reason for the more literal rendering here. Charles Perrot and Pierre Bogaert (1976, 85-86) suggest that Pseudo-Philo understands the "sons of God" to be descendants of Adam in line with those interpretations that relate them to the Sethites. This is striking since the author is clearly familiar with the fall of the Watchers and in 34:2-3 refers to them as *angeli*. Whatever understanding one favors, the influence of OGGen is very great in the *Liber antiquitatum biblicarum*.

Careful literary study of the works just surveyed indicates that their authors have often given distinctive twists to the Enochic traditions they have received. In the light of this, the fact that the authors and/or translators of three of these four works employ so much of the vocabulary of OGGen is even more striking.

We turn now to Greek Enoch. The Greek translation of Enoch has been dated variously. Matthew Black stated, "There is no reason to doubt that this Greek version, like other such Greek translations of intertestamental writings, was made by Christian scribes for Christians, in some cases probably for Jewish-Christian congregations" (Black 1985, 4). But we have shown elsewhere (Larson forthcoming, 209-14) that there is little basis for such an assertion, and to the contrary there are good reasons to see the translation as having been produced between 150 and 50 B.C.E. The evidence includes the quotation and allusions to Greek Enoch in the New Testament, the newly identified papyrus fragments of what seems to be a Greek translation of Enoch found in Qumran Cave 7, and the general translation characteristics of the book which share many similarities with the Old Greek translation of Daniel usually dated to this time.

With regard to Enoch's walk with God, not much is made of this detail in 1 Enoch. The words *euaresteō* and *euarestos* do not occur at all in Greek Enoch, nor does there seem to be any occasion when they would have been called for. In 1:2 Enoch is referred to as an *anthrōpos dikaios,* but this is the only place where much attention is placed on his character, unless one includes the phrase "scribe of righteousness," which could equally well refer to the nature of the works he writes (in 12:4 and 15:1). Again, the adjective may ultimately derive from the description of Noah in Genesis 6:9, though one does see something of a tendency in second temple literature to apply the adjective "righteous" to any biblical hero.

Concerning Enoch's translation, the clearest reference is in 1 Enoch 12:1-2. Here the verb *elēmphthē* is used, which is similar to *anelēmphthē* in Ben Sira 49:14 and perhaps also to the Greek that underlies Jubilees 4:23. Unfortunately, none of the Qumran manuscripts preserves the original Aramaic here, but whatever it was, the translator could surely have used *metetethē* as in OGGen if he had wanted to. Immediately after this the Greek states, "And no man knew where he was and what happened to him." This clearly corresponds to "and he was not" of MT, which in OGGen is rendered periphrastically as "and he was never found." It may also have some connection to material in 1 Kings 18:12 and 2 Kings 2:16-17, which refer to Elijah. Other references to Enoch's being taken up to heaven to see visions occur in 1 Enoch 14:8-9 and 81:5-6 and in 70:1-3 in the Similitudes. Only the first of these is preserved in Greek, where the verb *epēran* is used, though clearly again *metethēkan* could have been substituted had the translator desired.

Finally, I wish to address the matter of the angels in Genesis 6:2. Here we find that the translator of Greek Enoch often used the term "angels" to refer to the fallen Watchers (1 En 6:2; 8:1 [not in Syncellus]; 10:7; 14:4; 19:1-2; 21:10; 106:5-6, 12). Although none of these verses is preserved in the Aramaic, there is enough Aramaic preserved to be relatively sure that the word *ml'k* did not occur in the Aramaic Enoch texts as it does elsewhere in other Aramaic compositions from Qumran. Thus the usage would seem to derive ultimately from OGGen. Even if the Aramaic underlying these passages was not *bny shmy'* (cf. 6:2; 13:8; 14:3) but *'yryn,* the fact is that the translator could have used *egrēgoroi* as he does often elsewhere. While I suspect that the reason for the variation between *angeloi* and *egrēgoroi* is mainly stylistic, the fact that *angeloi* is used at all is likely due to the influence of OGGen.

George Nickelsburg (2001, 50, 58) has noted the curious fact that the Law of Moses does not play a central role in 1 Enoch. This is all the more remarkable since many current readings of the text suggest that priestly concerns underlie much of the imagery in the various Enochic works. Our study reveals that in spite of the many opportunities the translator of Greek Enoch had to use phraseology from OGGen, he passed almost all of them by.

The main conclusions from this brief study are as follows: (1) Of the five works surveyed, three show very strong influence from OGGen, namely, Ben Sira, the Wisdom of Solomon, and the *Liber antiquitatum biblicarum.* (2) Greek Enoch and the book of Jubilees, which are the only writings of those examined here dependent on the book of Enoch, show the least influence from OGGen. (3) But even these works seem to have felt the impact of OGGen in their use of "angels of God."

A Literary Dependency
of Jubilees on 1 Enoch?

Jacques van Ruiten

Jubilees is a rewriting of the biblical books of Genesis and Exodus 1–19. However, there are several deviations from the biblical texts. Sometimes the author
uses other theological texts and traditions. In a limited number of places he
seems to use Enochic texts and traditions (cf. Jub 4:15-26; 5:1-10; 7:20-39; 10:1-
17), especially with regard to the figure of Enoch and to the story of the
Watchers. In his study "Enoch Traditions in Jubilees and Other Second-
Century Sources," James VanderKam (1978) describes the relationship between
Jubilees and 1 Enoch. This work influenced his *Enoch and the Growth of an
Apocalyptic Tradition* (1984, 179-88) and formed the base of a chapter about the
relation between Jubilees and 1 Enoch in his book *Enoch: A Man for All Generations* (1995, 110-21). VanderKam relies to a certain extent on some of his predecessors, i.e., Robert H. Charles (1902, xliv, 36-39, 43-44), Pierre Grelot (1958, 5-
26, 181-210), and Josef T. Milik (1976), but surpasses them in many ways. His inventory of the parallels between Jubilees and 1 Enoch is quite impressive.
VanderKam is followed by others (Nickelsburg 2001, 71-76). I restrict myself to
the parallels mentioned with regard to Jubilees 4:17-25:

	References to 1 Enoch mentioned in VanderKam (1978)
Jub 4:17a	82:1-3; 92:1
	81; 82:1-3; 83:1; 94:1
	82:2-3; 92:1 (cf. 4QEn 1 ii 22-25)
	12:3; 82:1-3; 83:2
Jub 4:17b	72-82
	82:4-9

Jub 4:18	80-82
	81:6; 82:1; 82:4-9
	93:1-2 (4QEn^g 1 iii 18-22)
Jub 4:19	83-90
	92:1
	91:1
	93:2
	93:3; 91:15; 91:17
	81-82
	81:2; 81:6; 82:1-3
Jub 4:20	85:3
Jub 4:22	6-16
	7:1; 10:11
Jub 4:23-25	no affinities

Despite his caution and his hesitations, VanderKam concludes that the author of Jubilees is dependent on the *text* of 1 Enoch. He shows that Jubilees has knowledge of nearly all existing parts of the book (Vanderkam 1978, 1:241):

1 Enoch	*Jubilees*
Book of the Watchers (6–36)	4:15, 21, 22; 5:2, 6, 7, (9, 10); 7:21, (22), 23, 24, 27; 10:1-2
Astronomical Book (72–82)	4:17, 18 (?); 7:38-39 (?)
Dream Visions (83–90)	4:20; 5:(2, 6, 7), 9, 10; 7:(21), 22
Epistle of Enoch (91–105)	4:17 (?), 18, 19; 7:29; 10:17 (?)

According to VanderKam, the use of all existing parts of 1 Enoch points to the fact that Jubilees would have been composed after Dream Visions was written in 164 or 163 B.C.E. (VanderKam 1995, 117; 2001a, 21). I would like to question the literary dependency of Jubilees upon 1 Enoch. According to my opinion, the dating of Dream Visions is of no use for the dating of Jubilees because we cannot prove that the author of Jubilees is using the text of Dream Visions.

In many cases, especially for Dream Visions and the Epistle of Enoch, it is not clear that the author of Jubilees had direct access to the books of Enoch as we have them today. The verbal parallels are very small, often one or two words, which are moreover used in a different syntactical construction, words that often occur also elsewhere in 1 Enoch and sometimes even in other works of second-century Judaism. This is in sharp contrast to the biblical material the author of Jubilees is using, and which he often quotes verbatim.

In the cases when the author of Jubilees uses the biblical text, it is quite clear how he is referring to the biblical text, what he omits, adds, or modifies (Ruiten 2000). For the Enochic material, however, it is not clear. Parallels in thought or thematic parallels are often quite broad and do not point to a literary dependency. In this case one should decide that both are dependent on a common tradition. Both Jubilees and the later parts of 1 Enoch might be dependent either on a common text or on a common (Enoch) tradition. Although the author of Jubilees was certainly aware of many of the early traditions which surrounded Enoch, it is impossible to identify the source Jubilees is referring to. One can hardly speak about quotations from 1 Enoch in Jubilees. I focus on Jubilees 4:17-25 to illustrate my point (Ruiten 2000, 165-66).

1. Although 1 Enoch mentions in several places that Enoch was able to write (12:4; 15:1; 17–19; 20–36 [esp. 33:3]; 74:2; 81:6; 82:1; 83:2, 10; 92:11; 108:1), it is nowhere stated that he was the *first* who learned to write, as in Jubilees 4:17. Moreover, the exact wording in Jubilees differs from 1 Enoch. The mention of Enoch as the *first* writer may be a point the author of Jubilees himself is making: because Enoch was the first to write, and because he wrote his teachings in the company of God's angels, the teachings of Enoch transmitted to Noah and other patriarchs would have divine authority (Najman 1999, 385). The mention of Enoch as a writer may of course point to a *written* tradition. However, it is not clear to which book(s) the author of Jubilees is referring. It is by no means clear that he is referring to the whole composition of 1 Enoch as we know it.

2. One may point to the Epistle of Enoch, especially to 1 Enoch 93:1-2, as the background of Jubilees 4:18. In the introduction to the Apocalypse of Weeks, Enoch recounts passages from his book to his children. He received his information "in a vision of heaven, and from the word of the Watchers and holy ones" (cf. 4Q212 3:18-22), just as he received his information in Jubilees from the angels (cf. Jub 4:18g: "as we told him"), and in a vision (cf. 4:19ab). It is interesting that the heptadic structure of history is also the structural pattern of the Apocalypse of Weeks as it is in Jubilees. However, the exact wording in Jubilees differs from 1 Enoch. The other astronomical information in Jubilees 4:18 might also refer to several Enochic sources, especially from the Astronomical Book (1 En 81:6; 82:1; 83:2, 10; 92:11; 108:1) (Milik 1976, 11; Grelot 1975, 484-85). It is difficult, however, to point to an exact parallel.

3. The night vision of what had happened and what will happen unto the day of judgment (Jub 4:19) might refer to Dream Visions (1 En 83–90), which contains two dream visions, one about the past (85:3–88:3) and one about the future (83:3-5; 89:1–90:39) (Charles 1902, 38; Grelot 1975, 485; Milik 1976, 45). However, Jubilees knows only one vision, and it stops at the judgment, while 1 Enoch proceeds beyond the judgment (VanderKam 1978, 1:234-35). The wording is also quite different. Besides this, VanderKam points to 1 Enoch 81–82 (esp.

81:2; Vanderkam 1978, 1:234-35) and the Epistle of Enoch (esp. 92:1; 93:2; VanderKam 1995, 115) as the possible backgrounds to Jubilees 4:19. Moreover, here there are no verbal parallels.

4. In Jubilees 4:21b the author seems to betray his knowledge of the cosmological section of the Book of the Watchers (1 En 17–36) where Enoch, in company of the angels, views the heavenly and earthly things when he travels to the farthest end of the world (Milik 1976, 25; VanderKam 1978, 1:235; 1999, 156). However, no verbal parallel can be found.

5. With regard to Jubilees 4:22, one can point to the angelological part of the Book of the Watchers (1 En 6–16) (see esp. Jub 7:1; 10:11; cf. VanderKam 1999, 156, 169-70), but the exact wording is different.

6. In Jubilees 4:23-26, Jubilees has not very much affinity with 1 Enoch, which only briefly describes Enoch's translation from earth and the aftermath (VanderKam 1978, 1:235). The passage is of some importance for Jubilees' portrayal of Enoch.

In conclusion, one can say that Jubilees 4:17-26 reveals that the author of Jubilees knew much about the Enochic traditions. He is strongly influenced by this material. However, in my opinion it is not possible to say that Jubilees is dependent on the *text* of 1 Enoch. The wording of the two is too different.

Also, in other passages Jubilees (5:2, 6, 7, 9, 10; 7:21, 22) shows, according to VanderKam, influence of Dream Visions, though there seems to be no textual relationship. I refer to Jubilees 5:6-10, which is parallel to 1 Enoch 88. One can especially refer to the motifs of the sword and the binding of the angels. However, these elements occur also in the Book of the Watchers (esp. 1 En 10). As far as Jubilees 7:22 is concerned, one could relate the mention of the giants, the Naphillim, and the Elyo, with 1 Enoch 86–87. However, there is a closer parallel in the Book of the Watchers, i.e., 1 Enoch 7:2, which is perhaps the only case in which one could conclude for a dependency of Jubilees on 1 Enoch.

One may conclude that Jubilees has some parallels with Dream Visions. These parallels, however, do not point to a literary dependency of Jubilees on Dream Visions, but on a common tradition, which is probably to be found in the Book of the Watchers. It is not valid, therefore, to date Jubilees (relatively) after Dream Visions (i.e., after 164-163 B.C.E.) on the basis of the literary parallels between these two. The dating of Dream Visions is of no use for the dating of Jubilees, and vice versa. One should no longer say that Dream Visions is early *because* it is known to the author of Jubilees.

"Revealed Literature" in the Second Century B.C.E.: Jubilees, 1 Enoch, Qumran, and the Prehistory of the Biblical Canon

Annette Yoshiko Reed

The research of James VanderKam has done much to illumine the rich relationship between the book of Jubilees and the early Jewish writings preserved in 1 Enoch. With regard to topics such as the calendar, angelology/demonology, and Enoch's own life and writings, he has demonstrated Jubilees' dependence on various Enochic traditions and its author's familiarity with some early Enochic writings. He offers incisive analyses of reinterpretations of this material and departures from it (VanderKam 1978; 1984, 179-88; 1995, 110-21; 1999). On such matters his arguments are deservedly well known, oft cited, and much discussed. Their ramifications are helpful for our understanding of the Qumran community in which Jubilees itself seems to have been granted special authority alongside the early Enochic writings so cherished by its author.[1]

In this brief study I would like to draw attention to another aspect of VanderKam's research, an aspect which has received less attention than it deserves, namely, his exploration of the significance of Jubilees, as well as of the early Enochic pseudepigrapha, and their status at Qumran. This work is valuable for our understanding of the prehistory of the biblical canon and the char-

---

1. The discussion of the exact Enochic books known by the author of Jubilees has centered on Jub 4:17-22, which seems to refer to the Astronomical Book (4:17) and the Book of the Watchers (4:21-22) and perhaps also the Epistle of Enoch and/or the book of Dream Visions, depending on one's interpretation of 4:18-19; see, e.g., Charles (1902, xliv, lxviii-lxix), Grelot (1975), VanderKam (1995, 114-17), Nickelsburg (2001, 25-26); cf. Dimant (1974, 92-103). Jubilees' status at Qumran is inferred from the number of copies of this book (on which, see below) and the explicit reference and allusion(s) to it in the Damascus Document (CD 16:2-4; see also CD 10:7-10 as well as 4Q228); further Flint (2001, 96-103, 116-21).

acter of Jewish literary production prior to the canon's closure (VanderKam 2000a, 1-30; also 1995, 183-85; 2002, 105-7).[2]

The many thematic, ideological, exegetical, and theological strands that connect Jubilees with both 1 Enoch and the literature of the Qumran community are often approached solely as clues to the sociohistorical continuities between their respective authors/redactors. Yet, whether one feels confident speculating about the precise social realities that produced these connections, it remains that the intertextual relationships between these sources also tell us much about books and readers, as well as exegesis, scripturalization, and textual authority, in the second temple period. Jubilees' author is one of the earliest readers and exegetes of Enochic literature of whom we have knowledge. Likewise, the presence of multiple copies of Jubilees at Qumran, together with copies of early Enochic books, not to mention manuscripts that appear to attest early efforts at gathering Enochic writings into collections, provides us with evidence for an early Jewish community in which such books were read, copied, compiled, collected, and apparently treated as revelatory and authoritative.[3]

This is all the more important to note due to the now noncanonical status of Jubilees and 1 Enoch in Judaism and most varieties of Christianity. It is generally agreed that the centuries between the Babylonian exile and the destruction of the second temple saw the emergence of a concept of Holy Scripture, applied first to the five books of the torah but increasingly to other books, accompanied by the growth of a rich and varied tradition of scriptural exegesis. Some scholars, such as Roger Beckwith, have gone even further, proposing that the Jewish biblical canon was closed already in the second century B.C.E. According to Beckwith, the books in the present-day Tanakh, and hence the Protestant Old Testament in contrast to other Christian Old Testament canons, were officially accepted and promoted as the exclusive sources of authoritative, divine, written revelation by Judas Maccabeus himself in 164 B.C.E. (Beckwith 1985, 152-53; so too Leiman 1976, 29-30).

It is apt that VanderKam has taken Beckwith to task for this theory, inso-

---

2. Note that I here use the term "canon" in its most technical sense, to denote a closed group of writings that are commonly agreed to possess an exclusive level of authority within a group or tradition ("canon 2" in some scholars' schema, as opposed to the less fixed "canon 1" — writings or oral traditions that function as an authoritative guide — which I here term "Scripture"). On the importance of these distinctions, see discussions in, e.g., Barr (1983, 41-48), McDonald (1996, 6-21), Kraemer (1991).

3. As VanderKam notes, "Only Genesis (15), Exodus (15), Deuteronomy (25), Isaiah (19), and Psalms (30) are represented in more manuscripts" than Jubilees and the early Enochic pseudepigrapha now found in 1 Enoch (VanderKam 2000a, 25; see too Flint 2001, 118). For an in-depth discussion of the place of the Enochic literature in particular, see Nickelsburg (1999).

far as the argument involves, among other things, a rather idiosyncratic interpretation of Jubilees 2:23 that favors Syncellus's Greek over the Hebrew, Syriac,
and Geez witnesses (VanderKam 2000a, 18-19). With characteristically method-
ical analyses and judicious argumentation, VanderKam dismantles Beckwith's
arguments for a Maccabean-era closing of the canon in a manner that I personally find to be decisive. For our present purposes, however, the failure or success
of Beckwith's quest to pinpoint a pre-Christian date of canonization proves less
significant than the ways VanderKam's approach to the *pre*history of the biblical canon enriches our understanding of literary production, transmission, and
reception in the second century B.C.E.

Beckwith and others are forced to treat Jubilees' elevation of early
Enochic writings and the Qumranites' use of these so-called pseudepigrapha, as
well as the later acceptance of these and other so-called apocrypha in a variety
of Christian communities, as alleged deviations from an already-accepted ancient norm (Beckwith 1985, 395-405; see too VanBeek, 2000). By contrast,
VanderKam's approach allows him to recover a complex and dynamic reality:

> [A]t the early times in which the various parts of 1 Enoch and the unified
> book of Jubilees were written the term "biblical" would not have the preci-
> sion that was later given to it. Contrary to the view of R. Beckwith, it seems
> highly unlikely that the Hebrew canon had been closed in the time of Judas
> Maccabaeus; 1 Enoch and Jubilees themselves and the popularity of both at
> Qumran are eloquent testimony to the fact that other works billed them-
> selves as revelations and that their claims were accepted by at least some an-
> cient Jews. Which works the authors of these books may have considered
> authoritative are not entirely clear, although it is obvious that Genesis had a
> special appeal for them and that they valued many others. Thus the
> Enochic pamphlets and the book of Jubilees provide windows into the pro-
> cesses of interpreting older authoritative compositions at a time when the
> bounds of the Hebrew Scriptures were not set and when other writers were
> making revelatory claims for their literary efforts. (VanderKam 2000a, 227)

What I find helpful about this perspective is that it points to a productive
way to sidestep a set of traditional biases, which have been ingrained by what
Robert Kraft has termed the "tyranny of canonical assumptions." When investigating the writers, redactors, and earliest readers of so-called pseudepigrapha
like Jubilees and 1 Enoch, scholars have too frequently been influenced by what
we now know about the late antique, medieval, and modern reception histories
of these books. For instance, even despite what we now know about the diversity of second temple Judaism, the lack of any monolithic "normative Judaism"

at the time, and the inability of any one group or figure to lay down such norms, it is often assumed without argument that the original authors and readers of so-called pseudepigrapha must have been socially marginal figures, powerless visionaries masquerading as figures from the past to make fanciful claims to esoteric wisdom, poor prophets clustered in conventicles critiquing the status quo, disenfranchised scribes subverting "mainstream" culture and tradition.[4]

Furthermore, research on these texts often presumes a dichotomy between the practice of "biblical" pseudepigraphy and the practice of "biblical" interpretation. Rather than allowing for the possibility that their authors and redactors could be interested in "interpreting older authoritative compositions" that they cherish in common with other Jews at the same time as they "mak(e) revelatory claims for (their own) literary efforts," scholars sometimes interpret the latter as a sign of the rejection of now-canonical books and the intention to supplant rather than supplement older revelations; or alternately they assume that any author who values "biblical" books and seeks meaning in "biblical" exegesis could only deign to claim a secondary and derivative authority for his own work (e.g., Beckwith 1985, 395-405). In other words, the assumptions of canonical contexts are often imposed on authors and readers who appear to have operated in precanonical ones.

Yet, as VanderKam has shown, we may be able to learn much about these texts and the communities that transmitted them if we take seriously the prominence of "biblical" pseudepigraphy as a mode of literary production in second temple Judaism and the popularity of this new "revealed literature" in this period and beyond. Our evidence suggests that the boundaries of scriptural authority remained fluid in the second century B.C.E., and that a variety of texts continued to vie for elevated status, functioning as Scripture for some Jews but not for others. This is evident in the range of authoritative texts used by different groups, no less than in the dominant modes of literary production in second temple Judaism.

When seen from this perspective, it does not seem paradoxical that Enochic books like the Book of the Watchers can root their claims to record heavenly secrets in the "biblical" statements about Enoch, even as their expansions of Genesis are no less grounded in the "extrabiblical" claim of Enoch's status as revealer. Nor does it seem so odd that the author of Jubilees might seek to

---

4. I discussed these issues further in "Apocrypha, 'Outside Books,' and Pseudepigrapha: Ancient Categories and Modern Perceptions of Parabiblical Literature" (paper presented at the University of Pennsylvania, 10 October 2002); the text of the presentation is available on-line at http://ccat.sas.upenn.edu/psco/year40/areed1.html.

expand upon the books of the torah by using Moses' own voice, even if he wishes to supplement rather than supplant those cherished books (Reed 2002, 80-86). These books interpret the torah and simultaneously present themselves as equal in their status as revealed wisdom, but within the world of these authors/redactors perhaps neither stance made sense without the other.

Jubilees *and* 1 Enoch and the Issue
of Transmission of Knowledge

Eibert J. C. Tigchelaar

In this short contribution I want to touch upon two issues: first, in general, the variants in 1 Enoch and Jubilees with regard to modes of revelation and transmission of knowledge; and second, the treatment of the so-called Enochic material in Jubilees.

1 Enoch and Jubilees mention the same modes of revelation and carriers of knowledge, namely, angelic revelation, the heavenly tablets, visions and dreams, and the teachings of the Watchers. The human recipients transmit their knowledge by means of speech or books which they pass on to their sons.

Variants between Enoch and Jubilees concern the role of these phenomena within these texts. In 1 Enoch the heavenly tablets are more or less Books of Destiny and are read by Enoch (1 En 81:1, 2; 93:2; 103:2; 106:18). In Jubilees 32 Jacob reads seven tablets, which also are some kind of Book of Destiny (Jub 32:21), but no other human being, not even Enoch, reads the heavenly tablets in Jubilees. Compare Jubilees 4:19, where Enoch saw in a vision "what has happened and what will occur, how things will happen for mankind," and 32:21, where Jacob "read everything that was written in them — what would happen to him and his sons throughout all ages."

James VanderKam has argued convincingly, and this is corroborated in one case by the Qumran fragments, that even where the Ethiopic suggests that the angel *wrote*, the Hebrew said the angel *dictated* to Moses. At crucial points in Jubilees, namely, at the beginning, at the end, and at the conclusion of the eschatological chapter 23, it is made clear that the angel dictated to Moses from the heavenly tablets or, as stated in 1:29, "tablets of the divisions of the years."

Two things are important: (1) Nowhere in Jubilees is it suggested that the composition itself is a copy of the heavenly tablets; on the contrary, it refers at crucial points to the tablets. (2) Jubilees does not connect the heavenly tablets to books prior to Moses; Enoch has not read the tablets, and it may be no coincidence that with regard to Jacob the text refers only to an angel from heaven with seven tablets.

Important in Jubilees is the function of writing and books. Five times Jubilees refers to the learning of the art of writing, and four forefathers are credited with writing or transmitting books, namely, Enoch, Noah, Abraham, and Jacob (Jub 4:17 [Enoch]; 8:2 [Kainan]; 11:16 [Abram]; 19:14 [Jacob]; 47:9 [Moses]). It is important what Abraham and Jacob do with books: Abraham takes his forefathers' books, copies them, and studies them. Jacob reads aloud to his sons from the words of Abraham and gives all the books of his fathers to Levi in order that he would keep and renew them. This reflects a view on priestly scribal tasks, but also on the transmission of knowledge, that is, something passed on from generation to generation from father to son. I hesitate to follow, for example, Orval S. Wintermute, who suggests that this involves more than making new copies and that priests were commissioned to bring ancient traditions up to date.

In 1 Enoch there are few references to the transmission of books. In 81–82, the odd piece in the Astronomical Book, Enoch writes and gives the books to Methuselah, who is told to preserve them and deliver them to all generations. The section on books in 104:10-13 describes not the transmission but the writing of books in one's own words, and the giving of books. This may be compared to 1:2, where Enoch's words are meant for a remote generation. All in all, Enoch's books explicitly present themselves and envisage the sudden appearance of ancient books specifically meant for one's own time.

Secondly, what is the attitude of Jubilees toward 1 Enoch and/or the Enochic traditions? Apart from the description of Enoch's writings in Jubilees 4, there are two references to the words of Enoch, and these do not seem to fit with 1 Enoch. First, according to 12:27, his father's books were written in Hebrew; and second, according to 21:10, the command concerning the eating of the meat offerings was found in the words of Enoch and the words of Noah. Also interesting is 39:6, according to which the prohibition of adultery was written in the words of Abraham. One may take these references at face value and argue that Jubilees had access to additional books or sources. However, it is more likely that they represent a retrospective view on the books of the ancestors, namely, that these already contained part of the revelation given to Moses. It is important, I think, that there is no indication whatsoever that Moses himself read or studied these books. In fact, the revelation to Moses makes the previous books redundant.

A final aspect: in Jubilees a negative view on the teachings of the Watchers is mainly restricted to the study of the signs of the luminaries. Even so, the mere fact that Abram originally also indulged in astrology shows a nuanced view by the authors. Also, in the contents of Noah's books medicine overlaps with what is mentioned as teachings of the Watchers in the Book of the Watchers. Though Jubilees does not promote these sciences, it is also much less harsh than Enoch.

4Q390, the 490-Year Prophecy, and the Calendrical History of the Second Temple Period

Hanan Eshel

The first part of this chapter addresses the historical agenda of a scroll labeled 4Q390 (once identified as Pseudo-Moses Apocalypse, now known as Apocryphon of Jeremiah; see Dimant 1992, 2:405-47; 2001, 91-96), and particularly its connection to the 490-year prophecy in Daniel 9:24-27.[1] It exhibits no sectarian characteristics and was probably not composed by the covenanters.[2] Accusations against the priests for not adhering to the correct calendar, found in 4Q390, pave the way for a proposed chronology of the complex calendrical shifts that I conjecture took place in the second temple period. That is outlined in the second part of this chapter.

Daniel 9 updates Jeremiah's 70-year prophecies (Jer 25:8-14; 29:4-14), interpreting these prophecies as referring not to 70 years but rather to seven 70-year periods (weeks), or 490 years (see Dan 9:2; see Collins 1993, 347-49). This time span is subdivided into three periods: (1) seven weeks, or the 49 years of

1. Dimant holds that the nonsectarian writings predate the sectarian ones, because in her opinion no additional works reached the sect after its founding. She therefore tends to date all the works in the nonsectarian scrolls as early as the second century B.C.E. There is, however, no reason to reject the possibility that individuals joining the sect brought with them works that had been written after the sect came into existence. On the basis of the paleographical evidence, Dimant dates the copy of 4Q390 to between 30 and 20 B.C.E. (Dimant 2001, 236-37). Thus, nothing obviates the assumption that 4Q390 is a first-century B.C.E. update of the late part of Daniel, which was redacted in 165 B.C.E.

2. Regarding its provenance, Dimant noted the similarity in content between the Jeremiah Apocryphon (including 4Q390) and sectarian compositions, suggesting on this basis that the apocryphon belongs to an intermediate stage between nonsectarian and sectarian writings (Dimant 2001, 110-13).

the Babylonian exile;[3] (2) sixty-two weeks, or 434 years, from the rebuilding of Jerusalem until the reign of Antiochus IV; and (3) a week, namely, 7 years, for the first half of which sacrifices and meal offerings will cease because of abomination, and in the second half of which redemption will come (Grabbe 1987, 67-72; Dimant 1993, 58-61; Vermes 2003, 481-84). I submit that just as Daniel 9 updated Jeremiah's prophecy, 4Q390 is an update of the 490-year prophecy in Daniel 9.[4]

Column 1 of the text follows:[5]

4Q390 col. 1

2   [ ] ‬שבעים שנה [ ] וא[שוב [ונתתים] ביד בני אהר [ון‬
3   ‬ומשלו בנו אהרון בהמה ולא יתהלכו [בדר]כיאשר נצוק אשי‬
4   ‬תעיד בהם ויעשו גם הם את ארע בעוני ככל אשר עשו ושראל‬
5   ‬בימי ממלכתו הרישונים מלבד העולים רישונה מארץ שבים לבנות‬
6   ‬את המקדש ואדברה בהמה ואשלחה אליהם מעוה ויבנו בכול אשר‬
7   ‬עזבו הם ואבותיהם ומתום הדשר   ההוא ביובל השדיעי‬
8   ‬לחרבן הארץ ישכחו חוק ומועדושבת וברית ויפרו הכנל ויעשי‬
9   ‬הרע בעיני והסתרתי פני מהמה ונתתים ביד איביהם יהסגרת [ים]‬
10   ‬לחרב והשארתי מהם פליטים למען[ ] אשר לא י[כ]ל[ו] בחמתי [ו]בהסתר פני‬
11   ‬מהם ומשלו בהמה מלאכי המש[ט]מות ומ[אסתים ו]ישוב[ו]‬
12   ‬ויעשי [את] הרע בעינ[י] ויתהלכו בשר[י]רות לבם   [‬

2 [. . . and a]gain I shall [deliver them] into the hand of the sons of Aar[on] *seventy years* [ ];

3 the sons of Aaron shall rule over them, but they shall not walk [in] My [wa]ys which I am commanding you, so

4 you must warn them. And they also shall do evil before Me just as Israel did

5 in the days of the kingdom of their forefathers, except for those who are the first to go up from the land of captivity to rebuild

6 the Temple. I shall speak with them and send them a commandment, and they shall comprehend completely: namely, what

7 they and their fathers had forsaken. But at the end of that generation, in the *seventh jubilee*

---

3. Jerusalem was destroyed in 586 B.C.E. and Cyrus allowed the Jews to return to Judea in 538; thus Daniel 9's 49-year interval is historically accurate.

4. Although Dimant (1996, 40) correctly noted that 4Q390 divides history according to "weeks," she failed to observe that, like the Animal Apocalypse, it divides history into 490 years.

5. The Hebrew text is cited according to the official version published by Dimant (2001, 237-54), with the addition of a proposed reading for col. 2:1. The English translation is mine, as are the emphases.

8 after the destruction of the land, they shall forget *law, festival, Sabbath,* and covenant, and shall violate everything, and they shall do

9 evil before Me. So I shall hide My face from them, give them into the hand of their enemies and deliver [them] over

10 to the sword. But I shall cause a remnant of them to escape in order that they might not be completely [des]t[royed] in My wrath and when I turn [My face] away

11 from them. The angels of Mastemot will govern them and [. . . and they] shall again turn

12 and do ev[il] before [Me] and walk in the s[tubbornness of their heart . . .]

The historical survey continues in the next column:[6]

4Q390 col. 2

ויחללו] [	1
[את[ ]בית]י ומזבחי וא]ת מקדש הקד]ש	2
ו]ת[הי] [כי אלה יבואו עליהם] [נעשה כן]	3
וביובל ההוא יהיו] ממשלת בליעל בהם להסגירם לחרב שבוע שנים]	4
מפרים את כול חקותי ואת כל מצותי אשר אצוה א[ותם ואשלח בי]ד עבדי הנביאים	5
וי]ח[ל]ו] להריב אלה באלה שנים שבעים מיום הפר ה]אלה וה]ברית אשר יפרו ונתתרם	6
ביד מל]אכי המשטמות ומשלו בחם ולא ידעו ולא יביני כי קצפתי עליהם במועלם]	7
אשר עז]בוני ויעשו הרע בעיני ובאשר לא חפצתי בחרו להתגבר להון ולבצע]	8
ולחמס ואי]ש אשר לר]ע]הו יגזולו ויעוקו איש את רעהו ואת מקדשי יטמאו]	9
ואת שבתותי יחללו] את [מו]עדר יש]כח]ו ודדני [נכר] יחלל]ו] את זרעם כוהניהם יחמסו	10

1 [They profaned]

2 [My]house[and My altar and th]e Holy of Ho[lies]

3 done and thus [. . . all of] these things shall come upon them [. . .] and

4 the rule of Belial over them to hand them over to the sword for *a week of (seven) year*[*s . . . on*] that Jubilee they shall be

5 violating all My laws and all My commandments which I shall command t[hem sent by the han]d of My servants the prophets.

6 And they shall begin to contend with one another for *seventy years;* from the day that they violate the covenant. Then I shall give them

---

6. Dimant ascribes all the fragments attributed to Jeremiah to a single composition, which she entitles the Jeremiah Apocryphon. In its initial publication, Dimant (1992, 2:413) placed col. 2 immediately following col. 1. In the official publication of the text (Dimant 2001, 236) she suggests that there were intervening columns, which included various parts of the Jeremiah Apocryphon attested in other scrolls. As the extant texts do not overlap 4Q390, it is not certain that what appears in 4Q390 belongs to the same work that appears in the other scrolls. In her initial article, Dimant (1992, 2:412 n. 22) noted that Strugnell did not see a link between 4Q390 and the other scrolls. It then appears that col. 2 is the continuation of col. 1.

7 [into the hand of the ang]els of Mastemot and they shall govern them and they shall not know nor understand that I was angry with them for their unfaithfulness.

8 [. . . They shall fors]ake Me and do evil before Me. In that which I do not desire, they have chosen to enrich themselves by ill-gotten wealth and illegal profit

9 [. . .] they will rob, oppress one another, and they will defile My Temple

10 [*they will profane my sabbaths,*] *they will for[ge]t my [fes]tivals,* and with fo[reign]ers [t]he[y]will profane their offspr[ing].* Their priests will commit violence

The historical survey presented in the two surviving columns of 4Q390, a focal point of which is the harsh accusations against the second temple priests for various misdeeds, covers four periods. The first period, with which column 1 opens, is the 70-year rule of the priests during the Babylonian exile, when they did not walk in God's path.[7] Documented here is a historical perspective according to which the leadership passed from the House of David to the priests during the second temple period. Allusion is made to the fact that the priests sinned by continuing to follow what was accepted first temple period practice, "do evil before Me just as . . . in the days of the kingdom of their forefathers." Column 1:6 mentions prophets sent to the returned exiles ("I shall speak with them and send them a commandment"), apparently a reference to Haggai and Zechariah.

The return to rebuild the temple marked the beginning of a second, meretricious period during which the returnees recognized "what they and their fathers had forsaken" (ll. 6-7). This period lasted until the seventh jubilee counted from the destruction,[8] which I understand as a reference to the 343rd year since the destruction of the first temple (7 × 49 years). In the third 7-year period, evidently an allusion to the reign of Antiochus IV, the priests forgot "law, festival [and] sabbath" (l. 8); namely, they ceased to run the temple ac-

---

7. A similar accusation that the priests stopped pursuing the correct path during the Babylonian exile is documented in the Prayer of Joseph (preserved in 4Q371 and 4Q372, which states [ויחדל לוי] להבין לחקי אל וגם יהודה יחד עמו) (Schuller and Bernstein 2001, 157, 167; Eshel 1991, 125-29).

8. The calculation of dates according to jubilees or weeks was common in the second temple period. This notation is documented mainly in Jubilees and in the Apocalypse of Weeks (1 En 93 and 91:11-17) (Dimant 1993, 61-72). As I understand it, col. 1 of the Damascus Document states that the sect's history began when a group of Jews came from Damascus to the land of Israel, 390 years after the destruction of the first temple (Eshel 1997, 87). It appears that the Damascus Document and 4Q390 use different chronological methods, as there is evidence for placing the arrival of the returnees from Damascus ca. 170 B.C.E. Hence, the author of the Damascus Document believed that at 170, 390 years had passed from the destruction of the first temple, whereas the author of 4Q390 thought 343 years had passed from the destruction until the "week" that began with 167.

cording to the correct calendar.[9] Other accusations made against the priests are more sweeping; in addition to profaning the festivals, they have forgotten the covenant and violate everything. Because of these sins the Jews were delivered into the hand of their enemies (namely, Antiochus IV); nonetheless, God took care that they not be entirely destroyed.

Although column 2:2-4 is fragmentary, it appears likely that the "week of years" in which the people of Jerusalem were delivered to the sword is the one mentioned in Daniel 9:27: "For half a week he will put a stop to the sacrifice and the meal offering. At the corner [of the altar] will be an appalling abomination." I propose that both Daniel and 4Q390 refer here to the 3-year profanation of the temple by the introduction of an idol during the reign of Antiochus (167 to 164), as Daniel 11:31 states: "They will desecrate the temple, the fortress; they will abolish the regular offering and set up the appalling abomination" (see Collins 1993, 357-58).

I suggest reconstructing the end of the first line of column 2 as [ויחללו], reading "[they profaned . . . My] house and My altar and the Holy of Holies" (ll. 1-2). The text goes on to state that during this period the priests "shall be violating all My laws and all My commandments" (l. 5). This I understand as a reference to the Hellenized high priests, Jason, Menelaus, and Alcimus, who served in the sixties and seventies of the second century B.C.E. It is difficult to ascertain whether line 6's "And[t]he[y] shall be[gi]n to contend with one another" alludes to internecine high priestly quarrels, such as the one between Jason and Menelaus, or to the Hasmonean revolt.

The final historical stage described in 4Q390 is, in my opinion, the period of Hasmonean rule. Beginning after the "week" in which the temple was profaned, it will last for 70 years (l. 6), during which the people will be ruled by the "angels of Mastemot" (l. 7). Of the Hasmoneans the author states: "they shall not know nor understand" that God "was angry with them for their unfaithfulness" (מעל; l. 7). Unfaithfulness here seems to refer to fraudulent misuse of the temple funds,[10] for in the continuation the author notes that they have chosen "to pursue wealth and gain [and violence]" (ll. 8-9). In addition to accusing the

---

9. On the basis of Dan 7:25, it appears that Antiochus IV changed the calendar used in the Jerusalem temple: "He will think of changing times and laws." As we shall see below, 4Q390 alludes to this event. For the hypothesis that the verse in Daniel refers to a change from the solar to the lunar calendar in the Jerusalem temple during Antiochus's reign, see Jaubert (1953, 263), VanderKam (1981, 60), Boccaccini (2001, 2:311-28).

10. In its original biblical context, Lev 5:14-16, מעל means illicit enjoyment of temple property, a topic treated in the Mishnaic tractate *Meilah*. On the concept of מעל before and after the destruction of the second temple, see Bokser (1981, 557-74); on this meaning of מעל in the Dead Sea Scrolls, see Schwartz (1996, 76-77), Eshel (1996, 60).

Hasmoneans of mercenary aims, the author reprimands them for oppressing each other, defiling the temple, profaning the Sabbath, and forgetting the festivals (ll. 9-10). I read this final accusation as hinting at calendrical matters; that is, in the author's view the Hasmoneans ran the temple according to the wrong calendar. The passage concludes by noting that "they," the Hasmonean priests, profane their offspring with foreigners and violate the priesthood.

In view of the references to the various periods outlined above, I submit that 4Q390 is a historical interpretation of Daniel 9 (see Grabbe 1997, 595-611). In its update of Daniel's 490-year prophecy (see Milik 1976, 254-55), 4Q390 subdivided the 490 years found in Daniel 9:24 into four periods: (1) the 70-year Babylonian exile;[11] (2) the 343 years during which the returned exiles behaved correctly; (3) the 7-year period under Antiochus IV; and (4) the 70-year period of the Hasmonean reign.[12]

It appears likely that the author of 4Q390 believed that redemption would come at the end of the 490 years; he consequently assumed that the Hasmonean rule would last for 70 years. Whether 4Q390 counted the 70 years from the rededication of the temple by Judah Maccabee in 164 B.C.E., or from 152 when Jonathan ben Mattathias was appointed to the high priesthood, the period ends around the time of the Pharisee revolt against Alexander Janneus. I submit that by writing a composition showing that the Hasmoneans were about to leave the stage of history, 4Q390's author was trying to encourage Alexander Janneus's opponents.[13]

I have already noted 4Q390's harsh criticism of the second temple priests. I wish to call attention again to the fact that 4Q390 twice takes the priests to task for forgetting or profaning Sabbaths and festivals, that is, for their failure to follow the proper calendar, in this case the solar one: in 1:8, which I interpret as referring to the Hellenized priests serving in the temple prior to the Hasmonean revolt, and again in 2:10, which I understand as referring to the

11. Apparently the author of 4Q390 thought Jeremiah's prophecy called for the Babylonian exile to last 70, not 49, years.

12. There is a certain difficulty with this reconstruction, as the statement "in the seventh jubilee after the destruction of the land" (col. 1:7-8) appears to include the 70 years of the Babylonian exile in the 343-year period. If that was indeed 4Q390's intent, it is possible that it describes another 70 years after the Hasmonean period. Although most of col. 2 was not preserved, the remaining fragments perhaps support this proposal. In this column we find the following combinations: יחללו בה [ה] (1:10); ויזבחו בה [ה] (1:7); וברחמים לבק[ש] (1:8); ואשלח[ה] ואת המזבת (1:11; see Dimant 2001, 250). From the paleographical viewpoint Dimant determined that 4Q390 was copied between 30 and 20 B.C.E. (see n. 1 above); thus, it is possible that its author alluded to events after the Pompeian conquest. Nonetheless, in light of the proposal made below, this seems difficult to accept.

13. I thank Albert Baumgarten for this penetrating suggestion.

Hasmoneans, whose reign is here portrayed in a negative light. These accusations of not following the solar calendar support the interpretation of Daniel 7:25 as indicating a change in the temple calendar from a solar to a lunar one during Antiochus's reign.

On the basis of this supposition, I propose a tentative chronology of the complex calendrical shifts taking place in Judea and in the temple during the second temple period, submitting that these took place at two separate junctures: from a lunar to a solar calendar in a priestly propagated, relatively uncontested move in the third century B.C.E., and in the second century when Antiochus IV imposed a lunar calendar on the temple, and calendrical issues became actively debated.

During the first temple period, as attested by the biblical terms *yeraḥ* and *ḥodesh,* which relate to the moon, the Israelites followed a lunar calendar. (For attestation to *yeraḥ* in the Gezer Calendar, see Gibson 1971, 1-4; for *ḥodashim* in the Arad letters, see Aharoni 1981, s.v. חדש.) Such a calendar was suited to an agricultural, largely illiterate society, in which every person could determine the date via observation of the moon.

Because of the necessity to intercalate one month every 3 years to harmonize between the lunar and solar years, I posit the development of a viewpoint among the literate second temple priestly caste that the lunar calendar was inaccurate.[14] I conjecture that sometime during the third century B.C.E. the priestly temple leadership altered the temple calendar from a lunar to a solar one.[15] I further propose that the Astronomical Book in 1 Enoch reflects a priestly attempt to gain acceptance for this shift.[16] If we assume that this "quiet revolution" gained acceptance among the Jerusalem priests, this then paved the way for its acceptance by the majority, who now began to observe the festivals according to the

14. Since the verse in Daniel seems to allude to a change from a solar to a lunar calendar, Annie Jaubert and James VanderKam assumed that in the early second temple period the temple rites followed a 364-day liturgical calendar, namely, a solar calendar. See the summation in VanderKam (1998, 110-16).

15. The assumption that this process took place during the third century B.C.E. has two bases: first, that the roots of the solar calendar are to be found in Egypt and that this calendar was in use in the Ptolemaic Empire (see Bickerman 1968, 39-42). Because Palestine was under the Ptolemies in the third century B.C.E., I propose that under the influence of Egyptian rule the Jerusalem priests weighed whether to switch to a solar calendar. Second, Jewish writings dated to the third century B.C.E. attest to the use of a solar calendar (see following note). This suggestion is in opposition to Philip Davies' theory that early in the Babylonian exile the exiles abandoned the solar calendar in favor of the lunar one in effect there (Davies 1983, 88).

16. The Astronomical Book (1 En 72–82) is generally dated to the third century B.C.E. (Milik 1976, 7-22). Aramaic Levi, similarly dated to the third century, also documents use of a solar calendar (Stone 1988, 159-70).

solar calendar. At the same time, however, I suggest that Judean agricultural society continued to adhere to the time-honored lunar calendar.

The first half of the second century B.C.E. saw the development of a backlash against the worldview and behavior of the Hellenized priests among conservative elements in Judea, centered in the outlying villages near Jerusalem (see Tcherikover 1972, 121-31). This in turn led to a lessened reliance on the priests, which may also have encompassed criticism of their adherence to a solar calendar.[17] It is to this censorious atmosphere that I attribute Jubilees' defense of the solar calendar.[18]

I concur with the viewpoint of other scholars, Annie Jaubert, for example, who, on the basis of Daniel 7:25, infer that circa 175 a change took place in the temple calendar, when Antiochus IV imposed a shift from the solar to the lunar calendar (Jaubert 1953).[19] Furthermore, it seems that Gabriele Boccac-

---

17. Ps 104:19, "He made the moon to mark the seasons; the sun knows when to set," may reflect this criticism. This verse was not preserved in the Psalms Scrolls from Qumran (see Ulrich 2002, 198); thus we cannot determine how the sectarians read it. Clearly, Sir 43:7-9, preserved in a fragment found at Masada, gives expression to this critique. It reads: "Moreover, the moon prescribeth seasons/A r[ule of period and for an everlasting sign]/His the appointed season and from him feast/[?]/New moon as its name (betokens) rene[weth]/[How awe-inspiring is it in its changing!]" (Yadin 1965, 43 [Hebrew section], 46 [English section]). On the importance of these verses in the context of the intersectarian debates in Judea during the second temple period, see Rofé (1988, 43-45). VanderKam's attempt (1979, 407-9) to argue that the verses in Ben Sira refer to the role of the moon in establishing *rosh ḥodesh* and not in determining the date for festivals is difficult to accept. VanderKam retracted this claim in his book on the calendar (1998, 27). Note that, with the exception of these verses, Sirach preserves no evidence of a polemic against the solar calendar. Perhaps the explanation lies in the fact that Sirach edited his sayings after the Seleucid imposition of the lunar calendar on Judea in 175 B.C.E., to which Sirach already adhered.

18. In my view Jubilees dates to the first third of the second century B.C.E. For an exposition of this opinion, see Goldstein (1983, 63-86), Vanderkam (2000b, 1:434-38).

19. Moreover, I agree here with VanderKam's approach that 2 Macc 6:6-7 and 1 Macc 1:58-59 testify to the switch from the solar to the lunar calendar used by the Seleucids. 2 Maccabees and 1 Maccabees state that the Seleucids forced the Jews to celebrate the date on which Antiochus IV was born each month, which is possible only if the Jews followed the lunar calendar in effect in the Seleucid kingdom. In 2 Macc 6:6-7 we read: "No one was allowed to observe the Sabbath or to keep the tradition festivals or even to confess he was a Jew. On the monthly birthday of the king Jews were cruelly compelled to partake of the meat of pagan sacrifices." 1 Macc 1:58-59 relates: "Through their strength they acted against the Israelites who were found in the towns each month, as on the twenty-fifth day of the month they would offer sacrifices on the illicit altar which was upon the temple altar." On the monthly celebration honoring the king in the Hellenistic period, see VanderKam (1981, 64-68). This suggests that Dan 7:25 and the above-cited verses from Maccabees testify to the forceful imposition of the lunar calendar on the Jews by the Seleucids.

cini's (2001) attribution of Daniel to priestly circles adhering to the solar calendar, strong opponents of the return to the lunar calendar, is correct.[20] The Seleucid-imposed calendrical change did not appear to trouble the Hellenized high priests, Jason, Menelaus, and Alcimus. Others, such as Sirach and his circle, who supported the return to the lunar calendar in effect prior to the third century B.C.E., were certainly pleased by the change.

Without pursuing the fascinating but unanswerable question of who served as high priest from 159 to 152, and how the temple was administered during those years,[21] it appears that even if temple practice returned to the solar calendar, this was but a transient change. By the time Jonathan ben Mattathias was appointed to the high priesthood, the lunar calendar was in effect in the temple.[22]

As a result of the above-mentioned processes, the Teacher of Righteousness and his followers adhered to a solar calendar, whereas Jonathan ben Mattathias and the Hasmoneans followed the lunar calendar (see VanderKam 1981, 74). It appears that the temple rites continued to follow a lunar calendar from the appointment of Jonathan to the high priesthood in 152 until the destruction of the temple in C.E. 70. Throughout this period the Qumran sectarians called for the return to the solar calendar, which had been in effect in the temple during the third century and the first quarter of the second century B.C.E. Thus, 4Q390 not only provides an interpretative update of Daniel 9, via its harsh accusations against the priests for not observing the festivals correctly. It also sheds light on conjectured calendrical shifts in second temple Judea, providing background for the calendrical controversies so characteristic of the second temple period.

20. Although most of his conclusions are correct, his argument that the twenty-fourth day of the first month (mentioned in Dan 10:4) had to be determined according to the solar calendar so that it would fall on Friday, as just prior to the Sabbath is the best time for visions (Boccaccini 2001, 2:312-13), is unconvincing.

21. For the conjecture that the Teacher of Righteousness served as high priest between 161 and 152, see Jeremias (1963), Stegemann (1971), Murphy-O'Connor (1974, 215-44; 1976, 400-420; 1977, 100-124).

22. Several scrolls found at Qumran testify to this (including 4Q390, cited earlier). For the famous proof from Pesher Habakkuk, see Talmon (1951, 549-63). An accusation against the Hasmoneans for running the temple according to Gentile dates is found in Pesher Hosea[a] (4QpHos[a]), ll. 14-17: "And I shall put an end to all her joy, [her] pil[grimage,] her [new] moon, and her Sabbath, and all her feasts [Hosea 2:13]. The interpretation of it is that they make [the fe]asts go according to the appointed times of the nations. And [all] [joy] has been turned for them into mourning" (cited from Horgan 1979, 141).

Synchronizing Worship: Jubilees as a Tradition for the Qumran Community

Henry W. Morisada Rietz

Soon after the discovery of the first Dead Sea Scrolls, it was recognized that the calendar followed by the Qumran community differed from the 354-day lunar calendar followed by the establishment in the temple (VanderKam 1994). Annie Jaubert, following the suggestion of Domenique Barthélemy, identified the community's calendar as the 364-day solar calendar known earlier from 1 Enoch 72–82 and Jubilees (Jaubert 1953; 1957a; 1965; cf. Barthélemy 1952; VanderKam 1979). In addition to the biblical traditions, the most important traditions inherited by the Qumran community include 1 Enoch[1] and Jubilees.[2] This paper, which is in-

---

1. The traditional character of the Enoch material is indicated by a variety of evidence, including the number of manuscripts found at Qumran (4Q201-202, 4Q204-212). Influence of the story of the Watchers, which the Enochic material develops from Gen 6:1-4, is found in the Damascus Document (e.g., CD MS A 2:17-21) and the Interpretation concerning the Periods (4Q180 and possibly 4Q181).

2. That Jubilees was a tradition of the Qumran community is indicated by abundant evidence. Of the documents found at Qumran but not composed there, excluding documents later collected into the Tanakh, Jubilees leads the list of extant copies with at least fifteen manuscripts (1Q17-18; 2Q19-20; 3Q5 frg. 3; 4Q176 frgs. 19-20; 4Q176 frg. 21; 4Q216-224 [4Q223-224 are one manuscript]; cf. 4Q225-227 [4QPseudoJubilees[a-c]]; 4Q228; 4Q482-483). The dates of the manuscripts span the life of the community, and many evidence the scribal practices of the community. The first columns of the earliest manuscript (4Q216) are supplied by a later scribe, which may indicate the value ascribed to the document (J. T. Milik and J. C. VanderKam, in Attridge 1994, 1). Definitive evidence that Jubilees served as a formative tradition for the Qumran community is provided by the Damascus Document, which probably refers to Jubilees by its ancient title of the "the Book of the Divisions of the Times (ספר מחלקות העתים)," as an authoritative tradition (CD MS A 16:2-4 and 4Q271 [4QD[f]] frg. 4, 2:4-5; for the title, see 4Q216 [4QJub[a]] 1:11:

111

debted to James VanderKam's extensive work on Jubilees and its relationship to
the Qumran community, particularly with regard to its calendar and angelology,
explicates one important way in which the community appropriated the ideology of Jubilees and its devotion to a 364-day calendar.

As is well known, the 364-day calendar has several interesting features.
The number 364 is a multiple of 7, the number of days in a week; that is, 364 divided by 7 equals exactly 52, the number of weeks in a year. Therefore, any particular date of the year would fall on the same day of the week every year. Thus,
for example, the first day of the year always fell on the same day of the week.
The institution of the 364-day calendar was understood by the traditions of
1 Enoch and Jubilees as a commandment of God (1 En 18:14-16; 80:2-8; Jub 2:9;
cf. 6:30-32) modifying the tradition preserved in Genesis 1:14-19, where both the
sun and the moon are the determinants of the calendar: "The Lord appointed
the sun as a great sign above the earth for days, sabbaths, months, festivals,
years, sabbaths of years, jubilees, and all the times of the years" (Jub 2:9).[3] The
basis of the 364-day calendar also rests upon a concern to properly fulfill other
halakhot of the torah. By fixing the festival days on the same day of the week every year, the 364-day calendar avoids conflict between the commandments to
honor the Sabbath and commandments to celebrate the festivals. In Jubilees the
364-day solar calendar is emphatically opposed to the 354-day lunar calendar:

> There will be people who carefully observe the moon with lunar observa-
> tions because it is corrupt (with respect to) the seasons and is early from
> year to year by ten days.[4] Therefore years will come about for them when
> they will disturb (the year) and make a day of testimony something worth-
> less and profane a festival. Everyone will join together both holy days with
> the profane and the profane with the holy day, for they will err regarding
> the months, the sabbaths, the festivals, and the jubilee. For this reason I am
> commanding you and testifying to you so that you may testify to them be-
> cause after your death your children will disturb (it) so that they do not

---

מ]חלקות [העֹ]תים). Another document, 4Q228, also probably refers to Jubilees as an authority;
"for thus it is written in the division of [the times] (העתים] במחלקות כתוב כן כי)" (4Q228
frg. 1 1:9; cf. DJD, 13:179, pl. 12). The use of the formula -ב כתוב כן כי to refer to an authoritative
book is evidenced by 2 Chron 25:4, which refers to the torah, the book of Moses: ככתוב כי
בתורה בספר משה.

3. Translation of the Ethiopic version of Jubilees is from VanderKam (1989). This passage
is fragmentarily preserved in 4QJubᵃ (4Q216) 6:7-8; for the Hebrew text see Attridge (1994, 16-
17).

4. I.e., it is 10 days shorter than the true year of 364 days according to Jubilees, and thus
354 days.

make the year (consist of) 364 days only. Therefore, they will err regarding the first of the month,[5] the season, the sabbath, and the festivals. They will eat all the blood with all (kinds of) meat. (Jub 6:36-38)[6]

As in the book of Jubilees, the Qumran community was also concerned that the Sabbath regulations, which they interpreted quite literally, be strictly followed. Thus, for example, the community allowed only the burnt offering of the Sabbath to be performed on that day: "Let no one offer-up on the altar on the Sabbath, except for the Sabbath sacrifice (עולת השבת), for thus it is written, 'apart from your Sabbaths'" (CD MS A 11:17-18, interpreting Lev 23:38 [Talmon 1989, 171-73]; cf. 1QS 1:13a-15b; 3:9-11; 9:26-28). Thus, the following of the correct calendar had halakic significance: the times of worship have been commanded by God; failure to worship at the correct time violates God's torah.

The following of the 364-day solar calendar had not only halakic and thus social dimensions, but also cosmic dimensions. The book of Jubilees attests to the idea that the terrestrial worship of the Jerusalem temple was to be synchronized with the celestial worship in the heavens.[7] The holy day which dominates Jubilees is the weekly Sabbath.[8] Instructions concerning the Sabbath are found in Jubilees 2:17-33 and 50:1-13, which concludes the document. These two sections form a sort of *inclusio* to the book. Like the P writer, the author of Jubilees ties the institution of the Sabbath to the creation event (Jub 2:25; cf. Gen 2:1-4). However, distinct from the biblical tradition, the command to observe the Sabbath was first given to the angels (in the following passages referred to in the first-person plural) and the Sabbath is to be observed in heaven: "He gave us the sabbath day as a great sign so that we should perform work for six days and that we should keep sabbath from all work on the seventh day. He told us — all the angels of the presence and all the angels of holiness (these two great kinds) — to keep sabbath with him in heaven and on earth" (Jub 2:17-18). "On it [i.e., the seventh day] we kept sabbath in heaven before it was made known to all humanity that on it they should keep sabbath on earth" (Jub 2:30b) (trans. VanderKam 1989). The Sabbath was made known only to the chosen people of Israel (Jub 2:19-20, 30b; 50:9-10), and they were to observe it with the angels: "In this way he made a sign on it by which they, too, would keep sabbath *with us* on

5. Note that although Jubilees rejects the moon as a standard for calendrical purposes, it continues to celebrate the first of the month.

6. Translation of the Ethiopic version is from VanderKam (1989).

7. For the biblical antecedents of the worship in the heavens, see Isa 6; cf. Dan 7; 1 Kings 22:19-23; 1 En 14.

8. "It [the Sabbath] is more holy and more blessed than any day of the jubilee of jubilees" (Jub 2:30a). Cf. the section in CD MS A 10:14–11:18 "Concerning the sa[bba]th."

the seventh day to eat, drink, and bless the creator of all as he had blessed them and sanctified them for himself as a noteworthy people out of all the nations; and to keep sabbath *together with us*" (Jub 2:21) (trans. VanderKam 1989, emphasis added). In fact, the one who observes the Sabbath is comparable to the angels: "Everyone who observes (it) and keeps sabbaths on it from all his work will be holy and blessed throughout all times like us" (Jub 2:28).[9]

The idea of synchronicity between the human and angelic worship is attested at Qumran by the Songs of the Sabbath Sacrifice. While the exact function of the Sabbath Songs is disputed,[10] they provide clear evidence of a mirroring of heavenly and earthly worship.[11] The Songs of the Sabbath Sacrifice consist of songs for the first thirteen Sabbaths of the year according to the 364-day calendar. The first song calls the angelic priesthood[12] to praise God: "Praise [the God of . . .]*h*, O godlike beings of all the Most Holy Ones. And in divinity [. . .] among the eternally holy of the Most Holy Ones. And they have become for him priests of [the inner sanctum . . .]."[13] Later in the same song, reference is made to the "[G]o[d of] the divine beings, priests of the highest heights who [draw n]ear [. . .]."[14]

The Qumran sectarian Dead Sea Scrolls not only attest to a dualism of angels in the heavens and humans on earth, but also to the in-breakings of the angelic world on earth. Angels are present on earth in the community. The classic expressions of angelic presence are found in the form of prohibitions excluding certain people from some aspects of the community found in the Rule

9. Translation of the Ethiopic tradition is from VanderKam (1989). Cf. Jub 16:28, where Israel is circumcised and sanctified so that they may be in the presence of God and the angels who are also circumcised: "For this (i.e. circumcision) is what the nature of all of the angels of the presence and all of the angels of holiness was like from the day of their creation. And in front of the angels of the presence and the angels of holiness he sanctified Israel to be with him and with his holy angels." For discussion of biblical characters portrayed as angels in the documents collected in the Pseudepigrapha, see Charlesworth (1980).

10. Lawrence Schiffman (1982) suggests that it is an exegetical description of angelic worship. J. Maier (1992, 2:552-53) suggests that the recitation of the Sabbath Songs replaced the services of the defiled Jerusalem temple for the estranged community. Newsom (1985, 59) suggests that "the cycle of the Sabbath Shirot is a quasi-mystical liturgy designed to evoke a sense of being present in the heavenly temple"; more recently, see her comments in Newsom and Charlesworth (1999).

11. The question of direction of mirroring remains: Is angelic worship a reflection of human worship or is human worship a reflection of the angelic? While the latter is more probable, the question cannot be answered conclusively.

12. For discussion of the various terms used for angels and in the description of the heavenly temple, see Newsom (1985, 23-58).

13. Sabbath Song 1:1-5 (see Newsom and Charlesworth, 1999, 139).

14. Sabbath Song 1:20 (see Newsom and Charlesworth, 1999, 141).

of the Congregation (1QSa 2:3-10), the Damascus Document (CD MS A 15:15-17 and parallels in 4QD MSS), and the War Scroll (1QM 7:3-6 and possible parallel in 4QM1).[15] Although the context of the passages differs, the exclusion of certain individuals in each is based on the presence of angels. The broad context of the passage in the Rule of the Congregation[16] is provided by its incipit: "And this is the rule for the entire congregation of Israel in the latter days" (הימים וזה הסרך לכול עדת ישראל באחרית; 1QSa 1.1),[17] which provides instruction for, among other things, a messianic feast immediately following the exclusion passage (see 1QSa 2:11-22). The specific context of 1QSa 2:11-22 is, at the end of a passage which began in 1:25b-27, indicated by the *vacat* between 1:25a and b: "And when there will be a convocation of[18] the entire assembly for judgment, or for the council of the community, or for a convocation of war, they shall sanctify them(selves) three days so that everyone entering shall be pre[pared for the co]uncil." The participants in the various assemblies are instructed to "sanctify them(selves) three days"; the reason for this sanctification is eventually provided in 2:8-9: "for (the) angels of holiness (are) [in] their [coun]cil."

The similar exclusion passage in the Damascus Document (CD MS A 15:15-17) confirms that the belief in the presence of angels was operative during the community's existence. The context of the passage is a section in the "laws"[19] dealing with oaths (CD MS A cols. 15-16). The structure of the passage can be outlined as follows:

15:1-6a — oaths in general and the "oath of the covenant" (בשבועת הברית)

15. For earlier discussion of these passages, see Fitzmyer (1957-58) and Shemesh (1997).

16. The Rule of the Congregation is attested on only one extant manuscript, 1Q28, on which are also found the Rule of the Community (1QS) and Words of Blessing (1QSb). See Milik (1955, 107, and pls. XXII-XXIV).

17. Schiffman (1989, 12) understands this document as providing the rules for Israel at a future time when "[t]he entire community of Israel is to be identified with the sect in the end of days." The future reference is established by the reference to the Messiahs in 2:11-22 (cf. Talmon 1988). Stegemann (1993, 159-63; cf. Steudel 1993, 230-31) rightly points out that despite the presence of the Messiahs, the context is till the last days of an evil age since the final War is yet to occur (see 1QSa 1:21, 26). Although the document points to a future age, the specificity of the rules suggests that the Rule of the Congregation is not merely speculative. As Schiffman (1994, 35-36) suggests, the rules were probably practiced in the community in anticipation of the future.

18. Following the translation of Schiffman (1989, 29-30) here and later in the passage.

19. The Damascus Document comprises two large sections, often referred to as the "Admonition" and the "Laws." Cf. Rabin (1958). For an outline which includes the material from the Dead Sea Scrolls, see Baumgarten and Schwartz (1995, 5). Note that the "Laws" are introduced by "a catalogue of transgressions ending with an appeal to those who know to choose between the paths of life and perdition" (5).

15:6b-15a — (oath) "to return to the torah of Moses"; cf. 1QS 5 esp. 5:7-10
and the parallel vocabulary

15:15b-19[20] — exclusion of the physically and mentally impaired

16:1-6a — (oath) "to return to the torah of Moses" with reference to Jubilees

16:6b-20 — miscellaneous *halakhot* regarding oaths

In this passage the oath "to return to the torah of Moses" לשוב אל תורת משה
(CD MS A 15:9, 12; 16:1-2, 4-5) is compared (וכן in 15:6) to the "oath of the covenant" בשבועת הברית (15:5-6). The *halakhot* are directed "to everyone who
turns (השב)from his corrupt way" (15:7) and refer to the initiation into the sectarian community.[21] These *halakhot* are specifically for the present "wicked
time"; "And thus (also is) the precept during the entire wicked time" (וכן
המשפט בכל קץ הרשע; 15:6b-7). The passage claims that the correct interpretation of the torah of Moses has been revealed to the sectarian community:
"Should he err in any matter of the torah revealed to the multitude of the camp
(וכל אשר נגלה מן התורה לרוב המחנה), the Examiner shall ma[ke it known]
to him and enjoin it upon him, and te[ac]h (him) for (a minimum of) one complete year" (15:13-15).[22] After discussing the exclusion of the physically and mentally impaired, the passage returns to discussing the return to the torah of Moses:

> Similarly,[23] a man shall take upon himself (an oath) to return to the torah
> of Moses (יקום האיש על נפשך לשוב אל תורת משה), for in it everything
> is specified. And the explication of their times, when Israel was blind to all

20. A *vacat* between 15:6a and b signals the beginning of a subsection. That these instructions are for "the entire time of evil" is repeated in CD MS A 15:10//4Q266 frg. 8 1:1.

21. Cf. 1QS 5, esp. 5:7-11, which also deals with the initiation into the sectarian community, and the language parallels CD MS A 15:6b–16:6a. "He shall take upon his soul by a binding oath to return to the torah of Moses (ויקם על נפשו בשבועת אסר לשוב אל תורת מושה), according to all which he has commanded with all heart and with all soul (בכול לב ובכול נפש), according to everything which has been revealed from it to the Sons of Zadok, the priests who keep the covenant and seek his will, and according to the multitude of the men of their covenant who devote themselves to his truth and to walking in his will" (1QS 5:8-10; cf. 4QS MSS B and D which omit "according to all which he has commanded," thus providing a closer parallel to CD MS A 15:9-10).

22. Cf. 1QS 5:8-10, where the initiate swears "to return to the torah of Moses . . . according to everything which has been revealed from it to the Sons of Zadok (הנגלה ממנה לבני צדוק לכול. . .)."

23. Baumgarten translates כן as "therefore." כן probably functions comparatively, as in 15:6 where a comparison is made between the oath of the covenant and the (oath) to return to the torah of Moses. Here, in 16:1, the previous sentence ends with "with you a covenant and with all Israel" and כן marks a transition to the "(oath) to return to the torah of Moses."

these; behold it is specified in the Book of the Divisions of the Times in their Jubilees and in their Weeks.[24] And on the day when a man takes upon himself (an oath) to return to the torah of Moses (יקום האיש על נפשו לשוב אל תורת משה), the angel Mastema shall turn aside from after him, if he fulfills his words. (CD 16:1-5)

In this passage "the Book of the Divisions of the Times in their Jubilees and in their Weeks" is a reference to the ancient title of the book of Jubilees. Moreover, the reference to Jubilees is framed by the phrase אל תורת משה נפשכו לשוב יקום האיש על. The passage emphasizes that "in it (i.e., the torah of Moses) everything is specified" בה הכל מדוקדק.[25] Thus, the presence of angels is affirmed in the community which understands itself as returning to the torah, which includes the correct calendar.

The context of the third passage, from the War Scroll, is the final war between the Sons of Light and the Sons of Darkness. The War Scroll describes the time when "the congregation of divine beings and the assembly of men, the Sons of Light and the lot of Darkness, will war together" (חושך נלחמים יחד עדת אלים וקהלת אנשים בני אור וגורל; 1QM 1:10-11). The imagery of the War Scroll, however, attests to more than some sort of parallel universes with two separate battles occurring. Rather, as we have seen from the exclusion passage, the angels are said to be present on the side of the Sons of Light: "for the holy angels (are) together with their hosts" (כיא מלאכי קודש עם צבאותם יחד; 1QM 7:6). A copy of the War Scroll preserves a parallel tradition:[26] "for the holy angels (are) togeth[er] in their lines" (כיא מלאכי במצרכותמה יח]ד; 4Q491 frgs. 1-3 line 10).

This study seeks to explicate one of the ways in which the Qumran community developed the ideology of Jubilees associated with the 364-day calendar, namely, the way the observance of this calendar maintained their relationship with the angelic worship. Since the times of worship had been commanded by God, failure to worship at the correct time violates God's torah. Moreover, the Qumran community believed that the terrestrial worship of the Jerusalem temple was to be synchronized with the celestial worship in the heavens. From the point of view of the community, the Jerusalem establishment, by following the

---

24. This is the ancient title of Jubilees. See note 2, which discusses the evidence for Jubilees as a tradition inherited by the Qumran community.

25. Note that this is consistent with 1QS 5:9, where what has been revealed to the sons of Zadok "has been revealed from it" הנגלה ממנה (i.e., the torah of Moses in 5:8).

26. See the comments of J. Charlesworth and B. Strawn, PTSDSSP 2:110 n. 94 and 2:144 n. 16.

wrong calendar, severed the cosmic synchronicity, and thus the continuum between the heavens and the earth.

This led the community to believe they were living in the "latter days" of an evil generation predetermined by God and awaiting the appointed time when God would intervene on behalf of truth to eradicate deceit. By following the same calendar as the angels in the heavens, the Qumran community believed they maintained the synchronicity. The synchronicity between the angelic and human realms culminates in the conjoining of the heavens and the earth in the community's experience, with the community's affirmations that angels were present in their midst.

"The Days of Sukkot of the Month of Kislev": The Festival of Dedication and the Delay of Feasts in 1QS 1:13-15

Michael A. Daise

In two articles James VanderKam (1979; 1981; cf. 1994, 384-386; 1998, 113-116) proposed a historical context for the calendrical sentiments in Jubilees and the Qumran sectarian literature. Building primarily on the work of Annie Jaubert (1953; 1957ab; 1965), VanderKam argued that the concern for calendrical propriety in those works addressed the imposition of a lunisolar calendar upon the Jerusalem cult during the first decade and a half of the Maccabean Uprising. As VanderKam has it, the 364-day, solar calendar had been official to the cult until 167 BCE, when it was replaced by the Seleucid 354-day system to accommodate celebrations of Antiochus IV's birthday (VanderKam 1979, 402-410; 1981, 57-59). Maccabean success notwithstanding, the 364-day calendar remained marginalized from the cult until 160/159 BCE, due to the sustained tenure of pro-Seleucid high priests. It was then reinstated (or at least advocated from within the cult), perhaps by the Righteous Teacher, only to be ousted again, and this time for good, when Jonathan took the high priesthood in 150/149 BCE (VanderKam 1981, 60-74).[1] The calendrical polemics in Jubilees 6:32-38 and the Qumran

Along with the University of Michigan, for its sponsorship of the Second Enoch Seminar, I would like to thank the following for enabling my participation in it: the College of William and Mary for a Faculty Summer Research Grant and the Wendy and Emery Reves Center for International Studies, College of William and Mary, for a Faculty International Travel Grant.

1. VanderKam (1981, 72 nn. 61-63) follows the reconstruction inferred by Hartmut Stegemann (1971), corroborated by Jochen Gabriel Bunge (1975, 28-34, 39-43) and verified by Jerome Murphy-O'Connor (1976) that the Righteous Teacher held the high priesthood sometime between Alcimus (160/159 BCE) and Jonathan (150/149 BCE).

writings, contends VanderKam, championed the original cultic solar calendar against these intrusions, but each from a different period and social location: Jubilees from within the cult sometime between 159 and 150 BCE; the Qumran writings from outside it after 150 BCE (VanderKam 1981, 72-73).

VanderKam's proposal is, of course, one part of a larger debate. Not all agree that the 364-day calendar ever held official status in Jerusalem (see Davies, 1983; Wacholder 1995, 2-4; and, most recently, Stern 2001, 28-31, esp. 29 n. 130). And among those who do, VanderKam's is but one of several hypotheses for how that might have been so.[2] My purpose in this paper is not to engage that debate as it has been waged. Rather, taking VanderKam's scenario as essentially persuasive, I will make two observations which, when combined, suggest further developments in it.[3] The first concerns the resolve expressed in 1QS and perhaps two 4QD fragments that festivals not "be delayed" from the times appointed them; the second is the notion in 2 Maccabees that the Feast of Hanukkah was somehow an observance of Tabernacles in Kislev.

The Advance and Delay of Religious Festivals

One, possibly three, sectarian text(s) from Qumran carry an insistence that religious feasts not precede or lag behind their appointed times of observance. The best preserved is in the introduction to 1QS, at 1:13-15. After listing the aims for which the Rule has been designed (1:1-11), the introduction closes by stating the standards by which its adherents must live (1:11-15). Among them is absolute compliance with God's commands, elaborated, in part, as a commitment neither to "advance" nor "postpone" festal observance:

> And all who devote themselves to his truth
> shall bring all their knowledge, strength and wealth into the Community of God,
> to purify their knowledge in the truth of God's statutes,
> to issue their strength according to his perfect paths
> and all their wealth according to his righteous counsel;
> and not to step away, in any one (of them), from God's commands, in their scope:

2. See the summaries in Matthias Albani (1997, 112-115); as well as now Hanan Eshel's proposal in the contributions to this volume.

3. Nor are the implications to be drawn here incompatible with the hypothesis of Hanan Eshel, presented in this volume.

neither to anticipate their appointed times (ולוא לקדם עתיהם)

nor be delayed from any of their sacred feasts (ולוא להתאחר מכול מועדיהם);

And not to turn aside from his trustworthy statutes, so as to go to the right or to the left. (1QS 1:11-15)[4]

The idea may also appear in 4Q266 2 i 1-2 and 4Q268 1 4. Both texts roughly attest the same passage, which has no parallel in CD and would precede the first column of CD A by several lines.[5]

אין]לחת[ק]ד[ם ו]להתאחר ממועדיהם

(They are) not [to ad]va[nc]e nor be delayed from their sacred feasts. (4Q266 2 i 1-2)

אי]ן לקדם]ו[ל]א[חר ממועדיה]מה

And no]t to precede [nor] t[a]rry from th[eir] sacred feasts. (4Q268 1 4)[6]

The lines carry an ostensible affinity to 1QS 1:13-15, which, in the case of 4Q268, has not been lost on Baumgarten (1996, 120). Yet it must be conceded that an alternative interpretation is possible, on two bases. First, unlike 1QS, the 4QD lines have no extant subject that concretely links them to festal observance. Second, the context in which they are couched is explicitly eschatological. Though poorly preserved, it seems to concern the disclosure of the divine plan for history to the author's community: "The last things — shall they not indeed come?" (4Q268 1 1); "A wrathful end has been decreed for a people whom he does not know" (4Q266 2 i 3; 4Q268 1 5[7]); "[He fixed appointed times of goodwill (מועדי רצון) for those who see]k his commandment and walk in (his) perfect path" (4Q266 2 i 4; 4Q268 1 6-7[8]); "He uncovered their eyes unto hidden matters; and they opened their e]ar and heard profound things, and understood [all that occurs, even what will come upon them" (4Q266 2 i 5-6; 4Q268 1 7-8[9]). Also mentioned are the creation and eschaton, perhaps as they bracket the divine scheme for the ages: "What is its beginning? And what is its end?" (4Q268 1 2). These factors, together with the use in this context of מוער

---

4. The text is Burrows (1951). All translations in this article are mine unless otherwise indicated.

5. CD A column 1 would begin at 4Q266 2 i 6f. and 4Q268 1 9f., respectively.

6. 4QD texts here and below are from Baumgarten (1996).

7. 4Q268 1 5 reads "he decreed wr[athful] ends. . . ."

8. 4Q268 1 6-7 reads "his commandments."

9. 4Q268 1 7-8 reads "he opened their ear."

Michael A. Daise

for an eschatological period[10] (where it designates a sacred feast in 1QS), may suggest that מועד in these lines should not be translated "sacred feasts" but "appointed times," and that the phenomena not to be "hastened" or "postponed" here are not festal observances, but eschatological epochs. God has so fixed the "times of wrath" and the "times of goodwill" that the chronological thresholds between them (not festal *halakhah*) are "not [to ad]va[nc]e nor be delayed from their appointed times" (4Q266 2 1-2).

Such an interpretation would not void the observation being made here, since 1QS 1:13-15 clearly does have religious feasts in view: the context there is not the unfolding of eschatological eras but the keeping of God's commands, of which annual feasts are part and parcel. Yet a different meaning in the 4QD fragments would indeed narrow the basis of the present argument, and this will be remembered in all that follows.

The Advance of Feasts in the 354-Day Calendar

That feasts not "precede" their appointed times doubtless has the 354-day calendar in view. The 354-day system has shorter months than does the 364-day one: six of twenty-nine and six of thirty days to the solar calendar's eight of thirty and four of thirty-one days. Moreover, the 354-day calendar always plots the Waving of the ʿOmer, and hence the Feast of Weeks, earlier than the 364-day one. As Dominique Barthélemy (1952, 200-201) deduced, the solar calendar dates the Feast of Weeks at 3/15 and, therefore, the Waving of the ʿOmer at 1/26. The possible dates in the lunisolar calendar are more complex. The biblical rubric that the Waving of the ʿOmer is to occur "on the morrow of the sabbath" (Lev 23:15) could have designated the day following the first sabbath after Passover or, as was debated, may have meant the day following the first (Talmon, 2001, 5-6) or seventh days of Unleavened Bread (Charles 1902, 106-107; cf. VanderKam 1998, 30-32). In every case, however, the Waving of the ʿOmer and Feast of Weeks would have inevitably preceded their equivalents in the 364-day scheme: the former occurring anytime between 1/15 and 22; the latter anytime between 3/5 and 12. The combined effect of these factors would be that feasts in the 354-day scheme "advance" before their corollaries in the 364-day one. If both calendars were to start a year on the same day, their feasts of Passover and Unleavened Bread would coincide; but, from the Waving of the ʿOmer onward, those of the lunisolar would gradually "precede" those of the solar.

The chart below compares the two, using feasts likely shared between the

10. 4Q266 i 4/4Q268 1 6-7 above.

Qumran community and the Jerusalem cult. The calculations assume that the 354-day calendar alternates 29-day and 30-day months, beginning with the former, and that both calendars start the year on the same day. The advance of dates in the 354-day calendar would, of course, increase to the extent intercalation did not occur in subsequent years.

Feast	364-Day Calendar Date	364-Day Equivalent to 354-Day Calendar Date
Passover	1/14	1/14
Unleavened Bread	1/15(-21)[11]	1/15(-21)
Waving of 'Omer	1/26	1/15-22
Second Passover	2/14	2/13
Weeks	3/15	3/4-11
Remembrance/Trumpets	7/1	6/27
Day of Atonement	7/10	7/5
Tabernacles	7/15(-22)	7/10(-17)

In this respect, 1QS 1:13-15, and perhaps 4Q266 2 i 1-2 and 4Q268 1 4, echo the calendrical polemic in Jubilees 6:32-38. There, too, concern is expressed that Israelites "*neither omit a day* nor disturb a festival" (6:32), and the lunisolar calendar is disparaged, in part, because it "*is early from year to year* by ten days" (6:36).[12]

Hanukkah as the Feast of Tabernacles in Kislev

That feasts be "delayed" from their appointed times, however, is not an effect that the lunisolar calendar would have on the solar one. To be sure, the language perhaps ought not be pressed so far: it could be mere rhetoric on fidelity to the solar year (as suggested also by Stern 2001, 17); perhaps a hypothetical statement of principle; or even a historical censure of festal delays in biblical literature — Jeroboam's Feast of Tabernacles on 8/15[13]; or Hezekiah's Feasts of Passover and Unleavened Bread on 2/14-28.[14] A real and contemporary referent

11. Parentheses for intermediate days of multiple-day feasts are per Talmon's observation that these days are not registered in the Qumran calendrical texts (Talmon 2001, 11).

12. Translation VanderKam (1989); italics mine.

13. 1 Kings 12:32-33 (see Morgenstern 1948, 477-479; Talmon 1951, 557).

14. 2 Chron 30:1-27. In a comment that in some ways anticipates this paper, Jonathan Goldstein suggested that LXX 3 Kgdms 8:65 omitted (and MT 2 Chron 7:8-10 reworked) Solomon's seven-day extension of the Feast of Tabernacles in MT 1 Kings 8:65 because, like the Qumran Essenes (1QS 1:14-15), the writers could not accept a prolonged festival (Goldstein 1976, 279).

presents itself, however, in 2 Maccabees, where the feast later to be called Hanukkah is regarded as being, in some way, a celebration of Tabernacles in Kislev. Tabernacles was, of course, legislated to be observed on 15-22 Tishri, the seventh month; Kislev is the ninth month, implying a delay in that observance of some two months.

Whether or not 2 Maccabees presents Hanukkah as a surrogate or duplicate Tabernacles (Nodet 1986, 331-332; cf. Liber 1912, 21), it at least vests it with traits drawn from that feast.[15] Jason or his epitomator arguably cast it as such in chapter 10: if not by the flora carried[16] and hymns sung,[17] certainly by the eight-day duration[18] and exultant mood.[19] "They observed eight days with joy after the manner of Tabernacles, remembering how, a little while before, during the Feast of Tabernacles, they were dwelling in the mountains and caves like animals" (10:6).[20] Moreover, the two letters prefixed to the epitome virtually give the new feast the name "Tabernacles." This is clearest in the first letter (1:1-9), which closes with a bid to the Egyptian Jews "that you might observe the days of Tabernacles of the month of Kislev" (1:9). But it also emerges (albeit in

15. That Hanukkah is not a precise replica of Tabernacles in 2 Maccabees is clear, at the very least, from its lack of any reference to the making of booths (Neh 8:15-17); for this among other differences between the festivals (see Liber, 1912, 25-26; Vaux 1997, 512; VanderKam 1992b, 124).

16. 2 Macc 10:7; Lev 23:40; cf. also Jub 16.30-31; *L.A.B.* 13.7; *Ant.* 3.244-245; 13.372; and, for the *lulab* (see below), *m. Sukkah* 3.1-4, 8-9, 12-15; 4.1-2, 4, 7. Particularly noteworthy are the linguistic affinities between "ripened branches" (κλάδοι ὡραῖοι) and "palm fronds" (φοίνικες) in 2 Macc 10:7 and the flora prescribed in LXX Lev 23:40 (cf. Neh 8:15/2 Esdr 18:15). The θύρσοι in 2 Macc 10:7 could designate the *lulab* (Abel 1946, 543) but may also be an assimilated element of Dionysian rites; on these issues see Rubenstein (1992, 109-112, 132-134, 157-160; 1995, 63, 82, 94-97), and Ulfgard (1998, 183-185, esp. 184 n. 406 and the works cited there).

17. 2 Macc 10:7; 2 Chr 5:2-3, 11-13; 7:6; *Ant.* 8.100, 102; 11.154, 157; or more specifically, the *Hallel*: *m. Sukkah* 3.9-11; 4.1, 5, 8 (cf. Liber 1912, 25; Abel 1946, 541; VanderKam, 1992, 2:124).

18. 2 Macc 10:6; Lev 23:35-36; Num 29:12, 35-38; 1 Kgs 8:1-2, 65-66 (possibly); Neh 8:18; 2 Chr 5:2-3; 7:8-10; *Jub.* 32.1-2, 16-29 (cf. 31.3); *Spec.* 1.189; 2.204, 211-213; *Ant.* 3.244-245, 247; 11.154, 157; *m. Sukkah* 4.1, 8; 5.6. Relevant in this regard, but not assessed in this article, is the work of E. Regev (2001).

19. 2 Macc 10:6; Lev 23:40; Deut 16:14 ; 1 Kgs 8:1-2, 65-66; Neh 8:17; 2 Chr 5:2-3; 7:8-10; *Jub.* 16.20-21, 25, 27, 29, 31; 32.7 (cf. 31.3); *Ant.* 11.154-157; 15.50; *m. Sukkah* 4.1, 8; 5.1 (see Krauss 1895, 28-32).

20. For the text of 2 Maccabees see Kappler and Hanhart (1976). The extent to which parallels are seen between 2 Maccabees 10 and Tabernacles varies among scholars: Ulfgard (1998, 183 n. 400), for instance, sees a corollary between Lev 23:40 (and Neh 8:15) and the "palm fronds," but not the "ripened branches" of 2 Macc 10:7; Rankin (1930, 91-102), who further entertained similarities in sacrifices (2 Macc 10:3/Lev 23:36 [?]; Num 29:13-38 [?]) and light (2 Macc 1:18/ Hanukkah-lamps), ultimately suspected that these and all resemblances mentioned above were merely apparent.

eclipsed forms) in the second letter (1:10–2:18): at 2 Maccabees 1:18, "so that you yourselves might also observe (the days), as (days) of Tabernacles and of fire"; and at 2 Maccabees 2:16, "you, therefore, will do well to observe the days (of Tabernacles)."

This last point diverges somewhat from VanderKam's own work on Hanukkah. VanderKam is unconvinced 2 Maccabees goes so far as to name Hanukkah "Tabernacles," partly because, in 2 Maccabees 1:9, 18, the Greek term for Tabernacles, σκηνοπηγία, is not conjoined with the term "feast" (ἑορτή), as it is elsewhere in the LXX, but with the term "days" (ἡμέραι). The Egyptian Diaspora is asked to observe "the days of Tabernacles" (τὰς ἡμέρας τῆς σκηνοπηγίας), which, according to VanderKam (1987, 32-33; 1992, 2.124), is not quite tantamount to observing the "Feast of Tabernacles" proper (τὴν ἑορτὴν τῆς σκηνοπηγίας).[21] A significant, yet unconsidered factor in the discussion, however, is the designation given Purim in the Book of Esther. Esther was a peer to 2 Maccabees in its espousal of a new Jewish feast (Medico 1965; Momigliano 1975, 87-88; Goldstein, 1976, 551-57) and was known, if not to the authors of the prefixed letters (2 Macc 1:1–2:18), at least to Jason and/or the epitomator.[22] Relevant here is that, in Esther 9, where Purim is established, it is never designated by the term "feast" (גח, ἑορτή) but always with the phrase "days" or "days of." This appears tentatively at Esther 9:26, "thus they call *these days* Purim" (Esther 9:26)[23]; but becomes explicit at Esther 9:28 and, in the Hebrew only, 9:30-31:

> These days of Purim (וימי הפרים האלח) will not pass away from among the Jews,
> nor will their memory cease from their seed. (Esther 9:28)[24]

---

21. Not in dispute here are VanderKam's comments on 2 Macc 10:5-8; namely, (1) that 2 Macc 10:6 conveys only that participants celebrated "*after the manner* of Tabernacles" (not the feast of Tabernacles itself) and (2) that the theme of Tabernacles was introduced in these verses only to accentuate the missed celebration of it earlier in the revolt (not to transfer its title to the new feast). On this second point, see also Doran (1981, 5 n. 9).

22. The reference here is to 2 Macc 15:36, where Judas' defeat over Nicanor is dated relative to the non-Susan date of Purim in Esther 9:16-17: "And with a unanimous vote they all decreed to let this day in no way be effaced, but to hold eminent the thirteenth of the twelfth month — called Adar in the Syrian language — one day before the day of Mordekai." Bardtke (1971:103-109) traces the connection with 2 Maccabees to the movement behind the Greek additions to Esther.

23. Italics mine. The Greek of both LXX and Alpha (AT 8:49) texts reads the passive, "were called." For the LXX text see Hanhart (1983); for the Alpha text see Clines (1984, 244-47).

24. The LXX reads, "These days of Purim (αἱ δὲ ἡμέραι αὗται τῶν Φρουραι) will be observed for all time, and their memorial will not cease from their generations"; Alpha text 8:47, "And Mordekai wrote these words in a book and sent them to the Jews who were in Artaxerxes'

(Queen Esther, with Mordekai,) sent letters to all the Jews . . . establishing these days of Purim (לקים את־ימי הפרים האלה) in their appointed times. (Esther 9:30-31).

That the phrase "days of Purim" is here clearly used to designate the "Feast of Purim" — and this for a festival that is peer to Hanukkah in its novelty, in a book that was known to 2 Maccabees in its final redaction — suggests that the distinction between the two terms ought not be overstated. Hanukkah as "*the days* of Tabernacles of the month of Kislev" in 2 Maccabees 1:9 is likely synonymous to Hanukkah as "*the Feast* of Tabernacles of the month of Kislev." In view of the traits of Tabernacles given Hanukkah in 2 Maccabees 10, one may conclude that, in 2 Maccabees, Hanukkah is, in some sense, cast as a celebration of Tabernacles in Kislev — some two months after its "appointed time" in Tishri. And to return to the point at issue, the delayed observance implied in that conception makes it viable as a referent for the polemic issued in 1QS 1:13-15, as well as perhaps the 4QD fragments.

2 Maccabees and the Qumran Community

But was that, in fact, the case? That is to say, if these Qumran texts *could* have been addressing the idea of Hanukkah as Tabernacles in Kislev, how likely is it they actually *were?* Paucity of data prohibits a definitive answer[25]; but the distinct possibility of such a connection may be inferred from either of two lines of thought.

The first is the view, held by some, that Hanukkah did indeed begin as a Feast of Tabernacles in Kislev. In the array of hypotheses proposed for the feast's origins a number maintain that the account in 2 Maccabees is most accurate; that is, that the new feast was, from the beginning, a Tabernacles festival, of sorts.[26] Were this the case — following Stegemann (1971), Bunge (1975) and Murphy O'Connor (1976) — the earliest members of the Qumran community

---

kingdom . . . to establish these days, the fourteenth and fifteenth, with hymns and festivities instead of griefs and sorrows."

25. A tenuous connection between Hanukkah and Qumran was attempted by del Medico (1957, 467; 1965, 254 n. 1), who alleged the "glorious boughs" (לפארת כבוד) mentioned in 1QIIa xvi [Suk viii] 22 were part of a polemic against the "golden wreaths" used in the dedicatory ceremony at 1 Macc 4:57. The text used here is Sukenik (1955).

26. Though differing in details between them, see Krauss (1895, 28-32); Leszynsky (1911, 402-12); Liber (1912, 24-29); Abel (1946, 540-41); Bunge (1971, 492-495, 501-509); VanderKam (1987, 32-34); Ulfgard (1998, 183-85); as well as Goldstein (1976, 273-280), who, however, believed that, due to neglected intercalation, 25 Kislev was, in fact, actually 11 Tishri.

were bound to have known of it, since they were still integral to the mainstream priesthood. Even if a hiatus in observance of the festival occurred between its first celebration in 165/164 BCE[27] and Jonathan's assumption of the high priesthood in 150 BCE,[28] the feast still would have been established in Jerusalem during the period when the Righteous Teacher and his followers were directly interacting with the cult.[29]

But, even if the author(s) of 2 Maccabees invented the notion of Hanukkah as Tabernacles in Kislev sometime later, a case could still be made that the Qumran group was apprised of it. The date and provenance of 2 Maccabees are much debated: its sources being speculated to span from 164 BCE to the mid-1st century CE; and its provenance being traced from Judea/Jerusalem to Egypt/Alexandria (see Attridge, 1984, 177-78, 181-83; deSilva 2002, 269-70). A relative anchor in this sea, however, has been E. Bickermann's argument that the first prefixed letter (2 Macc 1:1-9) is authentic to its claims. Bickermann contended that the form of the letter quoted at 2 Maccabees 1:7c-8 reflected the subjugation under Demetrius II which it claimed, and that this period of subjugation was so brief (late fall 143 BCE to May 142 BCE) it would be absurd to think a forger had contrived it (Bickermann 1933, 237-41).[30] Significant for the issue at hand is that this first prefixed letter, as will be recalled, contains the most salient expression of Hanukkah as Tabernacles in Kislev. The new feast, at 2 Maccabees 1:9, is designated "the days of Tabernacles of the month of Kislev." Inasmuch as that letter claims to have hailed from "the Judean brethren in Jerusalem and in the land of Judea" (1:1) in "the one hundred and eighty-eighth year" of the Seleucid era (1:9) — that is, 124 BCE — its authenticity means this idea was circulating in Judea at the close of the 2nd century BCE. If one measures by manuscript evidence, this would have been just at or prior to the time the polemic against delayed feasts was emerging in Qumran circles. 4Q266 dates to the early or mid-first century BCE (Baumgarten 1996, 2, 26)[31] and, according to Joseph Baum-

---

27. For the precise date Hanukkah was inaugurated, see the discussion by VanderKam (1987, 24-31).

28. See, for instance, the speculations by Bunge (1971, 501-5); cf. also de Vaux (1997, 511).

29. Since Jubilees is innocent of any threat from "delayed feasts," such an early emergence of the notion that Hanukkah was Tabernacles in Kislev might also imply a date for the book earlier than the 150s BCE, when VanderKam (1977, 214-85) has it: perhaps 168 BCE, as per Nickelsburg (1984, 101-103), when the advancing effects of the lunisolar calendar threatened but Hanukkah had not yet been inaugurated. But even this is unnecessary if, after its first few observances, Hanukkah was not again celebrated until Jonathan's assumption of the high priesthood (Bunge 1971, 501-5; Vaux 1997, 511).

30. Further buttressing Bickermann's case was his deduction that the letter of 124 BCE had been translated from a Hebrew or Aramaic *Vorlage* (Bickermann, 1933, 245-246).

31. 4Q268 is dated to the early 1st century CE (Baumgarten 1996, 116-18).

garten and Ada Yardeni, appears to have been a personal draft or copy from a previous exemplar, suggesting a *terminus a quo* as early as the late second century BCE. But if that fragment does not, in fact, address festal observance (as per the caveat above), 1QS 1:13-15, which clearly does, dates circa 100-75 BCE (Metso 1997, 13-14; Alexander and Vermes, 1998, 9, 24).[32]

Implications for VanderKam's Scenario

If either of these correlations implies causation, they suggest a modification to VanderKam's hypothesis. Namely, more factors distinguished the calendrical polemics in Jubilees and the Qumran writings than time and social location. As was rehearsed at the beginning of this article, VanderKam proposed that both Jubilees and the Qumran sectarian literature championed the 364-day calendar, but at different periods and in different relationships to the Jerusalem cult. The observations made here suggest that an event occurring between the two writings differentiated them further. The inception or interpretation of Hanukkah as, in some way, a Feast of Tabernacles in Kislev compounded the lunisolar threat that feasts "precede" their appointed times with a new danger that feasts would "be delayed" from those appointed times. Qumran circles responded aptly, embellishing their stance against the 354-day calendar, which it shared with Jubilees, with a tandem posture against a delayed Feast of Tabernacles.

32. Following Metso (1997, 143-49), the introduction of 1QS does not seem to have been part of earlier extant recensions of the Community Rule.

Jubilees and Sectarianism

Martha Himmelfarb

The scholarly consensus views the book of Jubilees as a protosectarian work (e.g., VanderKam 2001a, 142-43). More manuscripts of Jubilees were found at Qumran, fourteen or fifteen (VanderKam 2001a, 16), than of any but the most popular biblical books, and the Damascus Document (16:3-4) appears to cite Jubilees as an authority. Jubilees vigorously advocates a 364-day solar calendar, and the embrace of a 364-day calendar is one of the features that sets the Qumran community apart from the Jewish establishment in Jerusalem. Yet, like the Book of the Watchers, which was also known and valued at Qumran, Jubilees lacks many aspects of the worldview characteristic of sectarian compositions. I argue here that a crucial difference between Jubilees and the sectarian literature is its attitude toward other Jews.

As a number of scholars have noted, one striking feature of Jubilees is the way it elevates the status of the people of Israel (e.g., Halpern-Amaru 1999; Kugel 1996; Werman 1995). Jubilees claims that God singled Israel out for special status long before the time of Abraham, on the sixth day of creation: "I will now separate a people for myself from among my nations. . . . I have chosen the descendants of Jacob among all of those whom I have seen. I have recorded them as my first-born son and have sanctified them for myself throughout the ages of eternity" (Jub 2:19-20, trans. VanderKam 1989).

Jubilees goes on to suggest a connection between the angels in heaven and the people of Israel on earth: both are to keep the Sabbath (2:21). Later it emerges that circumcision also serves to make the Israelites like the angels since the angels were created circumcised (15:25-27). Because the angels are the priests of the heavenly temple (31:14), the connection between Israel and the angels strengthens Jubilees' view of Israel as a kingdom of priests (Himmelfarb 1997).

In addition to claiming that the people of Israel are the earthly counterpart of the angels, Jubilees asserts that Jews are essentially different from Gentiles (Werman 1995, 255-57): "For there are many nations and many peoples, and all belong to [the Lord]. He made spirits rule over all in order to lead them astray from following him. But over Israel he made no angel or spirit rule because he alone is their ruler" (15:31-32; trans. VanderKam 1989).

For Jubilees membership in the holy people is a matter of ancestry. This explains Jubilees' interest in providing genealogies that make the wives of the patriarchs descendants of Shem and Terah (Halpern-Amaru 1999, 147-59). It also explains Jubilees' emphasis on the deceitfulness of the offer of Jacob and his sons to intermarry with the Shechemites if they first circumcised themselves. The biblical story (Gen 34) labels the account deceitful because in its telling Levi and Simeon clearly had no intention of abiding by the terms they laid down.

Jubilees is usually inclined to present the behavior of its heroes in the best possible light. Yet it insists more strongly than the biblical text on the deceitfulness of the offer because, from Jubilees' point of view, even circumcision would not have made the Shechemites appropriate marriage partners. Or, to put it in terms anachronistic from the point of view of the biblical text but not, perhaps, from that of Jubilees, conversion to Judaism is impossible (Hayes 2002, 73-81; Halpern-Amaru 1999, 155).

Several scholars have considered the implications of this picture of Israel for drawing boundaries between Jews and Gentiles (e.g., Endres 1987; Schwarz 1982). But there is another side to Jubilees' view of the essential and hereditary difference between Israel and the nations that requires consideration. The sectarians in whose library so many manuscripts of Jubilees were found understood membership in the holy people as a matter of merit, not of ancestry. They viewed most Jews, together with all Gentiles, as children of darkness. Only the sectarians themselves deserved to be considered members of the holy people, children of light. By insisting that membership in the people of Israel is hereditary, Jubilees rejects this division: all Jews are born into the holy people. Thus, while it denies anyone born a Gentile the opportunity to become a member of the holy people, from the point of view of those born Jews, Jubilees is radically inclusive.

The scholarly majority-view places Jubilees early in the Hasmonean era (VanderKam 2001a, 17-21). I prefer to place Jubilees somewhat later, sometime in the reign of John Hyrcanus (134-104), a date popular with scholars at the beginning of the twentieth century (Charles 1902, lviii-lxvi), but for somewhat different reasons. Under John Hyrcanus, Hasmonean conquest and ascendancy led neighboring Gentiles such as the Idumeans to identify as Jews (Rapaport 1965). This type of assimilation to Judaism, or at least to the Jewish people, helps to account for Jubilees' anxiety about intermarriage, a phenomenon otherwise little attested before or after the Maccabean revolt (Himmelfarb 1999). While marriage between a native Jew and an assimilated Idumean would surely have been accepted without any qualms by most contemporaries, Jubilees would have viewed such a union as intermarriage. Even formal conversion, if such a ritual existed at the time, would not have changed Jubilees' mind because its view of the difference between Jews and Gentiles made the transformation of Gentile into Jew impossible.

Finally, if Jubilees' insistence on the hereditary holiness of all Israel is understood as a response to sectarian understandings of the people of Israel, another advantage of the later date is that it allows more time for the sectarian rejection of most of Israel to have taken shape.

Denouncement Speech in Jubilees
and Other Enochic Literature

Jeff S. Anderson

One of the stated goals of the "Enoch and Jubilees" section of this volume is to explore the ideological relationship between Jubilees and other Enochic literature. One way to present this challenge is to ask what these texts can tell us about the constituent circles that produced this literature, or perhaps just as interestingly, about the communities that are opposed in these challenging texts. This raises the important issue of the extent and nature of the polemic in the book of Jubilees and in the Enochic literature roughly contemporaneous with it. To whom is the polemic directed, and how strong are these polemics? Certainly the Enochic works are rather opaque, as they do not typically point out specifically those adversaries with whom they disagree, thus making the problem of identifying the social reality behind these texts especially cumbersome (Wright 2002, 185; Levine 1978, 5-23). Nevertheless, the Enochic traditions of 1 Enoch, Jubilees, the Temple Scroll, and numerous sectarian texts from Qumran generously employ denouncement rhetoric, particularly texts containing performative curses.[1]

Curse rhetoric in the Mosaic torah ordinarily has a pronounced social function and can become a powerful tool of ideological rhetoric (Anderson 1998a, 223-27; 1998b, 1-13). As such, curses can be uttered as protective devices for contractual/covenantal agreements; they may be tools of social control or

---

1. To cite examples: 1 En 5:11-20; 6:2b-6; 27:1-4; 41:8; 80:2-8; 97:10; 98:4b; 102:3; Jub 9:14-15; 20:5-10; 22:16-20; 23:11-30; 24:28-29; 26:34; 30:14-15; 1QS 1:16–2:19; 4:12-15; CD 1:11-19; 8:5-6; 15:4; 1QM 13:4-5; 4QMMT 103-105; 4Q175; 4Q201; 4Q280; 4Q286-290; 4QpNah; 4Q377; 4Q473; 4Q505; 4Q509; Bar 1:15–2:19; TLevi 10:1-5; 14:1-5; 16:1-5; PsSol 4:14-25.

used to convey social values; they may be employed in legal judicatory matters, or as a private "law" protecting the vulnerable. Additionally, in some cases curses are uttered as polemical propaganda to exclude or at least marginalize one particular community, while at the same time legitimating the community that utters the curse. Consequently, it is worth considering how the use of curse rhetoric to marginalize other communities might relate to the book of Jubilees. To what extent is it demonstrable that the imprecations of this work are meant to ostracize contemporary competing communities or to demonstrate the superiority of the halakah of the circles that produced the book?

Several groups are the targets of rather heated polemical curse language in the book of Jubilees. Historically these peoples were infamously bitter enemies of Israel in the Mosaic torah. One targeted group is personified by Canaan and his descendants (Jub 9:14-15). In Jubilees' postflood account, Noah's sons divide the lands among themselves and bind each other by an oath, placing a curse on any son who might attempt to seize what had not been awarded equitably by lot. Canaan later intentionally breaks the oath, encroaches on territory that had not been awarded to him, and settles in Lebanon and along the Mediterranean coast, thereby inheriting the curse, "Cursed you are and cursed you will be more than all the sons of Noah" (10:32). Second, in 24:28-29 Isaac realizes he made a mistake when entering into a covenant with Abimelech, so he utters metonymical curse rhetoric against the Philistines: "Accursed be the Philistines, more than all the nations . . . may God make them a laughing stock and curse, an object of wrath and indignation."[2] In addition, Esau (and by implication the Edomites) is the object of a curse which clearly goes beyond the freely composed curse of Genesis 27:39-40. Like the biblical account, Jubilees alludes to Esau eventually "breaking the yoke" of his brother Jacob, yet with an additional cryptic judgment of that action: "it will be counted against you as a deadly sin, and your offspring will be uprooted from under heaven" (Jub 26:34). Other explicit curse formulae are directed against an unnamed evil generation that practices uncleanness, possibly a reference to Hellenized Jews (23:22-25), and anyone who takes a Gentile wife (30:14-15). All this derogatory language refers to contact with Gentile outsiders, but is there evidence to support the notion that certain elements within second temple Judaism might be the target of this rhetoric?

It is well known that the author of Jubilees is fond of reworking torah texts for his immediate purposes. The Pentateuchal curses the author elimi-

---

2. The same metonymical curse is employed in the prologue of 1 En 5, and by Christian redactors of the Testament of Levi: "and you will be scattered as captives among the gentiles and be a reproach and a curse and be trampled under foot. For the home which the Lord will choose shall be called Jerusalem, as it stands written in the book of the righteous Enoch" (10:4-5; see also 14:1-5; 16:1-5).

nates (Levi) are as interesting as those that are heightened (Philistines, Esau). Since the Canaanites, Philistines, and Edomites, as nation-states, were not imperial threats when Jubilees was written, do the allusions to these communities merely represent the stereotypical Gentile threat to the audience of Jubilees? If so, those Hellenizing Jews are by implication also suspect. This is the simplest and perhaps best answer.

If that is indeed the case, then these polemics are intended only secondarily to marginalize the Gentiles but are instead primarily uttered to garner resistance by the faithful against the dangers of Hellenization. Such polemical intent may be similar to language in the Temple Scroll regarding the Canaanite idolaters and their graven images: "so that you do not bri[ng] (this) abomination into your house and become accursed like it. (Rather), you shall utterly dete[st and abhor it, for] it is an accursed thing" (11QT 2:5-15). Lawrence H. Schiffman (1994, 263) suggests that this rhetoric may be targeting extreme Hellenizers of the early second century B.C.E.

Both of these texts, Jubilees and the Temple Scroll, function in much the same way. What the Temple Scroll does for halakic tradition, Jubilees does for narrative tradition, as the biblical traditions are rewritten for contemporary purposes. In these two works the common warning is against syncretism with Greek culture. The references to Philistines, Edomites, and Canaanites function primarily as a trigger to prod communal memory of the evils of these historical Gentile enemies of Israel.

Robert H. Charles (1902, 154-56), however, was suspicious that there might be more to it than this, at least in the case of the Philistines. He proposed a contemporary connection with the Philistines specifically, a reference to hostility in the second century B.C.E. between the Hellenist residents of the old Philistine cities and the new Maccabean rulers. James VanderKam (2001a, 60) has also noted that the author of Jubilees goes out of the way to completely ignore Abraham's covenant with the Philistines, thus severing any official relationship with this cursed Gentile people. The possibility that the Philistines typify a contemporary vilified community could perhaps be behind such an omission. This possibility is strengthened by the reference to the delivery of the Philistines into the hands of the sinful Gentiles and into the hands of the Kittim. "And whoever of them escapes the sword of the enemy and of the Kittim, may the righteous nation root him up in judgment from under heaven; for they shall be my children's enemies and foes in every generation on the earth" (Jub 24:28b-29). Martin Hengel (1974; 1980) has emphasized the role played by Phoenicia and Philistia as intermediaries of Greek culture to Judea, so it would be logical to assume that this fostered resentment among more conservative elements of second century B.C.E. Jewish culture.

George Nickelsburg also has argued that some of the other modifications that the author of Jubilees makes to the biblical tradition allude to the author's own time, in one case, the Idumeans. Chapters 35–38, for example, contain a lengthy expansion of the list of Edomite kings of Genesis 36:31-39. He suggests that such an expansion reflects contemporary Jewish-Idumean hostility, as these expansions explain the origins of the conflicts between these two peoples, stressing Jewish superiority (Nickelsburg 1980, 76-79). Such hostility reminds one of Ben Sira's scathing condemnation of Edom, Philistia, and Shechem, and reflects second century B.C.E. hostilities against the Samaritans, the Hellenistic cities of the western coast, and Idumea (Sir 50:25-26). Not everyone, however, assesses the relationships between Jews and Idumeans as problematic in the second century. Kasher (1988), for example, suggests that the relations between the Nabatean monarchs and the Hasmonean and Herodian dynasties were generally cordial.

Similar denouncement rhetoric is characteristic of the early booklets of 1 Enoch. Lars Hartman (1979) and Mark Elliott (2000; 2002) have both situated Enochic literature firmly in covenant theology, partly because of the connection between covenant making and blessings and curses. Hartman's treatment of the prologue suggests that 1 Enoch 1–5 serves primarily as a blessing to Israel, with inherent curses applied to those outside the covenant. The "you" and "they" terminology of the oracle in 1 Enoch 5:4-9 suggests clearly defined boundaries between the cursed and blessed communities. The Woe Oracles of the Epistles of Enoch also function like the blessings and curses of Deuteronomy. Elliott's treatment of the Book of Admonitions, for example, contends that this imprecatory rhetoric not only heightens dualisms between groups but also warns members against apostasy. The curses of the potential apostate not only protect the group's inner cohesion but also define, validate, and consolidate a fundamentally dualistic view of the covenant (Elliott 2000, 295-96).

Nickelsburg, however, argues that the Sinai covenant is not at all of central importance in 1 Enoch. He contends that the book is remarkably silent about the Mosaic covenant, and unlike Jubilees, actually contains very few legal parallels. He persuasively demonstrates that the curse rhetoric in 1 Enoch 5 is much closer to that in Isaiah 65–66 than to Deuteronomy 27–28 (Nickelsburg 2001, 50-51, 159). John Collins contends that Enochic literature, especially the Apocalypse of Weeks and the Animal Apocalypse, articulates the ideology of a movement that is essentially incompatible with the Maccabean revolt. In earlier Enoch literature, group identity was not prominent and there were no explicit polemics against mainline Judaism. The Apocalypse of Weeks and the Animal Apocalypse, however, show a heightened group identity more militant and directly critical of the temple and its leadership (Collins 1984, 70-74).

In spite of this mounting tension between Judaisms in the second century B.C.E., one does not observe the narcissism of small differences in Jubilees and the early Enochic literature to the extent that characterized later Qumran texts.[3] The Qumran texts are replete with traditional curse formulae and freely composed curses, most of which are uttered against fellow Jews who are antagonistic toward the community or those within the community itself who might consider leaving the group.

The recurring metaphor of border violations recalls the denouncement speech of covenant curses but gives them new contexts. The pejorative epitaphial designations of competing groups indicate that the outsiders are not only the Gentiles, but even fellow Jews who are not part of the *yaḥad*. Unlike the early Enochic literature, tensions between Jewish communities of the second century B.C.E. are made explicit in the sectarian texts from Qumran.

---

3. Martha Himmelfarb presses this point in her contribution to the present volume. She argues that for Jubilees, being a member of the holy community of Israel was hereditary, thus rejecting (at least implicitly) the division of fellow Jews into the Sons of Light and Sons of Darkness found in sectarian literature.

The Historical-Cultural Background
of the Book of Jubilees

Liliana Rosso Ubigli

With fourteen or fifteen attested copies, the book of Jubilees is undoubtedly one of the best-documented texts of the Qumran library. Moreover, it is cited as an authoritative source in a sectarian work, the Damascus Document (CD 16:2-4), and seems to have been equally important to the Qumran community. In fact, the community followed a solar calendar and apparently celebrated the festival of the renewal of the covenant on the occasion of the Festival of Weeks (1QS 1:16–3:12), which in the book of Jubilees is closely connected with the renewal of the covenant (Jub 6:17).

James VanderKam is undisputedly one of the greatest experts on the book of Jubilees, and with his new edition of the Ethiopic text and of the other surviving fragments, he has made a fundamental contribution to contemporary research (VanderKam 1989).

Jubilees and the Enochic Tradition

In his studies on Jubilees, VanderKam has pointed out the author's debt toward the earlier Enochic tradition, which Jubilees refers to explicitly (Jub 21:10; VanderKam 1995, 110). Most important are the Astronomical Book (1 En 72–82), the Book of the Watchers (1 En 6–36), and Dream Visions (1 En 83–90), the last of which serves as a sort of *terminus post quem* for establishing the date of the work. Jubilees 4:19 in fact makes reference to Dream Visions (VanderKam 2001a, 21). However, it is uncertain whether the author of Jubilees knew of the epistle.

Jubilees retells the story of Genesis-Exodus (chaps. 1–19), drawing upon both Enochic literature and, as VanderKam notes, the Aramaic Testament of Levi (VanderKam 2001b, 97). However, the writer introduces some changes with respect to the earlier tradition.

Particularly interesting from my point of view is the reelaboration of the myth of the Watchers; compared to the homonymous book, Jubilees contains important differences, although it is unknown whether these came from the author's pen or from other sources. At any rate, they are consistent with the ideas contained in the work. According to Jubilees, the Watchers came down to earth to perform a moral duty, "to teach mankind and to do what is just and upright upon the earth" (Jub 4:15); in fact, it was God himself who sent them to earth (5:6). With respect to the Book of the Watchers, the sin of the angels is understated, as are the consequences: only a tenth of the spirits of the giants, born from the union between the Watchers and women, will remain on earth to harm mankind (10:9).

According to VanderKam (1995, 120), this change in perspective is due, at least in part, to the author's rediscovery of the sin of Adam and Eve (Gen 3), which was still unknown in Dream Visions. However, it is also possible that the new viewpoint expressed in the Watchers episode can be attributed to the author's intention of placing more importance on human responsibility. In fact, Jubilees 5:15 states that everyone will be judged by his actions. In any case, Jubilees' retelling of the story of Adam and Eve with the particular halakah it contains (Jub 3; 31) can be seen as expressing the writer's reaction against the Hellenistic reform: "For this reason it has been commanded in the tablets regarding all those who know the judgment of the law that they cover their shame and not uncover themselves as the nations uncover themselves" (VanderKam 2001a, 21; cf. 1 Macc 1:14-15; 2 Macc 4:9, 12-15).

Furthermore, the insistence on observance of Sabbath and the rite of circumcision, which involves even the higher categories of angels (Jub 2:18), as well as observance of the solar calendar and the concurrent denunciation of the contamination of the temple are also consistent with the Antiochean crisis. The work lays particular stress on the danger of assimilation with non-Jews, which explains the recurring ban on mixed marriages (cf., e.g., Jub 30:11). Jubilees abandons the universalist viewpoint which characterized Enochic Judaism in its earliest phases, and as Gabriele Boccaccini observes in his book *Beyond the Essene Hypothesis,* a sort of compromise is established between Enochism and Zadokite Judaism (Boccaccini 1998, 89-90). A further consequence is the emergence of Israel into the foreground as the chosen people.

The Figure of Enoch: New Features

Another interesting aspect of VanderKam's studies is the attention he has devoted to Enoch. He observes that the author of Jubilees draws inspiration from the earlier tradition, but at the same time enriches the character with new features. Enoch had already appeared in the role of a scribe in the Book of the Watchers (1 En 12:3-4). The author of Jubilees, however, emphasizes that he was "the first of mankind . . . who learned (the art of) writing, instruction, and wisdom and who wrote down the signs of the sky," and so on (Jub 4:17).

From this standpoint the book of Jubilees is linked to the motif of *prōtos heuretēs* of Hellenistic literature, which was also a recurrent motif throughout the Judaic-Hellenistic authors. Pseudo-Eupolemus, for example, portrayed Enoch as the first astrologer/astronomer (VanderKam 1995, 112; Eusebius, *Praeparatio evangelica* 9.17.9: "The Greeks say that Atlas discovered astrology. Atlas and Enoch are the same"), whereas Eupolemus considered Moses the first sage and attributed to him the invention of writing (Eusebius, 9.26.1: "Eupolemus says that Moses was the first wise man and that he gave the alphabet to the Jews first"; cf. Clement of Alexandria, *Stromateis* 1.23; 153.4). Artapanus, albeit in a very particular context, attributed to Moses not only various technical inventions but also the discovery of philosophy (Eusebius, 9.27.4). Thus in the book of Jubilees Enoch acquires the features of a culture hero represented elsewhere by Moses (Najman 1999).

A new aspect of Enoch is his priestly role, which, as VanderKam points out, is not peculiar to him but pertains also to the other patriarchs (VanderKam 2001a, 141), particularly to Levi, who in Jubilees is not only the ancestor of the priests and Levites but is himself conferred with an eternal ministry and "acts as a priest" (Jub 30:18; 32:1, 3, 9; VanderKam 2001a, 141). According to the author of Jubilees, the priestly role is older than Aaron exactly as Moses' law is older than Moses himself.

This emphasis on the role of Levi is an element of continuity with the Testaments of the Twelve Patriarchs, but in my opinion it is less significant in relation to the Damascus Document, notwithstanding its reference to Levi (CD 4:15), and to the sectarian texts of Qumran, in which the Zadokites (1QS 5:2, 9; 9:11; cf. CD 3:21–4:4; 5:5) and Aaron (e.g., 1QS 8:6, 9; 9:7) come to the forefront (the role of the Zadokites in Qumran is discussed by Corrado Martone in his contribution to this volume). According to VanderKam, this emphasis on the prerogatives of Levi falls within the general plan of the work, which tends to attribute more recent "phenomena" to the earlier patriarchal era (VanderKam 2001a, 142). In any case, all of these elements prove that the author belongs to the priesthood.

Liliana Rosso Ubigli

The Chronology of Jubilees

A final point of interest is the particular chronological framework in which the narration is recorded. The periodization of history is characteristic of the historical apocalypses, implying that human events have been somehow preordained *ab aeterno*. However, there are various possible schemes, one being the scheme adopted by the Apocalypse of Weeks. Important for placing Jubilees in a historical context is the chronological system followed by the author. History is divided into periods of forty-nine years for a total of fifty jubilees, and each jubilee may be subdivided into smaller units (weeks of years and years).

VanderKam has pointed out the correlation between this chronological system and the law enounced in Leviticus 25, which states that at the end of a jubilee the landowner can repossess the land taken from him and the slave can regain his freedom. In Jubilees, however, this does not apply to individuals but to Israel as a whole. With reference to the exodus, one of the last events narrated in the work (Jub 49:23), the jubilee of jubilees framing history brings to mind the liberation from Egypt and the return to the Promised Land (50:4). But on another level the author meant a different kind of liberation: "freedom from foreign domination and Judean possession of their own land" (VanderKam 1997, 22).

Thus, added to the above elements is a further argument for placing the work against the background of the Antiochean crisis and the Maccabean struggles, regardless of the presumed references to these within the text. In any case, the writer is careful to trace a clear boundary between Jews and Gentiles with the intention of opposing dangerous assimilationist tendencies.

The Author

According to VanderKam, the author of Jubilees could have been an Essene, for two principal reasons: first, the predestinarian doctrine outlined in the reports of Flavius Josephus on the Essenes is shared by Jubilees, at least with regard to the course of history; and second, the idea that the body decays while the soul is immortal is also confirmed in Jubilees (23:30-31), as well as in Qumranic texts.

Based on these premises, it is worth reevaluating, together with the Enochic-apocalyptic components, the importance of the Antiochean crisis in the origins and development of Essenism and in the protohistory of the Qumran community.

Enoch and Jubilees

Ida Fröhlich

The ideological relationship between Jubilees and the Enoch literature as well as the relationship between the group that produced Jubilees and the group that produced the Enoch literature are questions of seminal importance in outlining spiritual tendencies in the Essene tradition. The two works were composed in various times, the later one being Jubilees and the earlier one being the Enochic collection.[1] Consequently, *similarities and differences can be clearly disclosed, and Enochic and other influences in Jubilees can be analyzed. In the following I try to draft some reflections on these questions by giving a brief survey of a characteristic literary tradition commonly used in both works and by giving a bird's-eye view of some basic concepts in the two works.

The Watcher Story

The Watcher story (1 En 6–11) is a seminal piece of the Enochic collection compiled from works of Jewish authors of the second temple period. Qumran Enochic manuscript fragments revealed that the original language of the work was Aramaic. The Watcher story is contained in the earliest manuscript tradition of the work going back to the beginning of the second century B.C.E.; that means the narrative itself may go back to the third century, or even earlier (Milik 1976).

---

1. For a date of 1 Enoch around the Maccabean crisis, see Rowley (1957). For a much older prehistory, see Beer (1900). Chaps. 37–71 are supposed to have been of Christian origin or a Christian reworking of earlier Jewish materials.

The story was composed, in all probability, well before the establishment of the Qumran settlement. It represents the oldest layer of the Essene literary tradition known by us, and had been present in Qumran tradition for a long time. Later pieces of the Enochic collection and other texts written in various ages refer to it, or retell it adding new details (a complete retelling is found in 1 En 85–90, the Animal Apocalypse). The popularity of the story lies in its seminal meaning. The Watcher story is a myth, a story which gives expression in nonconceptual language to some basic ideas of the spiritual circle in which it was composed.

1 Enoch 6–11 is a myth of the origin of evil (Delcor 1976).[2] According to the narrative, evil originated from deeds resulting in impurity of heavenly and human beings. Impurity defiled the earth, which finally "made the accusation against the wicked concerning everything which was done upon it" (7:5-6). The flood was a punishment for defiling the earth. The impure deeds by which the Watchers and humans defiled the earth were manifold, including the sexual relation of heavenly and earthly beings: in Jewish terms it could have been considered either as a case of *kilayim*[3] or as *zenut*, i.e., as transgression of any prohibition concerning sexual relations (7:1).[4] The Watchers taught humans magical practices (7:1).[5] The giants born from the union of heavenly and earthly beings brought bloodshed[6] and cannibalism to mankind. They sinned

---

2. On the centrality of the problem of evil in second temple literature, see Collins (1997, 30-51).

3. *Kilayim*, the violation of the boundaries raised between different groups, can be considered defiling. According to Lev 19:19: "You must observe my statutes. You may not allow two different kinds of animals to mate together. You are not to plant your field with two kinds of seed, nor to wear a garment woven with two kinds of yarn." The biblical examples of *kilayim* are listed in a series of sins in Lev 19–20 preceded and closed by the words of the Lord on Israel's sanctity (Lev 19:2; 20:26).

4. "The land is not to play the prostitute and be full of lewdness" (Lev 19:29).

5. The Mosaic laws condemn magic in several instances as defiling (in one instance, in Lev 19:26, it is mentioned together with the consumption of blood). "Do not resort to ghosts and spirits or make yourselves unclean by seeking them out. I am the Lord your God" (Lev 19:31). "I shall set my face against anyone who resorts to ghosts and spirits, and I shall cut that person off from his people" (Lev 20:6). "You must not allow a witch to live" (Exod 22:18). Deut 18:9-14 gives a long list of sorcerers. Their practices are abominable to the Lord, and "it is on account of these abominable practices that the Lord your God is driving them (i.e., the Canaanites) out before you." According to Deut 18:9-14, the Canaanites will be driven out by YHWH before the Israelites for this sin — this is the reason they will lose their land.

6. "You must not defile your land by bloodshed. Bloodshed defiles the land" (Num 35:33). Purification takes place when somebody is killed. If the murderer is unknown, the inhabitants have to take care of purification (Deut 21:1-9), which is also the case of someone who died in war (Num 31:19). The connection of blood and earth is apparent from the Lord's words in the story of Cain: "your brother's blood is crying out to me from the ground" (Gen 4:10).

against the world of animals and were guilty of violation of prescriptions concerning food, among them the prohibition of the consumption of blood (i.e., consumption of meat without draining the blood; cf. Lev 17:13-14).[7] The sinful teachings of the Watchers are in the complementary Asael story where they instruct humans in the various branches of metallurgy,[8] and the making of weapons and cosmetics, which are instruments of bloodshed and seduction. The Watchers' deeds have a common characteristic: they all are ethical impurities. All but one of these sins (that is, the breaking of dietary laws) are comprehended in the biblical mind as sins defiling the land. The perpetrators of those sins are to be wiped out of the land. Breaking of the dietary laws is comprehended in the Temple Scroll as defiling (11QT 48:6-11). The Watcher story is an alternative to the biblical story of the fall (Sacchi 1997, 211-32).[9] Genesis and Enoch offer two alternative explanations for the state of human existence. According to the one, evil was brought into the world by human choice, while the other shifts the responsibility onto the heavenly beings (who were conscious of the consequences of their deeds). The deeds of the Watchers bring about defilement in every sphere of creation, both humans and animal (birds, beasts, and reptiles) (Hanson 1977, 199-200). Human beings cannot control and impede the proliferation of sins and the defilement of the world.

Contrary to the popularity of the Watcher story in later Qumran (Enochic and other) tradition, the pericope of Gen 1–3 is never retold except in Jubilees. The afterlife of the Watcher story in later Enochic literature shows that retellings of the story and references to it were part of a process of elaboration of a "theoretical demonology." The afterlife of the Watcher story of 1 Enoch carries on in the Enochic collection itself. Enoch 15:8-12 contains information that is complementary to the narrative of chapters 6–11. According to that narrative, the giants were destroyed in the flood, but their spirit has remained in the world as evil spirits. The descendants of the Watchers and the daughters of men are evil spirits, demons called *nafsat* in the Ethiopic text and *pneumata* in the Greek version (1 En 15:8). These beings are spiritual in nature, having their fathers' characteristics: they do not eat, they are not thirsty, and they know no obstacles. Their destructiveness first and foremost affects children and women, as they were born of women.

7. The latter is an especially severe prescription: its punishment is that "whoever eats it is to be cut off," while transgressing against the former merely makes one unclean.

8. Bronze working was considered by ancient cultures to be an act of magic. For a study of the problem, see Eliade (1956).

9. Gen 2–3 is not represented in the Enochic collection. The antediluvian part (chaps. 1–5) is a hymnic description of the rules of creation without referring to the story of the fall. The introduction of the story of the Watchers is an antithesis of this regularity and order: "But you, you change your works."

Still, the Watcher story is not the exclusive source of the portrayal of spirits in 1 Enoch 15. The account is based on a folkloric figure well known in the ancient Near East, the baby-killer demons.[10] The author of 1 Enoch 15 may have been familiar with this widely popular belief. 1 Enoch 15 may have been written not later than the second century B.C.E., the date supposed for the composition of chapters 1–36 and 71–106 of the Enochic collection (Schürer 1973-87, 3.1:256). The Book of Giants known from the Enochic manuscript tradition from Qumran may have contained important information about the formation of beliefs concerning demons. Unfortunately, the present fragments of the work do not offer substantial information on this.

Jubilees is demonstrably later than the Enochic collection. Jubilees 4:17-19 alludes to the Book of the Watchers, the Astronomical Book, and Dream Visions. Enoch appears in Jubilees as a writer and revealer (4:17ff.), and Enochic traditions play an important role in Jubilees (VanderKam 1978). Jubilees is dated by James VanderKam (1992a) to the middle of the second century B.C.E.

Unlike the Enochic collection, Jubilees is an example of "rewritten Bible," a systematic retelling of the biblical tradition from the creation to the giving of the torah on Sinai. Its main character is Moses, not Enoch. Narratives of the book follow the order of the biblical pericopae, and it is only natural that the biblical story of the fall is part of the narrative. The Enochic tradition of the origin of evil was also built into the narrative on various points. From the perspective of Jubilees, the primeval history of humankind, similar to the biblical view, is a process of decline; the concept is adapted to later periods as well (Jub 23:8-23). Jubilees tries to harmonize Enochic and biblical traditions related to the material of Genesis 1–9. According to Jubilees, the angels that descended to the daughters of men originally came to the earth with the goal of teaching the humans, but their deeds became unintentionally the source of evil (Jub 4:15). The Watchers commingled with women and became defiled (Jub 4:22; 7:27; 20:3-6; 25:7). Demonic activity began immediately after the flood in the book of Jubilees: demons "leading astray" and killing babies (Noah's grandchildren are mentioned as the first victims). In response to Noah's prayer, God binds nine-tenths of the demons (Jub 10–14).

According to Jubilees, at the time of Abraham the world was ruled by unclean demons whose leader was Mastema.[11] These demons are said to be de-

10. Aramaic incantations against childbed demons are known from the Near East. 4Q560, an incantation text from Qumran, was written, among others, against childbed demons.

11. The name originates from the Hebrew verb *śtm,* "bear a grudge, cherish animosity, against" (Aram. *śtn*). In Hos 9:7, 8 it is employed as a common noun meaning "enmity." Job 1:6 mentions Satan in the assembly of the "sons of God" *(bny h'lhym).* Mastema, i.e., the Satan, is also mentioned in the (Greek) Acts of Philip chapter 13 (*Acta Apostolorum Apocrypha* 2, 1903, 7).

scendants of the "fallen angels" (cf. Jub 19:8-10). Abraham had power over the demons; the source of his power was his "righteousness." He was not only unwilling to sacrifice to idols while living in the city of Ur, but he set "the house of idols" on fire (12:12).[12] The biblical story of the binding of Isaac (*ʿaqedah*) is again reformulated in Jubilees: the attempt at sacrifice is made here upon the request of Mastema. He is the one who asks God to test Abraham's faith (17:16).[13]

In Jubilees the motifs connected with demons have three different sources:

1. Demons are said to be the offspring of the Watchers, and to lead people astray. The origin of these motifs is the Enochic story of the Watchers.
2. In the Noah pericope their characteristics are identical with those of the childbed demons of folk belief.
3. In the pericope of the *ʿaqedah* their leader Mastema appears as the instigator, a figure akin to Satan of the book of Job.

These characteristics of various origin are merged and incorporated in the figures of the demons in the book of Jubilees in a hierarchy and in a historical perspective.

The Background of Enoch and Jubilees and the Spiritual and Social Circle They Originate From

The Enochic story does not seem to be a haggadic midrash of Genesis 6:1-4, a paraphrase born from a "lust for narrative." In contrast with Genesis 6:1-4, which is rather an extract of a broader tradition or a series of glosses on a narrative with which the author was familiar, the Enochic story of the Watchers is an authentic, consistent, and knowingly constructed narrative. According to Paolo Sacchi, the narrative of Genesis 6:1-4 and the Watcher story are a parallel development of a common mythological heritage. The Watcher story is a myth on the origin of evil in the world and on the causes which led to the flood. The writing shows a strong interest in law and ethical purity. Although Priestly or

---

12. In the book of Judith, in Achior's speech (5:6-9) Abraham has to leave Mesopotamia because he refuses to worship the local deities. The core of this legend most likely came into being at the end of the second century B.C.E.

13. Similarly, Mastema is the prime instigator in one of the fragments of Pseudo-Jubilees (4Q225). The fragments called Pseudo-Jubilees (4Q225, 227) do not belong to any manuscript of the book of Jubilees.

Levitical themes are found, offerings are absent from the work.[14] On the other hand, the main interest of the work is concentrated on purity themes. Purity is meant not in a ritual but in an ethical sense, and is in some way related to the land. Supernatural elements (the relationship of heavenly and earthly beings; supernatural beings like the giants; and the all-devouring nature of the giants) serve as the literary vehicles of this tradition.

Jubilees is called the narrative parallel of the Temple Scroll. It is the interpretation of the biblical narrative tradition on the basis of the biblical legal tradition and halakic tradition of the Temple Scroll. Scribal traditions (motifs of the tradition of knowledge originating from Enoch, and motifs related to writing and the written tradition) are also present in the work. Enoch, Noah, Moses, and Jacob appear as revealers and bearers of special knowledge. Writing down revelations and all-inclusive knowledge through revelation are common themes in the work. Reference to tablets of heaven is often made. The author has a special interest in offerings, ritual, and Levitical tradition. The work's calendrical interest (a priestly duty in ancient societies) and its calendrical system (periods of jubilees and years of 364 days) are widely known. Besides Enochic and priestly traditions, the author of Jubilees is well acquainted with folk tradition related to demonology and other traditions concerning heavenly beings otherwise known from the book of Job. Jubilees tries to make a consistent system from this heterogeneous material.

The idea of purity is an overall theme in Jubilees. The realm of God and his angels is pure, that of Mastema, the idols, and the demons is impure. The actions of people fall within the one or the other. No impurity can occur in Israel since they are a holy people. Impurity is associated with the nations. However, by sinning and acting like the nations Israel may contract impurity. In particular, sexual sins are defiling (VanderKam 2001a, 131-32).

Jubilees' narrative contains many Enochic traditions. The work shows an attitude to purity very similar to that of the Enochic collection. Both of them work up popular tradition concerning the demons. In addition, Jubilees tries to comprehensively treat the various priestly traditions: ritual purity, offerings, and the "Zadokite" narrative tradition of Genesis. As to the relationship between the group that produced Jubilees and the group that produced the Enoch literature, it is hard to say anything because we have no information on determinative factors of groups (self-defining, location, habits, historical tradition, etc.). All we have are two works treating certain common traditions. Fortu-

---

14. Paolo Sacchi (1994, 89-104) maintains that Enoch was the work of a priestly opposition party, while Paul D. Hanson (1975) claims that Enochic literature came from nonpriestly circles.

nately both Enoch and Jubilees give some important information for those looking for groups behind them: the works reflect the legal attitude of their authors. The halakic system of both works is based, in all probability, on the Temple Scroll; thus their authors and readers may have followed a common legal practice. A legal practice and purity system based on a common *halakhah* was the basic determinative factor in establishing Jewish religious groups in antiquity; on that basis authors and readers of both the Enochic collection and Jubilees may have belonged to the same religious group. Differences between the two works reflect the particular interests of their authors.

Apocalypticism and the Religion and Ritual of the "Pre-Sinaitic" Narratives

Ithamar Gruenwald

Apocalypticism inserts itself into two major time spans in the wide context of biblical narrative. Several apocalyptic books, particularly the ones that belong in the Enoch cycle, place themselves in prediluvian times. Others, like 4 Ezra and Syriac Baruch, place themselves in a postdestruction situation. The Enoch literature, which constitutes the subject of the present volume, deals with events that span from the days preceding the flood to the end of days. Reading the eschatological message or testimony of 1 Enoch (10:17–11:2), one notices that the main concern is with the land and agricultural fruitfulness and blessing. Nothing is said about the body politic, or about a future king, not to mention the Messiah. I wish to contextualize this testimonial vision in the religious ethos of ancient Israel, particularly that of the book of Genesis into which the apocalyptic Enoch inserts its narrative.

It is virtually impossible to reconstruct the original settings and referents of biblical material and the extent to which any given text was originally intended to serve a religious purpose. Scholars have worked hard to establish in our mind the fact that the critical study of biblical texts exhausts itself on the axis connecting text-critical and historical-archaeological observations. In a broader sense, and when religious concerns were at stake, theological and hermeneutical issues, too, found their way to the center of the scholarly discussion. Little effort, though, has been invested to distill the existential import of Scripture. In this rather neglected area of scholarly discussion, I will place the cultural shaping factors that played an important role in the shaping of the biblical world, either by establishing a new cultural ethos or by adopting an existing one.

Special attention must be given in this respect to rituals in order to discern the full spectrum of the religious experience at hand. Ritual functions of texts, even at the prereligious ethos stage, are the practiced parts of communal behavior and shape the life of persons and communities. Ethos here is understood as the nonformalized phase of the religious history. It evolves in and directs the life of the people in pre-Sinaitic times (i.e., the book of Genesis and Exod 1–18). The telos or purposiveness in the ethos is what empowers it to become a culture-shaping lifestyle and eventually a religious, even theological, worldview.

Cain's ethos was that agriculture is good. It involved the building of a city (Gen 4:17), that is, urbanization, and urbanization in the land of Canaan was connected to monarchism (see Gen 14 and Joshua). Abel's ethos was that of sheepherding. It involved nomadism and implied the negation of urbanization. It was the essential factor in tribalism, the political ethos of ancient Israel. Although these cultural structures were prereligious, that is, they constitute the biblical narrative before the revelation on Mount Sinai, they persisted in many respects also after that revelation. They were life-shaping, in the full sense of the term.

A remarkable peculiarity of the Hebrew Bible lies in the fact that, while it moves from the garden to the city in its ideology and historical reality, the celebrated memory of the patriarchal progenitors and the words of the prophets idealize the nomadic culture. Furthermore, the Hebrew Bible perpetuates the conflict of ideologies between the two lifestyles and makes them resonate throughout the historical facts that are the trademark of monarchical urbanization. The forces at play in these contesting forms of ethos are expressive of natural drives rather than of following systemic cultural theories. They constitute the formative notions for those who are motivated by the desire to establish, by exempla rather than by an explicit theology, the right foundation of the sanctified.

The story of John the Baptist in the Gospels shows how far down in the history of ancient Israel this ethos goes. That story, which unfolds in the "wilderness" (Mark 1:3 and parallels), retrieves the ethos of ancient Israel, reviving the spirit of the prophets and their anti-urban ethos (see Isa 40:3). This is true for the ministry of Jesus as well, which culminates, in this sense, in the "Lament over Jerusalem" (Matt 23:37-39 = Luke 13:34-35) and the pronouncements on the destruction of the temple (Luke 19:39-48 and parallels). The special role of the desert, the Jordan River, and hermitic asceticism in ancient Christianity attests this ethos as well.

As a cultural notion rather than just a geographical place, the desert is a topos with its ethos. For ancient Israel and early Christianity, the sequence exodus–desert–land-flowing-with-milk-and-honey was a redemptive anti-urban metaphor, with *midbar* ("desert," "desolate place") standing in opposition to Jerusalem and its temple. Desert austerity and purity stand versus the social corruption of the monarchy, priesthood, and a temple turned into a "den of thieves."

John the Baptist, dressed as an ascetic and calling for return/repentance, established baptism as a ritual with transformative value. In its unique redemptive (rather than corporally purifying) function, it prepared the way to redemption through Jesus' alternative model of the self-sacrificial establishing of the kingdom of God. I view ritual as functional in bringing about transformation. The transformative events that John and Jesus established are the most essential aspects in the process of ritually launching Christianity as a fully functioning religion. Whether John and Jesus really did what the Gospels tell us is an immaterial question. It all belongs to what I have defined as the sphere of myth (Gruenwald 2003). I view myth as the context-endowing narrative of ritual, whether the narrative belongs in the pretheological ethos or the formally doctrinal religion. Myth gives rise to ritual and is the developed product of ritual.

Myth and ritual mutually contextualize. The community's hermeneutic consciously or unconsciously articulates the confessional character of the myth and ritual as an unfolding religious worldview headed toward theological formulation. For the narrative of John the Baptist, Isaiah's phrase "a voice calling in the wilderness" provides a hermeneutic stance in the context of which a myth is created. Consequently, its message is turned into a ritual. In its doctrinal setting this ritual evolves as a theological worldview. Ritual in this sense refers to the systemic, long-term principles that shape and organize the life of people in relation to their history, memory, and identity. Undoubtedly, Israel's memory is shaped by the sheep-desert ethos. The axis that links myth and ritual in this respect is a pivotal "event" that moves from the critique of urbanism through apocalypticism like the one that prevailed among the community of Qumran and that of early Christianity where it gave rise to the messianic notion of the "Lamb of God."

The Eden story is the paradigmatic myth. Adam and Eve ruined their idealized rural life, setting in motion a worldview in which righteousness and sin are configured as economic alternatives. Thus, through its link to ritual, a story receives its status as a myth and enforces an ethical norm or standard. The mythic narrative expresses and crystallizes the conscious and the subconscious ethos. Nomadic sheepherding life is pilgrimage through constant change and a dependence upon divine providence day by day, an authentic metaphor for life, while centralization and its urbanization are viewed as a Sisyphean attempt at denying this essential transitory nature of life and its direct dependence upon God.

Thus the former is good, natural, and potentially religious/sacred, and the latter is bad, contrived, and potentially secular, godless, and producing every sort of ungodliness. Once economy was conceived of in terms of an ethos, it became a key factor in the shaping of culture, changing practical behaviors into ideological norms. So the extra-urban status of Qumran and the Baptist made a real cultural and religious difference, and both created and were shaped by the ritual that arose from this ethos. By retrojection, this gave a new level of meaning and normativity to the patriarchal and exodus memories, making them key metaphors of cultural etiquette and religious truth.

The same paradigm is evident in the stories of Cain, Noah, the Tower of Babel, Enoch, Abraham, and Lot. In all these strata of Israelite memory-turned-myth, the same forces are at play. Three connected but distinct anti-urban channels are evident: anti-urban ethos per se, anti-urbanization linked to antimonarchianism, and the radical anti-urbanism of apocalyptic myth with its messianic and eschatological content. The third channel also signified radical spiritualization. In this respect it was ideally fitted, among other things, to propel processes that ended in the rise of Christianity in which a spiritual type of monarchic messianism prevailed. This channel also contributed to shaping the driving force behind the antitemple disposition of the Qumran community.

Thus, the cycle of patriarchal narratives idealizes a tribal-nomadic lifestyle which prevailed at least through the time of the judges when it began to shift to settled farming in a progressive movement toward urbanization and monarchy. The process was full of tension, as can be discerned in the Samuel stories. The ethos of the prophets was generally in opposition to city and kingship, and their ethos became a theology. This was a major issue in the ideology of the Qumran community with their predilection for the desert and a tribal cultural-political ethos. It follows naturally that the Baptist and Jesus idealized this nomadic lifestyle, assaulted the urban establishment, and were executed in what they condemned as the "godless" city — the godless city of the godless priests so aggressively opposed to what the "Essenes" of Qumran represented. Inevitably the basic Christian institution adapted the notion of pastoral leadership, shepherding a communal tribe of sheep, functioning always with considerable ambivalence regarding the established centralized urban culture of this world. In doing this it adopted, though sometimes in a transformed mode, a basic ethos of the Hebrew Scriptures.

3 Enoch and the Enoch Tradition

Lawrence H. Schiffman

In his pioneering work *3 Enoch, or the Hebrew Book of Enoch,* first published in 1928, Hugo Odeberg, in effect arguing for the validity of the name he had given the work with the authorization of Robert H. Charles (see Greenfield 1973, xxi), assembled a long list of comparisons between 1 Enoch and 3 Enoch (Odeberg 1928, 43-51).[1] After examining these parallels, he maintained (1) that 3 Enoch was dependent upon 1 Enoch and (2) that considerable development of these common ideas had taken place between the composition of 1 Enoch and the later 3 Enoch. We should remember that Odeberg (41) dated the main body of 3 Enoch to the second half of the third century C.E., a date most contemporary scholars would see as too early. Indeed, Heinrich Graetz (1859; cf. Odeberg 1928, 24-30) had dated the text to the Geonic period (seventh-eleventh centuries). Gershon Scholem (1965, 7 n. 9) dated the work to the fifth-sixth centuries. Josef T. Milik (1976, 123-35) dated it as late as the ninth-tenth centuries, but his view has not carried much weight. In light of other evidence for the diffusion of these ideas, Philip Alexander accepts the Scholem dating of the fifth-sixth centuries (Alexander 1983, 225-29).

Bearing in mind that the sources of 3 Enoch no doubt are to be dated earlier, and remembering the complex literary history of 1 Enoch (Milik 1976, 1-58; VanderKam 1984, 76-140), even if Odeberg has overstated their relationship, we should recall that George F. Moore postulated subterranean "channels of com-

---

1. On 3 Enoch see Gruenwald (1980, 191-208), Schäfer (1992, 123-38), and Mopsik (1989, 7-91), where a French translation and detailed commentary are presented. The manuscript evidence is available in Schäfer (1981).

munication if not literary acquaintance" (Moore 1927-30, 2:281). We today know so much more about second temple literature and its survival into the Middle Ages (Reeves 1994; Schiffman 1997-2001) that a reinvestigation of the relationship of 1 Enoch and 3 Enoch would seem to be in order. In this way we can extend the chronological limits of the thorough study of the Enoch tradition by James VanderKam (1995) that ended in 300 C.E. by discussing 3 Enoch. It is therefore to the relationship of this much later text to the earlier Enoch tradition that we devote this study.

Odeberg argued that the twin aspects of dependence and development were most apparent in the conception of Enoch. In 1 Enoch he is an ancient "saint-man" who was worthy of receiving disclosures about the future and celestial wonders, mostly in visions. He is the authority behind the secrets in the books bearing his name. Enoch's translation is also central. These aspects are said to occupy the Enoch-Metatron parts of 3 Enoch (Odeberg 1928, 51).

This view, argued Jonas Greenfield, is much oversimplified. Greenfield asserts that the decision to call the book 3 Enoch is in fact an error. The manuscripts uniformly call it *Sefer Hekhalot*, except for MS Oxford, which has a later addition, *Sefer Ḥanoch*, that Odeberg records as if it were in the same hand.

More importantly, Greenfield notes that Enoch does not appear as an independent entity in the book, but only as assimilated to Metatron, who delivers much *hekhalot* material to Rabbi Ishmael. Further, he draws a distinction regarding the role of Enoch-Metatron in 3 Enoch and the role of Enoch in 1 and 2 Enoch and in the Genesis Apocryphon (2:19-26) (Greenfield 1973, xxi-xxiii).[2] In these other works Enoch's translation to heaven and his vision, even his transformation into a companion of the angels, do not render him inaccessible to humans. In 1 and 2 Enoch he returns to earth. In the Genesis Apocryphon he is accessible to Methuselah. He never turns into an archangel or Prince of the Presence *(Sar ha-Panim)*. We may describe the journey of the "authentic Enoch" as "ascension (or vision) and return."

However, in 3 Enoch, Enoch is transformed into Metatron and cannot return to earth or to human fellowship. In other words, we may say, following Greenfield's observations, that the Enoch tradition, as it was absorbed into *hekhalot* circles, was later accommodated to *merkavah* traditions in that Enoch, already translated into heaven, was now translated into Metatron (Greenfield 1973, xxxii).

---

2. For the text of the Genesis Apocryphon passage, see Fitzmyer (1971, 52-55, 93-96).

Charles's Examples

We will begin by examining the original list of parallels between 1 Enoch and 3 Enoch provided by Charles (1912, lxxix-lxxxi). We need to bear in mind that Charles's knowledge of 3 Enoch was based on the partial edition of Adolph Jellinek (1967, 5:170-90) and an Oxford manuscript.[3]

1. According to 3 Enoch 4, Rabbi Ishmael ascends to heaven and receives revelations from Metatron, who says he is Enoch, son of Jared, translated into heaven at the time of the flood to be an eternal witness against sinful contemporaries. Of course, in 1 Enoch there is no Metatron and claims are made of revelation by Enoch. According to 1 Enoch 14:8, Enoch is borne to heaven, a notion also found in 70:2, but this notion is so widespread as to be of little significance for dependence. 3 Enoch 4 has Enoch-Metatron say he was lifted up to heaven to be a witness against the sinfulness of the generation of the flood. Charles points out allusions to this sinfulness in 1 Enoch 5:4-6 and 14:1-7, but these texts do not claim that Enoch was translated as a witness. Again, the sins of this generation are not a significant parallel.

2. According to Charles (1912, lxxx), Enoch-Metatron had been instructed by the Angel of Wisdom in the mysteries of the creation of heaven and earth, of past, present, and future, and of the world to come. Parenthetically, this list reminds us of the *razim,* "mysteries," of the Qumran books of Mysteries (Barthélemy and Milik 1955, 102-7; Schiffman 1997, 31-123) and other wisdom texts. In fact, 3 Enoch 8 makes God himself the teacher of wisdom who educationally transformed the young Enoch-Metatron. Charles cites as parallels to his approach 1 Enoch 93:10 (Apocalypse of Weeks), which alludes to the eventual instruction in such wisdom of the Elect — not a very close parallel.[4] Again, these works are not parallel here.

3. Charles pointed to the idea that until humans turned to idolatry, Adam and his generation beheld God's glorious presence, until the angels Aza and Azazel led humanity astray. In fact, 3 Enoch 5 says they simply went astray and the fallen angels appear only to object to Enoch's presence in heaven. Enoch is blamed for introducing idolatry. Only then did Uza, Aza, and Aziel teach them magical praxis. Charles's comparison to 1 Enoch 6:6 fails because it places the idolatry in the time of Jared, not Enosh or Enoch, and in 1 Enoch 6 the fallen angels caused the evildoing, they did not just teach magic, which indeed is a parallel motif in these texts. Both texts, by the way, associate wealth with stimulating the transgression. The evil machinations of Azazel are somewhat parallel, but this is also a reflection

---

3. Odeberg lists four Bodleian (Oxford) manuscripts that he used (17-18).
4. En 63:11-21, cited by Charles, does not exist.

of common exegesis of the scriptural Azazel demon (Lev 16:8, 10, 26). But in 3 Enoch it is humans who cause evil, whereas in 1 Enoch it is the fallen angels.

4. Charles notes that 3 Enoch describes the seven heavens, their hosts of angels, and the courses of the sun, moon, and stars.[5] At the outset we need to note that these chapters describe the angelic hierarchy in military terms[6] and that the heavenly aspect is discussed only from the point of view of the angelic hosts and their military ceremonial activity. Another dominant theme is the heavenly account books and their angelic scribes. Further, the overall theme is angelic support of the divine *merkavah*. 1 Enoch 72–82, cited by Charles (1912, lxxx) as parallel, is actually totally different. It consists of astronomical data and description, and Charles does not understand the "leaders" of 75:1 to be angels. Bottom line — 1 Enoch includes a calendar text and describes the heavens astronomically, and 3 Enoch is an angelic *merkavah* text similar to the *Sefer ha-Razim* (Margaliot 1966, 65-109), and has absolutely no astronomy in it. Further, the angelic hosts of the seven heavens and above are not described in 1 Enoch. Again, Charles's parallel is specious.

5. Charles points to the idea, at the end of a long description of the winds in 3 Enoch 23, that the winds enter Eden and absorb fragrant odors that are brought before the righteous in the end of days. He cites as parallel 1 Enoch 24:4–25:7. This text discusses one fragrant tree reserved for the end of days in what is essentially the Garden of Eden. As he notes in his commentary (Charles 1912, 53), this is the tree of life. There are no winds here and no mixed fragrances here. Again, this is not much of a parallel.

6. He then refers to 3 Enoch 24–26, which describe God's multiple chariots and then the Ophanim and Seraphim and their archangels. The presence of Ophanim and Seraphim with Cherubim in 1 Enoch 61:10 and 71:7 is quite minimal as an example of agreement, since none of the details of the accounts match and there is no multiplicity of chariots *(merkavot)* in 1 Enoch. While it is true that in both texts angels intercede for humans, in 3 Enoch 26 the Seraphim destroy the Satan's written indictments against Israel and in 1 Enoch 40:3-7 one of the four archangels intercedes for humanity to forefend against the Satans. Similarity, yes, but no real dependency can be observed.

7. A sort of heavenly librarian is described in 3 Enoch 27, who gives books and records to God and may read before him. 1 Enoch 89:61-64, 70-76 describes a divine recorder who is told to record and reads only his own records. 1 Enoch 98:7-8 and 104:7 refer to recording transgressions, but the parallel here is tenuous. In 3 Enoch there is no writing, only reading.

---

5. Charles refers to chaps. 18–22, but the account actually starts in chap. 17.
6. For this motif in early Jewish magical and mystical texts, cf. Levine (1970).

8. 3 Enoch 35–40 concerns camps of angels in the heavens reciting *qedushah,* the heavenly fiery stream, camps of the *shekhinah,* and the behavior of ministering angels and other parts of God's angelic retinue. These descriptions are widespread in *hekhalot* texts and in related ritual poetry *(piyyut)* (Altmann 1946). Enoch's praise of God in 1 Enoch 39:10-13 is not relevant, despite Charles's insistence to the contrary; but he also cites 1 Enoch 61:10-12. Here we have a description of the praise of God on the day of judgment, not daily praise in the present, as in 3 Enoch. But the doxology of this text has no relation to the Isaianic *trisagion* "Holy, Holy, Holy . . ." (Isa 6:3) that is the main theme of 3 Enoch in these chapters. So all that is parallel here is a brief reference to eschatological praise that hardly compares with the centrality of *qedushah* praise in 3 Enoch.

9. Charles (1912, lxxx-lxxxi) lists together a number of aspects of chapters 41–47 of 3 Enoch that we will look at one by one. Chapter 42 describes the repositories of rain, snow, hail, thunder, and lightning. 1 Enoch 60:11-21 is indeed parallel, except that the details of these accounts are different. In 3 Enoch 43–44 all the classes of righteous and evildoers are described in terms of their punishments and evil deeds. Then, in chapter 47 Metatron shows Rabbi Ishmael angels that are being punished for uttering praise of God at the wrong time or inappropriately. Charles compares 1 Enoch 18:11-16 and 1 Enoch 21, but here it is not angels but stars that are punished for coming out at the wrong time. This is referred to in 21:10 as the prison of the angels, and if the stars and angels are identical there is again some parallel, but no direct dependence. But in 1 Enoch 19:1 the punished angels have had relations with women, and none of these 1 Enoch texts mentions incorrect or poorly timed praise of God by the angels, the main offense in the 3 Enoch passage.

Metatron does show Rabbi Ishmael the ages of the world from Adam up through the messianic redemption (3 En 45), and the destruction of God's enemies (3 En 48a). 3 Enoch 45 mentions the messiah son of Joseph and the wars of "Gog and Magog." Charles cites 1 Enoch 56:5–57:2, which does talk about the end of days, but in very different terms. In fact, the specifics of this messianic vision have no parallels in 1 Enoch, despite some references Charles cites to the end of days.

What this detailed set of comparisons shows is that the initial assumptions about the relationship of these books were grossly exaggerated. In fact, I have so far found no evidence at all that the author of 3 Enoch was directly influenced by 1 Enoch.

Odeberg Parallels

I now turn to a detailed study of the parallels assembled by Odeberg (1928, 43-51) to show the dependence of 3 Enoch on 1 Enoch and its development of the ideas it supposedly inherited. In approaching this list I will not point out the irrelevance of examples but concentrate instead on trying to assemble some legitimate parallels. Whereas the Charles list proceeded in the order of 3 Enoch, Odeberg assembled his list in the order of 1 Enoch. I, however, have tried to group the phenomena under discussion.

1. *Angelic Designations.* Exceedingly common in 1 Enoch is the term "Watchers," which gives its name to an entire book of Enoch (1 En 6–36). It occurs in the phrase 'irin we-qadishin, "Watchers and Holy Ones," in 3 Enoch 28. Watchers and holy ones also appear in 1 Enoch, but seem to be derived there directly from Daniel 4:10, 14, and 20. Shemiúazah, the leader of the fallen angels in 1 Enoch, is not found in 3 Enoch. Asael and Azael do appear as part of the triplets Uzza, Azza, and Azziel in 3 Enoch 4–5, where two figures have been expanded to three in a fashion only possible if influence is indirect. Some angel names in 1 Enoch do appear in 3 Enoch, e.g., Berakiel (1 En 6:7, 8:3; 3 En 17).

According to 1 Enoch, there are four angels of presence — Michael, Uriel (or Penuel), Raphael, and Gabriel. 3 Enoch refers to four great princes over the camps of the divine presence *(shekhinah)*, but their names are not given. In 1 Enoch they are sometimes referred to without names (four presences) (Odeberg 1928, 50). 1 Enoch uses the term "angels of destruction," which is similar to 3 Enoch's *mal'akhe habalah*, "angels of destruction" (3 En 31; 33; 44). 1 Enoch 61:10-12 does enumerate types of angels, but the level of specificity of 3 Enoch is not even aspired to or imagined. Both texts, however, share the idea that the number of angels is enormous or even infinite, but this notion derives from a common source, Daniel, or its source. Both texts also work with systems of seven archangels and four angels of presence that have to be harmonized (cf. 1 En 20 and 87:2). This reconciliation is performed in totally different manners by the two texts.

2. *The Myth of the Fallen Angels.* We have already alluded to the different angelic leadership described in the two texts. Also, there is no full enumeration of the fallen angels in 3 Enoch. In fact, this myth is widespread in Jewish texts (Bamberger 1952; Jung 1974). As already mentioned, the role of the fallen angels is not the same in both texts. In 3 Enoch, after Enoch leads humanity astray, the angels, whose fall is not mentioned, teach humanity magic (3 En 5). The same angels oppose Enoch-Metatron (3 En 4). Odeberg (1928, 43) claims this as an example of a direct parallel, but it seems indirect to me.

3. *The Divine Throne.* 1 Enoch 14:8–15:1 is a chariot vision (cf. chap. 71). Both of these texts, like many others, build their *merkavah* visions on combin-

ing Ezekiel's (chaps. 1; 10) and Daniel's visions (7:1-14) of the world of the divine, and so parallels are to be expected. The almost equivalent quotations in 1 Enoch 15:3 and 3 Enoch 5 refer to different subjects. In 1 Enoch it is addressed to Enoch by God in a throne vision. In 3 Enoch the quotation is addressed by the ministering angels to God himself. In 1 Enoch 25:3 the throne plays a part in judgment, presumably at the end of days. This notion is also found in 3 Enoch (e.g., 26 [end]), except that it applies to the present, not to the end of days.

4. *Dramatis Personae.* The final comparison we will cite from Odeberg is that of the dramatis personae. Here I refer to the large amount of material about the Elect One in 1 Enoch (Puech 2000; Fitzmyer 1974).[7] Here Odeberg (1928, 47) notes that many of the features of the Elect One and Son of Man in 1 Enoch are transferred to Metatron in 3 Enoch. Enoch is indeed called an Elect One *(bahir)* in 3 Enoch 6. The term "Son of Man" does not occur in 3 Enoch. The Elect One, according to 1 Enoch 45:3 and the like, will sit on the throne of glory, and Metatron clearly derives from *meta thronos,* literally "along with the throne," despite the philological objections (Odeberg 1928, 125-42; Lieberman 1980). Metatron sits on a throne in 3 Enoch 10 *et alia,* but he never sits on the divine throne, as Odeberg notes (47).[8] 3 Enoch 48c, probably a later addition, does closely parallel 1 Enoch. There is one final central difference, not explicated by Odeberg: whereas Enoch appears in 1 Enoch as the revealer of hidden secrets, in 3 Enoch Rabbi Ishmael appears as an intermediary, always conveying what Enoch-Metatron told him in a vision. Thus, the role of Enoch/Enoch-Metatron is completely different in these works.

It is worth saying a few words to summarize our discussion of Odeberg's lists of parallels between 1 and 3 Enoch, remembering that our investigation was not comprehensive. Basically, we have found a few striking verbal parallels and some parallel ideas, along with a vast corpus of material that has both similarities and differences. All this seems to argue for a relationship less than that of dependence and calls for a much more cautious approach than the name 3 Enoch would imply.

Odeberg's 2 Enoch Parallels

Before drawing conclusions from what we have surveyed, it is worthwhile to look at the relationship of 2 Enoch to 3 Enoch. We can begin with Odeberg's

---

7. 4Q534 1 i 10 refers to *behir 'elaha,* "the elect of God" (Puech 2001, 133-34).

8. About this section of 1 Enoch, Odeberg comments that "the differences are, however, greater than the resemblances" (1928, 47).

summary discussion (Odeberg 1928, 60-63) after his fuller comparisons (52-60). He concludes that 3 Enoch is based on the same traditions as 2 Enoch "to a considerable extent." Moreover, he observes that in 3 Enoch the development of these traditions is further advanced than in 2 Enoch and (and this is most doubtful) "that, apparently, the conceptions of 3 Enoch in most cases are direct continuations on the lines of development begun by 2 Enoch" (60). To illustrate this assertion he discusses a number of topics.

1. *Angelology.* He says the tendency toward systematization in 2 Enoch, compared with 1 Enoch, has yielded the very complex schema of 3 Enoch. This need not be the case, since *Sefer ha-Razim* and a variety of *hekhalot* texts have similar angelology. Further, what these collections really share is the complex of heavens and angels, even of thrones, but the specifics are quite different, as he himself indicates in his detailed discussion.

2. *Concept of Enoch.* Odeberg argues that 2 Enoch represents a stage between 1 Enoch and 3 Enoch chronologically; "speaking metaphorically, [it is] on the straight line connecting 1 Enoch to 3 Enoch." This overstatement is one with which I clearly disagree; but he is correct that in 1 Enoch the essential feature is Enoch's visions and revelations, whereas in 2 Enoch the transformation of Enoch into a celestial being is central. Yet in 2 Enoch he is still below Michael. He is not yet ruler of all the angels and vice-regent of God. This is accomplished only with the identification of Enoch with Metatron in 3 Enoch. This is correct, but already points away from linear development to a more complex situation. It is only through the merger of a complex of Enoch traditions with those of Michael, Metatron, and other *hekhalot* archangels that 3 Enoch's approach comes about. This disproves Odeberg's linear, simplistic approach.

3. He correctly notes that regarding judgment and the fate of souls, 2 Enoch parallels 1 Enoch more closely than it follows 3 Enoch, which actually adheres to the rabbinic approach. But this is because of the general rabbinic milieu, even of the *hekhalot* texts such as 3 Enoch, that is sufficient to guarantee their general adherence or assimilation to rabbinic theological norms (Swartz 1996, 174-205). Perhaps most simplistic is Odeberg's statement that "2 Enoch must have been well known to the circle from which 3 Enoch originated."

4. *Close Parallels.* Several close parallels between 2 and 3 Enoch are striking and indicate at least indirect influence, if not Odeberg's "direct dependence."

a. 2 Enoch and 3 Enoch have three, not two, leaders for the fallen angels.
b. The heavenly librarian has the same name and function in 2 and 3 Enoch.
c. Both books have Enoch first instructed by angels, then by God himself (Odeberg 1928, 61).

Odeberg also notes that there are more of what he sees as later developments in 2 Enoch than in 3 Enoch, some of which are later additions, but some in our view are simply variant ideas.

After this roundabout tour and critique of the views of others, it is time to return to the work of our colleague James VanderKam. The notion of a developing literature of "booklets" that he has explored so carefully regarding 1 Enoch (VanderKam 1984, 17-101) is clearly the correct method with which to understand the eventual emergence of 2 and 3 Enoch as well. These works are composites of documents that were themselves put together from other minor protodocuments, a phenomenon clearly emerging from the results of VanderKam's detailed research, especially when coupled with Milik's approach to 1 Enoch, even if all of Milik's views are not accepted. The close relation of our official Enoch literature — or better, the various booklets — with other texts (not just traditions) highlights the value of this literary-historical model. Had I sought to work on 2 Enoch and its relation to 1 Enoch, this approach would have been enough to provide a model to understand the development of 2 Enoch.

There is another aspect, totally ignored by Odeberg, since it was not yet known in his time. It turns out that "booklets," or better, short treatises, are the building blocks of all the *hekhalot*-type texts, as shown by Peter Schäfer (1983). In fact, texts as we know them, independent compositions, are a misnomer for these "texts," since different manuscripts have different mixes of common, but not always present, building blocks. With this model in mind we can grasp that, like 1 Enoch and 2 Enoch, 3 Enoch is such a composite.

However, 3 Enoch is not just a composite of text traditions such as those found in 1 and 2 Enoch. The circle that produced, exported, composed, redacted, copied, and studied traditions like those in 1 Enoch and 3 Enoch produced various booklets which still circulated in different forms and in different languages after the so-called 1 and 2 Enoch came into being as redacted texts. Some of the original documents circulated in translation. These traditions somehow mixed with those of the *hekhalot* trend and were redomesticated as part of the emerging textual tradition of late rabbinic/early medieval Jewish esotericism. The results of this combination remain fully clear in the passages in 3 Enoch that harmonize the persona (if we can use this term) of Enoch with that of Metatron native to the *hekhalot* corpus. But let us not forget how Metatron himself, in this text, or better, in the booklets that preceded it, had inherited or superseded the roles of other heavenly figures, like Michael and Akatriel, all found in related *hekhalot* literature (Scholem 1965, 43-55).

What all this means is that any linear view of the relationship between 1 and 3 Enoch, let alone 1, 2, and 3 Enoch, is a gross oversimplification. Vander-

Kam's "booklet" theory holds for every one of these texts, but in the case of 3 Enoch the wide streams of both Enochic and *hekhalot/merkavah* traditions flowed together, just as streams had flowed together to create earlier Enoch materials. So VanderKam was right for his corpus, and to a great extent even for the later material, but for 3 Enoch the *merkavah* side cannot be minimized.

One final comment: Odeberg clearly should have realized this, in view of the detailed studies in his introduction and commentary that connect 3 Enoch to the *hekhalot* texts. But his desire to find another "pseudepigraphical" text — and to call it 3 Enoch — caused him to exaggerate the Enochic features.

A return to his detailed notes, even if based on out-of-date textual materials, will provide a gold mine for understanding how booklets of Enochic material and booklets of *hekhalot* material somehow were merged in a tradition that continued to have its impact on later Jewish mystical tradition.

Response: Jubilees and Enoch

James C. VanderKam

Let me begin by thanking the organizers of this volume for making it possible to engage in this published dialogue with scholars who have reacted to my work on Jubilees and 1 Enoch. I wish also to thank the fourteen scholars who have offered their reflections. Their kind words are gratefully received, while I have learned from the criticisms. Although the number of contributions is large, I will respond briefly to each one in the following pages.

1. Helge Kvanvig distinguishes two aspects of Jubilees as a literary production: narrative and story. *Narrative* for him refers to the framework of the book in which one is always at Sinai where Moses receives the revelation (a fact about which the author reminds the reader regularly); *story* designates the sequence of events from creation, through the patriarchs, to Moses and Mount Sinai. As a story Jubilees satisfies the Aristotelian criterion for artistry by having a well-structured beginning, middle, and end. The story and its intertextual relation with Genesis-Exodus have received much scholarly attention, but the narrative is the writer's unique creation. Through the narrative he conveys important points about this torah (Jubilees) vis-à-vis the scriptural torah (Genesis-Exodus). As Kvanvig puts it: "The author makes use of the words of the Pentateuch to make the torah of the Pentateuch disappear"; and here Moses "is placed at the start of the narrative as the ultimate witness of his own reduced significance" (the revelation to him is only the latest one, not the most important one). He finds that Jubilees, on issues such as torah, temple, and the role of the primeval age, mediates between the scriptural torah and Enoch's teachings, positioning itself closer to the latter in an intratextual sense.

The distinction between narrative and story (or whatever terms we choose) highlights a significant fact about Jubilees and allows us to address some issues more clearly. Yet we should not (and Kvanvig certainly does not do this) minimize the contribution of the author of Jubilees on the story level and the impressive manner in which he has rewritten an older text. His skills and theology are much in evidence here as well.

On the narrative level, the stance adopted by the author of Jubilees toward other texts (intratextuality) should attract plenty of expert attention. Here too we should be cautious about reducing Moses' role and overrating any opposition to the Pentateuch. An argument can be made that Moses' role is enhanced on the narrative level in comparison with his part in Genesis-Exodus in that all of this material is authoritatively revealed to him in Jubilees. The Pentateuch does not so much disappear as take its place within a broader setting provided by Jubilees' authoritative understanding of the tradition.

2. Erik Larson surveys five compositions that refer to Enoch and the descent of the Watchers to check for signs of influence from the Old Greek translation of Genesis. He concludes that three of the five (the Wisdom of Ben Sira, the Wisdom of Solomon, and Pseudo-Philo's *Liber antiquitatum biblicarum*) evidence significant influence from the Old Greek, while 1 Enoch and Jubilees show fewer marks of such influence in wording. Their phrase "the angels of God," however, suggests some impact from the Greek version.

My study of the text of Jubilees has led to a conclusion similar to Larson's — that the wording of the text was not affected by the renderings of Genesis-Exodus in the various languages into which it was translated (Greek, Latin, Ethiopic, and possibly Syriac). Translators rendered Jubilees; they did not accommodate the text to their versions of Genesis-Exodus. I would go further than Larson and argue that the phrase "the angels of God" (or "the angels of the Lord") in 4:15; 5:1, 6 should not, considering all the other evidence regarding the text of Jubilees, be interpreted as influence from Old Greek Genesis but as having arisen from one of two factors: Jubilees used a Hebrew text of Genesis that read מלאכי האלהים, not בני האלהים, in 6:2; or Jubilees embodies an exegetical tradition that מלאכי האלהים = בני האלהים, a tradition that also comes to expression in the Old Greek of Genesis 6:2. The former explanation is more likely.

3. Jacques van Ruiten questions the claim that the writer of Jubilees depended on a *text* of four Enochic booklets. An implication of Jubilees' use of a text of the Book of Dreams would be that it was written after the Book of Dreams, thus yielding a relatively precise terminus a quo for the composition of Jubilees. Van Ruiten holds that we cannot prove Jubilees had direct access to written forms of the Enoch material. The limited verbal overlap (especially with the Book of Dreams and the Epistle of Enoch) when compared with the extensive verbatim citations from Genesis-Exodus underscores the problem.

Both the Enochic authors and Jubilees may rather have been tapping into shared traditions. Jubilees may be drawing on written works, but if so we do not know which ones, as references in Jubilees could be to passages in more than one of the preserved booklets. Van Ruiten illustrates his point with several examples from Jubilees 4:17-26. The only exception he allows is Jubilees 7:22 // 1 Enoch 7:2.

Van Ruiten is correct to emphasize the uncertainty involved in identifying the specific Enochic booklets which Jubilees may be using in specific passages. But it does not follow from such a difficulty that the writer was not referring to particular written works (in whatever form he knew them). If we are not sure an item is from one book or another, it may still be from one or both of them.

We should not minimize the significance of the fact that Jubilees underscores that Enoch left written works behind. They included astronomical (4:17, 21), chronological (4:18), and predictive information (4:19). Enoch is even pictured as continuing his scribal labors after his removal from human society to the Garden of Eden. We may not have all the Enochic texts written in antiquity, but when the ones we do have correspond quite closely in theme if not in wording with the descriptions in passages such as Jubilees 4:17-26, it seems more economical to assume dependence on these written sources than to appeal to unknown ones.

4. Annette Reed addresses the intriguing subject of the prehistory of the biblical canon and calls attention to the ever present danger of imposing (wittingly or not) our own canonical assumptions on the meager evidence surviving from the period. She notes, for example, cases in which scholars assume that the authors and consumers of what we call pseudepigraphic literature were fringe characters, critiquing normative society from the margins; or ones in which experts start from the thesis that "biblical" pseudepigraphy (with its claims to revelation) and "biblical" interpretation were fundamentally different phenomena.

I applaud her clarification of such prior commitments and their baleful effects. We agree that the precanonical period included compositions and procedures that, with canonical hindsight, seem peculiar to us, pseudepigraphy being a prime example. Clearly we must evaluate it historically, using all the minuscule evidence at our disposal. As all recognize, our terms for some bodies of literature ("apocryphal," "parabiblical," etc.) do not help us to gain a more disciplined, historically attuned picture. While evidence is lacking for a canon at the time, there are indications aplenty of writers who claimed inspiration as the source for their books, and there are indications that some accepted these remarkable claims.

5. Eibert Tigchelaar provides some suggestive comments regarding differ-

ences between 1 Enoch and Jubilees respecting modes of revelation and the means for transmitting these disclosures. Though the two works appeal to the same forms of revelation (visions, dreams, celestial tablets, etc.) and tradition, one can distinguish variant features. Unlike 1 Enoch, Jubilees never speaks of a human reading the tablets of heaven, not even Enoch, Jacob (he reads other tablets), or Moses. Jubilees itself is not a copy of those tablets which apparently contain much more than the book does. Both works place the writing of books in primeval times and make provision for transmitting them through the generations, but 1 Enoch imagines ancient books appearing at the very time period they address. I find such observations challenging and hope to pursue them in future research. I doubt, however, that the method of transmission is really different in 1 Enoch and Jubilees. The latter speaks of handing books along in the priestly line and the former does not, but both say the books should be an inheritance from generation to generation.

His second point centers on the attitude adopted by Jubilees' author toward Enochic writings. There are two references (12:27 and 21:10) to compositions of Enoch which contain at least some items not in the extant works. Tigchelaar thinks the revelation to Moses (that is, Jubilees) makes "previous books redundant." Whatever the source(s) of the two stray allusions to Enoch's works, it seems too strong to say that Jubilees renders early writings no longer of value. A counterexample appears in Jubilees 30:12, where the angel refers the reader to Genesis for more details about the Shechem incident. Jubilees does not claim to have selected and reproduced everything useful in earlier books of Enoch. Jubilees is revelation that supplements rather than replaces previous disclosures. It is also doubtful whether Jubilees is less harsh than the Enoch texts regarding the sciences such as astrology and medicine. Jubilees roundly condemns what comes from the wrong source; even Abram erred (as he recognized) in attempting to read the weather forecast from the stars.

6. Hanan Eshel understands the chronology in 4Q390 as updating Daniel 9, just as Daniel 9 contemporized Jeremiah's 70-year prophecies. He assumes that the two relatively well preserved columns in the Qumran text are contiguous. In them the 490 years of Daniel 9 fall into four eras: 70 years of exile, 343 years of proper behavior by those who return, 7 years for the time of Antiochus IV, and a 70-year rule by Hasmoneans. As the last period leads to the time of Alexander Janneus, 4Q390 may have served to encourage his opponents by predicting an end to the Hasmoneans. It charges the Hellenizing and Hasmonean high priests with following the wrong calendar after Antiochus changed it from the correct solar arrangement. That solar calendar had been instituted by priests in the third century when they preferred it over the imprecise, unintercalated lunar calendar. The Astronomical Book of Enoch had at-

tempted to gain acceptance for the solar calendar. Opposition to this priestly system arose as the population countered the Hellenistic priests. Jubilees, a third-century work, defended the solar calendar within this debate.

A cloud of uncertainty hangs over this entire construct. Among its dubious points, these should be noted. First, we do not know how the fragments preserving the largest amount of 4Q390 relate to each other. Some have argued that their order is the reverse of the one Eshel accepts. If so, the chronology is seriously affected. Second, if the Herodian date assigned to the script of 4Q390 is accurate, an anomaly would result: a prediction of the demise of the Hasmoneans in the time of Janneus was still copied some 50 years or so after it was proved false. Third, what is column i.8 for Eshel seems contrary to his reconstruction. It predicts that in the seventh jubilee from the land's destruction (i.e., perhaps some point in the third century B.C.E.), "they" will forget law, festival, Sabbath, and covenant. This would supposedly be the time when the correct solar calendar was introduced, but it sounds as if what happened at that time is condemned, not applauded. Finally, much opposes and really nothing supports assigning Jubilees to the third century B.C.E.

7. Henry Rietz deals with one of the ways the Qumran community appropriated the ideology of Jubilees and shows how it has implications well beyond what one might expect. The item he has in mind is the solar calendar. Far from simply a convenient means for organizing time, the correct calendar insures that holidays (other than the ones lasting a week) will not fall on the Sabbath and allows a coordination of heavenly and earthly worship. Jubilees spends less time on this subject than a work such as the Songs of the Sabbath Sacrifice, but its teachings about Sabbaths and festivals observed in heaven make a similar point. The angels were understood to be present in the community which was returning to the torah, including the calendar, in the only correct way.

Rietz is certainly right to bring out these connections and also to identify them as developments of the heritage of Jubilees. Yet, while there are these points of contact, we should not allow them to obscure differences. It remains a puzzling fact that the writer of Jubilees could be so adamant that the only revealed calendar is the solar one of 364 days, while his heirs could reverse his stand on the lunar calendar of 354 days. In that move the calendarists of Qumran returned, of course, to the teachings of the Astronomical Book of Enoch.

8. Michael Daise writes that he accepts the key premises of my theory that a 364-day calendar prevailed in the Jerusalem temple until Antiochus IV forced a change to a lunar reckoning. During the *intersacerdotium* the matter was debated, with Jubilees arising from that debate. After the beginning of the Hasmonean high priesthood, the authorities settled on the lunar calendar, and

the Qumran writers opposed it from outside. That is, Jubilees and the Qumran writings are responses to calendar issues, although they differ in time and social location. Daise adds a nuance or development within this hypothesis. When the Rule of the Community 1:13-15 warns against advancing the timing of festivals, it is referring to ones incorrectly celebrated at an earlier date according to the shorter lunar calendar. However, when it condemns retarding the timing of festivals, Daise proposes that the writer refers to the Festival of Hanukkah which is referred to in 2 Maccabees as Sukkot in the month Kislev. The close identification between the two holidays could explain the warning about delaying the celebration of the festival.

I find this an intriguing proposal that gives concrete meaning to an expression in a sectarian legal text that may at first glance appear to be merely a rhetorical flourish. If the Festivals of Booths and Hanukkah were so closely associated that they could be confused, then the celebration of the latter in the ninth month could be viewed as a delay in the divinely commanded timing of the holiday. And, of course, there is no reference to Hanukkah in the Qumran lists of festivals. We should be cautious, though, about accepting the proposal because there are too many uncertainties. For example, 2 Maccabees is the only source that associates the two holidays, so we do not have a good way of gauging the extent of the tradition. Also, even in 2 Maccabees the two are not identified; rather, Hanukkah allowed for a tardy celebration of Booths on one occasion when it had not been possible to celebrate it at the correct time. Whether this would have inspired the sectarian writers to warn against a delay in these terms is uncertain.

9. Martha Himmelfarb argues that a crucial difference between the presectarian Jubilees and the sectarian texts of Qumran is their attitude toward other Jews. Jubilees exalts the status of the nation Israel in a variety of ways, including the implication that there could be no conversion to Judaism (e.g., by the Shechemites). For Jubilees membership in Israel is hereditary, whereas for the sectarians membership in the holy people was a matter of merit. She thinks Jubilees, written during the time of John Hyrcanus, shows great concern about intermarriage, which became a problem particularly with the Hasmonean conquests and expansions. She also suggests that Jubilees' teaching on the holiness of all Israel can be understood as a response to sectarian views about Israel.

Himmelfarb has isolated an important doctrine in Jubilees and a significant way in which it differs from the Qumran sectarian texts. Jubilees continues to operate with a pan-Israelite perspective, although the writer is concerned about those who do or may stray and thus deny their heritage. But should we view the book as a response to sectarian theories about the chosen or as preceding them? There is too much uncertainty about the early history of the community that eventually occupied Qumran to say much about when its texts were composed, but there seems to be little reason to date Jubilees later than these texts and some evidence that it precedes them. If so, Jubilees would not be antisectarian in the sense of opposing the Qumran sectarian works; but it could of course be antisectarian in reaction to other works which have not survived. And the problem of intermarriage hardly originated with Hyrcanus's conquests.

10. Jeff Anderson focuses attention on what he calls "denouncement speech" in Jubilees and other texts (some Enochic booklets, the Temple Scroll) in order to address the identity of those whom these works oppose. Curse language may have different settings. Anderson maintains that the curses against the nations (Edomites, Philistines, etc.) which were not threats at the time of Jubilees may represent a stereotypical Gentile danger to Jubilees' audience — specifically the evils of Hellenism and syncretism with pagan cultures. Yet he also thinks these references point to contemporary enemies and issues and that the imprecatory rhetoric serves to express a dualistic view of the covenant.

It is not easy to determine which imprecations of Jubilees are directed against contemporary nations and which might use those nations stereotypically. As Anderson indicates, there were problems at the time with people in the areas of Philistia and Edom. We could understand that the author would curse other nations, even if we cannot imagine that anyone from another nation would read Jubilees, so in the end, presumably the imprecations are for internal consumption and certainly do warn Israelites against mixing with those foreigners who were of such concern to the author.

11. Liliana Rosso Ubigli has chosen several themes from Jubilees, themes that can be detected by comparing it with the older Enoch literature. She notes the altered picture of the Watcher story and ties the changes to Jubilees' concern to emphasize personal responsibility. Also, through its ban on nudity, its use of the Eden story is tied directly to issues raised by Hellenism. Something similar may be said regarding its concern with circumcision, contamination of the temple, and assimilation with non-Jews. Enoch himself becomes a *prōtos heuretēs,* a common category in Hellenistic literature; and the book, through its chronology, stresses the importance of Israel's possession of its own land free of foreign domination. All these themes suggest the work should be read against an Antiochean backdrop. She ends by raising the important issue regarding the role of the Antiochean crisis in the origin and development of Essenism.

It is true that several features of Jubilees could have arisen in response to events associated with the difficult times in the 170s and 160s B.C.E. Whether we should see all the themes mentioned by Ubigli in such a context is another matter. Presumably the matter of nudity could have become more important then, but an issue such as personal responsibility could have suggested itself in many circumstances. Nevertheless, there is value in approaching both the Enochic and Jubilees material with Ubigli's questions in mind. After all, though we do not know enough about those years, we do know something about them — something we can hardly say for the preceding century of Jewish history.

12. Ida Fröhlich explores the story about the angels who fell as it comes to expression in the various parts of 1 Enoch and in Jubilees. She points out both shared elements and differences between the Enochic presentations and the one in Jubilees. She highlights the priestly concerns present in both and concludes that the halakic systems of the two are based on the Temple Scroll. That is, the writers of these works followed the same legal tradition. In this way their agreements can be explained, while their differences point to the specific concerns of their authors. The Enochic booklets and Jubilees arose from the same religious group.

Fröhlich's way of comparing the two works is the best one to take: isolate an important shared theme and study how it is developed in them. The angel story is especially suited to such a comparison. Whether the books of Enoch and Jubilees reflect the same halakic tradition is difficult to determine because there is much less pertinent material in the Enoch literature while Jubilees is filled with it. The fact that 1 Enoch and Jubilees, while they agree on much, differ so markedly about important matters such as the lunar calendar, the place of the Mosaic law, and the purpose for the angelic descent makes it difficult to describe what precisely their relationship may have been and to determine whether we can assign their writers to the same group at different times. The writers deal with similar themes but do so in markedly different ways.

13. Ithamar Gruenwald, noting that some apocalyptic writings like those associated with Enoch locate their hero in prediluvian times while others do not, ties this attribution with biblical traditions centered on land and agricultural plenty. He attempts to contextualize this ethos and to trace it in biblical traditions such as the patriarchal stories and the prophets as well as in Qumran, John the Baptist, and Christianity. That is, these varied expressions of an anti-urban stance are related to an ethos represented already by Seth, the third son of Adam and Eve. This particular ethos stands in opposition to the one represented by Cain — urbanization, centralization, and eventually monarchy and the like.

Careful efforts at contextualizing apocalyptic texts are much to be welcomed, since we know so little about the situation in which their authors produced them. Viewing the texts as parts of a more widely attested way of life and frame of mind is indeed a helpful way of reading them. But the pattern breaks down at points. While the eschatological picture in 1 Enoch 10:17–11:2 (to which

Gruenwald refers) concentrates on the land and fruitfulness, other passages in Enochic literature veer more toward the other option. So, for example, the Animal Apocalypse anticipates a messiah and a temple — elements that would not have been part of the ethos that comes to expression in the shepherding/wilderness traditions.

14. Lawrence Schiffman tackles the issue of the relation between the so-called 3 Enoch and 1 Enoch by checking the long list of parallels between them compiled by Robert H. Charles and Hugo Odeberg. As Schiffman shows, the lists are far less impressive than they may at first appear. Charles's list consists of minimal or specious similarities, while Odeberg's suffers from the same weaknesses. So, for example, the Enoch of 3 Enoch is transformed into Metatron and does not return to the places of human habitation, unlike his roles in 1 and 2 Enoch. Schiffman concludes that while there are some verbal parallels and other similarities, the evidence does not support a relationship of dependence. Schiffman prefers the "booklets" approach to the development of the Enochic works and notes that this is also the way the *hekhalot* texts evolved. Clearly, *merkavah* traditions were merged with varied Enochic ones in the formation of a text like 3 Enoch.

Schiffman and I agree on how these composite texts came into being and that it is simplistic to sketch the relationship as a purely linear one from 1 to 2 to 3 Enoch as Odeberg thought. The evidence at our disposal (much of it also available to Charles and Odeberg) indicates that the relationships were more complicated than a direct line of influence. It does appear as if the few Enochic compositions that have survived do not exhaust the richness of the traditions that grew up around this man. As those traditions grew and intermingled with others, new compilations gave expression to the themes found in those varied sources.

By way of concluding this response, let me say that I hope all the scholars who have been part of this discussion will continue to research the many facets of Jubilees and 1 Enoch. The more we study these works, the more it becomes evident that they are related yet hardly in complete agreement. Jubilees goes its own way on a number of central points. The book did, nevertheless, exercise a documentable influence on the sectarian texts found in the Qumran caves. Much remains to be done to clarify the literary relations between all of these texts and the sociological realities that lie behind them.

References to Part Two

Abel, Félix-Marie. 1946. "La fête de la Hanoucca." *RB* 53:538-546.

Aharoni, Yohanan. 1981. *Arad Inscriptions*. JDS. Jerusalem: Israel Exploration Society.

Albani, Matthias. 1997. "Zur Rekonstruktion eines verdrängten Konzepts: Der 364-Tage-Kalender in der gegenwärtigen Forschung." In *Studies in the Book of Jubilees*, edited by Matthias Albani, Jörg Frey, and Armin Lange, 79-125. TSAJ 65. Tübingen: Mohr Siebeck.

Alexander, Philip S. 1983. "3 Enoch." In *The Old Testament Pseudepigrapha*, edited by James H. Charlesworth, 1:223-325. Garden City, N.Y.: Doubleday.

Alexander, Philip S., and Geza Vermes. 1998. "4Q255-264: General Introduction." In *Qumran Cave 4. XIX: Serekh Ha-Yahad and Two Related Texts*, edited by Philip S. Alexander and Geza Vermes, 1-25. DJD 26. Oxford: Clarendon.

Altmann, Alexander. 1946. "Shire Qedushah be-Sifrut ha-Hekhalot ha-Qedumah." *Melilah* 2:2-24.

Anderson, Jeff S. 1998a. "The Social Function of Curses in the Hebrew Bible." *ZAW* 110:223-37.

———. 1998b. "The Metonymical Curse as Propaganda in the Book of Jeremiah." *BBR* 8:1-13.

Argall, Randal A. 1995. *1 Enoch and Sirach: A Comparative Literary and Conceptual Analysis of the Themes of Revelation, Creation, and Judgment*, 9-13. EJL 8. Atlanta: Scholars.

Attridge, Harold W. 1984. "Historiography." In *Jewish Writings of the Second Temple Period: Apocrypha, Pseudepigrapha, Qumran Sectarian Writings, Philo, Josephus*, edited by Michael E. Stone, 157-184. Philadelphia: Fortress.

Attridge, Harold, et al., eds. 1994. *Qumran Cave 4.VIII: Parabiblical Texts, Part 1*. DJD 13. Oxford: Clarendon.

Bal, Mieke. 1985. *Narratology: Introduction to the Theory of Narrative.* Toronto: University of Toronto Press.

Bamberger, Bernard J. 1952. *Fallen Angels.* Philadelphia: Jewish Publication Society of America.

Bardtke, Hans. 1971. "Der Mardochäustag." In *Tradition und Glaube: Das frühe Christentum in seiner Umwelt: Festgabe für Karl Georg Kuhn zum 65. Geburtstag,* edited by Gert Jeremias, Karl Georg Kuhn, and Hartmut Stegemann, 97-116. Göttingen: Vandenhoeck & Ruprecht.

Barr, James. 1983. *Holy Scripture: Canon, Authority, Criticism.* Philadelphia: Westminster.

Barthélemy, Dominique. 1952. "Notes en marge de publications récentes sur les manuscrits de Qumran." *RB* 59:187-218.

Barthélemy, Dominique, and Josef T. Milik. 1955. *Qumran Cave I.* DJD 1. Oxford: Clarendon.

Baumgarten, Joseph M., and Daniel R. Schwartz. 1995. "Damascus Document (CD)." In *Damascus Document, War Scroll, and Related Documents.* Tübingen: Mohr Siebeck; Louisville: Westminster John Knox.

Baumgarten, Joseph M. (with Stephen Pfann and Ada Yardeni). 1996. "4Q266 Damascus Document[a] (Pls. I-XVII)" and "4Q268 Damascus Document[c] (Pl. XXII)." In *Qumran Cave 4. XIII: The Damascus Document (4Q266-273),* edited by Joseph M. Baumgarten, on the basis of transcriptions by Józef T. Milik, with Stephen Pfann and Ada Yardeni, 23-93, 115-121. DJD 18. Oxford: Clarendon.

Beckwith, Roger. 1985. *The Old Testament Canon of the New Testament Church and Its Background in Early Judaism.* Grand Rapids: Eerdmans.

Beer, George. 1900. "Das Buch Henoch." In *Die Apokryphen und Pseudepigraphen des Altes Testaments,* edited by Emil Kautzsch, 2:224-26. 2 vols. Tübingen: Mohr.

Bickermann, Elias J. 1933. "Ein jüdischer Festbrief vom Jahre 124 v. Chr. (II Macc 1.1-9)." *ZNW* 32:233-254.

————. 1968. *Chronology of the Ancient World.* Aspects of Greek and Roman Life. London: Thames and Hudson.

Black, Matthew. 1985. *The Book of Enoch or 1 Enoch: A New English Edition.* In consultation with James C. VanderKam, with an appendix on the "Astronomical" chapters (72–82) by Otto Neugebauer. SVTP 7. Leiden: Brill.

Boccaccini, Gabriele. 1998. *Beyond the Essene Hypothesis: The Parting of the Ways between Qumran and Enochic Judaism.* Grand Rapids: Eerdmans.

————. 2001. "The Solar Calendars of Daniel and Enoch." In *The Book of Daniel: Composition and Reception,* edited by John J. Collins and Peter W. Flint, 2:311-28. VTSup 83/2. Leiden: Brill.

Bokser, Baruch M. 1981. "*Ma'al* and Blessings over Food: Rabbinic Transformation of Cultic Terminology and Alternative Modes of Piety." *JBL* 100:557-74.

Bunge, Jochen Gabriel. 1971. "Untersuchungen zum zweiten Makkabäerbuch: Quellenkritische, literarische, chronologische und historische Untersuchungen zum zweiten Makkabäerbuch als Quelle syrisch-palästinensischer Geschichte im 2. Jh. V. Chr." Ph.D. diss., Rheinischen Friedrich-Wilhelms-Universität, Bonn.

———. 1975. "Zur Geschichte und Chronologie des Untergangs der Oniaden und des Aufstiegs der Hasmonäer." *JSJ* 6:1-46.

Burrows, Millar. 1951. *The Dead Sea Scrolls of St. Mark's Monastery.* Volume II, Fascicle 2: *Plates and Transcription of the Manual of Discipline.* New Haven: American Schools of Oriental Research.

Charles, Robert H. 1902. *The Book of Jubilees; or the Little Genesis.* London: Black.

———. 1912. *The Book of Enoch or 1 Enoch.* Oxford: Clarendon. Reprint, Jerusalem: Makor, 1973.

Charlesworth, James H. 1980. "The Portrayal of the Righteous as an Angel." In *Ideal Figures in Ancient Judaism: Profiles and Paradigms,* edited by John J. Collins and George W. E. Nickelsburg, 135-51. SBLSCS 12. Chico, Calif.: Scholars.

Clines, David J. A. 1984. *The Esther Scroll: The Story of the Story.* JSOTSup 30. Sheffield: JSOT.

Collins, John J. 1984. *The Apocalyptic Imagination: An Introduction to Jewish Apocalyptic Literature.* Grand Rapids: Eerdmans.

———. 1993. *Daniel.* Hermeneia. Minneapolis: Fortress.

———. 1997. *Apocalypticism in the Dead Sea Scrolls.* London and New York: Routledge.

Cowley, Roger W. 1974. "The Biblical Canon of the Ethiopian Orthodox Church Today." *Ostkirchliche Studien* 23:318-23.

Davies, Philip R. 1983. "Calendrical Change and Qumran Origins: An Assessment of VanderKam's Theory." *CBQ* 45:80-89.

Delcor, Mathias. 1976. "Le mythe de la chute des anges et de l'origine des géants comme explication du mal dans le monde dans l'apocalyptique juive: Histoire des traditions." *RHR* 189:3-53.

deSilva, David Arthur. 2002. *Introducing the Apocrypha: Message, Context and Significance.* Grand Rapids: Eerdmans.

Dimant, Devorah. 1974. "The Fallen Angels in the Dead Sea Scrolls and in the Apocryphal and Pseudepigraphic Books Related to Them" (in Hebrew). Ph.D. diss., Hebrew University of Jerusalem.

———. 1992. "New Light from Qumran on the Jewish Pseudepigrapha." In *The Madrid Qumran Congress,* edited by Julio Trebolle Barrera and Luis Vegas Montaner, 2:405-48. Leiden: Brill.

———. 1993. "The Seventy Weeks Chronology (Dan 9,24-27) in the Light of New Qumranic Texts." In *The Book of Daniel: In Light of New Findings,* edited by Adam S. von der Woude, 57-76. BETL 106. Leuven: Peeters.

———. 1996. "The Four Empires of Daniel, Chapter 2, in the Light of Texts from Qumran" (in Hebrew). In *Rivkah Shatz-Uffenheimer Memorial Volume,* edited by Rachel Elior and Joseph Dan, 33-41. Jerusalem Studies in Jewish Thought 12. Jerusalem.

————. 2001. "4QApocryphon of Jeremiah." In *Qumran Cave 4. XXI: Parabiblical Texts,* part 4, 91-260. DJD 30. Oxford: Clarendon.

Doran, Robert. 1981. *Temple Propaganda: The Purpose and Character of 2 Maccabees.* CBQMS 12. Washington: Catholic Biblical Association of America.

Eliade, Mircea. 1956. *Forgerons et alchimistes.* Paris: Flammarion.

Elliott, Mark. 2000. *The Survivors of Israel: A Reconsideration of the Theology of Pre-Christian Judaism.* Grand Rapids: Eerdmans.

————. 2002. "Origins and Functions of Watchers Theodicy." In *The Origins of Enochic Judaism,* edited by Gabriele Boccaccini, 63-75. Turin: Zamorani [= *Henoch* 24].

Endres, John C. 1987. *Biblical Interpretation in the Book of Jubilees.* Washington, D.C.: Catholic Biblical Society of America.

Eshel, Hanan. 1991. "The Prayer of Joseph, a Papyrus from Masada and the Samaritan Temple on ARGARIZIN" (in Hebrew). *Zion* 56:125-36.

————. 1996. "4QMMT and the History of the Hasmonean Period." In *Reading 4QMMT: New Perspectives on Qumran Law and History,* edited by John Kampen and Moshe J. Bernstein, 53-65. SBL Symposium Series 2. Atlanta: Scholars.

————. 1997. "The History of the Qumran Community and Historical Details in the Dead Sea Scrolls" (in Hebrew). *Qadmoniot* 30:86-93.

Feldman, Louis. 1971. "Prolegomenon." In Montague R. James, *The Biblical Antiquities of Philo,* xxv-xxvii. New York: Ktav.

Fitzmyer, Joseph A. 1957-58. "A Feature of Qumran Angelology and the Angels of 1 Cor 11:10." *NTS* 4:48-58. Republished with postscript (1966) in *Paul and the Dead Sea Scrolls,* edited by Jerome Murphy-O'Connor and James H. Charlesworth, 31-47. Christian Origins Library. New York: Crossroad, 1990.

————. 1971. *The Genesis Apocryphon of Qumran Cave I: A Commentary.* 2nd ed. BibOr 18A. Rome: Biblical Institute.

————. 1974. "The Aramaic 'Elect of God' Text from Qumran Cave 4." In *Essays on the Semitic Background of the New Testament,* 127-160. Missoula, Mont.: Scholars.

Flint, Peter W. 2001. "Noncanonical Writings in the Dead Sea Scrolls: Apocrypha, Other Previously Known Writings, Pseudepigrapha." In *The Bible at Qumran: Text, Shape, Interpretation,* edited by Peter W. Flint. Grand Rapids: Eerdmans.

Gibson, John C. L. 1971. *Textbook of Syrian Semitic Inscriptions.* Vol. 1. Oxford: Clarendon.

Goldstein, Jonathan A. 1976. *1 Maccabees.* AB 41. Garden City: Doubleday.

————. 1983. "The Date of the Book of Jubilees." *PAAJR* 50:63-86.

Grabbe, Lester L. 1987. "The End of the Desolations of Jerusalem: From Jeremiah's 70 Years to Daniel's 70 Weeks of Years." In *Early Jewish and Christian Exegesis: Studies in Memory of W. H. Brownlee,* edited by Craig A. Evans and William F. Stinespring, 67-72. Homage 10. Atlanta: Scholars.

————. 1997. "The Seventy-Weeks Prophecy (Daniel 9:24-27) in Early Jewish Interpretation." In *The Quest for Context and Meaning: Studies in Biblical Inter-*

textuality in Honor of J. A. Sanders, edited by Craig A. Evans and Shemaryahu Talmon, 595-611. Biblical Interpretation Series 28. Leiden: Brill.

Graetz, Heinrich H. 1859. "Die mystische Literatur in der gaonaeischen Epoche." *MGWJ* 8:67-78, 103-18, 140-53.

Greenfield, Jonas C. 1973. "Prolegomenon." In Hugo Odeberg, *3 Enoch, or the Hebrew Book of Enoch.* Library of Biblical Studies. Reprint, New York: Ktav.

Grelot, Pierre. 1958. "La légende d'Henoch dans les apocryphes et dans la Bible. Origine et signification." *RSR* 46:5-26, 181-210.

———. 1975. "Hénoch et ses écritures." *RB* 82:484-88.

Gruenwald, Ithamar. 1980. *Apocalyptic and Merkavah Mysticism.* AGJU 14. Leiden: Brill.

———. 2003. *Rituals and Ritual Theory in Ancient Israel.* Leiden: Brill.

Halliwell, Stephen. 1995. *Aristotle: Poetics.* LCL 199. Cambridge: Harvard University Press.

———. 1998. *Aristotle's Poetics.* London: Duckworth.

Halpern-Amaru, Betsy. 1999. *The Empowerment of Women in the Book of Jubilees.* Leiden: Brill.

Hanhart, Robert. 1983. *Septuaginta.* Vol. 8/3: *Esther.* Göttingen: Vandenhoeck & Ruprecht.

Hanson, Paul D. 1975. *The Dawn of Apocalyptic.* Philadelphia: Fortress.

———. 1977. "Rebellion in Heaven: Azazel and Euhemeristic Heroes in Enoch 6–11." *JBL* 96:195-233.

Hartman, Lars. 1979. *Asking for Meaning: A Study of 1 Enoch 1–5.* ConBOT 12. Lund: Gleerup.

Hawthorn, Jeremy. 1994. *A Concise Glossary of Contemporary Literary Theory.* 2nd ed. London: Arnold.

Hayes, Christine E. 2002. *Gentile Impurities and Jewish Identities: Intermarriage and Conversion from the Bible to the Talmud.* New York: Oxford University Press.

Hengel, Martin. 1974. *Judaism and Hellenism: Studies in Their Encounter in Palestine in the Early Hellenistic Period.* Philadelphia: Fortress.

———. 1980. *Jews, Greeks, and Barbarians: Aspects of the Hellenization of Judaism in the Pre-Christian Period.* Philadelphia: Fortress.

Himmelfarb, Martha. 1997. "A Kingdom of Priests: The Democratization of the Priesthood in the Literature of Second Temple Judaism." *Journal of Jewish Thought and Philosophy* 6:89-104.

———. 1999. "Levi, Phinehas, and the Problem of Intermarriage at the Time of the Maccabean Revolt." *Jewish Studies Quarterly* 6:1-24.

Holladay, Carl R. 1983. *Fragments from Hellenistic Jewish Authors.* Vol. 1, *Historians.* SBLTT 20. Pseudepigrapha Series 10. Chico, Calif.: Scholars.

Horgan, Maurya P. 1979. *Pesharim: Qumran Interpretations of Biblical Books.* CBQMS 8. Washington, D.C.: Catholic Biblical Association of America.

Jaubert, Annie. 1953. "Le calendrier des Jubilés et de la secte de Qumrân. Ses origines bibliques." *VT* 3:250-64.

———. 1957a. "Le calendrier de Jubilés et les jours liturgiques de la semaine." *VT* 7:35-61.

———. 1957b. *La date de la Cène. Calendrier biblique et liturgie chrétienne.* Paris: Gabalda.

———. 1965. *The Date of the Last Supper.* Translated by I. Rafferty. Staten Island, N.Y.: Alba House.

Jellinek, Adolph. 1967. *Bet ha-Midrash.* Reprint, Jerusalem: Wahrmann Books.

Jeremias, Gert. 1963. *Der Lehrer der Gerechtigkeit, Studien zur Umwelt des Neuen Testaments* 2. Göttingen: Vandenhoeck & Ruprecht.

Jung, Leo. 1974. *Fallen Angels in Jewish, Christian, and Mohammedan Literature.* New York: Ktav.

Kappler, Werner, and Robert Hanhart. 1976. *Septuaginta.* Vol. 9: *Maccabaeorum liber II.* Göttingen: Vandenhoeck & Ruprecht.

Kasher, Aryeh. 1988. *Jews, Idumaeans, and Ancient Arabs.* TSAJ 18. Tübingen: Mohr.

Kraemer, David. 1991. "The Formation of the Rabbinic Canon: Authority and Boundaries." *JBL* 110:613-30.

Krauss, Samuel. 1895. "La fête de Hanoucca." *REJ* 30:24-43, 204-219.

Kugel, James. 1996. "The Holiness of Israel and the Land in Second Temple Times." In *Texts, Temples, and Traditions: A Tribute to Menahem Haran,* edited by Michael V. Fox et al. Winona Lake, Ind.: Eisenbrauns.

Kvanvig, Helge S. 2002a. "Gen 6:1-4 as an Antediluvian Event." *SJOT* 16:79-112.

———. 2002b. "Origin and Identity of the Enoch Group." In *The Origins of Enochic Judaism,* edited by Gabriele Boccaccini, 207-21. Turin: Zamorani [= *Henoch* 24].

Larson, Erik. Forthcoming. *The Translation of Enoch: From Aramaic into Greek.* Leiden: Brill.

Leiman, Sid Z. 1976. *The Canonization of Hebrew Scripture: The Talmudic and Midrashic Evidence.* Transactions of the Connecticut Academy of Arts and Sciences 47. Hamden: Archon Books.

Leszynsky, Rudolf. 1911. "Das Laubhüttenfest Chanukka." *MGWJ* 55:400-418.

Levine, Baruch A. 1970. "Appendix: The Language of the Magical Bowls." In *A History of the Jews in Babylonia.* V: *Later Sassanian Times,* edited by Jacob Neusner, 343-75. Leiden: Brill.

———. 1978. "The Temple Scroll: Aspects of Its Historical Provenance and Literary Character." *BASOR* 232:5-23.

Liber, Maurice. 1912. "Hanoucca et Souccot." *REJ* 63:20-29.

Lieberman, Saul. 1980. "Appendices." In Ithamar Gruenwald, *Apocalyptic and Merkavah Mysticism,* 235-41. AGJU 14. Leiden: Brill.

Maier, Johann. 1992. "Shîrê Ôlat hash-Shabbat, Some Observations on Their Calendric Implications and on Their Style." In *The Madrid Qumran Congress: Proceedings of the International Congress on the Dead Sea Scrolls, Madrid, 18-21 March 1991,* edited by Julio Trebolle Barrera and Luis Vegas Montaner, 2:543-60. STDJ 11. Leiden: Brill.

Margaliot, Mordecai. 1966. *Sefer ha-Razim, Hu' Sefer Keshafim mi-Tequfat ha-Talmud.* Jerusalem: American Academy for Jewish Research.

McDonald, Lee Martin. 1996. *The Formation of the Christian Biblical Canon.* Revised and expanded edition. Peabody, Mass.: Hendrickson.

Medico, Henri Edel del. 1957. *L'Énigma des Manuscrits de la Mer Morte.* Paris: Plon.

————. 1965. "Le cadre historique des fêtes de Hanukkah et de Purîm." *VT* 15:238-270.

Metso, Sarianna. 1997. *The Textual Development of the Qumran Community Rule.* STDJ 21. Leiden: Brill.

Milik, Josef T. 1955. "Annexes à la règle de la communauté." In *Qumran Cave I,* edited by Dominique Barthélemy and Josef T. Milik, 107-18. DJD 1. Oxford: Clarendon.

————. 1976. *The Books of Enoch: Aramaic Fragments of Qumrân Cave 4.* Oxford: Clarendon.

Momigliano, Arnaldo. 1975. "The Second Book of Maccabees." *Classical Philology* 70:81-88.

Moore, George F. 1927-30. *Judaism in the First Centuries of the Christian Era: The Age of the Tannaim.* 3 vols. Cambridge: Harvard University Press.

Mopsik, Charles. 1989. *Le Livre hébreu d'Hénoch ou Livre des Palais.* Collection "Les Dix Paroles." Verdier: Lagrasse.

Morgenstern, Julius. 1924. "The Three Calendars of Ancient Israel." *HUCA* 1:13-78.

————. 1948. "The Chanukkah Festival and the Calendar of Ancient Israel." *HUCA* 21:365-496.

————. 1955. "The Calendar of the Jubilees, Its Origin and Its Character." *VT* 5:34-76.

Murphy-O'Connor, Jerome. 1974. "The Essenes and Their History." *RB* 81:215-44.

————. 1976. "Demetrius I and the Teacher of Righteousness (I Macc X, 25-45)." *RB* 83:400-420.

————. 1977. "The Essenes in Palestine." *BA* 40:100-124.

Najman, Hindy. 1999. "Interpretation as Primordial Writing: Jubilees and Its Authority Conferring Strategies." *JSJ* 30:379-410.

Newsom, Carol A. 1985. *Songs of the Sabbath Sacrifice: A Critical Edition.* HSS 27. Atlanta: Scholars.

Newsom, Carol A., and James H. Charlesworth (with Brent A. Strawn and Henry M. Rietz). 1999. *Angelic Liturgy: Songs of the Sabbath Sacrifice.* PTSDSSP 4b. Tübingen: Mohr Siebeck/Westminster John Knox.

Nickelsburg, George W. E. 1977. "Apocalyptic and Myth in Enoch 6–11." *JBL* 96:383-405.

————. 1980. *Jewish Literature between the Bible and the Mishnah.* Philadelphia: Fortress.

————. 1984. "The Bible Rewritten and Expanded." In *Jewish Writings of the Second Temple Period: Apocrypha, Pseudepigrapha, Qumran Sectarian Writings, Philo, Josephus,* edited by Michael E. Stone, 89-156. CRINT II. Philadelphia: Fortress.

————. 1999. "The Books of Enoch at Qumran: What We Know and What We Need to Think About." In *Antikes Judentum und Frühes Christentum: Festschrift für*

Hartmut Stegemann zum 65. Geburtstag, edited by Bernd Kollmann, Wolfgang Reinbold, and Annette Steudel, 99-113. Berlin: De Gruyter.

———. 2001. *1 Enoch 1: A Commentary on the Book of 1 Enoch, Chapters 1–36; 81–108.* Hermeneia. Minneapolis: Fortress.

Nodet, Étienne. 1986. "La Dédicace, les Maccabées et le Messie." *RB* 93:321-375.

Odeberg, Hugo. 1928. *3 Enoch, or the Hebrew Book of Enoch.* Cambridge: University Press.

Perrot, Charles, and Pierre Bogaert. 1976. With the collaboration of Daniel J. Harrington. *Pseudo-Philon, Les Antiquités Bibliques,* 2 vols. SC 230. Paris: Cerf.

Puech, Émile. 2000. "Elect of God." In *Encyclopedia of the Dead Sea Scrolls,* edited by Lawrence H. Schiffman and James C. VanderKam, 1:240-41. 2 vols. Oxford: Oxford University Press,

———. 2001. *Qumrân grotte 4. XXII: Textes Araméens, Première partie, 4Q529-549.* DJD 31. Oxford: Clarendon.

Rabin, Chaim. 1958. *The Zadokite Documents.* 2nd rev. ed. Oxford: Clarendon.

Rankin, Oliver Shaw. 1930. *The Origins of the Festival of Hanukkah: The Jewish New-Age Festival.* Edinburgh: T&T Clark.

Rapaport, Uriel. 1965. "Jewish Religious Propaganda and Proselytism in the Period of the Second Commonwealth" (in Hebrew). Ph.D. diss., Hebrew University of Jerusalem.

Reed, Annette Yoshiko. 2002. "What the Fallen Angels Taught: The Reception-History of the Book of the Watchers in Judaism and Christianity." Ph.D. diss., Princeton University.

Reeves, John C., ed. 1994. *Tracing the Threads: Studies in the Vitality of Jewish Pseudepigrapha.* SBLEJL 6. Atlanta: Scholars.

Regev, Eyal. 2001. "Hanukkah, Succot and the Days of Milluim in II Maccabees" (in Hebrew). *Beit Mikra* 46:227-43.

Ricoeur, Paul. 1984. *Time and Narrative I.* Chicago: University of Chicago Press.

Rimmon-Kenan, Shlomith. 1989. *Narrative Fiction, Contemporary Poetics.* London: Routledge.

Rofé, Alexander. 1988. "The Onset of Sects in Postexilic Judaism: Neglected Evidence from the Septuagint, Trito-Isaiah, Ben Sira, and Malachi." In *The Social World of Formative Christianity and Judaism: Essays in Tribute to Howard Clark Kee,* edited by Jacob Neusner et al., 39-49. Philadelphia: Fortress.

Rowley, Harold Henry. 1957. *Jewish Apocalyptic and the Dead Sea Scrolls.* London: Athlone.

Rubenstein, Jeffrey L. 1992. "The History of Sukkot During the Second Temple and Rabbinic Periods: Studies in the Continuity and Change of a Festival." Ph.D. diss., Columbia University.

———. 1995. *The History of Sukkot in the Second Temple and Rabbinic Periods.* BJS 302. Atlanta: Scholars.

Ruiten, Jacques T. A. G. M. van. 2000. *Primaeval History Interpreted: The Rewriting of Genesis 1–11 in the Book of Jubilees.* JSJSup 66. Leiden: Brill.

Sacchi, Paolo. 1994. *Storia del Secondo Tempio: Israele tra VI secolo a.C. e I. secolo d.C.* Turin: Societa Editrice Internazionale.

———. 1997. *Jewish Apocalyptic and Its History.* Sheffield: Sheffield Academic Press.

Schäfer, Peter. 1981. *Synopse zur Hekhalot-Literatur.* TSAJ 2. Tübingen: Mohr Siebeck.

———. 1983. "Tradition and Redaction in Hekhalot Literature." *JJS* 14:172-81.

———. 1992. *The Hidden and Manifest God: Some Major Themes in Early Jewish Mysticism.* Translated by Aubrey Pomerance. Albany: State University of New York Press.

Schiffman, Lawrence H. 1982. "Merkavah Speculation at Qumran: The 4Q Serekh Shirot Olat ha-Shabbat." In *Mystics, Philosophers, and Politicians, Alexander Altmann Festschrift,* edited by Jehuda Reiharz and Daniel Swetschinski, 15-47. Duke Monographs in Medieval and Renaissance Studies 5. Durham, N.C.: Duke University Press.

———. 1989. *The Eschatological Community of the Dead Sea Scrolls.* SBLMS 38. Atlanta: Scholars.

———. 1994. *Reclaiming the Dead Sea Scrolls.* New York: Doubleday.

———. 1997. "Mysteries." In *Qumran Cave 4. XV: Sapiential Texts, Part 1,* edited by Torleif Elgvin et al., 31-123. DJD 20. Oxford: Clarendon.

———. 1997-2001. "Second Temple Literature and the Cairo Genizah." *PAAJR* 63:139-61.

Scholem, Gershon. 1965. *Jewish Gnosticism, Merkabah Mysticism, and Talmudic Tradition.* New York: Jewish Theological Seminary of America.

Schuller, Eileen M., and Moshe J. Bernstein. 2001. "4QNarrative and Poetic Composition[a-b]." In *Wadi Daliyeh II: The Samaria Papyri from Wadi Daliyeh and Qumran Cave 4. XXIII: Miscellanea,* part 2, edited by Douglas M. Gropp et al., 151-97, 371-72. DJD 28. Oxford: Clarendon.

Schürer, Emil. 1973-87. *The History of the Jewish People in the Age of Jesus Christ, 175 BC–AD 135.* Edited by Geza Vermes and Fergus Millar. 3 vols. Edinburgh: T. & T. Clark.

Schwartz, Daniel R. 1996. "MMT, Josephus and the Pharisees." In *Reading 4QMMT: New Perspectives on Qumran Law and History,* edited by John Kampen and Moshe J. Bernstein, 67-80. SBL Symposium Series 2. Atlanta: Scholars.

Schwarz, Eberhard. 1982. *Identität durch Abgrenzung: Abgrenzungsprozesse in Israel im 2. vorchristlichen Jahrhundert und ihre traditionsgeschichtlichen Voraussetzungen: Zugleich ein Beitrag zur Erforschung des Jubiläenbuches.* Frankfurt: Peter Lang.

Scott, James. 2002. *Geography in Early Judaism and Christianity: The Book of Jubilees,* 126-34. SNTSMS 113. Cambridge: Cambridge University Press.

Shemesh, Aharon. 1997. "The Holy Angels Are in Their Council: The Exclusion of Deformed Persons from Holy Places in Qumranic and Rabbinic Literature." *DSD* 4:179-206.

Skehan, Patrick, and Alexander Di Lella. 1987. *The Wisdom of Ben Sira.* AB 39. Garden City, N.Y.: Doubleday.

Stegemann, Hartmut. 1971. *Die Entstehung der Qumrangemeinde.* Bonn: Rheinische Friedrich Wilhelms Universität.

———. 1993. *Die Essener, Qumran, Johannes der Täufer und Jesus.* Freiburg: Herder.

Stern, Sacha. 2001. *Calendar and Community: A History of the Jewish Calendar, 2nd century BCE to 10th century CE.* New York: Oxford University Press.

Steudel, Annette. 1993. "Acharit ha-yamim in the Texts from Qumran". *RevQ* 16:225-46.

Stone, Michael E. 1988. "Enoch, Aramaic Levi and Sectarian Origins." *JSJ* 19:159-70.

Sukenik, Eleazar L. 1955. *The Dead Sea Scrolls of the Hebrew University.* Jerusalem: Magnes.

Suter, David W. 1979. "Fallen Angel, Fallen Priest: The Problem of Family Purity in 1 Enoch 6–16." *HUCA* 50:115-35.

Swartz, Michael D. 1996. *Scholastic Magic: Ritual and Revelation in Early Jewish Mysticism.* Princeton: Princeton University Press.

Talmon, Shemaryahu. 1951. "Yom Hakkippurim in the Habakkuk Scroll." *Bib* 32:549-63.

———. 1988. "Waiting for the Messiah — The Conceptual Universe of the Qumran Covenanters." In *Judaisms and Their Messiahs,* edited by Jacob Neusner, et al., 111-37. Cambridge: Cambridge University Press.

———. 1989. "The Calendar of the Covenanters of the Judean Desert." In *The World of Qumran from Within: Collected Studies,* 141-85. Jerusalem: Magnes.

Talmon, Shemaryahu (with Jonathan Ben-Dov). 2001. "Calendrical Documents and Mishmarot." In *Qumran Cave 4. XVI: Calendrical Texts,* edited by Shemaryahu Talmon, Jonathan Ben-Dov and Uwe Glessmer, 1-166. DJD 21. Oxford: Clarendon.

Tcherikover, Victor. 1972. "The Hellenistic Movement in Jerusalem and Antiochus' Persecutions." In *The Hellenistic Age: Political History of Jewish Palestine from 332 B.C.E. to 67 B.C.E.*" Vol. 6 of *The World History of the Jewish People,* edited by Abraham Schalit, 115-44. London: Allen.

Torrey, Charles C. 1945. *Apocalyptic Literature: A Brief Introduction.* New Haven: Yale University.

Ulfgard, Håkan. 1998. *The Story of* Sukkot: *The Setting, Shaping, and Sequel of the Biblical Feast of Tabernacles.* Beiträge zur Geschichte der biblischen Exegese 34. Tübingen: Mohr Siebeck.

Ulrich, Eugene. 2002. "Index of Passages in the Biblical Texts." In *The Texts from the Judaean Desert: Indices and Introduction,* edited by Emanuel Tov, 185-201. DJD 39. Oxford: Clarendon.

VanBeek, Lawrence. 2000. "1 Enoch among Jews and Christians; A Fringe Connection?" In *Christian-Jewish Relations through the Centuries,* edited by Stanley E. Porter and Birger A. Pearson, 93-115. Sheffield: Sheffield Academic Press.

VanderKam, James C. 1977. *Textual and Historical Studies in the Book of Jubilees.* HSM 14. Missoula, Mont.: Scholars.

———. 1978. "Enoch Traditions in Jubilees and Other Second-Century Sources." In SBLSP, edited by Paul J. Achtemeier, 1:229-51 [= VanderKam 2000a, 305-31].

———. 1979. "The Origin, Character, and Early History of the 364-Day Calendar: A Reassessment of Jaubert's Hypotheses." *CBQ* 41:390-411.

———. 1981. "2 Maccabees 6:7a and Calendrical Change in Jerusalem." *JSJ* 12:52-74.

———. 1984. *Enoch and the Growth of an Apocalyptic Tradition*. CBQMS 16. Washington, D.C.: Catholic Biblical Association of America.

———. 1987. "Hanukkah: Its Timing and Significance According to 1 and 2 Maccabees," *JSP* 1:23-40.

———. 1989. *The Book of Jubilees*. 2 vols. CSCO 510-11. Scriptores Aethiopici 87-88. Louvain: Peeters.

———. 1992a. "Jubilees, Book of." In *ABD* 3:1039-42.

———. 1992b. "Dedication, Feast of." In *ABD* 2:123-125.

———. 1994. "Calendrical Texts and the Origins of the Dead Sea Community." In *Methods of Investigation of the Dead Sea Scrolls and the Khirbet Qumran Site: Present Realities and Future Prospects*, edited by Michael O. Wise, Norman Golb, John J. Collins, and Dennis G. Pardee, 371-88. Annals of the New York Academy of Sciences 722. New York: New York Academy of Sciences.

———. 1995. *Enoch: A Man for All Generations*. Studies on Personalities of the Old Testament. Columbia: University of South Carolina Press.

———. 1997. "The Origins and Purposes of the Book of Jubilees." In *Studies in the Book of Jubilees*, edited by Matthias Albani, Jörg Frey, and Armin Lange, 3-24. TSAJ 65. Tübingen: Mohr Siebeck.

———. 1998. *Calendars in the Dead Sea Scrolls*. Literature of the Dead Sea Scrolls. London: Routledge.

———. 1999. "The Angel Story in the Book of Jubilees." In *Pseudepigraphic Perspectives: The Apocrypha and Pseudepigrapha in Light of the Dead Sea Scrolls; Proceedings of the International Symposium of the Orion Center for the Study of the Dead Sea Scrolls and Associated Literature, 12-14 January 1997*, edited by Esther G. Chazon and Michael E. Stone, 151-70. STDJ 31. Leiden: Brill.

———. 2000a. *From Revelation to Canon: Studies in the Hebrew Bible and Second Temple Literature*. JSJSup 62. Leiden: Brill.

———. 2000b. "Jubilees, Book of." In *Encyclopedia of the Dead Sea Scrolls*, edited by Lawrence H. Schiffman and James C. VanderKam, 1:434-38. 2 vols. Oxford: Oxford University Press.

———. 2001a. *The Book of Jubilees*. Guides to Apocrypha and Pseudepigrapha. Sheffield: Sheffield Academic Press.

———. 2001b. *An Introduction to Early Judaism*. Grand Rapids: Eerdmans.

———. 2002. "Questions of Canon Viewed through the Dead Sea Scrolls." In *The Canon Debate*, edited by Lee Martin MacDonald and James A. Sanders, 91-109. Peabody, Mass.: Hendrickson.

Vaux, Roland de. 1997. *Ancient Israel: Its Life and Institutions*. Translated by

J. McHugh. London: Darton, Longman & Todd. Reprinted Grand Rapids: Eerdmans.

Vermes, Geza. 2003. "Eschatological World View in the Dead Sea Scrolls and in the New Testament." In *Emanuel: Studies in the Hebrew Bible, Septuagint, and Dead Sea Scrolls in Honor of Emanuel Tov,* edited by Shalom M. Paul et al., 479-94. VTSup 94/1-2. Leiden: Brill.

Wacholder, Ben Zion (with Sholom Wacholder). 1995. "Patterns of Biblical Dates and Qumran's Calendar: The Fallacy of Jaubert's Hypothesis." *HUCA* 66:1-40.

Werman, Cana. 1995. "The Attitude towards Gentiles in the Book of Jubilees and Qumran Literature Compared with Early Tannaitic *Halakhah* and Contemporary Pseudepigrapha" (in Hebrew). Ph.D. diss., Hebrew University of Jerusalem.

Wright, Benjamin G. 1997. "Fear the Lord and Honor the Priest." In *The Book of Ben Sira in Modern Research,* edited by Pancratius C. Beentjes, 189-222. Berlin: De Gruyter.

———. 2002. "Sirach and 1 Enoch: Some Further Considerations." In *The Origins of Enochic Judaism,* edited by Gabriele Boccaccini, 179-187. Turin: Zamorani [= *Henoch* 24].

Yadin, Yigael. 1965. *The Ben Sira Scroll from Masada.* Jerusalem: Israel Exploration Society.

PART THREE

THE APOCALYPSE OF WEEKS

History as a Battlefield of Two Antagonistic Powers in the Apocalypse of Weeks and in the Rule of the Community

Klaus Koch

The scholarly debate concerning the growth of the Enoch literature is today mostly confined to a search for possible roots in earlier biblical traditions. Although there is a general agreement that the Enoch figure as a primeval sage and diviner was borrowed from the Mesopotamian tradition around Enmeduranki, only a few colleagues such as James VanderKam and Helge Kvanvig have attempted to pursue the relationship between the Akkadian and the Enochic texts.

Because the manuscripts of Enoch in the original Aramaic survived only among the literature of the exclusive *yaḥad* at Qumran, it is presupposed that the Mesopotamian precursor of the hero was of little interest to the concerns of 1 Enoch and that the latter originated within a group which cherished only the traditions of Israel. However, like other apocalypses of that time, 1 Enoch was written in Aramaic, and Aramaic was a lingua franca from Asia Minor to north India since the Persian period, a medium of communication not only for commerce and politics but also for an international exchange of ideas on astronomy and mythology.

The book of Daniel delivers a telling example. Not only its heroes, but also the authors seem to have been "taught the literature and language of the Chaldeans" (Dan 1:4), which in the second century B.C.E. probably already means Aramaic. The topics of the Nebuchadnezzar chapters have Mesopotamian or Iranian origins (Koch 1994, 126-38; 2001, 267-71).

I thank Charlotte Hempel for the thorough improvement of my English manuscript.

As far as 1 Enoch is concerned, in addition to the former Enmeduranki traditions a great deal of lore from the ancient Near East can be detected in the individual booklets. Thus, the Astronomical Book depends on the Akkadian MUL.APIN (Albani 1994; Koch 2003, 21-42), while the Book of Giants knows a dream of Gilgamesh (Stuckenbruck 1997, 72-74, 162-67). "Enochic traditions reveal central features and developments which parallel very closely the twofold nature of omens and their evolution in scientific and predictive directions in Mesopotamia . . . mantic traditions from Mesopotamia provided a considerable part of the context within which Enochic literature arose and grew" (VanderKam 1984a, 70).

Regarding the Apocalypse of Weeks, I would like to demonstrate that its leading motif — as well as some parallel utterances in the Qumran literature — also reflects a foreign source, in this case an Iranian one.

The seventeen verses of the short treatise comment on the course of world history from creation to an eschatological completion, but they do not tell a continuous story. The reader is expected to know the important stages according to traditions which may have been to some degree identical with biblical traditions but otherwise also with parabiblical texts (e.g., regarding chronology). These sources deliver the *bruta facta,* which are now alluded to in a coded manner. This basic framework is then supplemented with dualistic categories which are taken, as I hope to demonstrate, from outside the Israelite traditions. In the view of the author, the course of universal history needs to be taken into account from a metahistorical perspective.

Before I proceed, a remark concerning the language of the book is in order. The urtext of the apocalypse was doubtless written in Aramaic. The full text, however, is available only in the Ethiopic version. This translation, like its Greek forerunner, was not the result of an objective, philologically correct enterprise, but was determined by the worldview of the Ethiopic, Syrian, or Greek translators. The original meaning of the apocalypse of the second century B.C.E. comes to the fore only when we try to translate the Ethiopic text back into Aramaic. Therefore a historically oriented interpretation of a pre-Christian Enoch remains in many cases a hypothetical one.

The Chronological Frame

In the seventeen verses the past and future history of humankind is divided into ten units of seven. The word *shavua'* means any fixed seven-unit of time, normally the week but also the Sabbath year or a greater sabbatical cycle (Sokoloff 1990, 533; Koch 1996, 48). Each passage starts with the reference to the number of the epoch. The time of the world is not infinite and does not flow continuously. Rather, it is structured in finite and sevenfold entities since creation. The purpose of emphasizing the numbers was to enable the reader to be aware of his own situation and the time remaining before the end of the world. So *shavua'* must refer to a fixed number of years and not to a varying length of weeks.

Elsewhere I have tried to demonstrate that the author of the Apocalypse of Weeks reckoned 490 years for each unit, comparable with Jubilees, 4QMelchizedek and 4QPesher on the Apocalypse of Weeks (cf. DJD 26 [2000], 187-91, and Hanan Eshel regarding 4Q390 in this volume), although mostly in disagreement with the chronology of MT or LXX. Thus the 490 years for the third period can be presupposed even according to MT as the time between the procreation of Arpachshad after the flood and the procreation of Isaac as successor of Abraham (Gen 11:10–17:7, 21; 21:1).

The same number for the second period can be found in Samuel and Genesis for the fourth period if the 60 years of Isaac (Gen 25:26) were connected with the 430 years of the "sons of Israel" (including Jacob himself) in Canaan and Egypt (Exod 12:40). Concerning the fifth one, MT presupposes 500 years from the exodus to the dedication of the temple (1 Kings 6:1, 37f.; 7:1); the Apocalypse of Weeks sees the sum reduced to 10 × 49 years (cf. Koch 1996, 58-65, for the more complicated reckoning regarding the other periods). Such a search for the structure of time according to predestinated fixed numbers has its forerunners in Hebrew Scriptures but also parallels in Mesopotamia and Iran.

The author and the intended reader probably lived in the seventh week during the persecution of Antiochus IV Epiphanes, before the decisive change of destiny when sevenfold wisdom will be given to the righteous ones and the roots of wickedness will be destroyed (1 En 93:9f.). The desecration of the temple under Antiochus IV is not mentioned. Therefore a pre-Maccabean time for the author is often supposed (cf. Michael Knibb in this volume). Since that week started with the exile, the 490 years (cf. Dan 9:24) do not seem to be over yet. However, the awaited eschatological turn will not be a sudden one. There will be a considerable period of transition from the present constitution of the world to the eschatological completion taking up three more weeks. We find no imminent *Naherwartung* in this apocalypse.

Qushṭa as a Fundamental Power and Its Adversaries *Ḥamsa* and *Shiqra* in the Course of History

"The key concept of the Apocalypse" is the notion of *qushṭa* (indet. *qeshoṭ*), as George Nickelsburg (2001, 441) has recognized; but its effect changes in the sequence of the epochs because a pair of opposing forces are also at work, sometimes very actively. A survey of the catchwords displays the different content of the ten epochs according to the Ethiopic (E) and the Aramaic (A) versions:

Ethiopic version	Aramaic version

Prologue [1 En 93:1]:

Enoch began to speak	Enoch [took up] his *mantlâ*,
from the books . . .	saying,
Concerning the children of *ṣedeq*	Concerning the sons of *qushṭa*
+ the chosen of the *'alam*	+ the chosen of the *'alma*
and concerning the plant	[who have grown up] from the
of *ṣedeq warete*	sprout of *ysbt'* [*wqsh'* . . .]
(Revealed were to me:)	
. . . heavenly vision,	[. . . visions of heaven],
words of the holy angels,	word of the Watchers and
tablets of heaven	Holy Ones [. . .]

I Week: From Adam to Enoch (Gen 1-5) [1 En 93:3]:

| . . . *kuenane waṣedeq* endured[1] | until me *qushṭa* [endured?] |

II Week: From Enoch's Sons to the Flood and Noah (Gen 6-9) [1 En 93:4]:

. . . great *'eka waguelut* arises . . .	*shiqra weḥamsa* spring up
. . . a man saved . . .	
Afterwards(?) *'amasa* grows;	
The *sher'ata* was made for sinners	

III Week: From Noah's Sons to Abraham (Gen 10-25) [1 En 93:5]:

| Plant of *kuenane waṣedeq* chosen; | [. . . *nishbat qushṭa* . . .] |
| Out of it a plant of *ṣedeq la 'alam* | |

---

1. For "endured," cf. Knibb (1978, 2:224) and Nickelsburg (2001, 435[3b]) against the former translation "was delayed"; thus still Black (1985, 289).

IV Week: From Isaac to Sinai (?) (Gen 26-Exod) [1 En 93:6]:

Visions of the holy and righteous
sher'ata for all generations
and an enclosure (tabernacle) made

V Week: From the Exodus to the First Temple (1 Kings 6-8) [1 En 93:7]:

building of *sebhat wamangeshet*   [*bet rebuta wemalkuta*]
la'alam

VI Week: From the Kingdoms to the Exile (1 Kgs 11–2 Kgs 25) [1 En 93:8]:

Blindness of people, lack of wisdom,
A man ascends
House of *mangeshet*

VII Week: From the Return to Antiochus IV (?) (cf. Dan 9:24) [1 En 93:9-10, 11]:

Apostate generation . . .	
ṣadeqan chosen	Witnesses of *qeshoṭ 'alma* chosen
from the plant of *ṣedeq zala 'alam*	from the plant of *qeshoṭ 'alma*
get sevenfold teaching.	get sevenfold teaching and knowledge.
Rooting out of the roots	Rooting out of the foundations
of *'amasa.*	of *ḥamsa weshiqra*
Sinners destroyed by sword	to make . . .

VIII Week: Country Renewed [1 En 91:12-13]:

A week of *ṣedeq,*	A week of *qeshoṭ,*
Sword for *kuenane ṣedeq,*	Sword for *qashiṭin* for executing *din*
Sinners into the hand of *ṣedeqa,*	*qeshoṭ* from all *rashi'in*
Inheritance of houses because of *ṣedeqa,*	Getting riches in *qeshoṭ,*
House of the Great King	Temple of the kingdom of the Great
built in glory *la'alam*	built for all generations of *'alamin*

IX Week: Earth Renewed [1 En 91:14]:

kuenane ṣedeq revealed	*qeshoṭ* + *[din?] qeshoṭ* revealed
for the whole *'alam;*	for all children of the earth;
Deeds of *rashi'in* vanish,	Workers of *rashi'in* vanish
Destruction of *'alam,*	from the earth, thrown into the pit.
All men desire path of *rete*	All men [see] ways of *qeshoṭ 'alma*

X Week: Cosmos renewed and Great Judgment [1 En 91:15-16]:

kuenane la'alam	*din 'alma* and end of the great *din*
executed on the Watchers;	[executes among angels];
First heaven vanishes,	First heaven vanishes,
New eternal heaven appears,	New heaven appears,
Sevenfold light of powers	Sevenfold light of powers
of heaven *la'alam*	of heaven for all *'lmny[n*

Epilogue: "Weeks without numbers" [1 En 91:17]:

Emerging in goodness and *ṣedeq,*	*[. . . we] qushṭa* are done
Sin no more mentioned *la'alam*	

Surprisingly no direct divine activity is mentioned in this dramatic summary of the times of the world. God does not intervene either before or during the ten epochs. There is no "Lord of the sheep" who becomes active in times of danger as in the Animal Apocalypse (1 En 89:14ff.). Indeed, in the preamble (1 En 93:1) Enoch announces that he had heard the message as a *memar* of the watchers and holy ones and read it in the heavenly tablets, but God himself had not spoken to him. In the remainder of the Apocalypse of Weeks, even these otherworldly agents are not mentioned again.

Passive constructions dominate grammatically in nearly all the events within the ten weeks: a man will be saved (93:4), or men will be chosen (93:5, 10), a law will be made (93:4, 6), visions will be seen (93:10), an enclosure will be made, then a house of glory built (93:6f.), and later burned (93:8), but renewed with the eschatological fulfillment (91:13). The living ones will be blinded and thereafter the chosen root scattered (93:6, 8). With the turn of world history in the eighth week, first wisdom, then a sword will be given to the *qashiṭin* (93:10; 91:12). Neither God, nor his heavenly agents, nor his demonic adversaries come to the fore. Certainly, the reader ought to suppose that these sentences contain a *passivum divinum,* but the ultimate source of the development remains veiled. *Qushṭa* is presented as effective in the background, but it is more a field of power than a creator. Surprisingly, there is no explicit connection with God; there is no mention of God's *qushṭa*, nor is this phenomenon explicitly derived from creation.

On the other hand, neither does humankind determine the course of the periods. Even human actions are not referred to prior to the eschatological turn, unless the ascension of Elijah (93:8) should be seen as a sign of his own activity. Only with the seventh week will a generation with deeds of *ṭ'wt'* arise (93:9), if we follow Milik's reconstruction (1976, 265f.); but does "aberration, straying away" denote a conscious and deliberate action? Or is it an outcome produced by deceit and violence as the negative field of power in the world?

The righteous become particularly active in the eighth week. Now they will receive a sword to execute judgment over all the wicked and earn possession of the land, as descendants of the plant of Abraham (91:12f.; cf. 93:5). Thereafter the eternal temple will be built — this is no longer presented as a result of their initiative but pronounced with the *passivum*. In the ninth week judgment over the human beings without human agents is predicted all over the earth. The innocent — and therefore surviving — part of humankind will henceforth look on the path of *qushṭa* forever (91:14); but is this behavior a conscious decision which must be renewed again and again, or the result of the now overwhelming power of *qushṭa*? Regarding the final, tenth week, there is no reference to any human participation in actions. In the succeeding numberless weeks the doing of *qushṭa* will become a matter of course for human beings, with the dangerous alternative no longer a threat.

If history is made neither by God nor by humankind, what is its driving force? The Apocalypse of Weeks presents an antagonistic field of powers as responsible for the changing developments through the ages. A positive force, *qushṭa*, will always be active as the motor of progress, whereas its negative counterpart does not appear as a single entity but is represented chiefly by the pair deceit *(shiqra)* and violence *(ḥamsa)*, which bring about wickedness and disaster again and again. *Qushṭa* is the decisive force in the earliest history of the created world and its ultimate goal (cf. 10:16-19; 32:[3]; 77:3; 107:1).

Milik and Nickelsburg translate *qushṭa* as "righteousness," but this usage seems one-sided; the Ethiopic equivalent indeed is *ṣedeq*, but is often supplemented by a second noun (e.g., *rete'*). Others prefer "truth" (cf. the context in 13:10; 14:1) or *Wahrheit* (Beyer 1984, 687f.). The complex semantic problem is apparent in comparable texts, where a Hebrew *Vorlage* as well as an Aramaic translation are available. In the Targum of Isaiah *qeshoṭ/qushṭa* appears eleven times, as equivalent to Hebrew *'emet*, but eighteen times for *ṣedeq* (masculine), referring to a divine gift as a rule. Never does it appear, however, for *ṣedaqa* (feminine), which primarily means human behavior (Koch 2003, 65-90).

1. In the first week *qushṭa* is the earliest phenomenon worth mentioning, enduring until the time of Enoch (93:3). It was apparently established with creation (cf. Hebrew *ṣedeq* Ps 89:15 as foundation of the divine throne; cf. further Pss 97:2; 99:4). In the author's view it remained powerful in spite of the fall of Adam and the murder of Cain, if both episodes are presupposed. Its existence as a field of power precedes the actions of any individual. However, in the weeks after Enoch *qushṭa* is suppressed, comes to the fore only at specific situations. But in the last three weeks entire eras will be determined by it (1 En 91:12, 14).

2. In the second week the two opposing powers of deceit and violence, *shiqra* and *ḥamsa*, spring up and cause "the first end" in the sequence. After their emergence only one man (Noah) will not be contaminated by them, and he only will be saved. The same pair of nouns is used in the Aramaic Levi (DJD 31: Apocryphon of Levi[b]; 4Q541 9 i 7) as the sign of an evil generation. The second one alludes perhaps to Genesis 6:5, where the Hebrew equivalent is mentioned as the decisive cause for the flood. *Shiqra* may have had an even wider range of meaning, including evil intention, speech, and action, thus representing the closest counterpart to *qushṭa*.

According to 4QAmram (4Q 548 1 ii 8), the "sons of Shiqra" are in fact "sons of darkness." In these texts *shiqra* + *ḥamsa* appear as substantial forces independently of any angelic or human agents. The Apocalypse of Weeks offers no explanation for the origin of evil. It does not attribute the growth of the two antagonistic powers to a particular source. Is the fall of the watchers in the time of Enoch's father Jared presupposed? After the flood a law or covenant (Ethiopic *sher'ata*) is given to the surviving or future sinners, perhaps to enable them to lead a righteous life under new conditions. This gift is surely conceived as an outcome of the still-existing but weakened *qushṭa* set against the effectiveness of deceit and violence.

3. Regarding the third week, only its end is hinted at: a man (Abraham) will be chosen as the plant or sprout of *qushṭa*, not as an individual but as a source of uprightness for the duration of this world (or: forever?), i.e., as the origin of an enduring community characterized by this quality (within Israel or humankind as a whole?).

The image of the plant and its possible relation to historical or eschatological Israel has been discussed in detail by Patrick Tiller (1997) and George Nickelsburg (2001, 444f.). What I miss in the discussion so far is a differentiation between the meaning of "sprout of" and "full-grown plant" (*neṣer* versus *matta'* in Hebrew); the latter appears as the outcome of the former, but is not completely identical with it (cf. the sequence in 1QH 14[6]:15; 16[8]:6-11). The noun here was certainly *nṣbh* as in 1 Enoch 93:2[10]; in Genesis Apocryphon 2:15 it means embryo, thus Abraham seems more to be the *germ* of the transformation of the field of *qushta* into the whole of a human society than a final representation of it.

4. *Qushta* is again not mentioned in the fourth week, but at its end the reception of the visions of the holy and righteous ones (genitive subject or genitive object?), the making of a law (or covenant?), and the erection of a tabernacle (1 En 93:6) take place. At least the *sher'ata* doubtlessly has a close connection to *qushta*, although probably all three benefits are the results of its activity. While these phenomena clearly refer to the Sinai revelation, the man Moses does not get any attention. Contrary to some other parts of 1 Enoch, the Apocalypse of Weeks acknowledges a Sinai law or covenant, but the visions of that period (cf. Jubilees?) are more important.

5. The sole remarkable event in the fifth week will happen at its end (93:7): the building of a temple for the benefit of a glorious kingdom (certainly divine, not human) during the time of this world (probably not forever; cf. the following verse). This presupposes that the tabernacle mentioned in the previous week had a rather temporary relevance and is now replaced by a much superior institution. If we can assume that this development did not happen independently of the power of *qushta*, then the latter must have an essential connection with cult and sanctity in the eyes of the author (the plant of righteousness is connected with the building of the temple in Jub 1:16; cf. 1QS 8:5f.; 11:7-9).

6. The *sixth week* unfolds in purely negative terms (1 En 93:8). All living beings (in the country or on earth?) are characterized by blindness and lack of wisdom. *Shiqra* seems to be very effective. A single man (Elijah) ascends to heaven (as a reaction to the evil of his time?). The temple of the kingdom, built in the immediately preceding week (as an anchor of *qushta* on earth?), will be burned, and the whole race of the chosen root — which must be the root of the plant of *qushta* according to 93:5 — will be dispersed into exile.

7. At the end of the *seventh week* circumstances take a dramatic turn (93:9f.). Prior to this reversal the generations are characterized by aberration. The whole postexilic history is judged in a purely negative manner. The second temple is not mentioned at all. Not only is the process of Hellenization in the second century B.C.E. condemned, but even the times of Ezra and Nehemiah and all the high priests of these centuries. At its end, however, some witnesses of *qushta* will be chosen from this still-enduring plant. The righteous members of a minority group are separated from Israel as a whole (cf. Boccaccini 1998, 108). Now they are chosen for a specific function, to be witnesses, which perhaps means a missionary task among those people who do not yet belong to the outstanding plant. For that purpose they are equipped with sevenfold wisdom, which presumably surpasses all former human wisdom.

This will be followed by a turn of events which had not been possible before: with the appearance of this elect group the destructive powers *ḥamsa* and *shiqra* will be uprooted. We are not told how this will occur. This anticipation of the last judgment is also alluded to in other Enoch passages (91:5-11; 10:16). Thus the seventh week corresponds to the change in the field of supernatural powers in the second week, but has the opposite effect. The destruction of the foundations of the negative forces does not imply that their outgrowth, all the wicked men and institutions, also disappears. This will happen only in the following weeks. Will the elect take part in the first fundamental demolition? According to the Ethiopic text, they remain passive: "The roots of injustice will be cut." The Aramaic *wlhwn ʿqryn* was translated by Milik (1976, 266f.): "And they will have rooted out (the foundations)"; but the participle may be used in a nonpersonal manner: "And for their benefit (the foundations . . .) are rooted out"; cf. Daniel 3:4; 4:2; Ezra 7:19.

8. Now the way is open for the eighth week, the first week of complete *qushṭa*. Perhaps this is perceived as a return of the first week when no negative forces existed. However, a difference remains. Even if the sources of wickedness have disappeared, the wicked ones still remain. The *qashiṭin* become more active than in former times, make judgment, and come into possession (probably possession of the promised land of Israel). The temple of the kingdom, this time certainly the divine temple, will be built more glorious than before and stands now for all times and worlds. Salvation begins in the country of the plant of Abraham.

9. In the ninth week this transformation takes place all over the earth (with a "righteous law" for all? cf. Nickelsburg 2001, 434), the wicked part of humankind disappears into the abyss, and the remaining people adhere to the path of *qushṭa*, which is now not only one plant among others.

10. Cosmic change occurs in the tenth week: the angelic host will be judged, heaven vanishes, and a new heaven appears. Weeks without sins and filled with *qushṭa* will follow forever.

The specialty of this survey of world history with its concentration on *qushṭa* and the contrary field of *ḥamsa* and *shiqra* differs from the frame of the Enoch composition in which it is embedded now. Already the Aramaic redactor, who had presumably combined the Apocalypse of Weeks with the following Epistle of Enoch, had altered the concept of the decisive factors in the course of world history in certain regards. For him *qushṭa* remains an important category of moral conduct, but God and men are much more directly involved in history and act as responsible subjects. The text of the Apocalypse of Weeks is now continued by an epistle (93:1-107), written to the last generation before the eschatological turn and admonishing her to observe *qushṭa* for arising from sleep (death) and walking in its path forever, for God himself will be the judge at the end of times (92:4). For Enoch's children there is no obstacle to walk in the paths of *qushṭa* and to choose them and to keep away from the paths of violence and death (94:1-5).

Before the Apocalypse of Weeks stands a transitional passage (91:1-10, 18f.) linking it with the Animal Apocalypse (1 En 85–90) as a speech of Methuselah. Here also the Lord himself is announced, acting as the last judge. Moreover, the antagonistic character of the fields of *qushṭa* on the one side and the multiplicity of violence, impurity, blasphemy, perversity, uncleanness on the other side is much more accentuated concerning the power of the negative forces than in the Apocalypse of Weeks. The difference in comparison with the Animal Apocalypse itself is much greater. Although a survey of world history occurs in both texts, in the Animal Apocalypse the emphasis is on the good or evil actions of human nations depicted as animals and the frequent interventions of the Lord of the sheep, i.e., of Israel. However, no reference is made to *qushṭa* or the forces opposed to it.

The Two Antagonistic Spirits in the Rule of the Community

The Apocalypse of Weeks's antagonistic view of the world and history is clearly distinctive from the convictions of most of the other Judean movements in the Hellenistic period. The Aramaic description of *qushṭa* and its opponents as effective fields of power in the history of the world has a surprising Hebrew parallel in the famous treatise about the two spirits found at Qumran (1QS 3:16–4:26; Charlesworth 1996, 37f., 58-60), which may go back to an independent source (Lange 1995, 126).

According to this passage, God had created a spirit of *h'mt* and a spirit of *h'wl* in the beginning as supernatural forces. Since that time each one has been competing to influence human beings either to do good or to act wickedly, and thus to determine their corresponding destinies. The *toledot* of *'mt* had emanated from the spring of Light (the first divine creation), the *toledot* of *'wl* from the well of darkness. In the hand of the "prince of light," probably the hypostatic truth, is the dominion of all "sons of righteousness," whereas in the hand of the "angel of darkness" is the dominion of all the "sons of deceit." Fourteen vices are generated by the "spirit of deceit," while the "spirit of truth" illuminates the spirit of seven virtues for leveling the ways of righteousness. The sons of evil walk in the ways of darkness. The times of the dominions of the two leading spirits are appointed by God. He will directly intervene at the end of the time and ultimately destroy *h'wl* and its adherents. Then *h'mt* will reign in the world forever.

The word *'mt* is commonly translated as "truth," but in the Qumran literature the noun means "rarely . . . a verifiable body of knowledge." It otherwise refers either to faithfulness to God and his law as an important "characteristic of the identity and behavior of the community," or more often to God's dealing with humankind (Walck 2000). In the treatise it does not express human or divine qualities and actions but metaphysical forces intervening between the world above and the world below.

The relationship of this conception of the two primeval emanations — which act rather independently in the appointed periods of history until the eschatological revolution — with the *qushta-shiqra* opposition in the Apocalypse of Weeks is obvious. Certainly both texts mirror an older tradition, which presumably expressed the elitist consciousness of a pious minority eagerly expecting a future triumph over a hostile minority. But the treatise (from pre-Qumran times?) presents a more developed individualization. The ups and downs in the domination of the two opposite spirits do not primarily refer to different human parties within fixed epochs but to the moral struggles within each human heart. Especially concerning the end of times, the treatise is more theistic than the Apocalypse of Weeks. Nevertheless, the agreements are evident, being rooted in the same tradition.

Was this tradition originally an Aramaic one? The opposition *'mt-'wl* appears seldom in the Hebrew literature. In Aramaic Targums, however, *shqr* is not only the standard equivalent of Hebrew *'wl* but often used as the opposite of *qsht* as a translation of other Hebrew nouns (Lev 19:15, 35; Deut 32:4; Ezek 18:8, 24, 26). In the Aramaic Vision of Amram (4Q548 7-16, 31-34; Beyer 1994, 88f.), the same opposition is alluded to, but in most of the Qumran manuscripts the sharp division between truth and deceit is never to be taken for granted (Duhaime 2000). Some Hebrew texts may have their roots in a similar tradition, but their ethical principles are no longer seen as nearly self-existent entities. In the War Scroll a cosmic opposition is fundamental, however; the "sons of light" are not led by a hypostatic *'mt*, but by the well-known angel Michael, and the "sons of darkness" by the prince of the kingdom of darkness, viz., Belial along with his angels (1QM xvii 5-6).

The ancient Jewish writings, e.g., the Prophets and the Wisdom literature, are aware of a fundamental contradiction between *ṣdq* and *rsh'*, but the second noun means wickedness produced by a human society and not a demonic entity which determines as such the course of history (cf. however Zech 5:8).

The Aramaic *Qushṭa* outside the Bible and the Zoroastrian Roots of the Ontological Dualism

The decisive role of *qushṭa* as the order of life, as well as the source of righteous and true *behavior,* is a heritage of both the *ṣedeq* conception of the ancient writings of the Hebrew Bible and the adoption of *qushṭa* as a central notion of the worldview of the Aramaic-speaking koine of the Persian and Hellenistic epochs. As far away as India, King Ashoka (third century B.C.E.) introduced himself in the Kandahar inscription after his conversion to Buddhism as the king who promotes *qashiṭa,* a term that probably refers to the "Corpus der buddhistischen Lehre (dharma)" (Donner and Röllig 1968, 2:336). In later Mandaism *kushta* is praised as savior of humanity, "great radiance whose light is lovelier than all worlds" (Ginza 77A), and is "often personified as a celestial being" (Drower and Macuch 1963, 209). However, these Aramaic parallels only partially refer to opposing powers as is the case in the Apocalypse of Weeks and 1QS, although *shiqra* plays a role as a seducing force in Mandean literature (Drower and Macuch 1963, 463).

The kind of antagonism which dominates the Apocalypse of Weeks and 1QS texts seems much more related to Iranian sources, although there has been considerable discussion about this in the last fifty years (cf. Duhaime 2000, 218f.). In older Avestian and Old Persian texts, the antagonism of *asha/arta,* the "personification of the principle which orders and regulates the world," and *drug/drauga,* "deceit, denial of divine order and all that has power in itself," plays an important role. Zarathustra's Gathas and Achaemenid inscriptions presuppose a continuous struggle with the positive power in the cosmos throughout the redetermined epochs of human history. *Drug* is often accompanied by the arch-demon *Aeshma* "of the bloody club," the hypostatic Violence, "a savage ruffian" (Boyce 1982, 201-87). This figure is later called *Xeshm,* "Wrath," who with his demons will dominate in the last periods of world history according to the so-called *Bahman Yasht* (West 1880, 189-235; cf. Collins 1993, 163f.; Koch 1994, 131-34).

Here we come again across the hostile pair Deceit and Violence as the enemies of Righteousness/Truth. *Aeshma* was adapted in the second temple Jewish literature as *Asmodeus* (Hutter 1999). As in the Apocalypse of Weeks, these evil powers will be destroyed in the course of an eschatological transformation of the ages, often postulated for the tenth millennium (cf. Collins 1984, 50). I quote just one example concerning the coming of the victorious savior Astvathereta from the old *Yasht* 19, 93-95; I use a German translation where the Iranian names are transliterated (Wolff 1960, 297): "Dann wird er [the Savior] dort die *Drug* aus der Welt des *Asha* fortschaffen. Er wird mit den Augen der

Weisheit schauen. . . . Seine — des sieghaften Astvaereta — Genossen treten hervor. . . . Vor ihnen wird der das blutige Holz schwingende, übelberüchtigte *Aeshma* fliehen; überwinden wird das *Asha* die böse, häßlich anzusehende, finstere *Drug*." It was Darius I who transferred the conception of the *arta-drug* contrast to contemporary history. According to the Behistun inscription, the many rebellions against his kingship had the same source: "The Lie [*drauga*] made them rebellious so that these (men) deceived the people" (DB IV 34). After Cambyses had gone to Egypt, the *drauga* "waxed great in the Country" (DB I 34; Kent 1953, 117, 119, 129, 131). Even if the positive concept of *arta* was not explicitly mentioned, it "was clearly constantly present in Darius' thoughts" (Boyce 1982, 121). The king "sees this cosmic conflict only as it is manifest in his own empire" (Zaehner 1961, 157). A kind of dualistic worldview was also expressed by the name Artaxerxes, "Having dominion through Arta," of three of his successors.

Royal inscriptions like that of Behistun were translated into Aramaic and spread over all the provinces as demonstrated by the Behistun papyrus, found at Elephantine (Cowley 1923, 248-71). In these messages the Aramaic equivalents of *arta* and *drauga* probably were *qushṭa* and *shiqra*. Unfortunately, the corresponding passages are not preserved at Elephantine. The religious background of this king's ideology might have been interpreted by the magi who accompanied the Persian occupation of the West. Thus Aramaic translations were surely the bridge for the transfer of Iranian ideas to other cultures of the Near East.

In 1949 the emigrated German philosopher Karl Loewith published a book in the United States under the title *Meaning in History* in which he presented an overview of the many attempts to find meaning in the Western tradition during the past two thousand years. He concluded with the negative assessment that there will never be a convincing solution; there is no meaning in history! Loewith expressed a skepticism which had become a matter of course in the European mind after the two world wars.

Today the notion of evolution holds a prominent place with European scientists, but not with respect to human history. However, some implications of this issue seem to survive today beyond the Atlantic Ocean. Leading politicians in the United States are able to speak of infinite justice or enduring freedom as the ultimate goal of historical development, expected for the near future, as well as the destruction of a dangerous axis of evil. Such a program is reminiscent of eschatological ideas that were already expressed in the Enochic Apocalypse of Weeks two thousand years ago. Unlike contemporary propaganda, which seems to express these notions in a short-winded manner, the author of the Apocalypse of Weeks did so at some length and with considerable historical depth, reckoning the time till infinite justice is achieved not in decades but in centuries, if not millennia. This expectation could be convincing only if the intended reader was made aware of its roots in the past, even the remote past.

Reflection on Ideology and Date
of the Apocalypse of Weeks

Andreas Bedenbender

Compared with the central passages of the Mosaic torah, the Animal Apocalypse and likewise the Apocalypse of Weeks must appear odd, if not bewildering: in their retelling of the *Heilsgeschichte,* both texts, attributed to the antediluvian seer, manage to combine a highly schematized form with a strange
selection of content. They are, so to speak, boring and exciting at the same time.
While the Animal Apocalypse tacitly passes over the covenant of Mount Sinai
and the giving of the torah, the Apocalypse of Weeks seems to be ignorant of
the exodus. Forgetfulness is as implausible an explanation as underestimation.
The subjects are much too important for that.[1]

   If we take the omissions as intentional and accept the case of deliberate
deviation, every detail of both texts has to be pondered carefully. Do the texts
really fit the course of events known to us from the Mosaic torah? Never should
it be taken for granted that a certain biblical event, or biblical interpretation of
an event, must play a role in the Enochic apocalypses just because it is biblical.
Led by that reflection, interpretation must proceed more slowly. However, the
results are definitely worth the loss of time. The differences between the biblical
understanding of salvation history and its two counterparts in the Enochic
apocalypses can teach a lot about the respective ideological backgrounds from
which each of the visions of Enoch emerged. Each apocalypse came from a
background different from the other.

---

1. For a more detailed analysis of the theological signature of the Animal Apocalypse and
the Apocalypse of Weeks, see Bedenbender 2000, 126-42, and for the dating of the Apocalypse of
Weeks, 120-22 (with additional literature).

The starting point of the following consideration is 1 Enoch 93:6c. At the conclusion of the fourth week, "a *sher'ata* for all generations and a tabernacle will be made." Being an equivalent of Aramaic *qym'*, Ethiopic *sher'ata* has the meaning "covenant" as well as "law." In 93:4 the same word is applied to the time after the flood ("the first end"): "a *sher'ata* will be made for the sinners." In both instances it has to be asked which meaning is intended by the text. Are we informed about a "covenant for the sinners" and a "covenant for all generations," or about a "law for the sinners" and a "law for all generations"?

Interestingly enough, in his outstanding commentary on 1 Enoch George Nickelsburg draws a distinction between *sher'ata* in verse 4 and in verse 6. In translating verse 4 he opts for "law," while in 6 he uses "covenant" (Nickelsburg 2001, 434). As becomes obvious from his following interpretation, though, he does not intend to stress that distinction. For in the former case he explains: "verses 4-5 speak of a 'covenant' or a 'law' being made for the sinners," referring to Genesis 8–9 (444). And about the latter use of "covenant" he says "the translation 'law' is not excluded" (446). Here, he takes into account the possibility that "the author is referring to the whole of the exodus and the Sinai events," adding only casually: "this is the only explicit reference to the Mosaic covenant/torah in the whole Enochic corpus" (446).

Obviously Nickelsburg's indifference in the question of translation is connected to the correspondences he sees between Enoch and the Mosaic torah. As everybody knows, in Genesis 9:1-17 the giving of a law and the giving of a covenant appear side by side, and the same is the case at Mount Sinai according to the book of Exodus. Thus, to work with two rather global references to the biblical stories of Noah and of the exodus has the tendency, quite naturally, to blur the difference between the two possible meanings of *sher'ata* in 1 Enoch 93. If "law" naturally goes with "covenant," and "covenant" with "law," why should the translator be worried about the exact sense of the word?

But, as pointed out in the beginning, it is by no means clear that in the Apocalypse of Weeks "law" and "covenant" are really just two sides of the same coin. To find the meaning of 93:4, 6, the Mosaic torah can be used for formulating questions: Does the Apocalypse of Weeks speak, as the Mosaic torah does, of a law and a covenant connected to Noah? Does it speak, as the Mosaic torah does, of a law and a covenant connected to Mount Sinai? To use the Mosaic torah for finding the answers, also, would be circular. The answers have to be based primarily, if not solely, on the text of the Apocalypse of Weeks. And as will be shown in the next paragraphs, both the content and the structure of the Apocalypse of Weeks require in 93:6 as well as in 93:4 the translation "law." Neither in verse 4 nor in verse 6 is there left any place for the idea of a covenant.

In verse 4 the translation "covenant for the sinners" hardly would make sense. The sin of the "sinners" is not limited in any way in the Apocalypse of Weeks, and as a consequence the sinners could and would break every covenant made for them. Of course, the meaning could be: "a covenant which is made in spite of human sinfulness, a covenant triumphing over all human sins." But such an idea would be completely isolated within the Apocalypse of Weeks. "Law for the sinners," on the other hand, makes good sense. A law is not nullified by violation. If a law is broken by "the sinners," it still has the power to guide the judgment over the transgressors and to govern their fate.

A similar consideration can be made on verse 6. A "covenant for all generations," given at the end of the fourth week, would stand in tension with the sixth week, where everybody is going blind (v. 8), and also with the "perverse generation" of the seventh week (v. 9). Both expressions go rather with a broken than with an existing covenant. In addition, there would be an unclear relation between the "covenant for all generations" and the election of the "chosen" in week seven (v. 10).

So far it can be concluded that the biblical concept of a covenant between God and Israel is passed over not only in the Animal Apocalypse but also in the Apocalypse of Weeks. This feature is typical of the way the Apocalypse of Weeks deals with the biblical *Heilsgeschichte.* In it the ongoing history of the patriarchs and of Israel has been split into a chain of singular events, a chain with hardly any continuity. The election of the chosen ones in the seventh week (v. 10) is in no way the unfolding or the consequence of the election of Abraham in the third week (v. 5). Both events are simply analogous, just as the "first end," the flood (v. 4), is analogous to the coming end.

How can we explain the disappearance of the covenant of Mount Sinai, and even of a continuing relation between God and his people *(Heilsgeschichte),* in the Apocalypse of Weeks? If this apocalypse is dated in pre-Maccabean times, these strange features simply remain a riddle. But if we suppose it was written under the impression of the persecution of Antiochus, the riddle can be solved. The persecution was initiated, at least to a significant extent, by the Jewish high priest of Jerusalem, and a significant part of the Jewish population, threatened by death or convinced by new ideas, had given up torah. Persecuted by their own high priest and surrounded by Jewish apostates, or those thought to be apostates, the circles behind the Apocalypse of Weeks must have had reason enough to lose their trust in the unity of the Jewish people and in its inseparable connection to God.

The same holds true for the Animal Apocalypse, a text to be dated in Maccabean times in any case. In different ways both documents seem to face the same problem. They mirror the impossibility of any longer connecting the concepts which were combined with each other, fundamental for Jewish self-understanding in times before the persecution: (1) the election of the Jewish people, (2) the covenant with God, and (3) the gift of the torah. At the same time, both documents try to save at least essential parts of the tradition. But here we are confronted with a bifurcation.

The Animal Apocalypse abandons not only the conviction that God made a covenant with Israel at Mount Sinai but also that he gave a law to his people. By that means the apostasy of so many Jews during the persecution is less disturbing, and the Animal Apocalypse can keep the history of Israel as the basic system for all reflections.

The Apocalypse of Weeks, on the other hand, keeps the gift of the torah as an eternal norm. But the price is high. Confronted with the validity of the torah "for all generations," the apostasy during the persecution, and even in the time before, is getting an immense weight, and Israel can no longer be conceived as a unit. Consequently, the Apocalypse of Weeks avoids dealing with Israel or its history.

According to the Ethiopic version of 1 Enoch 93:2, the Apocalypse of Weeks is speaking about "the sons of righteousness, and . . . the chosen of eternity, and . . . the plant of truth" (Nickelsburg's translation). As 1 Enoch 93:5, 10 make clear, "the plant of truth" is meant to be Israel. The fragmentary Aramaic text, on the other hand, is reconstructed by Milik in the following way: "(the chosen of eternity) who have grown up from (the plant of truth)" (Milik 1976, 263s). The analysis given above can be taken in support of Milik's reconstruction: the "plant of truth," indeed, is not the subject of the Apocalypse of Weeks.

The Enochic Circles, the Hasidim, and the Qumran Community

Timothy H. Lim

In his stupendous commentary on 1 Enoch, George Nickelsburg has articulated what he regards as the possible relationship between the Qumran scrolls, Enochic texts, and pious rebels of the Maccabean revolt: "This commonality [i.e., the fact that the sectarian and Enochic texts are found together in multiple copies at Qumran] points one to the hypothesis that: (a) the Qumranians were descendants of the Hasidim; and (b) the lambs in the Animal Apocalypse were the Hasidim who made common cause with Mattathias and Judas" (Nickelsburg 2001, 363).

Such a suggestion, carefully advanced as it is by Nickelsburg as a mere possibility, raises a host of questions for which we have only uncertain answers. Who are the Hasidim and how are they related to the Qumran community? Are the literary parallels found between the Animal Apocalypse and the Apocalypse of Weeks on the one side and the Damascus Document on the other indicative of *more* than a common matrix of religious awakening? Is the militant concern about the torah attributed to the lambs in the Animal Apocalypse and the Hasidim, who became associated with Judas, compatible with the Damascus Document's description of the origins of the community? These issues have been previously discussed by scholars (Collins 1999, 48), not least by Nickelsburg himself (1982; 1986). What needs to be added here is the significance of 4Q306 for the present discussion. Nowhere is this text referred to in Nickelsburg's 1 Enoch commentary.

4Q306, entitled "4QMen of the People Who Err," is a badly mutilated and difficult to read text which appears to have been related to CD 1, the fledgling Qumran community, and possibly 4QMMT (Lim 2000). It comprises three fragments that do not join, whose arrangement as a text is based upon similarities of skin and script, and for fragments 1 and 2, also the right margin with stitching hole marks. It is unclear whether the six lines of fragment 3 belong to the same text.[1] The text is written in the highly variable script known conveniently as the "semicursive script" of the Hasmonean period. In such a case it is imprudent to date the text too precisely, and I have suggested a broad period between 150 and 50 B.C.E. for the copying of the text. There is no evidence that it was an autograph.

Much remains uncertain about these three badly mutilated and difficult to decipher fragments. There is no typically sectarian terminology like *yahad*, the Wicked Priest, Liar, Teacher of Righteousness, or similar. However, it does attest to the phrase ד]רך כמגששים, "gropers of the way," in fragment 2 line 4 ("and in all their soul they were as gropers of the wa[y"), a phrase found in CD 1:9 ("and they were as blind men and as gropers of the way for twenty years") and most likely derived from Isaiah 59:10 ("we grope as blind men along [or towards] a wall"). The context can be deduced only in part from the vestiges of this fragment: "the torah and the co[mmandments]" (line 3); and "the torah going forth" (line 5).

If the nine lines of fragment 1 also belonged to the same original column as fragment 2, then it could be suggested that in contrast to those who groped for the way were others "who will stray and not observe the commandments" (line 1) and who "will transgress [from day] to day and from month to mon[th]" (line 2). These latter may well be identical to those who groped for the way, as in CD 1, but we cannot be certain. Moreover, what these transgressions entailed cannot now be known with certainty; they appear to have been concerned with "dogs eating" (1:5), possibly bones dug up from within the temple area, and fresh oil (1:8). If this is the case, then it recalls the prohibition in 4QMMT CT B 58-62 against allowing dogs into "the holy camp, since they may eat some of the bones of the sanctuary while the flesh of the sacrifice is still on them" (Qimron and Strugnell 1994, 162-63). The Qumran-Essene avoidance of oil is attested in various places (Josephus, *War* 2.123; CD 12:16; and 11QT^a 49:12) (J. Baumgarten 1967).

Much remains uncertain about 4Q306, and one must not press the evidence. We do not have even one full preserved line. However, it is evidence that must be discussed in a comprehensive commentary that hypothesizes a relationship between the Hasidim, Enochic circles, and the Qumran community as Nickelsburg does in 1 Enoch 1. It appears to be related to CD 1 and the sect's own retelling of its emergence: "And they perceived their iniquity and recog-

---

1. See Lim (2000) for details.

Timothy H. Lim

nized that they were guilty men, yet for twenty years they were like blind men groping for the way" (ll. 9-10).[2]

As a foil 4Q306 highlights the difference between the Animal Apocalypse and CD 1. It is closer to CD 1 than to the Animal Apocalypse. There is no evidence of the militancy of the Enochic text. Rather it concerns the proper observance of the torah, the transgressions of people who err, and, one can only assume, the licit practices of the gropers of the way.

2. Translation from Vermes (1997, 127). Scholars sometimes regard this as secondary because it is prosaic rather than poetic (see discussion in Knibb 1987, 21-22).

The Apocalypse of Weeks and
the Architecture of the End Time

Matthias Henze

One of the characteristic features that defines apocalyptic thought is a distinct philosophy of history,[1] a particular way of giving meaning to the passage of time. Even the most casual reader of the Apocalypse of Weeks (1 En 93:1-10; 91:11-17) will notice that the organization of time was of principal concern to the author. What makes the Apocalypse of Weeks so impressive is not merely the use of the numbers seven and ten, for which there are numerous examples in apocalyptic literature (Collins 1998, 63-64; Koch 1983), but rather the fact that this deceptively simplistic architecture of the end time is predicated on more than one view of history. I would like to point to three such views, though there are undoubtedly more. The author of the Apocalypse of Weeks is aware of these different perceptions of time, yet does not consider them mutually exclusive but has them converge in his apocalypse. Moreover, for each of these views of history there is a precedent in biblical historiography, and sometimes these connections may not be fortuitous.

First, and on its most basic level, history is the linear progression of time as observed and recorded by the apocalypticists, ever unfolding in an orderly and entirely predetermined fashion in periods of ten weeks. History has a definite beginning in week 1, albeit not with Adam but with Enoch; and it has a definite goal in week 10. Then the finite and rather intentional structure of ten weeks will give way to an infinite succession of weeks: "After this there will be many weeks without number forever" (91:17). What matters in this schematization of time is that time can be measured and properly divided into periods,

---

1. Martin Hengel (1974, 1:183) speaks of a "theology of history."

and that the end of time becomes predictable. This understanding of history as the linear passage of time underlies, of course, most of biblical historiography, with only a few exceptions. It is commonly referred to as *Heilsgeschichte,* and it finds its most systematic expression in the Deuteronomistic History.

But for the apocalyptic mind history is not simply linear. Thus James VanderKam argues that the Apocalypse of Weeks is structured in pairs of weeks: the entire apocalypse is "arranged in an artful and symmetrical fashion." Weeks 1 and 10 form a certain parallelism in that both mention that something is seventh in order, weeks 2 and 9 speak of judgment and the annihilation of evil humans, weeks 3 and 8 form a parallelism in that they focus on the righteous, and so forth (VanderKam 1995, 65; 1984b). Gabriele Boccaccini makes a similar proposal. He speaks of "the chiastic structure of the Apocalypse," with the temple at the center of the composition in week 5, for Boccaccini a clear indication of the author's priestly roots. Unfortunately, Boccaccini then stops short of spelling out in greater detail how exactly the chiasm is maintained beyond the centrality of the temple (Boccaccini 1998, 107-8).

Both proposals, VanderKam's parallelism and Boccaccini's chiasm, work better in some parts of the apocalypse than in others. In other words, the symmetrical structure is not fully sustained throughout the entire composition of the apocalypse, but is employed in a somewhat loose manner. In his commentary on 1 Enoch, George Nickelsburg prefers a simpler and more obvious division of the apocalypse, not into pairs or chiasms but into two groups of weeks, with the obvious break after week 7, the point in time of the narrator. Nickelsburg speaks of the "complementarity of the two sets of weeks," namely, of weeks 1-7 and 8-10. "[W]eeks 8-10 depend on weeks 1-7. Specifically, week 8 is dependent on week 7, and the judgment of the wicked of week 7 is fully executed in week 8" (Nickelsburg 2001, 438).

The combination of a linear and a parallel structure in the architecture of time resembles the priestly creation account in Genesis 1 and the organization of the first six days of creation, cast both in linear and in parallel fashion. As has often been shown, days 1 through 3 with the creation of light, sky, and dry land provide the resource, and days 4 through 6 with the creation of the luminaries, fish and fowl, and the land creatures provide the utilizer.

It is the third view of history, however, that may well be the most intriguing one, the alternation between righteousness and sin: the time of righteousness in week 1 is followed by "deceit and violence" in week 2, then the choosing of "a man," presumably Abraham, "as the plant of righteous judgment" in week 3, and so on. The alternation of righteousness and deceit does not exactly coincide with the succession of weeks, to be sure, but the principle of descent and ascent is clear. The election of the chosen comes at the end of a period of utter corruption (Collins 1998, 64-65). Klaus Koch's comments about the concept of two antagonistic powers, which can be detected in the composition of the Apocalypse of Weeks, and which is also found at Qumran in the tractate of the opposing spirits (1QS 3:13–4:26), are especially pertinent here. Nickelsburg does not dwell on this pattern at any length in his commentary but has discussed it at an earlier date (Nickelsburg 1977).

The alternating pattern, reminiscent of the alternation between good and evil kings toward the end of the Deuteronomistic History (2 Kings 16–25), here becomes the ordering principle of all of history. The pattern is intriguing. It works well up to week 7, the focal point of the apocalypse, where it breaks off. Weeks 8, 9, and 10 present a threefold judgment and, in the words of Nickelsburg, "assert the ultimate triumph of righteousness" (Nickelsburg 2001, 438). The guiding principle in the pattern is human sin: with the perfect eradication of sin in week 10, "many weeks without number" merge and become eternity.

The perhaps closest analogy within the apocalyptic corpus to this architecture of time that combines a linear view of history with an alternating pattern of righteousness and sin is, as Nickelsburg notes (2001, 439), Baruch's vision of the cloud from which bright and dark waters alternately pour in the Syriac Apocalypse of Baruch (2 Bar 56–77). Baruch's vision is related to the Apocalypse of Weeks in form and genre — and may well have been composed with our text in mind. 1 Enoch and 2 Baruch are very different texts, to be sure. Even so, the parallels (a rigorous schematization of history; the alternating pattern of righteousness and sin; the continuation of time even after the proposed scheme is completed) as well as the differences (twelve rather than ten segments beginning with Adam, not Enoch)[2] invite close attention. Baruch's vision of the cloud is a further development of a particular genre, namely, that of the "historical apocalypse."

The Apocalypse of Weeks may well be the oldest surviving example of this genre (VanderKam 2001, 103). In his commentary Nickelsburg argues convincingly that the Animal Apocalypse (1 En 85–90) "is a massive elaboration of the Apocalypse of Weeks" (Nickelsburg 2001, 360). Baruch's vision of the cloud is yet another extended form of the same type, albeit no longer as an independent composition. It is well integrated into its literary context and modified to fit Baruch's particular emphases. Baruch's vision thus testifies to the continuous popularity of historical apocalypses in the postbiblical era.

---

2. The division of time into twelve distinct parts already occurs in 2 Bar 27–28. It seems doubtful that these chapters can shed any light on the original date of 2 Baruch, though it is striking that 2 Baruch replaces the ten with twelve segments; cf. Bogaert (1969, 288-89).

The Plant Metaphor in Its Inner-Enochic and Early Jewish Context

Loren T. Stuckenbruck

As George Nickelsburg has recently discussed in the first installment of his commentary on 1 Enoch (Nickelsburg 2001, 444-45, 448), the motif of a "plant" or "planting" as a metaphor for Israel in a way that signifies Israel's election, whether broadly or more narrowly, is widespread. Nickelsburg concludes that in the Apocalypse of Weeks at 1 Enoch 93:10, the ones chosen from the "eternal plant of righteousness" (which originates from Abraham in 93:5) compose a group within Israel, i.e., the author's community, who are Abraham's true descendants. But some questions need to be asked: How "open" or "closed" (i.e., sectarian) was this community? While the sevenfold instruction in verse 10 is yet to be given, is the community to be constituted by this disclosure or is it already a clearly definable entity from the perspective of the author? Can anything be inferred from comparisons made between the Apocalypse of Weeks and other Jewish literature?[1] My discussion focuses on what might be said by means of such comparisons. In so doing, I draw on the recent publications by Patrick Tiller (1997) and Torleif Elgvin (1998).

In addition to the Apocalypse of Weeks (93:5, 10), the plant metaphor is attested not only in the Book of the Watchers (10:3, 16), but also among the Dead Sea Scrolls materials (1QS 8:5; 11:8; 1QH 14:15; 16:6; CD 1:7-8), as well as in biblical tradition as an emblem of hope (esp. Isa 60:21; 61:3; cf. further Jub 1:16;

---

1. I ask these questions because it is not ultimately clear according to Nickelsburg whether the author is delineating an eschatological reconstitution of the plant or using the metaphor to describe what is already a reality, so that even now the community is, similar to that treated in Dead Sea documents (1QS 8:4-10), "a building that stands counterposed to this structure of deceit" (Nickelsburg 2001, 448; cf. 445).

16:26; 21:24; and 36:6, in which "righteous plant" denotes both the historically and eschatologically restored Israel). Nickelsburg discusses these and other texts, and his comparison leads him to regard the community behind the Apocalypse of Weeks as one yet to be constituted. What he does not address in his comparison, however, is the relationship between 4QInstruction (i.e., a probable reference to "eternal planting" in 4Q418 81:13) and the coded description of Abraham in 1 Enoch 93:5 as "the plant of righteous judgement." After all, in the Apocalypse of Weeks Abraham is regarded as progenitor of "the plant of righteousness forever and ever," which in turn is the nucleus from which the "chosen ones" (Eth. *xeruyan;* Aram. ‏ן[‏חירי‏]ב‏) are selected as those to whom the "sevenfold wisdom and knowledge" will be revealed (1 En 93:10). The comparison with 4QInstruction is especially apropos since, in addition to the Apocalypse of Weeks, it contains an apparent association between wisdom and the elect, understood as "eternal plant(ing)."[2] In short, this comparison raises the question whether or not the author of the Apocalypse of Weeks has a narrowly conceived community in view. The similarity of tradition has been noted by both Tiller (1997) and Elgvin (1998), but is worth investigating further (Stuckenbruck 2002, 249-57).

Tiller has devoted a thorough analysis to the plant metaphor in each of these texts. His approach has been comparative and makes no attempt to claim anything about a possible tradition-historical relationship between the occurrence of the metaphor in 4QInstruction and its usage in the Apocalypse of Weeks. Elgvin, on the other hand, suggests that the occurrence of the phrase "eter[nal] planting" in 4QInstruction (so for ‏למטעת עולם‏ in 4Q418 81:13; another passage in 4Q423 1-2.7 simply reads ‏ובמטע‏) reflects the direct influence of Enochic tradition. If Elgvin is correct, then 4QInstruction, tradition-historically, comes out as a close heir to the Apocalypse of Weeks. Briefly, I shall here supplement Nickelsburg's discussion by beginning with the texts from 4QInstruction before considering the Enochic traditions from which, according to Elgvin, its teaching has derived.

As in 1 Enoch 10:3, 16 and 84:6, the "plant" metaphor in the Apocalypse of Weeks is not made to carry the restricted sense of a "community of chosen ones." This stands in contrast to 4QInstruction, which contains an address to readers designated "chosen ones of truth" (‏בחירי אמת‏; so 4Q418 69:10).[3] Elgvin deduces from his hypothesis of influence that both documents are applying the

---

2. Nickelsburg is aware of Tiller's publication but does not draw on it in this respect.

3. A potential difficulty exists in that the plant metaphor in 4QInstruction does not occur in conjunction with the document's address to the "chosen ones of truth." I am, however, attempting to interpret the document as a whole.

Loren T. Stuckenbruck

notion of "eternal planting" in the same way: the authors' respective communities are similarly conceived as remnant communities which do not have "a clearly-defined role in history as do later sectarian writings"; indeed, "the designation 'eternal planting' indicates that the community is the nucleus of the future-restored Israel" (Elgvin 1998, 121; cf. 116). In other words, the similarity of expression is translated into a similarity of social location.

This correspondence, however, does not necessarily follow. Rather than analyzing the Enoch traditions and 4QInstruction in terms of linear influence in one direction, another possibility presents itself: both traditions emerge as attempts during the third and second centuries B.C.E. to come to terms with alternative interpretive possibilities with respect to the metaphorical usage of "plant(ing)" in Isaiah 5:7, 60:21, and 61:3. Whereas the Enochic texts seem to derive conceptually from Isaiah 5:7, in which God's "pleasant planting" is broadly identified with "the men of Judah," the sapiential work's narrowed usage seems more likely to have developed out of reflection on the passages from Trito-Isaiah.[4] To be sure, both the Apocalypse of Weeks and 4QInstruction correspond in having introduced something new vis-à-vis biblical tradition — the explicit notion that the plant(ing) itself is somehow eternal. Nonetheless, this shared feature does not have to be regarded as evidence for the influence of the Enochic upon the other tradition but may simply be explained against the apocalyptic backdrop that informed these later attempts to come to terms with a satisfactory interpretation of Isaiah. The Apocalypse of Weeks, like 4QInstruction, may have been composed within a community whose adherents understood themselves as a chosen group living penultimate to the eschatological transformation of the cosmos, but the "plant(ing)" imagery is being applied in very different ways. As a result, we are in a better position to pinpoint what the author of the Apocalypse of Weeks does and does not consider his community of "chosen ones" to be.

4. If Elgvin's thesis of influence were to hold at all, one would have to explain how the "plant" metaphor in one tradition has been much more narrowly reapplied in the other to a community that could be designated "chosen ones of truth."

212

The Apocalypse of Weeks
and the Epistle of Enoch

Michael A. Knibb

This chapter is devoted to a consideration of the Apocalypse of Weeks. The first question that must be asked is whether it is appropriate to treat the Apocalypse in isolation from its context in the Epistle of Enoch. The latter has traditionally been regarded as consisting of chapters 91–105 of the book of Enoch, but the limits and the unity of this text have both been disputed. Thus in recent years George Nickelsburg and Siegbert Uhlig have treated chapter 91 separately from the Epistle (Nickelsburg 2001, 24-25, 336, 410; Uhlig 1984, 673-74, 708-9). Further, in place of the widely held view that the Apocalypse was an earlier piece, later incorporated within the Epistle, Nickelsburg and Gabriele Boccaccini have both argued for the existence of a "proto-epistle" that did contain the Apocalypse but not the main body of the Epistle (Nickelsburg excludes 92 and 94:6–104:9; Boccaccini excludes 94:6–104:6). But whereas Nickelsburg (1982, 340; cf. 2001, 24, 336-37, 426, 441) regards the Apocalypse as a discrete unit, "a traditional piece," inserted into an early form of the Enochic corpus to provide a time frame for its eschatology, Boccaccini (1998, 104-6, 109-12, 131-36) regards it as integral within its context in the opening chapters of the Epistle. Finally, while Nickelsburg (2001, 414-15) believes that 93:11-17 was deliberately transposed in the Ethiopic to follow after 91:10, Boccaccini (104) believes that the transposition was accidental, and that the original order of his proto-epistle was 91:1-10, 92:3–93:10, 91:11–92:2, and 93:11–105:3 (without 94:6–104:6).

There are a number of headings and other markers that serve to structure the text of the Epistle of Enoch[1] and are perhaps an indication that the text has

---

1. Headings or introductory formulas are used in 1 En 91:1, 92:1, 93:1, 94:1, while within

grown by a process of accretion. But that does not mean that the different elements of which the Epistle is formed have a separate origin from one another; there are thematic links throughout chapters 91–105 that seem rather to point to its unity. These links are discussed further below; here the disputed passages are considered separately. First, with regard to chapter 91, Nickelsburg believes that 91:1-10 + 18-19 continue the narrative begun in chapters 81–82, and that the Epistle begins in chapter 92. Thus he suggests that the limits of the Epistle are indicated by the fact that the themes introduced in the superscription (92:1) are picked up in the conclusion (104:12–105:2); he also suggests that 91:1 has a different concept of revelation from that in 93:2, and that this may point to a different level of composition (Nickelsburg 2001, 24-25, 336-37, 410-11, 416).

Uhlig (1984, 673-74, 708-9) notes that chapters 92–105 are preceded in Lake Tana 9 by the numeral "5," that is, "(Book or Section) 5," and believes that 91:1-10 + 18-19 form the conclusion of the book of Dream Visions. However, while Lake Tana 9 is representative of the oldest form of the Ethiopic text of Enoch to which we have access, it is not clear that the fact that this manuscript marks the start of a new section of Enoch at the beginning of chapter 92 represents anything other than an inner-Ethiopic development. In any case, even if chapter 91 did originate separately from chapters 92–105, the fact that 91:18-19 is followed directly by 92:1-2 in 4QEn⁸ ar 1 ii 18-25 shows that chapter 91 was already linked to the Epistle by the end of the second century B.C.E., the date of the *Vorlage* of 4QEn⁸ ar (cf. García Martínez 1992, 90, 93).

Similar considerations apply to Nickelsburg's view that chapter 92 is part of a later redaction, apparently based solely on the grounds "that the title and introduction of Enoch's Epistle (chap. 92) are followed by a piece of narrative (93:1-3a) which belongs to the *setting* of Enoch's Epistle, *not to its contents*" (Nickelsburg 2001, 24; cf. 336). But the fact that the Apocalypse of Weeks should have a separate introduction is hardly surprising, while the evidence of 4QEn⁸ ar 1 iii shows that chapter 92 was already in place immediately before chapter 93 at a very early stage.

It has often been held in the past that the Apocalypse of Weeks is an older (pre-Maccabean) piece that was included in the later (post-Maccabean) Epistle. Recently, Nickelsburg (1982, 340 n. 23; cf. 346) has suggested that the absence from the remainder of the Epistle of the concept of election, which is central in the Apocalypse, may be an indication of different authorship. García Martínez

---

the main body of the Epistle (94:1–105:2) the blessing formula in 99:10 appears to mark some kind of conclusion. The smaller literary units of which the main body of the Epistle is composed are marked off by the use of a number of stereotyped expressions ("Woe to you . . . ," "Fear not . . . ," "I say to you . . . ," "I know . . . ," etc.); for these units and one possible analysis of the structure, see Nickelsburg 2001, 416-21.

has, however, pointed out that the absence is explained by the fact that while the theme of election properly has a central place in the Apocalypse, which provides a summary of the history of the nation, "the idea is less useful in the parenetic sections or in the admonitions" (García Martínez 1992, 83).[2] It is also not totally clear how such a brief text as the Apocalypse, which is cast in allusive language, might have functioned independently of its wider context.

One argument used by Nickelsburg (2001, 426) and Boccaccini (1998, 112, 132) in support of the view that the main body of the Epistle did not form part of the original appears to be the fact that it has not survived among the fragments of 4QEn^g ar or of 4QEn^c ar;[3] but the absence of this material among the fragments of the Aramaic Enoch does not constitute evidence for such a view. It may be accepted that 94:6–104:(6)9 does have a distinctive character within the Epistle in that it consists of a series of denunciations of the sinners and exhortations addressed to the righteous, including a refutation of the denial that the righteous will enjoy a blessed state after death, but again this distinctive character is not evidence that 94:6–104:(6)9 is secondary and is rather linked to the structure and purpose of the Epistle as a whole.

Nickelsburg (2001, 24; cf. 337, 426) seeks to support his argument by the suggestion that "if one brackets . . . 94:6–104:9, one finds in 104:10 an appropriate continuation of 94:5: 'For I know that sinners will tempt men to do harm to wisdom. . . . And now I know this mystery, that sinners will alter and copy the words of truth.'" The much abbreviated text that remains (81:1–82:4a; 91:1-10, 18-19; 93:1-10; 93:11–94:5; 104:10–105:2) forms in his view a literary unity in which the themes announced in 81:1–82:4a are taken up again for a final time in 104:10–105:2. However, the fact that 104:10 picks up the language of 94:5 is hardly evidence that the intervening material is secondary.

Constraints of space compel me to pass over the two additional arguments used by Boccaccini in support of his view that while his proto-epistle is presectarian, the main body of the Epistle, and hence the Epistle as a whole, is not merely postsectarian but also anti-Qumranic. I must simply state that I find neither argument convincing.

In contrast to the suggestions that the Epistle lacks unity, it is important to emphasize that there are expressions and motifs that bind the different parts of the Epistle together, as James VanderKam (1984a, 145) and García Martínez (1992, 83-84), who have provided detailed references, have pointed out. These

---

2. For a critical survey of the arguments used by older scholars in support of the view that the Apocalypse of Weeks is an earlier and independent piece incorporated in the Epistle, see García Martínez 1992, 80-83.

3. 4QEn^g 1 v breaks off in 94:2; 4QEn^c 5 I begins in 104:13.

include the basic contrast between the righteous and the sinners, the wise and the foolish, between the blessing in store for the former and the judgment awaiting the latter, references to the wisdom of the righteous and the folly of the sinners, references to the tablets of heaven, to the writings of Enoch, and to the fall and punishment of the Watchers. Here I would draw attention only to the expression "path(s) of righteousness" and its opposite, "path(s) of wrong-doing," which recur in all parts of the Epistle. The former occurs in 91:18, 19; 92:3; 91:14; 94:1; 99:10; 104:13; 105:2 (cf. 91:4, "good paths"; 94:4, "paths of peace"), the latter occurs in 91:18, 19; 94:1, 2, 3 (cf. 94:2, 3, "paths of death").

It is important also to observe that the different units of which chapters 91–105 are composed lead naturally from one into the other and in different ways reflect a common purpose: to encourage the righteous to persevere in right conduct in the face of oppressive circumstances, and to reinforce this message by the assurance of the certainty of the punishment that awaits the sinners at the judgment, and of the blessed state that awaits the righteous (cf. Nickelsburg 2001, 428-29). The basic message of the Epistle is already presented in the testamentary material in chapter 91, namely, in the admonition to love uprightness and not to associate with those of a double heart (vv. 3b-4). This is reinforced by the apocalypse of verses 5-10, which predicts the coming judgment, the ending of iniquity, and the resurrection of the righteous to whom wisdom will be given (v. 10). These themes, including the reference to wisdom (see 93:10; 99:10; 104:12), all recur throughout the remainder of the Epistle. The admonition of 91:3b-4 is picked up in verses 18-19, and this prepares the way for chapter 92, which marks the formal beginning of Enoch's letter.[4]

The Apocalypse of Weeks (93:1-10 + 91:11-17) then follows. Although seemingly out of place, it does have an important function just before the beginning of the main part of the Epistle. Nickelsburg suggests that one purpose is to provide "a time referent for the coming judgment, which elsewhere is mentioned without specific temporal reference" (Nickelsburg 2001, 419; cf. Koch 1983, 413, 429). But, as Lars Hartman (1975-76, 11-12) has pointed out, its purpose is not so much informative — and indeed, it is quite vague on details — as to provide comfort and encouragement. The Apocalypse identifies the author's group as the true heirs of Abraham and offers assurance of the ending of evil and the coming of the judgment.

The main part of the Epistle (94:1–105:2) begins with a further admonition to choose the paths of righteousness and not the paths of iniquity (94:1-5), and this is picked up toward the end by the command: "Fear not, O righteous, when

---

4. On the epistolary character of the material, cf. Milik 1976, 51-52. As García Martínez (1992, 79-80) observes, the work nonetheless still retains a testamentary character.

you see the sinners growing strong and prospering, and do not be their companions, but keep far away from all their iniquities, for you will be companions of the host of heaven" (104:6). The intervening material supports this admonition by offering encouragement to the author's group in the face of the oppression they were experiencing at the hands of the sinners. The whole passage is interspersed by a series of exhortations addressed to the righteous to persevere (95:3; 96:1, 3; 97:1; 102:4-5;[5] 104:2, 4, 6; 105:2), and the Epistle ends with a final address to the sinners (104:7-9) and a final revelation and promise for the righteous (104:10–105:2).

Thus what is argued here is that the different elements of which chapters 91–105 are composed all come from the same author and are directed toward a common end, and Nickelsburg himself ultimately seems to come close to a similar view when he suggests that, notwithstanding the use of traditional material in chapters 92–105, "their general unity of subject matter and their carefully crafted literary structure suggest that we may interpret the text as the product of a single author" (Nickelsburg 2001, 426). He is in any case surely right that 91:11-17 was deliberately moved to its location in the Ethiopic, as has been increasingly recognized (Knibb 1978, 2:218; Hartman 1975-76, 12; Uhlig 1984, 414-15). Here the contrast with the disruption caused in Sirach 30–36 by the accidental transposition of two pairs of leaves in the exemplar from which all the Greek manuscripts are derived is instructive.

Within the chronological limits set by the Epistle's use of the Book of Watchers and by the date of 4QEn^g and its *Vorlage,* the internal evidence of the Epistle can be related to more than one historical situation. But the fact that the Apocalypse does not refer to the persecution of Antiochus and the events that followed has been widely interpreted to mean that it dates from the pre-Maccabean period, perhaps about 170 B.C.E., and a date in the pre-Maccabean period for the Epistle as a whole, on the assumption that it is a unity, would make good sense (cf., e.g., García Martínez 1992, 90-91).

The seventh week, which is characterized by the emergence of an apostate generation, has almost universally been regarded as marking the period in which the author of the Apocalypse lived, but the only information about the group behind the apocalypse is contained in 93:10: "[At its end] will be chosen [the chosen] as witnesses of righteousness from the eternal plant of ri[ghteous]ness, [to] whom sevenf[old] wisdom and knowledge will be giv[en]." This sparse information may however be filled out by the statements made concerning the righteous and their opponents ("the sinners") in the main body of the Epistle, and it is worth observing that 94:2 contains a reference to the author's own group comparable to that of 93:10.

---

5. Addressed rhetorically to the righteous dead.

Within the main body of the Epistle the distinction between the righteous and the sinners is not primarily sociological, that is, between poor and rich, as suggested by Boccaccini (1998, 136-37). Socioeconomic issues clearly are important, but it is also clear that religious issues are important, and in this connection the passages describing the blasphemy, erroneous belief, idolatry, lack of wisdom, and false teaching of the sinners (e.g., 94:9; 98:4–99:2; 99:7-9, 12, 14; 102:6-11; 104:7-8, 9-10), and those describing the wisdom (91:10; 93:10; 99:10; 104:12) possessed by the righteous, are of particular interest; a helpful analysis of them has been provided by Nickelsburg (2001; 1982). The sinners are accused of writing "false words and words of error" through which they will lead many astray (98:15; cf. 104:9-10). They are also accused of altering the words of truth and perverting the eternal covenant (99:2) and of setting at naught "the foundation and the eternal inheritance of their fathers" (99:14).

In view of the parallel to the last of these passages in CD 1:16, and of parallels to the theme of leading astray in such passages as 4QpPs^a 1:26–2:1; 4QpNah 3–4 2:8-9; 1QpHab 2:1-4; 10:9-13, which are discussed by Nickelsburg (2001, 486-88), it seems clear that the accusation is of giving a false interpretation of the law. In 1 Enoch 99:14 the reference is most obviously to the Mosaic torah, and notwithstanding the setting of the book in the time before Moses, it seems hard to believe that for an author in the second temple period the same is not also true of other formulations such as "the words of truth" (99:2; 104:9), "the eternal covenant" (99:2), "the commandments of the Most High" (99:10), and "the words of the Most High" (104:9).[6]

In contrast to the error propagated by the sinners, the writings of Enoch are the source of righteousness and, according to the Ethiopic, of much wisdom (1 En 104:12). They may be seen, as Nickelsburg (1982, 342-43; 2001, 535) has pointed out, to embody the sevenfold wisdom given to the chosen in the seventh week (93:10) and to be equated with "the words of the wise" through which those who hear them learn to do the commandments of the Most High (99:10).

It is tempting to link what is said about "the chosen" from the eternal plant of righteousness (93:10) to what is said about the "root of planting" in CD 1:7-10, and beyond this to the group described in Jubilees 23:26 who "begin to study the laws, to seek out the commands, and to return to the right way." However, notwithstanding the likelihood of a connection between the three passages, it is not certain that they all refer to precisely the same group, or to events of precisely the same period. However, all three texts provide evidence of a

---

6. Nickelsburg (2001, 498, 532) accepts that 99:14 may refer to the Mosaic torah, but is doubtful whether other passages refer to it specifically.

movement for reform and renewal in the early second century B.C.E., and the Epistle itself may be attributed to what García Martínez has described as the "apocalyptic tradition," from which the Essene movement subsequently emerged.

Boccaccini (1998, xxi, fig. 1, and pp. 113-17) has suggested placing the Halakhic Letter (4QMMT) in what he describes as "the 'Qumran Chain' of Documents" between the Apocalypse of Weeks, as part of his proto-epistle of Enoch, and the Epistle as such. He has also suggested that "the attitude of the 'we' group [in 4QMMT] is similar to that of the Proto-Epistle of Enoch" (Boccaccini 1998, 117). It has already been argued that there is not a strong case for the existence of such a proto-epistle; but even if it were accepted that the Apocalypse of Weeks is an earlier document incorporated into the Epistle, it is not clear that there is any evidence to justify the interposition of 4QMMT between the Apocalypse and the Epistle in such a chronological chain of documents.

There is also very little information in the Apocalypse on which to suggest a commonality of attitude with 4QMMT. The Epistle and 4QMMT do both belong very broadly in the category of letters, and the question of the true and false interpretation of the torah is at issue in both. But the fact that 4QMMT is to a great extent taken up with specific halakic issues, while the Epistle speaks of the law almost entirely in general terms, suggests that any connection there may be between the Apocalypse of Weeks or the Epistle of Enoch and the Halakhic Letter is not close.

Evaluating the Discussions concerning the Original Order of Chapters 91–93 and Codicological Data Pertaining to 4Q212 and Chester Beatty XII Enoch

Eibert J. C. Tigchelaar

In an excursus "The Original Order of Chapters 91–93," George Nickelsburg briefly describes Josef Milik's reconstruction of 4Q212 (4QEn^g) and the general consensus regarding the original order of the text (91:1-10, 18-19; 92:1–93:10; 91:11-17; 93:11-14; followed by 94:1ff.) (Nickelsburg 2001, 414-15; Milik 1976). The main contestant was Daniel Olson (1993; followed by Boccaccini 1998), who suggested a different placement of 4Q212 fragment *a*, and argued for an original order 91:1-10, 92:3–93:10, 91:11–92:2, 93:11-14, 94:1ff. This order would have been changed due to an accidental displacement of a leaf. Nickelsburg questions Olson's reconstruction, but does not discuss the codicological aspects of 4Q212.

My questions are quite straightforward: To what extent do the manuscript evidence and codicological data of 4Q212 and the Chester Beatty Papyrus XII help us in tackling literary problems?

It is well known that 4Q212 column iv shows that weeks 8 through 10 followed immediately on the seventh week in the Apocalypse of Weeks, and that the strange order of the Ethiopic is not original. Yet 4Q212 also raises new problems with regard to the text.

The first major problem in 4Q212 is the placement of fragment *a* with remnants of 1 Enoch 91:18-19 and 92:1-2. Milik places this fragment in the column preceding 1 Enoch 92:5. He calculates the height of the columns on the basis of column iv, which should contain the text of weeks 3 to 10 of the Apocalypse of Weeks, but then he is forced to assume that all other sections in columns i-v were in the Aramaic two to three times more extensive than in the Ethiopic. Stated differently, at three different places in chapters 91–93 the Ethiopic has either lost portions of text or been drastically abridged.

Olson claims all problems are solved if one assumes a different original order and a different origin of fragment *a* in the manuscript, namely, after 91:17. I will not discuss Olson's other suggestions for the accidental dislocation of a page, but focus on the reconstruction of 4Q212 in relation to the Ethiopic and Greek texts.

From a purely material point of view, and inasmuch as can be determined from the photographs and Milik's description, there are no reasons to favor either placement. There are no unambiguous damage patterns which suggest a placement of fragment *a* at the bottom of the scroll, and there is no report of a clearly different appearance. One may object against Olson that fragment *b*, which in his reconstruction belongs to the first column of the scroll, has thread holes: hence another sheet was sewn to its right. This could have been a handle sheet, but I would not expect one with this particular type of nonofficial scroll. On the other hand, Olson's reconstruction, unlike Milik's, does not force us to assume major differences between the Aramaic and Ethiopic.

Nickelsburg in personal discussion of this point has referred to an examination by Stephen Pfann of the hair follicle patterns of fragments *a* and *c*, which would confirm Milik's placement and exclude Olson's reconstruction.[1] However, this most promising line of material approach needs to be corroborated by the research of other scholars.

What other evidence supports Milik's claim that the beginning of the composition was much fuller in Aramaic than in Ethiopic? First, the actually preserved materials of 4Q212 indicate at some places a text different from, and fuller than, the Ethiopic.[2] Milik himself refers to Campbell Bonner (1937), who would have calculated that the beginning of the *Epistolē Henoch* in the Chester Beatty papyrus was also longer in the Greek than in the Ethiopic version. However, this is a misunderstanding of Bonner's arguments.

In the Chester Beatty papyrus the first preserved page is page 15, which starts with 1 Enoch 97:6. It can be calculated that 1 Enoch 91:1 should start somewhere on page 7 or 8.[3] Yet, even if Milik is right that the beginning of the Epistle was much fuller than the Ethiopic, this still leaves some five pages of the Chester Beatty text unaccounted for. A small piece of evidence is the small Chester Beatty papyrus fragment which was published by Bonner as fragment 3 of the Apocryphal Ezekiel fragments. This preserves at its recto a text Milik identified as part of 91:3. The verso, however, shows a division mark, similar to

1. For the principles of this kind of examination, see DJD 20, 3-4.

2. Not only in lines 2-5 of fragment *a* (Milik 1976, 1 ii 14-17), but also where the Aramaic has more space than necessary for a retroversion of the Ethiopic, e.g., 1 ii 20, and 1 iii 16-17.

3. Cf. also Pietersma (1987, 44). Independently we arrive by the same method of calculation at the same results.

that which divides the Epistle from Melito's Homily. If Milik's identification is accepted, this would mean that almost one page preceded the Greek text of 91:3. In other words, I do not think Milik's reconstruction is altogether impossible.

I do think that both Milik and Olson overlooked two alternatives. First, both scholars proceed from the assumption that the missing text of the Apocalypse of Weeks corresponds more or less to that of the Ethiopic. On this assumption they calculate the height of a column as twenty-five to twenty-six lines. Yet, Milik also observes on the basis of the many mistakes that the scribe must have been very tired when copying this column. If one assumes, as a working hypothesis, that this tired scribe skipped by *homoioteleuton* from week 3 "at its end a man will be chosen as the plant of righteous judgment" to week 7 "at its end the chosen righteous will be chosen, from the plant of righteous judgment," then we would have much shorter columns (of sixteen lines) and we do not have to argue for extreme differences in size between the Aramaic and Greek.[4]

Second, both Olson and Milik do not really consider the possibility of additional materials at the beginning of the scroll. This need not of necessity be the Animal Apocalypse. It might also be text corresponding to Ethiopic Enoch 81 or 83–84. In fact, Milik suggests a blank column at the beginning of the sheet, presumably because he does not like the idea of a sheet with only two columns.

Here we should comment briefly on the manuscript. First, the manuscript seems to me to belong to the category of nonofficial or even private copies. The semicursive script, the irregular lengths of the lines, the crammed lines all are the opposite of the bookhands of the same period.

Secondly, Boccaccini's suggestion that the Qumran manuscripts contained only the proto-epistle cannot be verified or falsified on the basis of the present manuscripts (4QEn^c and 4QEn^g).

If one proceeds from calculations based on a height of twenty-five to twenty-six lines per column (thus both Milik and Olson), then Milik's 4Q212 (containing chaps. 91–105) probably consisted of fourteen columns (two meters), whereas Boccaccini's 4Q212 consisted of from four to six columns; only the proto-epistle according to Olson's reconstruction or perhaps the upper part of a fifth column for the shorter version, and the proto-epistle plus chapters 106–107 for the longer version.

These figures change if one follows my suggestion of a shorter column iv of circa sixteen lines. From a codicological point of view one cannot say anything more. However, especially if the columns were only sixteen lines high, I

---

4. Almost thirteen lines in Flemming's edition would be accounted for (Flemming and Radermacher 1901).

would be inclined to argue for a relatively short scroll, like the one Boccaccini argued for, that is, without the middle section.

Thirdly, with regard to Nickelsburg's suggestion of a testament in 4Q204 (4QEn^c) including chapters 81–82:4a but without 92, we have the problem that 4Q212 has a version of 92 attached (at least in part) to 91:18-19. It seems to me that a composition which begins abruptly with 91:1 is indeed problematic, but we cannot of course determine the form and extent of a missing introduction.

Another question concerning chapter 92 arises from the fact that it is clear that the crucial verse 92:1, which may seem to be either an introduction or a postscript, has different forms in Aramaic and Ethiopic, and perhaps even in Greek if the Chester Beatty fragment corresponds to the verse. Nickelsburg's criticisms of Olson are mainly based upon the Ethiopic text. Also, in 93:1 we see divergences between the Ethiopic and the Aramaic, which shows that at some stage the headings have been reedited. With regard to the few preserved elements of 92:1 in Aramaic, "and he gave to Methuselah," I would indeed suggest a postscript. Note that the idea of giving books or whatever to Methuselah is attested only in chapter 82.

The Greek Fragments of Enoch
from Qumran Cave 7

Peter W. Flint

One intriguing group of manuscripts found at Qumran are the Greek fragments published by Maurice Baillet in DJD 3 (1962). Since 1972 some scholars have attempted to identify verses from Mark and portions of other New Testament books in these fragments, giving rise to much discussion and controversy. This article will detail how some of the Cave 7 pieces contain portions from the Septuagint, assess whether others preserve New Testament writings, and show how several more contain material from 1 Enoch.

The Attempt to Identify New Testament Manuscripts at Qumran

Virtually all scholars agree that the scrolls found at Qumran were copied from before 250 B.C.E. to 68 C.E., which means several were copied during the lifetimes of Jesus and his apostles. Some scholars have thus wondered whether any New Testament writings are preserved in the caves at Qumran — which, if true, would have serious implications for New Testament scholarship on the writing and development of the New Testament.

In 1972 the Spanish scholar José O'Callaghan made the bold announcement that he had identified nine fragments containing parts of the New Testament from Cave 7 at Qumran (O'Callaghan 1972). O'Callaghan claimed to have identified Greek fragments of Mark, Acts, Romans, 1 Timothy, James, and 2 Peter, with varying degrees of certainty. He dated eight of these pieces within the Qumran period (the lone exception being 4Q4 at about 100 C.E.).

Manuscript	Contents	Identification	Date
7Q4	1 Tim 3:16; 4:1, 3	Certain	ca. 100 C.E.
7Q5	Mark 6:52-53	Certain	ca. 50 C.E.
7Q6.1	Mark 4:28	Certain	ca. 50 C.E.
7Q6.2	Acts 27:38	Probable	ca. 60 C.E.
7Q7	Mark 12:17	Probable	ca. 50 C.E.
7Q8	James 1:23-24	Certain	ca. 50-70 C.E.
7Q9	Rom 5:11-12	Probable	ca. 50-60 C.E.
7Q10	2 Pet 1:15	Possible	ca. 60 C.E.
7Q15	Mark 6:48	Possible	ca. 50 C.E.

If correct, O'Callaghan's identifications pose enormous problems for scholars of early Judaism and the New Testament. First, this would mean either that early Christians had contact with the Qumran community, or that Christians hid their documents in one of the Qumran caves after the community had been dispersed in 68 C.E. Second, it challenges long-held theories regarding the formation of the New Testament; if parts of Mark, Acts, and several epistles were actually found in Cave 7, it may be argued that many New Testament writings were completed far earlier than was previously supposed.

A Closer Examination of the Evidence

When we examine fragments 3-18 of the Cave 7 Greek scrolls (we shall return later to fragments 1-2, which were identified earlier), several problems arise to challenge O'Callaghan's proposal. First, we are dealing with very meager evidence, which is evident on the plate: the largest fragment is 4.2, which measures a mere 6.8 by 3.4 centimeters, while several more fragments are tiny and preserve just a few letters. Furthermore, only five complete words clearly survive, none of which is distinctive enough to aid in identifying the passages involved. There are two instances of καί on fragments 3 and 5, a single instance of τί on fragment 3, and two instances of τῶι on fragments 5 and 15. The second objection to O'Callaghan's thesis is his late dating of many manuscripts. The two Greek fragments from Cave 7 that were identified early on by scholars — 7Q1 and 7Q2 — are both dated at about 100 B.C.E. Moreover, some fragments listed by O'Callaghan are given earlier dates in the official edition (DJD 3): 7Q4 is dated at about 100 B.C.E., and 7Q5 at 50 B.C.E. to 50 C.E. (most are not given dates since they preserve so few letters) (Baillet 1962, 144-45). Like several other scholars who find alleged connections between the scrolls and the New Testament, O'Callaghan is obliged to date all the pieces listed by him to the mid–first century C.E. or later.

Third, the identifications made by O'Callaghan are tenuous and speculative. For example, his treatment of 7Q5, one of the largest fragments involved, relies on unconvincing evidence. In the facing transcriptions and translations of Mark 6:52-54 that follow, the traditional text of line 4 would be too long for a proper alignment in 7Q5; O'Callaghan's reconstruction thus omits ἐπὶ τὴν γῆν ("to the land") so that the words can line up correctly. This variant reading is not supported by any significant manuscript of the New Testament, only a medieval Latin one.

7Q5 (O'Callaghan)	*Mark 6:52-54*
[⁵²οὐ γὰρ]	⁵²οὐ γὰρ
[συνῆκαν] ἐ[πὶ τοῖς ἄρτοις],	συνῆκαν ἐπὶ τοῖς ἄρτοις,
[ἀλλ᾽ ἦν α]ὐτῶν ἡ [καρδία πεπωρω-]	ἀλλ᾽ ἦν αὐτῶν ἡ καρδία πεπωρω-
[μέν]η. ⁵³Καὶ τι[απεράσαντες]	μένη. ⁵³Καὶ διαπεράσαντες
[ἦλθον εἰς Γε]ννησ[αρὲτ καὶ]	ἐπὶ τὴν γῆν ἦλθον εἰς Γεννησαρὲτ καὶ
[προσωρμίσ]θησα[ν. ⁵⁴καὶ ἐξελ-]	προσωρμίσθησαν. ⁵⁴καὶ ἐξελ-
[θόντων αὐτῶν ἐκ τοῦ πλοίου εὐθὺς]	θόντων αὐτῶν ἐκ τοῦ πλοίου εὐθὺς
[ἐπιγνόντες αὐτὸν]	ἐπιγνόντες αὐτὸν
[⁵²For they did not]	⁵²For they did not
[understand] a[bout the loaves],	understand about the loaves,
[but t]heir [hearts were harden-]	but their hearts were harden-
[e]d. ⁵³And [when they had] cr[ossed over],	ed. ⁵³And when they had crossed over,
[they came to Ge]nnes[aret and]	they came to land at Gennesaret and
[moored the] boa[t. ⁵⁴And when they disem-]	moored the boat. ⁵⁴And when they disem-
[barked from the boat, people straightaway]	barked from the boat, people straightaway
[recognized him.]	recognized him.

Identifying the Greek Scrolls from Cave 7

Little Support for O'Callaghan's View

O'Callaghan found few followers for his thesis, with the notable exception of Carsten Peter Thiede, who agrees that several pieces from Cave 7 contain text from the Gospels or the Epistles (Thiede 1995, 189-97).

In particular, O'Callaghan's transcription of fragment 5 was questioned by several scholars, who offered different readings for certain lines. Two varying transcriptions of the surviving Greek letters appear as follows (Stanton 1995, 27):

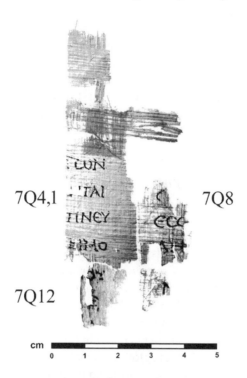

7Q4,1   7Q8

7Q12

cm
0   1   2   3   4   5

The Greek fragments 7Q3-18 (7QpapEn gr),
courtesy of the Israel Antiquities Authority

Published in 1962 by Maurice Baillet in DJD 3 (pl. XXX). Photograph used with permission of Thomas Nelson, Inc. This juxtaposition © 1997 by Ernest A. Munro, Jr. Not included here are a few additional Greek fragments: 7Q1 (Exod 28:4-7), 7Q2 (Ep Jeremiah vv. 43-44), and 7Q19 (six pieces that do not feature in O'Callaghan's identifications or the present discussion).

] . [	]ε[
] . τωι α . [	] υτωγη [
] η και τ . [	]η καιτι [
] γνη . [	] γνησ [
] θη . . [	] θησα [
S. Pickering and R. Cook	C. P. Thiede

Most scholars remained unclear as to exactly what texts the Cave 7 fragments do contain, but were united in rejecting any identification with New Testament texts. In 2000 the German scholar Stefan Enste devoted an entire book to whether the single fragment 7Q5 contains text from Mark 6:52-53 — and concluded that it does not (Enste 2000). The majority remained unconvinced both because of the challenges O'Callaghan's theory posed to traditional views on the formation of the New Testament, and because of the flimsy evidence on which it is based. To identify New Testament writings in tiny fragments such as 7Q6–7Q10 and 7Q15 seems speculative at best. It is fair to conclude that most scholars were agreed on what texts 7Q3-18 do *not* contain, but little solid evidence was offered on what these fragments *do* contain.

Portions of the Greek Bible

The first two pieces from this cave, 7Q1 and 7Q2, were identified by their editor as containing passages from the Septuagint: the Pentateuch (Exod 28:4-7) and the Apocrypha/Deuterocanonicals (Epistle of Jeremiah, vv. 43-44) (Baillet 1962, 143). It thus seemed reasonable to many scholars that most — perhaps even all — of the other Cave 7 fragments also preserve text from the Greek Bible. Accordingly, in the edition of the Cave 7 fragments (Baillet 1962, 143-44), editor Maurice Baillet classified 7Q3–7Q5 as "biblical texts (?)," and Emanuel Tov has more recently suggested that all fragments from this cave are probably from the Septuagint ("probably all biblical," Tov 2002, 150).

In 1992 the Spanish scholar Vittoria Spottorno proposed that 7Q5 preserves text from the book of Zechariah (7:3b-5), and provided a transcription to support her view (Spottorno 1992; the transcriptions of Baillet and O'Callaghan are provided for comparison):

] . [	]ε[	] τ [
] . τῷ α . [	] υτωγη [	] εγωγε [
] η καὶ τω [	] η καιτι [	] ς και π [
ἐγέ] γνησ [εν	] γνησ [	] γνησ [
] θηεσ [	] θησα [	] ωηεγ [
		] ε [
Baillet (1962)	O'Callaghan (1972)	Spottorno (1992)

Spottorno's identification, however, presents numerous problems, including doubtful readings of several Greek letters and variations from all known Greek texts of Zechariah 7:3-5. These variants include: (a) In verse 4 her lineup of letters requires Spottorno to omit "of hosts" to produce the shorter reading "the LORD" (compare NRSV, "the LORD of hosts"). (b) In verse 5 her reconstruction requires a longer text: "the priests of the land" (NRSV: "the priests"). (c) In the same verse, Spottorno proposes "in the fifth month" and "in the seventh month" (LXX: "in the fifth months" and "in the seventh months") (cf. Thiede 1995, 189-95). Compare the accompanying translation based on the Spanish scholar's reading of 7Q5 with the same passage adapted from the Septuagint.

Zech 7:3b-5 (Spottorno)	English Translation (LXX)
[3]. . . "Should I mourn and practice abstinence in the fifth month, as I have done for so many years?" [4]Then the word of **the Lord** came to me: [5]Say to all the people of the land and to **the priests of the land:** When you fasted and lamented in **the fifth month** and in **the seventh month,** for these seventy years, was it for me that you fasted?	[3]. . . "Should I mourn and practice abstinence in the fifth month, as I have done for so many years?" [4]Then the word of **the Lord of hosts** came to me: [5]Say to all the people of the land and to **the priests:** When you fasted and lamented in **the fifth months** and in **the seventh months,** for these seventy years, was it for me that you fasted?

Portions of 1 Enoch

A breakthrough was to come in the late 1980s and the 1990s — but in a direction that few expected. Many scholars had thus far focused on New Testament passages or especially Septuagint passages in the quest to identify the Greek fragments from Cave 7. Moreover, most researchers had viewed individual fragments as representing different books or separate parts of books. The new results were achieved only when other Jewish literature written in Greek was taken into account, and some of the Cave 7 fragments were pieced together or at least placed near to each other in reconstructing the original manuscript.

The German scholar Wilhelm Nebe and the French scholar Émile Puech concluded that several Cave 7 fragments are not from the New Testament or the Septuagint, but from the pseudepigraphical book of 1 Enoch. Nebe proposed that 7Q4.1 is part of 1 Enoch 103:3-4, that 7Q4.2 is from 98:11, and — with more reservation — that 7Q8 is from 103:7-8 (Nebe 1988).[1] For his part, Puech reiterated that 7Q4.1 contains text from 1 Enoch 103:3-4, but disagreed with Nebe's contention that 7Q4.2 is part of 98:11, preferring to place this fragment in 105:1.

---

1. Nebe points out that the association of 7Q8 with 1 En 103:7-8 is not assured since the fragment could also belong to Zech 8:8; Isa 1:29-30; Ps 18:14-15; Dan 2:43; Eccles 6:3; or Num 22:38. None of these six passages, however, is near a text that can serve as an identification for 7Q4.1 (Nebe 1988, 632-33 n. 26).

He further proposed that 7Q11 is part of 1 Enoch 100:12, that 7Q13 belongs to 103:15, and that 7Q14 preserves traces of 103:12 (Puech 1996; 1997).

Some of Nebe's and Puech's identifications were confirmed, and another was added, by the American sleuth Ernest A. Muro, who pieced together 7Q4.1, 7Q8, and 7Q12 and confirmed that they belong to 1 Enoch 103:3-8. As he studied the photographs of 7Q3-18, all written on papyrus, Muro's expertise in carpentry, different woods, and their grains caused him to focus on a distinctive physical characteristic common to some of the fragments: horizontal fibres with a characteristic downward slope to the right. While previous efforts to identify 7Q4.1, 7Q8, and 7Q12 had been hampered by the assumption that they were originally from different scrolls, Muro assembled on the basis of the matching papyrus fibers one ensemble consisting of three separate fragments. This enables the reader to treat 7Q4.1–7Q8–7Q12 as one large fragment (Muro 1997).

We may now reconstruct 7Q4.1, 7Q8, and 7Q12 as preserving portions of 1 Enoch 103:3-8 on two successive columns of a scroll classified as pap7QEn gr. These two columns must each have held about seventeen lines, with about twenty-four letter spaces to the line. This calculation is made possible by the blank top margin on fragment 4.1, the right margins on fragments 4.1 and 12, and the left margin on fragment 8. See the accompanying Greek transcription and an English translation; in both cases the letters actually preserved on the Cave 7 fragments are printed in bold type.

pap7QEn gr (1 Enoch 103:3-8)

top margin (col. I)

[ται και ἐγγέγραπται τ]**ῇ**   frg. 4.1
[ς ψυχῆς τῶν ἀποθανόν]**των**
[εὐσεβῶν· ⁴καὶ χαιρήσο]**νται**
[καὶ οὐ μὴ ἀπόλωται τὰ] **πνεύ**-
[ματα αὐτῶν οὐδε τὸ μν]**ημό**-
[συνον ἀπὸ προσώπου] **τοῦ**   frg. 12
[μεγάλου εἰς πάσας τὰς γ]ε-
[νεὰς τῶν αἰώνων. μὴ οὖν φο-]
[βεῖσθε τοὺς ὀνειδισμοὺς]
[αὐτῶν ⁵καὶ ὑμεῖς, οἱ νεκροὶ]
[τῶν ἁμαρτωλῶν, ὅταν ἀποθάν-]
[ητε ἐροῦσιν ἐφ' ὑμῖν, μακάρι-]
[οι ἁμαρτωλοὶ πάσας τὰς ἡμέ-]
[ρας αὐτῶν ὅσας εἴδοσαν ἐν]

English Translation *(APOT)*

top margin (col. I)

³[for good things and joy and honour have been prepared and written down for th]e [soul of the godly on]es **who** [have died. ⁴And they will rejo]ice, [and their] spi[rits will never perish, nor their me]**mo**[rial before the presence] **of** the [Great One for all g]e[nerations forever. So do not be afraid of their reproaches]. ⁵[But as for you, you corpses of sinners, when you die, people will say concerning you: "Blessed are the sinners; they have seen all their days, so many, in their

[τῆι ζωῆι αὐτῶν, καὶ ἐνδόξως]
[⁶ἀπεθάνοσαν, καὶ κρίσις]
[οὐκ ἐγενήθη ἐν τῆι ζωῆι αὐ-]

[top margin] (col. II)
[τῶν ⁷αὐτοὶ ὑμεῖς γινώσκ-]
[ετε ὅτι εἰς ἅϊδου κατάξου-]
σ[ιν τὰς ψυχὰς ὑμῶν,⁸καὶ ἐκεῖ]
ἔσο[νται ἐν ἀνάγκηι μεγά-]
λη[ι καὶ ἐν σκότει καὶ ἐ-]
ν[παγίδι καὶ ἐν φλογὶ καιομένηι],
[καὶ εἰς κρίσιν μεγάλην εἰσ-]
[ελεύσονται αἱ ψυχαὶ ὑμῶν]
[ἐν πάσαις ταῖς γενεαῖς τοῦ]
[αἰῶνος. οὐαὶ ὑμῖν, οὐκ ἔστ-]
[ιν ὑμῖν χαίρειν.   ]

frg. 8

lifetime, and in honour ⁶they have
died, and judgment has not taken
place in their lifetime."

[top margin] (col. II)
⁷(But) you yourselves realize that]
th[ey will drag your souls down to
Hades. ⁸And there] they w[ill be in
gr]ea[t anguish, and in darkness,
and e]n[trapped and in a burning
fire; and your souls will enter into
the great judgment for all generations forever. Woe to you, (for) you
are not able to rejoice!]

The identifications proposed by Nebe, Puech, and Muro all fall within the Epistle of Enoch (chaps. 91–107 of 1 Enoch). This particular section of the
pseudepigraphal book concerns the "two ways of the righteous and the sinner,"
and includes the Apocalypse of Weeks (91:12-17; 93:1-10) (Isaac 1983).

Progress Made So Far in Identifying the Cave 7 Fragments

By 2004 cumulative research has yielded several results, which are made clearer
when viewed in relation to O'Callaghan's original proposals:

Manuscript	O'Callaghan	Others
7Q4.1	1 Tim 3:16	1 En 103:3-4
7Q4.2	1 Tim 4:1, 3	1 En 98:11 or 105:1
7Q5	Mark 6:52-53	
7Q6.1	Mark 4:28	
7Q6.2	Acts 27:38	
7Q7	Mark 12:17	
7Q8	James 1:23-24	1 En 103:7-8
7Q9	Rom 5:11-12	
7Q10	2 Pet 1:15	
7Q11	—	1 En 100:12
7Q12	—	1 En 103:4

7Q13	—	1 En 103:15
7Q14	—	1 En 103:12
7Q15	Mark 6:48	

If the more recent identifications are correct, at least seven fragments belong to a manuscript which is classified as pap7QEn gr: four of these (7Q4.1, 7Q8, 7Q12, 7Q14) contain text from 1 Enoch 103:3-8, 12; one (7Q4.2) contains text from 98:11 or 105:1; one (7Q11) contains text from 100:12; and one (7Q13) contains text from 103:15.

But what of other fragments discussed by O'Callaghan that were not dealt with by Nebe, Puech, and Muro? These three authors have suggested identifications for only three pieces listed by the Spanish scholar — 7Q4.1, 7Q4.2, and 7Q8 — but have made no proposals for 7Q5, 7Q6.1, 7Q6.2, 7Q7, 7Q9, 7Q10, and 7Q15. Furthermore, to the best of my knowledge no one has offered proposals for 7Q3, 7Q16, 7Q17, or 7Q18.

Could some of these fragments preserve words from New Testament writings? Until they can be identified with certainty — which may never be possible for the smaller ones — it remains theoretically feasible that certain pieces may contain tiny portions of early New Testament books such as Mark. It is far more likely, however, that the unidentified Greek fragments from Cave 7 preserve text from the Septuagint (cf. frg. 1), the Apocrypha (frg. 2), or the pseudepigraphical book of 1 Enoch.

Significance of the Enoch Scroll from Cave 7

Although we are dealing with pieces of a damaged document, the existence of several Enochic fragments in Greek from Cave 7 is important for several reasons. (1) The recent identifications yield a "new" scroll (pap7QEn gr) from a group of previously unidentified fragments. (2) We now know that a Greek copy of 1 Enoch existed at Qumran; the others are all in Aramaic. (It is surprising that in his recent commentary on 1 Enoch George Nickelsburg [2001, 10-11] dismisses the notion that any of the Cave 7 fragments contain text from the pseudepigraphical book.) (3) This manuscript is a significant witness to the existence of the Epistle of Enoch in the scrolls (the only other being 4QQEn^g ar, which preserves text from 1 En 91:10 to 94). (4) This identification renders even more unlikely the existence of fragments containing New Testament passages in Cave 7. (5) Pap7QEn gr underscores the importance of 1 Enoch for the Qumran community (as it was for Jude, who cites 1 En 1:9 in vv. 14-15 of his epistle).

With the addition of pap7QEn gr, the total number of Enoch manuscripts found at Qumran rises to twelve (eleven from Cave 4 and one from Cave 7). The full list, with other pertinent details, is given in the accompanying table.

Manuscript	Number	Range of Contents	Date Copied
4QEn^a ar	4Q201	1:1 to 12:6	1st half 2nd c. B.C.E.
4QEn^b ar	4Q202	5:9 to 14:6	mid 2nd c. B.C.E.
4QEn^c ar	4Q204	1:9 to 107:2	last third 1st c. B.C.E.
4QEn^d ar	4Q205	22:13 to 89:44	last third 1st c. B.C.E.
4QEn^e ar	4Q206	18:15? to 89:30	1st half 1st c. B.C.E.
4QEn^f ar	4Q207	86:1-3	3rd quarter 2nd c. B.C.E.
4QEn^g ar	4Q212	91:10 to 94:2	mid 1st c. B.C.E.
4QEnastr^a ar	4Q208	73:1* to 74:9*	ca. 200 B.C.E.
4QEnastr^b ar	4Q209	73:1* to 82:13	early 1st c. C.E.
4QEnastr^c ar	4Q210	76:3 to 78:8	mid 1st c. B.C.E.
4QEnastr^d ar	4Q211	following 82:20**	2nd half 1st c. B.C.E.
pap7QEn gr	7Q4, 8, 11-13	98:11? to 103:15	ca. 100 B.C.E.

*4QEnastr^a ar and 4QEnastr^b ar contain material from the "synchronisitic calendar," the résumé of which is found in 1 En 73:1–74:9 (Milik 1976, 273-74). Although they may not preserve the precise text as indicated, they contain material akin to it.
**4QEnastr^d ar continues (with a description of winter) after the existing conclusion of the Ethiopic version (Milik 1976, 274, 297).

Response: Context, Text, and Social Setting
of the Apocalypse of Weeks

George W. E. Nickelsburg

The responses to my discussion of the Apocalypse of Weeks touch on many issues, some directly related to the topic of this volume, some inferentially so, and others uniquely related to the text itself. I shall focus mainly on the first two categories, treating them as they relate to the content and text of the apocalypse and, finally, to its social setting.

Content

Klaus Koch is correct that "righteousness" does not exhaust the meaning of Aramaic *qushṭa,* as I have indicated in my commentary. The double valence of *qushṭa* as "righteousness" and "truth" is matched in the apocalypse itself by its double antonyms, *shiqra* and *ḥamsa* ("deceit" and "violence"). It may also be indicated in the Greek and Ethiopic versions of the body of the Epistle, where the right path is qualified alternatively by *dikaiosynē* or *alētheia* and *ṣedeq* or *retʿ,* although the Hebraizing term *shevile ʾamit ʿalma* does occur in 1QapGen 6:2. But the problem remains how to translate the Aramaic. Would "uprightness" be better than "righteousness" because it has the connotation of straightness, which I take to be the basic meaning of *qushṭa?*

Koch's comparison of the apocalypse with 1QS 3:13–4:26 is especially fascinating and can be developed beyond what he has briefly indicated. First, both texts work with a polarity between what Koch calls two fields of power. In 1QS these are *ʾemet* and *ʿawel;* in the apocalypse they are *qushṭa* and *shiqra/ḥamsa.* In 1 Enoch 93:9 the Ethiopic root *ʿalawa* may reflect either Aramaic *shiqra* or

ʿawla. In 1QS ʾemet is connected with ṣedeq, similar to the dual valence of the Aramaic qushṭa.

Second, in both texts revealed wisdom and knowledge are central and related to righteousness. Third, both texts envision history moving from a beginning to an end. For the apocalypse the progression moves through a series of set periods. For 1QS there is an end, which comes at the moʿed (4:18, 20). For both, the end involves the annihilation of evil and the triumph of truth or righteousness, which is construed as a new creation, in one case cosmological, in the other anthropological. However, in 1 Enoch "all the glory of Adam" (1QS 4:23) has its counterpart in the companion piece to the Apocalypse of Weeks, the Animal Apocalypse (1 En 90:37-38). In broader context, we might note that 1QS 8:4-11 describes the community as both plant and building, and refers to the righteous as witnesses of truth for judgment, all of which finds a counterpart in 1 Enoch 93:10, 91:11. Finally, in the broader context of the Epistle one finds the repeated use of the image of the two ways (Nickelsburg 2001, 454-56), and there is one reference to the right way in the apocalypse (91:14).

While I do not wish to posit a direct literary dependence of 1QS 3:13–4:26 on the apocalypse, there is a parallel, polarized worldview in which truth and righteousness, on the one hand, and perversity or deceit and injustice, on the other hand, are reified and are characteristic of the community of the chosen, who are constituted by revelation. In 1QS 3:13–4:26 this reification is intensified to the point of positing two personal cosmic powers. While in 1 Enoch the antagonism of two opposing sets of angels appears only in chapters 6–11, there is a hint of the evil angel in the Epistle in 99:14, where a spirit of *error* (notably) pursues those who reject the foundation and eternal inheritance of the fathers. I think we could profitably pursue the comparison of the two texts.

Matthias Henze builds on Koch's analysis. He demonstrates that although the obvious structure of the Apocalypse of Weeks involves the progression of human history and its division into ten periods, the alternation of righteousness or truth and sin or deceit permeates and structures the author's view of history. Indeed, given the sketchy nature of the apocalypse, the repetition of this terminology is striking. This author sees the world in polarized, black-and-white terms, and given his identity of righteousness and truth with his own group — who are by definition the chosen — this is very much a we-against-them situation.

Michael Knibb takes up a number of issues. First, he is not convinced by my reasons for seeing the apocalypse as a preexistent piece of tradition that the author of the Epistle has integrated into his composition. He rightly notes that the absence of the body of the Epistle in 4QEnᶜ does not prove that it was not there. My point is this, however. Accepted wisdom states that MS c contained "the Epistle." Yet the preserved fragments attest only the very end of what is now in the Ethiopic version the very end of the Epistle, and I have argued that there are literary grounds for positing that these verses could have been the end of a collection that did not yet contain the body of the Epistle (Nickelsburg 2001, 335-37).

As to the relationship of the apocalypse's language of election with the lack of such in the body of the Epistle, I would make this point. I am less concerned with election as an ideology than I am with two different sets of terminology. In the apocalypse we have four references to the chosen (93:2, 5, 8, 10) and one to "the righteous," where they stand in opposition to "the wicked" (91:12). Yet the term "the chosen" appears nowhere in the body of the Epistle, and the verb and its adjectival form appear once, in the immediate context of the Epistle (94:4).

Instead one finds the proliferation of the terms "the righteous" and "the pious." That is, we have two alternative sets of terminology, one in the apocalypse and one in the body of the Epistle. Given dense, and almost exclusive use of the term in the apocalypse and its frequency in the Hebrew Bible, to say nothing of two other delineated sections of 1 Enoch (the introduction, chaps. 1–5, and the Parables, chaps. 37–71), I find its absence in the body of the Epistle and the presence of an alternative set of terms striking. If the Apocalypse of Weeks is the first part of a single composition by one author, I would expect the term "the chosen" to occur at least occasionally in the rest of the Epistle. Having said that, I should note that Knibb and I agree that the apocalypse is integrated with the Epistle and that, in a way, it provides not only a time referent but also a polarized conceptual framework for the Epistle.

Since the metaphor of the plant is central to the Apocalypse of Weeks (93:2, 5, 8, 10), it is not surprising that a number of my respondents have discussed the topic. As Stuckenbruck notes, I should have at least cited 4QInstruction, since 4Q418 81:13 is discussed by Tiller in the article that I consulted in my excursus (Nickelsburg 2001, 444-45). That I did not refer to it was an oversight. However, since a critical edition of that text was not available to me until the manuscript of my commentary was ready to go to press, I am not certain what I might have said about this particular passage. What I should have picked up is the association that Stuckenbruck finds between the prominent notion of wisdom in the passage and "the eter[nal] plant," though not with "the chosen" by that name, so far as I can see.

This association is important because it occurs also in a number of other passages, notably 1QS 8:4-7; CD 1:6-7; the related passage in 4Q306, cited by Lim; and 1 Enoch 10:2-3. Indeed, a number of these passages share a cluster of the same terms. Here I want to focus on the (eternal) plant and revealed wisdom or knowledge, which is sometimes connected with the notion of election.

The notion of revelation is especially prominent in the Apocalypse of Weeks. In addition to 93:10, where the chosen of the end time receive sevenfold wisdom and knowledge (which I take to be Enochic revelation), one finds the following: the law given at the time of Noah (93:4); Sinaitic revelation and, as Bedenbender probably rightly notes, the giving of the torah (93:6); the eschatological revelation of right law (91:14); and possibly the revelation of law to Abraham (93:5). In addition, there is the prominence of deceit *(shiqra),* which stands in contrast to it (93:4, 8, 11). Revealed wisdom is the special possession of the chosen, and of the righteous and pious (93:10), as 104:12-13 notes.

Without trying to collapse these texts into one, I suggest a common thread, which claims for certain people a special identity tied to revealed wisdom. I do not wish to claim that all these texts refer to the same group, and here I share the caution of both Tiller and Knibb, and I do not wish to apply the term "sectarian" to all of them. However, I suggest a common mentality that focuses on the claim of special knowledge and sometimes chosenness, which implies that certain other people are *not* the chosen and do *not* have this special knowledge (Nickelsburg 1985; cf. 1999; 2003b). In the Apocalypse of Weeks and, as I argue in my commentary, in one extended section in the body of the Epistle (98:9–99:10), these involve an exclusivist polarity between wisdom and deceit, the wise and those who lead many astray with their lies. The same worldview appears in 1QS; CD 1; the pesherim on Nahum, Psalms, and Habakkuk; as well as 1QH 12(4):5–13(5):4. In other texts the polarity is more muted or not at all evident. This is the case with 4QInstruction.

Where I do treat the relationship between this text and 1 Enoch — thanks to John Strugnell calling it to my attention — I state that "the text's epistemology, cosmology, and eschatology suggest that it represents a strand of Israelite sapiential tradition that also lies behind 1 Enoch" (Nickelsburg 2001, 59). Revealed wisdom comprises ethical and eschatological knowledge. What I think needs to be sorted out among these texts, and others in the sapiential tradition, are the content and nature, and the claimed or unclaimed source of revealed wisdom and knowledge, and the continuum along which the positing of such knowledge brings with it its foil: deceit and deceivers, lies and liars. The problem is perhaps not altogether different from the distinction one makes between gnosis and gnosticism.

Text

Peter Flint discusses the identification of certain Qumran Cave 7 fragments with text from the Epistle of Enoch as attested in the Chester Beatty–Michigan papyrus (CBM) (Bonner 1937, 65; Kenyon 1941, f. 11 r.). This identification attests the ingenuity and the papyrological and linguistic skills of the scholars who have proposed it, but I am skeptical of the identification for two reasons.

First, the meager size of the fragments. In the text reproduced by Flint, of a presumed twenty-eight lines and roughly 470 letters, the papyrus preserves a total of 26 letters, or 5 percent. These 26 letters occur in eleven groups of 1 to 4 letters, among which there is only one full word — the definite article *tou*. The only identifiable roots are *pneu[* = "spi[rits" (or "spiritual") and perhaps *eso[* = "[they] will be." Moreover, in line 1 the letter *eta* is read as part of the genitive singular article *t]ē[s,* where CBM reads the dative plural *tais*, in agreement with the Ethiopic. The tiny fraction of letters preserved in these scraps of papyrus raises a serious question about the validity of their identification as fragments of 1 Enoch 103:3-8.

Second, this question is exacerbated by an important text-critical problem that is not even addressed. CBM is a notoriously corrupt and defective text. To quote its first editor, "In addition to numerous irregularities in spelling and grammar, . . . almost every page exhibits errors of a more serious sort which show that the scribe was often drowsy or inattentive" (Bonner 1937, 17). To expand this observation, in comparison to the corresponding Ethiopic text, CBM has thirty-eight short readings, ranging from a few letters to several lines (Nickelsburg 1976). Given this propensity for short texts — some of them demonstrably omissions due to *homoioteleuton* or *homoiarchton* — the burden of proof for any short text in CBM lies with the person who accepts it as more original than its longer Ethiopic counterpart.

For 103:3-8 CBM has two such short readings. In the Ethiopic, verses 3-4 read (words unique to Ethiopic are in boldface type): "For all good and joy and honor have been prepared and written down for the spirits of those <u>who have died in righteousness,</u> **and much good will be given to you in the place of your labor, and your lot (will be) greater than the lot of the living. And they will come to life** — the spirit(s) of you <u>who have died in righteousness,</u> and they will rejoice **and be glad** and their spirits will not perish." In the Ethiopic, verses 5-6 read: "Blessed were the sinners; all their days <u>they have seen,</u> **and now they have died in goodness and wealth, and tribulation and slaughter <u>they have not seen</u>** in their life, but in honor they have died." Thus in the first seventeen lines of the reconstructed 7Q text, CBM, on which it is based, lacks two blocks of roughly twenty and twelve Greek words respectively, each block ending with a set of words identical with those at the end of the previous section (*homoioteleuton*).

If one accepts the Greek behind the Ethiopic as original, the restoration of 7Q is falsified after its second line and again after its thirteenth line. If one wishes to maintain, nevertheless, that the 7Q fragments do in fact preserve text from 1 Enoch 103, one must argue one of the following positions.

1. Despite the fact that the two long readings end in *homoioteleuton,* they are expansive, and despite CBM's propensity to have short and defective readings, these short readings are more original.

2. If one acknowledges that the short readings in CBM are defective, these defective readings were in place already in the first century, and the Greek manuscript from which the Ethiopic was translated, which did not have these omissions, derived from an archetype that was even earlier than the Qumran fragments.

If one asserts either of these positions, one must argue the case and not ignore the textual evidence. In my view it is methodologically questionable to resort to either of these hypotheses in order to support the restoration of a set of fragments that preserve a mere 5 percent of the alleged text being restored, and such fragile argumentation should not be used as the foundation of a theory about the presence of the Greek Epistle of Enoch at Qumran.

Communities and Social Settings

Finally I come to the sociological issue, which a number of my respondents have touched on and which I have implied at times in the earlier parts of this response. The key words are "groups" and "communities." I can only touch on a couple of points.

First, to follow through on Tiller's comments, what do we mean by "group" and "community"? Since the 1960s at least, there has been a tendency in biblical studies to ascribe texts to collective entities, often without any notion, much less description, of what these entities might be. We might learn something about this development from the sociology of knowledge: in New Testament studies the tendency was probably more theological than sociological, since this field of study had not yet discovered the social sciences. In some cases the development probably had a polemical theological or antitheological matrix. But this is another matter. I simply want to suggest that it is methodologically questionable to assume that a text or idea or group of ideas necessarily implies a group. However, if we posit a group, on what grounds do we do so, and what concretely do we imagine and mean when we use the term? What might we know about its structure or organization, its function(s), its origins, its membership, and its rules or discipline? In most cases precious little, with the exception of Philo's and Josephus's Essenes, the Qumran *yaḥad,* and to some degree the Pauline churches and Matthew's group. So that is one set of questions: Are texts always the products of groups, and if so, of what sort?

George W. E. Nickelsburg

The second major question relates to the identity of these groups. Here again we have been quick out of the gate to identify texts with Pharisees, Sadducees, Essenes, or Hasidim. What we have learned since the discovery of the scrolls is the greater complexity of Judaism in the centuries around the turn of the era (Nickelsburg 2003a, 160-82). Ithamar Gruenwald takes note of that, and among present company Albert Baumgarten (1997) has argued it at length.

Moving on from this, I want to make several points that relate to the Enochic corpus in general, and the Apocalypse of Weeks and related texts in specific. First, I think the writings comprised by 1 Enoch reflect some sort of ongoing communal existence. I find this a probable inference from the fact that the traditions in this corpus evolved and built on one another over the long course of three centuries. The traditions and the texts were transmitted through some sort of channel or channels, which had some sort of Enochic identification. For the most part, with the exception perhaps of the Astronomical Book (or Book of the Luminaries), there was a self-understanding of being the eschatological community of the chosen, constituted by revelation. This is evident in the Animal Apocalypse, the Apocalypse of Weeks, the body of the Epistle, and the Book of the Parables. That there was some sense of community is indicated by collective terms like "the chosen," "the pious," "the houses of his congregation" (1 En 46:8). To this we might add a few other particulars, but we know a great deal less about them than we know about Josephus's or Philo's Essenes or the Qumran yaḥad.

As to the identity of this group or these groups, we know little beyond their *Enochic* identity. Though Timothy Lim cites my association of the Animal Vision with hypotheses about the Hasidim, I put *"may be"* in italics (Nickelsburg 2001, 363). Similarly, I do not extrapolate from the Greek terms *eusebeis* and *hosioi* a Hasidic identity of the author of the Epistle. My principal problem is that we know very little for certain about the Hasidim. Although John Kampen (1988, 52-53) may be right that the transliteration in 1 and 2 Maccabees implies a group of that name, it is also probable that the term was sometimes used in a generic sense without reference to an organized group.

When we come to the specific topic of Enoch studies, I think we have to be very careful. There is no evidence that any of the Enochic books was composed at Qumran. Yet at least for a period they seem to have been held in considerable favor there. But how did they get there? Were they brought by some group of people, or by individuals at different times and from different places? The same question must be asked of other books held in favor at Qumran: Jubilees, the Temple Scroll, Aramaic Levi, and 4QInstruction.

Finally, what do we make of the community that seems to be implied in various texts that refer to the (eternal) plant? The matter has been treated in various ways by Tiller in his article and by Stuckenbruck and Knibb in their responses. How large a cluster of ideas and terms, and how fixed a form, must we have in order to posit a common tradition rather than natural interpretations and enhancements of a biblical term, metaphor, or image? And among the commonalities, where do we find differences and what do they imply sociologically? These are big questions!

For myself, I imagine some sort of reform movement in Judaism in the Hellenistic period, implied by the Animal Apocalypse, the Apocalypse of Weeks, the book of Jubilees, the Damascus Document, 1QS 8, and of course, other Qumran texts. I use the term "movement" advisedly. I do not imply an *organized, coordinated* movement, but a *proliferation* of individuals and groups, some of whom had some connection with one another. Among them I see a mentality that believes that things were not right in Israel and, specifically to some degree, in the temple. This mentality led in some cases to the formation of groups, though we know little about most of them. To me it is not so important to pin names on them, and to define interrelationships, though, as we have learned from the social sciences, we should do our best to be concrete and specific. In the final analysis we come a long way when we appreciate the individual contours in particular texts and the variegation among them. At the same time, we can guard against constructing hypotheses that are begotten of our desire to know more than the data allow us to know.

References to Part Three

Albani, Matthias. 1994. *Astronomie und Schöpfungsglaube. Untersuchungen zum astronomischen Henochbuch.* WMANT 68. Neukirchen-Vluyn: Neukirchener Verlag.

Baillet, Maurice. 1962. "Grotte 7: B. Fragments non Identifiés." In Maurice Baillet, Josef T. Milik, and Roland de Vaux, *Les 'Petites Grottes' de Qumran: Exploration de la falaise, Les grottes 2Q, 3Q, 5Q, 6Q, 7Q, à 10Q, Le rouleau de cuivre,* 1:143-45 (text) and 2:xxx (pl.). 2 vols. DJD 3. Oxford: Clarendon.

Baumgarten, Albert I. 1997. *The Flourishing of Jewish Sects in the Maccabean Era: An Interpretation.* JSJSup 55. Leiden: Brill.

Baumgarten, Joseph M. 1967. "The Essene Avoidance of Oil and the Laws of Purity." *RevQ* 6:183-93.

Bedenbender, Andreas. 2000. *Der Gott der Welt tritt auf den Sinai: Entstehung, Entwicklung und Funktionsweise der frühjüdischen Apokalyptik.* ANTZ 8. Berlin: Institut Kirche und Judentum.

Beyer, Klaus. 1984. *Die aramäischen Texte vom Toten Meer.* Göttingen: Vandenhoeck & Ruprecht.

———. 1994. *Die aramäischen Texte vom Toten Meer.* Supplementary volume. Göttingen: Vandenhoeck & Ruprecht.

Black, Matthew. 1985. *The Book of Enoch or 1 Enoch.* SVTP 7. Leiden: Brill.

Boccaccini, Gabriele. 1998. *Beyond the Essene Hypothesis: The Parting of the Ways between Qumran and Enochic Judaism.* Grand Rapids: Eerdmans.

Bogaert, Pierre. 1969. *L'Apocalypse Syriaque de Baruch.* SC 144. Paris: Cerf.

Bonner, Campbell. 1937. *The Last Chapters of Enoch in Greek.* London: Chatto and Windus.

Boyce, Mary. 1982. *A History of Zoroastrianism II.* HO 1,8,1,2,2A. Leiden: Brill.

Charles, Robert H. 1912. *The Book of Enoch or 1 Enoch.* Oxford: Clarendon.

————. 1913. *The Apocrypha and Pseudepigrapha of the Old Testament.* Oxford: Clarendon.

Charlesworth, James H., ed. 1996. *The Dead Sea Scrolls: The Rule of the Community.* Philadelphia: American Interfaith Institute.

Collins, John J. 1984. *The Apocalyptic Imagination: An Introduction to the Jewish Matrix of Christianity.* New York: Crossroad.

————. 1993. *Daniel: A Commentary on the Book of Daniel.* Minneapolis: Augsburg Fortress.

————. 1998. *The Apocalyptic Imagination: An Introduction to Jewish Apocalyptic Literature.* 2nd ed. Grand Rapids: Eerdmans.

————. 1999. "Pseudepigraphy and Group Formation in Second Temple Judaism." In *Pseudepigraphic Perspectives: The Apocrypha and Pseudepigrapha in Light of the Dead Sea Scrolls,* edited by Esther G. Chazon and Michael E. Stone, 43-58. Leiden: Brill.

Cowley, Arthur E. 1923. *Aramaic Papyri of the Fifth Century* B.C. Oxford: Clarendon.

Dexinger, Ferdinand. 1977. *Henochs Zehnwochenapokalypse und offene Probleme der Apokalyptikforschung.* SPB 29. Leiden: Brill.

Donner, Herbert, and Wolfgang Röllig. 1968. *Kanaanäische und Aramäische Inschriften II.* 2nd ed. Wiesbaden: Harrassowitz.

Drower, Ethel S., and Rudolf Macuch, eds. 1963. *A Mandaic Dictionary.* Oxford: Clarendon.

Duhaime, Jean. 2000. "Dualism." In *Encyclopedia of the Dead Sea Scrolls,* edited by Lawrence H. Schiffman and James C. VanderKam, 215-20. Oxford: Oxford University Press.

Elgvin, Torleif. 1998. "The Mystery to Come: Early Essene Theology of Revelation." In *Qumran between the Old and New Testaments,* edited by Frederick H. Cryer and Thomas L. Thompson, 113-50. Copenhagen International Seminar 6 and JSOTSup 290. Sheffield: Sheffield Academic Press.

Enste, Stefan. 2000. *Kein Markustext in Qumran.* Novum Testamentum et Orbis Antiquus 45. Freiburg: Universitätsverlag; Göttingen: Vandenhoeck & Ruprecht.

Flemming, Johannes, and Ludwig Radermacher. 1901. *Das Buch Henoch.* GCS 5. Leipzig: Hinrichs.

Flint, Peter W. 1998-99. "'Apocrypha,' Other Previously-Known Writings, and 'Pseudepigrapha' in the Dead Sea Scrolls." In *The Dead Sea Scrolls after Fifty Years: A Comprehensive Assessment,* edited by Peter W. Flint and James C. VanderKam, 2:24-66, esp. 42-43. 2 vols. Leiden: Brill.

García Martínez, Florentino. 1992. *Qumran and Apocalyptic: Studies on the Aramaic Texts from Qumran.* STDJ 9. Leiden: Brill.

Hartman, Lars. 1975-76. "The Functions of Some So-Called Apocalyptic Timetables." *NTS* 22:1-14.

Hengel, Martin. 1974. *Judaism and Hellenism: Studies in Their Encounter in Palestine during the Early Hellenistic Period.* Philadelphia: Fortress.

Hutter, Manfred. 1999. "Asmodeus." In *Dictionary of Deities and Demons in the Bible,* edited by Karel Van der Toorn, Bob Becking, and Pieter W. Van der Horst. 2nd ed. Leiden, Boston, and Cologne: Brill.

Isaac, Ephraim. 1983. "1 (Ethiopic Apocalypse of) Enoch." In *The Old Testament Pseudepigrapha,* edited by J. H. Charlesworth, 1:5-89, esp. 72-89. Garden City, N.Y.: Doubleday.

Kampen, John. 1988. *The Hasideans and the Origin of Pharisaism: A Study of 1 and 2 Maccabees.* SBLSCS 28. Atlanta: Scholars.

Kent, Roland G. 1953. *Old Persian.* AOS 33. New Haven: American Oriental Society.

Kenyon, Frederic G., ed. 1941. *The Chester Beatty Biblical Papyri; Descriptions and Texts of Twelve Manuscripts on Papyrus of the Greek Bible, Fasciculus VIII, Enoch and Melito.* London: Emery Walker.

Knibb, Michael A. 1978. *The Ethiopic Book of Enoch: A New Edition in the Light of the Aramaic Dead Sea Fragments.* 2 vols. Oxford: Clarendon.

————. 1987. *The Qumran Community.* Cambridge: Cambridge University Press.

Koch, Klaus. 1983. "Sabbatstruktur der Geschichte: Die sogenannte Zehn-Wochen-Apokalypse (1Hen 93,1-10; 91,11-17) und das Ringen um die alttestamentliche Chronologie im späten Israelitentum." *ZNW* 95:403-30. Reprinted in *Vor der Wende der Zeiten: Beiträge zur apokalyptischen Literatur.* Gesammelte Aufsätze 3, ed. Uwe Gleßmer and Martin Krause (Neukirchen: Neukirchener Verlag, 1996), 45-76.

————. 1986. *Daniel,* part 1. BKAT 22. Neukirchen-Vluyn: Neukirchener Verlag.

————. 1994. *Daniel,* part 2. BKAT 22. Neukirchen-Vluyn: Neukirchener Verlag.

————. 1996. *Vor der Wende der Zeiten. Beiträge zur apokalyptischen Literatur.* Gesammelte Aufsätze 3. Neukirchen-Vluyn: Neukirchener Verlag.

————. 1999. *Daniel,* part 3. BKAT 22. Neukirchen-Vluyn: Neukirchener Verlag.

————. 2001. *Daniel,* part 4. BKAT 22. Neukirchen-Vluyn: Neukirchener Verlag.

————. 2003. *Die aramäische Rezeption der hebräischen Bibel.* Gesammelte Aufsätze 4. Neukirchen-Vluyn: Neukirchener Verlag.

Kvanvig, Helge S. 1999. *Roots of Apocalyptic.* WMANT 61. Neukirchen-Vluyn: Neukirchener Verlag.

Lange, Armin. 1995. *Weisheit und Prädestination.* STDJ 18. Leiden: Brill.

Lim, Timothy H. 2000. "4QMen of the People Who Err." In *Qumran Cave 4. XXVI,* 249-54. DJD 36. Oxford: Clarendon.

Milik, Josef T. 1976. *The Books of Enoch, Aramaic Fragments of Qumrân Cave 4.* Oxford: Clarendon.

Muro, Ernest A. 1997. "The Greek Fragments of Enoch from Qumran Cave 7 (7Q4, 7Q8, & 7Q12 = 7QEn gr = Enoch 103:3-4, 7-8)." *RevQ* 18, no. 70: 307-12.

Nebe, G.-Wilhelm. 1988. "7Q4 — Möglichkeit und Grenze einer Identifikation." *RevQ* 13, nos. 49-52 (Carmignac Memorial): 629-33.

Nickelsburg, George W. E. 1976. "Enoch 97–104: A Study of the Greek and Ethiopic Texts." In *Armenian and Biblical Studies,* edited by Michael E. Stone, 112-35. Sion Supplements 1. Jerusalem: St. James Press.

————. 1977. "The Apocalyptic Message of 1 Enoch 92–105." *CBQ* 39:313-15.

————. 1982. "The Epistle of Enoch and the Qumran Literature." *JJS* 33:333-48.

————. 1985. "Revealed Wisdom as a Criterion for Inclusion and Exclusion: From Jewish Sectarianism to Early Christianity." In *To See Ourselves as Others See Us*, edited by Jacob Neusner and Ernest S. Frerichs, 73-91. Atlanta: Scholars.

————. 1986. "1 Enoch and Qumran Origins: The State of the Question and Some Prospects for Answers." In SBLSP, 341-60. Atlanta: Scholars.

————. 1999. "The Nature and Function of Revelation in 1 Enoch, Jubilees, and Some Qumranic Documents." In *Pseudepigraphical Perspectives: The Apocrypha and Pseudepigrapha in Light of the Dead Sea Scrolls, Proceedings of the International Symposium of the Orion Center for the Study of the Dead Sea Scrolls and Associated Literature, 12-14 January 1997*, edited by Esther G. Chazon and Michael E. Stone, 91-119. STDJ 31. Leiden: Brill.

————. 2001. *1 Enoch 1: A Commentary on the Book of 1 Enoch Chapters 1–36; 81–108*. Hermeneia. Minneapolis: Fortress.

————. 2003a. *Ancient Judaism and Christian Origins: Diversity, Continuity, and Transformation*. Minneapolis: Fortress.

————. 2003b. "Religious Exclusivism: A World View Governing Some Texts Found at Qumran." In *George W. E. Nickelsburg in Perspective: An Ongoing Dialogue of Learning*, edited by Jacob Neusner and Alan S. Avery-Peck, 1:139-61. 2 vols. JSJSup 80. Leiden: Brill. With a response by Carol A. Newsom (162-68).

O'Callaghan, José. 1972. "¿Papiros neo-testamentarios en la cueva 7 de Qumrân?" *Bib* 53:91-100. English translation by William L. Holladay: "New Testament Papyri in Qumrân Cave 7?" *JBL* 91 [Supplement] (1972): 1-14.

Olson, Daniel C. 1993. "Recovering the Original Sequence of 1 Enoch 91–93." *JSP* 11:69-94.

Pietersma, Albert. 1987. "New Greek Fragments of Biblical Manuscripts in the Chester Beatty Library." *BASP* 24:40-45.

Puech, Émile. 1996. "Notes sur les fragments grecs du manuscrit 7Q4 = 1 Hénoch 103 et 105." *RB* 103:592-600.

————. 1997. "Sept fragments de la Lettre d'Hénoch (1 Hén 100, 103 et 105) dans la grotte 7 de Qumrân (= 7QHén gr)." *RevQ* 18, no. 70: 313-23.

Qimron, Elisha, and John Strugnell. 1994. *Qumran Cave 4. V: Miqsat Ma'aseh Ha-Torah*. Oxford: Clarendon.

Sokoloff, Michael. 1990. *A Dictionary of Jewish Palestine Aramaic*. Ramat-Gan: Bar Ilan University Press.

Spottorno, Vittoria. 1992. "Una nueva posible identificacion de 7Q5." *Sefarad* 52:541-43.

Stanton, Graham. 1995. *Gospel Truth? New Light on Jesus and the Gospels*, 20-32. Valley Forge, Pa.: Trinity.

Stuckenbruck, Loren T. 1997. *The Book of Giants from Qumran*. TSAJ 63. Tübingen: Mohr Siebeck.

————. 2002. "4QInstruction and the Possible Influence of Early Enochic Traditions: An Evaluation." In *The Wisdom Texts from Qumran and the Development of*

Sapiential Thought, edited by Charlotte Hempel, Armin Lange, and Hermann Lichtenberger, 245-61. BETL 159. Leuven: Leuven University Press.

Thiede, Carsten Peter. 1995. *Rekindling the Word: In Search of Gospel Truth,* 189-97. Leominster, U.K.: Gracewing; Valley Forge, Pa.: Trinity.

Tiller, Patrick. 1997. "The 'Eternal Planting' in the Dead Sea Scrolls." *DSD* 4:312-35.

Tov, Emanuel. 2002. "The Biblical Texts from the Judean Desert — an Overview and Analysis of All the Published Texts." In *The Bible as Book: The Hebrew Bible and the Judean Desert Discoveries. Proceedings of the Conference Held at Hampton Court, Herefordshire, 18-21 June 2000,* edited by Edward D. Herbert and Emanuel Tov. London: British Library.

Uhlig, Siegbert. 1984. *Das Äthiopische Henochbuch.* JSHRZ V/6. Gütersloh: Gütersloher Verlagshaus Gerd Mohn.

VanderKam, James C. 1984a. *Enoch and the Growth of an Apocalyptic Tradition.* CBQMS 16. Washington, D.C.: Catholic Biblical Association of America.

———. 1984b. "Studies in the Apocalypse of Weeks (*1 Enoch* 93:1-10; 91:11-17)." *CBQ* 46:511-23.

———. 1995. *Enoch: A Man for All Generations.* Columbia: University of South Carolina Press.

———. 2001. *An Introduction to Early Judaism.* Grand Rapids: Eerdmans.

Vermes, Geza. 1997. *The Complete Dead Sea Scrolls in English.* London: Penguin Books.

Walck, Leslie W. 2000. "Truth." In *Encyclopedia of the Dead Sea Scrolls,* edited by Lawrence H. Schiffman and James C. VanderKam, 950-52. Oxford: Oxford University Press.

West, Edward William. [1880] 1977. *Pahlavi Texts I: Sacred Books of the East V.* Reprint, Delhi: Motilal Banarsidass.

Wolff, Fritz. 1960. *Avesta. Die heiligen Bücher der Parsen.* Strassburg: K. J. Trübner, 1910. Reprint, Berlin: De Gruyter.

Zaehner, Robert Charles. 1961. *The Dawn and Twilight of Zoroastrianism.* London: Weidenfeld and Nicolson.

PART FOUR

THE GRONINGEN HYPOTHESIS REVISITED

The Groningen Hypothesis:
Strengths and Weaknesses

Charlotte Hempel

The publication of the original Groningen Hypothesis (García Martínez 1988; 1995; García Martínez and van der Woude 1990) goes back more or less to the same time as my first encounters with the scrolls. So you could say that I belong to a generation of Qumran scholars who have not experienced the pre-Groningen Qumran era. I vividly remember reading it for the first time as a student and sensing that it struck a chord; the basic picture it painted seemed right. It immediately made a lot of earlier work on the Qumran community that I was reading seem a little dated. The basic notion of two communities having left their mark on the scrolls was of course not entirely new, and the monograph by Philip Davies on the Damascus Document, for instance, had pointed in the same direction (Davies 1982).

The Groningen Hypothesis has a great deal to commend it, and it has been very influential on my own thinking. Two key aspects of the hypothesis seem to me absolutely beyond doubt, and indeed have been confirmed by a close look at a number of texts that I have worked on over the last few years: (1) the nonbiblical corpus reflects more than one community as well as material from the forerunners of both communities; and (2) key documents are composite, and we must allow for the presence of material from different periods in the same composition.

In what follows I will discuss in turn each of the four stages of García Martínez's reconstruction. I will identify a number of aspects of his reconstruction with which I have difficulties. Moreover, those elements of his hypothesis that are convincing need to be correlated with the texts as we have them. García Martínez has outlined his position on a number of texts in his publications. So, for instance, he singles out two texts as compositions by the Teacher of Righteousness and considers them essential witnesses to the split of the Qumran group from the Essene parent movement: the Temple Scroll and MMT (García Martínez 1988). By contrast, I prefer to consider the Temple Scroll as well as the series of *halakhot* that make up the lengthy central section of MMT as belonging to the common halakic heritage of both groups (cf. García Martínez 1996a, 27, for a more nuanced view on MMT).

I have argued elsewhere that the author/compiler of MMT made use of a halakic source comparable to the material incorporated by the compiler/redactor of the Damascus Document (Hempel 2000). As for MMT's epilogue, it is far from certain in my mind that the emergence of the Qumran group is reflected in it. Rather, the concern with all of Israel and the conciliatory tone argue against such a view. I will suggest below some of my own correlations of texts to theory. My choice of texts is neither comprehensive nor normative. It reflects my own interests to date, and other texts may be added in due course.

I claim that García Martínez's attribution of the Temple Scroll and MMT to the Teacher of Righteousness is a very conservative segment in an otherwise progressive hypothesis. This throwaway remark deserves clarification. What I do not mean by that is that there was no Teacher and that he did not have followers and bear literary and other influence on Qumran. What I do mean is that, along with others, I am critical of the erstwhile fashion of a pan-Teacher approach to the scrolls, even to those texts that do not mention him such as the Temple Scroll, the Community Rule, and the Hodayot. Even if we find some statements in the Hodayot that might go back to him, it does not mean we can relate every allusion to suffering to the Teacher and his experience. Rather, like other strands in the scrolls, the Teacher strand is one among many. It is desirable to apply the motto Less Is More to the exploration of his influence in the scrolls. The pan-Teacher approach is speculative and distracts us from what we really can know about this shady figure or office. A clear focus on what is said about him in the few pieces of evidence we have might tell us quantitatively less than we want to know, but the quality of the information makes up for the shortfall.

Let me discuss, seriatim, the various stages identified in the Groningen Hypothesis.

Stage 1: The Palestinian Apocalyptic Tradition

I dislike this label because it opens up at least as many questions as it tries to answer. Two points that John Collins has highlighted in his publications seem to me relevant here:

1. Apocalyptic genres are not at all well attested among the scrolls (Collins 1990; 1997).
2. We need to allow for a plurality of groups among the bearers of apocalyptic literature (Collins 1999).

As far as the common background of the parent movement and the splinter group is concerned, I prefer to think of a multiform heritage, using Robert Kraft's terminology (Kraft 1975), drawing on liturgical, sapiential, and halakhic traditions that were cherished by the learned circles based around the temple. A group that turns its back on the temple because the temple is defiled must have a background and heritage that is close to the temple. There may well have existed differences of opinion among various groups, but these did not lead to the formation of a separate organized community. We will have to study these traditions in the context of the full spectrum of second temple Jewish literature beginning with the Hebrew Bible, comparing the promising approach to Qumran and biblical legal traditions outlined by Bernard Levinson at the 2002 SBL Annual Meeting in Toronto (Levinson 2002), and painting with a much broader brush Gabriele Boccaccini's work (Boccaccini 2002).

Stage 2: The Essene Parent Movement

The approach advocated by García Martínez of relying on the classical sources for information about the Essene movement is problematic. As Todd Beall has shown, more often than not the descriptions of the classical authors correspond to the *Serekh* which on the whole represents the organization of the Qumran community rather than its Essene parent movement (Beall 1988). Let me give just one clear example: Josephus's description of a complex and drawn-out admission process corresponds to what is laid down in 1QS 6:13b-23. A simpler procedure of admission which on my analysis refers to the parent movement and where the chief element is swearing an oath of the covenant is attested in CD 15. Thus, in this particular case the evidence of Josephus corresponds not with the parent movement, but with the more developed *yaḥad* procedure.

Let me briefly make a related point on the usage of the term "Essenes" and the adjective "Essene." García Martínez and others use the terminology to identify a parent movement over against an offshoot community. In my view this particular usage is somewhat misleading for the reasons given above. Exactly the opposite of what García Martínez means by the term "Essene" is the custom predominant in German scholarship and a smaller group of English scholars, that is, to use the term *essenisch* in the sense of sectarian and its counterpart, *vor-essenisch,* in the sense of presectarian (cf. Hempel 2003a).

All of this relates closely to John Collins's position. Maybe my own observations have clarified something, maybe they have added to the confusion, but we both agree there is an issue to be addressed here. I wonder whether Collins would go along with some of the substance of García Martínez's reconstruction of a parent movement and an offshoot if the Essene terminology were dropped from the former. My guess is maybe, because he himself frequently refers to a pre-Teacher stage in the development of the community, which might point in that direction.

In what follows I will focus on the scrolls themselves. Let me apologize at the outset that this is a broad look at some key texts as I read them for the purposes of thinking about the big picture. Only detailed exegetical discussion can persuade anyone of the individual building blocks of the structure I am erecting. In my defense I can refer to the more detailed individual studies I have published elsewhere. It has been helpful to me to stand back and try to put those discrete studies into a larger frame. I hope it might stimulate further discussion.

On my reading of the texts, key so-called sectarian documents reveal a great deal more about the parent movement of the *yaḥad* than commonly assumed. As I have tried to show in a number of my published works, several documents preserve remnants of the communal legislation of the parent movement of the *yaḥad*. These remains have been preserved, for the most part, in works that in their final form bear the marks of redaction by the *yaḥad*. Because this legislation differs considerably from the organization of the *yaḥad* as spelled out in the bulk of the Community Rule, we can try to connect the dots to reveal glimpses of a less rigidly structured yet nonetheless organized group. The following picture emerges:

1. We find a primitive communal setup portrayed in 1QS 6:1c-3a where like-minded Jews in all their dwelling places come together to eat, pray, and take counsel. This, the most primitive statement of communal activities, even lacks the reference to the role of priests mentioned in two subsequent additions (Hempel 2003b). The complexity increases exponentially elsewhere in the Community Rule where we have complex rules on sharing food and drink, proper conduct in meetings, and authority structures in the community.

2. Entry into the parent community took place in a relatively simple ceremony of swearing an oath to return to the law of Moses (cf. CD 15:5b–16:6a; 4QD^a 8 i; 4QD^e 6 i-ii; 4QD^f 4 ii and 1QS 5:7c-9a; 4QS$^{b \text{ and } d}$) rather than a prolonged process of admission in several stages (Hempel 1999a; cf., e.g., 1QS 6:13b-23; 4QS$^{b \text{ and } g}$). Apart from this very significant difference, a noteworthy shared feature that distinguishes both the parent movement and the offshoot from a number of otherwise related texts is that both groups lay down a formal procedure of admission.

3. The genre of the penal code originated with the parent movement of the *yaḥad,* and remnants of such a pre-*yaḥad* code are preserved in 4QD. The evidence of the penal codes is complex. I have spelled out my reading of the evidence of the Damascus Document and the Community Rule in the Cambridge Festschrift for Joseph Baumgarten (Hempel 1997; see also J. M. Baumgarten 1992; Hempel 1998, 141-48; Metso 2000; and Shemesh 2002).

4. The issue of women in the Dead Sea Scrolls has recently received renewed attention (cf., e.g., Brooke 2003; Crawford 2003a; 2003b; Schuller 1996; 1999). The following comments are restricted to the evidence on women in the parent movement of the *yaḥad.* Women played a role in the communal hierarchy of the parent movement though they were not equal to men. Compare the reference to the mothers of the congregation in CD's penal code (cf. Hempel 1997; see also Elwolde 2000; and Hurowitz 2002) as well as a text like 1QSa, which is replete with references to family life. Let me just summarize here my conviction that this framework seems to me to reflect a communal reality rather than a messianic vision. I have argued elsewhere that the core and bulk of 1QSa constitutes communal legislation of the parent movement that is now sandwiched into a messianic context. It originated separately from this setting and shows links with parts of the laws of the Damascus Document, and there is nothing messianic about the communal legislation component of this text (Hempel 1996; see also Davies and Taylor 1996).

5. The terminology used to refer to the parent movement is on the whole more scripturally based. We should note the prominence of camp and city language in the Damascus Document over against a preponderance of *yaḥad* language in the Community Rule (Hempel 1998, 191; for a slightly different view, see now Metso 2002).

6. Accounts of the emergence of the parent movement are found in the Damascus Document as well as works like Jubilees (see, e.g., Jub 1:16; 21; 24) and 1 Enoch (see the end of the seventh week in the Apocalypse of Weeks and the little lambs in the Animal Apocalypse). These accounts of the emergence of a righteous group within Israel were revised and updated by supplementing references to the Teacher and his followers who dismiss their forerunners as lacking in direction (CD 1; see Hempel 1999b).

7. Other questions that deserve to be addressed are the attitude to property (see Murphy 2002) and the temple in the parent group vis-à-vis the *yaḥad.*

Stage 3: The Formative Period

As I have argued elsewhere, I find the concept of trying to assign traditions and ideas to a formative period when the group was not yet sufficiently distinct from the Essene movement unrealistic (Hempel 1998, 5). Compare García Martínez's description of the formative period as presenting "a vision not yet clearly distinct from the Essenism from which they derive" (García Martínez 1995, 85). In the absence of clear-cut criteria for making such distinctions between the literary legacy of the formative period and the Essene movement, I find the category unhelpful.

Stage 4: Qumran Community

As far as terminology is concerned, I am more than a little uneasy about using the term "Qumran community" for the offshoot community. In light of the revised chronology of communal occupation of the Qumran site, i.e., late rather than mid–second century B.C.E., it is much more difficult to arrive at a neat synthesis of the archaeological evidence and the literary evidence (Laperrousaz 1986; Magness 2002, 63-72). Unless we use the term to distinguish a group of people who were associated with the Qumran settlement as opposed to others who were not, it is misleading to persist with this usage for the sake of convenience and habit. It may well be that the move to Qumran is a separate issue from the emergence of the offshoot group — especially if we still think of the split away by the *yaḥad* around the middle of the second century B.C.E.

On this issue see the comparable comments of Torleif Elgvin and Pierluigi Piovanelli in this volume. I am grateful to the former for further drawing attention in this context to S. Pfann's very early paleographical dating of the cryptic Rule of the Congregation manuscripts as well as 4Q298 (Pfann 2000, 522-33). I have great respect for Pfann's detailed analysis of the papyrus and his work on the cryptic scripts in DJD 36. However, as far as the paleographical dates are concerned, I feel a little uneasy. Given all the usual methodological caveats about paleographical dates, given that the pool of the cryptic texts is so small, and the amount of text preserved in each manuscript is rather limited, I do not think it is wise to build a strong case on the basis of these dates. Even in those cases where square titles are preserved, the amount of text of the title is also rather limited.

According to García Martínez, the calendar was one of the factors in the parting of the ways of the *yaḥad* from the parent group. Thus he comments on the basis of the Temple Scroll and MMT: "[T]he fundamental disputes within the Essene movement during the formative period of the sect centered on the question of the calendar and the resulting arrangement of the festival cycle" (García Martínez 1995, 93; for a slightly different view, see García Martínez 1996a, 27).

In contrast, and here I find myself in agreement with Mark Elliott, the calendar seems to me a shared concern between the parent group and the *yaḥad*. Or to put it differently, the calendar seems to have been an issue between the parent movement and society at large (see CD 3:17, which refers to all Israel going astray in these matters) that was shared with the *yaḥad* rather than a sticking point that drove the *yaḥad* apart from the parent group. If anything, the heat of the debate about the calendar seems to be cooling off at Qumran rather than the other way round. In this context, note Michael Knibb's observation that "observance of the proper calendar was a matter of concern to the Qumran community, but the impression given is that this was not quite such an issue as it was for the author of Jubilees" (Knibb 1989, 14).

Having offered a negative assessment of the calendar as an issue between the parent group and the offshoot, I would like to close with some brief positive suggestions. In an article that recently appeared in *Revue de Qumran,* I examined the prominence of references to a group called "the people of injustice" at defining moments in the community's emergence according to S (Hempel 2003c). It seems likely that some of the issues raised with reference to this group (mainly in the areas of *halakhah,* purity, especially with regard to sharing food, economic matters, and questions of authority) might hint at some of the causes that divided the *yaḥad* from its parent movement. The fact that this group of opponents is clearly a well-defined entity with close ties to at least some community members makes an assessment along such lines attractive.

The 1QS/4QS evidence of a Zadokite redaction of a "rabbim" tradition, on the other hand, testifies to internal leadership struggles which postdate the emergence of the *yaḥad* (see, e.g., Alexander 1996; Bockmuehl 1998; Metso 1997; and Vermes 1991).

Overall, although I disagree with some choices of terminology and texts, there is no doubt in my mind that the Groningen Hypothesis is still the best theoretical statement on the makeup of the Qumran library to date. It seems to me that when it was first published some fifteen years ago it was part of the avant-garde in Qumran thinking. Since then it has become part of the establishment of Qumran studies.

Reflections on the Groningen Hypothesis

Albert I. Baumgarten

This chapter is devoted to reflections on the Groningen Hypothesis from two perspectives, the one textual-philological, the other more abstract and theoretical. Alternating between these viewpoints, I believe the convergence of these two lines of analysis indicates that there is a better and more productive alternative to the Groningen Hypothesis that benefits from many of its advantages but suffers from fewer faults, requires the positing of fewer complex assumptions, and better explains a wider body of sources.

Marc Bloch on the Idol of Origins

Marc Bloch's place as one of the great historians of the twentieth century needs no argument or proof. He was a great creative force and one of the first to demonstrate the value of an interdisciplinary approach to the study of the past. In his reflections on the historian's craft, a fragment written in the dark years of World War II and published posthumously, Bloch devoted several pages to attacking the idol of origins (Bloch 1964, 29-35). This attack is a rare polemical section in an otherwise irenic, lucid, moderate, and judicious work. Bloch's disapproval of focus on origins had its own roots in the work of the economist F. Simiand (1903), who amplified arguments put forward by Durkheim against the way history was usually practiced at the turn of the twentieth century.

Of course, to point out the roots of Bloch's attack on the idol of origins in the work of Simiand and Durkheim is to offer Bloch himself on the altar of the very idol of origins he sought to demolish. One should therefore focus not on the roots of Bloch's attack on the idol of origins but on Bloch's own work. That contribution — best exemplified in his *Royal Touch: Sacred Monarchy and Scrofula in England and France* (Bloch 1973) and *Feudal Society* (Bloch 1961), his most Durkheimian study — stands as a monument to the way Bloch insisted one should study the past. It demonstrates the benefit derived from smashing the idol of origins (see further Burke 1990, 9-10, 12-27).

Bloch's principal argument is that discovering origins is not the ultimate objective of historical research. At best it is incidental and makes a minimal contribution to understanding. The latter is the real goal of historical inquiry, explaining phenomena in their context of time and place, understanding why an event took place when, where, and how it did, no place else, no sooner and no later. Bloch concludes by citing an old Arab proverb: "Men resemble their times more than they do their fathers." Disregard of this oriental wisdom has sometimes brought discredit to the study of the past (Bloch 1964, 35).

To put this conclusion in other terms, determining filiation has a place in historical study, but it is a mistake to assign establishing filiation the ultimate value. That is to be trapped by the generic fallacy. At best, determining filiation is a step on the way to understanding.

Bloch's attack on the idol of origins is worth taking seriously. When a historian of Bloch's stature warns that a particular approach has sometimes brought discredit to historical study, we should not take that caution lightly. These thoughts apply to the Groningen Hypothesis, a classic example of an attempt to trace the filiation of a number of sources and movements in Judaism of the second temple era.

The Groningen Hypothesis

Of all the attempts to determine the origins of the community that wrote the sectarian texts discovered in the caves around Qumran and that lived in accordance with these documents, the Groningen Hypothesis (conveniently summarized in García Martínez and van der Woude 1990) is clearly the best. With good reason, in one form or other, explicitly or implicitly, and with major or minor modifications, it is probably closest to being the scholarly consensus. The Groningen Hypothesis has the distinct advantage of utilizing the hints about the origins of the group at the outset of the Damascus Document in establishing an Essene stock from which the Qumran branch split off.

It posits that this pre-Qumran Essene stage is represented in the accounts of the Essenes in authors such as Philo, Josephus, or Pliny. These connections make these accounts of the Essenes relevant to the analysis of the Dead Sea

Scrolls. One body of sources illuminates the other. In this way the hypothesis also acknowledges that the classical authors and Qumran scrolls are not identical. It thus takes account of both similarities and differences between these sets of sources, and is not one of those simplistic theories that gives comparative work a bad name, necessitating apology (Patton and Ray 2000), focused only on the similarities (Davies 1990). The Groningen Hypothesis also asserts that works such as the Temple Scroll come from the pre-Qumran phase of the Essene movement. In doing so, it allows the explanation of the variety of works found in the caves as originating either with the Qumran movement or with their Essene predecessors.

Thus we need not assume the improbable notion of a thought police at Qumran that censored every work to make certain that it conformed perfectly to the ideology and law of the community. This idea was dismissed in the early days of DSS scholarship: "Even if we suppose that all books came from the official library, we cannot be sure that everything in the library reflected faithfully and directly the beliefs of its owners — that sort of absurd supposition should be left to the secret police" (M. Smith 1960, 347).

In fact, as recent research has shown, the community was willing to tolerate much more diversity than we might anticipate, even on issues that seem to us of central importance (A. Baumgarten 2002). Nor need we explain the variety of works found in the caves by the assumption that the Qumran collection is an arbitrary assemblage of second temple literature, deposited in the caves of the Judean desert by individuals with no connection to each other, in anticipation of the destruction of Jerusalem (Golb 1995).

However, for all its advantages, the Groningen Hypothesis is not immune to criticism on pure philological-historical grounds. As noted in several contributions to this volume (Hempel and Collins, in particular), a number of the closest parallels on which the hypothesis is built are between the Essenes as described by Philo and Josephus, and Qumran texts such as 1QS (Beall 1988; Davies 1990). Yet, as posited by the hypothesis, this is an overlap between the extremes, where we should expect the differences to be greatest. The Essenes of Philo and Josephus represent a continuation of the pre-Qumran phase of the original movement, from which the Qumran group broke off. They should not be so close to so quintessential a Qumran text as 1QS.

Has the Groningen Hypothesis reached the limits of its explanatory powers, such that it is ripe for replacement by some alternative, the inevitable fate of all human attempts to make sense of complex and messy reality? Replacement by better alternatives is also the basis for the unending progress of the sciences, human and physical (Lakatos 1978, 1-7). This is the conclusion for which I would like to argue. In particular, I would suggest that historians can "have their cake and eat it," that there is an alternative that allows many of the benefits of the hypothesis without the historical-philological disadvantages, and without the worship of the idol of origins.

Parallel Responses to the Same Circumstances

Cultural and social circumstances call forth a variety of attempts to deal with the issues of the time and place. These attempts bear important similarities to each other. This is not because of some generic analogy between phenomena that may be separated chronologically and culturally, what Marc Bloch called comparisons of the "grand sort" (Bloch 1967). Such comparisons are potentially fraught with difficulties, as the similarities on which they are based may turn out to be illusory, and resting on accidental or trivial points of contact that fade in importance on closer analysis.

The attempts to deal with the cultural and social circumstances I am discussing are similar because they are responses to the same set of issues, at the same time and place. Nonetheless, these responses are not necessarily similar because they are descended from each other. They are parallel (i.e., independent) responses to the same circumstances.

Comparison and contrast between these responses is essential, as any one attempt viewed in isolation is of limited value. Seen in seclusion, a particular answer will seem natural, the only possible way to deal with the issues of the era. Claims of authority or ultimate legitimacy made for that alternative may then go unchallenged. For as Bourdieu (among others) has noted: "Every established order tends to produce (to very different degrees and with different means) the naturalization of its own arbitrariness" (Bourdieu 1977, 164). Real insight is possible when several responses are compared to each other.

In other words, the ancient Jewish movements must be compared to each other. When that is done, each instance teaches us a good deal about itself and about the phenomenon in general, but without the need to make any claims of filiation. In particular, the Essenes of classical sources can help us understand Qumran texts such as 1QS without the need to posit any direct filial relationship between the groups. In Bloch's terms, one would then be comparing men of the same time to each other, whom they resemble most closely, without recourse to their fathers, whom they do not resemble as closely.

One example of the type of analysis I have in mind is the study of *ḥaverim* and Qumran sectarians offered by Lieberman in the early days after the discovery of the DSS (Lieberman 1951). Neither Lieberman nor any significant group of subsequent scholars argued for the identity or filial relationship of the *haverim* and the Qumran members.[1] And yet, thanks to the contribution of Lieberman, we understand the *haverim* in light of Qumran texts much better than we did before the discovery of the Qumran sources.

Perhaps I will be accused of simply wanting to turn the clock back to an earlier era when less was known, and of being unwilling to take advantage of fuller knowledge that allows greater precision in identifying the relationship between groups. I would reply to the contrary: in my view the detailed information about groups that we now have available indicates the differences between them, and should serve as a warning that we should not conflate them so easily. When we deal with small movements, the differences between them, easily overlooked or conflated by an outsider (our inevitable position as historians, thousands of years later), matter more than apparent similarities (A. Baumgarten 1994).[2] Furthermore, as Goodman has argued persuasively, the number of problematic and unproven jumps needed to connect one ancient group, usually known from only one set of sources, with another group, usually known from a different set of sources, is great (Goodman 1995; 2000). Thus, on pure philological-historical grounds, I would maintain that the Groningen Hypothesis has reached its limits and is ready for replacement by the alternative outlined above. That this alternative avoids worship of the idol of origins is an added bonus.

Biological Paradigms

Biology supplies many of the classificatory paradigms employed in the human sciences. The impulse to organize phenomena in a family tree, in which one is an offshoot of the other and each has its place in a branch coming off the trunk, has its basis in the biology of human experience. In that sense biology is at the root of the worship of the idol of origins attacked by Bloch.

In offering an alternative to the explanations based on filiation, I would want to note that the inclination to classify biological phenomena in strict monothetic family trees seems to be running its course in biology, and is being replaced by other organizational schemes (J. Z. Smith 1982, 3-5). Evolution is no longer understood as one long inexorable march upward from humble origins to complex life-forms. Rather, there were several key creative periods when

1. The suggestion of Chaim Rabin (1957) to connect the Qumran group with the Pharisees can be disregarded as a relic of an older era of scholarship.
2. Since writing that paper, I have learned that the formal name for the principle I called "the rule of the Martian" is "the narcissism of small differences."

many alternative life-forms arose, none of which could have been predicted in advance as possessing the characteristics that would make them best adapted to flourish in the circumstances that would prevail.

The path from any of these life-forms to those of later eras was complicated, incidental, and lacking intention. Unintended consequences may play a large part in the story. While the path from origins to outcome can be traced, it is much more important to understand how and why each small variation made a particular form best suited to its time and place than to lay out the complex, almost accidental, combination of circumstances that began with life-forms of one sort at one point and ended with life-forms of another sort later on, with human society organized one way at one time and in another way sometime later (Gould 1989).[3]

For all the reasons argued above, I suggest that we view the second temple era of Jewish history in the light of the new biological paradigm. It is one of those great creative times when numerous alternatives appeared on the stage of history. Which would survive and which would fail was unknown, to be determined by combinations of circumstances that could never be predicted. How these forms of religious life would change and adapt to the circumstances was far too complex and accidental to be meaningfully traced by a teleological historical method. What we can do, and should do, is try to understand these religious life-forms by comparison to each other, as evidence of their time and place, as parallel responses to the issues of a critical era. Real understanding is attainable in that direction. Attempts to establish filiation, by contrast, are less productive, more likely to prove futile and sterile and insoluble.

From this perspective, I am not surprised to find so much of the discussion of filiation of Enochic works in print and at Enoch conferences inconclusive and unsatisfying. It is fixed on the worship of the idol of origins and devoted to solving a problem that is not only beyond our abilities but also not that important, and thus much more heat than light is generated. We are therefore often able only to restate what we have written in the past rather than to convince each other. In terms suggested by Lakatos, this is a sign the research program has reached its limits (Lakatos 1978, 5-6). It is a degenerating program rather than a progressing one. More energy is spent in defending old conclusions than in including new evidence in a new program.

Hypotheses are being cooked up after the event to protect the theory

---

3. Gould's essay takes its title from the classic Frank Capra movie *It's a Wonderful Life* (1946). That film is an extended study of the unpredictable nature of events and of the role of unintended consequences. For a formal social scientific analysis of the same phenomena, see Merton (1936).

Albert I. Baumgarten

from the facts. Note, for example, the dismay that led to the intellectual acrobatics performed by some scholars when the possibility arose that archaeological evidence would indicate the presence of women in the Qumran community. Similar mental gymnastics are offered to help explain (away) the possible evidence that members of the Qumran community defecated at a latrine on site and not in the way described by Josephus (A. Baumgarten, forthcoming).

I therefore suggest that a fundamental change in perspective of the sort proposed above, away from the Groningen Hypothesis, would be most salutary. This is not a matter of adopting a "philosophical" perspective as an excuse for ignoring history.[4] Rather, it is good history, perhaps even historiography at its best, as pursued in accordance with the prescriptions of one of the greatest twentieth-century practitioners of the historian's craft.

4. If in the McCarthyite 1950s of my youth we were often reminded that patriotism is the last refuge of the scoundrel, I suspect that claims to a philosophical perspective, above history, are now the last refuge of the intellectually bankrupt.

Sealing Some Cracks in the
Groningen Foundation

Mark A. Elliott

The Groningen Hypothesis has many advantages over its precursor theories. It counters the impossible view that the exiled Qumran community represented the *whole* of the movement called Essenism, has helped push back the chronological origins of the original movement into the late third century B.C.E., and has tendered a consistent theory about the nature and purpose of the scroll library (García Martínez 1988, 113-16; García Martínez and van der Woude 1990, 521-26). This theory, or some form of it, remains the best of all attempts to explain the origins of Qumran to this time.

Two uncertainties remain, however, which any revised version of the theory must take into consideration: (1) The first concerns the methodology on which the historical reconstruction of the origins of the community is based. (2) The other concerns a presupposition about the social history and resulting theological conclusions which are based upon it.

Methodology

The problem with methodology relates to the use of data. That part of the theory which states that there was a breach in the party of the Essenes resulting directly in the formation of the community, to judge from its initial presentations, seems to be dependent in an excessive way on a short passage from the difficult and allusive Habakkuk Pesher, 1QpHab 2:3f., which, together with a similar passage, 1QpHab 5:9-12, serves as a springboard for other assumptions and conclusions. Such passages taken in isolation clearly do suggest a logical chain of links: (1) initially there was a larger group dedicated to the beliefs and goals shared by the Qumran community, but (2) through the influence of a certain "Man of Lies" many of them "turned back," reneged on their commitment, and rejected the Teacher of Righteousness, so that (3) the followers of the latter were compelled to make a break with the others, and accordingly (4) one can conclude that the Man of Lies was part of an originally much larger group which could only have been the Essenes.

In our view the potentially weakest point of the theory lies with the final link in the chain and with the notion that the sect separated chiefly from other Essenes prior to their exile (García Martínez 1988, 128; 1993a, 92-96; García Martínez and van der Woude 1990, 538). The foundation on which this point rests, namely, the identification of the Man of Lies of the Habakkuk Pesher with an Essene leader in conflict with the Teacher of Righteousness, is at least open to question. If it were not for the one doubtful association of this figure with the "traitors from the new covenant" in the partially reconstructed text 1QpHab 2:3f., the notion that this figure was an Essene would be completely unsustainable.

Even for this evidence, however, it ought to be remembered that most Jews could have rejected the idea of the new covenant and accordingly been termed "traitors." The Man of Lies, therefore, if not associated with one of the wicked priests in 1QpHab, could easily have been another *non*-Essene priest with teaching duties, or a Jewish leader of any kind. This could explain the absence of any clear references to the parent group elsewhere (since they were not really that important in the split),[1] and also why charges against opponents are more naturally understood as charges against Israel as a whole. Texts occasionally cited as examples of polemic against other Essenes, when considered in abstraction from the theory, appear more to be directed at all outsider Israelites or their leaders (4QMMT; 11QT; and esp. 1QpHab 1:16–2:10; 10:9-13; contrast García Martínez 1988, 121f.).

While the Habakkuk Pesher passages upon which this part of the Groningen Hypothesis rests are provocative and suggestive, to say the least, quite different results might have been attained had it relied more heavily on another text. For the sake of argument, why not start with CD 20:14f., which refers to "the men of war who turned back with the man of lies"? Of all the texts which reflect on the origins of the community in a split with another group, this is arguably the most distinctive and also, it might be added, the least evocative of the Essenes. If we allow CD 20:14f. to direct our assumptions and conclu-

---

1. The Hymn Scroll has similar references, but these are more or less the same, and no more point to a parent group than does the Habakkuk Pesher.

sions in a manner similar to the way 1QpHab 2:3f. has been allowed to do, we might come up with far different conclusions, such as the following.

1. To begin with, the term "men of war" sounds entirely like a reference to the Maccabean campaign, or perhaps to the later Hasmoneans. The argument that this phrase has no historical value but was borrowed from Deuteronomy 2:14 as part of the exegetical justification for the forty-year theme found here in the Damascus Document would be well taken, were it not that the modifying words "who turned back with the man of lies" is *not* found in Deuteronomy; and there is nothing in the biblical text to suggest such a connection, nor is any attempt made by the pesherist to identify another group, whether traitor Essenes or not, who filled the role of these war-making opponents. It would be, in that case, an inefficacious inclusion which, admittedly, might have meant something to the readers which we can no longer retrieve.

However, line 16 mentions the resultant judgment which is said to be "against *Israel*," and this suggests that the author was not preoccupied with traitors from his own movement primarily, or only, but with the whole nation in view of its being affected by a significant set of events such as those associated with the Maccabean uprising. "Men of war," it could at least be argued, is a deliberate allusion to a group or some leaders from whom the Qumranites separated and who in actual fact continued to take up arms, that is, probably the Maccabeans or their descendants and followers. That the term is borrowed from Deuteronomy 2:14 might not be accidental at all; the shoe fits.

2. In order to speculate on how more of this relates to the early Maccabean campaigns, one could conjecture that the "new covenant in the land of Damascus," to which the relevant texts refer, was not instituted originally at Qumran, for which "Damascus" would then be an anachronistic cipher. The conjecture would be that the new covenant was instituted in the region of Syrian Damascus, at some moment after the initial events of the Maccabean revolt.[2] This would place it perhaps in association with both the Maccabees and

2. We read of various gatherings during this watershed period; cf. 1 Macc 3:46-56 (at Mizpah); cf. also 1 Macc 5:9-23, which refers to an assembly in northern regions leading to the Gentile campaign. The possible choice of Damascus for a similar meeting conforms to an expectation, in line with the prophets, that an action from "the North" would result in a return of the exiles and of the nation to prosperity (cf. Jer 3:18; 31:2, 8; Ezek 8:5; the idea may be present in 1 Kings 20:34; 2 Kings 14:28; also cf. Amos 5:26f.). It is worthy of note that the testament of Mattathias sounds much like the prologue to a covenant or covenantal renewal (1 Macc 2:49ff.), suggesting that the self-assessment of the Maccabees' vision related closely to that of a new covenant in the scrolls. The conjectured association of the Damascus covenant with this type of meeting with the Maccabean company would of course suggest a period of longer reflection and planning than could have occurred in the preliminary ad hoc meetings.

their followers and "the volunteers for the law" we read about in 1 Maccabees 2:42f. These latter seem to have some connection with the crucial events indicated, and they are those who, it might be noted, wished to "maintain the covenant" with the others; cf. 1 Maccabees 2:27.[3] The new covenant would include those that later separated with the Teacher of Righteousness, but presumably also a much wider group, including Essenes and others.

3. The next step is to better define "covenant," by which might be intended not a "divine covenant" so much as a "human covenant," as admittedly false as such a distinction would have seemed to the original participants. The paradigm for making this new covenant, to judge by the terms used in the Damascus Document, would have been Nehemiah 9:38, the phrasing of which is repeated in CD 20:12 (cf. Neh 10:1ff., esp. 10:29, which even evokes the notion of "returning to the law of Moses" as in CD 15:5-30 et al.). The purpose of this new covenant was the reconstitution of Israel (neither an annual renewal nor a distinctively novel entity) in line with rededications which took place under Ezra or Nehemiah and which at points recalled the dedication of the Solomonic temple and the Josiah reforms when the nation was also called to renewed faithfulness. This would explain how the covenant could be considered "new" and yet amount to a renewal of the Mosaic covenant. As also suggested by the example of Nehemiah, the covenant, understood as a "pact," included aspects of an agreement as to how the reconstitution would take place in Israel's existential situation. We see evidence in 1 Maccabees 2:49ff. (cf. esp. v. 50) that Judas himself viewed the whole revolt as an attempt to reestablish covenant in Israel.

4. One could then speculate that twenty years following this binding agreement/covenant some betrayed the agreement. This happened at the instigation of the Man of Lies, who, according to the form of the title, was someone with political power and not an unknown Essene.[4] He was apparently one of

---

3. That this group included "Essenes," whether some or all of the Ἀσιδαῖοι or a related group, hardly demands that the Essene movement *began* with the Maccabean campaign. The 1 Maccabees text suggests that many groups were already in existence. See Elliott 2000, 203-13, and cited literature, which places this movement of protest at least as early as early postexilic Judaism and perhaps among the third-century anti-Hellenistic conservatives who penned the most ancient portions of the books of Enoch. See also García Martínez 1988, 118f.

4. It is noteworthy that Pompey is called a man of "insolence" in PsSol 2:25f., suggesting that such titles were reserved for political leaders who pretend much but deliver only disappointment, rather than for competing pietists or Essenes. That the Man of Lies is an Essene is, in any case, hardly "established" (García Martínez 1988, 126). One of the descriptions which refer to the Man of Lies building a city, 1QpHab 10:5-13, suggests Jonathan, who ruled from 152 B.C.E., although this interpretation is disputed and Groningen scholar Adam van der Woude (1982, 357) does not relate this figure to any priest; for similar conclusions about Jonathan, see Lim 1993, 422-24. If we locate the beginnings of the formation of the Dead Sea community in the

the Hasmoneans (cf. CD 19:22-24; 20:22-24). It took place in spite of protests of an unidentifiable Teacher of Righteousness. The motivation for the betrayal by these followers of the Man of Lies was the aspiration to choose expansion over piety, hence the derogation "men of war,"[5] and perhaps because this group tolerated sacerdotal ambitions which, even at as early a stage as the incumbency of Judas Maccabeus, became overt among non-Zadokite Hasmoneans. By pursuing such goals they not only broke with the practical aspects, but eventually also with the religious intentions, of the "Damascus Covenant,"[6] which may have included a clause that confirmed a place for the Zadokite priests in Jerusalem. The resulting departure by the Qumran sectarians, accordingly, did not involve a breach with other Essenes, but with a certain number of powerful individuals and their followers who started out in the movement of protest but surrendered their initial objectives because of what appeared to the followers of the Teacher of Righteousness to be selfish ambition.[7]

While this reconstruction is built on the foundation of one passage, it could be argued that the resulting theory has at least as much in its favor as does that part of the Groningen Hypothesis which is based largely on 1QpHab 2:3f. While space prevents it, it could be shown that this reconstruction also goes a long way toward explaining the diverse references in the other relevant texts, including CD 5:9-12, 19:13-35, 20:22-24, 1QS 2:11-14, 1QpHab 2:1-4, and 8:8-13. Although some have argued against individual points in this reconstruction,

---

new covenant and accordingly in the days following 15 Kislev 167 B.C.E. (although 1 Maccabees is not specific about the lengths of time involved; cf. ἐν ταῖς ἡμέραις 1 Macc 2:1), this would place the coming of the Teacher of Righteousness about 147 (cf. CD 1:9f.), the period of Jonathan. The "groping" in the twenty years of CD 1:9f. could refer to the events following the Antiochene desecration when Judaism was in disarray and lacking a sacerdotal authority, followed by the ascension to power of the non-Zadokite Hasmonean high priests. However, this could have begun even earlier during the period of Hellenization of Jerusalem.

5. The Teacher of Righteousness and his community, on the other hand, embraced the "theology of retreat" of the early Maccabees and saw it as their business to continue to stay in the wilderness (cf. 1QS 8:12-16; 9:19-21). This manifesto does not necessarily imply a break within the Essene movement itself.

6. One might be tempted to relate this breach already with the decision to fight on the Sabbath (1 Macc 2:41), a military expedient which apparently would not have been acceptable to the Qumranites (to judge by 1QpHab 11:5-8), but this goes beyond the evidence.

7. If this group included other Essenes, for example, if the Ἀσιδαῖοι are to be completely identified with Essenes, it does not imply that the main complaint was not with the Hasmoneans and with the mass of Israelites who accepted their incumbency. To judge by the probable reading of 2 Macc 14:6, the Hasidim appear more tolerant of the continuing Hasmonean movement than the Dead Sea sect does, but this coincidence hardly demands that we speculatively identify the followers of the Teacher of Righteousness with defecting Essenes, and Hasidim with continuing Essenes, as is sometimes done!

which in some respects is a return to the Maccabean theory without implying that Essenism was a new movement at the time, the exercise serves to prove that basing an important historical reconstruction on a single passage or type of passage can be risky to say the least.

Florentino García Martínez graciously responded to this proposed reconstruction by emphasizing that the Groningen Hypothesis was, after all, a "theory," and that he did not choose to argue with the point that it rests largely on a few closely related texts. I must respond that my alternative also can claim, at most, to be only a theory.

Social History and Theology

Social categorizations are often uncertain. With more historical data at our disposal, we might have concluded that there is little or no justification for naming the followers of the Teacher of Righteousness "Essenes" at all. Even given the historical data we have, however, the connection seems comparatively more defensible than the theory that an Essene split was determinative in the formation of the Dead Sea sect. I am convinced, in line with the Groningen Hypothesis, that there probably were continuing differences and probably also an initial practical division in which only some followed the Teacher of Righteousness, wherever he went after the initial dispute; archaeological data, and texts like 1QH 12[4]:8f., remain rather ambiguous about this. It seems apparent that few pursued the course of wilderness exile; but we cannot go so far as to accept that there were new and significant points of departure in beliefs between the former unified group of Essenes and the separatist Qumranites.

When the theory attributes to the continuing Essenes and separatist Qumranites differing positions on the calendar, the theology of determinism, and the like (cf. García Martínez and van der Woude 1990, 538), this leaves a lacuna in the logic. In regard to the calendar (cf. García Martínez 1988, 122f.; 1993b, 11), as one important example, this hiatus can be simply stated: While (1) apocalyptic Judaism defends the solar calendar rigorously,[8] and (2) the scrolls contained apocalyptic writings, according to the theory, (3) Essenes differed with Qumran over the calendar; leaving us to conclude that (4) either Essenism was not rooted in apocalyptic circles (as claimed; cf. García Martínez 1988, 116f., 120) or, even less likely, apocalyptic literature was a recent acquisition by the Qumranites. This problem is addressed somewhat in the development of the theory advanced by Boccaccini (1998). While evidence is taken from the his-

---

8. If there is any doubt about this, cf. Elliott 2000, 144-51, 154-59.

torical accounts about the Essenes that they, unlike the Qumranites, favored the official lunar or lunar-solar calendar, we find absolutely nothing in the accounts to lead to this conclusion.[9] It is more accurate to see that continuing Essenes and Qumran defectors alike remained essentially unified on such matters.

This brings to mind a related difference of opinion which on occasion has come to the surface during the Enoch Seminars and will perhaps be addressed more in the future. It is the notion that "Zadokite Judaism," which tended to feature Mosaic and covenantal theologies, had become separated and to a point even irreconcilable with another strand of Judaism usually associated with the "apocalyptic writings," which featured alternative non-Mosaic, noncovenantal ideas associated with wisdom categories.[10] This is often referred to by Enoch scholars as "Enochic Judaism." This dichotomy has yet to be fully endorsed by Enoch scholars. My personal view (cf. Elliott 2002a, 23-38, and to a somewhat lesser extent Elliott 2002b, 63-75) is that the Enochic literature, and other "apocalyptic" writings, do not clearly present a distinctive school of Judaism in quite so contrasting a fashion as is sometimes claimed.

My previous presentations revealed the way the authors of the Enochic material adapted Mosaic, particularly "Deuteronomistic," ideas in combination with Babylonian wisdom. The period of exile and settlement in Babylon suggests an obvious context for this combination. The latter ideas clearly served the former ideas.[11] This point needs more attention, but suffice it to say here that theories regarding distinctions among the groups, including the funda-

9. See Vermes and Goodman 1989, 16f. Nothing is said about the calendar in these sources, although in fact the editors refer to reverence for the sun and the Pentecontade calendar as common features between the Therapeutae, the Essenes, and the Qumran community. Our position assumes that living in Jerusalem and taking part in the cult, as some Essenes did, and accordingly being regulated by a lunar calendar, in no way contradict a theoretical preference for a solar calendar; the scrolls demonstrate that coordinating the calendars was considered an important task.

10. This distinction is clearly represented in Boccaccini 1998, especially 68ff., although it is consistent with other views of the differences between Zadokite and apocalyptic perspectives: "Enochic Judaism is the modern name for the mainstream body of the Essene party, from which the Qumran community parted as a radical, dissident, and marginal offspring" (16). I do not deny that disparate currents of thought and inherited loyalties were part of the history of Judaism, but to define the terms of departure of Qumranism from Essenism on such bases simply leaves too many problems. See Peursen (2001, 251): "We think that it is very doubtful that the biblical traditions were so exclusively Zadokite that Enochic and other non-Zadokite movements could ignore them till the Maccabean revolt."

11. The reason, in my mind, for the absence of references to Moses in 1 Enoch, for example, is simply that the author was being consistent with his literary fiction and with its dramatic context — according to which Moses had not yet been born. See Elliott 2002a, 38.

mental division between apocalyptic and Zadokite Judaism itself, do not yet appear to have been universally endorsed. Thus to imply that the division of the Essenes had something to do with major divisions already existing in Judaism is to beg the question. Differences in Judaism at this time had more to do with perceived levels of conformity to similar but not identically understood biblical and covenantal commands, than to differences of perspective born of political alliances, that is, Zadokite versus Enochic/apocalyptic Judaism.

This does not mean, on the other hand, that every Essene went to Qumran. The limitations of the Qumran site, for one thing, would hardly have permitted it. Nor does this mean that they all followed the same course of action following the breach of the Damascus Covenant in condoning the revelations of the Teacher of Righteousness. If there were differences within the Essenes, the evidence is not found so much in the historical allusions of the Habakkuk Pesher or the Hymns or in the legal material in 4QMMT, which appear to relate more to the rejection of the sect and their Teacher by the establishment in Jerusalem, but in the exclusive authority given to the revelations of the Teacher of Righteousness and expressed most unambiguously in the personal reminiscences by the Teacher in the Hymn Scroll. This evidence, coincidentally, is also proffered by the Groningen school (cf. García Martínez 1988, 124f.).

In other words, on sociological grounds we can safely advance the likelihood that many Essenes would not have followed the restrictive new options offered by the Qumran Teacher who, especially when the evidence of the Community Rule is taken into consideration, appears to have expanded the terms of the covenant when the sect became liberated from the confining attendance of the "traitors." Such additional material, however, does not appear to be legal or "doctrinal" or affect the chief motivations for protest shared by the whole Essene movement: calendar, cultic purity, interpretation of torah.[12] While others will assess the contents of the revelations given by the Teacher differently, those that most probably offended the nonfollowers of the Teacher of Righteousness relate to the enforcement of the rules of membership which were believed to anticipate conditions that would prevail during the period of Israel's restoration. 1QH 10[2]:13-15, 16[8]:16-26 suggest that a main function of the Teacher was to assess the suitability of candidates to join the movement. These membership rules were already being enforced at Qumran, and conceivably at least, even some Essenes would be unwilling to abandon their present circumstances of life to conform to them.

---

12. This is not to deny that some halakhic development eventually took place, as seems to be evidenced from differences in legal decisions between CD and 1QS, for example.

This probability aside, there is no material or documentary evidence for a schism in Essenism *itself* beyond the socioreligious postulate that new leaders with new rules tend to cause schisms even within closely knit groups. Perhaps then we can go only so far as to conclude that what defined the Qumran community over against Essenism, besides or in spite of differences of teaching or emphasis, was association with a rejected, estranged, isolated charismatic figure. In that case the Teacher himself will have been, sociologically speaking, the defining marker of the limits of the community, and novel aspects of his teaching will have tended to focus on that fact.[13]

If we were to characterize the ongoing relationship between the remaining Essenes and the dissident group, we would probably be wiser to speak in terms of an open relationship in which, in the eyes of the Qumran sectarians, the whole movement was represented in the exile to the desert and in the work of preserving the scrolls, even though only a minority participated in the retreat. While opportunity was given, initially at least, for all in Israel to join the covenant and the community, and this opportunity may have been refused even by some Essenes, material in the scrolls related to the ordering of the reconstituted and restored Israel suggests that the whole movement would be able to continue to practice its *halakhah* and could even live in towns outside of the headquarters of the sect if they followed the essential prescripts. There is no reason to deny that all Essenes continued to live in friendship, although the coming of the Teacher might have put considerable strain on this relationship.

It does not seem to have been noticed that part of the enigma of the surprisingly lengthy residence represented by the Qumran ruins can be explained, perhaps can *only* be explained, by appealing to a parent movement which continued to thrive in Palestine and Jerusalem. This parent movement supplied the community with personnel as well as with many material essentials, and it is only in this way that fluctuations in, and indeed even the continual survival of, the wilderness retreat can be adequately understood, from our point of view.

---

13. Note that the context of those passages which concern revelations given to the Teacher is replete with references to persecution and God's protection; e.g., 1QH 10[2]:8-19, 12[4]:5-29, 14[6]:2ff., 15[7]:6-25, and especially 16[8]:4-36. This position largely ignores the kind of revelation found in the pesherim. There is no proof that any of it comes from the Teacher, and internal chronological considerations tend to suggest that the pesherim were among the later writings of Qumran. Even so, again, the revelation found therein is not doctrinal but circumstantial. We have no way to ascertain whether the legal material in 4QMMT or the Temple Scroll, for example, was not also shared with the larger movement of Essenism or to what extent, if any, it was influenced by the Teacher. Legal positions would seem to change less over time than other matters. There is, of course, no doubt that the halakic ideals differed substantially from the practices of Judaism as a whole.

That parent movement might have been what we could call continuing Essenism, but in any event, evidence for a serious cleft in the parent movement out of which the Qumran settlement evolved is considerably depreciated by the manifest dependency of the desert settlement.

Thus we have potential evidence for a break within Essenism in the scrolls, but it is better deduced from the authority ascribed to, and claimed personally by, the Teacher of Righteousness than from any supposed decisive confrontation between the Teacher and the Man of Lies. It is not impossible that the Man of Lies was an Essene, in which case his debate with the Teacher certainly could have offered one factor in the break, but defending this is not essential and may be detrimental to the theory. The vital question remains "from whom" the Qumranites originally separated. This was primarily from apostate Israel, not primarily from other Essenes. The sectarians sought to escape from the problem raised by the rest of Judaism/Israel and from its compromised establishment and polluted cult, and thereby to avoid judgment. As it probably turned out, most Essenes did not follow them into exile.

Neither of these hesitations, it should be added, detracts from the genius of a very coherent theory which will serve to give direction for a very long time to the question of Qumran origins. While I have suggested two qualifications which seem overwhelming, it is certainly not unlikely that the Groningen Hypothesis will prove to be accurate in its main terms. Perhaps the above-mentioned qualifications will be explained by or otherwise integrated into the theory.

I want to add my congratulations to Florentino García Martínez and his associates for this hypothesis, and for many other indispensable contributions to the study of the Dead Sea Scrolls.

The *Yaḥad* Is More Than Qumran

Torleif Elgvin

In this chapter I will point to some obstacles for the Groningen Hypothesis with regard to dates and geography. In the Groningen Hypothesis the *yaḥad* is identified with the Qumran community and settlement, and with the Righteous Teacher establishing his stronghold at Qumran after a break with the wider Essene movement during the reign of Hyrcanus I. This movement to the desert is traditionally seen as a fulfillment of Isaiah 40:3.

Roland de Vaux tried to pull period Ia of Khirbet Qumran back to circa 135 B.C.E. or a little earlier (Vaux 1973, 5). One may suspect that this early dating was influenced by his reading of the scrolls and the consensus dating of the exodus of the Teacher and establishment of the *yaḥad* to 152. But Jodi Magness has convincingly argued that period I, the sectarian settlement, was established between 100 and 50, preferably later in this period (Magness 2002, 65). If she is right, it places the foundation of this center substantially after the copying of some central *yaḥad* scrolls, e.g., the oldest copies of the Community Rule, circa 125.

The establishment of the *yaḥad* (different from the center at Qumran) should perhaps now be dated to circa 175-150, preferably early in this period. The following reasons can be mentioned for such an early dating of the community.

1. Some of the scrolls copied in what Emanuel Tov has defined as the Qumran scribal school (characterized by orthography, morphology, and scribal practices: see Tov 1993) were copied long before the sectarian settlement at Qumran. The earliest are 4QQoh[a] and 4QDibMeor[a], copied in the mid–second century B.C.E. (according to personal communication from Tov). This scribal

school testifies to a socioreligious milieu (Essene or *yaḥad*) present at Qumran, but not only there.

2. Stephen Pfann argues that two sectarian cryptic texts must be dated to 190-140 B.C.E., preferably early in that period. Paleographical dating of the title in square script of 4Q249 *Midrash Sefer Moshe* places this scroll early in the second century, a date confirmed by carbon 14 examination. Pfann further dates the script of four cryptic copies of *Serekh ha'edah* (4Q249ᵃ⁻ᵈ) to the early second century (Pfann 2000, 522-34; 2001).

3. Enochic texts may point to an origin of the *yaḥad* early in the second century B.C.E. The Animal Apocalypse, written circa 164 (Charles 1912, 180-81; Milik 1976, 44; cf. Nickelsburg 2001, 361), ascribes the period of the Greeks to 360/59–199/98, from the accession of Philip II of Macedonia to the conquest of Coele-Syria by Antiochus III. The latter date marks the appearance of a new, elect, and righteous group (1 En 90:5-8), a fold of lambs, which probably should be identified with a parent group of the *yaḥad* (Dimant 1993, 65). The horn that appears after a lapse of time, by which the eyes of the sheep are opened (90:9-16), may be identified with the Teacher. If we follow the version of the Animal Apocalypse, the appearance of this pre-Essene group should be set to the first decade of the second century B.C.E. With a twenty-year period passing before the rise of the Teacher (cf. CD 1:5-11), the founding of the *yaḥad* would happen circa 170. Such an early dating of the origins of the *yaḥad* has been advocated by some scholars (Dimant 1982; Wacholder 1983; Kister 1986-87), and is now supported by other arguments.

4. A number of texts referring to the righteous planting may be dated to the first half of the second century B.C.E. This suggests that the planting of the *yaḥad* was shooting up well before 152. Here one may mention 1 Enoch 10:3 (Greek, Syncellus); 10:16; 84:6; 93:2, 5, 8, 10; 4QInstruction (4Q418 81:10-14), as well as the testing of the righteous remnant in 4Q215aTime of Righteousness 1 (Elgvin 2003). For this theme in writings of the *yaḥad*, see CD 1:7, 1QS 7:5-6, 11:8, 1QHᵃ 14(6):15, 16(8):4-26. In the sectarian writings the planting is used of a more defined entity (the community) than in 1 Enoch and 4QInstruction. At the same time, there are a number of similarities between all these planting passages. Thus, one should not postulate an excessively long time between the presectarian and sectarian planting texts.

According to Nickelsburg (and Dimant 2002, 234-37 as well), the poem referring to the planting in 1 Enoch 10:16–11:2 should not be pulled back to the third-century composite growth of 1 Enoch 6–11. It is rather a separate editorial unit added when chapters 6–10 were combined with 11–16, perhaps around 180-170 B.C.E. This passage is a repetitive interpretation of 10:3, 7. Chapters 11–16 do not repeat the themes of 10:16ff., which suggests that these chapters represent an interpretation of chapters 6–10 without this addition (Elgvin 2003; cf. Nickelsburg 2001, 24-26, 169-72, 224-28, 444-45).

If 1 Enoch 10:16 can be dated around 170, it would be close in time to the other Enochic references to the planting (84:6 in Dream Visions, 93:5 in the Apocalypse of Weeks). The similarities between 10:16–11:2 and the Apocalypse of Weeks (Nickelsburg 2001, 226 n. 38) can thus be explained by closeness in time and milieu.

In his contribution to the present volume, Stuckenbruck argues that planting passages in 4QInstruction and 1 Enoch need not have influenced each other. They may be parallel attempts to come to terms with the plant of Isaiah 5, 60, and 61 within an apocalyptic framework. In my opinion, it is hardly accidental that both traditions refer to an eternal planting (in, respectively, Aramaic and Hebrew). In the small milieu of pre-Hasmonean Yehud, apocalyptic exegetes would hardly operate without knowledge of each other or their close predecessors. So if there is no literal dependence one way or the other, a closeness in milieu seems likely (on the relation between 4QInstruction and Enochic material, see Elgvin 1997, 125-37, 168-72; Tigchelaar 2001, 212-17).

We have seen that the *yaḥad* cannot be identified with the Qumran settlement only; it predates the sectarian settlement at Khirbet Qumran by 50-120 years. Also after the establishment of the commune at Qumran the *yaḥad* was a wider entity. If the commune at Qumran indeed functioned as center of the *yaḥad,* one would expect to find membership rosters, financial records, and documents relating to disciplinary procedures. With two exceptions (4Q477 Rebukes Reported by the Overseer; 6Q26papAccount or Contract ar), such documents have not been identified. Yardeni argues for a provenance outside of Qumran (probably Seiyal/Hever) for seventeen documentary texts, 4Q342-360a (DJD 28, p. 283). The depository in the Qumran caves represents a religious library reflecting a close-knit organization, but probably not the center of this organization. Further, one needs a period of some years between the rise of the Teacher (CD 1:11) and the compilation of 1QSa as the earliest community order of the *yaḥad* (thus Stegemann 1973, 159-63, confirmed by Pfann's dating of 4Q249[a-d]).

With Magness's late dating of the settlement at Qumran, one should postulate a long pre-Qumranic period of the *yaḥad* to provide for a time span long enough to enable the complex editorial process of the S and D textual traditions, a process that took place before the end of Qumran period I. Also, with a differentiation between the *yaḥad* and the Qumran settlement, it is easier to comprehend the large textual differences that developed in the S and D traditions. In a scenario where *yaḥad* texts were used and transmitted at various locations in Judea, visitors or newcomers could easily bring their different versions with them to Qumran. If, however, the *yahad* was limited to this location alone during the period 150-31 B.C.E., it is difficult to perceive why a small and closely knit community would develop and keep largely different versions of the same basic documents. According to Metso and other scholars, 4QS manuscripts which preserve S editions that are earlier than 1QS are paleographically younger than 1QS. It is difficult to imagine such a complicated process of writing and transmission going on within the small scribal milieu at Qumran without causing serious headache for the scribe responsible for the archive.

The early dating of scrolls copied within the Qumran scribal school as well as two central sectarian writings (4QSa, 4Q249) puts a question mark to the traditional Essene Hypothesis identifying the Evil Priest with Jonathan or Shimon, dating the exodus of the Teacher from Jerusalem to 152 or 143. The Groningen Hypothesis suggestion that the designation *hakohen harashah* refers to a number of consecutive Hasmonean rulers/high priests from Judas Maccabee onward is also difficult to uphold if sectarian writings predate 150 by a number of years. Judas would be the latest possible candidate, but critics have questioned the historicity of Josephus's ascription of high priesthood to Judas (*Ant.* 12.414, 419, 434; Lim 1992, 465).

The suggestion of identifying *hakohen harashah* with Jason or Menelaos and *moreh hasedeq* with Onias III and the break in 174 (Pfann 2004) may be worth considering. But the short career of Onias III after 174 argues against this option.

One needs to discern between three sociological entities: (1) a wider Essene movement inspired by apocalyptic theology, such as in Enochic books and 4QInstruction; (2) the *yahad,* an elite movement among the Essenes; and (3) Qumran, one (but not the only) center of the larger *yahad.*

This picture is close to Qimron, who asserted that there were two separate groups in the Dead Sea sect (Qimron 1992, 292). He distinguished those who dwell in camps and conduct family life (CD 7:6-7) from the *yahad* members who had to be celibate. The *yahad* considered itself a substitute for the temple and therefore maintained a state of priestly temple purity for all members during the period of wickedness (Hebrew: *hamithalkim ba'elleh bitemim qodesh,* "walking in the perfection of holiness," CD 7:4-5; Qimron, 287-94). Qimron seems to identify the *yahad* with the Qumran dwellers, but does not make a clear statement on this issue. He adds that non-*yahad* sectarians dwelling in Jerusalem might have been permitted to marry as long as they kept their families outside the temple city, to avoid sexual contact there (cf. 11QT 45:7-12; 46:16-18; CD 12:1-2). Women and children are not mentioned in 1QS, which is the rule for the *yahad* only, while the Damascus Document refers to both groups.

There are many good points in Qimron's analysis. The material is, however, more easily explained if one allows for two kinds of lifestyles based on purity limitations within the *yaḥad*. 1QSa 1:25–2:9 describes the assembly of the *yaḥad* (Hebrew: ʿaṣat hayaḥad, 1:26; 2:2), where those of perfect behavior sanctify themselves for three days. There is no indication at all that the members of the assembly are different from the true Israelites portrayed in 1:2-25, who marry and conduct family life. In the movement founded by the Teacher there would be voluntarily celibacy from purity considerations, but celibate life or sexual abstention would normally be temporally limited. 4Q270 7:13 points in this direction (". . . the one who is fornicating when he lies with his wife contrary to the ordinance").

Recent research on the Qumran cemetery and excavated skeletons indicates that only males were interred in the main cemetery (Sheridan 2003). Zias concludes that Qumran represents a celibate community of males (Zias 2000). Zias seems to argue that all Essenes were celibate, and that Josephus, the only ancient writer reporting about a second order of Essenes with families, deliberately covered up the celibate image for a Jewish audience. However, Zias also refers to Pfann's edition of 4QSa, which confirms that there were both married and unmarried members of the community at an early stage of its history (Zias, 2000, 248; DJD 36, pp. 548, 558, 567). While some passages in the scrolls suggest sexual abstinence due to purity reasons, 1QSa and the Damascus Document clearly refer to families, thus supporting Josephus's picture of both married and celibate Essenes. It seems far-fetched to postulate, as Zias does, that the Essenes or the *yaḥad* could recruit enough members through initiation and adoption of minors to survive and flourish for more than two hundred years.

The main graveyard at Qumran was for men only, while texts related to the community at Qumran refer to families (1QSa 1:4-11; CD 4:20–5:2; 5:6-11; 7:6-9; cf. Schuller 1994). Thus, the men doing service at Qumran had close links to covenanters living a family life. The easiest way to interpret this material is to postulate a *yaḥad* organization which included Qumran but was not restricted to this settlement. As for the men living and serving at Qumran, they could have pledged a lasting celibate life or have volunteered for a service that entailed sexual abstention as long as they stayed at this holy camp.

There would be other centers of the *yaḥad*. One would probably find a center in or close to Jerusalem; cf. MMT B 29-31: "Jerusalem is the 'camp' . . . the encampment of their settlements"; 1QM 3:11 Hebrew: *haʿedah yerushalayim*; and the Qumran-style graveyard unearthed in Beit Safafa south of Jerusalem (Zissu 1998). One may note the centrality of Jerusalem also in a noneschatological text such as MMT. In this context the Essene Gate must also be mentioned (Bauckham 2003, 66-72).

Josephus (*Ant.* 18.21) and Philo (*Quod omnis probus liber sit 75*) number the Essenes in the land of Israel at 4,000, a number that includes only adult males, not their families. The number of *yaḥad* men living at Qumran may be calculated to 50–150, a fact that also points to the *yaḥad* as a movement larger than this settlement alone.

It is an open question whether the break between the Teacher and the Man of Lies is a schism within the *yaḥad* or the actual splitting of the *yaḥad* from the larger Essene movement. An early dating of the *yaḥad* could suggest that the community functioned for a certain period of time before such a bitter split occurred in its midst.

In the Qumran library/depository we can identify:

1. *Scrolls copied within the Qumranic scribal school, but not necessarily at this site.* Copying is different from authorship. A designation such as the *yaḥad* scribal school would be more fitting. The careless style of these scribes may be a purely conscious socioreligious feature. Alternatively, it could reflect lack of education. One may speculate that the Teacher did not convince the best scribes of Jerusalem to follow him. This school copied both biblical and extrabiblical scrolls. It presupposes a tight milieu of scribes from the mid–second century onward, so it rather belongs to the *yaḥad* than the larger Essene movement. A couple sectarian scrolls written in a different orthographic system do not cancel the larger picture. These scrolls could have been penned by scribes who had just joined the *yaḥad*. The *yaḥad* scribal school may have inherited some orthographical features from scribes or texts earlier than the *yaḥad*, but developed this tradition further as new facets were added in this milieu.

2. *Literary works authored within the* yaḥad. On criteria for classifying works as sectarian, see Newsom (1990), Chazon (1992), and Dimant (1995).

3. *Literary works from the "fathers" of the* yaḥad, which by different scholars are designated Essene (García Martínez and van der Woude 1990), Enochic (Boccaccini 1998), presectarian (Dimant 1995), apocalyptic (Nickelsburg 2001). There are many borderline cases, which may or may not stem from the *yaḥad*.

4. *Literary works from the wider Jewish (non-Essene) milieu.* Both the Groningen Hypothesis and Boccaccini are rather daring as to dating and allocating certain writings to specific milieus. Dimant and other scholars have designated a number of Qumran scrolls as presectarian. However, many of these may rather be extrasectarian, namely, contemporary with the *yaḥad* (cf. Tigchelaar 2000, 309: "can one classify documents both chronologically and ideologically?"). If so, the *yaḥad* with its Qumran center was less isolated than posited by the Groningen Hypothesis and Boccaccini. Works such as the prayer for King Jonathan in 4Q448 (which preferably should be related to Janneus) point to open communication channels between Qumran and other Jewish streams long after the establishment of the *yaḥad*. We should not forget that the

large majority of scrolls at Qumran represent not this narrow community but the wider Jewish literary heritage.

Further, there are scrolls which may place the roots of *hekhalot* mysticism close to the *yaḥad* and its predecessors. The Hymn to the Creator in 11QPs[a] is a precursor of the *hekhalot* psalms, built upon the throne visions of Isaiah and Ezekiel. The human worshipers are united with the angelic chorus and thus elevated to God's entourage (Chazon 2003, 93-94). 4Q301 (4QMyst[c]?) fragment 3 is a hymnic text describing God's majesty in a style similar to *hekhalot* hymns (Schiffman, DJD 20, pp. 114, 118), and fragments 4-6 represent the same kind of text. God's holy people on earth praise him who is exalted in the heavens and rules on the earth. Also, the Songs of the Sabbath Sacrifice prefigure the later *hekhalot* tradition, with a close identity between the singers and visionaries on earth and their heavenly counterparts (Schiffman 1987). More than the two other texts, these songs of praise describe the heavenly realms and actors in detail.

These compositions are not necessarily written within the *yaḥad*. Scholars such as Fletcher-Louis have argued for a sectarian provenance of *Shirot 'Olat Hashabbat*. The lack of *yaḥad* terminology and references to this narrow *ecclesiola* on earth makes it more probable to see it as a presectarian work widely used in the *yaḥad*. Thanks to Schiffman (DJD 20, pp. 99, 119), we note that 4QMysteries is not a *yaḥad* text. It may have its origins in circles close to the pre-Maccabean (Elgvin 2004; Tigchelaar 2003) or Maccabean temple milieu (Lange 1998, 131-34). 4Q301 may be a fourth copy of 1Q/4QMysteries (with 1Q27, 4Q299, 4Q300, thus Lange 1998, 131; Tigchelaar 2003: either the same work or a different edition of Mysteries). Alternatively, it is a separate but related writing from the same milieu (Schiffman, DJD 20, p. 113; Elgvin 2004).

I would like to suggest that also *Shirot 'Olat Hashabbat* and the Hymn to the Creator together with other nonbiblical psalms of 11QPs[a] and 4QPs[f] have their origin in a pre-Maccabean priestly or Levite milieu that saw the earthly temple as a counterpart to the heavenly one, with the celebrants below participating with the angels above. The Teacher and the priestly core of the *yaḥad* brought these hymnic traditions with them as part of their heritage. The image of the community as a spiritual temple facilitated their active use in the *yaḥad* (1QSb 4 and the Self-Glorification hymn are specific *yaḥad* contributions to this theological line). So far we know of these writings only through the library or depository of the *yaḥad*, except for the Sabbath songs found at Masada, perhaps brought there by Essenes during the revolt. The links between these texts and the later *merkavah* tradition point to a stronger *Wirkungsgeschichte* of this community than is often presupposed. This hymnic tradition underlines the priestly origin of the community and the essential place the temple occupies in its thinking.

Digging among the Roots of the Groningen Hypothesis

Lester L. Grabbe

My aim in this chapter is a simple, perhaps self-indulgent one: to look at some of the supports for the Groningen Hypothesis and make some observations that I think are pertinent. The comments are made in the spirit of constructive criticism.

The main "pillars" of the Groningen Hypothesis are the following (García Martínez 1988):

1. It makes a clear distinction between the origins of the Essene movement and those of the Qumran group.
2. The origins of the Essene movement lie in the Palestinian apocalyptic tradition before the "Antiochian crisis."
3. The Qumran group originated in a split within the Essene movement in which the group loyal to the Teacher of Righteousness eventually established itself in Qumran.
4. The term "Wicked Priest" is a collective one referring to different Hasmonean high priests in chronological order.
5. It highlights the importance of the Qumran group's formative period before its retreat to the desert, and makes clear the ideological development, the halakic elements, and the political conflicts taking place during this formative period and culminating in the break which led to the community's establishing itself in Qumran.

In this critique I wish to address the following issues: the "Wicked Priest," the question of the Hasidim, 4QMMT and the Sadducees, Qumran and its relationship to the Essenes.

When I first read an account of the Groningen Hypothesis, it sounded strangely familiar. It took me back to my graduate student days when I was studying with William Brownlee at Claremont Graduate School. Some aspects of the hypothesis were those he advocated from his long acquaintance with the scrolls, beginning with their discovery in 1947. I expected Brownlee's synthesis, interpreting the origin of the scrolls and their connection with the Qumran group and wider Jewish history, to be given in detail in his 4QpHabakkuk commentary on which he was then working. When his book, *The Midrash Pesher of Habakkuk,* eventually appeared, however, he had postponed a broader synthesis until he had time to rethink all aspects of it. The synthesis that finally emerged was published in a posthumous article in the *Jewish Quarterly Review,* in which venue Brownlee had many altercations with the *JQR* editor, Solomon Zeitlin, in the late 1940s and early 1950s.

One of the theses Brownlee had espoused, beginning already in a lecture in December 1948, and which he continued to maintain in his final article, was that the Wicked Priest was not a single individual but a succession of individuals in a particular office. Specifically, the term "Wicked Priest" designated several of the Hasmonean priest-rulers in Jerusalem in the late second and early first century B.C.E. In fact, Brownlee was one of the two scholars who independently proposed that "wicked priest" was a play on "high priest." This indebtedness to Brownlee's original proposal has often been overlooked, I think, though it is in fact acknowledged in van der Woude's article of 1982. In this particular case, I think the general principle advocated by Brownlee was correct. Consequently, I am happy to support the Groningen school in their view about the Wicked Priest.

Another area on which I agree with the Groningen Hypothesis is the critique of the thesis that derived Qumran from the Hasidim. This was always grasping at a chimera. Philip Davies' classic article on the Hasidim appeared in 1977, as did the statement of John Collins (1977, 201): "The party of the Hasideans has grown in recent scholarship from an extremely poorly attested entity to the great Jewish alternative to the Maccabees at the time of the revolt. There has been no corresponding growth in the evidence." That was true in 1977 and is still true. The "Asadeans" mentioned a couple times in the books of Maccabees simply do not have the characteristics foisted on them by scholars. The very brief description of them in these passages does not make them look like either Pharisees or Essenes; after all, they are described as "mighty warriors" (1 Macc 2:39-42); and there is the oft-ignored problem that Judas Maccabee is said to have been one of the Hasidim (2 Macc 14:6)! To make the Hasidim the parents of Qumran/Essenes and the Pharisees is not so much to lean on a broken reed as to lean on a nonexistent one.

I am also at one with García Martínez in arguing that 4QMMT does not support the Sadducean hypothesis, one of the reasons being the calendar differences between MMT and the Boethusians (= Sadducees?). I argued this in an article published in 1997, but he will be aware of this, since my article on the topic was in a volume he coedited (Grabbe 1997).

I also find appealing the idea that the Qumran community was a breakaway group of the Essenes. Based on my study of modern and ancient religious sects, it seems a priori a cogent explanation, and I have, in print, favored it as an explanation (Grabbe 2000, 204-5). Nevertheless, here the defenses of the Groningen Hypothesis are somewhat deficient. At least I have not seen any attempt by either Florentino García Martínez or the late Adam van der Woude to provide the necessary detailed textual study to demonstrate that the Qumran group came from the Essenes. There are some comments in the book *Los hombres de Qumrán/The People of the Dead Sea Scrolls* (García Martínez and Trebolle Barrera 1995), and an article looking at the contribution of new texts (García Martínez 1998), but these do not constitute a systematic argument to demonstrate that Qumran broke away from the Essenes. Therefore, I want to raise some of the central issues in this area, specifically on the question of the Man of Lies, the calendar, and eschatology.

The term "man of lies" (איש הכזב) is found in a number of passages, as well as what seems to have been an alternative form, "driveler or dripper of the lies" (מטיף הכזב). Unfortunately, most of the passages where the expression occurs are not decisive (1QpHab 2:2; 5:11; 10:9; 11:1 (?); 1QpMic frags. 8-10 4; 4QPs[a] 1:26-27; 4:14; CD 8:13; 19:26; 20:15), but some seem to be helpful:

> 1QpHab 2:2: "[The interpretation of the matter concerns] the traitors with the Man of Lies, for they did not [believe in the words of] the Teacher of Righteousness from the mouth of God."
>
> 1QpHab 5:9-12: "[Hab. 1:13b] Its interpretation concerns the House of Absalom and the men of their counsel who were silent at the reprimand of the Teacher of Righteousness and did not help him against the Man of Lies who rejected the law in the midst of all their counsel."
>
> 1QpHab 10:9: "Its interpretation concerns the Driveler of Lies who led many astray to build a worthless city through bloodshed and to establish a community in falsehood for his own glory to make many weary in vain labour." This passage has language reminiscent of 4QTestimonia 21-30, which quotes the Psalms of Joshua about an accursed man who would (re)build a city in bloodshed, just as the "Driveler of Lies" does here (cf. Brownlee 1982-83, 21). This has been interpreted as John Hyrcanus, who rebuilt the walls of Jerusalem after they had been

destroyed by Antiochus VII Sidetes (Josephus, *Ant.* 13.245-47; 1 Macc 16:23).

CD 20:13-15: "And from the day of the gathering (in) of the teacher of the Community [היחיד] until the end of all the men of war who turned (back) with the Man of Lies will be forty years." Here the Man of Lies leads men of war. If taken literally, it would easily apply to a Hasmonean ruler.

I would be the first to admit that we are dealing with highly allusive language. We cannot be sure that the expressions above are to be taken literally, but then can we be sure they are not to be taken literally? We should also keep in mind that the Wicked Priest may have been an associate of the Teacher of Righteousness at one time, or at least a member of the same group: 1QpHab 8:9 states that the Wicked Priest was "called by the name of Truth" at the beginning of his office, an expression likely to mean he was in some way associated with the group responsible for the pesher (cf. 1QpHab 7:10; Brownlee 1979, 134-36). It seems to me that the identification of the Man of Lies with one of the Wicked Priests is a reasonable interpretation of the evidence. Of course, arguing that Qumran split off from the main body of the Essenes does not require one to think that the Man of Lies was an Essene leader who in some way opposed the Teacher of Righteousness, but it has been given as a supporting thesis. If the Man of Lies was not the Essene leader, this fact would not be fatal to the theory, but it would remove one of its supports.

With regard to calendrical matters and eschatology, the reason for suggesting that they were not of interest to the Essenes is that they are absent from the accounts in the classical sources. But before taking this as a definitive answer, we have to consider the nature of our sources, primarily Philo and Josephus. Josephus claims to have tried out the Essenes, along with the other sects; but considering that he spent most of the three years of his trial period with a particular hermit, the time does not add up. Although it seems clear that he had personal knowledge of the Pharisees and Sadducees, his accounts of the Essenes seem almost certainly to have come from a written source or sources. In the *Bellum Iudaicum* he presents the various Jewish sects as philosophical schools. Similarly, Philo's interest is in illustrating a particular philosophical and moral approach to life by the use of a written source on the Essenes. Both Philo and Josephus were thus selecting from written sources the data that helped to support their point. This determined how they framed their description and also what they included and omitted. In the absence of their original source, we cannot know what they omitted; but we should be careful about too dogmatic an argument from silence.

A second general point about the calendar and eschatology is that I have not seen any criteria set out by the Groningen Hypothesis to distinguish literature of the Qumran group from the Essene writings that happened to be preserved in their library. How do we know a particular writing is by the Qumran group and not an earlier Essene writing if the only "Qumran" feature relates to the calendar or eschatology?

The Groningen Hypothesis argues that the fundamental disputes within the Essene movement during the formative period of the sect were centered on the question of the calendar and the consequent organization of the festive cycle, and on a particular way of understanding the biblical prescriptions relating to the temple, the cult, and the purity of persons and things (García Martínez 1988, 123). Yet calendar problems are not reflected in the classical accounts of the Essenes except with regard to the Therapeutae (123). It is therefore inferred that the Essenes agreed with the rest of Judaism in following a luni-solar calendar.

This is an argument from silence and, like all arguments from silence, can never be absolute. As already noted, if the classical descriptions were exhaustive, this would settle the matter, but I am not sure either Philo or Josephus would have regarded calendar questions of sufficient interest to include such information, even if they possessed it. Therefore, I cannot regard the silence of Philo and Josephus as the final word on the subject. The main reason for raising the issue of the calendar is that there are a number of writings among the Qumran scrolls that use a solar calendar yet do not seem to be the product of the Qumran group. My question is, what do we do about Jubilees and some parts of 1 Enoch? Are these definitely not Essene? Perhaps they are not, but the question needs to be addressed. Likewise with the Qumran calendrical texts surveyed by Professor García Martínez (1998, 199-204): Can we be sure they are Qumran compositions and not writings of the parent Essene group? There has been a disconcerting lack of coming to grips with this issue.

Now for the issue of eschatology: "Eschatology is precisely one of the elements which in classical descriptions of Essenism are not conspicuous, but it is prominent in the sectarian writings from Qumran and displays a clear development" (García Martínez and Trebolle Barrera 1995, 91). I think this argument does not stand up, and in this case we are not dealing with silence from the sources. First, Josephus in the *Bellum Iudaicum* (2.159) states that there are some among the Essenes who "profess to foretell the future, being versed from their early years in holy books, various forms of purification and apophthegms of prophets; and seldom, if ever, do they err in their predictions" (translation from LCL). In three of the four episodes involving individuals, an Essene makes a prediction or otherwise "reads" the future (*Ant.* 13.311; 15.373; 17.347-48). In each case the prediction involves a ruler or high official.

One could argue that this is not the same as setting out a full-blown eschatological scenario, but these are only allusions, not detailed expositions; we have to keep the nature of our sources in mind. Certainly, these statements are compatible with an Essene interest in eschatology. Furthermore, the question of whether some of the eschatological writings at Qumran might not be Essene in origin has to be considered. It seems to me that the case for denying eschatology to the Essenes has not been made at all.

These are not meant as nit-picking questions. I think they are fundamental for the Groningen Hypothesis, a hypothesis with which I have considerable sympathy, as already stated. But it seems to me that for it to be a viable hypothesis, some work needs to be done in putting some of these issues on a firmer basis.

One "Methodological Assumption" of the Groningen Hypothesis of Qumran Origins

Benjamin G. Wright III

In 1988 Florentino García Martínez sketched for the first time the Groningen Hypothesis of Qumran Origins. García Martínez and Adam van der Woude rearticulated this hypothesis in 1990 in *Revue de Qumran,* and in his book *The People of the Dead Sea Scrolls* García Martínez has provided perhaps his most complete articulation of his hypothesis. Essentially, as he puts it, "This new hypothesis proposes locating the ideological origins of the Essene movement in Palestinian apocalyptic tradition before the Antiochene crisis. In other words, before the Hellenisation of Palestine and the ensuing Maccabean revolt. It derives the Qumran community from a schism within the Essene movement and it tries to determine the many factors which initiated the rift and culminated in the setting up of the Qumran community" (García Martínez and Trebolle Barrera 1995, 77).

Underlying this hypothesis are a number of clearly set-out methodological assumptions, which have remained fairly constant since its initial publication in 1988. One of the most important for establishing the chronology of the separation of the Qumran group from its parent group is van der Woude's argument that the "Wicked Priest" of the Pesher Habakkuk is actually a series of six wicked priests who can be precisely identified. Timothy Lim has critiqued van der Woude's thesis in several publications, and I will not pursue that question here.

I want to raise some questions about one other "methodological assumption" of the Groningen Hypothesis. The third presupposition of the 1988 article, reiterated in the 1990 *Revue de Qumran* article and *The People of the Dead Sea Scrolls,* states, "the nonbiblical literature found in the various caves of Qumran is related either to the Qumran sect or to the ideological movement in which the sect has its roots" (García Martínez 1988, 116; cf. García Martínez and van der Woude 1990, 524-25; García Martínez and Trebolle Barrera 1995, 84-85). García Martínez is careful to say that this statement does not mean that all these works are of Qumranic origin, but that "in view of the character of the Qumran Community it seems to me out of the question that it should have preserved and made use of works incompatible with its own theology" (García Martínez 1988, 116), and that the presence of any work in the Qumran library "does assure us that the work in question was understood as compatible with its own ideology and its own *halakhah,* that is, coming from the Essene movement or from the apocalyptic tradition which inspired it" (García Martínez and van der Woude 1990, 525). Thus, these nonbiblical works serve as evidence for reconstructing the theology and ideology of the Qumran community and its formative stage, its Essene parent movement or the apocalyptic tradition that García Martínez sees as the matrix out of which the Essenes emerge.

While this kind of claim may seem fairly self-evident, it is actually more difficult to sustain than at first might appear. To assert that the community *understood* any work in the collection to be compatible with its theology is impossible to show, if there is no clearly sectarian comment on that work. One, of course, might speculate about how any particular work might fit, but in the absence of evidence beyond its presence in the collection, one is left with speculation only. The Qumran collection contains two works that I think can serve as examples of texts that would seem to problematize García Martínez's third methodological assumption: the Wisdom of Ben Sira (2Q18 [also the Masada scroll]) and 4Q448, the Prayer for the Health of King Jonathan.

On the surface of it, the presence at Qumran of a sapiential work like Ben Sira might seem fairly benign and unsurprising. In fact, one can see a fair number of similarities between it and 4QInstruction, a sapiential text that some might argue comes from the movement that produced the Qumran community. Yet, upon closer inspection several passages in Ben Sira set out positions that would seem to be opposed to the Qumran community's ideas and practice, and Ben Sira's broader perspective seems to argue against the "apocalyptic tradition" from which García Martínez claims that the Qumran community ultimately stems.

Perhaps the most important issue Ben Sira addresses is the calendar. While the Qumran community used a solar calendar, Ben Sira makes a fairly strong statement supporting a lunar calendar and, by implication, opposing a solar calendar. In 43:1-8 Ben Sira speaks of the sun and moon. For him the most important characteristic of the sun is that it is hot. Ben Sira nowhere in his book ascribes any calendrical function to the sun. When he describes the moon, however, he focuses almost exclusively on its function as a calendrical marker. It "marks the changing seasons, governing the times" (v. 6); the moon sets the festival days (v. 7).

Even more striking about Ben Sira's distinction between the blazing hot sun and the season-marking moon is that he differentiates their functions in contrast with the priestly account of creation, which he certainly knows, that gives the moon *and* sun cooperative responsibility for the calendar (Gen 1:14). Thus, one gets the sense that Ben Sira has eliminated any calendar significance for the sun deliberately, and 43:1-8 looks like a conscious criticism of those who followed a solar calendar, particularly Jewish groups like those that produced the Book of the Watchers (Wright 1997).

Other passages in Ben Sira may also reflect the author's critical attitude toward some aspects of "the apocalyptic tradition." Two in particular seem to criticize those who claim to receive revelation through dreams and visions and who seek knowledge that is beyond human ken. In 34:1-8 Ben Sira almost sarcastically dismisses receiving knowledge through dreams and visions. He calls the one who believes in dreams, one who "catches at a shadow and pursues the wind" (v. 2). Dreams are simply "a reflection" of what the dreamer wants to see (v. 3). Dreams deceive people, and "those who put their hope in them have perished" (v. 7). In 3:21-24 Ben Sira warns his students against seeking "what is too marvelous for you" (v. 21). "Hidden/secret things" and "things beyond you" should not be of concern. This passage is replete with language that in other places in Ben Sira indicates the wonders of God's creation and the secrets of the future. Ben Sira warns his charges to stay away from such dangerous speculations. They are to pay attention to those things that have already been entrusted to them, almost certainly for Ben Sira the torah (v. 23).

I have argued that these passages combined with Ben Sira's treatment of Enoch and his unflinching support of the Jerusalem priests suggest that he knew of apocalyptic traditions like those in the Book of the Watchers and Aramaic Levi criticizing the Jerusalem priests as defiled and corrupt and that he is addressing them in his book. That is, Ben Sira was aware of and intended certain passages in his book to respond polemically to complaints lodged against the Jerusalem priestly establishment and those who supported it. These complaints can be found in works like the Book of the Watchers and Aramaic Levi, which are roughly contemporary with Ben Sira. His strategy for addressing these complaints was (1) writing positively about the priesthood and encouraging Jews to pay the priests in the temple the honor due them, and (2) confronting some of the means by which his opponents legitimated or gave authority to their criticisms (Wright 1997, 191; cf. also Argall 1995, and Boccaccini 1991, who also suggest that Ben Sira and 1 Enoch are somehow interlocutors).

If Ben Sira does contain these kinds of criticisms of the apocalyptic tradition, then one might ask how Ben Sira fits with the ideology and theology of the Qumran community. Did those at Qumran who used Ben Sira simply ignore these issues? Could they not see them? Of course, we might be able to imagine possible ways the Qumran community overlooked these issues, but in the absence of any comment or exegesis of these passages we simply cannot know what the Qumran community made of them. We are left with García Martínez's presupposition that somehow the community made Ben Sira fit.

The second text is 4Q448, the so-called prayer for the health of King Jonathan, understood to be Alexander Janneus (E. Eshel, H. Eshel, and Yardeni 1998), a text that could be interpreted as a pro-Hasmonean document in the library of an anti-Hasmonean community. John Collins calls the text "anomalous" and argues that it represents a lack of consistency by the community. He suggests that it may represent temporary support for Janneus and might have been composed during a war against foreign enemies or during the conflict between the Pharisees (allied with the Seleucid Demetrius Akairos) and Janneus, the Qumran community disliking the Pharisees more than the king at this juncture (Collins 1997, 79-80; cf. Stegemann 1998, 133-34). Other scholars have suggested other occasions for the text's composition (H. Eshel and E. Eshel 1998; Flusser 1992). Yet, in the Nahum pesher, where Janneus is condemned for crucifying the Pharisees, there is no hint of support either for him or for the Pharisees inherent in the text. In fact, just prior to the mention of that incident the Pharisees are implicitly censured for collaborating with Demetrius. While Emmanuelle Main has argued that 4Q448 can be read as a prayer for God to fight against "Jonathan," this reading has not yet found acceptance among scholars.

In conclusion, texts such as Ben Sira and 4Q448 indicate that the presupposition that all the nonbiblical texts from Qumran are compatible with the community's ideology and theology contains some inherent difficulties. Of course, social and religious groups can preserve and use works that contain conflicting theologies or ideologies. The Jewish and Christian Bibles are evidence of that, but modern scholars have at least some evidence of the sifting and exegetical processes that went on in producing these collections. Modern Jewish and Christian Bibles also have the status of sacred scripture, which often necessitates finding ways of manipulating conflicting theologies to make them cohere.

What was the status of works like Ben Sira and 4Q448 at Qumran? Were they regarded as "scripture"? Were they authoritative in any way? I will not enter that discussion here, but it does seem to be a relevant problem/issue when looking at this methodological assumption of the Groningen Hypothesis.

While I see no reason to abandon the conclusion that the Qumran manuscripts must be connected to the group of people who lived at Qumran, at the very least Ben Sira and 4Q448 suggest that the contents of those manuscripts may not be as consistent as García Martínez presupposes, and thus not every text will necessarily provide details of Essene or Qumran theology and ideology.

The Translation of *NDMW* and Its Significance for the Groningen Hypothesis

Timothy H. Lim

The English translation of the key passage of 1QpHab 5:9-12 in Florentino García Martínez's article "Qumran Origins and Early History: A Groningen Hypothesis" requires one brief comment. The translation does not adequately draw out what is being intended: "Its prediction concerns the House of Absalom and the members of its council who were silent at the time of the reproof of the Teacher of Righteousness and gave him no help against the Liar who flouted the Law in the midst of their whole [congregation]" (García Martínez 1988, 124-25).

The ambiguity is centered on the phrase "who were silent at the time of the reproof of the Teacher of Righteousness." Did he mean that the House of Absalom and the members of its council were silent, in the sense that they did not speak up in support, during the reproof of the Teacher of Righteousness (Vermes 1997, 481)? That is to say, they remained guiltily neutral while the Righteous Teacher was chastised by the Liar. García Martínez's gloss on this passage seems to indicate otherwise: "that the majority of this community accepts the position of the Liar until the just rebuke of the Teacher of Righteousness reduces them to silence" (García Martínez 1988, 125).

The verb נדמו of 1QpHab 5:10 is derived from either the root דמה or דמם, since נדם is not attested as a triliteral root, and meaning "to be silent" (Williamson 1977-78). The נ is accordingly regarded as part of the prefix of the niphal conjugation, to be pointed as נִדְמוּ (Habermann 1952, 47) or נָדַמּוּ (Lohse 1964, 232). García Martínez's English translation renders this niphal in the middle voice, "were silent," whereas his explication gives it the active sense of "reduces them to silence." The latter gloss, however, is most likely to be a paraphrase rather than an unmarked citation.

I believe that García Martínez's explanation rather than his translation expresses his understanding of the passage. This is despite the fact that another translation that he and Eibert Tigchelaar published in their recent study edition of the scrolls renders the phrase "who kept silent when the Teacher of Righteousness was rebuked" (García Martínez and Tigchelaar 1997, 1:15). For the Groningen Hypothesis it seems it was the House of Absalom and members of its council whom García Martínez equates with "the majority of this community," who were reduced to silence.

The rendering of the niphal as passive rather than middle was previously suggested by Godfrey Driver (1965, 271-72) and Hugh Williamson (1977-78, 263-65). However, the translation by García Martínez of the ב of בתוכחת as a temporal preposition "at the time of the reproof (of the Teacher of Righteousness)" seems less likely than the *beth instrumenti* demanded by the passive (Williamson 1977-78, 264-65; cf. Kautzsch and Cowley 1983, §1190-q; Jouön and Muraoka 2000, §132e). Finally, he opts for "reproof" to render תוכחת, a noun whose semantic range overlaps with the synonym "chastisement" that is often used by English translators (Brownlee [1979, 93-94] sees distinct meaning in the words, but this is not so in current usage).

Clarifying this ambiguity will help one better grasp that according to the Groningen Hypothesis the Teacher of Righteousness not only opposed the Liar, but also rebuked a third party within the whole congregation, the group identified as the House of Absalom (Lim 2002, 74). What precisely is the relationship between the House of Absalom, its council, the Liar, and the whole congregation is not made clear.

The phrase תוכחת מורה הצדק has been understood either as the reproof that the Teacher of Righteousness himself bore or his castigation of either the Liar and/or the House of Absalom (Knibb 1987, 230). This ambiguity is familiar to us in grammar concerning the distinction between the subjective and objective genitive (Brownlee 1979, 93). If it is the latter, then the Teacher of Righteousness is the recipient of the reproof, whereas a translation like "the Teacher of Righteousness' reproof" would express the notion that it was he who chastised and censured others.

Vital to the view that the Teacher of Righteousness bore the reproof is the appeal to the context of the biblical lemma. Habakkuk 1:13b apparently describes "a wicked one who swallows up one more righteous than he." There has been some discussion on how to translate בלע, and it seems to me that one can hardly do better than "swallow," which conveys both a literal and figurative devouring of someone (Brownlee 1979, 94). But it is the analogical sense that is surely intended here as evidenced by its double use with a conventional phrase בכעס חמתו ("with the fury of his violence") and the parallel לכ[ה]שילם ("to make them stumble") in column 11:4-8.

On this view the biblical context of a wicked person swallowing up a more righteous person provides the clue to understanding תוכחת מורה הצדק. The reproof (תוכחת) of the comment corresponds to the swallowing up (בלע) of the lemma. Just as "a wicked one swallows up one more righteous than he," so also the Teacher of Righteousness was chastised by the Liar.

William Brownlee does not see these two elements in correspondence. Rather he argues that תוכחת מורה הצדק refers to the Righteous Teacher's reproof of the Liar which resulted in the former being swallowed up by the latter, precisely because of the House of Absalom's refusal to help (Brownlee 1979, 94). This explanation, however, reads historical information out of the biblical lemma and conflates it with the sectarian comment.

It seems to me more likely that the House of Absalom and its council were reduced to silence by the reproof of the Teacher of Righteousness. Jean Carmignac has shown that in biblical and Qumran usage תוכחת means "chastisement": "A Qumrân également, le verbe YKH et ses dérivés sont toujours pourvus d'une nuance favorable de justice et de bienfaisance" (Carmignac 1962, 509). It is hardly possible for the pesherist to apply the same term to a reproof whose object is the Teacher of Righteousness. Hugh Williamson (1977-78, 265) has suggested that the comment supplies the answer to the question posed by the biblical text: Why do the traitors remain silent? Because they were reduced to silence by the reproof of the Teacher of Righteousness.

Both these points bolster the case for the subjective genitive. However, they gloss over the grammatical solecism posed by the juxtaposition of a plural (תביטו) and singular (תחריש) verb in the biblical lemma. If the latter corresponds to נדמו in the comment, then it is possible that תחריש is a mechanical, scribal error for תחרישו. However, the MT attests to the singular "be silent" and the subject as YHWH, Elohay, Qedoshi: "Why do you (YHWH) look on the traitors and keep silent when a wicked one swallows up one more righteous than he?" The plural verb of the lemma ("why do you look") also points in the same direction (Lim 2000, 49).

The rather confused presentation of 1QpHab 5:9-12 detracts from our precise understanding of the Groningen Hypothesis. As I have observed previously, this is only a theory in the making (Lim 1992). What is needed is a comprehensive discussion of all the relevant issues, anchored as they should be on detailed exegesis.

Comments concerning the "Qumran-Essenes" Hypothesis

Shemaryahu Talmon

My conception of the community of "those who entered the renewed covenant" (CD 2:2; 9:2-3; et al.; cf. Talmon 1993) differs decidedly from the manner in which it is treated in the broad constructs of the "Qumran-Essene" hypothesis proposed by García Martínez and van der Woude (1990). My perspective holds that they are a *phenomenon sui generis,* a peripheral faction in second temple Judaism. In my view the *community* is the early second century B.C.E. crystallization of an apocalyptic millenarian *movement* that emanated in Palestine in the fifth or possibly already in the sixth century B.C.E. (Talmon 1994).

This movement predominantly comprised Ephraimites, namely, erstwhile citizens of the former Northern Kingdom (Jer 41:6-9), and possibly also some Judeans who had escaped exile during and after the conquest of Judah by the Babylonians in 597 and 586 (Jer 41:10–43:7). The local population, disparagingly designated עמ(י)/גויי הארץ/הארצות in the returnees' literature (Ezra 3:3; 4:4; 9:2, 11; cf. 9:14; Neh 9:30; 10:32; 2 Chron 13:9; et al.), clashed with the returning exiles who insisted on identifying themselves as בני הגולה (Ezra 4:1; 6:19, 20; 8:35; cf. 9:14; et al.), who descended from the tribes of Judah, Benjamin, and Levi (Ezra 1:5; 2:1; 6:8; 9:1; 10:7, 16; et al.), and who are the true Israel (Ezra 2:2; 3:1; 8:29; et al.) (Talmon 2001).

The movement also appropriated for itself the honorific designation יהודה and passed it on to the "community of the renewed covenant" (1QpHab 8:1; 12:4, 9; CD 4:3; 6:5; 1QM 1:2; et al.). At the same time, they implicitly present their opponents as survivors of the erstwhile Northern Kingdom whom disaster will befall, as prophesied by Isaiah: such as not experienced since the separation of Ephraim from Judah (Isa 7:17): יבוא(ו) עליך . . . ימים אשר (לא) באו מיום סור אפרים מעל יהודה (CD 7:11-12), whereas they, namely, the covenant-ers, will be saved from all evil: וכל המתהלכים באלה ברית אל נאמנות להם להנצילם מכל מוקשי שחת (CD 14:1-2).

The rivalry of the two communities who both claimed to descend from and to represent the biblical kingdom of Judah shows in the declaration of the author of the Damascus Document that "at the completion of the period of the (preordained) number of these years, there will no longer be any joining with the (other) house of Judah, rather each (of the two) will stand up on its watch-tower," ובשלום הקץ למספר השנים האלה אין עוד להשתפח לבית יהודה כי אם לעמוד איש על מצורו (CD 4:10-12).

The proposition that the "community of the renewed covenant," which consolidated itself at the height of the second temple period, should be consid-ered a *phenomenon sui generis* derives from specific and unique traits ascribed to it in documents authored by its own members and most probably locally committed to writing. This is quite different from its identity depending upon analogies or similarities which comparative research identifies in the concepts and traditions of other socioreligious factions in second temple Judaism. The pertinent information is primarily culled from foundation documents, such as various Rules, the Damascus Document, the War Scroll, the Temple Scroll, pesherim, 4QMMT, and diverse calendrical rota. These literary works, which all in all constitute a comparatively small part of the Qumran assemblage of manuscripts, do not contain any explicit or implicit reference to the Essenes or to their essential beliefs and doctrines, such as reported by Josephus, Philo, and Pliny the Elder, nor do they exhibit any trace of what has been named "Enochic Judaism" (Boccaccini 1998; Sacchi 1998).

As is well known, the larger part of the finds consists of writings which do not have a specific covenanters' profile, the corpus of biblical scrolls and frag-ments, wisdom, prayer texts, and the like; some of these are even marked by ideas that seemingly run counter to the covenanters' conceptual universe. In to-tal, the bulk of these variegated literary creations exemplifies the diversified lit-erary heritage of Judaism at large at the height of the second temple period. They were presumably brought to Qumran by novices who came from various strata of contemporary Jewry in order to join the community.[1]

In the present framework, only a few of the covenanters' unique charac-teristics clustered in the opening passage of the Damascus Document (1:1-10),

---

1. In parenthesis it may be said that because of its composition the collection of scrolls in the caves can hardly be termed a library by any definition of the term. However, at the same time, it is not an altogether happenstance assemblage.

which no ancient source ascribes to the Essenes or any other faction in second temple Judaism, can be brought under review.

The historical parameters of the *movement* turned *community* are spelled out in a pesherlike interpretation which confers a redemptive quality on an Ezekielian symbolic act signifying a 390-year period of woe for Israel (Ezek 4:4-5). Through investing this originally punitive prophetic symbol with a redemptive quality, the emergence of the *community* is dated 390 years after Nebuchadnezzar's capture of Jerusalem, namely, to the beginning of the second century B.C.E.

The restoration of Israel's fortunes thus is said to be realized exclusively in the covenanters' community, the only legitimate heir to biblical Israel. The reconstituted *politeia* is to be overseen by the (two) "shoots of planting" sprouting "from Israel and Aaron," who are prefigurations of the priestly and the Davidic "anointed" who together will lead in the future age (1QSa 2:11-15 et al.). This unparalleled bifurcation of the messianic idea derives from Zechariah's prophecies (chaps. 4 and 6), and in second temple Judaism was taken up and developed only by the covenanters.

When the foreordained *qeṣ* passed uneventfully, there arose the *moreh haṣedeq* who hammered the cluster of disappointed millenarians into a structured community (CD 1:5-6). The authors of the foundation documents apply to this community various appellations constructed with the term ברית, such as ברית היחד (1QS 8:16-17) and ברית ראשנים (CD 6:2) and the like. In this context the designation ברית חדשה (CD 1:4-5; 6:2-3, 19; 8:21; 1QpHab 2:3) is of signal significance. This biblical hapax legomenon occurs in an oracle proclaimed by Jeremiah after the destruction of Jerusalem in which the prophet predicts a future renewal of God's covenant with Israel (Jer 31:31). The *yaḥad* authors employ this term to present their community, and their community exclusively, as the youngest link in the biblical chain of covenant renewals. Unlike Jeremiah's oracles in which a restitution 70 years after the fall of Jerusalem is foreseen, his ברית חדשה prophecy is not dated, and therefore could easily be combined with Ezekiel's 390-years oracle of punishment turned promise.

I consider it most significant that in contrast to the fundamental import accorded to these prophecies of Jeremiah and Ezekiel in the covenanters' foundation documents, they are never referred to in sources relating to the Essenes, are only very seldom separately in the Apocrypha and rabbinic texts, and never in combination.

The Palestine-based, prophetically inspired *apocalyptic movement* clashed from the outset with the contingents of returnees from the Babylonian exile who in the Diaspora had developed a decidedly *rationalist* stance, although they conceived of their repatriation as the realization of Jeremiah's vision of a restitution of Israel's fortunes 70 years after the fall of Jerusalem to Nebuchadnezzar.

The controversy revolved around several issues, foremost being the right to rebuild the temple, and then there was the legitimacy of the officiating priesthood. These bones of contention possibly left traces in the quest of the "adversaries of Judah and Benjamin" to be given a share in the rebuilding of the temple, denied by "Zerubbabel and Jeshua (the high priest) and the heads of the families" (Ezra 4:1-5).

The collision occurred when Nehemiah ousted a scion of the high priest-hood (Neh 13:28-31). The local population that had escaped deportation ada-mantly refused to conduct their everyday life and have the sacrificial service in the temple executed in accord with the Babylonian lunar calendar which the re-patriates had adopted in the exile. The *'am ha'areṣ* insisted on adhering to their preexilic solar *ephemeris,* known in detail from the covenanters' calendrical documents.

Parallel with the development of the vaguely definable *movement* that af-ter some three centuries culminated in the establishment of the ברית היחד, the structured *community* of the renewed covenant, the returnees' party progres-sively consolidated to become *mainstream* Judaism at the height of the second temple period, and became *normative Judaism* in the first centuries c.e. The head-on collision about the calendar is indeed unequally socioreligious in the two communities. It can be traced in the covenanters' foundation documents, but is only occasionally and indirectly referred to in rabbinic sources.

The Essenes and Qumran,
the Teacher and the Wicked Priest,
the Origins

Émile Puech

Since the beginning of the Qumran studies, most scholars agree: (1) that the Qumranites were Essenes; (2) that the inhabited caves in the marl terraces, southwest and north of Khirbet Qumran (which is Sokokah of Josh 15:61 [with the old pronunciation of the LXX] and 3Q15), belong to the Qumran settlement; and (3) that the scrolls found there belong to that religious community. Already in the first decade of studies, scholars agreed that not all the scrolls were composed by the Essenes-Qumranites, distinguishing Essene writings from biblical and apocryphal works.

Different hypotheses have been proposed to explain the beginning of the movement and the settlement at Qumran, but only those which take into account all the data of archaeology, paleography, and the scrolls' content are acceptable, as Josef Milik put it (Milik 1959). The Groningen Hypothesis (García Martínez 1985a; 1987a; 1988; García Martínez and van der Woude 1990) emphasizes a clear distinction between the origin of the Essenes and the origin of Qumran, but its prehistory, pietist or apocalyptic, does not greatly affect our approach, except that Milik was right in designating the Hasideans of the Maccabean period, with their nationalism and religious messianic fervor, as the direct roots of the movement which crystallized and then split at the end of a twenty-year period of growth.

The period of the split and of the exile at Qumran is at the center of the debate. For the Groningen Hypothesis the origins of the movement must predate the pontificate of John Hyrcanus when the Qumran group was first established. However, this last point is not at all clear. After four-fifths of the coins had been identified, de Vaux (1973) concluded that it is difficult to explain how the period Ib began before John Hyrcanus, or how the period Ia may possibly have begun under his pontificate or one of his immediate predecessors, Simon or Jonathan. Since the period Ia was of brief duration, de Vaux favored Simon rather than Jonathan, but without any decisive archaeological arguments. It is not really legitimate scholarship to oppose these conclusions (Vaux 1973, 116; cf. Magness 2002); the preliminary reports in *Revue biblique* were written just after each season when only some coins were properly identified. That means that the Qumran settlement can have been established well before John Hyrcanus.

To determine the split, the study of the pesherim with some other scrolls is of the first importance, because the identification of the Wicked Priests can help us identify the Teacher at the center of the Qumran Essene movement.

Scholars generally agree that the wicked priest of 1QpHab 11:8ff. (in the future tense) is to be identified with Alexander Janneus (103-76), who ruled after the Teacher's death. Since the split took place during the Teacher's life, it must be dated well before the end of the second century B.C.E. This is in agreement with the archaeological data. Since the Teacher became old and died peacefully as it is written in the Damascus Document, he might have exercised his function during the second half of this century. The other five passages of 1QpesherHabakkuk dealing with the wicked figure have been interpreted by the Groningen Hypothesis in a chronological succession of (high) priests, from Judas Maccabeus to John Hyrcanus. This is very difficult to admit, since Judas never exercised the charge, as Timothy H. Lim (1993) has shown, and 1QpHab 9:16–10:5 applies much better to Jonathan, the builder of the city, than to Simon. This is in agreement with a large majority of scholars. Hence we propose the hypothesis of a unique figure of the past, Jonathan, following Vermes-Milik-Starcky-Stegemann, or Simon, with Cross–de Vaux, for the identification of the historical Teacher (Vaux 1973, 116ff.). A persecution of the Teacher by John Hyrcanus has no textual basis and cannot tell us anything about the beginning of the settlement at Qumran. In favor of the Jonathan hypothesis are many textual data, not only Flavius Josephus (*Ant.* 13.171, where the past tense *ēsan* is in a sentence about the last period of his leadership with no suggestion of previous decades). The second vision of the book of Dream Visions in 1 Enoch tells us that one of the white lambs was persecuted and killed (1 En 90:8, see Flavius Josephus, *War* 2.123 for the white garment of the Essenes). This seems to aim clearly at Onias III, killed in 171/70 B.C.E. A similar date is given by CD 1:5-12:

> And at the end of the wrath, three hundred and ninety years after giving them into the hand of Nabuchadnezzar, king of Babylon, God visited them and caused to grow out of Israel and Aaron a root of planting to inherit his

land and grow fat in the goodness of his soil. And they discerned their iniquity and knew that they were guilty people, and they were as blind as those who grope for a way for 20 years. But God discerned their works, that they sought him wholeheartedly, and he raised up for them the Teacher of Righteousness to guide them in the way of his heart.

As I showed in the Festschrift for Stegemann (Puech 1999), this calculation works very well if one adopts the computation still known and used by 2 Baruch 1:1ff., where the first siege of Jerusalem is dated in the twenty-fifth year of Jechonias (= 572 B.C.E.) and the fall of the city in 562. The growing of the root is then to be dated in (562-390 =) 172, precisely the year when Menelaus deposed Jason through the *gerousia,* asking Lysimachus his brother to take from the treasure of the temple the obligatory gift for the king (Denis 1977). Lysimachus was killed during this first popular revolt against the Hellenizing wicked priest, followed around one year later by the killing of Onias III.

Twenty years later, in 152, the decisive split took place when Jonathan Maccabeus took on himself the pontificate, thus deposing the priest in charge whose name is not preserved in Josephus's list. But there must have been a priest in the office after the death of Alcimus in 159 whose name had been erased by *damnatio memoriae,* because he was the one who went into exile in the desert as the central figure of the Qumranite Essenes, opposed to the main streams. In my hypothesis he was the son of Onias III who was still a child (*eti nēpios, Ant.* 12.237, and *pais, Ant.* 12.387) when Jason became high priest in 174, and he was not old enough when Menelaus died in 162 to take over the pontificate which went to another family, but this must have been possible in 159.

The Onias who went into Egypt to build a dissident temple was the son of Simon, the former provost of the temple, the brother of Menelaus of the Bilgah tribe (2 Macc 3:4), not the son of Onias III, as is generally too quickly accepted without any proof. This Onias was frustrated when Menelaus chose his brother Lysimachus as the priest of the second rank, to replace Simon, his father, who previously held the office, as second to Onias III. This explains much better why he flew into Egypt and began there another dissident Jewish cult. This Onias's temple in Egypt appears to have existed before 164, and this Onias had the grace of the Ptolemies. In any case, he could not have been the still-young, pious Zadokite, son of Onias III, whom I called "Simon" III by papponymy in use in this family as in many others in those centuries.

Then the 20 years of growing of a plant correspond precisely to this period of time from 172 to 152 before the exile of the high priest, the Teacher of Righteousness, who could have been and seems to have been persecuted later by Jonathan according to the Qumran texts. After his peaceful death, sometime around 120-110, another period of 40 years was counted for the eschatological war before the judgment of the wicked (CD 20:14ff.). Thus a jubilee of 490 years was completed, around 72. Such a chronological frame agrees well with the death of Alexander Janneus in 76, for the beginning of the end, the period of salvation (supposed to be around 72, according to their calculation), even if the composition of 1QpHab predated that death.

In consequence it is possible to know the names of both the Priest-Teacher of Righteousness (the son of Onias III, "Simon" III?) and the Wicked Priest, Jonathan Maccabeus[1] (Simon is excluded in 1QpHab 9:16–10:5). Precisely 4Q523 said something about robbed treasures in the temple by Jonathan's men, which with the change of calendars[2] could have precipitated the exile to the desert once the high priest was excluded from his office by Jonathan himself: hence the separation of the Hasido-Essenes from the Maccabeo-Hasmonean adherents, leaving the congregation of the Liar (Pharisees) to follow the wicked Hasmoneans.

This chronology explains much better some passages of the Hymns where the author-Teacher is said to have been an orphan. This also accounts for the absence in the Qumran library of any Pharisaic or pro-Sadducean composition after 152 (1-2 Maccabees, Psalms of Solomon, etc.) but the presence of MMT. MMT, after all, explains some halakic matters related to the separation, before, according to my chronology, any question about the statutes of the king arose. Then these statutes were included in the Temple Scroll, composed certainly after the death of Jonathan and most probably in the first years of John Hyrcanus. One must note the significance of the fact that it appears with the guard of the king on one side (11QT 57:5-11) and the succession of the royal house from father to son (11QT 59) on the other (Elledge 2004).

These texts must belong to the first decades of Qumran settlement, not to the formative period of the Groningen Hypothesis, neither to the pre-Antiochian crisis. The absence of the Hanukkah feast is better explained in a writing after the split than before, when the Hasido-Essenes were not totally opposed to the Maccabeo-Hasmoneans. Before the split in 152, Jonathan was

---

1. The paleographical dating of 4QSa and 4Q298 in the late Hasmonean–early Herodian scripts does not contradict this assumption, as Torleif Elgvin says in his comments on the Groningen Hypothesis (see above, "The *Yaḥad* Is More Than Qumran"). The suggestion of identifying the Wicked Priest with Jason, and the Teacher of Righteousness with Onias III, with a break in 174, has no support and is not worthy of consideration in my view.

2. The usage of calendars is of enormous importance for the regulation of the daily life and of course for the liturgical services and the fixed feast days in the years. In that I cannot totally agree with the view of Lester Grabbe (see above, "Digging among the Roots of the Groningen Hypothesis") on the use of the arguments from silence.

considered a faithful agent of the policy of independence begun by his father and brothers. Thus he was contributing to the ideal of the Hasidim, namely, that of restoring the kingdom of God, rebuilding the holy city, and fortifying the temple mount, as 4Q448 sings with its section of Psalm 154 praising that period. The king, Jonathan, as leader of the people of God in 4Q448, cannot be identified with Alexander Janneus, as has been said.[3] Such a composition would never have been accepted among the Hasidim. Then 4Q448 agrees with 1QpHab 8:8-10.

In conclusion, this solution agrees with all the data: archaeology, paleography,[4] literary texts and scrolls, chronology and history, and explains more easily the genesis of the main scrolls: *Serekh, Milhama,* Hymns, Covenant of Damascus, with the central role of the Teacher of Righteousness, the presence of the Epistle of Enoch in Cave 7, 4Q523, 4Q448, and the like.

Hence, Qumran cannot be a marginal Essene group; it is even the most important one, the center of the Essene movement (not a "sect" as it is too commonly said) where the Essene way of life was elaborated. The Hasideans belonged to the preformative period with roots in the prophetic, sapiential, and apocalyptic circles. Thus it is possible to explain their name, otherwise unexplained, "Essene" being the Aramaic nickname from Hebrew *hasid*,[5] as is also "Pharisee" for the separated congregation.

3. Benjamin Wright (see above, "One 'Methodological Assumption' of the Groningen Hypothesis of Qumran Origins") incorrectly follows the identification with Alexander Janneus. The paleography and content oppose such a conclusion. In that case, there is no lack of consistency (as Collins says) on the part of an anti-Hasmonean community, or of space for biased arguments. See Puech (1996).

4. The paleographical dating of 4QQoh[a], 4Q504 does not contradict the point. Part of the Qumran library is coming from the temple when the Teacher and other members left the temple with him. They did not leave with empty hands, but had copies of these imported books, and they composed other books for their proper use and needs. The paleographical dating of some cryptic texts by Stephen Pfann in the beginning of the second century B.C.E. cannot be accepted, and nothing contradicts the settlement at Qumran with the community, *pace* Torleif Elgvin. Contrary to Norman Golb's hypothesis and to James Davila (see below, "Enochians, Essenes, and Qumran Essenes"), the Essene groups did not transport much of their synagogue library to the caves of Qumran to hide them there in *genizot*.

5. This is the best philological explanation with Emil Schürer (1886-90, 2:558-61), notwithstanding the efforts of Geza Vermes in the English edition. I cannot follow the suggestion of Lester Grabbe (see above, "Digging among the Roots of the Groningen Hypothesis").

Qumran: The Headquarters of the Essenes or a Marginal Splinter Group?

Gabriele Boccaccini

Compared with most of the revisionistic hypotheses of the 1980s and 1990s, the Groningen Hypothesis shines for its soberness and balance. The research on the Dead Sea Scrolls is fascinating enough without the tricks of pretended surprises and only-announced-and-never-fulfilled revelations. To me, and to many young scholars of my generation, the Groningen Hypothesis taught that it was possible to go beyond the Essene Hypothesis and build a new understanding of Qumran moving forward and not backward, beyond and not against the accomplishments of decades of research (Boccaccini 1998, 1-17).

The Groningen Hypothesis accepted without reservations the two major tenets of the Essene Hypothesis: (1) the ruins of Qumran were of a religious community who owned the scrolls and authored part of them; and (2) that community was an Essene community. Yet the Groningen Hypothesis also showed that the Essene Hypothesis was only a starting point, as many essential questions were still largely unsolved, in particular concerning the role of Qumran within the Essene movement. Now that the long process of restoration and publication of the scrolls has finally ended, we are just at the very beginning of the no less complex process of historical interpretation of the evidence.

From ancient Jewish sources, notably Philo (*Quod omnis probus liber sit* 75) and Josephus (*Ant.* 18.21), we know that the Essenes were a large and popular movement of at least 4,000 adult members, while the archaeology of Qumran tells us that only around 150 Essenes could live in the harsh desert environment there. Obviously, the overwhelming majority of Essenes did not live at Qumran. If Qumran was indeed an Essene community and the Essene movement was indeed a much larger movement, what was the relationship between the Qumran community and the rest of the Essene movement?

We face three possibilities: either the community of Qumran was (a) simply one of the many Essene communities existing in Israel in the late second temple period; (b) a leading group, perhaps even the headquarters of the Essene movements; or (c) a splinter, marginal group.

Each of these hypotheses has profound ramifications for our understanding of the scrolls in relation to the Essene movement and more generally to the diverse world of second temple Judaism.

If the community of Qumran was indeed one of the many Essene communities, we may use the Dead Sea Scrolls as evidence of both the way of life and the ideology of the Essenes. In this case the terms "Essene" and "Qumran" are perfectly interchangeable.

If instead the community of Qumran was the headquarters of the Essenes, we may not use the Dead Sea Scrolls as evidence of the way of life of non-Qumran Essenes, although we may still use them as evidence of the ideology (or at least of the ideals) of all Essenes. In this case the terms "Essene" and "Qumran" may or may not be interchangeable.

If the community of Qumran was a splinter group, we may not use the Dead Sea Scrolls as evidence of either the way of life or the ideology of the Essenes, unless some similarity between the two groups is positively proved. The terms "Essene" and "Qumran" are not interchangeable.

Let us now examine briefly each of these hypotheses.

Qumran as an Ordinary Essene Community

The possibility that Qumran was simply one of the many Essene communities existing in Israel in the late second temple period goes against archaeological and historical evidence. We have not found in Israel anything comparable to the Qumran settlement. This could be accidental. After all, we would have never identified Qumran as the ruins of an Essene communal center if the scrolls had not been found. However, the uniqueness of Qumran is also confirmed by literary data. If we contrast the description of the Essene settlement near the Dead Sea provided by non-Jewish authors (Pliny and Dio) with the description of the Palestine communities provided by Jewish authors (Philo and Josephus), we find the same elements in and out of Qumran, but at Qumran they are always characterized by a high degree of intensity (Boccaccini 1998, 21-49).

Dio of Prusa claims that the Essenes lived in a city *(polis)* near the Dead

Sea — a situation confirmed by the archaeology of Qumran. On the contrary, Philo and Josephus say the Essenes did not form their own cities but lived as "colonists" in villages and towns. The Essene movement was essentially a phenomenon of urban colonies spread in villages and towns of Israel.

Pliny claims that the Essenes lived in isolation *(gens sola)* — a situation confirmed by the archaeology of Qumran. On the contrary, Philo and Josephus describe a sociologically complex setting. The Essenes had their own rituals and meetings, but they spent most of their life among non-Essenes. They lived, worked, preached, and during the Jewish war, even fought side by side with non-Essenes.

Pliny describes a self-sufficient and self-sustained society *(sine pecunia)* — a situation confirmed by the archaeology of Qumran. On the contrary, Philo and Josephus describe a situation in which the Essenes shared part of their wages for communal needs, after providing for themselves and their own families.

Pliny claims the Essenes lived without their wives *(sine ulla uxore)* — a situation confirmed by the archaeology of Qumran. On the contrary, Philo and Josephus offer a much more complex picture of the relations between men and women, husbands and wives, parents and children, within the Essene movement.

In short, all evidence — historical and archaeological — points to the fact that Qumran was a special, perhaps unique Essene community characterized by radical views. This leaves open either of the other two hypotheses.

Qumran as the Center of the Essene Movement

That Qumran was the headquarters of the Essenes is the hypothesis held by many distinguished specialists (see, above, Puech). This is what the frequent definition of Qumran as a "monastic" community also suggests. A monastery in Christianity is a place where people retreat to live a more perfect way of life than ordinary believers. A choice for the few makes these few leaders and models of a superior way of life. If the Qumranites were indeed "Essene monks," they must have been the leaders of the Essene movement. As such, we would expect them to be admired and highly respected within the larger Essene movement, as those who have chosen a more perfect way of life than that of the ordinary members. But was this the case?

There are two major difficulties.

First, neither Philo nor Josephus mentions Qumran (or any Essene community living in the desert or near the Dead Sea). Whether they were unaware

Gabriele Boccaccini

of the existence of Qumran or consciously avoided any reference to it, they chose the Palestinian communities as the best representatives of the Essene movement. As insiders, they chose what they believed was theologically and sociologically more important and representative. But Pliny and Dio, who were merely in search of sensational elements, chose what modern archaeology confirms was more peculiar and distinctive. Philo and Josephus might have been ill informed or biased, but contrary to what we now do in our scholarly publications, in the first century it was perfectly reasonable to offer a picture of the Essene movement without even mentioning Qumran.

The second clue comes from the very structure of the Qumran library. When the Dead Sea Scrolls were first discovered, it was natural to label the material according to our previous knowledge of it. In accordance with modern canonical categories, the scrolls were classified as "biblical" or "pseudepigraphic," while everything not previously known was assumed to be "sectarian," i.e., representative of the ideology of the Qumran group.

The first collections of the scrolls were selections of previously unknown "sectarian" documents (Vermes 1962). The "biblical" and "pseudepigraphic" texts became footnotes in the modern editions of the already established corpora of the Hebrew Bible (the *Biblia Hebraica Stuttgartensia*) and of the Old Testament Apocrypha and Pseudepigrapha. In one case only, the Damascus Document, which was already known as "Fragments of a Zadokite Work" from the Cairo Geniza (Schechter 1910) but whose sectarian features seemed too obvious to be overlooked, the overlapping was solved by removing the document from the corpus of the Pseudepigrapha, in which it had been included (Charles 1912-13, 2:785-834; Riessler 1928, 920-41), and moving it into the Dead Sea Scrolls.

Classifying the material according to our knowledge of it was a practical yet hardly scientific criterion. Modern editions of the scrolls are struggling to overcome such anachronistic assumptions and promote a more inclusive and comprehensive approach to the entire material discovered in the caves (Charlesworth 1994-; Vermes 1995; García Martínez 1996b). A new, more "neutral" taxonomic consensus is emerging that groups the scrolls ideologically in three categories:

1. a core group of rather homogeneous sectarian texts composed by the people of Qumran (like the Damascus Document, the Community Rule, the War Scroll, the pesherim, etc.).
2. a group of semisectarian texts (like 1 Enoch, Jubilees, the Temple Scroll, etc.) that have only some sectarian features and yet are compatible with the complex of ideas characteristic of the sectarian texts.

3. a group of nonsectarian texts in which sectarian elements are marginal or totally absent, the most obvious examples being, of course, the "biblical" texts.

Now, none of the sectarian texts authored by the Qumran community appears to have had any impact in the development of second temple Jewish thought. In vain one searches for a quotation in any of the ancient documents of Judaisms, other than Qumranic, or for a translation in Greek, Syriac, or any other ancient language. "None of the works connected to the Qumran community was transmitted by other channels" (Dimant 1995, 32). This phenomenon is even more striking when one considers the success that the nonsectarian texts preserved among the Dead Sea Scrolls enjoyed outside Qumran, in Christianity and elsewhere. I refer not only to the "nonsectarian" scrolls but also to some of the major "semisectarian" scrolls (like 1 Enoch or Jubilees). The popularity of these documents is in inverse proportion to their proximity to the sectarian literature. In short: the more sectarian a text is, the less known it is.

Such a phenomenon cannot be accidental. The experience of Christian monasticism proves that even the most isolated group can provide a strong intellectual leadership, becoming a center of theological production. What kind of leadership was the one provided by the Qumran community, which produced a vast corpus of documents that nobody read, and elaborated a highly sophisticated theology that nobody knew! A community that lived isolated in the desert and for more than two centuries went unnoticed in contemporary Jewish sources and was not able to "export" a single document and make it part of the theological and intellectual discourse of second temple Judaism can hardly be considered a leading group.

Qumran as a Marginal Splinter Group of Essenes

The Groningen Hypothesis has made a strong case that Qumran was a splinter group from the larger Essene movement. The hypothesis is based on the analysis of passages in the scrolls (especially from the Damascus Document and the pesherim) which seem to allude to an internal split within the parent movement from which Qumran was born.

I maintain that another clue is offered by the Enochic tradition. The Enoch literature provides evidence of at least a major stream of thought and a major group that originated long before Qumran and played an important role in Qumran origins, so much so that the Qumran community can be described as "a latter-day derivative of or a successor to the community or communities that authored and transmitted the Enochic texts" (Nickelsburg 2001, 65; cf. Boccaccini 1998). Then something must have happened to separate the Enoch and the Qumran groups. In the library of Qumran, which preserved and cherished all Enoch books composed before the birth of the community, the later literature of Enoch is conspicuous by its absence; not only the Parables of Enoch but also, probably, significant portions of the Epistle of Enoch are missing (Boccaccini 1998; cf. Nickelsburg 2001). This suggests the existence "outside Qumran . . . [of] circles that transmitted" the ancient Enoch literature (Nickelsburg 2001, 77). Furthermore, in the later Enoch literature we read statements and see the development of ideas that seem openly to contradict the principles of the sectarian literature of Qumran.

As Enoch lost touch with Qumran, at the same time Qumran lost its interest in the Enoch literature (Charlesworth 1980, 227; Collins 1997, 35-36; Boccaccini 1998, 129-31). The last quotation of Enoch is in the Damascus Document, therefore at a very early stage in the life of the community. The more the community strengthened its dualistic and predeterministic worldview, the more it lost interest in a literature that maintained that "evil originated not with God's permission, but as the result of a rebellious conspiracy that was hatched behind God's back" (Nickelsburg 2001, 47).

The split between Qumran and the Enoch group is evidence of a larger phenomenon. The distinction within the Dead Sea Scrolls between non-sectarian, semisectarian, and sectarian texts is not only ideological but chronological. The more ancient a text is, the less sectarian it is. And even more strikingly: not a single document, not even one, produced outside the community of Qumran after their withdrawal into the desert managed to find its way into the Qumran library.

Such a phenomenon cannot be accidental. Once again, Christian monasticism proves that even the most isolated community can participate actively in the cultural life of its own time. What kind of leadership was provided by the Qumran community that shut its doors and ceased to listen to and interact with the society at large, including the outside members of its own group? A community that lived isolated in the desert and for more than two centuries went completely unnoticed in ancient Jewish sources and neither "exported" nor "imported" a single document can hardly be considered a leading group.

In conclusion: the community of Qumran and its sectarian literature cannot be taken as representatives of the entire Essene movement, of Essene theology and way of life; the terms "Qumranic" and "Essene" are by no means interchangeable. The Qumranites were not ordinary Essenes; their uniqueness, however, did not make them leaders of the Essene movement. On the contrary: in their radical position the Qumranites were outcasts even within their own movement.

The implications are monumental, in particular for Christian origins. When the scrolls were discovered there was a lot of excitement about the possibility of finding Christian texts and/or references to Christian characters. Despite the popular, recurring success of fanciful theories about the Christian origins of the scrolls, it soon became clear that none of these expectations was to be fulfilled.

The distinction between Essenes and Qumranites may now allow us to recognize a close relationship between the Essene and the Christian movement, while continuing to see many major differences between the New Testament and the sectarian literature of Qumran. There was no need for John the Baptist or Jesus to go to Qumran to be familiar with the principle of the Essene movement. "Jesus was closer to the non-Qumran Essenes than to the strict and withdrawn Essenes living in the desert of Judah" (Charlesworth 1992, 40).

When the Dead Sea Scrolls were discovered, the voice of the Essenes was obscured by the voice of their most radical members — a very small group but with a large and outstanding library. It has taken some time to realize that the Qumran library comprised not only the documents of a marginal sectarian community but also a substantial body of Essene literature from the second temple period, independent of Qumran. As the Essene Hypothesis before, the Groningen Hypothesis also is only a starting point. The task of defining the theology and way of life of the thousands of Essenes who lived outside Qumran as well as their contribution to second temple Judaism and Christian and rabbinic origins is before us as one of the most fascinating and urgent goals of contemporary research.

Response: The Groningen Hypothesis Revisited

Florentino García Martínez

I would like, first of all, to thank all those who have "revisited" the Groningen Hypothesis, for their thoughtful contributions and particularly for having forced me, through their insights, to revisit the hypothesis myself. What was almost the accidental result of a passionate love affair with the scrolls appears now to me, with the approaching of old age, as a typically adolescent endeavor, overconfident and immature, but with the resilience and buoyancy typical of youth.

In this response I will briefly comment on the points that have attracted my attention. I confess without any shame that I have not reread the publications in which I have put forth my part of the Groningen Hypothesis. Not because of lack of time to do my homework (which is also true), but because in my opinion it all boils down to a matter of perception. It is not what I have said or intended to say that is important, but what others have perceived in the Groningen Hypothesis.

Charlotte Hempel

I also dislike the label "Palestinian apocalyptic tradition." I used it for lack of a better phrase to designate what appears to me as a reality. If we put the emphasis on "tradition" (and not on a community or on several organized communities), I have no doubt that within the Jewish literature of the time we can reasonably speak of an apocalyptic worldview as clearly distinct from the prophetic or wisdom tradition, even though we cannot pinpoint its sociological background. Labels are commodity designations, and I do not mind using the "apocalyptic" label as a shorthand reference to what appears to be an essential though certainly anterior component of the "sectarian scrolls."

We may consider it problematic to rely on the classical sources for information about the Essene movement, but they are the only sources that speak of the Essenes without ambiguity. The Groningen Hypothesis grew out of the simple fact that while some elements of the classical descriptions are present in the sectarian scrolls, other elements that are equally present are clearly incompatible. Hempel has admirably summarized some of the differences that appear on the final *yaḥad* redacted form of the Serekh and the Damascus Documents and considers them characteristic of the "parent" movement. Her reasoning seems to imply a reversal of the labels of the Groningen Hypothesis, and she postulates the application of the "Essene" label to the *yaḥad* group, not to the parent movement. I beg to disagree, among many other reasons, because her description of the key elements of the parent movement sounds very much like Josephus's and Philo's descriptions of the Essene movement.

I would not mind abandoning the "Qumran" label to designate the *yaḥad* community if there were not a very real risk of forgetting the most concrete data available (the tombs, the caves, the ruins, the cisterns, the pottery) and of making the community a utopian ideological construct, existing only in our texts. It may be possible that the move to the "desert," and concretely to Qumran, is a separate issue from the emergence of the splinter group, but the move did happen and provides us with a firm anchorage to reality.

As for the calendrical controversy, it is obvious that it has its climax in Jubilees, is present in compositions that I attribute to the "formative period," and is a matter of fact, both in the sectarian and nonsectarian texts of Qumran. But, if I am not mistaken, the calendrical controversy plays no role at all in the classical description of the Essenes, which as far as we know had no quarrels with the calendar of society at large. This can be dismissed as negative evidence, but in my opinion and in view of the importance of the matter for the cult, such a dismissal would be unwise.

The excellent article in the *Revue de Qumran* to which Hempel refers is (if I have not misunderstood it completely) a clear vindication of a key element of the Groningen Hypothesis: the presence in the sectarian scrolls of references to a split within the parent movement as the immediate origin of the Qumran community. Thus, even if we differ in the labeling, we seem to agree in the essentials.

A final word is due on the Temple Scroll and the Halakhic Letter (MMT). Although I am still inclined to place both documents in the unfortunate "formative period," it seems evident that both were not originated at the same time.

The "we," "you," and "they" perspective of MMT is totally absent from the Temple Scroll.

Albert Baumgarten

I humbly acknowledge that I have worshiped "the idol of origins" and committed the sin of being "obsessed with origins" (I even, in my youthful enthusiasm, organized a whole conference on the issue of "Qumran *Origins* and Early History"). My only excuse is that this "obsession with origins" was a sickness of the times (the late eighties) in Qumran research (something like AIDS could be considered the sickness of the nineties, or SARS the sickness of our present days, using biological paradigms). However, this disease did bring forth, quite by accident, a good result: the creation of the International Organization for Qumran Studies (IOQS) during that conference at Groningen in 1989. But of course, we should not consider the Groningen Hypothesis, or any other attempt to establish filiations, as the ultimate value. Even at the risk of being "only able to restate what we have written in the past," I cannot avoid the temptation to quote the conclusion of an article I wrote in 1984: "I am not convinced that the ideological heritage should always follow a straight line of transmission. Sometimes grandchildren or cousins are those who inherit the most" [Je ne suis pas convaincu que l'héritage idéologique doive suivre toujours une ligne droite de transmission. Quelquefois ce sont les neveux ou les cousins qui reçoivent la meilleure part] (García Martínez 1987b, 57). This quotation is still in the conceptual frame of a family tree, and as such is outdated and far from the biological paradigm Baumgarten proposes; but it shows that establishing genetic filiations was not the only impulse of the Groningen Hypothesis.

I think that attention to the context is essential, and that ancient Jewish movements should be compared to each other in order to understand the way they respond to the same set of issues. On this matter I have no quarrel endorsing the old Arab proverb Baumgarten cites. I think we can learn much also from comparison with similar movements in completely different historical and cultural contexts, because similar responses in different contexts may reveal some fundamental structures. And I also think the biological paradigm Baumgarten proposes as a hermeneutic tool is most promising, and I look forward to the results of its application on a large scale. But, as an old-fashioned Darwinian, I am also convinced that genetics play an important role in all ancient Jewish movements (in which I include early Christianity), and that genes transmit information. In all ancient Jewish movements we find not only responses to the issues of their era, but also a hereditary component that informs all of them: the foundational text of the Hebrew Bible. Its different interpretations, transformations or manipulations, also inform the different religious outlooks we encounter in the texts.

Mark Elliott

The point on methodology is well taken, and I will not deny that the Groningen Hypothesis looks somehow like an inverted pyramid, with all the risk of breaking down if one of the anchorage pillars proves to be defective. For Elliott the weakest of these anchorage points is number four in the logical chain he describes: the conclusion that the Man of Lies was part of an originally much larger group to which the Teacher also belonged. He may of course be right, but for me this was not perceived as a logical conclusion but as a starting point, clearly imposed by the text itself (1QpHab 5:9-12). It is true that the manuscript is partially broken. Following Brownlee and most of the earliest commentators, I read עצתם in *The Dead Sea Scrolls Translated* ("their whole community") and עדתם in *The Dead Sea Scrolls Study Edition* ("their whole council"). The reading "community" or "council" can be twisted, but what cannot be disputed is the third-person plural suffix. And the suffix refers to the nearest antecedents, the Teacher of Righteousness and the Man of Lies. They were thus both members of an entity (the "House of Absalom" in the terminology of the pesher) in which the dispute took place. This reference to the council or the community in which both the Teacher and the Man of Lies were members, the reference to the "reproof" of the Teacher in the council of the House of Absalom, and particularly the clear reference not only to the city but also to "erecting a community with deceit for his own glory" were for me of such importance at the moment of formulating the Groningen Hypothesis that I did not give due attention to the military language of the Damascus Document.

Elliott has made very sensible remarks on social history and theology, particularly the emphasis he puts on the influence of the figure of the Teacher and on the "association with a rejected, estranged, isolated charismatic figure" that we can read in the Hodayoth as a defining marker of the limits of the community. But I will not so quickly dismiss "the kind of revelation found in the pesherim." The apocalyptic and end-time expectations and the prophetic interpretation of the Scripture attached to his person are too important and characteristic to be overlooked.

Florentino García Martínez

Torleif Elgvin

It is impossible to do justice to the many points of detail touched upon by Elgvin without going to undue length. If I have understood correctly the thrust of his argument, Elgvin dissociates the *yaḥad* (I assume he refers to the community described in the *Serekh*) from Qumran and dates the establishment of this *yaḥad* community early in the second century B.C.E. I leave to others the evaluation of Elgvin's discussion of the Enochic texts and the manuscripts referring to the "righteous planting." Instead, I will comment on only two points — both paleographical — that for him are essential: the date assigned (mid–second century) to two manuscripts copied according to the "Qumran scribal school" and the date assigned by Pfann to the cryptic manuscripts.

On the first, I will simply say that I am rather skeptical of the value of arguments extracted from the so-called Qumran scribal school to build great theories. We can easily see that certain Qumran manuscripts dated to different periods, be they biblical, sectarian, or nonsectarian, have been copied with a particular orthography and according to certain scribal conventions, and that other manuscripts, be they biblical, sectarian, or nonsectarian, have not. But since we have no other evidence outside Qumran on this matter, we cannot determine with precision whether these scribal conventions were peculiar to the site of Qumran (which is the conclusion of Tov, and is explicit in the name he has given to the "scribal school") or were also used in other places. Besides, we should not forget that there are many other manuscripts copied not according to any sort of scribal conventions but penned by untrained hands. In any case, I do not think the scribal characteristics of a manuscript can tell us anything about the origin of the *yaḥad* circa 175 B.C.E.

I am equally skeptical of an argument that depends on Pfann's dating of several copies of the *Serekh ha'edah* to the early second century B.C.E. I am not convinced that among the cryptic fragments nine copies of this composition have been found. With due respect for Pfann's work on those snippets of cryptic texts, a dispassionate look at plates XXXV-XXXVII of DJD 36 will make my point clear. And even a cursory reading of the pages dedicated to the paleographic dating of the cryptic manuscripts in DJD 20, 35, and 36 shows the fragility of all attempts to build an argument upon an assumed typology.

The postulate (I am afraid I cannot use another term) that the "*yaḥad* (different from the center at Qumran) should perhaps now be dated to circa 175-150, preferably early in this period," seems to me not only unsubstantiated, but also difficult to align with other known facts.

Lester Grabbe

I fully agree with the observation of Grabbe that I have not put forth a systematic argument for the Groningen Hypothesis (and I strongly doubt I ever will). The three concrete points are important and highly relevant. The predictive gifts of the Essenes may be compatible with an interest in eschatology, but in this case I do not think the categories of prophecy and eschatology should be confused. In the episodes cited from Josephus, we are dealing with predictions in the life of individuals, whose realization serves as proof. This seems to be something entirely different from Daniel's prophetic reinterpretation of Jeremiah's prediction, for example. As for the calendar, my reasoning was indeed from silence, always a very delicate argument. However, I am convinced that calendrical matters are one of the most discernible signs of difference, and festival calendars, with their consequences for participation or not in the temple cult, even more. It seemed to me that these matters should not be ignored even in nonexhaustive descriptions. After all, Josephus gives us several details of the daily prayers, a topic closely related to the calendar.

Also, the first point on the "Man of Lies" is well taken, and has already been raised by Elliott, who fully exploits the military language associated with this figure in the Damascus Document. I need to reconsider the whole matter carefully, not because I mind one "Wicked Priest," but because the expressions associated with the Man of Lies in the Pesher Habakkuk were for me one of the strongest indications of a rift, which I still consider the basis for the origins of the Qumran community.[1] Again with reference to Elliott's suggestions, I must confess that I did not give due attention to the military language of the Damascus Document. However, if I ever put forth a systematic argument for the Groningen Hypothesis, I will certainly consider this point as well.

Benjamin Wright

I love methodological discussions. I am thus most grateful for the opportunity Wright gives me to explain one of the "assumptions" I have been working with, which we could for the occasion label "the assumption of compatibility." I will

---

1. My contribution to this aspect of the Groningen Hypothesis was an article that has been unnoticed — I do not know if it has been because it was published in Spanish or because it appeared in an obscure Festschrift (García Martínez 1985b) — in which I suggested that Judas Maccabeus could also have been perceived as high priest, and could thus have completed the series of Wicked Priests.

attempt to clarify this assumption with respect to the two examples cited by Wright: Ben Sirach and the so-called Prayer for King Jonathan.

Regarding Ben Sirach, who attacks the apocalyptic tradition and yet is preserved within the Qumran collection of books, I need not refer to the even greater diversity of thought and clearly contradictory statements within the collection of books we call Bible (indeed, for example, Ben Sirach and Enoch coexist peacefully in the Ethiopic Bible). Instead, I have a ready answer provided in the discussions on precisely this topic at the 2002 Colloquium Biblicum in Leuven, whose proceedings are already published (García Martínez 2003, xxxiv and 491). 4QInstruction provides us precisely the sort of combination of both strands of apparently contradictory thought. Thus, in this case my "assumption of compatibility" has been proved with the publication of 4QInstruction.

Regarding 4Q448, with all due respect to the work of E. and H. Eshel, Flusser, Main, Lemaire, and many others, and in spite of the conclusion one may draw from the transcription and translation of the study edition, I confess that I have not been able as yet to make up my mind on the proposed readings or the different interpretations suggested. I cannot thus make any claims at the moment on its "compatibility" with the rest of the collection.

Émile Puech, Shemaryahu Talmon, Gabriele Boccaccini

Profoundly different as they are, the contributions of Puech and Talmon have in common the fact that they do not "revisit" the Groningen Hypothesis, but they simply restate and put forth with more or less details the understanding of the Qumran phenomenon of the two distinguished scholars. Since I am not prone to polemic, and a close examination of the two comprehensive hypotheses is well beyond the possibilities of the cadre of a short "response," I will leave their assertions without an answer. I will simply express my admiration for the effort they both have undertaken to state in a clear, concise, and forceful way their own views as an alternative to the Groningen Hypothesis. The evaluation is up to the reader.

As for Gabriele Boccaccini's remarks, they articulate better than I could, with more inner logic, stronger arguments, and in incomparably better English, some of the implications of the Groningen Hypothesis. I can thus only say thanks.

References to Part Four

Alexander, Philip S. 1996. "The Redaction-History of Serekh ha-Yaḥad: A Proposal." *RevQ* 17:437-53.

Argall, Randal A. 1995. *1 Enoch and Sirach: A Comparative Literary and Conceptual Analysis of the Themes of Revelation, Creation, and Judgment.* EJL 8. Atlanta: Scholars.

Bauckham, Richard J. 2003. "The Jerusalem Church, Qumran, and the Essenes." In *The Dead Sea Scrolls as Background to Post-Biblical Judaism and Early Christianity,* edited by James R. Davila, 63-89. Leiden: Brill.

Baumgarten, Albert I. 1994. "The Rule of the Martian as Applied to Qumran." *Israel Oriental Studies* 14:121-42.

———. 2002. "But Touch the Law and the Sect Will Split: Legal Dispute as the Cause of Sectarian Schism." *Review of Rabbinic Judaism* 5:301-15.

———. Forthcoming. "Who Cares and Why Does It Matter? Qumran and the Essenes, Once Again!" *DSD.*

Baumgarten, Joseph M. 1992. "The Cave 4 Versions of the Qumran Penal Code." *JJS* 43:268-76.

Beall, Todd S. 1988. *Josephus' Description of the Essenes Illustrated by the Dead Sea Scrolls.* Cambridge: Cambridge University Press.

Bloch, Marc. 1961. *Feudal Society.* Translated by L. A. Manyon. Chicago: University of Chicago Press.

———. 1964. *The Historian's Craft.* Translated from the French by Peter Putnam. New York: Vintage.

———. 1967. "A Contribution towards a Comparative History of European Societies." In *Land and Work in Medieval Europe: Selected Papers by Marc Bloch,* 44-81. Berkeley: University of California Press.

————. 1973. *Royal Touch: Sacred Monarchy and Scrofula in England and France.* Translated by J. E. Anderson. London: Routledge & K. Paul.

Boccaccini, Gabriele. 1991. *Middle Judaism: Jewish Thought, 300 BCE to 200 CE.* Minneapolis: Fortress.

————. 1998. *Beyond the Essene Hypothesis: The Parting of the Ways between Qumran and Enochic Judaism.* Grand Rapids and Cambridge: Eerdmans.

————. 2002. *Roots of Rabbinic Judaism: An Intellectual History, from Ezekiel to Daniel.* Grand Rapids: Eerdmans.

Bockmuehl, Marcus. 1998. "Redaction and Ideology in the Rule of the Community (1QS/4QS)." *RevQ* 18:541-60.

Bourdieu, Pierre. 1977. *Outline of a Theory of Practice.* Translated from the French by Richard Nice. Cambridge: Cambridge University Press.

Brooke, George. 2003. "Between Qumran and Corinth: Embroidered Allusions to Women's Authority." In *The Dead Sea Scrolls as Background to Postbiblical Judaism and Early Christianity,* edited by James R. Davila, 157-76. Leiden: Brill.

Brownlee, William H. 1979. *The Midrash Pesher of Habakkuk.* Missoula, Mont.: Scholars.

————. 1982-83. "The Wicked Priest, the Man of Lies, and the Righteous Teacher — the Problem of Identity." *JQR* 73:1-37.

Burke, Peter. 1990. *The French Historical Revolution: The Annales School, 1929-1989.* Stanford: Stanford University Press.

Carmignac, Jean. 1962. "Notes sur les Peshârîm." *RevQ* 3:505-38.

Charles, Robert Henry. 1912. *The Book of Enoch.* Oxford: Oxford University Press.

————. 1912-13. *The Apocrypha and Pseudepigrapha of the Old Testament.* 2 vols. Oxford: Clarendon.

Charlesworth, James H. 1980. "The Origins and Subsequent History of the Authors of the Dead Sea Scrolls: Four Transitional Phases among the Qumran Essenes." *RevQ* 10:213-34.

————. 1992. "The Dead Sea Scrolls and the Historical Jesus." In *Jesus and the Dead Sea Scrolls,* edited by James H. Charlesworth, 1-74. New York: Doubleday.

————, ed. 1994-. The Princeton Theological Seminary Dead Sea Scrolls Project. 12 vols. Tübingen: Mohr.

Chazon, Esther G. 1992. "Is *Divrei ha-me'orot* a Sectarian Prayer?" In *The Dead Sea Scrolls: Forty Years of Research,* ed. Devorah Dimant and Uriel Rappaport, 3-17. STDJ 10. Leiden: Brill; Jerusalem: Magnes.

————. 2003. "The Use of the Bible as a Key to Meaning in Psalms from Qumran." In *Emanuel,* edited by Shalom M. Paul et al., 85-96. Leiden: Brill.

Collins, John J. 1977. *The Apocalyptic Vision of the Book of Daniel.* HSM 16. Atlanta: Scholars.

————. 1990. "Was the Dead Sea Sect an Apocalyptic Community?" In *Archaeology and History in the Dead Sea Scrolls,* edited by Lawrence H. Schiffman, 25-51. Sheffield: Sheffield Academic Press.

————. 1997. *Apocalypticism in the Dead Sea Scrolls.* London and New York: Routledge.

————. 1999. "Pseudepigraphy and Group Formation in Second Temple Judaism." In *Pseudepigraphic Perspectives: The Apocrypha and Pseudepigrapha in Light of the Dead Sea Scrolls. Proceedings of the International Symposium of the Orion Center for the Study of the Dead Sea Scrolls and Associated Literature, 12-14 January 1997,* edited by Esther G. Chazon and Michael E. Stone with Avital Pinnick, 43-58. Leiden: Brill.

Crawford, Sidney White. 2003a. "Mothers, Sisters, and Elders: Titles for Women in the Second Temple Jewish and Early Christian Communities." In *The Dead Sea Scrolls as Background to Postbiblical Judaism and Early Christianity: Papers from an International Conference at St. Andrews in 2001,* edited by James R. Davila, 177-91. Leiden: Brill.

————. 2003b. "Not according to Rule: Women, the Dead Sea Scrolls and Qumran." In *Emanuel: Studies in Hebrew Bible, Septuagint, and Dead Sea Scrolls in Honor of Emanuel Tov,* edited by Shalom M. Paul et al., 127-50. Leiden: Brill.

Davies, Philip R. 1977. "Hasidim in the Maccabean Period." *JJS* 28:127-40.

————. 1982. *The Damascus Covenant: An Interpretation of the "Damascus Document."* Sheffield: Sheffield Academic Press.

————. 1990. Review of *Josephus's Description of the Essenes Illustrated by the Dead Sea Scrolls,* by Todd S. Beall. *JTS* 41:164-69.

Davies, Philip R., and Joan Taylor. 1996. "On the Testimony of Women in 1QSa." *DSD* 3:223-35.

Denis, Albert-Marie. 1977. "L'historien anonyme d'Eusèbe (Præp. Ev. 9,17-18) et la crise des Macchabées." *JSJ* 8:42-49.

Dimant, Devorah. 1982. "History according to the Animal Apocalypse" (in Hebrew). *Jerusalem Studies in Jewish Thought* 2:18-37.

————. 1993. "The Seventy Weeks Chronology (Dan 9,24-27) in the Light of New Qumranic Texts." In *The Book of Daniel in the Light of New Findings,* edited by Adam S. van der Woude, 57-76. BETL 106. Leuven: Peeters.

————. 1995. "The Qumran Manuscripts: Contents and Significance." In *Time to Prepare the Way in the Wilderness. Papers on the Qumran Scrolls by Fellows of the Institute for Advanced Studies of the Hebrew University, Jerusalem, 1989-90,* edited by Devorah Dimant and Lawrence H. Schiffman, 23-68. STDJ 16. Leiden: Brill.

————. 2002. "1 Enoch 6–11: A Fragment of a Parabiblical Work." *JJS* 53, no. 2: 223-37.

Driver, Godfrey. 1965. *The Judaean Scrolls: The Problem and a Solution.* Oxford: Oxford University Press.

Elgvin, Torleif. 1997. "An Analysis of 4QInstruction." Ph.D. diss., Hebrew University of Jerusalem.

————. 2003. "The Eschatological Hope of 4QTime of Righteousness." In *Wisdom and Apocalypticism in the Dead Sea Scrolls and in the Biblical Tradition,* edited by Florentino García Martínez, 89-102. Leuven: Peeters.

————. 2004. "Priestly Sages? The Milieus of Origin of 4QMysteries and 4QInstruction." In *Sapiential Perspectives: Wisdom Literature in Light of the Dead Sea Scrolls,* edited by John J. Collins et al., 67-87. STDJ 51. Leiden: Brill.

Elledge, Casey D. 2004. *The Statutes of the King: The Temple Scroll's Legislation of Kingship (11Q19 LVI 12–LIX 21).* CahRB. Paris: Gabalda.

Elliott, Mark A. 2000. *The Survivors of Israel: A Reconsideration of the Theology of Pre-Christian Judaism.* Grand Rapids: Eerdmans.

———. 2002a. "Covenant and Cosmology in the Book of Watchers and the Astronomical Enoch." In *The Origins of Enochic Judaism. Proceedings of the First Enoch Seminar, University of Michigan, Sesto Fiorentino, Italy, June 19-23, 2001,* edited by Gabriele Boccaccini, 23-38. Turin: Zamorani [= *Henoch* 24:23-38].

———. 2002b. "Origins and Functions of the Watchers Theodicy." In *The Origins of Enochic Judaism. Proceedings of the First Enoch Seminar, University of Michigan, Sesto Fiorentino, Italy, June 19-23, 2001,* edited by Gabriele Boccaccini, 63-75. Turin: Zamorani [= *Henoch* 24:63-75].

Elwolde, J. F. 2000. "RWQMAH in the Damascus Document and in Ps. 139:15." In *Diggers at the Well — Proceedings of a Third International Symposium on the Hebrew of the Dead Sea Scrolls and Ben Sira,* edited by Takmitsu Muraoka and John F. Elwolde, 65-83. Leiden: Brill.

Eshel, Esther, Hanan Eshel, and Ada Yardeni. 1998. "4Q448, Apocryphal Psalm and Prayer." In *Qumran Cave 4. VI: Poetical and Liturgical Texts, Part 1,* edited by Esther Eshel et al. DJD 11. Oxford: Clarendon.

Eshel, Hanan, and Esther Eshel. 1998. "4Q448, Psalm 154 and 4QpIsa^a" (in Hebrew). *Tarbiz* 67:121-30.

Flusser, David. 1992. "Some Notes about the Prayer for King Jonathan" (in Hebrew). *Tarbiz* 61:297-300.

García Martínez, Florentino. 1985a. "Orígenes apocalípticos del movimiento esenio y orígenes de la secta qumránica." *Communio: Commentarii Internationales de Ecclesia et Theologia* 18:353-68.

———. 1985b. "¿Judas Macabeo, Sacerdote Impío? Notas al margen de 1Q pHab viii, 8-13." In *Mélanges bibliques et orientaux en l'honneur de M. Mathias Delcor,* edited by André Caquot, Simon Legasse, and Michael Tardieu, 169-81. AOAT 215. Neukirchen-Vluyn: Kevelaer.

———. 1987a. "Orígenes del movimiento esenio y orígenes qumránicos. Pistas para una solución." In *Il simposio bíblico español,* edited by Vicente Collado Bertomeu and V. Villar Hueso, 527-56. Valencia-Córdoba: Fundación bíblica española. Also printed as "Orígenes del movimiento esenio y de la secta qumránica," in Florentino García Martínez and Julio Trebolle Barrera, *Los Hombres de Qumrán* (Madrid: Trotta, 1993), 91-117.

———. 1987b. "Essénisme qumrânien: origines, caractéristique, héritage." In *Correnti Culturali e movimenti religiosi del Giudaismo. Atti del Y Congresso internationale dell'AISG. S. Miniato, 12-15 novembre 1984,* edited by Bruno Chiesa, 37-57. Associazione Italiana per lo Studio del Giudaismo, Testi e Studi 5. Rome: Carucci.

————. 1988. "Qumran Origins and Early History: A Groningen Hypothesis." *Folia Orientalia* 25:113-36.

————. 1993a. "The Origins of the Essene Movement and of the Qumran Sect." In *The People of the Dead Sea Scrolls*, edited by Florentino García Martínez and Julio Trebolle Barrera, translated by Wilfrid G. E. Watson, 92-96. Leiden: Brill.

————. 1993b. "The Dead Sea Scrolls." In *The People of the Dead Sea Scrolls*, edited by Florentino García Martínez and Julio Trebolle Barrera, translated by Wilfrid G. E. Watson. Leiden: Brill.

————. 1995. "The Origins of the Essene Movement and of the Qumran Sect." In *The People of the Dead Sea Scrolls*, edited by Florentino García Martínez and Julio Trebolle Barrera, translated by Wilfrid G. E. Watson, 77-97. Leiden: Brill.

————. 1996a. "4QMMT in a Qumran Context." In *Reading 4QMMT: New Perspectives on Qumran Law and History*, edited by John Kampen and Moshe J. Bernstein, 15-27. Atlanta: Scholars.

————. 1996b. *The Dead Sea Scrolls Translated.* 2nd ed. Leiden: Brill.

————. 1998. "The History of the Qumran Community in the Light of Recently Available Texts." In *Qumran between the Old and New Testaments*, edited by Frederick H. Cryer and Thomas L. Thompson, 194-216. JSOTSup 290. Copenhagen International Seminar 6. Sheffield: Sheffield Academic Press.

————, ed. 2003. *Wisdom and Apocalypticism in the Dead Sea Scrolls and in the Biblical Traditions.* BETL 168. Leuven: Peeters.

García Martínez, Florentino, and Julio Trebolle Barrera. 1995. *The People of the Dead Sea Scrolls.* Translated by Wilfrid G. E. Watson. Leiden: Brill. ET of *Los hombres de Qumrán: Literatura, estructura social y concepciones religiosas, Coleccion Estructuras y Procesos,* Serie Religión (Madrid: Trotta, 1993).

García Martínez, Florentino, and Eibert J. C. Tigchelaar. 1997. *The Dead Sea Scrolls. Study Edition.* Leiden: Brill.

García Martínez, Florentino, and Adam S. van der Woude. 1990. "A 'Groningen' Hypothesis of Qumran Origins and Early History." In *The Texts of Qumran and the History of the Community: Proceedings of the Groningen Congress in the DSS 3,* edited by Florentino García Martínez, 521-41. Paris: Gabalda (= *RevQ* 14).

Golb, Norman. 1995. *Who Wrote the Dead Sea Scrolls? The Search for the Secret of Qumran.* New York: Scribner.

Goodman, Martin. 1995. "A Note on the Qumran Sectarians, the Essenes and Josephus." *JJS* 46:161-66.

————. 2000. "Josephus and Variety in First-Century Judaism." *Israel Academy of Sciences and Humanities, Proceedings* 7, no. 6: 201-13.

Gould, Stephen J. 1989. *Wonderful Life: The Burgess Shale and the Nature of History.* New York: Norton.

Grabbe, Lester L. 1997. "4QMMT and Second Temple Jewish Society." In *Legal Texts and Legal Issues: Proceedings of the Second Meeting of the International Organization for Qumran Studies, Cambridge 1995, Published in Honour of Joseph M.*

Baumgarten, edited by Moshe J. Bernstein, Florentino García Martínez, and John Kampen, 89-108. STDJ 23. Leiden: Brill.

―――. 2000. *Judaic Religion in the Second Temple Period: Belief and Practice from the Exile to Yavneh.* London: Routledge.

Habermann, Abraham Meir. 1952. *'Edah ve-'edut.* Jerusalem: Mahbarot le-sifrut.

Hempel, Charlotte. 1996. "The Earthly Essene Nucleus of 1QSa." *DSD* 3:253-67.

―――. 1997. "The Penal Code Reconsidered." In *Legal Texts and Legal Issues: Proceedings of the Second Meeting of the International Organization for Qumran Studies, Cambridge 1995, Published in Honour of Joseph M. Baumgarten,* edited by Moshe J. Bernstein, Florentino García Martínez, and John Kampen, 337-48. STDJ 23. Leiden: Brill.

―――. 1998. *The Laws of the Damascus Document: Sources, Traditions, and Redaction.* Leiden: Brill.

―――. 1999a. "Community Structures in the Dead Sea Scrolls: Admission, Organization, Disciplinary Procedures." In *The Dead Sea Scrolls after Fifty Years: A Comprehensive Assessment,* edited by Peter W. Flint and James C. VanderKam, 2:67-92. Leiden: Brill.

―――. 1999b. "Community Origins in the Damascus Document in the Light of Recent Scholarship." In *The Provo International Conference on the Dead Sea Scrolls: Technological Innovations, New Texts, and Reformulated Issues,* edited by Donald W. Parry and Eugene C. Ulrich, 316-29. Leiden: Brill.

―――. 2000. "The Laws of the Damascus Document and 4QMMT." In *The Damascus Document: A Centennial of Discovery,* edited by Joseph M. Baumgarten, Esther G. Chazon, and Avital Pinnick, 69-84. Leiden: Brill.

―――. 2003a. "Kriterien zur Bestimmung essenischer Verfasserschaft von Qumrantexten." In *Qumran kontrovers,* edited by Jörg Frey and Hartmut Stegemann, 71-85. Paderborn: Bonifatius.

―――. 2003b. "Interpretative Authority in the Community Rule Tradition." *DSD* 10:59-80.

―――. 2003c. "The Community and Its Rivals according to the Community Rule from Caves 1 and 4." *RevQ* 21:47-81.

Hurowitz, Victor A. 2002. "hmqwr in Damascus Document 4QD^e (4Q270) 7 i 14." *DSD* 9:34-37.

Joüon, Paul, and Takmitsu Muraoka. 2000. *A Grammar of Biblical Hebrew.* Rome: Pontificio Istituto Biblico.

Kautzsch, Emil, and Arthur E. Cowley, eds. 1983. *Gesenius' Hebrew Grammar.* 2nd ed. Oxford: Clarendon.

Kister, Menahem. 1986-87. "Concerning the History of the Essenes: A Study of the Animal Apocalypse, the Book of Jubilees and the Damascus Covenant" (in Hebrew). *Tarbiz* 56:1-18.

Knibb, Michael A. 1987. *The Qumran Community.* Cambridge: Cambridge University Press.

———. 1989. *Jubilees and the Origins of the Qumran Community.* London: published privately.

Kraft, Robert. 1975. "The Multiform Jewish Heritage of Early Christianity." In *Christianity, Judaism, and Other Greco-Roman Cults: Studies for Morton Smith at Sixty,* edited by Jacob Neusner, 3:174-99. Leiden: Brill.

Lakatos, Imre. 1978. *The Methodology of Scientific Research Programmes: Philosophical Papers Volume 1,* edited by John Worrall and Gregory Currie. Cambridge: Cambridge University Press.

Lange, Armin. 1998. "In Diskussion mit dem Tempel, Zur Auseinandersetzung zwischen Kohelet und Weisheitlichen Kreisen am Jerusalemer Tempel." In *Qohelet in the Context of Wisdom,* edited by Antoon Schoors, 113-59. BETL 136. Leuven: Peeters.

Laperrousaz, Ernest-Marie. 1986. "Brèves remarques archéologiques concernant la chronologie des occupations esséniennes de Qoumrân." *RevQ* 12:199-212.

Levinson, Bernard M. 2002. "What Pentateuchal Theory Might Learn from the Temple Scroll, and How Biblical Studies Might Contribute to the Study of 11 QTemple." Paper read at the Joint Session on Biblical Law and Qumran, Annual Meeting of the Society of Biblical Literature, Toronto, Canada.

Lieberman, Saul. 1951. "The Discipline in the So-Called Dead Sea Manual of Discipline." *JBL* 71:199-206.

Lim, Timothy. 1992. "The Qumran Scrolls: Two Hypotheses." *SR* 21, no. 4: 455-66.

———. 1993. "The Wicked Priests of the Groningen Hypothesis." *JBL* 112, no. 3: 415-25.

———. 2000. "The Wicked Priest or the Liar." In *The Dead Sea Scrolls in Their Historical Context,* edited by Timothy H. Lim et al., 45-51. Edinburgh: T. & T. Clark.

———. 2002. *Pesharim.* Sheffield: Sheffield Academic Press; London: Continuum.

Lohse, Eduard. 1964. *Die Texte aus Qumran.* Munich: Kösel.

Magness, Jodi. 2002. *The Archaeology of Qumran and the Dead Sea Scrolls.* Grand Rapids: Eerdmans.

Merton, Robert K. 1936. "The Unanticipated Consequences of Purposive Social Action." *American Sociological Review* 1:894-904.

Metso, Sarianna. 1997. *The Textual Development of the Qumran Community Rule.* Leiden: Brill.

———. 2000. "The Relationship between the Damascus Document and the Community Rule." In *The Damascus Document: A Centennial of Discovery,* edited by Joseph M. Baumgarten, Esther G. Chazon, and Avital Pinnick, 85-93. Leiden: Brill.

———. 2002. "Qumran Community Structure and Terminology as Theological Statement." *RevQ* 20:429-44.

Milik, Josef T. 1959. *Ten Years of Discovery in the Wilderness of Judaea.* SBT 26. London: SCM.

———. 1976. *The Books of Enoch.* Oxford: Clarendon.

Murphy, Catherine M. 2002. *Wealth in the Dead Sea Scrolls and in the Qumran Community.* Leiden: Brill.

Newsom, Carol A. 1990. "Sectually Explicit Literature from Qumran." In *The Hebrew Bible and Its Interpreters*, edited by William Henry Propp et al., 167-87. Winona Lake, Ind.: Eisenbrauns.

Nickelsburg, George W. E. 2001. *1 Enoch 1: A Commentary on the Book of 1 Enoch, 1–36; 81–108*. Minneapolis: Fortress.

Patton, Kimberly C., and Benjamin C. Ray. 2000. *A Magic Still Dwells: Comparative Religion in the Postmodern Age*. Berkeley, Los Angeles, and London: University of California Press.

Peursen, Wido Th. van. 2001. "Qumran Origins: Some Remarks on the Enochic/Essene Hypothesis." *RevQ* 20:241-53.

Pfann, Stephen J., et al. 2000. *Qumran Cave 4. XXVI: Cryptic Texts and Miscellanea, Part 1*. DJD 36. Oxford: Clarendon.

———. 2001. "The Character of the Early Essene Movement in Light of the Manuscripts Written in Esoteric Scripts from Qumran." Ph.D. diss., Hebrew University of Jerusalem.

———. 2004. "The Historical Implications of the Early Second Century Dating of the 4Q249-250 Cryptic A Corpus." In *Things Revealed: Studies in Early Jewish and Christian Literature in Honor of Michael E. Stone*, edited by Esther G. Chazon, et al., 171-86. JSJSup 89. Leiden: Brill.

Puech, Émile. 1996. "Jonathan le prêtre impie et les débuts de la Communauté de Qumrân. 4QJonathan (4Q523) et 4QPsAp (4Q448)." In *Hommage à Józef T. Milik*, edited by Émile Puech and Florentino García Martínez. *RevQ* 17:241-70.

———. 1999. "Le grand prêtre Simon (III) fils d'Onias III, le Maître de Justice?" In *Antikes Judentum und Frühes Christentum. Festschrift für Hartmut Stegemann zum 65. Geburtstag*, edited by Bernd Kollmann, Wolfgang Reinbold, and Annette Steudel, 137-58. Berlin and New York: De Gruyter.

Qimron, Elisha. 1992. "Celibacy in the Dead Sea Scrolls and the Two Kinds of Sectarians." In *The Madrid Qumran Congress*, edited by Julio Trebolle Barrera and Luis Vegas Montaner, 289-94. Leiden: Brill.

Rabin, Chaim. 1957. *Qumran Studies*. London: Oxford University Press.

Riessler, Paul. 1928. *Altjudisches Schriftum ausserhalb der Bible*. Augsburg: Filser.

Sacchi, Paolo. 1998. "Enochism: Qumranism and Apocalyptic: Some Thoughts on a Recent Book." *Hen* 20:357-65.

Schechter, Solomon. 1910. *Fragments of a Zadokite Work*. Cambridge: Cambridge University Press.

Schiffman, Lawrence H. 1987. "Sifrut hahekhalot wekitve Qumran." *Jerusalem Studies in Jewish Thought* 6:121-38.

Schuller, Eileen M. 1994. "Women in the Dead Sea Scrolls." In *Methods of Investigation of the Dead Sea Scrolls and the Khirbet Qumran Site: Present Realities and Future Prospects*, edited by Michael O. Wise et al., 115-27. New York: New York Academy of Sciences.

———. 1996. "Evidence for Women in the Community of the Dead Sea Scrolls." In

Voluntary Associations in the Graeco-Roman World, edited by John S. Kloppenborg and Stephen G. Wilson, 252-65. London and New York: Routledge.

———. 1999. "Women in the Dead Sea Scrolls." In *The Dead Sea Scrolls after Fifty Years: A Comprehensive Assessment,* edited by Peter W. Flint and James C. VanderKam, 2:117-44. Leiden: Brill.

Schürer, Emil. 1886-90. *Geschichte des jüdischen Volkes im Zeitalter Jesu Christi.* Leipzig.

Shemesh, Aharon. 2002. "Expulsion and Exclusion in the Community Rule and the Damascus Document." *DSD* 9:44-74.

Sheridan, Susan G. 2003. "Analysis of the Skeletal Remains from Qumran: The French and German Collections from the DeVaux Excavations." Paper presented at SBL Annual Meeting, 23 November 2003.

Simiand, François. 1903. "Methode historique et sciences sociales." *Revue de Synthèse Historique* 6:1-22.

Smith, Jonathan Z. 1982. *Imagining Religion.* Chicago and London: University of Chicago Press.

Smith, Morton. 1960. "The Dead Sea Sect in Relation to Ancient Judaism." *NTS* 7:347-60.

Stegemann, Hartmut. 1973. *Die Essener, Qumran, Johannes der Täufer und Jesus.* 4th ed. Freiburg: Herder.

———. 1992. "The Qumran Essenes — Local Members of the Main Jewish Union in Late Second Temple Times." In *Proceedings of the International Congress on the Dead Sea Scrolls, Madrid, 18-21 March 1991,* edited by Julio Trebolle Barrera and Luis Vegas Montaner, 83-166. STDJ 11. Leiden: Brill.

———. 1998. *The Library of Qumran.* Leiden: Brill.

Talmon, Shemaryahu. 1993. "The Community of the Renewed Covenant: Between Judaism and Christianity." In *The Community of the Renewed Covenant: The Notre Dame Symposium on the Dead Sea Scrolls,* edited by Eugene Ulrich and James C. VanderKam, 3-24. Notre Dame: Notre Dame University Press.

———. 1994. "Qumran Studies: Past, Present, Future." *JQR* 85:1-31.

———. 2001. "Exile and Restoration in the Conceptual World of Judaism." In *Restoration — Old Testament, Jewish and Christian Perspectives,* edited by James M. Scott, 107-46. Leiden: Brill.

Tigchelaar, Eibert J. C. 2000. "Review of *Beyond the Essene Hypothesis,* by Gabriele Boccaccini." *JSJ* 31:308-11.

———. 2001. *To Increase Learning for the Understanding Ones: Reading and Reconstructing the Fragmentary Early Jewish Sapiential Text 4QInstruction.* STDJ 44. Leiden: Brill.

———. 2003. "Your Wisdom and Your Folly: The Case of 1–4QMysteries." In *Wisdom and Apocalypticism in the Dead Sea Scrolls and in the Biblical Tradition,* edited by Florentino García Martínez, 66-88. Leuven: Peeters.

Tov, Emanuel. 1986. "The Orthography and Language of the Hebrew Scrolls Found at Qumran and the Origin and Language of These Scrolls." *Textus* 13:31-57.

———. 1988. "Hebrew Biblical Manuscripts from the Judaean Desert: Their Contribution to Textual Criticism." *JJS* 39:6-37.

———. 1993. "The Qumran Scribal School" (in Hebrew). In *Studies in Bible and Exegesis: Moshe Goshen-Gottstein — in Memoriam,* edited by Mosheh Bar-Asher et al., 135-54. Ramat Gan: Ramat Gan University.

———. 1995. "Letters of the Cryptic A Script and Paleo-Hebrew Letters Used as Scribal Marks in Some Qumran Scrolls." *DSD* 2, no. 2: 330-39.

———. 1996. "Scribal Markings in the Texts from the Judean Desert." In *Current Research and Technological Developments on the Dead Sea Scrolls,* edited by Donald W. Parry and Stephen D. Ricks, 41-77. STDJ 20. Leiden: Brill.

———. 1997a. "Further Evidence for the Existence of a Qumran Scribal School." In *The Dead Sea Scrolls Fifty Years after Their Discovery, Major Issues and New Approaches, Proceedings of the Jerusalem Congress, July 20-25, 1997,* edited by Lawrence H. Schiffman, 199-216. Jerusalem: Israel Exploration Society.

———. 1997b. "Tefillin of Different Origin from Qumran." In *A Light for Jacob: Studies in the Bible and the Dead Sea Scrolls, in Memory of Jacob S. Licht,* edited by Yair Hoffman and Frank H. Polak, 44-54. Jerusalem: Bialik Institute.

Vaux, Roland de. 1973. *Archaeology and the Dead Sea Scrolls.* Oxford: Oxford University Press.

Vermes, Geza. 1962. *The Dead Sea Scrolls in English.* Baltimore: Penguin Books.

———. 1991. "Preliminary Remarks on Unpublished Fragments of the Community Rule from Qumran Cave 4." *JJS* 42:250-55.

———. 1995. *The Dead Sea Scrolls in English.* 4th ed. Sheffield: Sheffield Academic Press.

———. 1997. *The Complete Dead Sea Scrolls in English.* London: Penguin Books.

Vermes, Geza, and Martin D. Goodman, eds. 1989. *The Essenes according to the Classical Sources.* Sheffield: JSOT.

Wacholder, Ben Zion. 1983. *The Dawn of Qumran: The Sectarian Torah and the Teacher of Righteousness.* Cincinnati: Hebrew Union College Press.

Williamson, Hugh G. M. 1977-78. "The Translation of 1QpHab V, 10." *RevQ* 9:263-65.

Woude, Adam S. van der. 1982. "Wicked Priest or Wicked Priests? Reflections on the Identification of the Wicked Priest in the Habakkuk Commentary." *JJS* 33:349-59.

———. 1996-97. "Once Again: The Wicked Priests in the Habakkuk Pesher from Cave 1 of Qumran." *RevQ* 17:375-84.

Wright, Benjamin G. 1997. "Fear the Lord and Honor the Priest: Ben Sira as Defender of the Jerusalem Priesthood." In *The Book of Ben Sira in Modern Research,* edited by Pancratius C. Beentjes, 189-222. Berlin: De Gruyter.

Zias, Joseph E. 2000. "The Cemeteries of Qumran and Celibacy: Confusion Laid to Rest?" *DSD* 7, no. 2: 220-53.

Zissu, Boas. 1998. "'Qumran Type' Graves in Jerusalem: Archaeological Evidence of an Essene Community." *DSD* 5, no. 2: 158-71.

PART FIVE

THE ENOCHIC-ESSENE
HYPOTHESIS REVISITED

Theodicy and the Problem
of the "Intimate Enemy"

David W. Suter

In *The Origin of Satan,* Elaine Pagels describes Satan as "the intimate enemy —
one's trusted colleague, close associate, brother. He is the kind of person on
whose loyalty and goodwill the wellbeing of family and society depend — but
one who turns unexpectedly jealous and hostile" (Pagels 1995, 49). Satan thus
becomes ideally suited to reflect social conflict within the community, a way of
stigmatizing an insider gone astray. The fundamental assumption behind this
point is that the history of ideas and social history are linked, and that we can
use one to examine the other.

Pagels's concept and assumption provide a starting point for an examination of Gabriele Boccaccini's work in *Beyond the Essene Hypothesis.* Boccaccini
cites Pagels in developing his argument for the parting of the ways between
Enochic Judaism and the Qumran community: "In the face of the harshness of
this evil world, concepts such as dualism, individual predestination, and self-
segregation strengthened the identity and unity of the group, provided a way of
explaining the suffering of the chosen and the opposition of outsiders, and targeted the adversaries as the devil's party according to a pattern that would be repeated often with tragic results in the history of religion" (Boccaccini 1998, 155).

Boccaccini uses ideology, primarily theodicy, to examine Jewish writings
of the Persian, Hellenistic, and Roman periods to construct chains of texts with
a common ideological basis, following what he calls systemic analysis
(Boccaccini 1998, 8-11). For Boccaccini the ideological connections rather than
the common use of traditional material become the clues to an underlying social movement (Boccaccini 2002, 30). His work on these chains of texts has led
him to locate the roots of the subsequent history of Jewish sectarianism in a

dispute within the larger priestly community between the Zadokites, who create the high priesthood and use it to take control of government, and Enochic Judaism, priestly dissidents left on the outside with the Zadokite seizure of power (Boccaccini 2002, 43-60, 89-103). In Boccaccini's reconstruction the Maccabean revolt and subsequent events lead to the emergence of a separatist community that uses the two-spirit ideology to stigmatize its opponents as the "devil's party." Other elements of Enochic Judaism give birth to the Essenism represented in the classical sources (Boccaccini 1998, 119-62).

I am interested in his project for two reasons. The first is that I have a more general interest in theodicy that leaves me fascinated by myths of the origin of evil (see Suter 1992). Second, the implication of my own work, beginning with "Fallen Angel, Fallen Priest" (Suter 1979), is that the roots of the emergence of sectarianism, reflected particularly in the Damascus Document (CD) and 4QMMT (see Himmelfarb 1999), are in an intrapriestly dispute in which the presenting symptoms are charges related to the purity of priestly marriages. Boccaccini's Enochic Judaism, particularly as developed in *Roots of Rabbinic Judaism* (Boccaccini 2002, 89–103), provides a context for an analysis of 1 Enoch 6–16 as a polemic against priestly marriage practices in the Persian or early Hellenistic period. It is when I turn to the analysis of *Beyond the Essene Hypothesis* that I have problems with the method, and I would like to explore the problems by responding to three questions. My exploration will use primarily the lens of theodicy, or the philosophy of evil, recognizing at the same time that Boccaccini's case is broader.

a. The first question, dealing with the relationship between the Essene and the Enochic movements, is the one that presents the greatest challenge to scholarship, since the leap from the early Enochic literature to the classical descriptions of the Essenes in Josephus and Philo should appear somewhat daunting to anyone appreciative of the issues involved. Boccaccini's case rests on his method involving the construction of chains of texts through systemic analysis and the relation of the results of that investigation to the results of his historiographic assessment of the classical sources in Josephus and Philo. The results of the systemic analysis are impressive, but the method itself also raises questions since it depends on the subjectivity of interpretation, which is not an exact science, to construct the chains of texts. Moreover, there is the great difficulty one faces in dating these documents conclusively.

There is something within me that asks for some element to give a sense of continuity between the earliest exemplars of the proposed movement and the results of Boccaccini's historiographic assessment of Josephus and Philo, since Boccaccini's method involves the tracking of subtle developments from document to document over a significant period of time. Perhaps the connection between beginning and end is to be found in the linking of a critique of the purity of the temple and the marriage practices of its priesthood in the Book of the Watchers, to a concern for the purity of the temple and distinctive teachings and practices regarding marriage in the classic descriptions of the Essenes. These are issues that George Nickelsburg and I developed some years ago (Nickelsburg 1981; Suter 1979). As Boccaccini puts it in summing up his case: "The same attitude toward the Jerusalem temple is manifest in Enochic literature [as is found in the description of the Essenes in Josephus]. The second temple was for the Enochians a largely impure temple, led by a sinful priesthood; but while criticizing the actual functioning of the temple and awaiting its future restoration, they never questioned its existence and centrality" (Boccaccini 1998, 184).

At the same time, one must recognize that the critique of the temple and its priesthood changed over time. The concern with the purity of the temple in the earlier layers of material appears to be with the purity of priestly marriages, while following Boccaccini's analysis of Josephus, the issue at the later end of the spectrum is with the sacrificial system itself (Boccaccini 1998, 183-85). A key mediating passage is the discussion of the three nets of Belial in CD 4:15-17, which lists *zenut* (or whoredom), wealth, and "defilement of the sanctuary" as the chief sins of the priestly establishment. While "defilement of the sanctuary" is left largely undefined in the Damascus Document, perhaps it could be seen as foreshadowing the concern with the sacrificial system itself in the classical sources. 4QMMT and the Temple Scroll also reflect a concern with the sacrificial system and the operation of the temple (Boccaccini 1998, 98-104, 113-17), but like the Damascus Document, they are in the middle of Boccaccini's chain of texts and not at the beginning.

The other change lies in the understanding of sexual morality. As I have argued in "Fallen Angel, Fallen Priest," *zenut* in the Damascus Document does not refer to the visiting of prostitutes and other more conventional forms of sexual immorality, but to marriages contracted in violation of an interpretation of the rules of priestly marriage in Leviticus 21:7, where marriage with a *zonah* is prohibited.[1] The examples in CD 4:20-21 and 5:7-10 have to do with marriage with a niece and bigamy, while 4QMMT B 75-82 suggests that marriages between priests and the laity are an example of *zenut*. In 1 Enoch 12–16 the marriage of Watchers with human women is problematic first of all because it violates sacred boundaries between heaven and earth and spirit and flesh, much

---

1. In addition to my article (Suter 1979, 125-31), see the discussion of the prohibition of the marriages between priests and the daughters of Israelites in 4QMMT B 75-82 by Elisha Qimron and John Strugnell (1994, 171-75), a passage that seems to advocate a radical form of endogamy. Martha Himmelfarb is the first to posit a connection between 4QMMT and the discussion of the myth in 1 Enoch (Himmelfarb 1999).

like the marriage of priests and laity in 4QMMT, where the law of mixed fruits is systematically cited to rule it out.

On the other hand, in the classical sources there appears to be a much more conventional interest in sexual immorality, for which the burden of responsibility seems to be placed on the character of women themselves (note Boccaccini 1998, 179). Perhaps the common thread is that in each case the choice of a spouse or sexuality is seen not as an expression of individual desires and tastes but rather as essential to communal well-being. At this point I consider the case for a connection between Enochic Judaism and Essenism as described in the classical sources as open and in need of further testing. We can document critiques of temple and priesthood over a long period of time, but does that translate into any single movement? I do think there are reasons to attempt to create global theories regarding the complex period with which we deal, but the developer has to be prepared for the critics, many of whom make valid points.

b. The second question is: What was exactly the contribution given by Enochic Judaism to Qumran origins? A response to this question forces us to ask whether the transformations involved between Enochic Judaism and the Qumran sectarian literature are evolutionary or revolutionary. At either end of the spectrum there are discontinuities. As Boccaccini has described it, Enochic Judaism presents a theodicy that understands evil as a cosmic aberration imposed upon humanity as a consequence of the sins of the Watchers, good creatures gone bad whose sins corrupt the entire world order (Boccaccini 1998, 71-74), while the Qumran sectarian documents reflect the two-spirit theodicy that attributes all to God and emphasizes individual predestination (59, 63). One could perhaps argue that Enochic Judaism raises the problem of evil, which the Qumran community seeks to solve in a dramatically different fashion, but for me it is this dramatic break in theodicy in what appears to be a community of texts that needs more explanation.

My problem with Boccaccini's approach to Enochic Judaism is that he tends to treat the myth of the fallen angels as a cipher, always carrying the same meaning: "A group of rebellious angels [is] ultimately responsible for the spread of evil and impurity on earth" (72). Myths, however, are stories susceptible to different interpretations. Boccaccini himself recognizes the problem in *Roots of Rabbinic Judaism* when he comments, "Ideas are not systems of thought. The same ideas or traditions often happen to play completely different roles in different documents" (Boccaccini 2002, 30). However, while his treatment of the nuances of thought in the different documents of Enochic Judaism is well developed, he does have a tendency to take the myth of the fallen angels as an idea rather than a myth.

I would identify two possibilities in the myth of the Watchers that exist in tension with each other as the story is told and retold (see Suter 1979, 116-17). One possibility is that it represents an etiology of the origin of evil: all evil in the world stems from a single event. This is the possibility reflected in Boccaccini's interpretation and would appear to be dominant in the Animal Apocalypse. The other is that the myth functions as a paradigm of the origin of evil: the myth presents the way in which evil emerges time after time as good creatures depart from the divinely established cosmic order. This approach is inherent in CD 2:16-18, where the story of the Watchers functions at the beginning of a list of great sinners, who go astray individually by walking "in the stubbornness of their hearts" or through "thoughts of a guilty inclination and lascivious eyes" (García Martínez 1996). The approach in the book of Jude in the New Testament is similar. The implication involved in the use of lists of sinners is that each generation goes astray in the same manner, pointing toward a paradigmatic use of the myth.

To the extent that the myth in 1 Enoch 6–16 (or even at the very least in 12–16) functions as a polemic directed against the Zadokite priesthood, the paradigmatic meaning is dominant: like the angels, the priests have departed from their appointed place in the divinely sanctioned order. In actuality, the Book of the Watchers is ambiguous about the distinction between etiology and paradigm. On the one hand, it pictures the flood as purifying the earth and reestablishing the conditions of paradise, implying that it needs to be interpreted paradigmatically as a reflection on how evil emerges when good creatures — the Watchers — go astray.

On the other hand it attributes all sin to Asael and speaks of the spirits that come forth from the giants continuing to plague humankind, pointing toward an etiological interpretation. This latter interpretation opens the door for the subsequent development of the two-spirit theodicy, but does not necessarily explain in and of itself why the sectarian literature at Qumran takes such a revolutionary departure.

The distinction between paradigm and etiology makes a difference in understanding Enochic Judaism. The paradigmatic interpretation would emphasize the responsibility of each generation for a departure from the divinely ordained order, ascribing responsibility for sin to the Zadokites, who are typologically parallel to the Watchers. The etiological interpretation already introduces a sense that sin is the consequence, at least in part, of forces that originate beyond the human person, contradicting the Zadokite theology in Genesis, which emphasizes the goodness of creation.

Perhaps we can best get at the juxtaposition of the approaches to theodicy between what Boccaccini calls Enochic Judaism and Qumran by noting that the Damascus Document and the Community Rule follow a similar form in prefacing rules for communal life with an ideological statement dealing with the origin or nature of evil. For CD 2:14–3:12 it is the story of the Watchers, which is treated as a paradigm for the repeated emergence of evil in the angelic and human community. As good creatures choose to go bad, they become something other than what they were created to be.

For the Community Rule 3:13–4:1 it is the two-spirit doctrine, which treats the origin of evil as divinely ordained — sinners are what they are as a consequence of their created nature. The Community Rule will occasionally use language suggestive of the Damascus Document's theodicy (sinners are sometimes said to walk "in the stubbornness of their hearts"; see 2:25), indicating that there is some carryover from one to the other. All in all, the break is revolutionary and seems to point toward some sort of social transformation.

On the other hand, Jubilees provides a potential approach to understanding the evolution of the theodicy of the Book of the Watchers into that of what Boccaccini classifies as the sectarian literature (see Suter 1993). It contains both the story of the Watchers and the role of Prince Mastema (see Jub 10:1-9; 11:5), which I see as an anticipation of the evil spirit of the two-spirit theodicy in the sectarian documents. In Jubilees Prince Mastema clearly is in a position to make a claim on God for personnel to carry out his responsibilities, while in the Community Rule and the War Scroll the evil spirit is described in terms of enmity, *mastema* (1QS 3:23; 1QM 14:9; cf. CD 16:5; 4Q388a frag. 1, 2:6; 4Q390 frag. 1, 11; frag. 2, 1:7; and 11Q11 2:4). In developing this argument, one should also note that the seventy shepherds of the Animal Apocalypse in 1 Enoch 85–90 anticipate the formation of the two-spirit theodicy. One might say that the fingerprints of Enochic Judaism are definitely to be found upon the Qumran theodicy, but that in the process there has been a radical transformation.

In my estimation Enochic Judaism is a viable hypothesis, but it represents a somewhat diverse movement without the ideological clarity that comes through with the two-spirit theodicy in the Qumran literature. The story of the Watchers represents a common thread, but one that is susceptible to various interpretations. Let me also add, somewhat parenthetically, that I find Enochic Judaism, at least as exemplified by the Book of the Watchers, more syncretistic than Boccaccini allows, reflecting developments in theology, angelology, and divination current in Hellenistic Syria and Phoenicia (see Suter 2003). Perhaps it needs to be evaluated in light of Morton Smith's distinction between the older syncretistic worship of YHWH and the YHWH-only party of Jerusalem (M. Smith 1971).

c. The third question is: Do we have evidence that a split occurred between Qumran and the Enochic movement? It appears to me that what we have is evidence for a revolutionary ideological transformation in the area of theodicy between the literature of the Enochic movement and what Boccaccini terms the sectarian Qumran literature. Jubilees may point the way to understanding some of the intellectual steps that lead from one theodicy to the other, but we still do not quite understand the underlying social realities that led to the transformation. What we have is the disappearance or displacement of the Watcher theodicy. Boccaccini speaks simply of its abandonment (Boccaccini 1998, 154). It would be helpful in order to identify a split between the two groups to be able to find a polemic directed against the Watcher theodicy.

It is possible that the incident of the Liar mentioned in the Habakkuk Pesher 2:1-10 represents the point of departure, as Boccaccini argues, but the context of the report of that incident suggests to me that the dispute is over the failed interpretation of prophecy by the Teacher of Righteousness, with nothing said about theodicy (see 1QpHab 7:1-14). One possible case of a critique of the story of the Watchers is found in the Epistle of Enoch (cf. 1 En 98:4); although if one follows Boccaccini's interpretation (131-38), the polemic in the passage is directed against the two-spirit ideology, providing an argument directed against the Qumran ideology from the side of Enochic Judaism. However, the ambiguity of the passage with regard to the object of its critique only serves to demonstrate the difficulty of basing systemic analysis upon hermeneutics.

It appears to me that we have rather tantalizing evidence for the transformation of social ideologies related to the nature of evil in which there is a movement from a perspective that treats evil as the departure of good creatures from their appointed place in the cosmos to one that makes the division between the righteous and the wicked one of divine predetermination. The second perspective does appear to reflect a social division in which the group's opponents have become the "devil's party" or the "intimate enemy," to use language of Boccaccini and Pagels cited at the beginning. I find the argument plausible that it serves to support a separated group with a sense of certainty about the nature of good and evil in the world, but continue to be puzzled over the apparent silencing or abandonment of the story of the Watchers without the trace of a polemic directed against it.[2]

---

2. One issue deals with whether ideology or theodicy could be used to write social history. Lawrence Schiffman has observed that Jewish texts are capable of containing radically divergent theodicies. The example he gave was the book of Job. Schiffman's point is well taken, although with some reservations. The argument above is that the theodicies implied by the use of the myth of the Watchers in texts belonging to Enochic Judaism are significantly more complex than Boccaccini allows, indicating a more divergent movement. However, the two-spirit theodicy of the sectarian texts from Qumran seems more consistent within the texts designated by Boccaccini, suggesting some sort of ideological coherency. Moreover, the extent to which these texts demonize their opponents suggests a sectarian mentality, even if it is not easy to identify the groups involved.

Interrogating "Enochic Judaism":
1 Enoch as Evidence for Intellectual History, Social Realities, and Literary Tradition

Annette Yoshiko Reed

Whatever disagreements one might have with Gabriele Boccaccini's Essene-Enochic Hypothesis, one cannot contest the fact that his ideas compel a stimulating, much-needed discussion about the social, intellectual, and religious landscape of Judaism(s) in the second temple period (further Jaffee 2002-3; Kraft 2003, 88-90; also Schwartz 2001, 81). Any synthesis so broad, sweeping, and original is bound to provoke criticisms. Admirably, Boccaccini anticipates this, tackling the task of generalization with a sharp sense of the necessity of this scholarly practice combined with an awareness of its inherent and inevitable shortcomings. Just as he offers us his ideas in the spirit of an academic discourse in which conventional wisdom must be ever-tested and every new consensus wrought in the heat of debate, so it is in this same spirit that I would like to raise a couple of constructive questions about the use of 1 Enoch in his reconstruction of "Enochic Judaism" (see esp. Boccaccini 1998, 12-16, 70-79, 165-70; 2002, 89-103).

From 1 Enoch to "Enochic Judaism"

The concept that "1 Enoch is the core of an ancient and distinct variety of second temple Judaism" lies at the heart of Boccaccini's hypothesis about the relationship between the Enochic literature, the Essene movement, and the Qumran community (1998, 12). Central to his understanding of 1 Enoch is the approach to the problem of evil first found in the Book of the Watchers (= 1 En 1–36; see esp. 6–16), whereby the fallen angels seem to be held responsible for the very origins of human sin and suffering (1998, 70, 76, 185; also 2002, 89-103).

Contrasting this supernatural explanation of evil's origins with the more orderly concept of the cosmos in the torah and most other texts now collected in the Tanakh (1998, 68-70; 2002, 73-82), Boccaccini suggests that the Enochic version of the angelic descent myth represents a radical departure from biblical tradition (cf. Gen 6:1-4). In this disjuncture he sees a clue to a broader phenomenon: the emergence of "Enochic Judaism," a distinctive system of thought that had as its "generative idea . . . a particular conception of evil, understood as an autonomous reality antecedent to humanity's ability to choose" (1998, 12). Rightly seeking to root this theological development in concrete historical circumstances and social settings, he further proposes that Enochic Judaism originated among priests in the fourth or third century B.C.E. as an alternative to the so-called Zadokite Judaism of temple authorities and biblical tradents (1998, 12-13, 71-79; 2002, 89-103).

Boccaccini's account of the development of Judaism(s) in the following centuries is largely the tale of the competition and conflicts between these two philosophical opposites and religious rivals. In light of the generalized nature of his comments and the schematic character of the contrast between Enochic Judaism and Zadokite Judaism, it is notable that he does not merely replicate the traditional dichotomy between an allegedly marginal apocalyptic ideology and an allegedly monolithic mainstream Judaism; nor does he fall back on the familiar and facile contrast, common in much past scholarship on 1 Enoch, between charismatic powerless visionaries and the powerful pragmatic priests that their pseudepigraphical writings purportedly critiqued (see esp. 1998, 75-76). Instead, Boccaccini builds on recent scholarship about the complex attitudes toward the priesthood in 1 Enoch to suggest that Enochic Judaism originated in an inner-priestly "movement of dissent" (2002, 89; also 99-103; 1998, 77-78). Moreover, he cites the widespread influence of early Enochic texts and traditions to depict this movement as a major factor in Jewish society; rather than being relegated to the margins, Enochic Judaism is said to have developed and flourished alongside Zadokite Judaism in the centuries between the Maccabean revolt and the destruction of the second temple (esp. 1998, 186-91).

To trace the trajectory of its development, Boccaccini uses a method of systematic analysis borrowed from the history of philosophy, and he filiates the textual evidence for Enochic Judaism primarily on the basis of his analyses of approaches to evil's emergence, effects, and ends (1998, 59-162 passim). The main structure for the chain of documents he thus constructs is provided by the five books now collected in 1 Enoch, the dates of which roughly span the period between the third century B.C.E. and the turn of the common era. Into this structure are inserted aligned works from the so-called Old Testament Pseudepigrapha and Dead Sea Scrolls: Aramaic Levi, Jubilees, the Temple Scroll, 4QMMT, and the Testaments of the Twelve Patriarchs.

By interpreting their patterns of ideological similarity and difference in terms of social continuity and religious innovation, Boccaccini uses these documents to describe a development and diversification of ideas about evil that mirrors the development and diversification of a distinct religious movement. More specifically, he argues that (1) Enochic Judaism was a movement with broad-based appeal, (2) this movement stands behind ancient references to the Essenes, and (3) the Qumran community was a splinter group from these Essenes/"Enochians." In his words, he posits that "Enochic Judaism is the modern name for the mainstream body of the Essene party, from which the Qumran community parted as a radical, dissident, and marginal offspring" (1998, 16).

Just as the pivotal source for Boccaccini's reconstruction of the origins of the movement is one of the earliest subdocuments of 1 Enoch (i.e., the Book of the Watchers, 1 En 1–36), so the latest source in 1 Enoch, the Similitudes (1 En 37–71), proves central to his treatment of the fate of Enochic Judaism after the Qumranite schism (see esp. 1998, 144-49). Consistent with this text's celebrated affinities with the New Testament literature, he suggests that its nonsectarian stream flowed into the Jesus movement. In effect, he posits that mainline Enochic Judaism constitutes the Jewish roots of Christianity in much the same way that he depicts Zadokite Judaism as the roots of rabbinic Judaism.

Before taking issue with any specific aspect of Boccaccini's theory, I should stress that his overall approach to 1 Enoch is in many ways a model of methodological care. I noted above his judicious treatment of attitudes toward the priesthood in 1 Enoch and his avoidance of a canonical bias whereby the present status of texts ("biblical," "apocryphal," "pseudepigraphical") is anachronistically assumed to reflect the social position of their ancient authors and audiences. In a broader sense the Essene-Enochic Hypothesis embodies a timely corrective to the scholarly tendency to downplay the significance of 1 Enoch and other extracanonical texts for our understanding of the major trends in ancient Judaism. Not only does Boccaccini acknowledge the importance of this text as a collection of materials spanning most of the second temple period, but he takes on the challenge of bringing all of its constituent parts to bear on philosophical and sociohistorical as well as literary and religious history.

It is indeed a pressing task at this point in the history of scholarship to revisit, revise, and perhaps even rewrite our "master narratives" about the parties, trends, and trajectories of second temple Judaism(s). A wealth of new and revolutionary insights has emerged from the study of the Dead Sea Scrolls and other, now noncanonical texts. Recent years have also seen major advances in research on the relationship between second temple and rabbinic Judaism as well as the Jewish background of the New Testament and early Christianity. Boccaccini's books rightly answer the need to integrate these data into our overall picture of ancient Jewish and Christian history, working toward a generalist account that responsibly reflects the results of recent specialist research and exploring the possibility that new findings might necessitate a completely new framework.

Precisely because of the timeliness and importance of Boccaccini's project, it proves critical that we interrogate his ideas about Enochic Judaism, considering their ramifications for research on second temple Judaism, Jewish history, and Christian origins, as well as 1 Enoch more specifically. With these broader aims in mind, I would like to offer a few reflections about (1) what is assumed and implied by the manner in which Boccaccini uses the texts now collected in 1 Enoch to reconstruct a distinctive movement, and (2) what is assumed and implied by his choice to describe this movement as "a Judaism" rather than merely a movement, group, community, school of thought, or literary tradition within Judaism.

Using 1 Enoch as a Source for "a Judaism"

Boccaccini is hardly the first to interpret the shared Enochic pseudepigraphy of the writings preserved in 1 Enoch, the thematic cohesion and ideological continuities between them, the very fact of their compilation as evidence for a distinctive ideological stream in Judaism (see Sacchi 1997a; Schwartz 2001, 74-87), and/or a cohesive and clearly delineated social entity, movement, community, group, or school (Nickelsburg 2001, 64; Tiller 1993, 116-26; Collins 1998, 72). For this the reasons are clear: 1 Enoch is not a single book penned by a single author, but rather a collection of writings that are "closely related to one another through a consistent internal system of literary connections, metaphors, allusions, and quotations" (Boccaccini 1998, 12). Moreover, these writings owe their present forms and their settings in 1 Enoch to the labors of a long series of authors, redactors, tradents, copyists, translators, and anthologists, such that the collection itself is an artifact of the continued cultivation of Enochic traditions in the second temple period and well beyond.

It is agreed, then, that the texts in 1 Enoch should be read in terms of a continuity of some sort; the question is what kind(s) of continuity: sociohistorical, religious, philosophical, literary, and/or intertextual. What stands out about Boccaccini's theory is that he draws all these elements into a reading of 1 Enoch as a record of the evolving ideology of "a Judaism" with a solid sociohistorical basis in a clearly delineated communal identity (i.e., the Essenes). Just as his equation between "Enochic Judaism" and the Essene movement rests on the claimed correspondence between philosophical trends in our literary evidence and explicit statements in our historiographical sources, so his use of 1 Enoch to construct this Enochic Judaism is based on the assumption that we can write social history on the basis of the history of ideas. In fact, he himself cites the correlation of the two as a major benefit of his theory: "Enochic Judaism . . . ceases to be a mere intellectual phenomenon, an ingenious yet monstrously bodiless soul, and becomes flesh and blood in the sociology of the Essene group, a group that has left substantial evidence in ancient historiography" (1998, 195).

As with any attempt to reconstruct sociohistorical realities from ideological and thematic affinities in literary sources, his approach raises a number of methodological issues. Foremost are questions pertaining to his principles of selectivity, interpretation, and taxonomy. Boccaccini chooses to privilege the problem of evil when defining and distinguishing "Judaisms," as well as in tracing their development. Although his focus on theodicy proves fascinating and productive from the perspective of the history of ideas, one might ask: How would his reconstruction of the social history of second temple Judaism have differed if he had focused on another issue? Is it plausible to base hypotheses about historical connections so heavily on evidence for common beliefs and concepts, as opposed, most notably, to common rituals and practices? Was the problem of evil really so pressing for Jews of this period that opinions about the origins of human sin and suffering determined inclusion and exclusion from groups?

Furthermore, Boccaccini's reading of 1 Enoch privileges the version of the angelic descent myth in the Book of the Watchers, treating its supernatural etiology of evil as the "generative idea" that unites, motivates, and defines Enochic Judaism. This choice, however, raises another problem: 1 Enoch itself is far from univocal on the topic of the Watchers and their role in the origins of human sinfulness. As I have demonstrated in detail in my recent dissertation (Reed 2002, esp. 108-19), the earliest stage in the reception history of the Book of the Watchers is characterized by a striking reticence toward its assertion that human sin and suffering originated in a supernatural sphere; accordingly, its version of the angel descent myth was reinterpreted, redeployed, and/or suppressed even in texts that were otherwise shaped by its influence. Interestingly, this trend is even evident in Dream Visions and the Epistle of Enoch, two second century B.C.E. works now collected in 1 Enoch. The authors/redactors of these texts self-consciously work within a tradition of Enochic pseudepigraphy and are deeply indebted to the Book of the Watchers in other ways. Nevertheless, they depart from the earlier Enochic book in downplaying the Watchers' culpability for the origins of evil, omitting all reference to their corrupting teachings, and casting these creatures almost solely in paradigmatic terms as sinful creatures akin to wicked humans.

This divergence proves significant, in my view, shedding doubt on Boccaccini's use of a supernatural etiology of evil as a criterion for distinguishing Enochic Judaism and on his use of theodicy as the primary taxonomic principle for sorting different second temple "Judaisms." On the one hand, the variety of viewpoints among the earliest Enochic authors highlights the difficulty of culling information about social groups from the diverse material now found in 1 Enoch. On the other hand, its inclusion of texts with different perspectives on evil points to the interpretive problems raised by reconstructing a sociohistorical movement from a textual collection.

Indeed, even if we accept that Enochic Judaism can be resurrected in body and soul, and even if we concur that the authors, redactors, and readers of 1 Enoch should be fleshed out with secondhand statements about the Essenes, we might do well to stop and ask whether 1 Enoch can be used to tell the story of the evolving spirit of a single entity. Are the affinities among the materials in this collection so strong that the differences can only be interpreted in terms of developments within a single, distinctive movement? To what degree does the unity within 1 Enoch reflect the production of its parts within a single socioreligious sphere, and to what degree is the appearance of unity created retrospectively by the act of collection?

At first glance, 1 Enoch's anthological character would seem to exempt us from (at least some of) the infamous historiographical and interpretative problems raised by modern scholarly attempts to reconstruct ancient communities from individual texts. As is clear from the example of Enochic approaches to the problem of evil, however, the situation is a bit more complex. With regard to canonical collections such as the Tanakh and New Testament, and modern anthologies such as the "Old Testament Pseudepigrapha," Boccaccini rightly stresses that "documents need to be freed from the cages of their anachronistic corpora" (2002, 29; so also 28-32; 1998, 56-57). The same might be said of 1 Enoch: collections and compilations can tell us much about the *Nachleben* of their constituent texts, but we should be wary lest we read those (earlier) texts through the lens of the (later) collection, internalizing the values of the anthologist and harmonizing rather than analyzing difference.

I do not mean, of course, to downplay the many commonalities among the texts in 1 Enoch. I only wish to note the importance of distinguishing the whole from the parts (and the parts from the parts), especially when using this source to reconstruct social realities in the second temple period. It is easy to forget that 1 Enoch as a collection survives only in an Ethiopic form that goes back to the fourth or fifth century c.e. at the very earliest. Given the first-century date of the Similitudes and our lack of evidence for its later reception history, it is likely that even the ultimate *Vorlage* of 1 Enoch postdates the second temple period. Although the practice of compiling Enochic materials has many earlier precedents and the materials themselves are early in date, the collection could still be late antique in origin (see further Reed 2003). Moreover, just as the Enochic compilations at Qumran (esp. 4QEnoch^c) seem to reflect the understanding and use of these documents in this particular community, so the selection and arrangement of material in 1 Enoch appear to embody and express a different, even later perspective.

For me these factors problematize Boccaccini's understanding of 1 Enoch as "the core of an ancient and distinct variety of second temple Judaism" (1998, 12). Personally I am wary of reconstructing a single, cohesive, and distinctive second temple "Judaism" from what is a particular collection of texts, with its own particular principles of selectivity and arrangement, which have been shaped by a historical context that differed from the Enochic authors/redactors of second temple times. Although I may be too cautious in this regard, I am concerned about what we might overlook if we leap too quickly from insights about literary, thematic, and ideological connections to conclusions about sociohistorical realities. I worry lest our relative lack of evidence for the period tempt us into a misleading conflation of intertextual connections, philosophical trends, and communal identities.

"Enochic Judaism" as "a Judaism"

In light of the diversity of the material in 1 Enoch as well as the widespread diffusion of Enochic traditions in other texts of the time (Reed 2002, 88-170), I still have my doubts about whether we can even extrapolate a social group from 1 Enoch in any direct fashion, let alone "a Judaism" that is discrete, distinctive, or bounded in any meaningful fashion.

The redaction histories and reception histories of now-canonical (i.e., retrospectively "biblical") books bespeak the great creativity and flexibility with which second temple Jewish readers reinterpreted texts and recast their relevance, such that the same books could be used for different purposes by different exegetes, groups, and authors, and in differing times and settings. Likewise, the commonalities between the writings in 1 Enoch, as well as the affinities shared by them with other texts of the time, need not reflect only the evolving ideas of a single movement that can be readily distinguished from other "Judaisms." Rather, they might evince the broad-based influence of early Enochic texts and traditions, and their use and reinterpretation in multiple settings.

In light of the evidence of 2 Enoch and so-called 3 Enoch in particular, as well as the long, rich, and winding reception histories of the books now collected in 1 Enoch in both Christianity and post-70 Judaism (Reed 2002, 171-364), I also wonder whether we might be better off accounting for the commonalities and continuities among Enochic pseudepigrapha in more fluid, dynamic, and permeable terms, such as in terms of an Enochic literary tradition which crossed the boundaries of different groups and influenced different streams of tradition in different ways.

Space does not permit a consideration of broader questions about the benefits of describing multiple second temple "Judaisms" as opposed to distinct varieties within a single "Judaism," or one "Judaism" that was by definition a variegated continuum rather than a monolithic whole or a collection of separate parts. For our present purposes the issue of "religions" and their boundaries proves pertinent inasmuch as it points to one of the most wide-reaching ramifications of Boccaccini's hypothesis: by reconstructing an "Enochic Judaism" that distinguished itself from "Zadokite Judaism" already in the fourth or third century B.C.E., he provides a model for approaching rabbinic Judaism and Christianity as equal heirs to second temple Judaism. He does so, however, by giving each a separate heritage, reconstructing a different "Judaism" at their respective roots. The result is a bifurcation of second temple tradition into proto-Christian and protorabbinic parts. Consequently, even despite his explicit efforts to encompass both Judaism and Christianity within a single intellectual system (esp. Boccaccini 1991), his reconstruction of second temple history has the effect of reinscribing their "Parting of the Ways" and, moreover, placing this "Parting" even prior to the birth of Jesus.

Those familiar with Boccaccini and his work will realize just how ironic this is. Recent research on the New Testament, early Christianity, and post-70 Judaism has shed doubt on whether, when, and where we can discuss the relationship between Judaism and Christianity in terms of the interaction between two separate entities (Boyarin 1999; Becker and Reed 2003), and Boccaccini himself has had an influential role in these discussions. This irony, however, may be instructive, inasmuch as it reminds us of the special difficulties involved in writing the religious, social, and intellectual history of the Jews in the second temple period.

With so little evidence and so much at stake, we must be especially careful not to read our data retrospectively through our knowledge of later developments. Yet we also cannot avoid the fact that this period is the shared prehistory of rabbinic Judaism and early Christianity, such that any reconstructions have ramifications that ripple well beyond 70 C.E. Furthermore, later developments may sometimes shed light on earlier trends and trajectories. This is clearly the case with 1 Enoch; even if we must seek to avoid anachronism when reading its constituent parts, we surely cannot ignore the ongoing influence of this literature in late antiquity and the Middle Ages. For, among other things, the lively *Nachleben* of the early Enochic literature starkly highlights the problem with reading 1 Enoch through the lens of its present status, sheds further doubt on the common assumption that these books were somehow marginal in their own times, and buttresses Boccaccini's efforts to bring 1 Enoch to center stage in the study of second temple Judaism(s).

Only time will tell whether the Essene-Enochic Hypothesis succeeds in shaping a new consensus about ancient Jewish sectarianism and whether Boccaccini's concept of "Enochic Judaism" holds up as a heuristic framework for analyzing texts and trends. In any case, the contribution of his work and the importance of his project remain unassailable. Whatever criticisms we might have, we should be thankful that he has taken on the challenge of navigating the path to a new, more integrated history of second temple Judaism, so generously offering us inventive ideas, thoughtful analyses, and timely correctives which resonate both within and beyond the study of ancient Judaism.

Enoch, the Dead Sea Scrolls, and the Essenes: Groups and Movements in Judaism in the Early Second Century B.C.E.

John J. Collins

In his stimulating book *Beyond the Essene Hypothesis,* Gabriele Boccaccini proposes the thesis that "Enochic Judaism is the modern name for the mainstream body of the Essene party, from which the Qumran community parted, as a radical, dissident, and marginal offspring" (Boccaccini 1998, 16). This suggestion is not entirely without precedent. At one point in the history of research it was customary to associate all references to elect groups in the books of Enoch, Daniel, and Jubilees with the Hasidim, and regard them as the forerunners of the Essenes (and Pharisees) (Hengel 1974, 1:175-80). In 1984 Devorah Dimant suggested that the Animal Apocalypse was an early sectarian work, and refers to the appearance of the Teacher of Righteousness (Dimant 1984, 544-45). In 1987 Philip Davies, who a decade earlier had debunked the all-embracing portrayal of the Hasidim (Davies 1977), threw caution to the winds and declared that it seemed "unnecessarily pedantic" not to call the authors of the Enochic texts and Jubilees "Essenes" (Davies 1987, 109) and proceeded to equate the terms "pre-Qumran" and "Essene" (30). Davies also promoted the view that the Damascus Document reflected "the organization of the parent community, from which the Qumran group emerged," and that the latter group originated in a schism not with Judaism as a whole but with the parent "Essene" group (18-19).

The "Groningen hypothesis" advanced by Florentino García Martínez in 1990 also tried "clearly to distinguish between the origins of the Qumran group and the origins of the parent group, the Essene movement, and to trace back to the apocalyptic tradition of the third century BCE the ideological roots of the Essenes." García Martínez also sought "the origins of the Qumran group in a split which occurred within the Essene movement in consequence of which the group loyal to the Teacher of Righteousness was finally to establish itself in Qumran" (García Martínez and van der Woude 1990, 537).

Boccaccini, then, is building on the results of earlier scholarship, although one cannot speak of a consensus on these issues. In my view, however, there are serious problems with this reconstruction of Essene origins, and the resulting identification of Enochic Judaism as Essene is at best an oversimplification. There are, to be sure, clear lines of continuity between the Enoch literature and the Dead Sea sect that are not in dispute. These include the common solar calendar, division of history into periods, and an interest in the angelic world that involves life after death, as well as the fact that the Enoch literature, like the Damascus Document, speaks of the emergence of an elect group late in the second temple period. But these affinities must be seen in perspective of what we know of the Essenes, of continuities with other literature, and of the range of interests that characterize the sectarian scrolls.

The Essenes

Let us begin with the issue of terminology. I still believe that the community, or communities, described in the Community Rule and Damascus Rule should be identified with the Essenes described in the Greek and Latin sources, despite some troubling discrepancies, particularly about the question of celibacy (Collins 1992). But it is important to remember the basis of the identification. This is primarily the similarity in community organization and process of admission. There are also some similarities in religious ideas, such as the Essene belief in determinism and the description of life after death, but I doubt that these would be sufficient to sustain the identification without the community structures. The closest parallels are found in the Community Rule.

If, then, we are justified in speaking of Essenes in connection with the DSS at all, the *yaḥad* of the Community Rule should be our primary example of an Essene community. If we share the common assumption that this *yaḥad* was the Qumran community, then that community is our touchstone of what it meant to be an Essene. If we compare what is said about the "lambs" in the Animal Apocalypse or about the "chosen righteous" in the Apocalypse of Weeks with the accounts of the Essenes in Josephus, Philo, or Pliny, we find that they have almost nothing in common. The Enochic texts do not attest the kind of separatist community that is central to the classical accounts. It seems to me, then, that to speak of the tradents of the Enoch literature as Essenes is to sow confusion.

Now it may be objected that I am overlooking the evidence of the Damascus Document, which has been taken to reflect a middle ground between the Enoch literature on the one hand and the Community Rule, which is taken to reflect the Qumran community, on the other. CD 7 legislates for people who live in camps according to the order of the land and marry and have children. These people are often identified with "the marrying Essenes" who are mentioned by Josephus as another branch of the sect (*War* 2.160). Josephus says they were in agreement with the other Essenes on the way of life, usages, and customs, and differed only with respect to marriage. We may suspect that people who married and had children cannot have lived the same kind of communal life as those who did not. But even if they did not, the mere absence of communal life is hardly sufficient grounds for identifying them with Enochic Judaism. In the end, the case for such an identification stands or falls on the degree of similarity that we find between the Damascus Document and the Enoch literature.

The Alleged Schism

Before I turn to that question, however, I want to comment on the relation between the two orders of Essenes, and between the Damascus Document and the Community Rule. Josephus gives no hint that the existence of the two orders of Essenes was due to a schism. Quite the contrary. He suggests that they differed only with respect to marriage. The best evidence for a distinction of two orders in the scrolls is found in CD 7, which can be taken to distinguish between those who "walk in perfect holiness" and those who live in camps and marry (J. Baumgarten 1990). The passage can also be construed so that those who live in camps are a subgroup of those who walk in holiness. But here again there is no suggestion of a schism. The Damascus Document legislates for both. Whether the people of the *yaḥad* in the Community Rule were celibate is much disputed, especially in light of new evidence about the cemetery (Zangenberg 1999). But in any case, the people who are said to go into the desert to prepare the way of the Lord in 1QS 8 are not schismatics but people set aside within the community for a life of holiness. There is no indication that the Community Rule and the Damascus Document represent different sides in a schism. Both texts are preserved at Qumran. The Damascus Document, it should be noted, pays explicit homage to the Teacher, who is not mentioned in the supposedly Qumranic Community Rule. It seems to me, then, that the two orders of Essenes represented different options within the sect, not dissenting factions. Equally, the Damascus Document represents both the "men of perfect holiness" and those who live in camps as loyal followers of the Teacher of Righteousness.

The idea of schism within the parent movement is based above all on the references in the Damascus Document to the "Scoffer" (CD 1:14) and to those who turned back with the Man of the Lie (CD 20:15) (Stegemann 1971, 48-52). It is clear that some people rejected the Teacher and broke with his community. One may well argue, then, that the whole Essene sect arose as the result of a schism within a wider movement (such as the Hasidim), and this was in fact the usual argument in the earlier phase of research on the scrolls. But there is no reason to suppose that the people who settled at Qumran were the only ones loyal to the Teacher; CD 7 clearly regards those who lived in camps as members of the same movement. I see no justification for referring to those who left with the Man of the Lie as Essenes.

As a first step toward reducing confusion, therefore, I suggest that the word "Essene" be restricted to the followers of the Teacher of Righteousness, whether celibate or married. Those who turned back with the Man of the Lie ceased to be Essenes, and may have become Pharisees (Stegemann 1971, 257), but I see no evidence of any schism between two parties who remained Essene. I might add that I would not object to a complete moratorium on the word "Essene" in connection with the Dead Sea Scrolls. It is inevitable that we discuss the identification of the sect, but the information provided by the Greek and Latin sources is suspect anyway, and does not add anything reliable to what can be gleaned from the scrolls themselves.

The Damascus Document and the Enoch Literature

But leaving aside the term "Essenes," can we say anything about the identification of the "plant root," the community that existed for some twenty years before the arrival of the Teacher? Was this community identical with the "chosen righteous" and "small lambs" of the Enoch literature?

The argument for the identification is clear enough: one should not multiply sectarian groups without cause. Since the Enoch literature was known and influential at Qumran, and it indicates the rise of an elect group late in the second temple period, why not identify this group with the "plant root" of the Dead Sea sect? Moreover, they have in common allegiance to the solar calendar, which set them at odds with the Jerusalem temple, and they shared ideas of reward and punishment after death. Even the metaphor of planting figures prominently in 1 Enoch (Tiller 1997). These factors certainly show that there was some connection between the Enoch group and the plant root of the Damascus Document. Are they enough to establish the identification?

I think not. The concept of covenant and the torah of Moses are absolutely central to the Damascus Document. As we have seen repeatedly, neither is at all prominent in the early Enoch literature. Conversely, while the Damascus Document knows the story of the Watchers, it never appeals to the authority of Enoch as a revealer, although it does appeal to Levi, and cites Jubilees. It also attaches major importance to issues of purity, which are not especially prominent in the Enoch literature. There is then an ideological gulf between the Enoch literature and the Damascus covenant.

Boccaccini tries to bridge that gulf by appeal to the book of Jubilees. Here we have a revelation that was allegedly given to Moses and is greatly concerned with halakic issues. It also draws on the Enoch tradition, notably on the myth of the Watchers, and attaches great importance to the solar calendar. Boccaccini concludes that "the Book of Jubilees gives us evidence that after the Maccabean crisis, the Enochians, or at least some Enochians, now considered the Mosaic revelation as no longer a competitive revelation to pass over in silence, as Dream Visions did, but as a common heritage that could neither be ignored nor dismissed" (Boccaccini 1998, 88). But is the book of Jubilees necessarily a product of Enochians? Might one not equally well suppose that some people who venerated Moses no longer regarded Enochian revelation as competitive; or indeed that some people who were devoted to the torah of Moses became aware of the Enoch literature and tried to incorporate it into "Mosaic religion"? There is a fusion of traditions in Jubilees, but can we be so confident that the people doing the fusing were the so-called Enochians?

The impulse to apply Occam's razor to the identification of groups in second-century Judaism is commendable up to a point, but it can be carried to excess. The Enoch literature and the Damascus Document are not the only texts from this period that speak of the emergence of an elect group. We also have the *maskilim* in Daniel, and remnants in the pseudo-Daniel writings, that do not seem to me to come from the same source as the canonical book (Collins 1999). Daniel was also known and influential at Qumran, and like Enoch had a great interest in the angelic world and hoped for an angelic afterlife. But as Boccaccini recognizes, Daniel cannot be subsumed into Enochic Judaism. Now we must also add 4QInstruction to the list (Strugnell and Harrington 1999). This wisdom text is addressed to "people of the spirit" who are sharply distinguished from "the spirit of flesh." It has been suggested that this text too was influenced by the Enoch literature, especially by the Epistle (Elgvin 2000), but it never refers to Enoch, nor to distinctively Enochic themes like the fall of the Watchers. In each of these cases, Enoch, Daniel, and 4QInstruction, there are clear lines of continuity with central writings of the sectarian scrolls (Lange 1995, 69-79). But they cannot be reduced to a single parent movement.

It seems to me that the safest conclusion from this evidence is that the

Dead Sea sect drew its inspiration from various quarters. One of these was certainly the Enoch literature. Another was the wisdom tradition attested in 4QInstruction. Daniel was another, and the torah of Moses was yet another. The reduction of all these to a single line of tradition is a temptation that should be avoided. Rather than being a splinter movement, an offshoot of a branch, it seems to me that the sectarian movement reflected in the scrolls involved a synthesis of traditions, Enochic and Mosaic, sapiential and apocalyptic. It was still a sectarian movement, but it drew together traditions, and probably also people, from various sources. If the people who settled at Qumran were originally Enochians, I would expect Enoch to play a larger role in the sectarian writings. This is not at all to deny the important continuities between Enoch and Qumran, but these continuities must be seen in the broader context of elect communities in Judaism in the second century B.C.E.

From "Communities of Texts" to Religious Communities: Problems and Pitfalls

Jeff S. Anderson

One of the focuses in the work of Gabriele Boccaccini, particularly in his three monographs tracing the intellectual history of second temple Judaism (Boccaccini 1991; 1998; 2002), has concerned the relationship between the Essenes, Qumran, and Enochic groups. Broadly based, wide-ranging studies such as his are absolutely necessary. It is important that they be done, and Boccaccini's contributions are noteworthy. But these types of studies are beset with pitfalls and carry considerable risk. Boccaccini is well aware of these problems as he details them in the methodological discussions in the early pages of his most recent work, *Roots of Rabbinic Judaism*. There he challenges the single-Judaism model as anachronistic and presents four scholarly approaches to the problem of the definition of common Judaism (Boccaccini 2002, 8-14). To put it simply, if articulating a definition of common Judaism is elusive, then how could one ever conceivably hope to define Enochic, Essene, or Zadokite Judaism? Speaking of multiple Judaisms has always been an attractive alternative, but it carries a weakness in that it solves one problem only to create another, more fundamental problem, namely, exactly what makes any Judaism a Judaism (Cohen 1999; Neusner 1998)?

Enochic scholars are well aware of these difficulties. To speak of Enochic literature is to speak of a community of texts which share a socioreligious worldview. There is danger enough in the parallelomania that often accompanies a search for commonalities among disparate literary works, but moving from communities of texts to actual religious communities is a particularly giant leap — not that it is an impossible task, but there are monumental dangers. These dangers can perhaps be described along a hypothetical vertical axis. As one moves up the vertical axis, the danger is essentially one of elevation: elevation from an ideal type to a social reality. As one moves down the axis, the danger is reductionism: moving from those texts with a shared literary perspective to an oversimplified, coherent, socioreligious community, which produced that perspective.

One particular pitfall of studying texts as opaque as these is the elevation of ideal types to social reality. Max Weber (1930; 1952) proposed the ideal type as an analytical construct to enable the observer of social history to measure similarities and differences in social phenomena. As such, an ideal type is intentionally a one-sided accentuation of one or more points of view, or a synthesis of a great many points of view with the goal of obtaining this analytical construct. Weber was careful to point out that an ideal type never corresponds directly to or mirrors a specific social reality but always remains one step removed from that reality. The danger, therefore, is to ignore that separation and make an explicit identification of the ideal type with a specific social reality.

The problem is pronounced in second temple Jewish literature. For example, when a community of texts appears rather uniformly to criticize a religious phenomenon, it doesn't necessarily mean that criticism constitutes a coherent socioreligious movement. It certainly does not justify jumping to the conclusion that this one particular criticism is what an entire movement was all about. Specifically, it is attractive to appeal to the origin of evil as the basis for two distinct and divergent forms of Judaism, Zadokite and Enochic. A simple summary of Zadokite Judaism and Enochic Judaism is as follows: For Zadokite Judaism, the world as basically good and evil arose from the sin of Adam and Eve in the Garden of Eden. The heart of Zadokite Judaism is the torah, with Moses as its esteemed lawgiver, the Jerusalem temple, its priesthood. Rituals are of central importance for observing the sacred boundaries that keep the cosmos in order. For Enochic Judaism, however, evil arose when fallen angels seduced human women, resulting in a hopelessly corrupt evil world order. Enochic Judaism has a lukewarm regard for Moses, while instead, Enoch assumes center stage in the literature. While certainly interested in the priesthood, Enochic Judaism is largely hostile to the second temple and its rituals.

Certainly these diverse viewpoints correctly qualify as Weber's ideal types. As an ideal type, it is helpful to accentuate certain disparate points of view or synthesize others. But it is, perhaps, too big a step to argue that they reflect two socially distinct Jewish movements or groups, at least with the present evidence. The criticism of the priesthood is another example that illustrates the dangers of elevating ideal types to social realities. Most scholars would agree that the Enochic tradition criticizes the temple establishment of the second century B.C.E. (Suter 1979, 115-35; Nickelsburg 1981, 575-600), but what are the implications of that criticism? Does such a critique necessarily denote competitive movements? Might this critique instead represent two distinct views within the same priestly establishment? It is not impossible to imagine that those within the priesthood could criticize that institution just as effectively as priests who had been marginalized by those with priestly power.

Moving down the hypothetical vertical axis, the opposite problem is one of reductionism. Actually, one could argue that all the excesses confronted here are essentially reductionistic. Difficult lessons learned in the twentieth century should inform us that scholars of the second temple period simply cannot relate every development to two or three or four groups. Recent trends in Qumran studies have recognized this, as do scholars of the Jesus movement and early Christianity. This complexity is also at the heart of the dilemma to define common Judaism(s) in the second temple period. Although I have used the terms "Zadokite Judaism" and "Enochic Judaism," I am admittedly uneasy about the appropriateness of such designations (Anderson 2002). Furthermore, there is great danger in the default methodology that reduces nearly everything that is not categorized as Enochic Judaism to Zadokite groups, just as in earlier generations the dichotomy was between Pharisees and sects.

One might argue that it is more reasonable and certainly safer to simply discuss the relationships between texts and not groups at all. But the fascination with sociological groups has always been a part of the study of the Hebrew Bible, and such an enterprise has its rightful place. Scholars have unashamedly written of prophetic movements, wisdom schools, priestly circles, the kerygma of the Yahwist, the theology of P, and countless other expressions denoting movements or groups. For second temple scholarship specifically, Michael Stone reflects the ideal of scholarly aspiration: "the task of trying to infer the existence of groups or trends in society from opinions in literary works is, of course, hazardous. We must try, however, for all the issues are very central, but caution must be employed" (Stone 1988, 167).

The adage that came up repeatedly in discussions of the Enoch Seminar, "groups don't write books," is a truism that is only partially accurate. When written, a literary work is either passed down or it is not. If it is not, there is nothing really to discuss. If, however, it is passed down, that work is either passed down as is or is redacted in some way. Generally, as a community finds a literary work useful and convincing, they pass down the work through the process of transmission and editing. Consequently, groups really do write books, and the search for evidence of communities behind texts is a legitimate enterprise. That being the case, there are several examples in the Enochic literature that provide evidence of the circles that produced and transmitted this literature. These examples include: the use of collective titles or eponymous names, the adoption of we/you/they terminology, the use of denouncement speech rhetoric, and the adoption of (or aversion to) a specific calendar.

Within the category of collective titles and eponymous names should be mentioned epithetical self-descriptions and descriptions of one's enemies. The sectarian literature at Qumran is replete with such examples: the Teacher of Righteousness, the Sons of Light and the Sons of Darkness, the Liar, the Men of Violence, the Breakers of the Covenant, the House of Absalom, the Wicked Priest, the Spouter of Lies, and numerous other designations which refer to a leader of a group or to a community itself. Such rhetoric betrays a rigid dualism of insiders and outsiders. Early Enochic literature does not nearly reflect the inner-group, in-group, out-group boundaries as at Qumran, but terms like "the righteous," "the holy," and "the chosen" all indicate a consciousness of community (Nickelsburg 2001, 64). Twice Enoch denounces "those who change or distort the words of truth and write books in their own words" (1 En 104:10; 98:15). The Epistle of Enoch also refers to "those who build their houses with sin." Such references may reflect a community identity.

A second example is the use of personal pronouns to refer to constituent communities. This we/you/they terminology is exemplified in 1 Enoch 1–5 and 4QMMT. In 1 Enoch the "you" group has apparently turned aside from the commandments of God (5:2, 4) and will inherit the curse (5:5-7), while the "they" group which carries out God's word will inherit the earth and spend their days in peace (5:6-9) (Nickelsburg 2001, 157-64). Likewise, the "we" circle responsible for 4QMMT seeks to convince the "you" recipients to disassociate themselves from the views of the "they" party. Such terminology does not necessarily designate the identity of outsiders, but it does demonstrate a group consciousness and a propensity to erect boundaries between socioreligious circles.

I argue that denouncement speech can be used as a means of propaganda to marginalize outsiders while exercising control over the behavior of insiders. The early Enochic literature and, to a greater degree, the sectarian texts from Qumran generously employ imprecations for such purposes.

Participants in the Enoch Seminar agree that calendrical issues were an important means of demarcating between religious communities. For many years Shemaryahu Talmon has argued that the acceptance or rejection of a calendar is one of the primary ways of erecting boundaries between religious communities (Talmon 1986). During the second temple period the sacred calendar became an important concern and a magnet for controversy. Jubilees is an excellent example of this preoccupation, depicting the sacred mandates of the faith as invalid if performed on incorrect dates. Such a calendar was given by God to Moses at Sinai, and its recipients were warned that following a lunar calendar rendered that particular group illegitimate. The Habakkuk Commentary's allusion to the Wicked Priest's appearance on the Day of Atonement is informative, in that an alternative calendar reveals why this priest would journey to Qumran on the holiest day of the cultic year.

Despite the opaque nature of the Enochic texts, and despite the thorny dilemma regarding the demarcation of boundaries between the Judaisms of the second century B.C.E., evidence remains of religious communities behind these enigmatic texts. To speak definitively, however, about Enochic and Zadokite groups, *as groups,* is an oversimplification of the complexities present in these traditions.

Enochians, Essenes, and Qumran Essenes

James R. Davila

Gabriele Boccaccini has provided us with an extraordinarily useful framework for understanding the Dead Sea Scrolls in his book *Beyond the Essene Hypothesis*. Taking the scrolls on their own terms and attending closely to what they actually say, he has also placed them in their ancient historical and literary context in a falsifiable reconstruction that has great explanatory power.

Briefly, Boccaccini postulates two competing lines of tradition stemming from Ezekiel: the Zadokites and the Enochians. The Enochians produced the earlier Enoch literature, the Book of the Watchers, the Astronomical Book, and the Animal Apocalypse, along with Aramaic Levi. They were a priestly, anti-Zadokite movement centered on Enoch and his revelations rather than on Moses and his torah.

The Enochic movement gradually came to terms with some Zadokite elements and was transformed into the earliest manifestation of the Essene movement. The transition into Essenism is documented by the book of Jubilees, the Temple Scroll, the Halakhic Letter, and the Proto-Epistle of Enoch, the last of these four having the Apocalypse of Weeks embedded in it.

At least two factions developed in the later Essene movement. The more radical, indeed extremist, is represented by the Essenes who lived in a small, quasi-monastic, celibate community at the site where the ruins of Qumran now stand. They produced the sectarian texts such as the Damascus Document, the Community Rule, the War Scroll, the Hodayot, and the pesherim.

The mainstream or less extreme branch of the Essene movement produced other surviving literature, including the Epistle of Enoch, the Testaments of the Twelve Patriarchs, and the Similitudes of Enoch, none of which,

Boccaccini asserts, were found in the Qumran library. The library also omitted "Pharisaic" material (the Psalms of Solomon), pro-Hasmonean works (1 Maccabees and Judith), Hellenistic Greek Jewish texts (the Letter of Aristeas, 3 Maccabees, the Wisdom of Solomon, and works of Philo), and early Christian documents. The first-century Jewish writers Philo and Josephus seem to concentrate on mainstream Essenism in their comments, while the non-Jewish authors Pliny and Dio refer to the celibate group at Qumran.

I find much of this reconstruction highly persuasive. One could perhaps debate whether early Enochic Judaism really rejected the Mosaic/Zadokite traditions to the degree argued by Boccaccini (1998, 68-79) and George Nickelsburg (1998), or how helpful it is explicitly to identify the sectarians with the "Essenes" rather than taking them purely on their own terms, but these are issues for other papers. For the purposes of this one, I will accept Boccaccini's reconstruction up to the point of the origins of Qumran Essenism. From that point on, a number of problems occur to me.

First, although it is indeed possible that the ruins at Qumran are those of a celibate, extremist Essene community, this is by no means proven. The archaeological evidence appears to be consistent with this hypothesis, but the case falls well short of proof (Magness 2002). If Joseph Zias is correct in concluding that graves of women and children in the cemetery result from modern Bedouin burials, this at least dislodges a major obstacle to the hypothesis of a celibate group (Zias 2000). But the fact remains that there is no mention of celibacy anywhere in the scrolls. It is possible to read the Community Rule as the constitution for a celibate cenobitic group, but I would prefer to read it as the charter for something more like a Victorian men's club that met in each other's houses to study the scriptures and have meals together, no doubt not cooked by the men.

Second, Boccaccini's assertion that late, nonextremist Essene literature was censored out of the Qumran library is not convincing. If we accept Émile Puech's reconstructive work on the Greek Enoch manuscripts from Cave 7, which seems convincing to me, then one of these Greek manuscripts contains the final recension of the Epistle of Enoch, not just the proto-epistle (Nebe 1988; Puech 1996; 1998; Muro 1998; and the contribution of Flint to this volume). One could perhaps argue that this cave is a separate hoard from the Qumran Essene library, but this smacks of special pleading.

As for the Testaments of the Twelve Patriarchs, I do not grant that it is a first-century Essene work. The form we have now is that of a Christian work of the second century C.E. or later, and I remain to be persuaded that it is not in fact a Christian composition that drew, to a greater or lesser degree, on earlier Jewish sources. It is instructive to note that this is the view of Marinus de Jonge, who has been working on the document for many decades (Jonge 1975; 2003, 69-177), and of Robert Kugler, who in his recent Sheffield Guide has retracted his earlier view that there was a Jewish Greek Testaments of the Twelve Patriarchs (Kugler 1996a; 2001, 7 and passim).

The date of the Similitudes of Enoch remains debatable, and it is entirely possible that it is missing from the Qumran library because it was composed either in the late first century after the library was hidden or late enough in the first century that copies of it were not widespread, and either none happened to make it into the library or only a few did and these did not happen to survive destruction in the caves.

Third, there are problems with regarding the Qumran finds as a single library in itself. The collection reflects a bewildering variety of scribal hands; scarcely any of them are represented in more than one manuscript (Golb 1995, 97-98, 151). There are variant recensions of both Enochic works (the Proto-Epistle and Epistle of Enoch) and sectarian works (the Community Rule, the Hodayot, and perhaps the War Scroll), and multiple recensions of some biblical books as well (such as Exodus, Numbers, and Psalms).

With all this in mind, let me present an alternative interpretation of the Qumran library. It is possible that there was an extremist Essene conclave at Qumran. But the library is an Essene library in general, the library of a movement that included a broad range of utopian ideologies, probably none of which were implemented in full (Davies 1992b; 1994; cf. Collins 2003). During the war with the Romans the Judean Essene groups or congregations cooperated at least enough to transport many of their (synagogue? personal?) libraries to the caves of Qumran and to hide them there. These various libraries contained somewhat different collections and recensions of sectarian works, which had somewhat different, but related, technical terminology and doctrines.

To take a case or two in point, the pesherim are highly hostile to the Jerusalem priesthood and it is hard to imagine that their writers worshiped in the temple. The Community Rule presents the community as a spiritual temple, but it always has struck me as an overreading to assume that this precludes worship at the actual temple. The Damascus Document and the War Scroll take worship at the temple for granted, as do other texts that refer to the sanctuary (e.g., the purification liturgies 4Q414/4Q512). The Damascus Document and some pesherim treat the Teacher of Righteousness as their founder, while the Community Rule, the Hodayot, the War Scroll, and other sectarian texts never mention him (Davies 1991). The calendrical texts use a solar calendar, but some of them seem to coordinate it with the luni-solar calendar (VanderKam 1998, 71-86; Davila 2000, 208-38 [on 4Q503]).

None of the libraries stored at Qumran include either Zadokite literature that was hostile to Essene views or Hellenistic literature. Most of them contained only Hebrew and Aramaic works, but at least one library was in Greek. Boccaccini's allegedly late mainstream Essene texts either do not appear in the corpus or else were written too late for inclusion.

In short, we need not read the Qumran library as an internally consistent collection by an extremist sect, and I do not believe it does the evidence justice to do so. Rather, I find it more useful to regard it as a hastily assembled collection of libraries belonging to utopian groups within a broadly cohesive but multifaceted and internally inconsistent Essene/sectarian movement.

Beyond *Beyond the Essene Hypothesis:* Some Observations on the Qumran Zadokite Priesthood

Corrado Martone

As far as I know, the first scholar to establish a clear-cut connection between the Qumran sect and apocalyptic literature was Paolo Sacchi in 1979. In his *Jewish Apocalyptic and Its History* — a collection of studies written between 1979 and 1989 and then translated into English (Sacchi 1990; 1997a) — Sacchi points out that the author of the Book of the Watchers expressed some ideas which were new for the Jewish culture. Then he analyzed how these concepts were acknowledged by this same culture and developed especially within Essene circles.

Sacchi identified in this way a link between the apocalyptic tradition and some of the main themes of the Qumranic ideology. This later led the way to new stimulating hypotheses concerning the origins and the development of the sect of Qumran. Both in the apocalyptic tradition and in the sect of Qumran the theme concerning the nature and the origin of evil can be found, which Sacchi examined within the development of Jewish thought, pointing out the original way the Qumranic Essenism modified ideas already present in the Book of the Watchers. He drew attention particularly to the concept that humankind is contaminated and as such can only depend on a free gesture of pardon by God for salvation. The Essenism of Qumran took this ideology to its extreme by completely denying the freedom of humans, as can clearly be seen in the well-known "instruction on the two spirits" (1QS 3:13–4:26).

A turning point in Qumran studies is represented by the so-called Groningen Hypothesis first put forward by Florentino García Martínez in 1988 and reassessed by him and Adam Simon van der Woude in 1990. In my opinion, the main merit of this hypothesis is to make a distinction between the origins of the Essene movement and the origins of the Qumran sect. Essenism, as described in the classical sources, is, to quote García Martínez, "a Palestinian affair, which has its ideological roots within apocalyptic tradition" (García Martínez 1996, liii). The Qumran community's origins have to be found in a rift that occurred within the Essene movement. In this way the Groningen Hypothesis accounts not only for the analogies between Essenism as described in the classical sources and the Qumran sect but also for the undeniable and equally important differences between the two entities.

Gabriele Boccaccini moves *Beyond the Essene Hypothesis* (Boccaccini 1998). In his view the Essene movement from which the Qumran sect emerged is to be identified with Enochic Judaism. To this movement are to be ascribed those apocalyptic works that may be defined "Enochic," since Enoch is their main character. On the other hand, Boccaccini notes the absence in the Qumran corpus of some apocalyptic works that focus on human responsibility and that accordingly deny the angelic origin of evil.

This would mean that the Qumran community refused those works that did not fit with its own ideology, centered, as noted above, on a radical denial of human freedom. Undoubtedly this Enochic/Essene hypothesis has many merits, which Boccaccini himself summarizes in the final pages of his book (191-96). It allows us to see in a new light not only the Qumran community, but also the "main Jewish union of the late second temple times" (Stegemann 1992) that otherwise would have disappeared forever. We see from this quick outline that the search for the origins of the Qumran community is a work in progress as well as that many pieces of the jigsaw puzzle are gradually finding their proper place.

I would like to attach another piece to the puzzle, and I will start from a question: Why did a Zadokite group originate from an anti-Zadokite movement? I will not repeat here the many, and as a whole, convincing arguments put forward by Boccaccini to define the Enochic/Essene movement as an anti-Zadokite movement (Boccaccini 1998, 68-79). On the other hand, in my opinion it is highly probable that the Qumran sect was a Zadokite group for the following reasons.

1. The only self-definition of the sect which can be somehow related to history is "sons of Zadok," that is "Zadokites." According to a well-established Jewish tradition, the "sons of Zadok" were the only legitimate Jerusalem high priests. The following is a brief outline of the Zadokite descent as reported by biblical and nonbiblical sources.

In Chronicles we find the genealogy of the descendants of Zadok to Jehozadak at the time of the Babylonian exile: "Zadok [became the father] of Ahimaaz, Ahimaaz of Azariah, Azariah of Johanan, and Johanan of Azariah (it was he who served as priest in the house that Solomon built in Jerusalem).

Azariah became the father of Amariah, Amariah of Ahitub, Ahitub of Zadok, Zadok of Shallum, Shallum of Hilkiah, Hilkiah of Azariah, Azariah of Seraiah, Seraiah of Jehozadak; and Jehozadak went into exile when the LORD sent Judah and Jerusalem into exile by the hand of Nebuchadnezzar" (1 Chron 6:8-15 [5:34-41]). The prophet Haggai links together Jehozadak and Joshua, the last preexilic and the first postexilic high priest respectively: "Yet now take courage, O Zerubbabel, says the LORD; take courage, O Joshua, son of Jehozadak, the high priest" (Hag 2:4). Nehemiah provides us with the Zadokite genealogy from Joshua to Jaddua: "Jeshua was the father of Joiakim, Joiakim the father of Eliashib, Eliashib the father of Joiada, Joiada the father of Jonathan, and Jonathan the father of Jaddua" (Neh 12:10-11). Josephus links Jaddua to Onias I ("About this time it was that Jaddua the high priest died, and Onias his son took the high priesthood"; *Ant.* 11.8) and provides us with the Zadokite genealogy up to Onias III (for Josephus's translation, see Whiston and Maier 1980). First, it was Simon the Just ("when Onias the high priest was dead, his son Simon became his successor; he was called Simon the Just"; 12.2); then Simon's brother Eleazar ("When [Simon] was dead, and had left a young son, who was called Onias, Simon's brother Eleazar, of whom we are speaking, took the high priesthood"; 12.2); Manasseh, Eleazar's uncle ("after Eleazar's death, his uncle Manasseh took the priesthood"; 12.4); Onias II ("and after [Manasseh] had ended his life, Onias II received that dignity"; 12.4); Simon II ("Onias died [about this time], and left the high priesthood to his son Simeon"; 12.4); and finally Onias III ("And when [Simeon] was dead, Onias III his son succeeded him in that dignity"; 12.4).

2. A number of Qumran texts ascribe the greatest importance to the Zadokite element, seen as the elite of the sect itself. This makes at least plausible the identification of the community's elite with a group which no longer acknowledges the Jerusalem priesthood as the legitimate priesthood after the end of the Zadokite descent (Garbini 2003, 133-37).

3. The Community Rule has an interesting variant reading: 1QS 5:1-4 reads as follows (for DSS translations see García Martínez 1996):

> This is the rule for the men of the Community who freely volunteer to convert from all evil and to keep themselves steadfast in all he prescribes in compliance with his will. They should keep apart from men of sin in order to constitute a Community in law and possessions, and acquiesce to the authority of the sons of Zadok, the priests who safeguard the covenant and to the authority of the multitude of the men of the Community, those who persevere steadfastly in the covenant. By its authority, decision by lot shall be made in every affair involving the law, property and judgment, to

achieve together truth and humility, justice and uprightness, compassionate love and seemly behaviour in all their paths.

In the 4QS^b and 4QS^d manuscripts we find no reference to the sons of Zadok. The same passage in 4Q256 5, in fact, runs as follows: "Midrash for the Instructor concerning . . . what he commands. They should keep apart from the congregation of [the men of sin] according to the authority of the Many in every affair involving the law, [property and judgment, to achieve together truth and humility, justice and uprightness,] compassionate love and seemly behaviour in all their paths," and in 4Q258 1 I as follows: "Midrash for the Instructor concerning the men of the law who freely volunteer to revert from all evil and to keep themselves steadfast in all he prescribes. They must keep apart from men of sin in order to be together in the law and in possessions and acquiesce to the authority of Many in every affair involving the law and possessions. They must exercise humility, justice and right, compassionate love and se[emly behav]iour in all their paths."

It should be noted as well that both 4Q manuscripts represent an earlier stage than the one represented by 1QS in the redaction of the Community Rule (Martone 1995; Metso 1997a; 1997b).

4. This variant reading may well be the link between the Sacchi–García Martínez–Boccaccini interpretive line and the one discussed here: at some point a group of Zadokites takes over the Essene-Enochic tradition because of its eschatological elements. After the death of Onias III, in fact, the Zadokites are definitely removed from the historical scene and only these eschatological elements may offer a last hope to see the legitimate priesthood reestablished in its office. This shift of the Zadokite priesthood from a historical to an eschatological level is pointed out in CD 3:12–4:3:

But with those who remained steadfast in God's precepts, with those who were left from among them, God established his covenant with Israel for ever, revealing to them hidden matters in which all Israel had gone astray: his holy sabbaths and his glorious feasts, his just stipulations and his truthful paths, and the wishes of his will which man must do in order to live by them. He disclosed (these matters) to them and they dug a well of plentiful water; and whoever spurns them shall not live. But they had defiled themselves with human sin and unclean paths, and they had said: "For this is ours." But God, in his wonderful mysteries, atoned for their failings and pardoned their sins. And he built for them a safe home in Israel, such as there has not been since ancient times, not even till now. Those who remained steadfast in it will acquire eternal life, and all the glory of Adam is for them. As God established for them by means of Ezekiel the prophet, saying (Ezek 44:15): "The priests and the levites and the sons of Zadok who maintained the service of my temple when the children of Israel strayed far away from me, shall offer the fat and the blood." The priests are the converts of Israel who left the land of Judah; and the levites are those who joined them; and the sons of Zadok are the chosen of Israel, "those called by name" who stood up at the end of days.

The scriptural passage quoted here is Ezekiel 44:15, which is a bit different, however: "But the levitical priests, the descendants of Zadok, who kept the charge of my sanctuary when the people of Israel went astray from me, shall come near to me to minister to me; and they shall attend me to offer me the fat and the blood, says the Lord GOD."

The Damascus Document quotation subtly and skillfully plays with the conjunctions and reads "the priests and the levites and the sons of Zadok who maintained the service of my temple." In my opinion, it is clear that our text aims at a distinction of the Zadokites from other priests. This way the Zadokite priests are provided with a central role; they are no less than the "the chosen of Israel, 'those called by name' who stood up at the end of days."

So it comes as no surprise to see the Zadokite priesthood raised to an eschatological level and given a central role in a well-known passage of 1QSa 1:1-3: "And this is the rule of the congregation of Israel in the final days, when they gather [in community to wa]lk in accordance with the regulation of the sons of Zadok, the priests, and the men of the covenant who have turn[ed away from the pa]th of the people."

This same concept is in my opinion even more patent in 4Q174 (4QFlor), fragment 1-2, column 1:16-17: "And this (refers to) those about whom it is written in the book of Ezekiel, the prophet, that (Ezek 37:23) '[they should] not [defile themselves any more with all] their filth.' This (refers to) the sons of Zadok and to the men of their council, those who seek jus[tice] eagerly, who will come after them to the council of the community."

In this passage Ezekiel's prophetic dream of a reunited Israel is interpreted in the sectarian text as referring only to the בני צדוק. I would like to recall that the verse from Ezekiel preceding the one quoted in our text runs as follows: "Never again shall they be two nations, and never again shall they be divided into two kingdoms" (Ezek 37:22).

5. In sum: the 4QS reading is more ancient and represents a first stage in the community's development, whose origin has been outlined by the Sacchi–García Martínez–Boccaccini interpretive line. At some point after the Oniads fled to Egypt the Zadokite element enters (and gains the power in) this com-

munity. As noted above, however, these Qumran Zadokites, far from changing radically the Enochic-Essene tradition, took it over. This new stage is represented by the 1QS reading (see also Kugler 1996a; 1996b; 1999b).

One more concluding remark is appropriate. I have tried to shed some light on a historical problem by shedding some light on a philological problem. That is why I would like to dedicate this brief contribution to Paolo Sacchi, who first taught me that the history of the culture within which a given text originated may not be kept separate from the history of the text itself (e.g., Sacchi 1997a, 140-49).

Some Archaeological, Sociological, and Cross-Cultural Afterthoughts on the "Groningen" and the "Enochic/Essene" Hypotheses

Pierluigi Piovanelli

The so-called Groningen Hypothesis, originally put forward by Florentino García Martínez in 1988, considers the Qumran community a sectarian and schismatic group that appeared during the high priesthood of John Hyrcanus (134-104 B.C.E.). The Qumranites would have split off from a mainstream Jewish religious movement, the Essene *hairesis*, which had its ideological roots in the pre-Maccabean Palestinian apocalyptic tradition. According to Gabriele Boccaccini (1998), such an Essene matrix should be more precisely identified with the group that produced the earliest Enochic literature, hence the "Enochic/Essene" label of his complementary approach (for an adequate overview, see Peursen 2001).

Both hypotheses must be praised for their ability to account for the discrepancies, probably more apparent than real, between the literary descriptions of the Essenes and the textual and archaeological data from Qumran. In fact, the "Groningen Enochic/Essene" hypothesis, as we could rename it, is the best response to some alternative counterreconstructions that have flourished in the 1980s and 1990s, denying, as Norman Golb (1995) does, that the Qumran texts are either Essene or sectarian. Accordingly, I would clarify that the following archaeological, sociological, and cross-cultural remarks should be considered more constructive and sympathetic to, rather than critical of, such a "parting of the ways" theory.

The Initial Establishment of the Qumran Settlement

If we take into account the methodological approaches followed by García Martínez and Boccaccini, we note that both scholars have been especially committed to the study of the literary texts. In the wake of Paolo Sacchi, Boccaccini's aim is to draw an "intellectual history" of second temple Judaism, while García Martínez is perhaps more sensitive to the "real life" of the Qumranites as well as to their own version of reality. However, as the reading of the classical works of Geza Vermes (1956), Josef Milik (1959), Frank Cross (1958), Roland de Vaux (1973), or Ernest-Marie Laperrousaz (1976) constantly reminds us, any historical reconstruction of the Qumran community should be the result of a global understanding of both the textual *and* the archaeological records, each set of data illuminating and, up to a certain point, confirming or correcting the other. The human remains found in the cemeteries, for example, may corroborate the presence of a small group of women at Qumran, but not the existence of a family life on the spot. Needless to say, this does not imply that archaeologists should dig keeping an eye on the book, or that exegetes are supposed to carry out literary criticism with the help of the pottery.

We are fortunate enough to have two recent provisional syntheses of the archaeology of Qumran, Jean-Baptiste Humbert's reexamination of the site as a templelike "sacred space" (1994; 1998) and Jodi Magness's overall survey (2002). Both deserve careful consideration. In both cases one of the most interesting novelties is the proposal that we adopt a shorter chronology for the sectarian occupation of the site, thus renouncing an early foundation date for the Qumran settlement. This was already suggested by Laperrousaz and is indicated by Magness: "This [the numismatic evidence] and the apparent absence of second-century pottery types suggest that the sectarian settlement was established later than de Vaux thought. Based on the abundant finds and significant architecture associated with the first phase of Period Ib, . . . it is reasonable to date the initial establishment of the sectarian settlement to the first half of the first century B.C.E. (that is, *some time between 100-50 B.C.E.*)" (Magness 2002, 65, emphasis mine).

It is evident that if the archaeologists are right, either the Teacher of Righteousness did not personally lead his first followers to Qumran, or he lived a few generations later, as Michael Wise (2003) and André Dupont-Sommer (1954) argued. This chronological shift has some impact on the proposed reconstruction, and if the presence of such a catalytic figure as the Teacher is still essential for the foundation of a dissident settlement, his career seems now to be more distant from the dynastic concerns supposedly provoked by Jonathan Maccabee's "usurpation" and much closer to the real turmoil of King Alexander Janneus's period.

The Sociology of Sectarian Groups

From the very beginning, the literature on the Qumran community frequently employed terms and concepts such as "sect/sectarian," "schism," "alienation," "social marginality," or "millennialism" in a rather generic way, without providing any exact definition of the sociological categories underlying them. Among the rare exceptions was Philip Davies' empirical attempt to define, in 1994, what he considers a "sect," before applying this category to the social realities we can notice behind the Damascus Document (Davies 1994; 1996, 163-64), as well as Albert Baumgarten's broad definition of Maccabean sectarians as those Jews who *"treated other Jews as outsiders of a new sort"* (A. Baumgarten 1997, 5-15).

Of course, it remains true that amid all this terminological imprecision in the literature regarding Qumran, most scholars have generally given preference to the more specific notion of "apocalypticism" in their work. Nonetheless, when we go through the few social scientific analyses of the Qumranic materials published to date, we cannot but share George Nickelsburg's disenchanted appraisal: "As things stand, the practitioners of the social scientific methods primarily occupy themselves with the canonical texts" (1999, 94). John Peristianys' anthropological categories of "honour and shame," Mary Douglas's "grid and group" model, Charles Glock's relative rather than absolute deprivation notion (in spite of the criticism voiced by Cook 1995, 35-46), and Leon Festinger's cognitive dissonance theory are just a few of the most useful approaches in social scientific studies. All these analytical and heuristic tools are conspicuously absent from the literature on the Qumran sectarian landscape. A few excellent exceptions, such as Schmidt (2001), confirm the general trend.

To complicate things, a young Finnish scholar, Jutta Jokiranta, has recently pointed out some methodological difficulties in applying a social-scientific sect typology to the Qumran texts (2001). In spite of the correctness and relevance of her observations, we should remember three things especially. First, the reconstruction of the world of Qumran is by no means limited to the textual evidence. Second, even if the typology of new religious movements is one of the most debated topics in contemporary social-scientific studies, the majority of the sociologists today agree on the heuristic usefulness of a set of theoretical ideal-types such as "church," "denomination," "sect," or "cult." Third, historical phenomena are always different from and more complex than the abstract categories of the theoretical paradigms we use for analytic purposes. Bryan Wilson (1982, 89-120) discusses other apparent limitations inherent to modern sect typologies, such as the risk of ethnocentricity and circularity. If we take into account his definition of the ideal sect, we will notice many parallels with the Qumran situation, as well as some minor disagreements.

> He [Wilson] characterizes the sect as a voluntary association with a strong sense of self-identity. Membership depends upon merit or some kind of qualification such as knowledge or acceptance of doctrine or of conversion evidenced by some form of religious experience. The sect is exclusive and regards itself as an elite in sole possession of the truth. It is separated from the wider society and at odds with prevailing orthodoxy. Certain standards of behaviour are required of members and expulsion may follow any serious or persistent failure to live by them. Regular procedures for expulsion will exist. The commitment of the sectarian is always more total than that of the non-sectarian and he or she is always more distinctly characterised in terms of religious affiliation. The sect has no distinct or professional ministry. (As summarized by Hamilton 1995, 197-98; cf. Saldarini 2000, 2:854)

A fourth point should be made, therefore, as Wilson aptly reminds us that classification in itself is but the first step of the analytic process that helps us put different questions to the set of data at our disposal.

> It is a futile occupation to spend time on deciding whether a particular movement should be called a "sect" or not. Ideal types are not empty boxes into which the sociologist drops appropriate cases; they are, rather, to be used to make us aware of the specific historical, organizational, compositional, or other features of a sect that depart from our hypothetical system of logical relationships. The type should always turn us back to historical or empirical data so that we can explain those features of a case that contradict our hypothesized common-sense assumptions. (Wilson 1982, 105)

Accordingly, a sectarian classification can be helpful to understand not only the circumstances and the mechanisms of the schism that gave birth to the Qumran community, but also the rather obscure trajectories of its subsequent development. After the passing away of the first sectarian generations, what kind of routinization path was followed by the members of the group? Did they search for an accommodation with the surrounding society, institutionalizing their sect, or did they radicalize their positions, eventually developing a peculiar form of mysticism? How did they respond to the various dissonances that they certainly experienced during the turbulent times from 63 B.C.E. to 68 C.E.? If the community had scarce family ties, or none at all, from where came the influx of new converts necessary to insure its survival? What was the social and religious function of such a group? After the initial persecutions, if any, were they tolerated, and why? Were they supported, and by whom? In other words, in spite of its original breakaway, was the Qumran sect really thoroughly isolated from the rest of second temple Judaism?

This is a short sample of the questions a sociologist of sectarian movements could formulate and address to the textual and archaeological remains of the Qumran community, especially, for example, the rules and penal codes.

The Books on the Shelves of Sectarian Libraries

One of the most debated topics is the exact nature and function of the different libraries, rather than *genizot,* stored in the Qumran caves. Devorah Dimant has provided the clearest classification of the approximately 800 manuscripts and 200 to 300 works discovered and identified so far. According to her original taxonomy of the literary manuscripts, 223 manuscripts contain biblical texts (30 percent), 192 contain texts with a clearly sectarian terminology (25 percent), 249 texts have no such terminology (33 percent), and 96 are unidentified texts (12 percent) (Dimant 1995, 57-58).

If we are ready to accept the working hypothesis that this collection stems from the library of a sectarian group, we should be able to import some relevant insights from other sectarian milieus and apply them to the Qumran situation. A general question we could address is: How selective are the criteria applied by a group that has so strong a concern, as the Qumran community apparently did, regarding its various ideological boundaries?

If we take a cross-cultural look at similar cases, we notice that among the different works copied in the codices of the Nag Hammadi collection, there are some Gnostic editions of early Christian (e.g., the Gospel of Thomas) or even originally Jewish ("Sethian") texts (e.g., Melkizedek), a certain number of Hermetic texts (e.g., the Discourse on the Eighth and Ninth), and even an excerpt of Plato's *Republic* (588A-589B). Nevertheless, the main content and the overall outlook of this small library are both undeniably "Gnostic," however we define this controversial category (Williams 1996).

Then, when we turn our attention to the collections of the dissident and almost schismatic monastic movements of the Stefanites and the Eustathians in fifteenth-century Ethiopia, we find similar patterns of library organization: approximately one-third of the codices contain biblical and parabiblical texts, one-third are devoted to the special production of each movement (e.g., the Acts of the founder and his main collaborators), and the last third to liturgical and devotional texts inherited from the common stock of Ethiopian literature. In a single exceptional case, we even know how the gift of such an official text as the Book of the Light of the Emperor Zär'a Ya'qob was received, in 1457-58, in the Eustathian library of Däbrä Bizän (Eritrea): all the critical passages concerning the Eustathian dissidence, corresponding to a dozen pages of the printed edition, have been systematically erased (see Bausi 1997, 30-31, 33-34, 48, figs. 1-6). Such censorship is analogous, mutatis mutandis, to the cut of sexually explicit love scenes from some movies broadcast to the members of contemporary "puritan" religious denominations.

When we consider such behavior by some historical "sectarian" movements, we can better understand the nature of the first third of Qumran manuscripts in Dimant's taxonomy. Both the biblical texts and a large number of the nonsectarian works are part of a common heritage that includes not only truly Enochic/Essene writings but also some "external" texts such as Sirach, the book of Daniel, and the second edition of Jeremiah. This Jeremiah edition, incidentally, has a long addition, 33:14-26, representing in Adrian Schenker's opinion a religious recognition of the Maccabean power. I agree with Schenker.

The end of the spectrum of this group of non-Essene inherited works probably occurred around 100 B.C.E. Then the truly sectarian texts began to flow, while such other first-century productions as the book of Judith, the Psalms of Solomon, or the Parables of Enoch were ignored. If we think of the presence of the apparently anomalous Prayer for the Health of King Jonathan (4Q448), an early appraisal for the "Lion of Wrath," the one who will persecute the "Seekers of Smooth Things" (4Q169 3+4 i 6-8), and contrast it with the absence of Judith, a text probably written on behalf of Alexandra Salome (Patterson 2002), the royal patroness of the antagonist Pharisee party (Ilan 2001 argues that the pesherim were responding to such propaganda), we will begin to understand the principles of the organization of the Qumran sectarian library.

Afterthought

As a final and personal afterthought, I would like to note that the sociological category "sect" is a scientific and neutral one, without any pejorative connotation. To apply it to the Qumran case does not automatically lower the Qumran community, placing it among the "freakiest" phenomena of religious history. In my opinion, in spite of the apocalyptic parallels found by James Tabor (1998) and others, the social condition of the Qumran sectarians was quite different from the situation of the Branch Davidians of Waco. If I had to compare the Qumranites to a contemporary religious "sect," I would rather suggest the example of the Jehovah's Witnesses, the members of the Watchtower community, a world-renouncing, puritanical, and millennial movement founded in 1872 by a group of former Millerites and Seventh-Day Adventists (for an ethnographic approach, see Holden 2002). Or better, adopting a suggestion proposed by Joel Marcus (1996), I would resort to the Habad or Lubavitcher movement (for other cross-cultural comparisons, see Regev 2004). After all, who claimed that "[o]ur post-rabbinic world mirrors the pre-rabbinic world of antiquity"?

Complicating the Notion
of an "Enochic Judaism"

John C. Reeves

Gabriele Boccaccini's *Beyond the Essene Hypothesis* (Boccaccini 1998) advances a boldly provocative reconstruction of the social and literary history of second temple Judaism. Fusing the purportedly historical *testimonia* to Jewish sectarianism contained in contemporary apologists like Josephus and Philo with the contents of a number of the legendary, programmatic, and exegetical texts recovered from the caves at Qumran, Boccaccini posits the existence of a so-called Enochic Judaism out of which the Essene movement described in Josephus and Philo later emerged. This alleged Enochic strain of Judaism is so named because he closely identifies it with a distinctive religious ideology he discerns undergirding the contents of what eventually is incorporated within the Ethiopic Book of Enoch or 1 Enoch, more primitive portions of which have been recovered in Aramaic from Qumran. He isolates what he considers to be the defining contours of this particular ideology: a mythopoeic interpretation of early human history, a theodicy at variance with what he portrays as the normative biblical one, a deterministic understanding of the progression of historical events, and a devotion to the antediluvian figure of Enoch as the paramount medium of divine revelation.

Enochic Judaism, according to Boccaccini, competed alongside and against other varieties of second temple Judaism such as Zadokite Judaism and Samaritanism for the allegiance of the populace at large, and eventually gave birth to what Boccaccini terms mainstream Essene Judaism, a social movement out of which and in reaction to which the peculiar sectarian community of Qumran emerged. Long-recognized discrepancies between the contents of the Qumran texts and the reports about the Essenes found in Jewish and classical sources can be resolved by ascribing the descriptions found in the latter works to the broader antecedent mainstream movement, whereas the Qumran evidence attests the existence of a sectarian rift within Essenism which attempts to harmonize the competing "Enochic" and "Zadokite" currents.

Such, *in nuce,* is the wide-ranging thesis of Boccaccini. There are many attractive features to his arguments, not least among which is his elegant solution to the vexing problem, as Norman Golb (1995) put it, of who wrote the Dead Sea Scrolls. Nevertheless, as I see it there are at least three major conceptual difficulties with his broad thesis which will each require some extended rehearsal in the present context.

The first difficulty relates to the generation de novo of an Enochic Judaism (retrojecting Essenism) out of the exceedingly murky religio-historical situation of the postexilic Achaemenid province of Yehud. A second problem is his overly positivistic reading of Hellenistic and Roman era Jewish Enochic literature through the restrictive and distorting lens of one post-Christian expropriation and arrangement of this material. The third and perhaps most important problem involves his uncritical acceptance of the category Essene as a meaningful label for actual religious behavior within the Judaism of the late second temple era.

a. Basing himself almost exclusively on the literary witnesses recovered from Qumran, Boccaccini confidently constructs an Enochic Judaism as a distinct ideological movement which emerges within the second temple period of Jewish history. It arises in conscious opposition to what he labels Zadokite Judaism, another construction, which he defines as the religious program sanctioned by the priestly elite who controlled the Jerusalem temple cultus. Enochic Judaism thus forms a nonconformist priestly tradition (Boccaccini 1998, 71) designed to subvert Zadokite textual and social hegemony.

Boccaccini holds that the library of texts recovered at Qumran can be mapped across these two polarities. Zadokite literature "includes most of the so-called biblical texts [excepting Esther and Daniel] and also apocryphal texts such as the Epistle of Jeremiah, Tobit, and Sirach" (68). Enochic texts, on the other hand, are represented in the Qumranic library by the Aramaic fragments of the Astronomical Book (1 En 72–82), the so-called Book of the Watchers (6–36), and the Aramaic Levi document.

To delineate the interests and claims of each group, Boccaccini isolates a series of characteristic elements or motifs which he argues can serve as markers to locate a particular text within an Enochic or Zadokite literary orbit. According to Boccaccini, Zadokite Judaism operates within the confines of an ordered universe which establishes clearly demarcated boundaries between binary categories like good and evil, holy and ordinary, and pure and impure. Disruptive or destructive forces can be controlled or deflected provided these boundaries remain inviolate. The maintenance of these boundaries, and indeed, of the very cosmos itself, is overseen by the Jerusalem priesthood and the rituals performed by them in the temple. By contrast, Enochic Judaism holds that present existence is characterized by cosmic disorder, a disruption occasioned by supernatural forces and agencies acting in rebellion against the creator deity. Evil and impurity lie largely outside human control, and the restoration of a primal harmony must await divine intervention (Boccaccini 1998, 68-74).

Leaving aside for the moment the pertinent question of whether his dual schematic ordering and conceptual appraisal actually do full justice to the multiple ideologies and variegated contents of the Qumran corpus, it should perhaps first be asked whether the physical evidence collected from a single rural encampment in Judea can bear the rhetorical weight with which Boccaccini invests it. Qumran affords us a snapshot view of at least one and perhaps several Jewish textual communities during the late second temple period. Can we legitimately extrapolate from this limited perspective a wide-angle view that will shed light on the ideological currents coursing through all Jewish textual communities for the entire second temple period? Such a wide-angle view would also need to take into account the various regional centers of intellectual culture and their relatively sparse *testimonia* to both literary and behavioral trends and activities. Can we, for example, trace Enochic and/or Zadokite trajectories or tensions among the literary products of Alexandrian Judaism? Or among those, assuming they can be securely identified, of Babylonian Judaism? Or perhaps, most importantly, among that corpus of largely Hebrew-language texts which constitute what will eventually be labeled scriptural, namely, the Tanakh?

We must not forget that the second temple period during which Boccaccini contextualizes his Enochic and Zadokite movements is also the era when Jewish scripturalism emerged as a vital social force. Those texts which eventually became Tanakh were being promulgated, redacted, and shaped at the very same time that Boccaccini claims the Enochic and Zadokite *Tendenzen* were struggling for influence. Given the fairly rigid boundaries governing literacy in ancient Near Eastern societies, it is arguably the very same groups — Zadokites, Enochites, and the like — that were also involved in *this* authorial and editorial process.

Boccaccini is of course cognizant of this cultural development. As stated above, he situates most biblical literature among the Zadokite camp. His classification of biblical texts, however, betrays a kind of uncritical assumption about the age and authority of the Bible in the second temple world, an assumption he rightly criticizes in another place (57), but which he inexplicably reverts to when isolating his Enochic and Zadokite Judaisms. It is a slippage of the kind that Robert Kraft has jocularly labeled the tyranny of canonical consciousness; namely, the common, almost unconscious, yet anachronistic and hence unwarranted retrojection of the later canonical conceptions formed within classical Judaism and Christianity into the then inchoate literary productions of the second temple period.

Boccaccini expends very little effort in trying to connect his alleged movement with the onset of early Jewish scripturalism, a phenomenon which arguably was inaugurated with the mission of Ezra and which eventually achieved dominance over all currents of Judaism that flourished during the Roman period, both in *Eretz Israel* and in the Diaspora. The question which must be asked, it seems to me, is: How does an alleged Enochic Judaism relate to the construction and promulgation of the Pentateuch and other scriptural collections? A simple polarity of Bible versus Enoch, which is what I read Boccaccini to be saying, brushes over some essential issues which need more careful study before being swept aside.

I must confess that despite both the character and the work or content of Enoch showing undeniable connections with Mesopotamian lore (Jansen 1939; Grelot 1958a; 1958b; VanderKam 1984; Reeves 1998), I am very sympathetic to the general tenor, if not always the specific points, of the arguments advanced in the past by Jonathan Smith (1975), Margaret Barker (1980; 1987), and Robert Murray (1985). These points have been most recently revived and solidified by Seth Schwartz (2001). They situate the Enochic legends among the autochthonous mythical lore associated with the royal cultus of the first temple; in other words, the very social circles from which Boccaccini derives his Zadokite group, the supposed adversaries of Enoch.

I agree with Boccaccini that the figure of Enoch and most Enochic literature have deep roots in priestly traditions (Jub 4:25; 7:38-39; 21:10; cf. Stone 1978, 489-90; VanderKam 1984, 185-86), but I suspect they are not as nonconformist as Boccaccini seems to think. I would add that the speculative cosmogonical and cosmological wisdom characteristic of the earliest layers of our extant Enochic sources and which continue to resurface up to a millennium and a half later in medieval Jewish, Christian, and Muslim texts,[1] should be associated with the intermediate redactional stages of the Pentateuchal source labeled by modern source-critics as the Priestly or P source. I suspect that Milik (1976, 30-32) may be brilliantly prescient in his recognition that what we now know as 1 Enoch 6–11 is actually more primitive than and presupposed by Genesis 6:1-4;

1. For an initial cataloguing of these texts, see my *The Recovery of the Enochic Library* (Reeves, forthcoming).

I would even be willing to endorse the Enochic passage as an integral component of an earlier rendition of the Priestly narrative of antediluvian events, and hence of the biblical book of Genesis itself.

b. The book now referred to by scholars as 1 Enoch exists in this integral form only within the Ethiopic scriptural tradition. This is a circumstance which has gone largely unappreciated by most students of second temple and Roman era Jewish literature. Hence I will restate this proposition in a more provocative way: the work referenced by scholars as 1 Enoch is not a Jewish book; rather, the surviving textual evidence indicates it is a Christian compilation. 1 Enoch 1–108 occurs as a textual unit only within the Ethiopic Christian biblical canon. Smaller consecutive portions of what eventually becomes 1 Enoch are extant in several Greek manuscripts, and isolated chapters or citations occur among Greek, Latin, Coptic, and Syriac witnesses, but again only within what are blatantly Christian contexts, the longest of which do not seem to predate the fourth or fifth century C.E.

The 7Q Greek fragments which purportedly stem from an early Greek recension of the Epistle (1 Enoch 91–105) are, in the words of Michael A. Knibb, "too small for any certain identification to be possible" (Knibb 2001, 401). The Akhmim or Panopolis manuscript transmits a recognizable form of 1 Enoch 1:1–32:6, and a duplicate version of 19:3–21:9, together with excerpts from the Gospel and Apocalypse of Peter. The Chester Beatty–Michigan papyrus gives us 97:6–107:3 (sans chap. 105), together with Melito's Homily on the Passion. The Byzantine chronographer George Syncellus (Mosshammer 1984, 11.19; 24.10; 27.8; 34.18) provides four separate quotations from works which he or his source(s) termed "the first book of Enoch about the Watchers," "the word of Enoch," or simply "Enoch's book." Most of these excerpts overlap with what eventually becomes 1 Enoch (6:1–9:4; 8:4–10:14; 15:8–16:1), but one of them is apocryphal.

This latter circumstance is suggestive. When coupled with the similar appearance of Enochic apocrypha at Qumran (Stuckenbruck 2000, 3-7) and the dozens of instances of putative Enochic citations or references to be found within later Jewish, Christian, Gnostic, and Muslim works (e.g., Reeves 2003, 44-52), it serves to remind us that producing books of Enoch was a cottage industry in the Near East during late antiquity and the medieval eras. Were we to take the words of Slavonic Enoch seriously (10:2, 5-7; Vaillant 1952), we could read a different book of Enoch every day for almost an entire year!

It is undeniable that the bulk of the content of what eventually becomes 1 Enoch possesses a Jewish origin. The Aramaic (and arguably Hebrew)[2] frag-

---

2. Note 1Q19, whose true status as either translation of or source for its Aramaic parallel has yet to be satisfactorily resolved.

ments recovered from Qumran indicate this much, even though they do not come anywhere close to mirroring the eventual contents of Ethiopic Enoch. Seven distinct manuscripts preserve various parts of 1 Enoch 1–36, 85–90, and 91–107, and four additional manuscripts relate to 72–82. Multiple copies of other allied compositions, such as the Book of Giants, are also attested (Reeves 1992; Stuckenbruck 1997; 2000; Puech 2001), and it is unclear how they might factor into the creation of an ancient Enochic library.

It seems likely that Enochic apocrypha were a staple of pseudepigraphic forgery even at this early stage. Knibb estimates that perhaps just under one-fifth of the Ethiopic version is represented at Qumran, and then qualifies this assessment by stating that "the Aramaic fragments which have survived are severely damaged; mostly we have to do with quite small pieces of text, and in no case do we have anything approaching an entire column from one of the manuscripts" (Knibb 1978, 2:12). This being the case, I think we need to be wary about ideological reconstructions and especially codicological arrangements which automatically assume that one particular post-Christian editorial scheme should govern our understanding of how physically isolated and scribally distinct portions of the Enochic corpus relate to one another.

The surviving Aramaic fragments provide meager evidence for the primitive joining of one Enochic subdivision to another, namely, the placement of 1 Enoch 1–5 prior to 6–36 or the Book of Watchers (Milik 1976, 4QEn[b] 1 ii lines 1-2 or pl. VI).[3] There is even less compelling evidence for the linkage of the Noah birth story (1 Enoch 106–107) to the final lines of the so-called Epistle (91–105) in 4Q204 (4QEn[c] ar) 5 i fragment a (Milik 1976, pl. XIV; Tov 1993a, PAM 43.202). Further assumptions or pronouncements about the placement of the other Enoch subdivisions (e.g., Similitudes, 1 Enoch 37–71) or even apocrypha (e.g., Book of Giants) are completely speculative.

Ideological reconstructions such as those advanced by Boccaccini need to acknowledge the complicated shape of the reception history of Enochic literature when formulating their hypotheses about its intellectual background and interests. For example, it is only within this external context that one can speak intelligibly of an alleged Enochic pentateuch which was supposedly designed to subvert its Mosaic rival. Crucial components like the Similitudes (i.e., 37–71) are nowhere attested in second temple literature and should probably be banished henceforth from such discussions.

c. A final soft point in Boccaccini's construction of an Enochic Judaism

---

3. Note, however, that line 1 contains only the bottom stroke(s) of one or two letters (read by Milik and those following him as ומי[']), which is hardly enough to guarantee that this line indeed concluded with what corresponds in later versions to 1 En 5!

involves his uncritical embrace of the existence of a sect called Essenes among the expressions of Judaism during the Hellenistic and Roman eras. He assigns writings purportedly advocating the ideology of the Enochic party, in effect practically all of the nonbiblical writings recovered from the caves at Qumran, to the mysterious Jewish sect termed Essenes, discussed by Philo, Josephus, and other pagan and Christian authorities (Adam and Burchard 1972). The category Essene, invariably conflated with its presumed historical referent, forms a crucial component of Boccaccini's argument. A close analysis of the most important Greek and Latin sources describing this group constitutes the first major section of his book (Boccaccini 1998, 21-49). He repeatedly invokes these testimonies as touchstones for assessing the alleged Enochic and/or Essenic propensities of various apocryphal and pseudepigraphic works. On the basis of these reports, together with a selective utilization of information gleaned from the Dead Sea Scrolls, he confidently delineates the historical and ideological vicissitudes of a religious trajectory within second temple Judaism, which he terms mainstream Essenism. Mainstream Essenism, according to Boccaccini, was the cultural locus for the expression of Enochic Judaism.

Since the initial decade of the scholarly study of the Dead Sea Scrolls, it has been largely accepted as a scholarly axiom that these recovered writings are to be associated in some fashion with the Essenes. The so-called Essene Hypothesis, signaled in Boccaccini's title, holds that the community apparently resident at Qumran and presumably responsible for generating and depositing the scrolls found near that site, should be identified with the Jewish sect of the Essenes mentioned in the Greek and Latin sources. Boccaccini endorses this suggested correlation as compelling and conclusive (165). A number of comparative studies of the Qumran texts alongside the classical reports about Essenes have isolated some admittedly intriguing correspondences between the two groups of texts, but they have also identified a number of important differences. There is no need to list those items here, since the standard discussions of the Qumran site and its associated scrolls treat this topic in some detail.

Accordingly, most scholars who accept this correlation have devised ingenious ways to argue an Essene identity for the Qumran sect despite these discrepancies, and Boccaccini is no exception. For him the Qumran writings should be associated with an internal schism within mainstream Essenism which led to the establishment of a dissident outpost of Essene sectaries in the desert of Judea. Josephus and Philo do not speak of the desert site at Qumran because they are providing a generic portrait of mainstream Essenism. Conversely, Qumran does not correspond in all particulars with the descriptions supplied in the Greek and Latin sources because its library allegedly attests to a small and ultimately ineffectual splinter movement within mainstream

Essenism, a fissure effected by the so-called Teacher of Righteousness and his small band of followers.

Leaving aside for the moment the writings from Qumran and their posited affinities with one or more of the religious groups supposedly operative in second temple Judaism, I think a pertinent question worth posing is whether in fact there was any such thing as an Essene sect. I want to be perfectly clear, and hence I will proceed deliberately. I am not questioning the notion of the Greco-Latin semantic marker "Essene," one which when wielded by writers like Josephus, Philo, or Pliny served to invoke a very specific network of ideas and cultural competencies within the minds of a discerning imperial readership. That notion or category is undeniably present and meaningful when read within its proper ethnographic context. I am much less confident, however, about whether the label Essene corresponded in point of fact to an actual party, group, or movement within second temple Jewish society. There are several factors here which prompt my skepticism.

1. There is not a single extant Palestinian or Syro-Mesopotamian Jewish writing authored in either Hebrew or Aramaic during the Achaemenid, Hellenistic, Roman, Byzantine, or Sassanian periods which mentions an Essene sect, categorizes a tradition or practice as Essene, or employs the label Essene in a recognizable way.

2. A superficial perusal of the table of contents of a comprehensive collection of the classical (i.e., Greek and Latin) descriptions of the Jewish sect of the Essenes can leave an unwary reader with the mistaken impression that the primary sources for a scholastic reconstruction of Essene ideology are manifold and grounded on an extensive series of empirical observations and experiences. In actual fact, though, it is extremely improbable that any of the extant tradents who speak of a Jewish sect of Essenes, including our earliest authorities, Philo and Josephus, write on the basis of such knowledge.

3. Finally, and more speculatively, I would like to suggest that modern scholars have been unduly credulous about the actual existence of a Jewish Essene sect. Since the era of Hecataeus and Herodotus, a popular *Tendenz* in classical ethnography was the description of a number of elite or secretive castes of religious and/or intellectual functionaries supposedly flourishing among various barbarian peoples who inhabited the fringes of the Greco-Roman *oikoumenē*.

Prominent examples of such castes would be the Druids of Gaul and ancient Celtic society, the magi of Persia, the Chaldeans of Mesopotamia, and the so-called naked philosophers, or gymnosophists, of India. At times they dwell interspersed among their respective *ethnoi;* but sometimes they exist in segregated isolation from their respective societies, and there are occasionally instances of groups who can be found in the far reaches of the inhabited world where they constitute utopian conventicles (Mendels 1979). Regardless of their alleged physical location within or apart from their societies, Greek and Latin accounts about these groups exhibit a general family resemblance: members of these groups typically experience a marvelous longevity of life, they are dedicated to lives of piety and holiness, they are cultural repositories of priestly and philosophical wisdom, and they are adept in a number of useful arts, crafts, and technologies, among which the oracular sciences are prominently numbered. The Essenes and Philo's Therapeutae are clearly marketed by their publicists as the Jewish representatives of this ethnological trope.

Students of early Christian and medieval Muslim heresiography and historiography are thoroughly familiar with this literary tactic. The premodern historians of these religions will sometimes fabricate artificial sects in order to provide a communal framework for certain disreputable ideas or practices, or invent fictive heresiarchs so as to assign blame for critical disputes and schisms. One thinks of shadowy groups or figures like the Simonians, the Sethians, Dustai, and Ebionites. The Qur'ānic *Ṣābi'ūn* (Q 2:62; 5:69; 22:17) can be fit within this scheme. Medieval Muslim heresiography constructs the Barahima, a sect which supposedly denied the validity of prophecy, and the Jewish Maghariyya, "so called," Qirqisānī says, "because their writings were found in a cave" (1939-43, vol. 1, 12.1; Wasserstrom 1998, 127-54; Reeves 1999, 161-62).

Utopian currents are visible as well in these later literatures. The wicked Nimrod becomes adept in and an apostle of magical mysteries after his three-year sojourn on the eastern shore of Okeanos among the people of Yonton, the fourth son of Noah (Ri 1987, 208-17; Gero 1980, 321-30). According to the hermit Zosimus, the prophet Jeremiah's Rechabites are able to maintain their strict regimen in the guise of Christian monks living in a blessed land located at the ends of the earth (Charlesworth 1982).

One wonders, then, how much credence should be granted such analogous *testimonia* about the formal existence of a pietist elite within second temple Jewry. I would counsel, very little. To be sure, I would in no way deny that individual pietists were active within or at the margins of Jewish society. I am questioning only the existential status of a distinctive social aggregate bearing the name Essene. To sharpen this point and to urge caution among those who would blithely accept the historicity of a Jewish Essene sect solely on the basis of one or more literary source(s), I introduce here for consideration a series of semi-anthropological, descriptive excerpts taken from a medieval account about a Jewish group, allegedly to be found somewhere east of Palestine, who are most frequently called the *beney Mosheh* (Arabic *banū Mūsa*) or "the people of Moses" (Jellinek 1853-77, 2:103-5; 3:9-11; 5:18-20; 6:15-16; Albeck 1940, 124; Ox-

John C. Reeves

ford Bodl. Ms. Opp. 603, 41b-42a; Shahrastânî 1951-55, 1:507; Qazwīnī *apud* Wüstenfeld 1848-49, 2:18). The account, which enjoyed great popularity in medieval folkloristic and apocalyptic collections, belongs among a group of writings associated with the mysterious figure of Eldad ha-Dani, a traveling messianic agitator (Epstein *apud* Habermann 1949-56, 1:1-211, 357-90; Neubauer 1888-89; Shochat 1971) of the eighth or ninth century:

> the levitical *beney Mosheh:* they are encamped east of the River Sa(m)bat-yon . . . no unclean animal or bird or creeping thing can be found among them; they have with them (only) their flocks and cattle. Six springs are there whose waters they have collected into a pool which they constructed, and they irrigate their land from the pool. All types of pure fish flourish in it (the pool), and by the springs and the pool flourish all kinds of pure waterfowl. They enjoy all kinds of fruits: (the fertility of the land is such that) whoever plants one seed harvests a hundredfold. They are religiously observant, each of them learned in Torah, Bible, Mishnah, and Aggadah. They are "pure pietists" (טהורים חסידים). None of them ever swears a false oath. They live to be one hundred and twenty years old, and a son or daughter never dies during the lifespan of their father: they witness the succession of three or four generations. They construct their own houses and do their own sowing and harvesting because they have no slaves or maidservants. They never lock their doors at night. A very small child might go and tend their cattle for a number of days, and no one will be in the least bit anxious, for there are no thieves or dangerous wild animals or pests, and there are no demons or anything that might cause harm. Because they are holy and persist in the sanctity revealed by our teacher Moses, He (God) has granted all this to them and chosen them . . . and they will remain there until the time of the Eschaton. (Yassif 2001, 220-21)

I would suggest that it might prove instructive to begin situating and studying the classical accounts about the Essenes in tandem with the recurrent testimonies and traditions we find in late antique and medieval Jewish, Christian, and Muslim sources about utopian pietist groups like the *beney Mosheh,* the Rechabites, and the Maghariyya. Zeev Safrai (1979) has already pointed to some interesting connections linking the biblical and rabbinic discussions of the adherents of Yehonadab b. Rekhab with behavioral and doctrinal aspects of the Essene and Qumran sects. Patristic sources, Nilus of Ankara, the Byzantine *Suda,* probe the Essene-Rechabite axis even further, and there are versions of the Eldad ha-Dani legend which link the Rechabites with the *beney Mosheh* (Friedlaender 1910-11).

It does not require a trained eye to see that there exist a number of conceptual and thematic similarities between the descriptions provided by classical sources of the Essenes, or barbarian utopian communities, and that of Eldad ha-Dani of the people of Moses. Yet to my knowledge no responsible post-Enlightenment thinker has ever seriously maintained that the latter group really existed, or sought to attribute any Jewish literature to their creative pens. Why then should the Essenes be so uncritically privileged?

Enoch, Moses, and the Essenes

William Adler

The problem that inspired Gabriele Boccaccini's book is well-known, namely, the much discussed distinction between the descriptions of the Essenes provided by ancient witnesses and the self-representation of the Qumran community found in the scrolls themselves. While not abandoning what he calls the Essene Hypothesis, he urges scholars to reexamine their approach to the subject and to look at the Qumran community within the broader pluralistic context of early Judaism.[1]

I would like to begin by commending Boccaccini for writing a book that I consider one of the most lucid recent works on the Dead Sea Scrolls. The book owes its clarity in large part to a useful distinction that the author draws at the very outset of his discussion. He distinguishes between two forms of analysis: what he calls "systemic analysis" and "historiographical analysis." Applied to the study of the Dead Sea Scrolls, historiographical analysis encompasses the testimony about the Essenes from ancient witnesses like Josephus, Philo, and Pliny. By mentioning communities, parties, or documents whose existence might otherwise be unknown from primary documentary evidence, these witnesses enable us to fill in gaps in our knowledge of early Judaism. But there are limitations as well. Modern historians make it their business to draw connections and relationships between communities and documents. Trying to tease

1. As an aside, I ask Boccaccini's forgiveness in continuing to use the nomenclature "early Judaism" and not "middle Judaism" (Boccaccini 1991). Certain habits are hard to dislodge. But let me assure everyone that whether it is "early" or "middle," we're both talking about the same thing.

this kind of informational evidence out of a Josephus or Philo is a thankless undertaking, so the author wisely decides upon another course: Only ask from these sources what they are willing to tell you.

Systemic analysis proceeds in a different way. Here one takes the relevant documents and attempts to analyze and group them according to their system of thought. If the connections are tight enough and it is possible to date them, then it might even be possible to establish a genetic relationship, as Boccaccini does so effectively in his book. It might even be possible, with this sort of analysis, to reconstruct the historical stages in the development of a religious community and the conflicts and tensions within it. But systemic analysis, taken alone, has its own inadequacies, which the author does well to point out. Here is what he has to say on the subject:

> Through systemic analysis, we group the documents according to their different systems of thought, thus identifying and describing a certain number of middle Judaisms. But documents are often silent about the historical and sociological context of the group behind the author(s). . . . In addition, a large quantity of documents surviving from one group may make the ideological system of that group seem more prevalent than actually was the case, and therefore modern interpreters may overestimate it, while they underestimate other systems because of the lack of or loss of their documents. (Boccaccini 1998, 10)

This is a valuable observation, and I very much endorse Boccaccini's decision to keep the two approaches, historiographic and systemic, separate and distinct. It makes for pleasurable reading and it keeps the arguments clean. Only at the very end of the work does the author correlate the findings of the two analytical methods to determine if the results generated actually converge.

I turn now to the author's major arguments. In his historiographical analysis Boccaccini makes what seems to me the completely sound assertion that Essenism was fairly widespread and influential and not entirely uniform. The Qumran community represented only a minority group within the larger Essene movement. Greek and Roman writers focused on this community simply because their extreme behavior satisfied an interest, characteristic of the Hellenistic period, in the eccentric customs of Eastern peoples. On the other hand, Jewish writers like Philo and Josephus express little interest in this fringe sect, because their intentions are to present the Essenes as a wider, more mainstream movement in Palestinian Judaism. This observation seems completely reasonable and intuitive. What religious or political group can impose an ironclad uniformity on its members?

In his systemic analysis of the relevant documents from Qumran, Boccaccini sets forth a complex argument about the taxonomy of the Qumran documents, the development of their sectarian ideology, and the way in which the community created and preserved its library. While allowing that the Qumran documents are not homogenous, he argues that there is an underlying "generative idea," namely, the superhuman origin of evil, that makes it possible to link these texts together. This idea, he argues, arose out of a conflict in Jewish priestly circles between pro- and anti-Zadokite factions. But while this concept remains the ideological constant, older documents, like the books of Enoch, expressed it in a less sectarian, exclusivistic way. As a schismatic group became progressively estranged from the parent community (what the author calls Enochic Judaism), it began to express this doctrine in more radical terms. In the author's view this development accounts for several peculiarities in the Qumran library. The texts from Qumran, he contends, must be read diachronically. On the one hand, the Qumran sectarians preserved the older documents, like the books of Enoch, because they understood them as foundational and legitimizing texts attesting the prehistory of their group. But sources of their own day were more rigorously scrutinized for their ideological purity.

At the end of his investigation Boccaccini returns to the impasse that inspired his study. This is the problem that has bedeviled scholarship since the scrolls were discovered. How can we reconcile ancient historiography about the Essenes with the witness of the scrolls themselves? He grants what is by now an uncontested point: namely, that the description of the Essenes provided by Philo and Josephus is not entirely consistent with the self-representation of the Qumran sectarians. The reason for this divergence, he argues, can be explained in light of the development of the group itself. What Josephus and Philo describe are the doctrines of the more moderate parent group (what Boccaccini calls Enochic Judaism), not the fringe group that came to settle in Qumran.

In concluding my remarks, I would like to pose a few questions for discussion.

1. My first question concerns what Boccaccini calls the generative idea of Essenism or Enochic Judaism, namely, the superhuman origin of evil. He does a very creditable job in tracing both the origin of this idea in the disputes with the Zadokite priesthood and its subsequent evolution and refinement within the Essene community. At the end of the book he examines how this idea outlived the group itself. But may I respectfully question his assertions that this idea represents the unique contribution of Essenism, and that it is the inspiration for Christian and quasi-Christian thinking from Augustine to the Branch Davidians (190-91)? One could make this case very persuasively for the Manichees. Like the Essenes of Qumran, they were radical dualists, knew and

read the Enoch literature, and even considered parts of it canonical. But after that the lines of influence become increasingly attenuated. Exclusivism and the attribution of evil to superhuman agency are natural religious impulses, especially in embattled sectarian communities, and I doubt whether such groups ever needed much intellectual prodding to come up with it.

2. I would also like to ask from Boccaccini precisely in what sense he uses the term "Enochic Judaism." If the term is simply one that the author employs to describe the dualism of the Essene parent group, I have no serious objection to that. But it seems clear that by this term he wanted to suggest that the books of Enoch were both a foundational document for the Essene movement and a statement of its alienation from the Zadokite priesthood. If this is so, I think we need to explain why there was not a more vigorous discussion of the meaning and significance of this work within and without the Essene community. Boccaccini maintains that the Qumran community regarded Enoch as in some sense legitimizing and that it opposed another branch of Enochic Judaism, reflected in the Epistle of Enoch and the Testaments of the Twelve Patriarchs. I think he makes a good case that the Qumran redaction of the Enochic literature has an ideological basis, but if all of this is correct, one might have expected to find a more lively controversy and direct discussion of the meaning of the work within the Qumran literature itself.

The same observation holds true for the status of Enoch outside of the Qumran community. The work is occasionally mentioned in other documents, like the Testaments of the Twelve Patriarchs. It is even possible that other Jewish writings of the period, among them Ben Sira, wage a silent polemic against it. But Philo and Josephus, our principal Jewish witnesses, are another matter. They know that the Essenes read secret books, and there are instances in which their descriptions of Essene practices correspond with portions of Enoch. But neither writer says anything about Enoch or his writings in their discussion of the Essenes, or at all. They do assert, however, that the Essenes honored Moses. Despite the author's best efforts to explain the problem, I still find their testimony discordant with Boccaccini's assertions about the centrality of the Enoch literature.

These questions should in no way detract, however, from Boccaccini's highly original and ambitious reconstruction of the Essene movement and its prehistory. Before reading his book, I knew very little about the theoretical roots of systemic analysis. But if any subject cries out for this kind of approach, it is the Essenes, Qumran, and the Dead Sea Scrolls. By applying this method, Boccaccini has gotten behind the ancient sources to reveal a fascinating and formative stage in the development of Jewish pluralism, especially as it involves conflicts over priesthood and authority in Judaism of the third and second centuries B.C.E.

Too Far Beyond the Essene Hypothesis?

James C. VanderKam

In *Beyond the Essene Hypothesis* Gabriele Boccaccini attempts to place the Qumran community and the texts found in its library in a larger and intellectually more satisfactory context than scholars have proposed to date. He sets for himself the ambitious agenda of describing the two major traditions in second temple Judaism, the Zadokite and the Enochic brands of Judaism, with a special focus on the latter. This Enochic Judaism is in his view the type of Judaism Josephus and Philo associated with the name Essene and depicted in considerable detail in their writings. Qumran, it turns out, was a splinter group that broke away from the larger Essene movement. The significance of the word "Beyond" in the title of his book is that the theory presented in it, while resting on the results of the work of other scholars, adds to the familiar Essene theory about the Qumranites by situating it within this larger Enochic/Essene hypothesis.

The method Boccaccini has chosen to approach his subject is to combine historiographical analysis with systemic analysis. The results obtained from the two types of analysis, which are done separately, are then compared in the third section of the book. Historiographical analysis involves study of what the ancient sources say about the Essenes. The Jewish sources are Josephus and Philo, and the non-Jewish ones are principally Pliny and Dio. Boccaccini maintains that Josephus and Philo describe a larger group (about 4,000 members) that was not radically segregated from the rest of Jewish society but lived among other Jews. The non-Jewish writers deal with a much different phenomenon — the Qumran community, which was isolated and living in a single place on the shores of the Dead Sea.

Systemic analysis "studies groups, and maps out the ideological remains of middle Judaisms: the documents" (Boccaccini 1998, 10). This section, which occupies about one-half of the book, derives from the texts in the Qumran library an overview of the theological or ideological development of Enochic Judaism. Boccaccini divides the works from the Qumran library into nonsectarian and sectarian for this purpose. In the sectarian texts he finds a cosmic dualism, predeterminism, an identification of impurity with evil, and a picture of a community apart. This unique combination arose at the end of a long history that can be traced in the texts. The earliest phases of that history lie primarily though not exclusively in one of the two Judaisms of the second temple period. Those two Judaisms are the Zadokite and the Enochic brands. The Zadokite literature turns out to be virtually everything that eventually made its way into the Hebrew Bible (excluding later works such as Daniel and Esther) and a few others (e.g., Sirach); all of this is Zadokite in the sense that it underwent a Zadokite revision at some time early in the second temple era (68). There is no evidence that these texts underwent a sectarian revision at Qumran, apart from an addition to Sirach 15:14. The earliest Enochic texts, and here the central one is the Book of the Watchers, show a markedly different approach. Boccaccini considers it a literature that arose from a nonconformist priestly tradition. The Zadokite literature (e.g., Gen 1) sets forth a teaching about creational bounds that were not to be transgressed, about the temple as representing the cosmos, about the goodness of creation, and about priestly control of an uncorrupted order. "The ideology of the authors of the Enoch documents directly opposed that of the Zadokites. The catalyst was a particular concept of the origin of evil that portrayed a group of rebellious angels as ultimately responsible for the spread of evil and impurity on the earth" (72). For the authors of the Enochic tradition the original order cannot be restored; the only hope is for a decisive intervention by God.

Boccaccini adds a comment about a phenomenon other scholars have also noted — the "Enochians completely ignore the Mosaic torah and the Jerusalem temple, that is, the two tenets of the order of the universe. In addition, the attribution to Enoch of priestly characteristics suggests the existence of a pure prediluvian, and pre-fall, priesthood and disrupts the foundations of the Zadokite priesthood, which claimed its origin in Aaron at the time of the exodus, in an age that, for the Enochians, was already corrupted after the angelic sin and the flood" (74). Here the Aramaic Levi, with its focus on Leah and Jacob's third son, is also brought into the picture. Enochic Judaism springs from anti-Zadokite priestly circles.

The early period was followed by a formative age best glimpsed from the Dream Visions in 1 Enoch 83–90, Daniel, Jubilees, the Temple Scroll, the Proto-

Epistle of Enoch (that is, the Epistle of Enoch less 94:6–104:6), and 4QMMT. These texts manifest interesting developments within both traditions (or at least the influence of the Zadokite on the Enochian), but especially in the Enochic one. Jubilees, for example, combines the principal tenets of Enochic Judaism with one of the major features of the Zadokite tradition — the Mosaic torah. Furthermore, its author identifies impurity with evil and, at least on Boccaccini's reading, claims the world was purified after the flood (Jub 5:12 is supposed to support this conclusion). In this general context Boccaccini claims that the early Maccabees were the ones who succeeded in making the Zadokite torah the torah of all Jews. Advocates of Enochic Judaism, people who addressed the entire Jewish nation, had hopes at this time that with the demise of the Zadokites they would become the dominant force in Jewish thought and practice; but this was not to be the case. The Proto-Epistle of Enoch shows that by this time Enochic Judaism was a minority and its adherents were now embracing a theory of double election.

Boccaccini views the schism between Enochic Judaism and Qumran through the lens of the Damascus Document, which bears witness to the existence of a special group, an elite segment of Enochic Judaism, gathered around the Teacher of Righteousness. They could thus be termed sectarians, and they believed they took the place of Israel as the elect of God. The dates of the copies of Enochic writings in the Qumran library show a decreasing interest in the older Enochic books which were not copied at a later time in the occupation of the site; furthermore, the library lacks altogether the later literary efforts of Enochic Judaism such as the full Epistle of Enoch, the Testaments of the Twelve Patriarchs, and the Similitudes. Some sort of break seems to have occurred.

The sectarian works from Qumran also demonstrate that the members of this small, withdrawn body were hostile to people they regarded as traitors within the larger Enochic movement. The Teacher of Righteousness had called for a more radical separation from Israel and the temple, and few within the movement responded favorably to his call. Dualism became Qumran's answer to its members' progressive isolation from others. Nevertheless, by isolating themselves at Khirbet Qumran they also denied themselves virtually any possibility of influencing larger segments of society. The major cause of the disagreement between Enochic Judaism and Qumran was the latter's denial of angelic and human freedom, points affirmed by Enochic Judaism.

After this rapid survey of Boccaccini's truly interesting and impressive accomplishment in the book, let me highlight several points that I found to be the strengths of *Beyond the Essene Hypothesis*. After making these positive statements, I will raise a few objections to some of the conclusions and claims in the book.

First, I find it refreshing, in a time when parts of verses are the subjects of learned essays and a paragraph can be the subject of entire tomes, to find an author who tackles a large body, or rather bodies, of literature and goes to work uncovering the historical and ideological connections between them. Not only is the task a large one to cover in 200 pages, but the approach Boccaccini takes is also intriguing. Building upon the work of Paolo Sacchi and others, including his own earlier book *Middle Judaism* (Boccaccini 1991), Boccaccini writes a history of ideas, a study of what one might call the systematic (or not so systematic) theologies that lie in each of the works examined. How did one ancient author expand upon or otherwise alter the ideas found in an earlier work? The ideological trajectories he presents can be helpful in placing the different texts of second temple Judaism in their place on a map of Jewish thought.

Second, the book serves well in putting Qumran within realistic bounds. Despite the massive interest its library has attracted in the last fifty years and the virtually innumerable publications on it, the group itself must have been small and nonrepresentative. In his dealing with the Dead Sea Scrolls and in his efforts to move beyond the currently regnant hypothesis, Boccaccini also does not so much oppose the work of most scholars as begin with it and attempt to do more.

While many additional positive points could be said about his book, there are reservations and disagreements that I would like to raise for discussion. First I will mention a few relatively minor ones, and then move to some more basic questions.

Minor Matters

First, Boccaccini claims that "[e]ven today, for many scholars, and certainly for the general public of non-specialists, the people of Qumran are not only members of an Essene community — they are the Essenes . . . the terms 'Essene' and 'Qumranic' have become virtually interchangeable" (Boccaccini 1998, 7). This is puzzling insofar as it includes "many scholars"; I wonder who those scholars are who supposedly have missed the rather obvious point that there were about 4,000 Essenes and if Qumran could accommodate no more than about 200 at most, there must have been a lot of Essenes who were not at Qumran. The distinction between the Essene party and the Qumran branch of it may not always receive the attention it deserves, but I doubt the charge that many scholars identify the two is true. Furthermore, I doubt we needed the Groningen Hypothesis, with its thesis about multiple Wicked Priests, to bring home to us that there was a distinction between the larger Essene party and the Qumran group.

Second, I found the term "Zadokite" a little too malleable for comfort. The word is used appropriately to refer to the dominant priestly clan and to whatever may have been associated with them. But Boccaccini uses it more broadly to refer to the non-Enochic Judaism of the second temple period, a type of Judaism whose views are expressed in the torah and whose interests centered around the temple. That may be accurate, although it is difficult to be sure of much in the Persian and early Hellenistic periods. His definition of Zadokite literature illustrates the problem: it includes nearly all the texts that eventually made their way into the Hebrew Bible (excluding late books such as Daniel and Esther), with works such as the Letter of Jeremiah, Tobit, and Sirach. They are Zadokite in the sense that they were "collected, edited, and transmitted" by temple authorities (68). I wonder whether it would not be better to speak of the common heritage of almost all Jews at this time rather than to put the tag "Zadokite" on all of this literature which is quite diverse in content. I suspect that Enochic Judaism, too, embraced most of the books that became the Hebrew Bible, even if its earlier adherents gave less prominence to Moses (whose writings they did use) and questioned (at least at times) the purity of the temple cult in Jerusalem.

More Substantive Issues

First, the major problem I have with Boccaccini's case that Enochic Judaism equals Essenism (note his formulation: "If the Enochians were not Essenes, they were their twin" [170]) is that the information derived from our sources of information about the Essenes does not fit all that well with what we find in the Enochic texts. I am not denying that there are points of agreement; Boccaccini has highlighted a number of these. The root problem is that the heart of Enochic Judaism — the story about the angels who sinned (a tale that appears in several forms) and thus about a supernatural source of sin — receives no mention in Josephus's and Philo's lengthy accounts of the Essenes and their beliefs. These two authors know about the angel story and deal with it in their writings, but they do not discuss it in connection with the Essenes and certainly do not tell us it was a central Essene belief. True, Josephus does inform us that the Essenes were interested in the writings of the ancients, but he does not mention Enoch in such contexts. The sources for the Essenes emphasize their predestinarian views and their unusual way of life. We do find predestinarian statements in Enochic texts, but the peculiar Essene ways of conducting their lives receive no mention in the Enoch texts. Boccaccini is, of course, aware of this problem and attempts to deal with it. He does succeed in isolating some noteworthy examples, such as the correspondence between teachings of the Book of the Watchers and aspects of what Josephus says about the Essene view of the afterlife. However, as we know, the Essene beliefs in this regard are hotly debated because of a discrepancy in the sources. Despite Boccaccini's valiant efforts, I found this essential part of the argument unconvincing. It seems rather that Josephus and Philo, in talking about Essenes, described a group that shared a number of traits with the Enochians but was not identical with them.

A second substantive objection has to do with whether the essence of Enochic Judaism, if it really was a single trajectory, is properly depicted in *Beyond the Essene Hypothesis*. We may agree that the angel story, in its multiple forms, is central to Enochic Judaism, especially as it comes to expression in the Book of the Watchers. It seems less essential in other Enochic texts such as the Astronomical Book and Dream Visions (where the angel story certainly does not account for the origin of evil); the same may be said about the Epistle of Enoch, whatever its original form may have been, and the subsequent works Boccaccini places in this tradition (e.g., Jubilees). It appears prominently in several of the later texts, but not as centrally as in the Book of the Watchers. Perhaps a more central teaching in these books is that terrible consequences follow from violating the created orders and boundaries, although ironically Boccaccini considers this a distinctive Zadokite doctrine.

Third, I did not find the explanation for Qumran origins very convincing. For Boccaccini the Qumran group separated not so much from the Jewish nation in general as from the Essene movement in particular. It is true that some sectarian works mention splits that seem to have taken place within the community, but they also bear witness to conflicts with authorities such as the Wicked Priest, who certainly does not seem to have been an Enochian/Essene. Also, was the central problem only that the Teacher of Righteousness advocated a stricter separation from others as a corollary of his dualistic theology, a separation that only a few accepted? Or did he have fundamental halakhic differences with those in control of the temple, and did he underscore his views with a claim for his own unique authority? Such matters, it seems to me, are more likely to have been the cause for the move of his group into a form of exile. Whether that exile under the leadership of the Teacher was to Qumran is another question to which we have no answer.

There is much more to discuss (e.g., the impurity = sin issue), but it is more appropriate to thank Gabriele Boccaccini at this point for writing a stimulating book and for giving even those of us who are happy with the Essene Hypothesis much to ponder.

Some Remarks on the Partings of the Ways

Benjamin G. Wright III

Gabriele Boccaccini's *Beyond the Essene Hypothesis: The Parting of the Ways between Qumran and Enochic Judaism* is an ambitious undertaking. It proposes nothing less than the resolution of several fundamental issues that lie at the heart of identifying the group who lived at Qumran and used the collection of scrolls discovered in the nearby caves. In short, Boccaccini's solution is to propose that the Qumran community was a sectarian group who separated from a larger, more mainstream movement within Judaism that he calls Enochic and that ancient sources called Essene. Who and what that larger, more mainstream movement was and why the Qumran community broke away from it are the central foci of Boccaccini's study.

His method is largely twofold. He first looks at the ancient sources that speak about the Essenes in order to see exactly what they thought this movement was about (historiographical analysis). Second, he examines the textual remains themselves to see what clues they give about the groups who produced them (systemic analysis). He then combines these two separate analytical approaches to construct the larger picture that he seeks.

Generally this approach seems to work well. When he looks at the ancient sources that provide evidence about Essenism, Boccaccini concludes that there must have been two "orders" of Essenes. One was a "widespread movement of communities in Palestine, whose complexity was well known by Jewish authors, such as Philo and Josephus" (Boccaccini 1998, 47). The other was a particular Essene settlement by the Dead Sea "with such peculiar characteristics as to draw attention and curiosity of non-Jewish authors, such as Pliny and Dio" (47).

Boccaccini's subsequent analysis of the texts leads him to the conclusion that the group at Qumran withdrew from Jewish society after the Maccabean crisis. This isolation resulted not from conflict and opposition with the temple authorities in Jerusalem, as has often been suggested, but as the consequence of an internal crisis within Enochic/Essene Judaism precipitated by the anonymous "teacher of righteousness" and his followers whose criticisms were directed against the broader Enochic movement.

Such a conclusion in and of itself is not revelatory. Several scholars have suggested that the Qumran community represents a small sectarian group of Essenes who left a larger Essene parent movement (Davies 1992a; García Martínez and Trebolle Barrera 1995). But Boccaccini's analysis is not simply intended to provide more substantive argumentation for such a conclusion. He wants to step back and look at the larger social and theological matrix of second temple Judaism with an eye toward explicating the origins and development of what he calls Enochic/Essene Judaism. By understanding the growth of the parent movement we learn more about the origins and nature of the community that removed itself to Qumran.

It may be helpful at the outset to summarize what Boccaccini concludes about his Enochic movement before proceeding to the particular questions his arguments raise.

According to Boccaccini, Enochic Judaism was a "nonconformist priestly tradition" that stood diametrically opposed to the other major priestly tradition, Zadokite Judaism, which held control of the temple cult up to the Maccabean period. The origins of both groups can be traced to the biblical book of Ezekiel, but they produced different literatures and were governed by different theological understandings of the world. Zadokite literature included almost all of what we now know as biblical literature, except for Esther and Daniel. In addition, apocryphal texts such as the Epistle of Jeremiah, Tobit, and Sirach stem from Zadokite Judaism (Boccaccini 1998, 68). For the Zadokites the Jerusalem temple "was a visual representation of the cosmos itself" (72); both were ordered and uncorrupted. The Zadokites claimed to be the custodians of this divinely created order.

Enochic ideology, on the other hand, was directly opposite that of the Zadokites. Enochic Judaism held to a view that the world had been and was still corrupted by the original sin of the angels/Watchers who had transgressed the boundary between the heavens and the earth, had sexual intercourse and offspring with human women, and subsequently divulged secret heavenly knowledge to human beings. This corruption was not restored after the flood as the Zadokite worldview maintained, but it continued in the form of evil spirits which were the souls of the offspring of those illegitimate sexual unions killed in the deluge. There was, as a result, no way for human beings to stem the tide of evil and impurity in the world, and the holy and the profane could not be kept separate as the Zadokites understood themselves doing in the temple ritual and cult. Only intervention by God could rectify this situation.

Enochic Judaism drew its assessment of the cosmic condition from a literature that completely differed from that of the Zadokites. They "completely ignore" the Mosaic torah of the Zadokites and rely on works like 1 Enoch and Aramaic Levi which articulate this type of worldview. Boccaccini dates the origins and separation between Zadokite Judaism and Enochic Judaism in the fourth or third century B.C.E. But the essential understanding for Boccaccini is that "Enochic Judaism arose out of anti-Zadokite priestly circles that opposed the power of the priestly Zadokite establishment" (77).

Enochic Judaism, however, was not characterized by an isolationist, sectarian mentality. In Boccaccini's words, "[W]e have no evidence that the Enochians formed a schismatic community, in Palestine or elsewhere. The Enochians were an opposition party within the temple elite, not a group of separatists" (78). It is conflict within this "opposition party" that Boccaccini attempts to chronicle in the literature found at Qumran, and that he argues led to the withdrawal of the Qumran people into the desert.

Up until this juncture I am completely sympathetic with Boccaccini's view. I have argued independently of him that 1 Enoch and Aramaic Levi represent a priestly tradition that is at odds with the Jerusalem priestly establishment. One of Boccaccini's Zadokite works, the Wisdom of Ben Sira, provides evidence that in pre-Maccabean Jerusalem priests, or in the case of Ben Sira himself people close to the priests, were aware of this anti-Jerusalem polemic and were responding to it. Indeed, the priesthood posed a problem that was apparently quite contentious for quite a while (Wright 1997). I also argued that the wisdom Enoch is granted in 1 Enoch "is handed down as a sort of counter wisdom to that offered by teachers like Ben Sira. For the authors of 1 Enoch this wisdom has chronological precedence to that given to Moses in the Sinaitic Law" (219). The fact that Ben Sira polemically engages ideologies like that found in 1 Enoch or Aramaic Levi probably confirms Boccaccini's notion that his Enochic Jews (those who produced these works) did not remove themselves from Jewish society. Despite their critical stance, they may well have participated to a degree, or at the very least they did not physically separate themselves into sectarian communities like that at Qumran.

Several works that Boccaccini includes as Enochic testify to the beginnings of a sectarian mentality that would ultimately result in the schism that led to the settlement at Wadi Qumran. These pre-Qumranic works provide evidence for what Boccaccini calls the "formative age" of the community, and they are positioned, according to him, between what could be called normative Enochic Judaism and the Damascus Document, perhaps the foundation document of the isolationist breakaways. They are composed during or shortly after the Maccabean crisis. Boccaccini argues that these works — Dream Visions, Jubilees, the Temple Scroll, the Proto-Epistle of Enoch,[1] and 4QMMT — display elements such as a developing notion of certain Jews being "the chosen among the chosen" who possessed a special revelation and have "separated" from the majority even though it may not have been a physical withdrawal. Although these works argue against their Zadokite antagonists, they do not contain the idea that they have replaced Israel as the chosen people, as the Damascus Document later does. MMT, for example, has a very conciliatory tone and expresses the expectation that its addressees would in fact come to agree with its positions on the law — not the stuff of isolationism and rejection.

Into this mix Boccaccini adds the book of Daniel. He understands this apocalypse as mediating between Zadokite and Enochic Judaism. Daniel is "sympathetic to the principles of Zadokite Judaism" but was not a supporter of the Zadokite priesthood (Boccaccini 1998, 85). Yet Daniel is not Enochic in that it does not share the Enochic view of evil, and it "defends the tenets of Zadokite Judaism: the Mosaic torah and the legitimacy of the second temple" (83). It is canonized in later Judaism because of its covenantalism, but the people at Qumran read it avidly because of its Enochic emphasis on the continuing of the exile and the expectation that Israel's exile will end only via God's intervention.

In his discussion of Jubilees Boccaccini makes a statement in an almost matter-of-fact way that points to an important issue in his reconstruction of this formative age. He argues that Enochic Judaism originates in anti-Zadokite priestly circles that "ignore" the Mosaic torah. He apparently sees the Maccabean crisis and its immediate aftermath as the catalyst for a dramatic change in that approach. About Jubilees he says, "The book of Jubilees gives us evidence that after the Maccabean crisis, the Enochians, or at least some Enochians, now considered the Mosaic revelation as no longer a competitive revelation to pass over in silence, as Dream Visions did, but as a common heritage that could neither be ignored nor dismissed" (88).

For Jubilees this means making Moses part of the same tradition of revelation that began with Enoch. Enoch, Noah, Abraham, Jacob, and now Moses become a chain of people who reveal information contained in heavenly tablets which they saw. Each is incomplete and inexact, but divine revelation nonetheless.

---

1. Boccaccini (1998) argues that the people at Qumran preserved a shorter version of the Epistle of Enoch that contained the traits of this growing sectarian mind-set and was expanded later in Enochic Judaism before being included in the book of 1 Enoch as we now have it.

The incorporation of Moses into the chain of revealers in Jubilees makes sense in Boccaccini's reconstruction, but the importance of the Mosaic torah to the documents he places in his "formative age" requires more explanation. Three of the works Boccaccini includes here, Jubilees, the Temple Scroll, and MMT, see the event of Mosaic revelation as fundamental to their view of the world. Boccaccini claims that Jubilees "opened the path not only to a harmonization between Zadokite and Enochic literature, but also to the production of 'pseudo-Zadokite' or 'pseudo-Moses' texts" (98). This rapprochement is apparently possible because of the fall from power of the Zadokite high priesthood and the rise of the Hasmoneans in the events before, during, and immediately after the Maccabean revolt.

I find it difficult to envision, however, how all this happens. Enochic Judaism initially, and for quite a while, "ignores," indeed even rejects, the Mosaic torah. The Zadokite priesthood falls; Daniel articulates an anti-Zadokite but pro-Mosaic torah position; the Hasmoneans apparently convince a large segment of Jews that "the Mosaic torah could be restored even without restoring the Zadokite priesthood" (91); and Enochians welcome the Mosaic torah with open arms. Boccaccini remarks, "It was through the experience of the Maccabean revolt that the Zadokite torah became the Jewish torah *tout court* as the essential element of Jewish national identity" (91). What was it about that experience that convinced even Boccaccini's Enochians that this should be so? How do we get from Boccaccini's picture of a pre-Maccabean Judaism divided, at least in part, over acceptance or rejection of the Mosaic torah to an immediate post-Maccabean Judaism where that same torah becomes the quintessential statement of Jewish nationalism?

My sense of Boccaccini's argument here is that the ability of the Hasmoneans to dissolve what had been heretofore a firm link between the revelation of Moses at Sinai and the Zadokite priesthood convinces Enochians that they can adopt the torah as well. I am just not convinced that the short time between the events of the Maccabean revolt and the writing of MMT, for example, in which proper fulfillment of the Mosaic torah is the bone of contention between the "we" party of the document and the "you" to whom the letter is addressed, can accommodate such a decisive about-face. By the time one gets to the Qumran literature, the Mosaic torah is woven into the very fabric of those works used by the community. This can be seen throughout, but even and especially in the document that according to Boccaccini forms the bridge between the "formative age" literature and the "schism" between Enochic Judaism and the Qumran community, the Damascus Document. I suspect that the relationship between Enochic Judaism and the Mosaic torah is more complex than Boccaccini describes it, since the issue as we see it in these texts is not acceptance of the Mosaic torah — that seems assumed — but its interpretation and proper fulfillment.[2]

Boccaccini then comes to the matter of the schism between Qumran and its larger parent movement, Enochic Judaism. He paints a picture of a small group led by the Teacher of Righteousness that insists on a separation from larger Israel and the temple because of its impurity and its unwillingness to follow the law properly. Tensions increasingly mounted as the Teacher of Righteousness attempted unsuccessfully to gain control of the Enochic movement. In the separation each group left the other behind. Boccaccini tries to show how later Enochic literature — works like the Epistle of Enoch (in its later Enochic redaction), the Testaments of the Twelve Patriarchs, the Similitudes of Enoch — even though it displays similarities to ideas found in the Qumran sectarian documents, evidences a clear difference from and even an opposition to them. The ways had truly parted.

In Boccaccini's arguments concerning this split, the Groningen Hypothesis plays a large role in determining why certain books were or were not found in the Qumran library. He notes on several occasions that "no writing has been found [at Qumran] that contradicts the basic ideas of this community or represents the ideas of a group opposed to it" (129; cf. García Martínez and Trebolle Barrera 1995, 9). I have no doubt that the scrolls found in the caves near the settlement at Qumran belonged to that community and represent an intentional collection of works rather than a haphazard accumulation of some kind. But there seem to be a couple flies in the ointment.

Boccaccini recognizes one of them when he tries to account for the presence of 4Q448, the so-called "prayer for the health of King Jonathan," which could be interpreted as a pro-Hasmonean document in the library of an anti-Hasmonean community. He relies on the explanation given by John Collins, who argues that the text represents a lack of consistency by the community and suggests that it may represent temporary support for the king and might have been composed during a war against foreign enemies or during the conflict between the Pharisees (allied with the Seleucid Demetrius Akairos) and Alexander Janneus, the Qumran community disliking the Pharisees more than the king at this juncture (Boccaccini 1998, 129-30; Collins 1997, 79-80). Collins, however, does call the text "anomalous." I find this explanation difficult at best, since, if Boccaccini is right and the community at Qumran thought of the remainder of Jews as traitors, the sect would presumably have no inherent inter-

---

2. See, for example, Alexander, who sees 1 Enoch as dependent on the biblical book of Genesis. He concludes that "[t]he relationship of 1 Enoch to the biblical text seems primarily exegetical" (Alexander 1998, 90).

est in supporting any Jewish group or individual outside of itself. In the Nahum Pesher where Alexander Janneus is condemned for crucifying the Pharisees, there is no hint of support either for him or for the Pharisees inherent in the text. In fact, just prior to the mention of that incident, the Pharisees are implicitly censured for collaborating with Demetrius.

The other problematic text is Ben Sira. As I noted above, I have argued that Ben Sira is engaged in some kind of polemical confrontation with Enochic Jews, to put it in Boccaccini's terms. A number of aspects of his book would not seem to fit with the Groningen Hypothesis. Perhaps the clearest is his discussion of the sun and moon in 43:2-8, which forms an argument for the lunar calendar and against a solar one. Ben Sira clearly makes the case for the moon, to the exclusion of the sun, as the body responsible for calendar setting, a position contrary to that of the Qumran community. In addition, he counsels against inquiring into the secrets of the universe (3:21-24) and against trusting in dreams and visions (34:1-8), things Enochic Judaism claimed Enoch did (Wright 1997). There may indeed be aspects of Ben Sira's book that appealed to the Qumran community. Ben Sira, for example, puts Enoch at the head of his Praise of the Ancestors (Wright 1997, 214-15). They may have been drawn to some of the wisdom proverbs and perhaps to the message that wisdom is embodied in torah (chap. 24). But despite passages such as these, it seems very difficult to argue that Ben Sira is consistent with the worldview of the Qumran community. The Qumran covenanters would have had to overlook a fair number of problematic passages to make Ben Sira fit in.

In the end, whether or not one agrees fully with Boccaccini's construction of "Enochic" Judaism, his thesis is provocative and attractive, and he has brought into much clearer relief some of the most important issues that divided Jews in the second temple period. That the Qumran group broke away from a larger parent movement that had the characteristics of Boccaccini's Enochic Judaism seems to me largely convincing. His proposals have the additional and distinct advantage of incorporating and correcting a number of the approaches that scholars recently have taken to the problem of the prehistory and origins of the Qumran sect. Like any attempt to draw a large-scale historical picture, Boccaccini's book helps to answer some questions while at the same time raising others. It should provoke both conversation and debate. Boccaccini is to be congratulated for producing such a challenging and insightful study.

History of the Earliest Enochic Texts

Paolo Sacchi

Here I attempt to trace the history of the earliest Enochic texts, from the Book of the Watchers (BW) through the book of Dream Visions (DV) and the book of Jubilees. In doing so I will refer to the Groningen and the Enochic-Essene hypotheses.

A further point to be examined here is a reconsideration of early research in the field of Qumran. The point of departure for this research was the information that could be drawn from Jewish Hellenistic sources such as Philo and Josephus, in order to identify those texts that were previously unknown. In the opinion of the majority of the first Qumran scholars, the newly discovered texts belonged to the Essene movement. The Qumran texts and the Jewish Hellenistic sources do not agree on all the details, but in general terms this was accepted and has been fundamentally confirmed through the years.

Given that we have reached a good level of knowledge of Jewish literature during the last centuries before the advent of Christianity, I feel we can now compare the Jewish pre-Christian movement(s) we have discovered with the information found in the Jewish Hellenistic sources. This is a reverse process, by which we could find out what Jewish culture of the first century c.e. knew of its own past, and what it had forgotten, or perhaps wanted to forget.

The Book of the Watchers and the Astronomical Book

The Book of the Watchers contains a revelation whose contents display sapiential features. The worldview of the author is cosmic rather than historical. His thought is based on the cosmic structure; therefore he uses his astronomical knowledge to understand the universe and God. Enoch lives in the "in-between world" (Sacchi 2000, 125-29) and speaks to the sinner angels and to God. He then makes a journey through the entire cosmos and thus obtains knowledge of all things.

The main points of the author's theology are the following:

1. In the Book of the Watchers there is no trace of the Mosaic law, of any law.

2. The origin of evil in the world lies in an angelic sin that contaminated the whole world. Since the world is not as God desired it, it is a disorder, not a cosmos. However, in the introduction (chaps. 1–5), which is later than the text, the world is already considered an order (cf. 2:1). Also, in the almost contemporary Astronomical Book the world is conceived of as an order. This signifies that the development of Enochic thought was very fast.

3. The author of the Book of the Watchers never refers to the temple. He has no dispute with the priests of Jerusalem or of any other place; he simply ignores them. It seems that he does not understand the value and functions of the temple. On one hand he refuses the reality of the temple functions. On the other hand, in this book there is a strong search for God, which could perhaps be called mystical. Contact with the divine is not institutionalized, but it is possible, at least for some chosen ones, who can enter into contact with the divine world through their own ascesis. In chapter 14 an ascent into heaven is described. This was a real experience for the author, who reached ecstasy through opposite extreme physical sensations: extreme heat and extreme cold. The text narrates, with tongue of flesh, what is beyond physical experience. The author's scientific knowledge is the basis of his piety; he seeks God in the structure of the universe.

4. As a consequence of the lack of the Mosaic torah in the Book of the Watchers, there is no mention of purity laws. The sole exception is that of eating blood (1 En [BW] 7:5).

5. The impure truly exists in nature as an outcome of angelic sin. Impurity is the root of evil in history. Besides, the devil continues his work in this world. (Cf. 1 En [BW] 10:8; 19:1; 10:7, 8, 22; 12:4; see the sin of the seven stars in 18:15; 21:3.)

6. The author of the Book of the Watchers believes in the existence of a human soul, which can be separated from the body and live in another dimension after the body's death.

7. Paradise and hell exist (1 En [BW] 18:14; 19:1; 21:3; 22:10-11; 25).

8. The Astronomical Book proposes a 364-day annual calendar, which is merely a theological development of the earlier calendar where the year was

composed of 360 days plus 4. The earlier form was still in use in the book of Daniel (Sacchi 1997a, 128-39; Boccaccini 2001).

9. As concerns messianism, there is no trace of it in the Book of the Watchers.

10. We find the heavenly tablets for the first time in the Astronomical Book. Everything concerning human knowledge is written on these tablets, but it is not explicitly said that the laws are inscribed there as well.

11. Some problems arise from the texts of chapter 8 and 32:5-6, where knowledge itself is condemned. In chapter 8 astronomy is taught by a demon, and in chapter 32 the old tree of knowledge appears, the tree from which "ancient father and ancient mother" ate and were driven from Eden. It seems, however, that here only knowledge concerning the human state is dealt with, not knowledge itself: "They knew that they were naked and therefore they were driven from the garden."

There are very few parallels between the Book of the Watchers and the Zadokite torah. The author of the Book of the Watchers seems to know the stories of Adam and Eve, the patriarchs, the flood, and he even refers to Abel. However, he deals with these topics in a very different manner than does the Zadokite torah.

Summarizing: the Book of the Watchers bears witness to the existence of a Judaism that was very different from Zadokite Judaism. Given the name of the revealer, the term "Enochism" is very apt to this current of Judaism.

The Book of Dream Visions

This book is nearer to Zadokite Judaism than is the Book of the Watchers. It narrates a history of the world and Israel from the very beginning through the time of the author. The author follows the Bible's narration, but with some particularities with a strong conceptual value.

1. Adam was a righteous man. He was never introduced into Eden, where according to the biblical account he sinned. Therefore it is very clear that the origin of evil lies in angelic sin. A first star fell on the earth and began to cause humankind and other angels to sin. It is perhaps the earliest figure of the devil we know of.

2. In BW the absence of any reference to the law could be explained as a lack of any direct interest in the law, whereas DV clearly rejects the Mosaic torah. Moses went up on the mount to meet God, but he did not receive any law. When he came back to the Israelites, he punished the blind sheep and then he built a house for the Lord of the sheep. In other words, Enochism accepted

the old temple of Solomon as the true temple, in accordance with God's will, but it did not acknowledge the contemporary temple. Enochism acknowledged the value of the temple but did not recognize any value for the temple of that time (1 En [DV] 90:28). Besides, the value itself of Solomon's temple is relative. Moses built the tabernacle because the Israelites were afraid to see God, who lived among them and guided them directly (1 En [DV] 89:27-32). The temple is the consequence of the refusal to live with God. Also, Moses' mediation is a consequence of this refusal. The ideal of the author of the Book of the Watchers is clear: humankind shall return to live with God, who will come upon the earth *again* into his true temple at the end of the historical time. In this book there is a universalistic feature as well. The future true temple seems to be for the whole world. God will create the new temple where all peoples of the world will come together (1 En [DV] 90:33).

3. Messianism is still missing. A possible messianic figure appears at the end of the book, the king of the future world, who shall govern it on behalf of God. But this figure has no functions of salvation. We can consider him as a Messiah only because he was a king, the eternal (?) king of the entire world.

Jubilees and the Book of Daniel

The steps leading Enochism toward contact with Zadokitism reach their height in the book of Jubilees, which I think was written in the mid–second century B.C.E. We now find that Enochians were thinking about the law. Jubilees explicitly acknowledges the law of Moses, though considering it subordinate to the laws of the heavenly tablets which are eternal (cf. 1 En [Epistle of Enoch] 99:2). Zadokite tradition is accepted, but it is inserted into the Enochic theology. It is clear that the author's aim in Jubilees is to unify the theologies of Enochism and Zadokitism.

If Dream Visions were the last book having the figure of Enoch as revealer, we could believe that the book of Jubilees marks a great turning point in the history of Enochism; but since other Enochic books appear in the following times, the Epistle of Enoch, the Book of Parables, and Slavonic Enoch, we must infer that a new form of Judaism arose with the book of Jubilees, a form occupying a space between Enochic and Zadokite Judaism. Works such as the Testaments of the Twelve Patriarchs or the Psalms of Solomon belong to this new Jewish movement. Some scholars have begun to outline the history of this third Jewish movement, but I feel we still have a great deal to do.

Regarding the book of Daniel, I believe it bears witness to the existence of a movement whose goal was to bring Enochism and Zadokitism together, but which remained substantially within Zadokite circles.

Qumran Movement

The Qumran movement was very particular. It assumed topics from all of the Jewish tradition, revising and modifying them in an original manner. But it remained closed in on itself. It is not clear if any ideas born in Qumran ever reached other Jews directly. In contrast with Enochism, the people of Qumran accepted the Mosaic law absolutely. Thus they did not know or recognize any law written on the heavenly tablets. Regarding ethics, Mosaic law contained all that was necessary. Again in contrast with Enochism, Qumran accepted the value of the temple; in Qumran there was a temple, or rather, *the* temple, because it was already the eternal cosmic temple. However, this temple was not the temple of the Zadokites.

In contrast with Enochism, Qumran developed a strong belief in messianism.

Following and modifying Enochic historical predeterminism (this, however, was not exclusively typical of Enochism, since it also exists in the book of Daniel), Qumran produced an absolute, i.e., personal predeterminism; human thinking itself was determined by God (cf. 1QH 9 [1], 18-29). Thus the origin of evil becomes a mystery lying in the will of God. In Qumran there is no room for the myth of the fallen angels.

Comparison with Hellenistic Information

From the Jewish Hellenistic sources we can gather the following scheme concerning Essenes in the first century c.e.

1. Essenes were either a *hairesis* or a philosophy. To become a member of this *hairesis* an admittance rite was necessary. Only at Qumran do we find such a rite.

2. They lived in groups scattered throughout all of Palestine. On this point the western sources give us discordant information: according to them, they lived in a single place on the shores of the Dead Sea. The Jewish sources do not fit with what we know of the Qumranites.

3. They had great respect for legal authority. This fits with Qumran.

4. They were extremely pious. This too fits with Qumran.

5. They honored Moses very much. This means they also honored the torah and observed it. Again, this fits with Qumran. At this point we can no longer consider Enochism an Essene movement, because they did not have Moses' law. Even the ethic of the last Enochic work we know, the Slavonic Enoch, is not based on Moses' law.

6. They believed in the immortality of the soul. This topic has no value in the comparison because it is shared by almost all Jewish movements. It is not clear to me why this topic is given such great importance in the Jewish Hellenistic sources. Perhaps there is something here we do not know.

7. They considered events more a manifestation of God's will than a consequence of human actions. This feature of Hellenistic Essenism was interpreted by the scholars who began to study Qumran as an indication that the sources spoke of absolute predeterminism. Thus this topic became a central point leading scholars to consider the Qumranites as Essenes (see Dupont-Sommer 1954). This issue was a commonly held opinion until the criticism of Boccaccini. He is correct when he refuses to consider the Hellenistic predeterminism spoken of in the sources as absolute. This means that the Hellenistic writers did not have the Qumranites in mind when they spoke of the Essenes. Besides, it is doubtful that historical predeterminism is unique to Enochism. Historical predeterminism is shared by Daniel and the Apocalypse of the Weeks, by the Fourth Book of Ezra, and by the Syriac Apocalypse of Baruch. Thus we cannot assume that this idea is a feature capable of singling out one movement.

On the basis of this scheme we can conclude that the texts which fit best with Hellenistic Essenism are those derived from Jubilees.

Qumran and Enochism were ignored or totally rejected by the Hellenistic authors. We cannot consider Enochism a part of the Essene movement because it lacks the torah and the temple. When the temple was acknowledged by Dream Visions, it was recognized only as a means of maintaining the contact with God that people had interrupted during the period in the desert. Each of these features is too important to allow Enochism to be considered an internal stream of a single movement.

In summary: initially (fourth century B.C.E.) there were two main currents in Israel: Enochism and Zadokitism. The book of Jubilees gave birth to a third form of Judaism, and this last form seems to fit best with the information we have from the Jewish Hellenistic sources of the first century C.E. Therefore, the information we find in the Hellenistic sources must be read independently from Qumran and Enochic texts.

Now a new question clearly arises: Why did the Jewish Hellenistic authors of the first century C.E. ignore those movements we call Qumran and Enochism?

I consider three solutions possible:

1. Qumran and Enochism were not known. This may fit with Qumran, whose people lived separated, but it is quite impossible for a text as widespread as the Book of the Watchers.

2. The name Essene was used in a very broad sense, so that all that was not Pharisaic could be indicated by the term "Essene." It is possible, too, that the common root of the three movements was still acknowledged. It is a fact that Pliny knew that people lived at Qumran, whose name reached him as Essenes. He knew nothing of their theology, but he knew they were Essenes.

3. Qumran and Enochism were already rejected by the theologically and politically correct movements. Qumran was condemned because of its predeterminism (see R. Aqiba); Enochism was condemned because of its belief in the existence of "two powers in heaven" or because of its lack of belief in Moses' torah.

In my opinion the third hypothesis seems the most probable one. But Pliny's information supports the second solution.

Different Bibles for Different Groups?

Torleif Elgvin

I agree with many facets of the Enochic-Essene Hypothesis. But there are elements in this hypothesis which cannot be proved or disproved. It seems to me that Boccaccini too easily makes the jump from documents to sociologically defined groups. First, referring to my other chapter in this volume ("The *Yaḥad* Is More Than Qumran"), "*yaḥad* Judaism" would be a better designation than Boccaccini's "Qumranic Judaism"; and the *yaḥad* should be seen as a larger entity encompassing also the Qumran settlement. In the following paper I will touch on two major areas of disagreement with the Enochic-Essene Hypothesis.

Torah and Prophets Are a Common Heritage in Third-Century Judaism

It is problematic to uphold the Mosaic torah and most of the biblical texts as belonging only to Zadokite Judaism until the Maccabean revolt (Boccaccini 1998, 68ff.), postulating Jubilees and Daniel as bridging documents. The evidence rather suggests that Moses and the prophets were a common authority in Judea not later than 200 B.C.E., and probably substantially before that time, long before Jubilees. The following arguments should be considered in this context.

1. The Samaritans brought with them the Mosaic torah as an authoritative document when they split off in the fourth century B.C.E. Both sides of this split related to the torah as a formal authority. Why should it be different for the Enochians?

2. Ben Sira (24:23-28; 46–49) takes the authority of Moses and the prophets generally for granted. He does not argue polemically for their acceptance. This is quite different from his opposition to those who rely on visions and revelations (3:21-24; 18:4-7; 34:1-8; 43:31-32; cf. Wright 1997, and his contribution to the present volume). At the meeting of the Enoch Seminar in Venice, Philip Davies argued that Genesis 2–4 is a late anti-Enochic unit that makes evil the responsibility of man, not of angels. Such a late dating is speculative. There is strong evidence for dating the Eden story to circa 500 B.C.E. (Stordalen 2000, 206-13 and passim). Further, Ben Sira does not seem to know about recent censorship of Genesis or any disagreement as to what the Genesis text should contain. It is easier to see 1 Enoch 6–11 as a parabiblical text elaborating Genesis 6:1-4 as an already authoritative text than the other way around (Nickelsburg 2001, 166-70; Dimant 2002).

3. 4QInstruction (early second century B.C.E., with an apocalyptic worldview) has many thematic links with Enochic literature (Elgvin 1997, 125-37, 168-72; Tigchelaar 2001, 212-17). It once refers explicitly to Moses as an authority (4Q418 184/4Q423 11), and contains many allusions to texts from the later prophets, Psalms, and even Proverbs.[1] Also, other apocalyptic writers, including Enochic authors, found evidence for their worldview and view of history in the Prophets and Psalms. They are a crossbreed of sapiential and prophetic tradition.

4. Moses is a self-evident authority in the (apocalyptically influenced) *yaḥad*.

5. The pesherim show that the Psalms and Prophets are a self-evident authority in the *yaḥad*.[2]

There is an ambiguity in the Enochic tradition regarding the Mosaic torah, but Enochic writers in the late third and early second centuries could not deny its authority. Sacchi argues that they interpreted the Pentateuch as history and not as law (Sacchi 1998, 360). Enochic circles had to accept the Mosaic torah (cf. 1 En 93:6; 99:2, 14), but had their own prophetic/apocalyptic inspiration and writings in addition — thus the ambiguity. I suggest that there was no ambiguity regarding the prophets and Psalms, where the Enochians could find

---

1. The following are among the clear scriptural allusions in 4QInstruction: 4Q416 2 ii 12 (Jer 17:9); 2 ii 13 (Mal 3:17); 2 iii 15-16, 19 (Exod 20:12); 2 iii 21–iv 1, 4 (Gen 2:24); 2 iv 9-10 (Num 30:6-14); 4Q417 1 i 6 (Josh 1:8; Ps 1:2); 1 i 15 (Mal 3:16); 1 i 23-24 (Prov 6:29); 1 i 27 (Num 15:39); 1 ii 12 (Gen 6:5); 2 i 1 (Prov 25:17); 2 i 15-16 (Nah 1:6; Isa 61:3, 7); 2 i 18 (Ps 107:30); 2 ii 7-8 (Isa 58:13); 4Q418 81 3 (Num 18:20; Deut 10:9); 81 7-8 (Exod 20:5-6); 103 ii 6-9 (Deut 22:9-11); 126 ii 15 (Job 1:10); 4Q423 1-2 i 1-3 (Gen 2:15; 3:6, 18); 3 1 (Lev 26:20).

2. Cf. the evidence for dating the *yaḥad* before 150 B.C.E. (see my chapter in part 4 of this volume).

many proof texts for their worldview and hope for the future. It would indeed be a strange picture if these circles accepted the prophets, David, and Solomon as authorities, but not Moses.

The Dating of the Schism

The Enochic-Essene Hypothesis dates the schism between Enochic and Qumran Judaism to the early first century (Boccaccini 1998, 187). I have argued that the foundation of the *yaḥad* occurs well before 150 B.C.E. A schism between Enochic Judaism and *yaḥad* Judaism should therefore be dated much earlier than postulated in the Enochic-Essene Hypothesis.

Furthermore, it is problematic to enlist 4QMMT in the Enochic-Essene chain. The majority dating of MMT to circa 150 B.C.E. is not self-evident. Internal evidence from MMT itself does not point to the mid–second century B.C.E., and all copies are written in Herodian script. Has circular reasoning led scholars to put the needed missing link into a preconceived picture of sectarian history? MMT might just as well be an internal Essene or *yaḥad* tractate from the first century B.C.E. The offering of wheat of the Gentiles (4Q394 3-7 i 6) would make better sense in the time of Antiochus III or after Pompey than in the period 170-63 B.C.E.

The Evidence of the Biblical Scrolls

My last point refers to the biblical scrolls from the Judean desert, which may have implications for our study of different ideological milieus in Judea in the second century B.C.E. Among the biblical scrolls from Qumran, four main types can be discerned, three of which reflect a conscious ideological attitude toward the biblical text in the second century (25 percent of the scrolls are nonaligned and do not fit into any of these types) (Tov 2001, passim).

1. The Proto-Masoretic School (Cross: "Proto-Rabbinic School")

To some extent the earliest proto-Masoretic textual tradition elaborates on earlier Septuagintal texts they want to replace (Tov 2003, 138). However, at a certain stage of the textual transmission the scribes of this school demonstrate a conservative attitude toward the transmission of their sacred text, and copy it faithfully without adding new features. Tov suggests master scrolls in the temple as prototypes of the scrolls of this school, perhaps as early as the third century (oral communication; cf. 138-41). Forty percent of biblical scrolls from Qumran and all the biblical scrolls from the Judean desert outside Qumran represent this tradition. While the Qumran manuscripts exhibit some variation within this group of texts, the biblical scrolls from Masada and Bar Kokhba insurgents are identical with the medieval Masoretic Text. A process of minute standardization is thus evident in the first century C.E., at least in circles connected to the temple (138-41) — and the rebels deliberately chose the text of the temple since it was their spiritual center. Since this is the biblical text chosen by the rabbis (used by Targum, Talmud, and the midrashim), Tov has suggested it should be ascribed to Pharisaic circles (1996b). However, the rabbis should not too easily be designated as the successors of the Pharisees. One should remember that in the first century C.E. the temple establishment was primarily Sadducean, not Pharisaic. The *tannaim* and *amoraim* clearly received and transmitted the textual tradition of the master scrolls of the temple before 70 C.E., and we should not designate these scrolls as Pharisaic.

2. The Yaḥad Scribal School

This school took a free attitude to the text and had a more careless style (cf. Tov 1986; 1988; 1993b; 1995; 1996a; 1997a; 1997b). This free style may be conceived as a protest against the temple scribes of the proto-Masoretic school. For *yaḥad* scribes the spirit was as important as the letter; they did not feel bound by scribal procedures authorized in the temple. Alternatively one may hypothesize that the Teacher of Righteousness got only second-class scribes to join his exodus from Jerusalem. While 25 percent of the biblical scrolls from Qumran fall into this category, no extra-Qumranic biblical scrolls do.

3. The Harmonizing School, Often Called Proto-Samaritan

The scribes of this school believed that inconsistencies in the Pentateuch diminish the text's sanctity and endeavored to smooth out the text transmitted to them. They therefore added secondary features to the text (cf. recently Eshel and Eshel 2003). Esther and Hanan Eshel list fifteen harmonizing texts from the last two hundred years of the second temple period, including five biblical scrolls, biblical paraphrases or *testimonia*, mezuzot, and phylacteries. Apart from the Nash papyrus, all texts were found at Qumran. In the second century B.C.E. the Samaritans chose five scrolls of this wider Judean text type as basis for their version of the Pentateuch. After correcting the text to make it conform to the Samaritan faith, their scrolls were henceforth accurately transmitted, while Jewish scribes in the land continued to develop the harmonistic process into the next century (Eshel and Eshel 2003).

4. The (Hebrew) Septuagint Text Type

This type often preserved the earlier version or edition of the book in question (Tov 2003, 143 n. 65). I suggest that this textual tradition was marginalized in Judea and Jerusalem during the second century B.C.E. *after* the translation of books such as Jeremiah and Ezekiel into Greek (cf. 137-43). It stands to reason that the translators chose a textual version with a good name also in Jerusalem in their days (*pace* Tov: "Clearly the circles or persons who sent or brought the manuscripts of the torah to Alexandria were *not* Eleazar the High Priest and the sages, as narrated in the Epistle of Aristeas 176" [140]). In the temple circles of the second century the shorter and older version of Ezekiel and Jeremiah had to give way for the proto-Masoretic version of these two books. The ascension to power of the proto-Masoretic text tradition may be connected with the Hasmonean temple establishment.

Type 1 above would fit well with the Zadokite stream of the Enochic-Essene Hypothesis, while type 2 could be Enochic-Essene but is more probably Qumranic in Boccaccini's terminology. Another group that crosses the categories above is the paleo-Hebrew scrolls. Four of these belong to group 1, one to group 3, and one is nonaligned (Tov 1996b). Following Diringer (1950), Tov suggests that the paleo-Hebrew proto-Masoretic scrolls came from the Sadducees, who ascribed much importance to the authenticity of the ancient characters. Rabbinic tradition forbids this script for biblical scrolls (*m. Yad.* 4.5; *b. Sanh.* 21b). Tov's identification of Pharisaic and rabbinic tradition is important in his chain of arguments: proto-Masoretic scrolls written in square script are Pharisaic, since they were adopted by the rabbis. The paleo-Hebrew texts do not exhibit Qumranic scribal features and are carefully written and transmitted. Thus they must come from a major religious source other than the Pharisees and the *yaḥad* — the only alternative seems to be the Sadducees (Tov 1996b, 1:367-70).

While I disagree with this part of Tov's argument, I tend to support his conclusion. One may hypothesize that the Sadducees influenced the Maccabees to revive the ancient script (cf. the script of the Hasmonean coinage). The careful scribal practice evidenced in these paleo-Hebrew scrolls reflects a well-trained scribal milieu that may have been connected to the temple. MMT has demonstrated close links between Qumran *halakhah* and the Sadducean *halakhah* described in rabbinic writings. The Teacher and some of the early members of the *yaḥad* had their roots in the temple milieu, so the *yaḥad* and the Sadducees had common grandparents. The four paleo-Hebrew scrolls in question would then be spoils from the temple (and Boccaccini's Zadokites), coming from a scribal school supported by the Sadducees. However, the use of paleo-Hebrew script on coinage in the two Jewish revolts weakens Tov's theory. The Zealots were close to the Pharisees, and hardly fans of the Sadducees. Thus, Tov's Pharisees supported paleo-Hebrew on nationalistic coinage but not on biblical scrolls.

More study is needed to see to what extent groups of biblical texts from the Judean desert may be related to different socioreligious streams among the Jewish people in the last three centuries of the second temple period.

Essenes, Qumran, and Christian Origins

Claudio Gianotto

As a historian of Christian origins, I would like to make some observations on the legacy of the Enochic-Essene tradition, especially within early Christianity. Gabriele Boccaccini deals with this problem in the third part of his *Beyond the Essene Hypothesis* ("Comparative Analysis"). I agree with him that the clear distinction between mainstream Essenism and Qumran, required by the Enochic-Essene Hypothesis, calls for an urgent reassessment of the Essene (and Qumranic) contribution to Christian origins (Boccaccini 1998, 189). In this respect I would like to highlight three points in the legacy of the Enochic-Essene tradition that emerge from Boccaccini's comparative analysis but are not specifically referred to in relation to Christian origins.

Mythology

The first point concerns the story of the fallen angels and of the consequent introduction of evil into the human world and history. This story, which exonerates both God and the humans from direct responsibility in the origin of evil, has important consequences at the soteriological level because it rules out the possibility that humans achieve their salvation relying on their own resources. The logic of the story requires that if humans are not entirely and directly responsible for their sinful condition, they cannot be the authors of their own salvation but need help from outside.

This thought fascinated Paul and influenced his soteriology, in particular his idea of the necessity of the work of a superhuman mediator, Jesus Christ, for the salvation of the whole of humankind. Moreover, if it is true that mainstream Christianity has reintroduced the common idea of the responsibility of humans in the achievement of their salvation, the theme of what historians of religions like the late Ugo Bianchi called *colpa antecedente* (previous guilt) has been characteristic of many groups which developed at the margins of early Christianity, such as the Gnostics.

Religious Ideas

The second point concerns the belief in both the immortality of the soul and the resurrection of the body. Generally, this double belief in early Christianity is explained as the result of a double cultural influence: that of Greek (especially Platonic) philosophy regarding the immortality of the soul, and that of Jewish thought regarding belief in the resurrection of the body. Now we see that this double belief was already characteristic of the Enochic-Essene tradition, although it had developed within that tradition in different times and ways. We can say that the roots of early Christian thought on individual and collective eschatology lie here.

Social Practices

The third and last point concerns the attitude of suspicion and distrust toward sexuality. When you read what Boccaccini writes with reference to the Testament of Issachar 2:1-3, "They despised [sexual] intercourse, yet they married and mated for the sake of children and not for fondness for pleasure" (Boccaccini 1998, 180), certainly you find here not only a statement representative of the attitude of the Enochian Essenes toward sexuality but also a brilliant synthesis of Christian morals in the field of marriage and sexuality up to Vatican II. This would be true particularly for post-Tridentine Roman Catholic moral codes. From a certain point of view, we can say that the roots of Christianity are encratite; surely this statement cannot be generalized, but we know that in the first centuries celibacy was required, in some areas, especially Syria, before receiving baptism, which was conceived as the introduction to a sort of *angelikos bios* where sexuality and procreation have no place.

We have here a cluster of themes which are common to Enochic-Essene and Christian traditions. Now we have to go beyond this simple observation and ask ourselves, further, whether it is possible to trace a genetic trajectory from one tradition to the other. Some work has already been done in this field, but much is still to be done. Gabriele Boccaccini has given us a wise, scientific, and well-ordered beginning on this quest in his three important volumes: *Middle Judaism: Jewish Thought, 300 B.C.E. to 200 C.E.* (1991); *Beyond the Essene Hypothesis: The Parting of the Ways between Qumran and Enochic Judaism* (1998); and *Roots of Rabbinic Judaism: An Intellectual History, from Ezekiel to Daniel* (2002).

Response:
Texts, Intellectual Movements,
and Social Groups

Gabriele Boccaccini

The value of a hypothesis lies in its capability of making the scholarly community reflect on a possible way of reassembling proven yet scattered pieces of evidence within a broader framework to form a new picture of a familiar scene. A hypothesis always goes "beyond" accepted paradigms and in its most challenging perspectives even dares to be provocative and controversial, provided it remains consistent to its methodological, philological, and historical premises *(iuxta sua propria principia)*. If the discussion produces tangible results and contributes to advance our knowledge in the field and even shape a new consensus, a hypothesis may claim to have scored a major goal (perhaps, its major goal).

Under this aspect I think that for the last seven years the Essene-Enochic Hypothesis has served honorably. It has generated dozens of remarkable responses from specialists all around the world and has made scholars think about the very existence of an ancient variety of Judaism ("Enochic Judaism") and of a social group (the "Enoch group"). It has drawn attention to the contribution given by this movement (and this group) to Qumran origins and raised some challenging methodological issues. We may not agree on what Enochic Judaism was or on who the Enochians were, yet scholars now recognize the presence since pre-Maccabean times of an intellectual tradition that was at odds with the Jerusalem priestly establishment ("Enochic Judaism"), corresponding to a still ill-defined yet actual social entity (the "Enoch group"). We may not agree on what relation this movement of dissent had with the Essene movement and the Qumran community, yet we have become aware that the mystery of both Essene and Qumran origins is largely hidden in the Enoch literature.

417

Gabriele Boccaccini

The dialogue here engaged with such a distinguished group of specialists is yet another important opportunity, thanks to their thoughtful insights, to advance our knowledge of the period — beyond my *Beyond*. While I thank all the contributors for their kind words of appreciation and their constructive criticism, the complexity of the problems they raised does not allow me to articulate a comprehensive and detailed response. My *Beyond the Essene Hypothesis* was planned as only one stage in a broader project of reconstruction of the development of Jewish thought in second temple Judaism — a project that started with *Middle Judaism: Jewish Thought, 300 B.C.E. to 200 C.E.* (Minneapolis: Fortress, 1991) and *Portraits of Middle Judaism in Scholarship and Arts* (Turin: Zamorani, 1992) and has now been expanded with the publication of *Roots of Rabbinic Judaism: An Intellectual History, from Ezekiel to Daniel* (Grand Rapids: Eerdmans, 2002), to which *Rabbinic Origins: An Intellectual History, from Daniel to the Mishnah* (Grand Rapids: Eerdmans, forthcoming) and other publications dealing with each of the many intellectual trends of the time will soon be added. In this brief response I have the opportunity to touch upon only a few major issues.

The Methodological Dilemma; or, From Communities of Texts to Groups and Movements

A methodological question resurfaces over and over again through this entire volume: How can we move from "books" to "people" or from "communities of texts" to "communities of people"?

A book is a book, not an intellectual movement or a social group. But "texts are historical artifacts, created in time and space, by real human beings" (Nickelsburg 2001, 2). We have to look at ancient documents not only as testimonies of Judaisms but also as artifacts of Judaisms — the equivalent of ruins in archaeology. Behind any book (like behind any wall) there is an author (or authors), and as Helge Kvanvig also noticed in his contribution to this volume, where there is a "family of books" there is a "family of people" who handed them down.

"The good historian resembles the ogre of the fairy-tale; where he scents the human flesh, he knows that his prey is there" (Bloch 1949, 35). Marc Bloch's witty remark reminds us that ours is a dirty job that has not to do with anonymous and aseptic "intellectual phenomena" but with the actual lives and temperamental behavior of flesh-and-blood people. In the words of Eugenio Garin, the intellectual historian's task is "to be aware of the plurality of philosophies, understand the many voices, put them in context, identify the relations with the social groups in which they emerged, assess what they meant for these groups, how they acted if they acted, how they changed, and how they declined — human thoughts, how they were created by people, how they changed people" (Garin 1959, 41). Although difficult to detect, movements and social groups do exist. The historian can't give up this task, no matter how hard and complex it may be.

The status of second temple Jewish literature reminds me of the old box where my grandmother used to put, higgledy-piggledy, the pictures of her huge family (eleven siblings, and an uncounted number of uncles and aunts, great-uncles and great-aunts, cousins, friends and relatives — all smiling together). In the box there were, along with a large number of scattered pictures, also some albums containing collections or "canons" of pictures that my grand-mother had put together according to the most diverse reasons (format, her fa-vorite choices, inheritance from some other relatives, or just chance).

Since I was a child, I was captivated by the curiosity of reconstructing the genealogical tree of my family. By instinct I tried first to free the pictures from the cages of their corpora and put them in a single line according to the chro-nological order. But even so, they did not make much sense, as the pictures por-trayed neither one nor many individuals but generations of individuals who of-ten lived simultaneously. I had to group together the pictures that portrayed the same individuals if I wanted those individuals to become alive again. It was not a simple task, as I realized immediately. The pictures portrayed people at differ-ent stages of their lives, and it was not easy to recognize in that shy baby the bold officer and pilot who died in World War I, or to find any resemblance be-tween that old severe lady and the young girl full of life and beauty. The family likeness only complicated the situation and many times made me mistake one character with another.

I soon created my own (tentative) "communities of pictures," which re-placed my grandmother's old albums of blessed memory and gave some order to the messy picture collection. In some cases I was able to supply the informa-tion I received from the pictures with what I knew from family stories or other sources. When none of my relatives could reveal to me the identity of forgotten characters, I used nicknames, which soon became as familiar to me as real names. In some cases an individual became very much alive, as if his or her pic-tures could be put in motion; in other cases he or she remained only a pale im-age. Sometimes I had a lot of pictures of individuals who apparently were very popular in their own time but now seemed just forgotten. Sometimes I met people who had left enthusiastic memories of themselves in the family oral tra-dition, but only a few pictures of themselves or no pictures at all; maybe they just did not like to have pictures taken of themselves, or maybe their pictures were all lost when my great-aunt's house was bombed during World War II. In every family, then, there is always a black sheep (in my family actually two or three) who made his or her fortune or misfortune elsewhere; the few surviving pictures showed them undoubtedly to be "bone of our bones and flesh of our flesh" in spite of any conspiracy of silence. Finally, there were pictures that I could attribute only tentatively to a character, and others I was never able to figure out to whom they belonged, and doubt that I ever will. I am in my forties, and I still enjoy playing with that messy box and those dear old pictures.

Writing an intellectual history of second temple Judaism is very much like reconstructing the genealogical tree of a large family. We have documents instead of pictures, and historical accounts instead of family stories. Documents, like family pictures, must be studied each on its own terms, within the broader social and intellectual framework provided by other sources. A common-denominator approach would only conflate data from different documents to shape a single, eclectic subject (the theology of second temple Judaism) that never existed, while dismissing the individual traits (the conflicting pieces of evidence) as marginal and negligible phenomena, only because they do not conform to the majority. On the other hand, an excessive emphasis on diversity would lead us to the opposite extreme of seeing documents in isolation from each other, as representatives of as many diverse subjects, not as portraits of the same subjects at different stages of their existence. We face neither a single subject nor an incalculable number of subjects, but genealogies of subjects (the diverse and competing theologies of second temple Judaism). We should not be misled by the family likeness or the abundance of parallels. This was well stated by E. P. Sanders: "One may consider the analogy of two buildings. Bricks which are identical in shape, color, and weight could well be used to construct two different buildings which are totally unlike each other" (Sanders 1977, 13). The identification of "chains of documents" or "communities of texts," representing the diverse and competing trajectories of thought in second temple Judaism, is the major goal and the major challenge in the study of the period. It is not an easy task. We meet so many cases of false resemblance, forgetfulness, mistaken identity, and rejection (first of all, the anachronistic separation between Jewish and Christian documents). Yet, it is an inescapable task, if we want to understand the diversity of Jewish thought in the second temple period.

I maintain that a clear methodological distinction between "intellectual movements" (or Judaisms) and "social groups" is the basis for any sound reconstruction of the history of Jewish thought. A Judaism is not a single social group but, as also George Nickelsburg points out in his contribution to the present volume, a proliferation of individuals and social groups.

The chain of documents I identified in my *Beyond the Essene Hypothesis* does not mean that the same social group wrote, one after the other, Dream Visions, Jubilees, the Temple Scroll, the Epistle of Enoch, the Halakhic Letter, the Testaments of the Twelve Patriarchs, and the Similitudes of Enoch. What I identified in my book is an intellectual movement or a Judaism, not a single social group. Only in the case of Enochic literature and of the sectarian literature of Qumran, the sources themselves provide some evidence that each set of documents was the product of a single social group. The "Qumran chain of documents," however, shows that the Enoch group and the Qumran group were components of the same, broader intellectual trend.

The Problem of Origins and Influences

The problem of Qumran origins (like the one of Christian origins) cannot be easily dismissed simply by arguing multiple influences. In history there is no such thing as a group or movement that suddenly emerges from nowhere, taking a little from everywhere. We can get around the problem and delude ourselves, but in the end it will keep haunting us. Would we say that Christianity was not born from Judaism, as it was so heavily influenced by Hellenic thought and religion? Of course, Christianity was influenced by Hellenic thought and religion; nevertheless, it was born from Judaism. The problem of origins is not coincidental with the problem of influences. In the case of Qumran, it is apparent that the sectarian literature was influenced by both Enochic and Zadokite thought; yet the Enochic idea of demonic origin of evil, not the Zadokite covenantal theology, is the prime suspect as the trajectory of thought from which the Qumran predestinarian theology emerged. What would have been the point of maintaining that the angels are in fact responsible for the behavior of human beings only to stress that it was God who created both the good and the evil angels and so indirectly that God was ultimately the one who predetermined the destiny of each individual? Why was it necessary to state the presence of angels in the chain of cause-effect elements that determine the destiny of each individual? Only if the myth of the fallen angels was in fact the starting point upon which the Qumranites built their predestinarian system of thought, would such a twisted theology about the origin of evil make sense.

The Enoch literature provides evidence of a major stream of thought and a major group of dissent that originated long before Qumran. In the aftermath of the Maccabean revolt the Enochic movement proliferated in a series of social groups, each of them reinterpreting the generative idea of the demonic origin of evil in its particular way. In spite of any other influence, the relationship be-

3

2642

tween the Enochic literature and the sectarian scrolls is so close that it seems appropriate to describe the Qumran community as "a latter-day derivative of or a successor to the community or communities that authored and transmitted the Enochic texts" (Nickelsburg 2001, 65; cf. Boccaccini 1998).

Enochians, Essenes, Qumranites

The relationship between Enoch and Qumran was not limited to the period of the origins of the community, but is far more complex and fascinating. After Enochic Judaism played such an important role in Qumran origins, something happened to separate the Enoch and the Qumran groups. In the library of Qumran, which preserved and cherished all Enoch books composed before the birth of the community, the later literature of Enoch is conspicuous by its absence; not only the Parables of Enoch but also, probably, significant portions of the Epistle of Enoch are missing (Boccaccini 1998; cf. Nickelsburg 2001). This suggests the existence "outside Qumran . . . [of] circles that transmitted" the ancient Enoch literature (Nickelsburg 2001, 77). Furthermore, in the later Enoch literature we read statements and see the development of ideas that openly contradict the principles of individual predeterminism held by the sectarians of Qumran.

The Parables of Enoch are a case in point. The superhuman nature of the Messiah Son of Man enables him to defeat the angelic forces responsible for the origin and spread of evil, a task that no human messiah (either priestly or kingly) could ever accomplish. The anti-Qumranic implications of such an idea of the Messiah are obvious. Why should God be concerned about conversion and deliverance from evil if individuals are what they are by God's choice? The idea of a savior from heaven does not make any sense at Qumran. Why should God send God's angelic savior if good and evil are from God and are given according to God's unchangeable decision? That the Parables are missing from the Qumran library is no surprise: it is the logical consequence of the schism between Qumran and Enochic Judaism.

As Enoch lost its touch with Qumran, at the same time Qumran lost its interest in the Enoch literature (Charlesworth 1980, 227; Collins 1997, 35-36; Boccaccini 1998, 129-31). The last quotation of Enoch is in the Damascus Document, therefore at a very early stage in the life of the community. The more the community strengthened its dualistic and predeterministic worldview, the more they lost interest in a literature that maintained that "evil originated not with God's permission, but as the result of a rebellious conspiracy that was hatched behind God's back" (Nickelsburg 2001, 47).

It seems obvious to conclude that after generating the Qumran community the Enoch group did not lose its ideological and sociological identity. Clearly we are now facing two distinct and somehow competing social groups. Does the term "Essene" apply to both?

Paolo Sacchi suggests that we limit the term "Essene" to the urban Essenes and the literature related to them, and not apply it to the Qumran community or the Enoch group; the problem is that Pliny and Dio apply it to the Qumran group, too. John Collins would rather limit it to Qumran; the problem is that Philo and Josephus apply it to the urban Essenes, too. None of the ancient sources speaks of the Enochians or connects them to the Essene movement. Systemic analysis, however, shows that the Enoch group, the urban Essenes, and the Qumran community, although distinct social groups, were all part of the same trajectory of thought. As the ancient sources apply the term "Essene" to two of the major components of this movement, it seems to me reasonable to use the term "Essene" or "para-Essene" to denote the entire movement. After all, ancient historians also seem to be aware that "Essenism" was not a single social group but rather a large and diverse movement. Josephus speaks of different groups of urban Essenes; Pliny and Dio apply the same term to the secessionists of Qumran; Philo seems to encompass under the same label even the Egyptian Therapeutae. The link among these groups is so close that we would need anyway to create a common term to denote collectively the entire movement to which they all belong.

I therefore happily and unrepentantly stick to my claim that the Enochians were Essenes, yet I would not say they were *the* Essenes or the parent group from which the community of Qumran split. The Enochians were and remained a single social group, while the term "Essene" denotes the much larger intellectual movement that historically manifested itself in a proliferation of different social groups such as the Enochians, the Qumran community (perhaps the Therapeutae), and later the Jesus movement.

Conclusion

While we have to fight against oversimplification, we have also to fight against overskepticism. To say that today in the United States there are two major political parties (the Democratic Party and the Republican Party) and three major religions (Christianity, Judaism, and Islam) is an oversimplification. Even without considering the presence of significant religious or political minorities, each of these major movements is in reality a proliferation of social groups and individuals, often in competition or disagreement with one another, and each of them bears evidence of multiple influences. It may even happen that the worldview and way of life of some Democrats are much closer to those of some Republicans than to those of some of their fellow Democrats. And the world-view and way of life of a Reform Jew are probably closer to the worldview and way of life of a Presbyterian than to those of a Hasidic Jew. To say that in the United States there are two major political parties and three major religions is an oversimplification; it is confusing, easy, simplistic, dangerously reductive, yet nevertheless, there are two major parties in the United States (the Demo-cratic Party and the Republican Party) and three major religions (Christianity, Judaism, and Islam).

The 1934 Nobel Prize–winning Italian playwright and novelist Luigi Pirandello would have taught us that even the fifty contributors to this volume are actually twenty-five hundred, because each of us is at least fifty characters (what I think I am, and what each of the others thinks that I am). Besides, our opinions are continuously changing, and I am not sure myself that I have today the same opinion of myself that I had yesterday or I will have tomorrow. Dur-ing these years in which we have being working on this project, I have also ac-quired a better understanding of many of my colleagues, and I have to assume that they also have acquired an opinion of me that is different from what they had before. This means that the world is becoming more and more (almost dangerously) crowded with thousands of (old and new) characters to make it impossible to say who each of us is. Being surrounded by hundreds of Gabriele Boccaccinis (some familiar, some so bizarre as to be almost unrecognizable), the very idea of the existence of an individual called Gabriele Boccaccini starts to look to me like an oversimplification. Before I fall victim to a desperate crisis of identity, let me reiterate that I do exist as an individual, even though compel-ling and conclusive philosophical reason should probably convince me that I do not.

At the end it is a matter of sense and balance. We need names and catego-ries to explain reality, even though we are aware that reality is always more complex than our categories. We need the category of Judaism, even though we know there are several Judaisms. We need the categories of Zadokite Judaism, Enochic Judaism, Sadduceeism, Pharisaism, Essenism, Christianity, Hellenistic Judaism, Qumranism, etc., even though we know these are merely labels and there are many more groups and subgroups, and at the end there are individu-als with their ever changing opinions. As it has happened to the "canonical" cat-egories we have inherited from our religious traditions — categories we have used and do not need anymore — some of these categories will probably soon become obsolete, and will need to be replaced or adjusted. The problem is not to use categories but to identify useful categories, which can help us advance in our research. In this discussion we may have not reached any agreement on who the Enochians, the Essenes, and the Qumranites were and on what their relation to each other was, but the Essene-Enochic Hypothesis has served well to make us rethink and reshape our categories. Not a little accomplishment.

References to Part Five

Adam, Alfred, and Christoph Burchard, eds. 1972. *Antike Berichte über die Essener.* Berlin and New York: De Gruyter.

Albeck, Chanoch, ed. 1940. *Midrash Bereshit Rabbati.* Jerusalem: Mekitze Nirdamim.

Alexander, Philip S. 1998. "From Son of Adam to Second God: Transformation of the Biblical Enoch." In *Biblical Figures outside the Bible,* edited by Michael E. Stone and Theodore A. Bergren, 87-122. Harrisburg, Pa.: Trinity.

Anderson, Jeff S. 2002. *The Internal Diversification of Second Temple Judaism.* Lanham, Md.: University Press of America.

Barker, Margaret. 1980. "Some Reflections upon the Enoch Myth." *JSOT* 15:7-29.

—————. 1987. *The Older Testament: The Survival of Themes from the Ancient Royal Cult in Sectarian Judaism and Early Christianity.* London: SPCK.

Baumgarten, Albert I. 1997. *The Flourishing of Jewish Sects in the Maccabean Era: An Interpretation.* Leiden: Brill.

Baumgarten, Joseph M. 1990. "The Qumran-Essene Restraints on Marriage." In *Archaeology and History in the Dead Sea Scrolls,* edited by Lawrence H. Schiffman, 13-24. Sheffield: Sheffield Academic Press.

Bausi, Alessandro. 1997. "Su alcuni manoscritti presso comunità monastiche dell'Eritrea (Parte seconda)." *Rassegna di Studi Etiopici* 39:25-48, pls. I-V.

Becker, Adam H., and Annette Y. Reed, eds. 2003. *The Ways That Never Parted: Jews and Christians in Late Antiquity and the Early Middle Ages.* TSAJ 95. Tübingen: Mohr.

Bloch, Marc. 1949. *Apologie pour l'histoire.* Paris: Colin.

Boccaccini, Gabriele. 1991. *Middle Judaism: Jewish Thought, 300 B.C.E. to 200 C.E.* Minneapolis: Fortress.

—————. 1997. "E se l'essenismo forse il movimento enochiano? Una nuova ipotesi circa il rapporto tra Qumran e gli esseni." *Ricerche Storico Bibliche* 9, no. 2: 49-67.

————. 1998. *Beyond the Essene Hypothesis: The Parting of the Ways between Qumran and Enochic Judaism.* Grand Rapids: Eerdmans.

————. 2001. "The Solar Calendars of Daniel and Enoch." In *The Book of Daniel: Composition and Reception,* edited by John J. Collins and Peter W. Flint, 2:311-28. Leiden: Brill.

————. 2002. *Roots of Rabbinic Judaism: An Intellectual History, from Ezekiel to Daniel.* Grand Rapids: Eerdmans.

Boyarin, Daniel. 1999. *Dying for God: Martyrdom and the Making of Christianity and Judaism.* Stanford: Stanford University Press.

Charlesworth, James H. 1980. "The Origins and Subsequent History of the Authors of the Dead Sea Scrolls: Four Transitional Phases among the Qumran Essenes." *RevQ* 10:213-34.

————. 1982. *The History of the Rechabites.* Vol. 1, *The Greek Recension.* Chico, Calif.: Scholars.

Cohen, Shaye J. D. 1999. *The Beginnings of Jewishness: Boundaries, Varieties, Uncertainties.* Berkeley: University of California Press.

Collins, John J. 1992. "Essenes." In *ABD* 2:619-25.

————. 1997. *Apocalypticism in the Dead Sea Scrolls.* London: Routledge.

————. 1998. *The Apocalyptic Imagination: An Introduction to the Jewish Apocalyptic Literature.* 2nd ed. Grand Rapids: Eerdmans.

————. 1999. "Pseudepigraphy and Group Formation in Second Temple Judaism." In *Pseudepigraphic Perspectives: The Apocrypha and Pseudepigrapha in Light of the Dead Sea Scrolls,* edited by Esther G. Chazon and Michael E. Stone, 43-58. Leiden: Brill.

————. 2001. *Seers, Sibyls, and Sages in Hellenistic-Roman Judaism.* Leiden: Brill.

————. 2003. "Forms of Community in the Dead Sea Scrolls." In *Emanuel: Studies in Hebrew Bible, Septuagint, and Dead Sea Scrolls in Honor of Emanuel Tov,* edited by Shalom M. Paul et al., 97-111. VTSup 94. Leiden: Brill.

Cook, Stephen L. 1995. *Prophecy and Apocalypticism: The Postexilic Social Setting.* Minneapolis: Fortress.

Cross, Frank M. 1958. *The Ancient Library of Qumran.* Garden City, N.Y.: Doubleday.

Davies, Philip R. 1977. "Hasidim in the Maccabean Period." *JJS* 28:127-40.

————. 1987. *Behind the Essenes: History and Ideology in the Dead Sea Scrolls.* BJS 94. Atlanta: Scholars.

————. 1991. "Communities at Qumran and the Case of the Missing Teacher." *RevQ* 15:57-58, 275-86.

————. 1992a. "The Prehistory of the Qumran Community." In *The Dead Sea Scrolls: Forty Years of Research,* edited by Devorah Dimant and Uriel Rappaport, 116-25. Leiden: Brill.

————. 1992b. "Redaction and Sectarianism in the Qumran Scrolls." In *The Scriptures and the Scrolls: Studies in Honour of A. S. Van Der Woude on the Occasion of His Sixty-Fifth Birthday,* edited by Florentino García Martínez et al., 152-63. Leiden: Brill.

————. 1994. "Communities in the Qumran Scrolls." *PIBA* 17:7-20.

————. 1996. *Sects and Scrolls: Essays on Qumran and Related Topics.* Atlanta: Scholars.

Davila, James R. 2000. *Liturgical Works.* Eerdmans Commentaries on the Dead Sea Scrolls 6. Grand Rapids: Eerdmans.

Dimant, Devorah. 1984. "Qumran Sectarian Literature." In *Jewish Writings from the Second Temple Period,* edited by Michael E. Stone, 483-550. CRINT 2/2. Philadelphia: Fortress.

————. 1995. "The Qumran Manuscripts: Contents and Significance." In *Time to Prepare the Way in the Wilderness: Papers on the Qumran Scrolls by Fellows of the Institute for Advanced Studies of the Hebrew University, Jerusalem, 1989-1990,* edited by Devorah Dimant and Lawrence H. Schiffman, 23-58. Leiden: Brill.

————. 2002. "1 Enoch 6–11: A Fragment of a Parabiblical Work." *JJS* 53, no. 2: 223-37.

Diringer, David. 1950. "Early Hebrew Script versus Square Hebrew Script." In *Essays and Studies Presented to S. A. Cook,* edited by D. Winton Thomas, 35-49. London: Taylor's Foreign Press.

Dupont-Sommer, André. 1954. *The Jewish Sect of Qumran and the Essenes: New Studies on the Dead Sea Scrolls.* Translated by R. D. Barnett. London: Vallentine, Mitchell & Co.

Elgvin, Torleif. 1997. "An Analysis of 4QInstruction." Ph.D. diss., Hebrew University of Jerusalem.

————. 2000. "Wisdom and Apocalypticism in the Early Second Century BCE — the Evidence of 4QInstruction." In *The Dead Sea Scrolls Fifty Years after Their Discovery,* edited by Lawrence H. Schiffman, Emanuel Tov, and James C. VanderKam, 226-47. Jerusalem: Israel Exploration Society in cooperation with the Shrine of the Book, Israel Museum.

Eshel, Esther, and Hanan Eshel. 2003. "Dating the Samaritan Pentateuch's Compilation in Light of the Qumran Biblical Scrolls." In *Emanuel: Studies in Hebrew Bible, Septuagint, and Dead Sea Scrolls in Honor of Emanuel Tov,* edited by Shalom M. Paul et al., 215-40. Leiden: Brill.

Friedlaender, Israel. 1910-11. "The Jews of Arabia and the Rechabites." *JQR,* n.s., 1:252-57.

Garbini, Giovanni. 2003. *Mito e storia nella Bibbia.* Brescia: Paideia.

García Martínez, Florentino. 1988. "Qumran Origins and Early History: A Groningen Hypothesis." *Folia Orientalia* 25:113-36.

————. 1996. *The Dead Sea Scrolls Translated: The Qumran Texts in English.* 2nd ed. Leiden: Brill.

García Martínez, Florentino, and Julio Trebolle Barrera. 1995. *The People of the Dead Sea Scrolls.* Leiden: Brill.

García Martínez, Florentino, and Adam S. van der Woude. 1990. "A Groningen Hypothesis of Qumran Origins and Early History." *RevQ* 14:522-41.

Garin, Eugenio. 1959. "Osservazioni preliminari a una storia della filosofia." *GCFI* 38:1-55.

Gero, Stephen. 1980. "The Legend of the Fourth Son of Noah." *HTR* 73:321-30.

Golb, Norman. 1995. *Who Wrote the Dead Sea Scrolls? The Search for the Secret of Qumran.* New York: Scribner.

Grelot, Pierre. 1958a. "La legende d'Hénoch dans les apocryphes et dans la Bible: Origine et significance." *RSR* 46:5-26, 181-210.

————. 1958b. "La géographie mythique d'Hénoch et ses sources orientales." *RB* 65:33-69.

Habermann, Abraham Meir, ed. 1949-56. *Kitvey R. Avraham Epstein.* Jerusalem: Mosad ha-Rav Kook.

Hamilton, Malcolm. 1995. *The Sociology of Religion: Theoretical and Comparative Perspectives.* London: Routledge.

Hengel, Martin. 1974. *Judaism and Hellenism.* Philadelphia: Fortress.

Himmelfarb, Martha. 1999. "Levi, Phinehas, and the Problem of Intermarriage at the Time of the Maccabean Revolt." *Jewish Studies Quarterly* 6:1-24.

Holden, Andrew. 2002. *Jehovah's Witnesses: Portrait of a Contemporary Religious Movement.* London: Routledge.

Humbert, Jean-Baptiste. 1994. "L'espace sacré à Qumrân: Proposition pour l'archéologie." *RB* 101, no. 2: 161-214.

————. 1998. "Qumrân, esséniens et architecture." In *Antikes Judentum und frühes Christentum: Festschrift für Hartmut Stegemann zum 65. Geburtstag,* edited by Bernd Kollmann, Wolfgang Reinbold, and Annette Steudel, 183-196. Berlin: De Gruyter.

Ilan, Tal. 2001. "Shelamzion in Qumran: New Insights." In *Historical Perspectives: From the Hasmoneans to Bar Kokhba in Light of the Dead Sea Scrolls. Proceedings of the Fourth International Symposium of the Orion Center for the Study of the Dead Sea Scrolls and Associated Literature, 27-31 January 1999,* edited by David M. Goodblatt, Avital Pinnick, and Daniel R. Schwartz, 57-68. Leiden: Brill.

Jaffee, Martin S. 2002-3. "[On] Gabriele Boccaccini, *Roots of Rabbinic Judaism: An Intellectual History, from Ezekiel to Daniel,* Grand Rapids: Eerdmans, 2002." *Journal of Hebrew Scriptures* 4.

Jansen, H. Ludin. 1939. *Die Henochgestalt: Eine vergleichende religionsgeschichtliche Untersuchung.* Oslo: Dybwad.

Jellinek, Adolph, ed. 1853-77. *Bet ha-Midrasch.* Reprint, Jerusalem: Bamberger and Wahrmann.

Jokiranta, Jutta M. 2001. "Sectarianism of the Qumran Sect: Sociological Notes." *RevQ* 20, no. 2: 223-39.

Jonge, Marinus de. 1975. *The Testaments of the Twelve Patriarchs: A Study of Their Text, Composition, and Origin.* Amsterdam and Assen: Van Gorcum.

————. 2003. *Pseudepigrapha of the Old Testament as Part of Christian Literature: The Case of the Testaments of the Twelve Patriarchs and the Greek Life of Adam and Eve.* SVTP 18. Leiden: Brill.

Knibb, Michael A. 1978. *The Ethiopic Book of Enoch: A New Edition in the Light of the Aramaic Dead Sea Fragments.* Oxford: Clarendon.

————. 2001. "Christian Adoption and Transmission of Jewish Pseudepigrapha: The Case of 1 Enoch." *JSJ* 32:396-415.

Kraft, Robert A. 2003. "The Weighing of the Parts: Pivots and Pitfalls in the Study of Early Judaisms and Their Early Christian Offspring." In *The Ways That Never Parted: Jews and Christians in Late Antiquity and the Early Middle Ages,* edited by Adam H. Becker and Annette Y. Reed, 87-94. TSAJ 95. Tübingen: Mohr.

Kugler, Robert A. 1996a. *From Patriarch to Priest: The Levi-Priestly Tradition from Aramaic Levi to Testament of Levi.* Atlanta: Scholars.

————. 1996b. "A Note on 1QS 9:14: The Sons of Righteousness or the Sons of Zadok?" *DSD* 3, no. 3: 315-20.

————. 1999a. "The Priesthood at Qumran: The Evidence of References to Levi and the Levites." In *The Provo International Conference on the Dead Sea Scrolls: Technological Innovations, New Texts, and Reformulated Issues,* edited by Donald W. Parry and Eugene C. Ulrich, 465-79. STDJ 30. Leiden: Brill.

————. 1999b. "Priesthood at Qumran." In *The Dead Sea Scrolls after Fifty Years: A Comprehensive Assessment,* edited by Peter W. Flint and James C. VanderKam, 2:93-116. Leiden: Brill.

————. 2001. *The Testaments of the Twelve Patriarchs.* Guides to Apocrypha and Pseudepigrapha 10. Sheffield: Sheffield Academic Press.

Lange, Armin. 1995. *Weisheit und Prädestination.* Leiden: Brill.

Laperrousaz, Ernest-Marie. 1976. *Qoumrân, l'établissement essénien des bords de la Mer Morte, histoire et archéologie du site.* Paris: Picard.

Magness, Jodi. 2002. *The Archaeology of Qumran and the Dead Sea Scrolls.* Grand Rapids: Eerdmans.

Marcus, Joel. 1996. "Modern and Ancient Jewish Apocalypticism." *JR* 76:1-27.

Martone, Corrado. 1994. "Nuovi testimoni qumranici della Regola della comunità." *Hen* 16:173-87.

————. 1995. *La Regola della Comunità. Edizione Critica.* Turin: Zamorani.

Mendels, Doron. 1979. "Hellenistic Utopia and the Essenes." *HTR* 72:207-22.

Metso, Sarianna. 1997a. *The Textual Development of the Qumran Community Rule.* STDJ 21. Leiden: Brill.

————. 1997b. "The Textual Traditions of the Qumran Community Rule." In *Legal Texts and Legal Issues: Proceedings of the Second Meeting of the International Organization for Qumran Studies, Cambridge, 1995: Published in Honour of Joseph M. Baumgarten,* edited by Moshe J. Bernstein, Florentino García Martínez, and John Kampen, 141-47. STDJ 23. Leiden: Brill.

————. 2000. "The Redaction of the Community Rule." In *The Dead Sea Scrolls: Fifty Years after Their Discovery. Proceedings of the Jerusalem Congress, July 20-25, 1997,* edited by Lawrence H. Schiffman, Emanuel Tov, and James C. VanderKam, 377-84. Jerusalem: Israel Exploration Society in cooperation with the Shrine of the Book, Israel Museum.

Milik, Josef T. 1959. *Ten Years of Discovery in the Wilderness of Judaea.* Translated by John Strugnell. Naperville, Ill.: Allenson.

————. 1976. *The Books of Enoch: Aramaic Fragments of Qumrân Cave 4*. Oxford: Clarendon.

Mosshammer, Alden A., ed. 1984. *Georgii Syncelli: Ecloga Chronographica*. Leipzig: Teubner.

Muro, Ernest A., Jr. 1998. "The Greek Fragments of Enoch from Qumran Cave 7 (7Q4, 7Q8, & 7Q12 = 7QEn gr = Enoch 103:3-4, 7-8)." *RevQ* 18, no. 70: 307-12.

Murray, R. 1985. "Disaffected Judaism and Early Christianity: Some Predisposing Factors." In *"To See Ourselves as Others See Us": Christians, Jews, "Others" in Late Antiquity*, edited by Jacob Neusner and Ernest S. Frerichs, 263-81. Chico, Calif.: Scholars.

Nebe, G. Wilhelm. 1988. "7Q4 — Möglichkeit und Grenze einer Identifikation." *RevQ* 13:49-52, 629-33.

Neubauer, Adolf. 1888-89. "Where Are the Ten Tribes? II. Eldad the Danite." *JQR*, o.s., 1:95-114.

Neusner, Jacob. 1998. *The Four Stages of Rabbinic Judaism*. London: Routledge.

Nickelsburg, George W. E. 1981. "Enoch, Levi, and Peter: Recipients of Revelation in Upper Galilee." *JBL* 100:575-600.

————. 1998. "Enochic Wisdom: An Alternative to the Mosaic Torah?" In *Hesed Ve-Emet: Studies in Honor of Ernest S. Frerichs*, edited by Jodi Magness and Seymour Gittin, 123-32. Atlanta: Scholars.

————. 1999. "Currents in Qumran Scholarship: The Interplay of Data, Agendas, and Methodology." In *The Dead Sea Scrolls at Fifty: Proceedings of the 1997 Society of Biblical Literature Qumran Section Meetings*, edited by Robert A. Kugler and Eileen M. Schuller, 79-99. Atlanta: Scholars.

————. 2001. *1 Enoch 1: A Commentary on the Book of 1 Enoch, Chapters 1–36; 81–108*. Hermeneia. Minneapolis: Fortress.

Pagels, Elaine H. 1995. *The Origin of Satan*. New York: Random House.

Patterson, Dilys Naomi. 2002. "Honoured in Her Time: Queen Shelamzion and the Book of Judith." Ph.D. diss., University of Ottawa.

Peursen, Wido Th. van. 2001. "Qumran Origins: Some Remarks on the Enochic/Essene Hypothesis." *RevQ* 20, no. 2: 241-53.

Puech, Émile. 1996. "Notes sur les fragments grecs du manuscrit 7Q4 = 1 Hénoch 103 et 105." *RB* 103:592-600.

————. 1998. "Sept fragments grecs de la Lettre d'Hénoch (1 Hén 100, 103 et 105) dans la grotte 7 de Qumrân (= 7QHéngr)." *RevQ* 18, no. 70: 313-23.

————. 1999. "Le grand prêtre Simon (III) fils d'Onias III, le Maître de Justice?" In *Antikes Judentum und frühes Christentum: Festschrift für Hartmut Stegemann zum 65. Geburtstag*, edited by Bernd Kollmann, Wolfgang Reinbold, and Annette Steudel, 137-58. BZNW 97. Berlin and New York: De Gruyter.

————. 2001. "Livre des Géants." In *Qumrân Grotte 4. XXII: Textes araméens, première partie, 4Q529-49*, 9-115. Oxford: Clarendon.

Qimron, Elisha, and John Strugnell. 1994. *Qumran Cave 4. V: Miqsat Maʿase Ha-Torah*. Oxford: Clarendon.

Qirqisānī. 1939-43. *Kitâb al-anwâr wa'l-marâqib*. New York: Alexander Kohut Memorial Foundation.

Reed, Annette Y. 2002. "What the Fallen Angels Taught: The Reception-History of the Book of the Watchers in Judaism and Christianity." Ph.D. diss., Princeton University.

———. 2003. "The Textual Identity, Literary History, and Social Setting of 1 Enoch: Reflections on George Nickelsburg's Commentary on 1 Enoch 1–36; 81–108." *Archiv für Religionsgeschichte* 5, no. 1: 279-96.

Reeves, John C. 1992. *Jewish Lore in Manichaean Cosmogony: Studies in the Book of Giants Traditions*. Cincinnati: Hebrew Union College Press.

———. 1998. "Enoch, Books of." In *Encyclopaedia Iranica* 8.5, 453-55.

———. 1999. "Exploring the Afterlife of Jewish Pseudepigrapha in Medieval Near Eastern Traditions: Some Initial Soundings." *JSJ* 30:148-77.

———. 2003. "Some Explorations of the Intertwining of Bible and Qur'ân." In *Bible and Qur'ân: Essays in Scriptural Intertextuality*, edited by John C. Reeves, 43-60. Atlanta: Society of Biblical Literature.

———. Forthcoming. *The Recovery of the Enochic Library*. Leiden: Brill.

Regev, Eyal. 2004. "Comparing Sectarian Practice and Organization: The Qumran Sect in Light of the Regulations of the Shakers, Hutterites, Mennonites and Amish." *Numen* 51:146-81.

Ri, Su-Min, ed. 1987. *La Caverne des Trésors: Les deux recensions syriaques*. Louvain: Peeters.

Sacchi, Paolo. 1990. *L'apocalittica giudaica e la sua storia*. Brescia: Paideia.

———. 1997a. *Jewish Apocalyptic and Its History*. Translated by William J. Short. JSPSup 20. Sheffield: Sheffield Academic Press.

———. 1997b. "A New Step Towards a Deeper Knowledge of the Jewish Second Temple Thought: Review of John J. Collins, *Apocalypticism in the Dead Sea Scrolls*." *Hen* 19, no. 3: 367-72.

———. 1998. "Enochism, Qumranism and Apocalyptic: Some Thoughts on a Recent Book." *Hen* 20, no. 1: 357-65.

———. 2000. *The History of the Second Temple Period*. Sheffield: Sheffield Academic Press.

———. 2003. "The Theology of Early Enochism and Apocalyptic. The Problem of the Relationship between Form and Content of the Apocalypses: The Worldview of Apocalypses." In *The Origins of Enochic Judaism. Proceedings of the First Enoch Seminar. University of Michigan, Sesto Fiorentino, Italy, June 19-23, 2001*, edited by Gabriele Boccaccini, 77-85. Turin: Zamorani [=*Henoch* 24].

Safrai, Zeev. 1979. "The Sons of Yehonadav ben Rekhav and the Essenes." *Bar Ilan Annual*, 16-17, 37-58.

Saldarini, Anthony J. 2000. "Sectarianism." In *Encyclopedia of the Dead Sea Scrolls*, edited by Lawrence H. Schiffman and James C. VanderKam, 2:853-57. Oxford: Oxford University Press.

Sanders, E. P. 1977. *Paul and Palestinian Judaism*. Philadelphia: Fortress.

Schmidt, Francis. 2001. *How the Temple Thinks: Identity and Social Cohesion in Ancient Judaism.* Translated by J. Edward Crowley. Original in French, 1994. Sheffield: Sheffield Academic Press.

Schwartz, Seth. 2001. *Imperialism and Jewish Society, 200 B.C.E. to 640 C.E.* Princeton: Princeton University Press.

Shahrastânî. 1951-55. *Kitâb al-milal wa'l-nial.* Cairo: Matba'at al-Azhar.

Shochat, Azriel. 1971. "Eldad ha-Dani." In *Encyclopaedia Judaica* 6, 576-78.

Smith, Jonathan Z. 1975. "Wisdom and Apocalyptic." In *Religious Syncretism in Antiquity,* edited by Birger A. Pearson, 131-56. Missoula, Mont.: Scholars.

Smith, Morton. 1971. *Palestinian Parties and Politics That Shaped the Old Testament.* New York and London: Columbia University Press.

Stegemann, Hartmut. 1971. *Die Entstehung der Qumrangemeinde.* Bonn: published privately.

———. 1992. "The Qumran Essenes — Local Members of the Main Jewish Union of the Late Second Temple Times." In *The Madrid Qumran Congress: Proceedings of the International Congress on the Dead Sea Scrolls, Madrid, 18-21 March 1991,* edited by Julio Trebolle Barrera and Luis Vegas Montaner, 83-166. Leiden: Brill.

Stone, Michael E. 1978. "The Book of Enoch and Judaism in the Third Century BCE." *CBQ* 40:479-92.

———. 1988. "Enoch, Aramaic Levi, and Sectarian Origins." *JSJ* 19:159-70.

Stordalen, T. 2000. *Echoes of Eden: Genesis 2–3 and Symbolism of the Eden Garden in Biblical Hebrew Literature.* Leuven: Peeters.

Strugnell, John, and Daniel J. Harrington. 1999. *Qumran Cave 4. XXIV: Sapiential Texts, Part 2. 4QInstruction.* DJD 34. Oxford: Clarendon.

Stuckenbruck, Loren T. 1997. *The Book of Giants from Qumran: Texts, Translation, and Commentary.* Tübingen: Mohr Siebeck.

———. 2000. "4Q201 2-8 and Book of Giants Fragments." In *Qumran Cave 4,* XXVI: *Cryptic Texts . . . and Miscellanea, Part I,* edited by Stephen J. Pfann et al., 3-94. Oxford: Clarendon.

Suter, David W. 1979. "Fallen Angel, Fallen Priest: The Problem of Family Purity in 1 Enoch 6–16." *HUCA* 50:115-35.

———. 1992. "Of the Devil's Party: The Marriage of Heaven and Hell in *Satanic Verses.*" *South Asian Review* 16, no. 13 (January): 63-78.

———. 1993. "[On] Maxwell J. Davidson, *Angels at Qumran: A Comparative Study of 1 Enoch 1–36, 72–108 and Sectarian Writings from Qumran.*" *IOUDAIOS Review* 3, no. 19 (August).

———. 2002. "Fallen Angels Revisited." In *The Origins of Enochic Judaism,* edited by Gabriele Boccaccini, 137-42. Turin: Zamorani [= *Henoch* 24].

———. 2003. "Why Galilee? Galilean Regionalism in the Interpretation of 1 Enoch 6–16." *Hen* 25:167-212.

Tabor, James D. 1998. "Patterns of the End: Textual Weaving from Qumran to Waco." In *Toward the Millennium: Messianic Expectations from the Bible to Waco,* edited by Peter Schäfer and Mark Cohen, 409-30. Leiden: Brill.

Talmon, Shemaryahu. 1986. *King, Cult, and Calendar in Ancient Israel.* Jerusalem: Magness.

Tigchelaar, Eibert J. C. 2001. *To Increase Learning for the Understanding Ones: Reading and Reconstructing the Fragmentary Early Jewish Sapiential Text 4QInstruction.* STDJ 44. Leiden: Brill.

Tiller, Patrick A. 1993. *A Commentary on the Animal Apocalypse of I Enoch.* Atlanta: Scholars.

―――. 1997. "The 'Eternal Planting' in the Dead Sea Scrolls." *DSD* 4:312-35.

Tov, Emanuel. 1986. "The Orthography and Language of the Hebrew Scrolls Found at Qumran and the Origin and Language of These Scrolls." *Textus* 13:31-57.

―――. 1988. "Hebrew Biblical Manuscripts from the Judaean Desert: Their Contribution to Textual Criticism." *JJS* 39:6-37.

―――. 1993a. *The Dead Sea Scrolls on Microfiche: A Comprehensive Facsimile Edition of the Texts from the Judean Desert.* Leiden: IDC and Brill.

―――. 1993b. "The Qumran Scribal School" (in Hebrew). In *Studies in Bible and Exegesis: Moshe Goshen-Gottstein — in Memoriam,* edited by Mosheh Bar-Asher et al., 135-54. Ramat Gan: Ramat Gan University Press.

―――. 1995. "Letters of the Cryptic A Script and Paleo-Hebrew Letters Used as Scribal Marks in Some Qumran Scrolls." *DSD* 2, no. 2: 330-39.

―――. 1996a. "Scribal Markings in the Texts from the Judean Desert." In *Current Research and Technological Developments on the Dead Sea Scrolls,* edited by Donald W. Parry and Stephen D. Ricks, 41-77. STDJ 20. Leiden: Brill.

―――. 1996b. "The Socio-Religious Background of the Paleo-Hebrew Biblical Texts Found at Qumran." In *Geschichte — Tradition — Reflexion, Festschrift für Martin Hengel,* edited by Hubert Cancik et al., 1:353-74. Tübingen: Mohr Siebeck.

―――. 1997a. "Further Evidence for the Existence of a Qumran Scribal School." In *The Dead Sea Scrolls Fifty Years after Their Discovery: Major Issues and New Approaches. Proceedings of the Jerusalem Congress, July 20-25, 1997,* edited by Lawrence H. Schiffman et al., 199-216. Jerusalem: Israel Exploration Society.

―――. 1997b. "Tefillin of Different Origin from Qumran." In *A Light for Jacob: Studies in the Bible and the Dead Sea Scrolls. In Memory of Jacob S. Licht,* edited by Yair Hoffman and Frank H. Polak, 44-54. Jerusalem: Bialik Institute.

―――. 2001. *Textual Criticism of the Hebrew Bible.* 2nd ed. Minneapolis: Fortress.

―――. 2003. "The Nature of the Large-Scale Differences between the LXX and MT S T V, Compared with Similar Evidence in Other Sources." In *The Earliest Text of the Hebrew Bible: The Relationship between the Masoretic Text and the Hebrew Base of the Septuagint Reconsidered,* edited by Adrian Schenker, 121-44. Leiden: Brill.

Vaillant, André. 1952. *Le livre des secrets d'Hénoch: Texte slave et traduction française.* Paris: Institut d'études slaves.

VanderKam, James C. 1984. *Enoch and the Growth of an Apocalyptic Tradition.* Washington, D.C.: Catholic Biblical Association of America.

————. 1998. *Calendars in the Dead Sea Scrolls: Measuring Time.* New York: Routledge.

Vaux, Roland de. 1973. *Archaeology and the Dead Sea Scrolls.* Rev. ed. London: Oxford University Press.

Vermes, Geza. 1956. *Discovery in the Judaean Desert.* New York: Desclee.

Wasserstrom, Steven M. 1998. "Šahrastānī on the Maġāriyya." *Israel Oriental Studies* 17:127-54.

Weber, Max. 1930. *The Protestant Ethic and the Spirit of Capitalism.* New York: Charles Scribner's Sons.

————. 1952. *Ancient Judaism.* New York: Free Press.

Whiston, William, and Paul L. Maier, eds. 1980. *The New Complete Works of Josephus.* Peabody, Mass.: Hendrickson.

Williams, Michael A. 1996. *Rethinking "Gnosticism": An Argument for Dismantling a Dubious Category.* Princeton: Princeton University Press.

Wilson, Bryan R. 1982. *Religion in Sociological Perspective.* Oxford: Oxford University Press.

Wise, Michael O. 2003. "Dating the Teacher of Righteousness and the *Floruit* of His Movement." *JBL* 122:53-87.

Wright, Benjamin G. 1997. "Fear the Lord and Honor the Priest: Ben Sira as Defender of the Jerusalem Priesthood." In *The Book of Ben Sira in Modern Research: Proceedings of the First International Ben Sira Conference, 28-31 July 1996, Soesterberg, Netherlands,* edited by Pancratius C. Beenties, 189-222. BZAW 255. Berlin: De Gruyter.

Wüstenfeld, Ferdinand, ed. 1848-49. *Zakarija Ben Muhammed Ben Mahmud el-Cazwini's Kosmographie.* Reprint, Wiesbaden: Martin Sändig.

Yassif, Eli, ed. 2001. *Sefer ha-Zikronot hu' Divrey ha-Yamim le-Yerame'el.* Tel Aviv: Tel Aviv University.

Zangenberg, Jürgen. 1999. "The Final Farewell: A Necessary Paradigm Shift in the Interpretation of the Qumran Cemetery." *Qumran Chronicle* 8:273-78.

Zias, Joseph E. 2000. "The Cemeteries of Qumran and Celibacy: Confusion Laid to Rest?" *DSD* 7:220-53.

Summary and Conclusions:
The Books of Enoch or 1 Enoch Matters:
New Paradigms for Understanding Pre-70 Judaism

James H. Charlesworth

ויהי כל־ימי חנוך חמש וששים שנה ושלש מאות שנה
ויתהלך חנוך את־האלהים ואיננו כי־לקח אתו אלהים

All the days of Enoch amounted to 365 years.
And Enoch walked continuously with God [or the angels];
then he was no more, for God took him. (Gen 5:23-24)

Introduction

At the invitation of the University of Michigan, a group of scholars highly trained in second temple Judaism and Christian origins, and most experts on the books of Enoch (= 1 Enoch),[1] have agreed to convene biennially in various sites in Italy (Florence 2001, Venice 2003, Camaldoli 2005 . . .).

We meet and discuss the problems confronted by one or more of the books of Enoch. So far the sessions have been organized according to the chronological order in which these books were composed. In spite of the presence of different approaches and sensitivities, we have worked together harmoniously. We tend to listen to one another, even when we often disagree. Intolerance of another's opinion has been replaced characteristically by an impressive appreciation.

---

1. "1 Enoch" or "Ethiopic Enoch" is the term that has been used to designate this apocalyptic work; to clarify that the work is composite and consists of at least five books that were composed by different Jews over more than two centuries at least, I have chosen, except when citing the history of scholarship, to use the more appropriate term the "books of Enoch."

436

I am pleased to present here my own summary of what has been accomplished in the most recent symposium and assess how and in what ways knowledge has been advanced. In the present work I shall thus focus, inter alia, upon four main questions: (a) What are the most important achievements of the international Enoch Seminar? (b) How has an understanding of second temple Judaism been advanced by the discussions among many of the world's leading authorities in this area of research? (c) Have any new perspectives opened? (d) What new challenges are becoming clearer?

The Importance of the Books of Enoch

At the outset it is prudent to focus on the importance of the books of Enoch. During the nineteenth and twentieth centuries, before the discovery of the Qumran scrolls, some experts rightly elevated the books of Enoch, but they often did so by celebrating a shining light perceived as being outside the canon and apocryphal. Note these quotations:

> That the author was uninspired, will be scarcely now questioned; but, although his production was apocryphal . . . it may nevertheless contain much moral as well as religious truth; and may be justly regarded as a correct standard of the doctrine of the times in which it was composed.[2]

> 1 Hénoch est . . . un des plus célèbres des livres apocryphes.[3]

> The influence of 1 Enoch on the New Testament has been greater than that of all the other apocryphal and pseudepigraphal books taken together.[4]

> The Book of Enoch is for the history of theological development the most important pseudepigraph of the first two centuries B.C. Some of its authors — and there were many — belonged to the true succession of the prophets.[5]

---

2. R. Laurence, *The Book of Enoch* (Oxford: J. H. Parker, 1833), xlvi. In the early nineteenth century Laurence was obviously overshadowed by forces that celebrated the dominance of the canon. The situation no longer is so apposite for specialists. I shall limit footnotes to classic work, such as the book by Laurence, and the most recent publications.

3. J.-B. Migne, *Dictionnaire des apocryphes, ou collection de tous les livres apocryphes* (Paris, 1858), vol. 2, col. 223.

4. R. H. Charles, *The Book of Enoch or 1 Enoch* (Oxford: Clarendon, 1912), xcv.

5. R. H. Charles, *APOT* (1913), 2.163. Charles seems to take back with one hand what he gave in the other.

1 Enoch was comprehended in terms of the canon. Also, interest in it was almost always as a precursor of Jesus and Christianity, which was defined as distinct. Judaism was not appreciated and honored in and for itself, a malady that continues in many seminaries in the United States and elsewhere. Even Charles referred to "the evil character of the period," which meant the Judaism of the time that produced 1 Enoch (*APOT* 2.163).

Even after portions of the Aramaic text at Qumran were made available in the 1950s, specialists of second temple Judaism and Christian origins have largely continued to ignore the work. Particularly in the case of the Parables of Enoch, they were usually afraid the work, or a major section of it, was a Christian composition or represented Christian reworking of an earlier Jewish document.[6]

One example of this attitude alone must suffice. E. P. Sanders makes use of the books of Enoch except for the Parables of Enoch which are "omitted" in his discussion. Sanders is convinced that this book is "probably post-Christian in origin." He considers it likely that Milik is correct that the Parables of Enoch, which he calls the Similitudes, replaces the Book of the Giants. He judges "unusually cogent" J. C. Hindley's argument that the Parthian invasion, mentioned in 1 Enoch 56:5-7, should be dated to the period between 115 and 117 C.E. Sanders rightly points out that the absence of the Parables of Enoch among the Qumran fragments may be an accident, but much more significant is his correct perspective of "the paucity of even possible references to the Similitudes in the New Testament and early fathers." Sanders wisely refers to the "remarkable role played by the Son of Man" in the Parables of Enoch, and states that the "Christian ring of the passages about the Son of Man sitting on the throne of his glory (e.g. 62.5) seem easier to explain on the hypothesis of a post-Christian date than not."[7]

Most members of the Enoch Seminar would rather hear the sound of this "Christian ring" within the orchestra of second temple Judaism. In my own judgment they are correct, and we are beginning to explore — by focusing on

---

6. That opinion has been virtually a consensus among members of the Studiorum Novi Testamenti Societas, even at times by members of the Pseudepigrapha Seminar and the Seminar on the Pseudepigrapha and Christian Origins — two seminars that ran, with about a five-year interruption, from 1976 to the present. I have firsthand knowledge of this fact, since I was the convener of the first seminar and the coconvener of the second. Without disappointing redundancy I have been told by the leading NT scholars that 1 Enoch, or at least the Parables of Enoch, should not be included in an assessment of second temple Judaism or even in terms of the development of New Testament theology.

7. E. P. Sanders, *Paul and Palestinian Judaism* (Philadelphia: Fortress, 1977), 346-48, 377, 564.

the books of Enoch and related Jewish documents — just what might be meant by the Jewishness of Jesus and the fact that the Palestinian Jesus movement was one of the early Jewish groups.

It is only in the last few decades that leading scholars have been willing to affirm that the books of Enoch are the most important of the documents composed during second temple Judaism — and traditionally collected within the Old Testament Apocrypha and Pseudepigrapha. The books of Enoch are not branded as apocryphal — a perspective I find refreshing among the members of the Enoch Seminar. Note the following selections from experts on the books of Enoch:

> Insieme coi Giubilei e coi Testamenti dei Dodici Patriarchi . . . il libro di Enoc forma un'ottima trilogia per la conoscenza del mondo giudaico precristiano.[8]

> Nach der überwiegend fruchtlosen Diskussion um die Quellen der Bilderreden hat sich die Henochforschung stärker den traditionsgeschichtlichen Fragen und dort insbesondere denen um die Messiasgestalt zugewandt. Dabei gewinnt im Lichte der Jesusforschung das Problem der Datierung dieses Traktates große Bedeutung.[9]

> Certainly, if Daniel can be called the classic Jewish apocalypse, 1 Enoch does not come far behind, and may even have equal claim to classical status in intertestamental literature; and if the so-called Parables of Enoch did, in fact, precede the Gospels, they constitute a remarkable *praeparatio evangelica.*[10]

> 1 Enoch is . . . arguably the most important text in the corpus of Jewish literature from the Hellenistic and Roman periods.[11]

> 1 Enoch is a collection of apocalyptic (revelatory) texts that were composed between the late fourth century B.C.E. and the turn of the era. The size of the collection, the diversity of its contents, and its many implications for the study of ancient Judaism and Christian origins make it arguably the

8. P. Sacchi, *Apocrifi dell'Antico Testamento* (Turin: Unione Tipografico-Editrice, 1981), 1:423.

9. S. Uhlig, *Das äthiopische Henochbuch,* JSHRZ 5.6 (Gütersloh: Gerd Mohn, Gütersloher Verlagshaus, 1984), 574.

10. M. Black, *The Book of Enoch or I Enoch,* SVTP 7 (Leiden: Brill, 1985), 1.

11. G. W. E. Nickelsburg, *1 Enoch* (Minneapolis: Fortress, 2001), 1.

most important Jewish writing that has survived from the Greco-Roman period.[12]

These comments are distinct from those offered by scholars in the nineteenth century and early twentieth century, which (as we have seen) are dated by the assumption that what is apocryphal is always inferior and uninspired compared to the canon. In my judgment the books of Enoch seem, in some ways, even more important than Daniel. This canonical text is certainly exceptionally important, but it is basically an anonymous text, composite, and divided into two poorly related sections (with Hebrew and Aramaic sections mixed within each):[13] chapters 1–6, stories about Daniel, and 7–12, apocalyptic visions.[14] In no way does it denigrate Daniel to recognize genius and perhaps "revelation" also in the books of Enoch. Specialists should not be afraid of the power of the canon (the Hebrew canon), which clearly was not closed before 70 c.e..[15] The new wind blowing into academic studies is invigorating. Its freshness contrasts with an old (perhaps too perennial) breeze that brands many early Jewish texts as "apocryphal," marginal, and primarily important because they help us understand Christian origins.[16]

The study of 1 Enoch often was tinged by anti-Judaism (or anti-Semitism). The quotation from Charles presented earlier is both disappointing and enlightening. What was outside the "Christian canon" must be judged to be inferior. In the past it was almost always Christians who were showing interest

12. G. W. E. Nickelsburg and J. C. VanderKam, *1 Enoch: A New Translation* (Minneapolis: Fortress, 2004), vii. I obtained a set of the uncorrected proofs of this work from Bob Todd of Augsburg Fortress on the day I was completing this paper. I am grateful to him for this assistance.

13. While this comment on Daniel may seem shocking to some, I am only trying to describe the nature of the edited work, which is clearly composite. Also see the comments by John Collins and Florentino García Martínez in the present volume.

14. John Collins, in the present volume, reiterates a point that should have become axiomatic for the leading experts; that is, the noun "apocalyptic" makes sense in German but not in English, where it often obfuscates.

15. See the discussion of Annette Reed's points by VanderKam in the present volume.

16. An example of the misperception of 1 Enoch is found in J. Y. Campbell, "The Origin and Meaning of the Term Son of Man," *JTS* 48 (1947): 145-55. Also, see Boccaccini's introduction in the present volume. The new current is obviously not only a distinction of the Enoch Seminar. It is represented by the Princeton Theological Seminary Dead Sea Scrolls Project; for example, with James Sanders I decided to shift the name of some psalms from "apocryphal" to "non-Masoretic." Thus, they are no longer presented in terms of some canon. See J. A. Sanders, J. H. Charlesworth, and H. Rietz, "Non-Masoretic Psalms," in *Pseudepigraphic and Non-Masoretic Psalms and Prayers,* ed. Charlesworth with Rietz, PTSDSSP 4A (Tübingen: Mohr Siebeck; Louisville: Westminster John Knox, 1997), ad loc.

in the so-called Jewish apocryphal books. All too frequently scholars continued their theological agendas in studying these texts, perhaps in an attempt to clarify the uniqueness of Jesus or Christian theology. Research was intermittently undermined by an assumption that Christianity must be distinct from and superior to Judaism. Some of the authors studying 1 Enoch even harbored the belief that Christianity had superseded Judaism. As Gerd Theissen and Dagmar Winter point out, research on Judaism and Christian origins has suffered from two main ideologies: confessionalism and anti-Semitism.[17]

While only a few Jews were formerly devoted to the study of the so-called Pseudepigrapha, now many leading Jewish scholars are active in this area of research. Space will permit mentioning only a select number, including Alan Segal, Michael Stone, Devorah Dimant, Albert Baumgarten, Esther Eshel, Lawrence Schiffman, Hanan Eshel, Ithamar Gruenwald, and Shemaryahu Talmon. More importantly, reading the papers of scholars reveals a shared methodology and no evidence of the precommitments of the authors. In fact, one should not be concerned who argues what but what is being argued.

How important are the books of Enoch? The books conveniently labeled the books of Enoch were pseudonymously attributed to the wise and experienced Enoch. Most likely, in my judgment, they are the most important and creative collection of documents produced in second temple Judaism. The collection's cohesiveness, complex thoughts, development of earlier traditions, and sheer mass distinguish it from all other compositions of the time. The corpus is important because it is full of brilliant insights and reflections, is one of the major apocalypses ever written, and ultimately, in the final composition or book, elevates Enoch as the Son of Man.

What is the provenience of this collection of writings? A group of Jews gathered, perhaps in Galilee near Mount Hermon, probably sometime after Alexander the Great's conquest of ancient Palestine in the late fourth century B.C.E., and began to compile and write new compositions. They attributed their insights and claims to new revelations linked to, and perhaps received from, the antediluvian Enoch. This pseudepigraphical attribution was a wise choice. Enoch is introduced in the first book in the Tanakh (the Hebrew Bible, or Old Testament) as a special character who "walked continuously with God [or the angels]; then he was no more, for God took him" (Gen 5:23-24). Moreover, in the Hebrew Bible (but not the LXX) Enoch is listed in a significant position; he is seventh after Adam.

Enoch was lauded in later Jewish communities, including those in which

---

17. See G. Theissen and D. Winter, *The Quest for the Plausible Jesus,* trans. M. E. Boring (Louisville and London: Westminster John Knox, 2002), esp. 76.

Jesus of Nazareth was proclaimed the Messiah: "By faith Enoch was taken up so that he should not see death" (Heb 11:5). The author of Jude quoted from the books of Enoch, using the Greek verb to denote "prophesy," and shifting the prophecy in the attempt to prove predictions about the coming of "our Lord Jesus Christ": "Enoch prophesied of these things also in the seventh generation from Adam, saying, 'Behold, the Lord came with his holy myriads, to execute judgment on all, and to convict all the ungodly of all their deeds of ungodliness which they have committed in such an ungodly way, and of all the harsh things which ungodly sinners have spoken against him'" (Jude 14-15). The quotation of Enoch 1:9 by the author of Jude, in a slightly different form than in Greek, has been recovered in an earlier Aramaic form from the Qumran caves.[18]

Portions of the books of Enoch were saluted as important by early Jews and Christians. This list is impressive and includes the following selection: the authors of Jubilees, the Testament of Moses, the Testament of Simeon (5:4), the Testament of Levi (10:5; 14:1; 16:1), the Testament of Dan (5:6), the Testament of Jude (18:1), the Testament of Zebulon (3:4), the Testament of Naphtali (4:1), the Testament of Benjamin (9:1 [B]), the Testament of Reuben (5:1-6), 2 Baruch (perhaps), 4 Ezra (conceivably), Barnabas (4:3; 16:5-6), Justin Martyr *(Apologia breviore)*, Irenaeus *(Adversus Haereses* 4), Tertullian *(De idololatria)*,[19] Clement of Alexandria *(Eclogae Propheticae, Stromata)*, Origen (esp. *Comm. in Joannem* and *Contra Celsum;* but he offered contradictory advice),[20] and others.[21]

Eventually the books of Enoch were branded by rabbinic Jews and Christians as apocryphal and pushed aside. For rabbinic Jews as well as post-Nicene Christians the doctrines and perspectives developed by the Enoch scribes did not harmonize with what was deemed authoritative and revealed. In contrast to the Ethiopic church, the books of Enoch were not included in the canon of Scripture. Two leading forces behind this decision were Rabbi Judah the Prince, who compiled the Mishnah, and Jerome, who considered the book apocryphal.[22] The compiler of the *Apostolic Constitutions* did not consider the work canonical.

---

18. For a photograph of 4QEn[c] li, see J. H. Charlesworth, *Jesus within Judaism,* Anchor Bible Reference Library (New York: Doubleday, 1988), illus. 3, between pp. 46 and 47.

19. Esp. see the comments by Laurence, *The Book of Enoch,* xv-xvii.

20. For the Greek texts of some of these passages, see A.-M. Denis in *Apocalypsis Henochi Graece,* 10-14.

21. For Greek and Latin texts, see J. A. Fabricius, *Codex pseudepigraphus veteris testamenti* (Hamburg: Theodori Christoph. Felginer, 1722), 1:160-99. For an English discussion see Charles, *Book of Enoch,* lxx-xcv.

22. Jerome, *De viris illustribus* 4: "Et quia de libro Enoch, qui apocryphus est. . . ." Augustine judged against the books of Enoch. See Charles, *Book of Enoch,* xci-xcii.

Why would earlier Jews and "Christians" deem the books of Enoch important? If Enoch did not die but "was taken up," then he can reveal mysteries and secrets to God's faithful Jews now living on earth. The length of his life stimulated reflections on God's calendar; it was not lunar but solar, consisting of 365 units (for Enoch years, for each year "days").[23] The corpus is creative because there are many new and surprising concepts, such as the significance of the so-called solar calendar,[24] the dualism,[25] the relation between the Messiah and the Son of Man,[26] the knowledge that the moon receives its light from the sun, the minute observations of the sun's movement, the high moral insights, the development of the origin of sin (due to the fall of God's angels), and the perspectives of a future blessed day.

In these reflections the Jewish intellectuals who bequeathed to us the books of Enoch showed that they were versed not only in Tanakh but also in the discoveries made by Babylonians, Persians, Egyptians, and Greeks. The significance of the books of Enoch, which are often assumed (sometimes uncritically) to constitute five books like the five books of Moses (the Pentateuch), is placarded by the recognition that these books were composed from about 300 B.C.E. to sometime during the time of Herod the Great (40-4 B.C.E.) and even conceivably later. Thus, these compositions cover at least three centuries, and they took shape during the time second temple Judaism was developing perspectives and traditions that would be determinative for all forms of Judaism that survived the two great Jewish revolts of 66–73/74 and 132-35/36 C.E.

The books of Enoch were once labeled Ethiopic Enoch since they were extant partially in Greek[27] and primarily, and in some sections even today, only in Ethiopic. In 1773 James Bruce brought three Ethiopic manuscripts of Enoch

23. See VanderKam's response to Henry Rietz in the present volume.

24. The importance of calendrical debates within second temple Judaism is clear; they are certainly reflected in the books of Enoch. Observation of the laws and festivals demanded by the torah depends on following either the lunar or the solar calendar, not both. It seems that the solar calendar is older and the lunar calendar appeared within Judaism sometime in the early decades of the second century B.C.E. and defined the temple cult during the remainder of second temple Judaism.

25. Both 1QS and the Apocalypse of Weeks are shaped by dualism, if presented in different terms. See the response to Klaus Koch by Nickelsburg in his "Response: Context, Text, and Social Setting of the Apocalypse of Weeks" in the present volume.

26. In the present volume Collins argues that the Messiah in the books of Enoch (viz., 48:10; 52:4) is a heavenly figure described in language borrowed from Dan 7 in which the son of man appears.

27. Syncellus preserved excerpts of 6:1–10:14 and 15:8–16:1. Quotations are also found in the early church fathers, and Greek manuscripts have now been found. For a critical text see M. Black, ed., *Apocalypsis Henochi Graece,* PVTG 3 (Leiden: Brill, 1970).

from Ethiopia to England.[28] Since that time many manuscripts of Enoch in Ethiopic have been discovered, but the earliest is from about the fourteenth century C.E.[29] The late medieval date of these manuscripts caused careful historians to hesitate using the books of Enoch to comprehend pre-70 Jewish thought.

Prior to World War II, in attempting to re-create the thought world of pre-70 Judaism, scholars focused on the New Testament documents, Josephus's works, and the tractates in the Mishnah. Sometimes specialists glanced at the apocryphal compositions, including the books of Enoch; but these works were suspect since most had been transmitted only by Christian scribes and were judged nonessential for describing the world of second temple Judaism. Such documents were usually deemed marginal since they did not represent a putatively normative and orthodox Judaism.

Since at least 1970 scholars presuppose that the New Testament, Josephus's works, and the Mishnah were transmitted to us edited, altered, and with misleading perspectives. Virtually no specialist working in the Enoch Seminar talks about "orthodoxy" and "normative Judaism" in pre-70 Judaism. With the discovery in the Qumran caves of Aramaic fragments of all portions of Enoch, except the Parables of Enoch, specialists have a better understanding of the antiquity of these books. Some manuscripts date from about 200 B.C.E.[30] Even though the Aramaic manuscripts found near Qumran are disappointingly fragmentary, we can study them and obtain a better guide to what had been written and comprehended in second temple Judaism.

Four Main Questions

a. What are the most important achievements of the Enoch Seminar?

Contemporary research has still a long way to go until the value of the Pseudepigrapha and the Dead Sea Scrolls is fully recognized. It is disappointing to notice how the knowledge of "noncanonical" texts as well as of the archaeological work is still occasional and marginal even among many scholars of the period.

28. See E. Ullendorff, *The Ethiopians*, 3rd ed. (Oxford: Clarendon, 1973), 11-13.

29. Ephraim Isaac called me when the present work was almost completed. He informed me that a fourteenth-century manuscript of Enoch has been discovered in Ethiopia. I also know about a fragment of 1 En 8–9 that was probably found in Cave 4 but is unknown to scholars.

30. 4QEn[a] "seems to have been made from a very old copy, dating from the third century at the very least." See J. T. Milik, *The Books of Enoch: Aramaic Fragments of Qumrân Cave 4* (Oxford: Clarendon, 1976), 141.

In this regard I wish to stress some significant achievements of the Enoch Seminar. First is the focus on the most important document composed during second temple Judaism. The books of Enoch are finally receiving the detailed examination and exposure they deserve.

Second is the gathering of scholars — Jews and Christians — who are trained in this area to discuss together the books of Enoch and related texts in the attempt to move beyond the previous analysis that has characterized the study of this period in search of some synthesis. The Enoch Seminar represents a movement from analysis and myopic focus on one text to a synthesis based on the books of Enoch.

Third, there is widespread recognition that this book is really a library of books which represent numerous communities, over at least three centuries in ancient Palestine. The members of the Enoch Seminar should have removed any doubts that the books of Enoch are a library of books composed over many centuries. These works are thus clearly composite, and there is editing of sources and traditions in many of them.[31] The group of Jews who wrote, collected, and revered the books of Enoch obviously elevated one person above all others in the history of salvation. He is Enoch. Thus, there is more than a theological dimension to these writings. The Enochians, if that is an appropriate term, rejected as inferior those who revered Moses, David,[32] and Ezra; and that would include the priests, and high priests,[33] who controlled the sacerdotal aristocracy in the Jerusalem cult.

Fourth, most members of the Enoch Seminar wisely avoid labeling any of the Jewish documents usually placed in the Old Testament Apocrypha and Pseudepigrapha as if they were composed by Pharisees, Sadducees, Essenes, or Zealots. Most members of the seminar concur that Josephus's division of Jewish thought into four "philosophies" is misrepresentative. As many of us have warned for decades, we have no Zealot or Sadducean document, and we cannot

---

31. In the middle of the nineteenth century Migne rightly pointed out that "Enoch" is "hétérogènes." Migne, *Dictionnaire des apocryphes,* vol. 2, col. 224.

32. In the present volume John Collins insightfully points out that the books of Enoch and Daniel show a lack of interest in the Davidic monarchy.

33. See the important study by James C. VanderKam entitled *From Joshua to Caiaphas: High Priests after the Exile* (Minneapolis: Fortress; Assen: Van Gorcum, 2004). This is the first major study of the fifty-one high priests who often controlled political life in Palestine from 515 B.C.E. to 70 C.E. (sometimes as "heads of state"). VanderKam's tome completes what was begun by Schürer, Bevan, and Jeremias. The "Joshua" in the title is Joshua (Jeshua), the son of Jehozadak, who was a descendant of the last high priest in Solomon's temple. Joshua returned from Babylon to Palestine and reestablished the temple cult in 520 B.C.E. He is the first high priest of the second temple (cf. esp. Ezra 2:2 and 3:2 and Hag 1:1).

claim to possess a Pharisaic document that antedates 70 (though some still mislabel the Psalms of Solomon as Pharisaic).[34]

Fifth, it is certainly obvious to all members of the Enoch Seminar that we must no longer imagine a monolithic Judaism prior to 70 C.E.[35] Various concepts have not appealed to most members of the Enoch Seminar, among them the concept of chaos, the image of many detached Judaisms,[36] and the assumption of a "common Judaism."[37] The members of the Enoch Seminar tend to agree that we should talk about the numerous varieties of thought and action (praxis) within second temple Judaism. Clearly, it is agreed that one of the most important of these voices — actually numerous voices — is heard from the books of Enoch.

Sixth, quite surprisingly the members of the Enoch Seminar agreed on the probable date of the earliest composition among the books of Enoch. The consensus is now that the Book of the Watchers was composed by the early Hellenistic period and may reflect the struggles of the Diadochi after the death of Alexander the Great in 323 B.C.E. Thus, the writings now called the books of Enoch originated before 200 B.C.E., and conceivably as early as the end of the fourth century B.C.E.

b. How has an understanding of second temple Judaism been advanced?

It seems clear that the canon, which often shaped the study of second temple Judaism anachronistically, is no longer the defining force it was in the past. The "fear of the canon" became apparent when we reviewed the celebration of the importance of the books of Enoch. For example, Laurence, who prepared the

---

34. See Charlesworth, "A Rare Consensus among Enoch Specialists: The Date of the Earliest Enoch Books," in *The Origins of Enochic Judaism: Proceedings of the First Enoch Seminar: University of Michigan, Sesto Fiorentiono, Italy, June 19-23, 2001,* ed. G. Boccaccini, Henoch 24.1-2 (Turin: Silvio Zamorani Editore, 2002), 225-34.

35. See the following recent publications: Nickelsburg, *Ancient Judaism and Christian Origins: Diversity, Continuity, and Transformation* (Minneapolis: Fortress, 2003); J. S. Anderson, *The Internal Diversification of Second Temple Judaism* (Lanham, Md.: University Press of America, 2002).

36. J. Neusner, *The Judaism the Rabbis Take for Granted* (Atlanta: Scholars, 1994); see esp. 12 and 18.

37. "Common Judaism" was coined by E. P. Sanders. See Sanders, *Paul and Palestinian Judaism;* Sanders, *Jesus and Judaism* (Philadelphia: Fortress, 1985); and Sanders, *Jewish Law from Jesus to the Mishnah* (Philadelphia: Trinity, 1990); Sanders, *Judaism: Practice and Belief, 632 BCE–66 CE* (Philadelphia: Trinity, 1992). For a critique of his position, see M. Hengel and R. Deines, "E. P. Sanders' 'Common Judaism,' Jesus, and the Pharisees," *JTS,* n.s., 46 (1995): 1-70. J. Neusner has also been critical of Sanders, but Neusner's works are so well known to those who will read this report that mentioning them would be otiose.

first English translation of the work, felt compelled to refer to the "apocryphal Book of Enoch." Laurence was convinced that the "Book of Enoch," which he seems to have assumed was a unity, was written during the reign of Herod the Great and completed at "an early period" of that reign (37-4 B.C.E.).[38] Yet, while Laurence knew that the book was extremely important, he felt compelled to stress that it was only apocryphal. Note the full title of his publication: *The Book of Enoch, the Prophet: An Apocryphal Production.*

The documents composed during second temple Judaism have been customarily studied in terms of false barriers or imprecise categories and labels.[39] As I have pointed out repeatedly since the seventies, the categories in which early Jewish documents have been traditionally placed were never adequately examined in terms of cohesive criteria. Some collections were compiled in antiquity (sometimes before 70 C.E.); most important in this category would be the Hebrew Bible, the Septuagint, the Apocrypha, Philo, Josephus, the New Testament, and the early Mishnah (and Tosephta). Other documents have been separated from these roughly contemporaneous documents and categorized according to the place in which they were found; among these would be the Qumran scrolls, the Naḥal Ḥever manuscripts, the Masada manuscripts, the Naḥal Ṣe'elim manuscripts, the Samaritan manuscripts (the Wadi ed-Daliyeh documents), and the Wadi Murabba'at manuscripts (cf. also the Nag Hammadi codices). Even other categories resulted from modern decision, even if such collections were based on early lists of writings; most important among such would be the Pseudepigrapha and the Jewish magical papyri. Most members of the Enoch Seminar, as other experts, have tended now to include in their purview all early Jewish writings — regardless of categories — that are important for comprehending the history of composition represented by the books of Enoch.

A continuing sensitivity to methodology remains a hallmark of the Enoch Seminar. We all agree that it is a daunting task to make sense of the varied data before us. On the one hand, we do not want to impose some order that is not representative of all extant sources, literary and nonliterary. On the other hand, we recognize that there is some coherence within second temple Judaism. The members of the Enoch Seminar have felt the freedom to explore what that coherence might entail, and such explorations should become a part of future agendas.

While it is clear that the temple and the cult tended to unite Jews living in

---

38. Laurence, *The Book of Enoch*, xxxv.

39. See Charlotte Hempel's work in this volume and García Martínez's response to her about the use of "Palestinian apocalyptic tradition."

the Diaspora and those living in Palestine, it is also clear that the temple created diversity. Some excesses in the cult ruled by the sacerdotal aristocracy were criticized by the compilers of the Mishnah, explain the exodus of Aaronites and Levites to Qumran, help us comprehend some aspects of the Palestinian Jesus movement, and bring into focus the fact that the Samaritans are not to be ignored in our historical work — surely the Samaritan Pentateuch is virtually identical to the received Pentateuch in the *Biblia Hebraica Stuttgartensia* (except for the elevation of Gerizim and other clearly Samaritan redactions).

c. Have any new perspectives begun to appear?

We alluded to the treatment of documents being studied in terms of their own integrity, and not according to the category in which they may be found. What is so attractive now is the treatment of canonical books without giving them pride of place, as we have seen with Daniel. For example, no longer is Daniel perceived as the earliest Jewish work that contains a reference to the resurrection of those who have died; this honor now is clearly bestowed on the earliest sections of the books of Enoch.

The members of the Enoch Seminar conclude (or assume) that the books of Enoch were composed somewhere in Palestine (with many earlier experts including Migne [1.596]), and not in the Diaspora (*pace* Laurence). They see many conceptual links with the Qumran scrolls and the Essenes, but would not want to attribute the documents to Essenes (*pace* Jellinek). While many experts attribute the latest document, the Parables of Enoch, to the time of Herod the Great (viz., Sacchi, Nickelsburg, Charlesworth), they would stress, against Laurence and Hoffmann, who dated the entire work to that period, that the books of Enoch represent many books composed over at least three centuries.

Some new perspectives seem to appear in the use of terminology. More attention is being given to the groups and communities that have shaped or collected some of the early Jewish documents. Most important are the references to the Qumranites, Jesus' followers, and the Enoch groups. A consensus seems to be emerging that we can talk about a community or group of Jews behind the books of Enoch.[40] The degree to which the texts allow us to reconstruct the sociology of such a group and groups will always remain problematic.[41] Sociologists are not trained to work with texts, and it has proved impossible to present a sociology of any early group, including the Palestinian Jesus movement.

40. See esp. Nickelsburg, *1 Enoch,* esp. 46.
41. See esp. Nickelsburg's "Response" in the present volume.

Now, some experts follow the lead of Gabriele Boccaccini, who in 1998 introduced the term "Enochic Judaism." This is a new term but it has antecedents.[42] The first to refer to an "Enoch circle" seems to be Charles Albeck, who in 1930 perceived a group of Jews represented by 1 Enoch, Jubilees, 2 Enoch, and the Testaments of the Twelve Patriarchs.[43]

Albeck did point to some similarities that need to be explored in light of the refinement of methodology and perceptions since 1930, the recovery of the Qumran scrolls, and especially the evidence of Aramaic manuscripts of Enoch from the Qumran caves. While 1 Enoch and Jubilees represent similar but not identical groups within second temple Judaism,[44] the Testaments raise many issues and questions, even though the early Jewish traditions in them are linked somehow with those who produced 1 Enoch and Jubilees. To include 2 Enoch is problematic, since it is not a pre-70 composition and it is difficult to perceive the early Jewish source or tradition behind the extant Slavonic texts.

Boccaccini claims that the origins of the Essene community at Qumran can be discerned in Jewish groups that antedate the establishment of the community. He posits a special type of Judaism that existed since pre-Maccabean times; he calls it "Enochic Judaism." He contends that this type of Judaism represented by the books of Enoch clarifies the origins of the Qumranites. Further, he avers that after the Maccabean revolt, without losing its identity as a social group, this form of Judaism developed into the larger movement that our ancient authors called "the Essenes."

Scholars have often talked about two types of Essenes, those who married, represented by the Damascus Document, and those who were stricter and perhaps did not marry, represented by the Rule of the Community. These historians appeal to Josephus's comment that the Essenes were bifurcated (*War* 2.160).[45] Boccaccini claims to move this distinction further and with what he is convinced is new, more precise terminology. The Enochic community represented by the Qumran scrolls broke away from the Essenes living in towns and

42. The term is also used by Boccaccini's teacher, Paolo Sacchi. But he is now clearly influenced by Boccaccini. Both talk about "Zadokites" and "Enochians," "Zadokite Judaism" and "Enochic Judaism." See Sacchi, *The History of the Second Temple Period,* JSOTSup 285 (Sheffield: Sheffield Academic Press, 2000), esp. 18.

43. Charles Albeck, *Das Buch der Jubiläen und die Halacha,* BHWJ 47 (Berlin, 1930). See the review by L. Finkelstein in *MGWJ,* n.s., 76 (1932): 525-34.

44. See esp. J. C. VanderKam's "Response: Jubilees and Enoch" in the present volume. In particular, see his response to Martha Himmelfarb.

45. Josephus reported that "there is also another order of Essenes *(heteron Essenōn tagma),* which at one with the rest in its mode of life, customs, and regulations, differs from them in its views on marriage" (*War* 2.160).

villages, and so from "mainstream Enochic Judaism." Thus, for him Essenism embraces three phenomena: Qumran Essenes, urban Essenes, and "Enochians." The main difference seems to be that Jews represented by the urban Essenes and Enochic Judaism tended to believe in free will while the Qumran Essenes believed not only in historical determinism but also in individual predestination.[46] Boccaccini argues that, faithful to their Enochic roots, the Qumranites despised everything about the historical Zadokites, the dynasty of high priests who ruled the temple up to the eve of the Maccabean revolt. Thus, he imagines that the terms "sons of Zadok," which the Qumranites applied to themselves, may have been a topos, a supersessionistic reading of Ezekiel, and not a genealogical term.[47]

According to Boccaccini, the foreshadowing of Qumran thought can be traced back to a period prior to a movement to Qumran. Subsequently, there was a split within this larger group of Jews. The Qumranites split from the larger Enochic-Essene movement represented by the urban Essenes and the Enochic group.[48] Evidence of such a movement is provided by numerous pre-Qumranic texts such as Jubilees, the Temple Scroll, the Proto-Epistle of Enoch (including the Apocalypse of Weeks), and the Halakhic Letter (MMT), and by the production of non-Qumranic texts, such as the Epistle of Enoch, the Testaments of the Twelve Patriarchs, and the Parables of Enoch, which parallel the sectarian literature of Qumran.

David R. Jackson also uses the term "Enochic Judaism." He obtains this term from studying the self-understanding of the authors who composed, compiled, and edited the Enoch books found in the Qumran caves. Jackson includes within Enochic Judaism both those who produced the books of Enoch

---

46. See esp. Boccaccini, *Beyond the Essene Hypothesis* (Grand Rapids and Cambridge: Eerdmans, 1998), 170. Boccaccini hypothesizes that the earliest dimensions of Christianity should be traced to Enochic Judaism and that its origins should also be sought in the Essene movement outside of Qumran. In *Roots of Rabbinic Judaism* (Grand Rapids: Eerdmans, 2002) Boccaccini claims that rabbinic Judaism should be traced back to Zadokite Judaism through the Pharisaic movement. Also, see Boccaccini's "Response: Texts, Intellectual Movements, and Social Groups" and his other publications noted in his introduction to the present volume.

47. The possibility of a topos was suggested already by Philip Davies; see Boccaccini's introduction in this volume.

48. A schism within groups prior to the establishment of a community at Qumran has been a consensus among the leading scholars for decades. Even the advocates of the Groningen Hypothesis posit a split within the movement that was "parent" to the Qumran group. I think García Martínez is correct to point out that the Temple Scroll and MMT represent, in their early form (I would add), the early or formative stages of the group that is known to us from 1QS, and that such terms as "we," "you," and "they" which are found in MMT distinguish it from the Temple Scroll.

and those who "accepted" this tradition.[49] It is not clear how and in what ways his use of "Enochic Judaism" is distinct from that of Boccaccini.

In the past I have referred, on the one hand, to the pre-70 Enoch groups or circles that produced the books of Enoch over three centuries, and on the other to the Enoch cycle of texts, which includes the books of Enoch, the Book of the Giants,[50] and later compositions, including 2 Enoch, the Coptic texts (some edited by Walter E. Crum and others by Henri Munier), the Armenian Vision of Enoch the Just, and 3 Enoch.[51] While I am convinced we should avoid labeling all these texts as representative of something like a movement, they do represent a cycle of thought that is devoted to reflections grounded in, and attributed to, Enoch.

Clearly, we may talk about a circle or group of Jews in second temple Judaism that are devoted to or significantly influenced by Jewish reflections on Enoch. This becomes clear from studying the development of thoughts within the books of Enoch, studying Jubilees, and reflecting critically on the Testaments of the Twelve Patriarchs, as well as studying testaments attributed to the sons of Jacob within Qumran. Mosheh D. Herr rightly refers to the "Enoch circle," but it is not obvious that one should now describe it as "a very small circle within Second Temple Judaism."[52] While I wish to defer to others in assessing the size of the Enoch group or circle, and while I cannot yet judge its influence, I have no doubt about its importance for the development of Jewish thought within second temple Judaism, as well as the emergence of the theology within the Palestinian Jesus movement and perhaps within Jesus' own self-understanding.

It is clear that some of Boccaccini's terminology is being used, and sometimes modified, by other scholars, who may or may not be willing to use such terms as "Zadokite Judaism" and "Enochic Judaism." More important than labels and terms, however, is the perception of the types of Judaism within second temple Judaism. It is certain that many forms of Judaism thrived in Palestine before 70 C.E., and that one of the major and influential groups is

49. D. R. Jackson, *Enochic Judaism*, Library of Second Temple Studies 49 (London and New York: T. & T. Clark International, 2004).

50. See L. T. Stuckenbruck, *The Book of the Giants from Qumran: Texts, Translation, and Commentary*, TSAJ 63 (Tübingen: Mohr Siebeck, 1997).

51. See, e.g., Charlesworth, "1 (Ethiopic) Enoch [and Enoch Cycle]," the Pseudepigrapha and Modern Research with a Supplement, SCS 7S (Chico, Calif.: Scholars, 1981), 98-99. 3 Enoch reflects a very different time and place from 1 Enoch. See VanderKam's discussion of Schiffman's judgments in the present volume.

52. M. D. Herr, "The Calendar," in *The Jewish People in the First Century*, ed. S. Safrai and M. Stern, CRINT 1.2 (Assen and Amsterdam: Van Gorcum, 1976), 2:834-64; see esp. 839.

represented by the books of Enoch, which preserve Jewish thought from about 300 B.C.E. to the end of the first century B.C.E., and perhaps into the first century C.E.

Within a world of scholarship in which synthesis was shunned in favor of analysis, becoming ever more focused on one text or even one section of a document, Boccaccini's Essene-Enochic Hypothesis (and he admits it is a working hypothesis)[53] has proved stimulating and has helped to reveal that analysis must not continue hand and glove with an outmoded perception of the whole. Clearly all members of the Enoch Seminar would reject concepts like a monolithic normative pre-70 Judaism.

While concurring with that perception, I would still hold to a powerful form of Judaism being promulgated and enforced by the high priests and other powerful thinkers in and near the temple cult. Recall that Jesus of Nazareth was spied on by "scribes" (Mark 3:22; 7:1), or "Pharisees and scribes" (Matt 15:1; cf. Luke 5:17) who *had been sent out from Jerusalem.* Equally significant for comprehending the social dynamic in pre-70 Judaism and the power of the Jerusalem-based authorities is the report that "priests and Levites from Jerusalem" (John 1:19) were sent to interrogate John the Baptizer.

d. What new challenges are becoming clearer?

It is clear that the proper approach to second temple Judaism and Christian origins should be free from the limitations of a closed canon that dictates what is important and what is marginal. It is also clear that scholars cannot, and do not wish to, separate texts and perspectives into clear categories of "Jewish" or "Christian." I am convinced that a scholar should not describe first century C.E. phenomena with any of the following terms: "Christian," "church," "orthodoxy," and "heresy."

The learned group of experts of the Enoch Seminar are exploring how and in what ways the Enoch books, most of which were found in the Qumran caves, help us understand the origins and development of the Qumran community. It is not yet clear, and may never be resolved, how significant and powerful were the Jewish groups represented by the books of Enoch.

Among the multitude of questions yet to be explored, five seem fundamentally important. They are the following:

1. How reliably do the late Ethiopic texts and Greek texts of 1 Enoch represent the Semitic texts composed before 70 C.E. by Jews?

---

53. See Boccaccini's "Response" in the present volume.

2. Can one discern the social groups behind the books of Enoch;[54] and should they be described, among many options, as representative of a Judaism that antedates the Mosaic torah as normative, or as priests who have forsaken the Jerusalem temple?[55]

3. Can we be more precise about the provenience or location of the Enoch groups, and to what extent they represent Galilean thought?[56]

4. How early and Jewish are the Parables of Enoch, and what is the explanation of the fact that they are not quoted by the early scholars of the church and are not clearly reflected in the New Testament documents?

5. Is the mind of Jesus, as represented in the intracanonical Gospels, grounded in the post-Easter community of the Palestinian Jesus movement, as so many from Martin Kähler to Hans Conzelmann concluded, or in the Jewish theology of ancient Palestine before the destruction of 70 c.e.?

In proceeding further we should be clear on one point: If the Qumran scrolls (except for the Copper Scroll) help us define the Qumranites, and if we can be certain of the topographical setting of the Qumranites,[57] we know nothing like that for the Enoch groups. That is, we have neither a clear definition of them nor a geographical location that would allow us to define their origin and setting. While the Rule of the Community clarifies the organization and theological ideas of the Qumranites that lived near where it was found, we have nothing similar from which to define and comprehend the location of the Enoch groups.

54. Inter alia, see the comments by Patrick Tiller in this volume and especially John Collins's response to him. Most important in searching for an identity of the Enoch groups and their relation to the *maskilim* is Stephen Pfann's claim that the *maskilim* are much older than Qumran and may move the origins of Qumran (at this time in history an anachronism) back to about 200 B.C.E. See his Ph.D. dissertation at Hebrew University, Jerusalem (unpublished as of now). Also, see García Martínez's critique of Pfann's work in the present volume.

55. In the present volume Helge Kvanvig rightly argues that behind a family of books like the books of Enoch lie a family of people. Esp. see the comments by Nickelsburg in *1 Enoch*, 67. There can be no doubt that many groups within second temple Judaism reacted against and sometimes were shaped by antitemple rhetoric; this is a consensus in research (see notably the works by Paul Hanson, John Collins, Doron Mendels, Ithamar Gruenwald, Martha Himmelfarb, and Michael Stone). Also see Boccaccini, "The Priestly Opposition: Enochic Judaism," in *Roots of Rabbinic Judaism*, 89-103.

56. One may learn a lot about attempts to reconstruct the worldview of the Enoch groups by studying the comments by Armin Lange in this volume and especially Collins's critique of him. Indeed, scholars need to clarify the difference between a "worldview" and a milieu.

57. García Martínez rightly warns against missing the point that the Qumran community does not exist only as a utopian ideal; there are real pots, coins, ruins, and caves that define this community; see his "Response: The Groningen Hypothesis Revisited" in this volume.

Conclusion

The deliberations of the members of the Enoch Seminar not only help us understand the origins of the books of Enoch. They involve also the reassessment of what is meant by Judaism before 70 c.e., which includes a better understanding, inter alia, of the emergence of "Christianity" and the mind of Jesus, who was a deeply devout Jew. In addition to the specialists convening in Italy, others will be interested in how and in what ways Jews, including Jesus, may have been influenced by the Enoch groups, or Enochic Judaism, and to what extent. To what extent was the Jewish genius before 70 shaped by the Enoch groups? To what extent was Jesus' own self-understanding impacted by ideas, concepts, perceptions, and terms developed by those who composed the books of Enoch?

While some in the Bultmannian school claimed that the Son of Man concept was illegitimately attributed to Jesus by the post-Easter community (viz., Conzelmann), some scholars may begin to imagine that when we delve into the mind of Jesus we have already entered into a Jewish world of thought that antedated him.

Contemporary research focused on describing the world of second temple Judaism is paradigmatically distinct, in many ways, from research published before 1970. Work on the Qumran scrolls stimulated research on the so-called Old Testament Pseudepigrapha. Out of this focused research comes a renewed and challenging appreciation of the genius of the early Jews. Surely, the appreciation of the world of thought and social movement represented by the books of Enoch signifies an advance not only in scholarship but also in a more pellucid perception of the origins of Western civilization.

About five years ago Gene Shalit sent me his book that is attractively entitled *Laughing Matters*.[58] I was impressed with the double entendre. Surely, today all members of the Enoch Seminar agree that 1 Enoch matters.[59]

---

58. G. Shalit, *Laughing Matters: A Celebration of American Humor* (New York: Barnes & Noble, 1993).

59. Jacob Neusner, in contrast, can refer to the "exemplary figures in the emergence of Judaism" without mentioning Enoch; he moves from God to Abraham and then to Isaac, Rachel, Moses, and so forth. See Neusner, *The Emergence of Judaism* (Louisville and London: Westminster John Knox, 2004). Neusner, of course, would agree with the perspective that pre-Mishnaic Judaism was complex and many-faceted — which is the perspective of the members of the Enoch Seminar.